STUDY GUIDE

AN
INVITATION
TO
FLY

Basics for the Private Pilot

THIRD EDITION

DOCUMENTS NEEDED IN AIRPLANE

A IRWORTHINESS

R EGISTERATION

R
O } RADIO STATION

W EIGHT, CG

ANNUAL INSPECTON ; 100 HR INSP — RENTAL

For further information about ordering or adopting this Study Guide or accompanying material, write or call Anne Scanlan-Rohrer, Wadsworth Publishing Company, Belmont, CA 94002, (415) 595-2350.

Accompanying Materials

Textbook and partial San Francisco Sectional Chart (packaged together)

Instructor's Manual (complimentary to instructors on adoption of the textbook for classroom use)

Videotapes (30 half-hour color tapes)

Viewer's Guide (integrates the videotapes with the textbook and Study Guide)

Flight Maneuvers Manual for Private Pilots

Computerized testing system for the FAA (Airplane) Exam and the Study Guide

Student Electronic Study Guide for the FAA (Airplane) Exam
(See Appendix E)

STUDY GUIDE

AN INVITATION TO FLY

Basics for the Private Pilot

THIRD EDITION

GEORGE B. SEMB
UNIVERSITY OF KANSAS

DONALD E. TAYLOR
SAN DIEGO MESA COLLEGE

WADSWORTH PUBLISHING COMPANY
BELMONT, CALIFORNIA
A DIVISION OF WADSWORTH, INC.

Aviation Education Editor: Anne Scanlan-Rohrer

Composition: Trilogy Systems, Inc.

ISBN 0-534-09391-4

Printed in the United States of America

1 2 3 4 5 6 7 8 9 10 -- 93 92 91 90 89

CONTENTS

Appendices

PREFACE

TO THE STUDENT

This Study Guide contains answers and explanations to *all* of the items that may appear on the FAA Private Pilot Written Exam (Airplane) published in the Private Pilot Question Book (FAA-T-8080-1B). The FAA questions are fully integrated with the appropriate chapter in this Study Guide. Appendix B contains a cross-referenced list of FAA exam questions.

This Study Guide is designed to accompany An Invitation to Fly: Basics for the Private Pilot, Third Edition, by Dennis Glaeser, Sanford Gum, and Bruce Walters. It can also be used to review and prepare for the Federal Aviation Administration (FAA) Private Pilot Written Exam (Airplane). The Study Guide is based on principles, regulations, and practices that were current at the time it was printed.

The Study Guide requires the use of the same supplemental materials as the text, including:

1. San Francisco Sectional Chart (partial)
2. Navigation plotter
3. Flight computer
4. Calculator (optional)

The Study Guide is designed primarily to help you learn the basic information necessary to become a safe, competent private pilot. Each chapter includes: a summary of the main points in the text, vocabulary and technical exercises to make certain you know the "language" of piloting, and discussion questions and review exercises that emphasize the important concepts. Many of the discussion questions and review exercises are similar to questions you will encounter on the FAA Private Pilot Written Exam (Airplane). Questions that will actually appear on the FAA Private Pilot Written Exam (Airplane) are listed by the same question number that appears in the Private Pilot Question Book. Furthermore, each FAA question is cross-referenced to the Private Pilot Question Book. This Study Guide contains answers and explanations to *all* of the items that the FAA uses for the airplane exam. It also has several other items that reinforce concepts stressed on the FAA exam. Answers to all discussion and review questions, plus an analysis of the questions and answers on the FAA exam, appear at the end of each chapter. Finally, there is a computer software package for the IBM-PC at the back of this book, The Electronic Study Guide, that enables you to practice taking sample FAA written exams. See Appendix E for complete instructions about how to use this helpful software package.

As a general guide to studying the text and using this Study Guide, begin by thoroughly reading the chapter in the text. Next, read the main points in the Study Guide. These summarize and review material presented in the text. Once you are familiar with the material, it is time to become actively engaged in learning it. Try to do all of the vocabulary and technical exercises without referring to the text for help. Once you have attempted them all, refer to the text to check your answers and to restudy those items you missed. Next, answer the discussion questions and review exercises, again without referring to the text until you have attempted all of them. Answer all of the questions before you look up the answers at the end of the chapter. Finally, complete the FAA exam questions at the end of the chapter. Do not look up the answers until you have finished answering all of the FAA items.

If you follow these guidelines you should be able to correctly answer most of the review questions. Further, you should have a good grasp of the material covered in the chapter. One of the most important parts of this process is your attempt to answer the questions before looking up the answers. Learning specialists have argued for a long time that active involvement in Study Guide exercises promotes effective learning and retention, and research has shown them to be correct. Therefore, this Study Guide is designed to encourage you to actively participate in the learning process.

PREPARING FOR THE FAA PRIVATE PILOT WRITTEN (AIRPLANE) EXAM

The FAA Private Pilot Written Exam (Airplane) is not an easy test. Nor is it a terribly difficult one, *if* you are well prepared. One purpose of this Study Guide is to help you prepare for it. Refer to Appendix D for complete instructions on how to take the exam, how questions are scored, and how to retake it if you do not pass it the first time. Many of the instructions are also repeated in what follows here.

Answers and explanations to all of the items that appear on the FAA written exam for private pilots (airplane) are included in this Study Guide and in the Electronic Study Guide (Appendix E). Everything you need to master the FAA Written Exam (Airplane) is contained right here!

Before you can take the test, Federal Aviation Regulations (FARs) require that you: (a) have satisfactorily completed a ground-instruction or home-study course signed off by a Certified Flight Instructor (CFI), Ground Instructor, or by a General Aviation District Officer, (b) present an airman certificate, driver's license, or other official document as proof of identification, and (c) present a birth certificate or other official document showing that you meet the age requirement. For complete details, refer to Part 61.103-105 of the Federal Aviation Regulations in Chapter 11.

For written test purposes, you will be required to use the Private Pilot Question Book provided by the testing center or the designated written test examiner. The test administrator will give you an "assignment" sheet listing the 50 questions you are to answer. You will have four hours to complete the test. Each question is to be answered by selecting a single *best* alternative. You may take the following equipment with you to the test center: a protractor or plotter and a flight navigation computer. Textbooks and notes are forbidden, and the test administrator will provide papers, answer forms, and special pencils. You may also use a calculator; however, there are several regulations concerning its use. First, the test administrator will instruct you to turn the calculator on and off before and after the test to ensure that any data stored in it are destroyed. If your calculator is one that stores data even when the switch is off, the administrator may ask you to demonstrate that all memory registers are empty. Second, if your calculator produces hard copy, all printouts must be surrendered to the administrator at the end of the test. Third, you will not be allowed to use any written instructions pertaining to the calculator during the test.

The feedback you will receive will be in the form of an Airman Written Test Report (AC Form 8080-2) that includes not only the test score but also the subject matter knowledge codes (see Appendix D) in which you missed items. Please note that a subject matter code is identified whether you miss one or more items in the code. That is, whether you miss one, two, three, or more items in a particular code, the code is listed only once.

Besides reading the text and completing the Study Guide, you will find it valuable to simulate examination conditions whenever possible. One way you can do this is to consider the review questions at the end of each chapter as a mini-examination. Set a time limit of four minutes per question and answer all of them before looking up the answers. Making the simulated exercises as similar as you can to the actual exam conditions will greatly aid in your preparation for the FAA written exam and may also help you reduce your anxiety.

One of the best ways to prepare yourself for the actual exam is to be well rested. Staying up late and "cramming" the night before the test often leads to anxiety, fuzzy thinking, and careless errors. So, get a good night's sleep the day before the exam. Next, make a checklist of the things you will need for the exam (plotter, calculator, and so on). Use the checklist, much as you would before you started a flight, to be certain that you take all of the required paraphernalia. It is easy to become flustered when you discover that you have forgotten something important, so use your checklist. Finally, arrive at the test center early to acquaint yourself with the setting. Find the restroom. Ask about the availability of beverages. Remember, too, that you are usually not allowed to bring food, so eat a good meal before your test.

The multiple-choice questions on the FAA exam have one answer that is considered *most* correct. Each item is independent of other items. This means that an answer to one item in no way depends upon or influences the answer to another item. However, as you read through a series of questions on the same subject, you may find answers to one question in the stem or body of another.

The minimum passing grade will be specified by the test administrator on the written test sheet you receive. Before you begin the exam, read the directions carefully. If you have questions, ask the administrator.

Many questions on the exam may appear tricky. Some of the questions may in fact be tricky, but careful analysis of most of them reveals that they are not tricky per se but rather that they require subtle discriminations. For example, a question that asks you to discriminate between 3,500 ft. MSL (above sea level) and 3,500 ft. AGL (above ground level) is attempting to make certain that you understand the difference between two ways of referring to altitude. Although such subtle discriminations are sometimes difficult to learn, they are extremely important in flying.

You will be asked to answer only 50 of the questions that appear in the FAA test bank. You will be given a *Question Selection Sheet* listing the

questions you are to answer and an *Answer Sheet* on which to circle the
correct answer. The questions you are to answer will be specified as follows:

CORRESPONDING NUMBER ON ANSWER SHEET	QUESTION NUMBER
1	1002
2	1113
3	1267
4	1333

A common mistake many students make is to place an answer beside the wrong
item number on the *Answer Sheet*. Because you are permitted to write on the
Question Selection Sheet, we recommend that you first write all of your
responses on the *Question Selection Sheet* between the item number and the
question number as shown below.

(your answer)

	(your answer)	
1 .... **2**	1002
2 .... **3**	1113
3 .... **4**	1267
4 .... **3**	1333

After you have answered all the questions and rechecked your responses,
carefully transfer your answers to the *Answer Sheet.*

Read each question thoroughly and carefully before selecting an
alternative. If the statement refers to a general rule, do not look for
exceptions to the rule unless the question specifically asks you to do so.
Once you have read and understood the question, carefully evaluate each of the
alternatives. Treat each one as a true-false statement and eliminate those
you know to be obviously incorrect. Then concentrate on those (if any) about
which you are uncertain. When answering multiple-choice items like those that
appear on the FAA written exam, keep a list of the alternatives about which
you are uncertain, so that when you return to the question later, it will be
easy to see exactly where ambiguities still exist. Finally, if time remains,
go through the test a second time.

In general, do not spend a great deal of time on any single question.
If, after you have spent more than two minutes on a question, you still do not
understand what is being asked, go on to the next question. At some point
later in the exam, you may discover an item that has a direct bearing on what
you did not comprehend earlier or one that jogs your memory. When that
happens, answer the question you are working on, then return immediately to
the one you did not understand earlier. Keeping a "tally sheet" of questions
about which you are uncertain while taking the exam makes retracing your steps
an easy task.

Once you have attempted all of the questions, return to the items about
which you were uncertain. Count how many items there are in the "uncertain"
category and divide the number of unanswered questions into the time
remaining. This will give you an idea of how much time to spend on each
question. Attempt to answer each of the remaining questions, checking

occasionally to be sure that you are not spending too much time on any one item.

When you are confident all of your answers are correct, stop and cross-check the answer sheet with your tally sheet. If there are any discrepancies, check to see which answer is the one you want and make certain the answer key is marked the way you want it. We cannot emphasize *the rechecking process* enough. Our research has shown that as many as 10 percent of the answers students record on the answer sheet do not correspond with their tally sheet, so cross-check your answers thoroughly. Finally, if you left any answers blank, make your best guess and record it. There is no penalty for guessing, so choose the alternative that you think best answers the question being asked.

If you do not pass the test the first time you try it, you were not adequately prepared. You will have to wait 30 days from the time you last took the test to reapply, unless an authorized instructor certifies in writing that appropriate instruction has been given and that he or she finds you competent to pass the test, in which case you can reapply before the 30-day limit has elapsed.

One final comment about the written test concerns cheating. If you cheat you are cheating yourself as well as others. It is something that simply cannot be tolerated. Federal Aviation Regulation 61.37 is presented here for you to read.

FAR 61.37 Written tests: cheating or other unauthorized conduct

(a) Except as authorized by the Administrator, no person may

(1) copy, or intentionally remove, a written test under this part;
(2) give to another, or receive from another, any part or copy of that test;
(3) give help on that test to, or receive help on that test from, any person during the period that test is being given;
(4) take any part of that test in behalf of another person;
(5) use any material or aid during the period that test is being given; or
(6) intentionally cause, assist, or participate in any act prohibited by this paragraph.

(b) No person whom the Administrator finds to have committed an act prohibited by paragraph (a) of this section is eligible for any airman or ground instructor certificate or rating, or to take any test thereof, under this chapter for a period of one year after the date of that act. In addition, the commission of that act is a basis for suspending or revoking any airman or ground instructor certificate or rating held by that person.

We hope the information provided here helps you achieve a high score on the FAA written exam. If you find other preparation techniques helpful, please send a description of them to me so we can incorporate them into future editions of this study guide. Address your correspondence to: George B. Semb, Department of Human Development, University of Kansas, Lawrence, Kansas 66045.

UNUSABLE FAA TEST QUESTIONS

Periodically, the FAA designates questions as unusable for test purposes and removes them from the Question Selection Sheets. Deleted items are noted by an * next to the FAA item number. Because many of these items have educational value, they are also included in this Study Guide.

PRACTICAL TEST STANDARDS

To standardize the practical tests for certification of private pilots, the FAA published the Private Pilot Practical Test Standards, which became effective in 1985. Pilot examiners are required to "conduct practical tests in compliance with these standards." These include assessing the student's ability by means of oral questions and demonstrations of skill and judgment. The oral questions may be given on the ground before flight and/or integrated into the flight test. The typical oral examination is three to five hours long, followed by the flight portion of the practical test.

It is recommended that you purchase the Practical Test Standards Airplane (Single-Engine Land) booklet to study the questions you must be able to answer and the procedure you will be required to demonstrate. These booklets are available at most flight schools.

ABOUT THE AUTHORS

George B. Semb is professor of human development at the University of Kansas. He holds a B.S. degree from the University of Washington, an Sc.M. degree from Brown University, and a Ph.D. degree from the University of Kansas. All of his degrees are in the field of psychology, with particular emphasis on the design and evaluation of instructional systems. He received his private pilot's license in 1966 and has flown actively since that time. He has written study guides for textbooks in psychology, child development, and biology. His primary area of research is instructional systems, where he has published and presented over 100 papers in the last decade.

Donald E. Taylor is head of the Aviation program and Chief Ground Instructor of the pilot ground school at San Diego Mesa College. He holds a B.S. degree in psychology from Purdue University. Mr. Taylor is a retired Naval Aviator who first soloed in 1960. During his 25-year naval career he was a ground instructor, a flight instructor in single-engine and twin-engine airplanes, and an Aviation Safety Officer. Mr. Taylor holds the following FAA ratings: Airline Transport Pilot, Certified Flight Instructor, Instrument Airplane, and Advanced Ground Instructor. He has written study guides for a variety of aviation courses.

ON BECOMING A PILOT

MAIN POINTS

1.   The **aviation community** consists of three sectors: commercial airlines, military aviation, and general aviation. Included under general aviation are student-pilot training, air taxis, crop dusters, business aircraft, and numerous other activities.

2.   The **Federal Aviation Administration (FAA)** regulates aviation in the United States. It issues and enforces **Federal Aviation Regulations (FARs)**, operates **Flight Service Stations (FSS)**, and coordinates traffic flow at busy airports through **air traffic control** facilities.

3.   **Aircraft** are classified by category, class, and type. **Category** refers to the method of staying aloft and means of propulsion, **class** refers to aircraft with similar operating characteristics, and **type** refers to model and make. **Lighter-than-air aircraft**, the first category, includes balloons and airships. **Rotorcraft**, the second category, includes helicopters and gyroplanes. **Gliders**, the third category, are unpowered aircraft with wings and a tail, such as a sailplane. An **airplane** is a powered aircraft with wings and a tail. There are four classes of airplanes: single-engine land, single-engine sea, multi-engine land, and multi-engine sea. Common airplane **types** include the Cessna 152, the Beechcraft Bonanza, the Piper Tomahawk, and the Boeing 767.

4.   This chapter explains how to obtain Student and Private Pilot (Airplane) Certificates as detailed in Part 61 of the Federal Aviation Regulations (FARs).

5.   There are no minimum or maximum ages for taking flight lessons. However, you must be at least 16 to fly solo and at least 17 to receive the Private Pilot Certificate.

6.   Flight instruction (sometimes referred to as **dual instruction**) must be performed by a **Certified Flight Instructor (CFI)**. Your training will also include **ground instruction**. Businesses that provide services for general aviation at airports and where flight instruction is frequently available are

called **fixed-base operators (FBOs)**. Fees associated with the various aspects of training will include the instructor's fee, airplane rental charges, and any fees associated with ground school such as enrollment and texts.

7.   To receive a **Student Pilot Certificate**, you must be at least 16; be able to read, speak, and understand English; and hold at least a **Third Class Medical Certificate**. The Student Pilot Certificate is on the same form as your medical certificate. It is required to fly an airplane solo and must be carried when flying solo. The Student Pilot Certificate is valid for 24 months; it expires after two years at the **end of the month** in which it was issued.

8.   To fly solo as a student pilot (by yourself--no passengers allowed), a Certified Flight Instructor (CFI) must determine that you are familiar with visual flight rules (VFR)--Part 91 of the FARs--and must enter an endorsement in your logbook and on your Student Pilot Certificate. The solo endorsement does not entitle you to fly cross-country; each cross-country flight must be endorsed separately.

9.   To apply for the Private Pilot (Airplane) Certificate, you must be at least 17; be able to read, speak, and understand English; hold at least a Third Class Medical Certificate; pass the Private Pilot Written Exam (Airplane); have completed at least 20 hours of dual instruction, including 3 hours of cross-country and 3 hours in preparation for the flight test within 60 days of the test; and have completed 20 hours of solo time, including 10 hours in airplanes and 10 hours of cross-country flight. Flying at night requires separate training and endorsements, but it is not required to obtain a private pilot's certificate. FAR Part 141-approved schools can recommend students with a minimum of 35 hours (20 dual, 15 solo). If instruction was conducted under FAR Part 61, 40 hours is required (20 dual, 20 solo).

10.   Requirements for the **FAA Private Pilot (Written) Exam** are discussed in the **Preface** to this study guide, together with suggested study techniques.

11.   Once you satisfy the above requirements, you are ready for the practical test. It includes oral and skill portions. The skill portion is a flight test that includes the demonstration of basic flying techniques and cross-country flying. Passing the test results in your being awarded the **Private Pilot Certificate**. This certificate is issued without an expiration date.

12.   There are two types of flight rules, **visual flight rules (VFR)** and **instrument flight rules (IFR)**. VFR pertain to flight free of clouds and in areas of adequate visibility. IFR pertain to aircraft operating in weather conditions below VFR minimums.

13.   Like other fields, aviation has many terms and abbreviations. One of your tasks as a student pilot will be to learn several of them such as CFI, FCC, FAA, VOR, TRSA, ADF, FBO, POH, ARSA, IAS, CAS, MSL, AGL, and many more. The dictionary of aeronautical terms located in the back of the text provides definitions of abbreviations and terms.

KEY TERMS AND CONCEPTS

Match each term or concept (1-16) with the appropriate description (A-N) below. Each item has only one match.

___ 1. airplane **type**
___ 2. sixteen
___ 3. VFR
___ 4. CFI
___ 5. aircraft **category**
___ 6. FBO
___ 7. IFR
___ 8. Third Class

___ 9. designated examiner
___ 10. FARs
___ 11. basic flying technique
___ 12. airplane **class**
___ 13. twenty
___ 14. pilot-in-command
___ 15 FAA
___ 16. cross-country flight

A. person who must endorse logbook for solo flight
B. DC-10
C. one part of the private pilot **flight** test
D. minimum age for solo flight
E. flight free of clouds and in areas of adequate visibility
F. type of medical certificate required of student and private pilots
G. minimum number of hours of instruction required for private pilot certification
H. rules that apply to weather conditions below VFR minimums
I. government branch responsible for civil aeronautics
J. rotorcraft
K. business that provides services at airports
L. civilian flight instructor authorized by the FAA to give the practical test
M. regulations governing all aspects of aviation
N. individual responsible for operation of an aircraft
O. single-engine land
P. a flight of more than 50 NM from your home airport

DISCUSSION QUESTIONS AND REVIEW EXERCISES

1.   What three sectors constitute the **aviation community?**

2.   Distinguish among **category, class,** and **type** of aircraft. Identify four **categories** of aircraft, name four **classes** of airplanes, and identify what type you fly or intend to fly.

3. What are FARs? Who issues and enforces them?

4. What is a CFI? Name at least three activities he or she performs.

5. What three requirements must you meet before you can obtain a Student
Pilot Certificate?

6. What document(s) must be in your possession whenever you fly solo?

7. What is a supervised solo flight? What must a CFI do before each solo
cross-country flight?

8. What restrictions apply to flying at night?

9.   According to FAR Part 61, how much time must you accumulate, and in what categories, before you can take the private pilot practical test?

10. Briefly describe the two parts of the private pilot practical test.

11. Distinguish between VFR and IFR.

12. What age must you be to be eligible to receive a Private Pilot (Airplane) Certificate?
     1--15 years of age.
     2--16 years of age.
     3--17 years of age.
     4--There is no minimum age.

13. Of the following items (a, b, c, and d), which are you **required** to carry with you when you are flying solo as a student pilot? (a) Student Pilot Certificate; (b) Social Security card; (c) valid driver's license; (d) pilot logbook.
     1--a.
     2--a, b.
     3--a, c.
     4--a, d.
     5--b, c.
     6--b, d.
     7--c, d.
     8--a, b, c.
     9--a, c, d.
     10--b, c, d.
     11--a, b, c, d.

14. According to FAR Part 61, how many total hours are required, both with a flight instructor and solo time, before you can take the private pilot flight test?
    1--20 hr.
    2--30 hr.
    3--40 hr.
    4--50 hr.

15. A hot-air balloon is classified as a/an
    1--airplane.
    2--glider.
    3--lighter-than-air aircraft.
    4--rotorcraft.

16. Which of the following is an example of a **class** of aircraft?
    1--Boeing 747.
    2--Multi-engine sea.
    3--Glider.
    4--Airplane.

17. Which of the following is an example of a **category** of aircraft?
    1--Single-engine land.
    2--Glider.
    3--Helicopter.
    4--Ultralight.

18. An unpowered aircraft with wings and a tail is classified as a/an
    1--airplane.
    2--glider.
    3--lighter-than-air craft.
    4--rotorcraft.

19. A DC-10 is a _____ of aircraft.
    1--category
    2--class
    3--kind
    4--type

20. Which government agency issues and enforces federal air regulations?
    1--CFI.
    2--FAA.
    3--FBO.
    4--IRS.

21. A powered aircraft with wings is classified as a/an
    1--airplane.
    2--glider.
    3--lighter-than-air craft.
    4--rotorcraft.

FAA EXAM QUESTIONS

1. (FAA 1597) Which is a category of aircraft?
   1--Balloon.
   2--Gyroplane.
   3--Rotorcraft.
   4--Single-engine land.

2. (FAA 1598) Which is a class of airplane?
   1--Turbojet.
   2--Multi-engine land.
   3--Helicopter.
   4--Glider.

3. (FAA 1599) Which is a rotorcraft class?
   1--Helicopter.
   2--Airship.
   3--Turbojet.
   4--Turboprop.

4. (FAA 1600) Which is a class of lighter-than-air?
   1--Airship.
   2--Gyroplane.
   3--Airplane.
   4--Ultralight.

ANSWERS AND EXPLANATIONS

Key Terms and Concepts

1. B	5. J	9. L	13. G
2. D	6. K	10. M	14. N
3. E	7. H	11. C	15. I
4. A	8. F	12. O	16. P

Discussion Questions and Review Exercises

1. Commercial airlines, military aviation, and general aviation. You, as a student pilot, will be part of the general aviation community.

2. See Study Guide Main Point #3.

3. Federal Aviation Regulations (FARs) are issued and enforced by the Federal Aviation Administration (FAA).

4. A CFI is a Certified Flight Instructor. They provide ground instruction and flight instruction, sign-off your log book for solo and cross-country flights, and perform many other duties.

5. See Study Guide Main Point #7.

6. Student pilot certificate and pilot logbook showing the appropriate endorsements.

7. See Study Guide Main Point #8.

8. See text page 15.

9. See Study Guide Main Point #9.

10. Oral test and flight test.

11. VFR refers to visual flight rules (flight free of clouds and in areas of adequate visibility) and IFR refers to instrument flight rules (pertains to aircraft operating in weather conditions below VFR minimums).

12. 3--You must be at least 17 to obtain a Private Pilot Certificate.

13. 4--You are required to carry your Student Pilot Certificate and your pilot logbook with the appropriate endorsements. Remember, your Medical Certificate also serves as your Student Pilot Certificate.

14. 3--Under FAR Part 61, 40 is the required minimum, 20 hr. of which must be dual instruction and 20 hr. of which must be solo.

15. 3--Lighter-than-air is a **category**. A balloon is a **class** within that category.

16. 2--A Boeing 747 is a **type** of aircraft. Airplanes and gliders are **categories** of aircraft. Multi-engine sea is a **class** of airplanes.

17. 2--Gliders are a category; the rest are classes, with the exception of ultralights, which the FAA classifies as a "vehicle."

18. 2--Of the four categories named, an unpowered aircraft is classified as a glider.

19. 4--A **type** refers to a specific make and model.

20. 2--Federal Aviation Administration (FAA).

21. 1--Airplanes are a category of aircraft; they are powered and have wings.

FAA Exam Questions

1. 3--The categories of aircraft are Lighter-than-air, Glider, Rotorcraft and Glider.

2. 2--The Airplane category has four classes: single-engine land, multi-engine land, single-engine sea and multi-engine sea.

3. 1--The Rotorcraft category has two classes: gyroplane and helicopter.

4. 1--The Lighter-than-air category has two classes: balloon and airship.

THE PRACTICAL SCIENCE OF FLIGHT

MAIN POINTS

1.   You should be able to label an airplane, including the following common structures: **wings**, including ailerons and flaps; the **fuselage**; the tail **assembly** or **empennage**, including the vertical stabilizer, rudder, horizontal stabilizer, and elevator; **engine, propeller,** and **cowl**; and, **undercarriage,** including the nose wheel (if any) and main landing gear. The angle at which the wing root leaves the fuselage forming a slight "V" is called the **dihedral**.

2.   The four forces of flight are **lift, weight, thrust,** and **drag.** The general rule is: Lift opposes weight and thrust opposes drag. Gravity acts on weight to cause airplanes to go down. Thrust, the force developed by the airplane's engine, acts in the same direction as the airplane's flight path. Lift and drag are forces produced by the motion of the airplane through the air. Lift acts perpendicular to the flight path and drag acts parallel to it. The four forces are in equilibrium when the aircraft is in unaccelerated, or steady-state flight, which can be straight and level, in a climb/descent, or in a turn.

3.   Airplanes have several **airfoils** such as the wings, elevator, and propeller. The airfoil that produces the greatest effect is the **wing.**   It has a rounded leading edge and a sharp trailing edge. The imaginary line passing through the leading and trailing edges is called the chord line. The angle that the chord line makes with the **relative wind** defines the **angle of attack.** The relative wind is exactly opposite the flight path of the airfoil.

4.   An airplane creates **lift** by redirecting passing air downward. Newton's third law of equal and opposite reaction applies. The action of redirecting air downward creates the reaction of lift. The wing causes this redirection of air because its airfoil shape causes air passing over the wing to accelerate while causing air passing below it to slow down. As Bernoulli observed, when you increase velocity, there is a lower pressure. Thus there is a lower pressure area on top of the wing, which draws passing air downward, creating downwash. Higher pressure under the wing and the deflection of air

striking the lower surface of the wing also contribute to downwash. Finally, lift consists of two primary forces—horizontal and vertical. The differential interaction of these two forces causes an airplane to turn.

5.   That proportion of lift parallel to the flight path is called **induced drag**. Remember that forces perpendicular to the flight path produce lift, while those parallel to it produce drag. Another type of drag is called **parasite drag**. This refers to the effect of air molecules that run into parts of the airplane such as the landing gear, wing struts, and windshield.

6.   Four variables influence the aerodynamic features of an airplane: (1) its size and shape, (2) air density, (3) the wing's angle of attack, and (4) how fast it is moving through the air. Increasing the angle of attack increases both lift and induced drag. But there is an upper limit to how large an angle the wing can support. It is similar to the limit set on how much weight you can lift. As the angle of attack increases, the air flowing over the top of the wing begins to separate from the upper surface. The amount of separation increases as the angle of attack increases, until lift begins to decrease. At this point, the wing is **stalled**. The angle of attack at which the stall begins is called the **critical angle of attack**. The only way to recover from a stall is to reduce the angle of attack. We put a great deal of emphasis on stalls because they are a leading cause of accidents. **Stalls can occur at any airspeed and in any attitude!** All you need to do is exceed the critical angle of attack. Airplanes are usually designed to cause stalls to occur close to the fuselage and then work their way out the wing.

7.   An airplane has three axes of rotation: **lateral**, **longitudinal**, and **vertical**. Rotation about the lateral axis is referred to as **pitch**, as when the nose of the airplane goes up or down; it is controlled by the **elevator**. For example, when you push the control column or yoke forward, the trailing edge of the elevator (another airfoil) moves down, which in turn produces lift on the elevator surface. The result is that the tail goes up and the nose goes down. Rotation about the vertical axis is called **yaw**, as when you turn right or left; it is controlled by the **rudder**. For example, when you push the right rudder pedal, the rudder moves to the right. Once again, the forces of lift operate, this time to move the tail of the airplane to the **left** and the nose of the airplane to the **right**. Rotation about the longitudinal axis is called **roll**, as when the control wheel is turned left or right (banking); it is controlled by the **ailerons**. For example, when you turn the control wheel to the left, the left aileron goes **up** and the right aileron goes **down**; this increases the angle of attack of the right wing, which in turn produces more lift (the right wing goes up), and the plane banks to the left. Go through these axes, their controlling surfaces, and your actions several times until you can <u>visualize</u> what is happening.

8.   **Load factor** is the ratio of total lift to the weight of the airplane. As you bank the airplane, total lift increases; therefore, so does the load factor. In a 60° banked level turn, the wings must produce <u>twice</u> the lift (a load factor of 2). Load factors are expressed in terms of G units, which refer to gravitational force. Angle of bank also affects the minimum speed in level flight at which the wings will stall. In level, turning flight, **the steeper the bank, the higher the stall speed.**

9. Every airframe has a maximum load it can handle without damage. The **maneuvering speed** is the maximum speed to use during maneuvers or in turbulent air, so as not to exceed the maximum load limit of the airplane. If sudden increased lift occurs at faster than maneuvering speed, damage can occur, but at slower than maneuvering speed, the airplane simply stalls. You can recover from a stall, but not from loss of a wing. Maneuvering speed decreases when the plane is operated at light weights.

10. Two other important control surfaces are **wing flaps** and **trim tabs**. When wing flaps are lowered, the wing produces more lift and more drag. Thus, they increase the stall angle of attack of the wing. During landing, flaps allow the fuselage to assume a more nose-down attitude; during low speed flight, they allow a steeper glide path and lower approach and touchdown speeds. Trim tabs are fine-tuning control surfaces located on a primary control surface such as the elevator. Some airplanes also have trim tabs for the rudder and ailerons, again to fine-tune the aerodynamic features of the airplane and allow the airplane to fly "hands off."

11. **Stability** refers to the airplane's tendency to return to the trimmed condition following a disturbance such as turbulence or control movement. Stability may be **positive** (return to the original trim condition), **neutral** (stay in the same condition), or **negative** (move away from the original condition). Stability may also be classified as static or dynamic. Finally, it also applies to the three axes of rotation: longitudinal (pitch), directional (yaw), and lateral (roll).

12. Operating an airplane near the ground affects the airflow over the wings. This is referred to as **ground effect**. The effect is most pronounced when the airplane is less than half the wing span from the ground. Ground effect allows the airplane to start flying at lower than normal airspeeds and may cause the plane to travel farther (float) when landing.

13. **Wake turbulence** is caused by tornado-like **wingtip vortices**, which are the result of the production of lift. It is strongest behind aircraft that are heavy and slow and that have landing gear and flaps retracted. As a general rule, stay above the flight path of larger aircraft! On takeoff, lift off well before the point the previous large aircraft did and stay upwind of its flight path. On landing, stay above the glide path and land farther down the runway. Wait **at least** two minutes before departing after a large aircraft.

14. Several **propeller effects** lead most planes to display a left-turning tendency under certain conditions. First, the tendency of the airplane's propeller to produce unbalanced thrust, thereby inducing a yaw force to the left, is called the **P-factor**. This force can be counteracted by applying the right rudder. Second, the propeller also produces **torque**, which induces a left-rolling movement. Third, raising or lowering the tail of the airplane when the propeller is spinning produces a gyroscopic effect called **precession**. Finally, the high-speed rotation of the propeller causes a spiraling motion to the air-flow behind it. This spiraling motion affects vertical control surfaces and is referred to as the **slipstream effect**.

15. We return to **stalls** now because of their importance. Most airplanes have **stall warning devices** to help the pilot detect impending stalls. Stall recovery involves these steps: lower the angle of attack (control wheel forward); simultaneously add full engine power and level the wings. Return to level flight as soon as possible to minimize altitude loss.

16. If a yawing force is present when an airplane stalls, a steep corkscrew path, called a **spin**, results. There are several ways to produce yaw, such as uncoordinated use of the rudder, adverse yaw from the ailerons, and turbulence. In general, spin recovery involves several steps: close the throttle, neutralize the ailerons, add full rudder opposite to the direction of the spin, move the control column forward to break the stall, neutralize the rudder, level the wings, and recover smoothly from the resulting dive.

KEY TERMS AND CONCEPTS, PART 1

Match each term or concept (1-20) with the appropriate description (A-T) below. Each item has only one match.

___	1. neutral stability	___	11. up
___	2. angle of attack	___	12. left
___	3. flaps	___	13. down
___	4. gravity	___	14. Bernoulli's Principle
___	5. airfoil	___	15. Newton's third law
___	6. lift	___	16. load factor
___	7. pitch	___	17. yaw
___	8. roll	___	18. thrust
___	9. right	___	19. maneuvering speed
___	10. wake turbulence	___	20. P-factor

A. force of attraction between the earth and the airplane
B. rotation about the airplane's longitudinal axis
C. direction the left aileron moves when the control wheel is turned left
D. force that opposes gravity
E. direction the elevator moves when the control column is pushed in
F. principle that explains the area of reduced pressure created above the surface of an airplane's wing
G. rotation about the airplane's vertical axis
H. tendency to remain in conditions produced by a disturbance
I. direction of roll with right aileron up and left aileron down
J. shape designed to obtain lift from air that passes over and under it
K. direction the rudder moves when making a left turn
L. force created by a power plant that gives the airplane forward motion
M. allows slower approach speeds
N. ratio of total lift produced to the airplane's weight
O. principle that explains the force obtained from the creation of downwash
P. rotation about the airplane's lateral axis
Q. strongest behind heavy, slow aircraft
R. angle between the airfoil's chord and the direction of the relative wind
S. decreases as the airplane's weight decreases
T. unbalanced thrust that produces yaw to the left

KEY TERMS AND CONCEPTS, PART 2

Match each term or concept (1-20) with the appropriate description (A-T) below. Each item has only one match.

___ 1. parasite drag
___ 2. tricycle
___ 3. flaps
___ 4. spin
___ 5. induced drag
___ 6. static flight
___ 7. relative wind
___ 8. trim tab
___ 9. stall recovery
___ 10. ground effect
___ 11. critical angle of attack
___ 12. positive stability
___ 13. stall
___ 14. camber
___ 15. adverse yaw
___ 16. conventional landing gear
___ 17. empennage
___ 18. coordinated flight
___ 19. dihedral
___ 20. precession

A. motion of air **parallel** to an airfoil flight path, opposite direction
B. speed that increases as the angle of bank increases in a level turn
C. type of landing gear with a nose wheel and two main gears on the wings or fuselage
D. angle at which the wing root leaves the fuselage
E. cushion created by downwash from the wing
F. force that pushes the nose of the airplane opposite (away from) the direction of a turn
G. allow a steeper glide path
H. flight in which yawing and slipping motions are not produced by the pilot
I. simultaneously applying forward pressure to the control column and adding full engine power
J. tail assembly of an airplane
K. force that slows the forward movement of an airplane through the air due to frontal areas and undercarriage resistance
L. proper use of aileron and rudder
M. fine-tuning controls for primary control surfaces
N. type of landing gear with a tail wheel and two main gears on the wings or fuselage
O. curvature of an airfoil
P. occurs when yaw is induced in a stalled airplane
Q. tendency to return to the original trimmed condition
R. retardant force produced when lift is being produced
S. a stall will occur when this is exceeded
T. gyroscopic effect

DISCUSSION QUESTIONS AND EXERCISES

1. Label each part of the airplane shown in Figure 2.1.

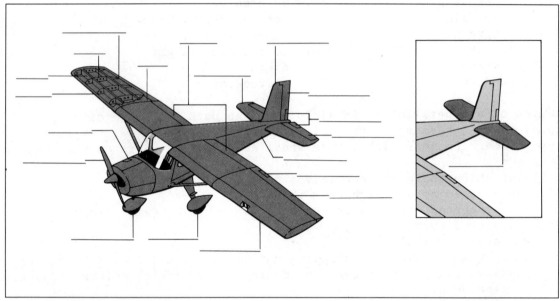

Figure 2.1

2. What are the four forces that affect flight? Explain the relationship among these forces.

3. T F Drag opposes lift and thrust opposes gravity.

4. Explain how lift works when you turn the control column of the airplane to the right.

5. Distinguish between **parasite drag** and **induced drag**.

6. Describe in **your own words** what happens when the wing of an airplane **stalls**. How is a stall related to the **angle of attack** of the airfoil? How is it related to the airplane's airspeed and attitude?

7. Define **pitch, yaw, and roll**. Give an example of each, being certain to explain how each relevant control surface moves and to describe the resultant change in the airplane's attitude.

8. T F When you push the left rudder pedal, the rudder moves to the right and the airplane moves to the left.

9. T F When you push the control column forward, the elevator moves down and the tail of the airplane goes up.

10. T F When you turn the control column to the right, the right rudder moves up and the left rudder moves down, resulting in the airplane rolling to the right.

11. Define **maneuvering speed.** How is this speed related to the airplane's weight? Under what flight conditions is it important?

12. Explain how lowering the **flaps** affects each of the following: takeoff distance, glide path, landing distance, landing speed, and lift.

13. What are **trim tabs**? For what are they used? Give at least one example of the use of trim tabs.

14. T F Elevator trim tabs control movement about the airplane's lateral axis.

15. Define **load factor** and explain how it is related to the stalling speed of the airplane. Using Figure 2.2 find the load factor in G units for banks of (a) 30°, (b) 60°, and (c) 75°.

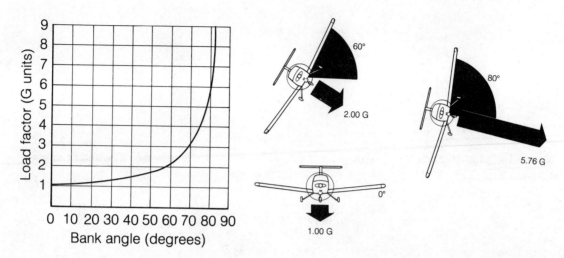

Figure 2.2

16. Explain the relationship among the following terms: relative wind, flight path, angle of attack, and stall.

17. T F Relative wind is in the same direction as and parallel to the flight path of the airplane.

18. T F <u>Lift</u> is the term used to express the relationship between an airfoil's chord and its encounter with the relative wind.

19. T F The point along the trailing edge of an airfoil at which smooth airflow breaks away is called the stalling point.

20. T F The greater the angle of bank is, the lower the stalling speed will be.

21. T F Ground effect often causes an airplane to settle to the surface immediately after becoming airborne.

22. T F An airplane will enter a spin when the elevators lose their effectiveness due to a decrease in the velocity of the relative wind.

2 - 9

23. What is **wake turbulence**? Under what conditions is it most likely to occur? Identify at least three things you should do as a pilot to avoid it.

24. What is the **P-factor**? What is **torque**? How do each of these forces affect the airplane?

25. Briefly describe how you enter a **spin**. Describe the general procedures you are to follow to recover from one.

26. The back edge of the wing is called the _____ edge.
    1--elevated
    2--horizontal
    3--leading
    4--trailing

27. Air resistance over the wings of an airfoil is called
    1--drag.
    2--gravity.
    3--lift.
    4--thrust.

28. When the angle of attack increases, as in a climb or a turn,
    1--induced drag increases.
    2--induced lift increases.
    3--induced thrust increases.
    4--parasite drag increases.

29. What airplane control surface is responsible for movement about the longitudinal axis of rotation?
    1--Aileron.
    2--Elevator.
    3--Flap.
    4--Rudder.

30. What direction does the right aileron move when the control wheel is turned right?
    1--Down.
    2--Left.
    3--Right.
    4--Up.

31. Elevator trim tabs influence movement about the airplane's _____ axis.
    1--elevated
    2--lateral
    3--longitudinal
    4--vertical

32. As the angle of attack increases, induced drag _____ and power must be _____ to fly slower.
    1--decreases; decreased
    2--decreases; increased
    3--increases; decreased
    4--increases; increased

33. Recovering from a stall necessitates
    1--increasing drag.
    2--increasing lift.
    3--reducing thrust.
    4--reducing the angle of attack.

34. Suppose you are crossing the flight path of a large jet airplane that is ahead of you at the same altitude. To avoid wake turbulence, you should
    1--descend and adjust speed to maneuvering speed.
    2--descend and fly parallel to the jet's flight path.
    3--descend below the jet's flight path.
    4--fly above the jet's flight path.

35. Air pressure decreases when the speed of an airflow increases. This principle helps explain the creation of
    1--drag.
    2--lift.
    3--gravity.
    4--thrust.

36. The forward edge of the wing is called the _____ edge.
    1--elevated
    2--horizontal
    3--leading
    4--trailing

37. What airplane control surface is responsible for movement about the lateral axis of rotation?
    1--Aileron.
    2--Elevator.
    3--Flap.
    4--Rudder.

38. What airplane control surface is responsible for movement about the vertical axis of rotation?
    1--Aileron.
    2--Elevator.
    3--Flap.
    4--Rudder.

39. In what direction does the trailing edge of the elevator move when the control column is pushed in?
    1--Down.
    2--Left.
    3--Right.
    4--Up.

40. In what direction does the rudder move when you push the right rudder pedal?
    1--Down.
    2--Left.
    3--Right.
    4--Up.

41. When flaps are lowered, they _____ the camber of the wing.
    1--decrease
    2--increase
    3--reflect
    4--have no effect on

42. When flaps are lowered, they _____ drag and _____ lift.
    1--decrease; decrease
    2--decrease; increase
    3--increase; decrease
    4--increase; increase

43. Changes in the elevator trim tabs lead to changes in the airplane's
    1--camber.
    2--pitch.
    3--roll.
    4--yaw.

44. When the airflow over the wing cannot follow the airfoil surface
    1--lift changes erratically and unpredictably.
    2--lift is created.
    3--lift is destroyed.
    4--lift remains constant.

45. The greater the angle of bank, the _____ load the wings have to support and the _____ the stalling speed.
    1--less; higher
    2--less; lower
    3--more; higher
    4--more; lower

46. As the angle of bank increases, stalling speed
    1--changes erratically and unpredictably.
    2--decreases.
    3--increases.
    4--remains constant.

FAA EXAM QUESTIONS

(Note: All FAA Figures are located in Appendix C)

1. (FAA 1084) The four aerodynamic forces acting on an airplane are
    1--power, velocity, gravity, and drag.
    2--power, velocity, weight, and friction.
    3--thrust, lift, gravity, and weight.
    4--thrust, lift, weight, and drag.

2. (FAA 1086) What is the relationship of lift, drag, thrust, and weight when the airplane is in straight-and-level flight?
    1--Lift equals drag and thrust equal weight.
    2--Lift, drag, and weight equal thrust.
    3--Lift and weight equal thrust and drag.
    4--Lift equals weight and thrust equals drag.

3. (FAA 1085) When are the four aerodynamic forces that act on an airplane in equilibrium?
    1--When the aircraft is at rest on the ground.
    2--When the aircraft is accelerating.
    3--While the aircraft is decelerating.
    4--During unaccelerated flight.

4. (FAA 1087) What makes an airplane turn?
    1--Centrifugal force.
    2--Rudder and aileron.
    3--Horizontal component of lift.
    4--Rudder, aileron, and elevator.

5. (FAA 1090) The term angle of attack is defined as the
    1--angle between the wing chord line and the direction of the relative wind.
    2--angle between the airplane's climb angle and the horizon.
    3--angle formed by the longitudinal axis of the airplane and the chord line of the wing.
    4--specific angle at which the ratio between lift and drag is the highest.

6. (FAA 1089)   Refer to Figure 7.   The acute angle A is the angle of
   1--dihedral.
   2--attack.
   3--camber.
   4--incidence.

7. (FAA 1111)   The angle of attack at which an airplane wing stalls will
   1--increase if the CG is moved forward.
   2--change with an increase in gross weight.
   3--remain the same regardless of gross weight.
   4--decrease if the CG is moved aft.

8. (FAA 1112)   As altitude increases, the indicated airspeed at which a
   given airplane stalls in a particular configuration will
   1--decrease as the true airspeed decreases.
   2--decrease as the true airspeed increases.
   3--remain the same as at low altitude.
   4--increase because the air density becomes less.

9. (FAA 1096)   The purpose of the rudder on an airplane is to
   1--control the yaw.
   2--control the overbanking tendency.
   3--maintain a crab angle to control drift.
   4--maintain the turn after the airplane is banked.

10. (FAA 1098)   The amount of excess load that can be imposed on the wing
    of an airplane depends upon the
    1--position of the CG.
    2--speed of the airplane.
    3--abruptness at which the load is applied.
    4--angle of attack at which the airplane will stall.

11. (FAA 1099)   During an approach to a stall, an increased load factor will
    cause the airplane to
    1--stall at a higher airspeed.
    2--have a tendency to spin.
    3--be more difficult to control.
    4--have a tendency to yaw and roll as the stall is encountered.

12. (FAA 1100)   Which basic flight maneuver increases the load factor on an
    airplane as compared to straight-and-level flight?
    1--Climbs.
    2--Turns.
    3--Stalls.
    4--Slips.

13. (FAA 1091)   Refer to Figure 8.   If an airplane weighs 2,300 lb., what
    approximate weight would the airplane structure be required to support
    during a 60° banked turn while maintaining altitude?
    1--3,400 lb.
    2--4,600 lb.
    3--2,300 lb.
    4--5,200 lb.

14. (FAA 1092)   Refer to Figure 8.   If an airplane weighs 3,300 lb., what approximate weight would the airplane structure be required to support during a 30° banked turn while maintaining altitude?
    1--3,100 lb.
    2--3,960 lb.
    3--1,200 lb.
    4--7,220 lb.

15. (FAA 1093)   Refer to Figure 8.   If an airplane weighs 5,400 lb., what approximate weight would the airplane structure be required to support during a 55° banked turn while maintaining altitude?
    1--5,400 lb.
    2--6,720 lb.
    3--9,180 lb.
    4--10,800 lb.

16. (FAA 1094)   Refer to Figure 8.   The maximum bank that could be made during a level turn without exceeding the maximum positive load factor of a utility category airplane (+4.4 G units) is
    1--71°.
    2--73°.
    3--77°.
    4--83°.

17. (FAA 1088)   One of the main functions of flaps during the approach and landing is to
    1--decrease the angle of descent without increasing the airspeed
    2--permit a touchdown at a higher indicated airspeed.
    3--increase the angle of descent without increasing airspeed.
    4--decrease lift, thus enabling a steeper-than-normal approach to be made.

18. (FAA 1097)   A purpose of wing flaps is to
    1--enable the pilot to make steeper approaches to a landing without increasing airspeed.
    2--relieve the pilot of maintaining continuous pressure on the controls.
    3--decrease wing area to vary the lift.
    4--inject low pressure air into the boundary layer.

19. (FAA 1101)   An airplane said to be inherently stable will
    1--not spin.
    2--be difficult to stall.
    3--require less effort to control.
    4--not overbank during steep turns.

20. (FAA 1118)   Floating caused by the phenomenon of ground effect will be most realized during an approach to land when
    1--at less than the length of the wingspan above the surface
    2--at twice the length of the wingspan above the surface.
    3--a higher-than-normal angle of attack is used.
    4--at speeds approaching a stall.

21. (FAA 1115) Ground effect is most likely to result in which problem?
    1--Settling to the surface abruptly during landing.
    2--Becoming airborne before reaching recommended takeoff speed.
    3--Inability to get airborne even though airspeed is sufficient for
       normal takeoff needs.
    4--A rapid rate of sink and absence of normal cushioning during
       landings.

22. (FAA 1116) Which phenomenon must a pilot be aware of as a result of
    ground effect?
    1--The increase in wingtip vortices.
    2--It results in the least significant reduction of thrust required.
    3--Wing downwash on the tail surfaces increases.
    4--The induced angle of attack and induced drag decreases.

23. (FAA 1117) After takeoff, and after leaving ground effect, the pilot
    will need to
    1--decrease the angle of attack to maintain the same lift coefficient.
    2--increase thrust due to an increase in induced drag.
    3--increased pitch attitude due to a nose down change in moment.
    4--increase thrust to correct a decrease in indicated airspeed.

24. (FAA 1424) Wingtip vortices, the dangerous turbulence that might be
    encountered behind a large aircraft, are created only when that aircraft
    is
    1--operating at high airspeeds.
    2--heavily loaded.
    3--developing lift.
    4--using high-power settings.

25. (FAA 1427) The greatest vortex strength occurs when the generating
    aircraft is
    1--light, "dirty," and fast.
    2--heavy, "dirty," and fast.
    3--heavy, "clean," and slow.
    4--light, "clean," and slow.

26. (FAA 1425) Wingtip vortices created by large aircraft tend to
    1--sink below the aircraft generating the turbulence.
    2--rise into the traffic pattern.
    3--rise into the takeoff or landing path of a crossing runway.
    4--accumulate at the beginning of the takeoff roll.

27. (FAA 1426) When taking off or landing at a busy airport where heavy
    aircraft are operating, one should be particularly alert to the hazards
    of wingtip vortices because this turbulence tends to
    1--rise from a crossing runway into the takeoff or landing path.
    2--rise into the traffic pattern areas surrounding the airport.
    3--sink into the flightpath of aircraft operating below the aircraft
       generating the turbulence.
    4--accumulate at the beginning of the takeoff roll.

28. (FAA 1429) When departing behind a heavy aircraft, the pilot should avoid wake turbulence by maneuvering the aircraft
1--below and downwind from the heavy aircraft.
2--above and upwind from the heavy aircraft.
3--below and upwind from the heavy aircraft.
4--above and downwind from the heavy aircraft.

29. (FAA 1428) The wind condition that requires maximum caution when avoiding wake turbulence on landing is a
1--light, quartering headwind.
2--strong tailwind.
3--strong headwind.
4--light, quartering tailwind.

30. (FAA 1430) When landing behind a large aircraft, the pilot should avoid wake turbulence by staying
1--above the large aircraft's final approach path and landing beyond the large aircraft's touchdown point.
2--below the large aircraft's final approach path and landing before the large aircraft's touchdown point.
3--above the large aircraft's final approach path and landing before the large aircraft's touchdown point.
4--below the large aircraft's final approach path and landing beyond the large aircraft's touchdown point.

31. (FAA 1095) The left turning tendency of an airplane caused by P-factor is the result of the
1--clockwise rotation of the engine and the propeller turning the airplane counterclockwise.
2--propeller blade descending on the right, producing more thrust than the ascending blade on the left.
3--gyroscopic forces applied to the rotating propeller blades acting 90° in advance of the point the force was applied.
4--spiral characteristics of the slipstream air being forced rearward by the rotating propeller.

32. (FAA 1107) P-factor causes the airplane to
1--be unstable around the lateral axis.
2--yaw to the left when at high angles of attack.
3--yaw to the left when at high speeds.
4--be unstable around the vertical and lateral axes.

33. (FAA 1110) In what airspeed and power condition is torque effect the greatest in a single-engine airplane?
1--Low airspeed, high power.
2--Low airspeed, low power.
3--High airspeed, high power.
4--High airspeed, low power.

34. (FAA 1114) In what flight condition must an aircraft be placed in order to spin?
1--Partially stalled with one wing low.
2--Placed in a steep diving spiral.
3--Stalled.
4--Placed in a steep nose-high pitch attitude.

35. (FAA 1113) During a spin to the left,
    1--both wings are stalled.
    2--neither wing is stalled.
    3--the left wing is stalled and the right wing is not stalled.
    4--the right wing is stalled and the left wing is not stalled.

ANSWERS AND EXPLANATIONS

Key Terms and Concepts, Part 1

1. H	5. J	9. I	13. E	17. G
2. R	6. D	10. Q	14. F	18. L
3. M	7. P	11. C	15. O	19. S
4. A	8. B	12. K	16. N	20. T

Key Terms and Concepts, Part 2

1. K	5. R	9. I	13. B	17. J
2. C	6. H	10. E	14. O	18. L
3. G	7. A	11. S	15. F	19. D
4. P	8. M	12. Q	16. N	20. T

Discussion Questions and Exercises

1. See text Figure 2.1.

2. See Study Guide Main Point #2.

3. F--Drag opposes thrust and gravity opposes lift.

4. See Study Guide Main Point #7.

5. See Study Guide Main Point #5.

6. See Study Guide Main Points #6 and #15.

7. See Study Guide Main Point #7.

8. F--The rudder moves to the left.

9. T--The nose also goes down.

10. F--If you substitute aileron for rudder, the answer is true.

11. See Study Guide Main Point #9.

12. See Study Guide Main Point #10.

13. See Study Guide Main Point #10.

14. T--Trim tabs on the elevator influence the airplane's <u>pitch</u> (movement about the lateral axis).

15. See Study Guide Main Point #8 and Figure 2.2. Read <u>up</u> from the bank angle (in degrees) until you intersect the curved function line. Then read <u>over</u> to the load factor (G units). (a) 30° produces a load factor of about 1.2 G units; (b) 60° produces a load factor of 2.0 G units (you should commit this relationship to memory; and (c) 75° produces a load factor of about 4.0 G units.

16. See Study Guide Main Point #6.

17. F--It is in the <u>opposite</u> direction and parallel to the flight path.

18. F--This defines the <u>angle of attack</u>.

19. F--It is called the <u>separation</u> point.

20. F--Stalling speed <u>increases</u> as the angle of bank increases.

21. F--The ground effect frequently causes an airplane to become airborne <u>before</u> sufficient airspeed is obtained to maintain flight above the ground effect level.

22. F--A spin occurs when <u>yaw</u> is induced in a stalled airplane.

23. See Study Guide Main Point #13.

24. See Study Guide Main Point #14.

25. See Study Guide Main Point #16.

26. 4--The rounded, front edge is called the leading edge.

27. 1--Drag opposes thrust and weight opposes lift.

28. 1--When the angle of attack increases, this leads to an increase in induced drag due to greater air resistance.

29. 1--The ailerons control bank, or the amount of roll.

30. 4--The right wing goes down when the airplane rolls right; the aileron goes up to help produce this movement, while the left aileron goes down.

31. 2--Elevator trim tabs are the fine-tuning control surfaces that influence the airplane's pitch (movement about the lateral axis).

32. 4--This is the principle of **slow flight**. Induced drag increases; and to maintain slow flight with an increased angle of attack, more thrust (power) must be added.

33. 4--The first thing to do when you encounter a stall is to reduce the angle of attack while simultaneously adding power (thrust).

34. 4--Stay above the jet's flight path to avoid encountering wake turbulence. The effect created by the wing tips falls toward the ground and moves with the direction of the wind, so flying below the jet may lead to an unexpected encounter.

35. 2--This is Bernoulli's Principle; it helps explain how lift is produced.

36. 3--The back edge is the trailing edge.

37. 2--Rotation about the lateral axis is referred to as pitch.

38. 4--Rotation about the vertical axis is referred to as yaw.

39. 1--Pushing the control column forward results in a downward movement of the trailing edge of the elevator. This produces lift on the elevator surface, and the result is that the tail goes up and the nose goes down.

40. 3--Pushing the right rudder pedal moves the rudder to the right. Once again, the forces of lift operate, this time to move the tail of the airplane to the <u>left</u> and the nose of the airplane to the <u>right</u>.

41. 2--Lowering the flaps increases the wing area, which leads to an increase in both lift and drag.

42. 4--Lowering the flaps increases the wing area, which leads to an increase in both lift and drag.

43. 2--The elevator influences movement about the airplane's lateral axis of rotation (pitch).

44. 3--This is referred to as the separation point, and lift begins to dissipate.

45. 3--Increasing the angle of bank increases the load on the wings and thereby leads to higher stalling speeds.

46. 3--Increasing the angle of bank increases the load on the wings and thereby leads to higher stalling speeds.

FAA Exam Questions

1. 4--These are the four forces.

2. 4--The four forces are balanced in unaccelerated flight. This can be in a climb, in a descent, or in a turn.

3. 4--The four forces are balanced in unaccelerated flight. This can be in a climb, in a descent, or in a turn.

4. 3--An airplane turns because the lifting force is divided into horizontal and vertical components when in a bank.

5. 1--This is the definition of angle of attack.

6.   2--Angle of attack is measured between the chord line and the relative wind.

7.   3--The airplane will stall whenever the critical angle of attack is exceeded. The critical angle of attack is the same for all conditions.

8.   3--As altitude increases, air density decreases. This affects lift, thrust and drag, reducing performance. But it also affects airspeed indications. Although the TRUE AIRSPEED will be greater, the INDICATED AIRSPEED remains the same for all stall and performance figures.

9.   1--Yaw about the vertical axis is controlled by the rudder.

10. 2--The excess load depends upon the excess lift available above stalling speed. High speeds provide more excess lift. A sudden increase of lift, as from wind gusts or sharp control movements, could provide lift in excess of the strength of the airframe causing structural damage.

11. 1--An increased load factor requires more lift, thus the airplane's stall speed is increased.

12. 2--In turns, centrifugal force joins gravity to increase the effective weight which the wings must support.

13. 2--Find the bank angle along the bottom. Proceed vertically to the load factor curve, then horizontally to note the load factor in G units. 60° of bank has a load factor of 2. 2 X 2,300 lb. = 4,600 lb. of force to be supported by the wing.

14. 2--Find the bank angle along the bottom. Proceed vertically to the load factor curve, then horizontally to note the load factor in G units. The load factor for 30° bank angle is about 1.2. 1.2 x 3,300 = 3,960 lb.

15. 3--Find the bank angle along the bottom. Proceed vertically to the load factor curve, then horizontally to note the load factor in G units. The load factor for 55° bank angle is about 1.7. 1.7 X 5,400 = 9,180 lb.

16. 3--In this problem, find 4.4 G on the left, proceed horizontally to the curve, then vertically down to determine maximum bank angle of 77°.

17. 3--Lowering flaps increases the angle of attack, increasing lift at low speeds without increasing the pitch angle.

18. 1--Lowering of the flaps increases angle of attack, increasing lift without increasing speed.

19. 3--When displaced, a stable airplane tends to return to the condition for which it was trimmed.

20. 1--Ground effect occurs when the wing is about one-half of the wingspan distance above the surface.

21. 2--Ground effect may occur when the wing is no more than one-half the wingspan distance from the ground. The airplane gains extra lift from the cushion of an allowing flight at slower speeds.

22. 4--In ground effect the wingtip vortices are reduced and both induced angle of attack and induced drag is decreased.

23. 2--When climbing out of ground effect, induced drag increases and thrust requirements to counter the drag is increased.

24. 3--Wingtip vortices result when lift is being produced. They are stronger when the lift generated is greatest, when airplanes are heavy and slow with gear and flaps up. When an airplane is on takeoff or landing roll there are no vortices.

25. 3--Wingtip vortices result when lift is being produced. They are stronger when the lift generated is greatest, when airplanes are heavy and slow with gear and flaps up. When an airplane is on takeoff or landing roll there are no vortices.

26. 1--Wingtip vortices sink below the aircraft, move with the wind and move outward when striking the ground.

27. 3--Wingtip vortices sink below the aircraft, move with the wind and move outward when striking the ground.

28. 2--Wingtip vortices sink below the aircraft, move with the wind and move outward when striking the ground.

29. 4--Wingtip vortices sink below the aircraft, move with the wind and move outward when striking the ground. Light quartering tailwinds require maximum caution because the vortices may be moved forward over the runway.

30. 1--Wingtip vortices sink below the aircraft, move with the wind and move outward when striking the ground.

31. 2--When the thrust line of the engine-propeller is not aligned with the flight path, the descending and ascending blades are producing different amounts of lift in the plane of flight. At high angle of attack the descending blade is producing more lift, causing the left turning tendency.

32. 2--When the thrust line of the engine-propeller is not aligned with the flight path, the descending and ascending blades are producing different amounts of lift in the plane of flight. At high angles of attack the descending blade is producing more lift, causing the left turning tendency.

33. 1--As the propeller turns clockwise (as viewed from the cockpit), Newton's law of "for every action, there is an equal and opposite reaction" causes the airplane to try to roll left. When on the ground this results in left yaw. Torque has a greater effect at high power and at low speed when aerodynamic effects are less to counter the torque.

34. 3--For an aircraft to spin, the wing must be stalled and a yawing force must be present.

35. 1--In a spin both wings are stalled, but not equally. The outer wing produces more effective lift.

THE POWER PLANT AND ITS SYSTEMS

MAIN POINTS

1. **Reciprocating engines**, the power plant of most general aviation airplanes, produce rotary motion, or **torque**, to do work, which is measured in horsepower. Fuel and air mixed in the **carburetor** flow into the engine's cylinders through intake valves (the intake stroke). Once inside the cylinder the mixture is compressed by the piston (the compression stroke) and ignited by electrical sparks provided by two separate ignition systems. The resulting force (the power stroke) forces the piston downward, producing torque. As the piston continues to move, this time upward (the exhaust stroke), the exhaust valve opens and exhaust fumes are expelled through the **exhaust manifold**. The four strokes of the piston give the engine its name: the **four-stroke cycle**. Piston movement is translated into torque by a series of **connecting rods** that attach to the **crankshaft**. A crankcase encloses the crankshaft and connecting rods. The **propeller** is at the end of the crankshaft. Although some aviation engines are liquid-cooled, most are air-cooled.

2. **Propellers** convert engine torque into forward thrust. Each propeller blade is airfoil-shaped with decreasing angles of attack from the hub (where the propeller attaches to the crankshaft) to the tip. There are two types of propellers, **fixed-pitch propellers**, whose blade angles cannot be changed, and **constant-speed propellers**, whose blade angles can be changed by the pilot during flight. The position of constant-speed blades is controlled by a governor that is connected to the propeller control in the cockpit.

3. Engine power depends upon the rotational speed (RPM) of the propeller (indicated on the **tachometer** in the cockpit) and the pressure of the air/fuel mixture (**manifold pressure**). Power changes are made by moving the **throttle control**. In fixed-pitch airplanes, the amount of power is directly related to RPM and is indicated on the tachometer. Lower air density at higher altitudes leads to a decrease in manifold pressure; this decrease means that **if engine power is held constant, RPM must increase with altitude** (fixed prop only). Airplanes with constant-speed props have both a tachometer and a manifold pressure gauge. When increasing power with a constant-speed prop, first increase RPM and then increase manifold pressure. When decreasing power, first decrease manifold pressure and then decrease RPM.

4.   Some airplanes have liquid engine-cooling systems, but most are air-cooled. Some high-horsepower engines have movable **cowl flaps** to aid cooling during low-speed, high-power flight. A **cylinder head temperature** gauge registers engine temperature in the cockpit.

5.   Engine oil removes internal engine heat and coats the moving parts of the engine. There are two types of engine oil--**nondetergent**, which is typically used during break-in, and **detergent** (ashless-dispersant) oil. Oils are also categorized by their viscosity. The oil system gauges include the **oil pressure gauge**, which should show movement within 30 seconds after a normal engine start and should stay within the green arc during flight, and the **oil temperature gauge**, which should also operate within the green arc during flight.

6.   Aviation gas (avgas) is identified by its **octane number**, which is a measure of how fast it burns. Higher octane fuel burns more slowly and more controlled, thus leading to less rapid, uncontrolled combustion (**detonation**). Various grades of fuel are color-coded for positive identification. The color dyes are typically designed to cancel each other out if different grades are mixed; however, if you mix 80-octane and 100-LL, the resultant color is purple. You can use a **higher** grade of fuel if the proper grade is not available, but **never use a lower grade**. While detonation is one form of abnormal combustion, **preignition** is another. Preignition causes fuel to ignite **before** the spark from the spark plug and creates high pressures in the cylinder. It is often caused by operating at excessively high engine temperatures.

7.   You should make sure that an airplane is **grounded** before starting to fuel it to prevent fire caused by static electrical discharge. You should also make sure that fuel vents are clear and that the fuel is of the proper grade and not contaminated by sediment or water. To help avoid water accumulation in the gas tanks from condensation, it is best to keep the tanks full, particularly when the airplane is left overnight. Furthermore, it is the pilot's responsibility to visually check for the presence of water by draining fuel from the **sumps** located at the lowest point on each tank and from the **fuel strainer**, which is at the lowest point of the engine's fuel system. On low-wing aircraft, the tanks are lower than the engine, thus the need for fuel pumps.

8.   The purpose of the fuel system is to provide the engine with an uninterrupted flow of fuel. All airplanes have **fuel gauges** to indicate fuel levels in each tank, but you should also check visually to determine before a flight how much fuel you have on board. There are two types of fuel systems in light airplanes: **gravity systems**, which are common in high-wing airplanes, and **pump systems**. Fuel pumps may be driven by either the accessory pad or the electrical system. Primary pumps are typically engine driven, while backup or boost pumps are typically electrical. A **fuel selector valve** allows the pilot to select from which tank gas is to flow. (Note: never run a tank dry before switching as this may cause vapor lock.) The **engine primer** allows the pilot to inject fuel directly into the cylinders before starting, a common practice when the engine is cold.

9.   Air and fuel are mixed in the **carburetor**. Opening and closing the throttle adjusts the **throttle valve** (butterfly valve) in the carburetor. As the liquid fuel evaporates into the intake air, it cools rapidly and may

condense and freeze any moisture in the air. The butterfly (throttle) valve area of the carburetor is most susceptible to this type of icing. Carburetor ice is most likely to occur in high humidity when the temperature is between 20°F and 70°F. The first sign of carburetor ice is a loss of RPM (fixed-pitch prop) or a decrease in manifold pressure (constant-speed prop). You may also suspect carburetor ice if airspeed decreases during level flight. The carburetor heat system removes ice from the carburetor by sending heated air into the carburetor and melting the ice that has accumulated. As the ice melts, the engine runs rough as the water goes through the engine. (Note: use of carburetor heat reduces air density, thus the mixture becomes richer and engine power is less than normal.) Since warm air is necessary to melt ice, the engine must be developing power to provide warm air. If your POH recommends using carb heat before landing, apply it before reducing the throttle. Remember that outside air is not filtered, so avoid using carb heat on the ground, particularly in dusty conditions.

10. An alternate way to mix fuel and air without a carburetor is through a fuel injection system, which delivers fuel directly to the cylinders. Such systems are more common with high horsepower engines. They provide a more uniform flow of fuel, provide quicker acceleration, and are not subject to icing. However, they are most costly and they are subject to vapor lock.

11. The mixture control allows you to adjust the ratio of air to fuel. As altitude increases, the mixture becomes more fuel-rich. The mixture control allows you to reduce (lean) the fuel/air ratio. You should change the mixture whenever you change altitude or power settings. Rich mixtures cause the engine to run cooler, but with higher fuel consumption rates. The heat of a too-lean mixture may cause damage.

12. Ignition occurs between the compression and power strokes. The ignition system includes a source of high voltage, a timing device, a distribution system to the cylinders, spark plugs, control switches, and shielded wiring. The airplane's ignition system is the magneto, which typically runs off the engine accessory pad and produces a high-voltage electrical pulse. Airplanes have two magnetos, and each cylinder has two spark plugs (the concept of redundancy). Further, the entire ignition system is independent of other systems and can be stopped only by grounding the magneto or stopping engine rotation. The chances of losing power because of ignition system failure are remote because each magneto has independent spark plugs. Ignition and starter operations are controlled by a single switch with the following settings: Off, R (right magneto), L (left magneto), Both, and Start. An important part of the preflight runup is the magneto check to verify that both magnetos are operating properly. You should expect a small drop in RPM when each magneto is switched off (within allowable limits). If the engine begins to die or you lose more than the allowable RPM, you have a problem. Similarly, if there is no drop in RPM, it may mean that the magneto is not grounded and that any movement of the propeller could start the engine. The proper way to stop the engine is to pull the mixture control to full lean to burn any remaining fuel out of the cylinders.

13. The airplane's electrical system operates on direct current (DC). Voltage is initially provided by a DC battery to get the engine started, and then by the alternator, which is driven by the accessory drive pad. The ammeter measures electrical current flowing into or out of the battery. Some airplanes have load meters that measure the electrical load being placed on

the alternator or generator. The electrical system has a **master switch** that
must be on to activate any of the electrical components. Further, each piece
of equipment has an independent **circuit breaker** or **fuse**, which turns the
equipment off in the event of a malfunction. Circuit breakers can be reset in
flight, but they should never be held in place manually. Fuses must be
replaced with a fuse of the **same or lower** amperage. Always carry extra fuses.

KEY TERMS AND CONCEPTS, PART 1

Match each term or concept (1-24) with the appropriate description (A-X)
below. Each item has only one match.

___	1.	cowl flaps	___ 13.	amps
___	2.	oil	___ 14.	carb heat
___	3.	fuel selector valve	___ 15.	carburetor
___	4.	power stroke	___ 16.	mixture control
___	5.	fuel strainer	___ 17.	manifold pressure gauge
___	6.	fuel injection	___ 18.	preignition
___	7.	master switch	___ 19.	volts
___	8.	exhaust valve	___ 20.	AC
___	9.	alternator	___ 21.	crankshaft
___	10.	throttle valve	___ 22.	ammeter
___	11.	magnetos	___ 23.	float chamber
___	12.	pitch	___ 24.	constant-speed

A. these open and close to control air flowing over the engine
B. part of the carburetor most susceptible to icing
C. located at the lowest point of the engine's fuel system
D. system that counteracts carburetor icing
E. device that controls power to all electrical components
F. measures the amount of stored electrical potential
G. device that allows the pilot to control the air/fuel mixture
H. valve used to select fuel from one tank to another
I. hot carbon particles cause spark plugs to fire early
J. the air/fuel mixture is ignited during this stroke
K. this measures the flow of electrons
L. electron current that flows in cycles
M. an engine-driven, alternating-current generator
N. device that displays air/fuel mixture pressure in the intake air passages
O. system in which fuel goes directly into the cylinders
P. terminology describing propeller blade angle
Q. residual gases leave the cylinder through this
R. device where air and fuel are mixed together
S. heart of most airplane ignition systems
T. product that lubricates the internal parts of an engine
U. propellers whose blade angles can change
V. fuel enters the carburetor and is deposited here first
W. device that measures the alternator's electrical output
X. the propeller is attached directly to this part of the engine

KEY TERMS AND CONCEPTS, PART 2

Match each term or concept (1-24) with the appropriate description (A-X) below. Each item has only one match.

___ 1. connecting rods
___ 2. ground
___ 3. circuit breaker
___ 4. exhaust manifold
___ 5. accelerating system
___ 6. intake valve
___ 7. octane number
___ 8. horsepower
___ 9. tachometer
___ 10. accessory drive pad
___ 11. DC
___ 12. vapor lock

___ 13. detonation
___ 14. oil pressure gauge
___ 15. fixed-pitch
___ 16. primer
___ 17. ashless-dispersant
___ 18. fuel boost pump
___ 19. RPM
___ 20. intake stroke
___ 21. piston
___ 22. leaning
___ 23. two
___ 24. cylinder head gauge

A. capability of suppressing detonation (antiknock value)
B. gears where the crankshaft ends
C. device through which residual gases exit from the engine
D. propellers that cannot change their blade angle
E. bubbles of gas that block the fuel line
F. provides fuel pressure for starting some airplane engines
G. what you should do to prevent fire when refueling an airplane
H. gas burns too rapidly in the combustion chamber
I. free-swinging device attached to the bottom of a piston
J. measure of the speed of the crankshaft's rotation
K. type of oil used in most general aviation airplanes
L. air/fuel mixture enters the cylinder through this
M. air/fuel mixture enters the cylinder during this stroke
N. capacity for doing work
O. electron current that comes in a constant flow
P. device that controls power to a particular airplane instrument
Q. displays pressure of oil being sent to lubricate the engine
R. carburetor system that compensates for sudden throttle movements
S. device that directs raw fuel directly into the cylinder
T. device that displays crankshaft revolutions per minute
U. movable plunger that fits inside the cylinder
V. procedure used to reduce the fuel/air ratio
W. number of magnetos found on most airplanes
X. displays engine temperature in the cockpit

DISCUSSION QUESTIONS AND EXERCISES

1. Briefly explain how piston movement translates into propeller movement.

2.   Distinguish between fixed-pitch and constant-speed propellers. Explain how each operates.

3.   Briefly describe the functions of the tachometer and the manifold pressure gauge. Describe the procedure you should follow when increasing and decreasing power with a constant-speed prop.

4.   Briefly describe the importance and proper use of the oil pressure and oil temperature gauges.

5.   Distinguish among vapor lock, detonation, and preignition.

6.   If your airplane uses 100-octane aviation fuel, would it be acceptable to use 80-octane fuel if 100-octane were not available? Why or why not?

7.   What are the two general types of fuel systems? Why is it important to
check the fuel strainer and wing tank sumps before each flight?

8.   What are the two primary functions of the carburetor? Briefly describe
how a fuel injection system differs from a carburetor system.

9.   What is carburetor icing and where in the carburetor does it typically
occur? Specifically, how does it affect RPM and manifold pressure? Describe
the procedure you should follow if you encounter carburetor icing.

10.   What does the mixture control mechanism do? What is **leaning**?

11. Briefly describe the ignition switch and its proper use for starting and stopping the engine.

12. Describe the preflight procedure for checking the operation of the magneto system. What are **two** indications of a magneto that is malfunctioning?

13. Briefly describe the components and functions of the engine's electrical system. Include a discussion of the master switch, ammeter, voltage regulator, circuit breakers, and alternator.

14. T F If the specified grade of aviation fuel is not available for your airplane, it is best to use a slightly lower octane, but <u>never</u> a higher octane.

15. T F Detonation occurs in a reciprocating aircraft engine when the unburned air/fuel mixture in the cylinder explodes rather than burning evenly.

16. T F It is generally considered good operating practice to check for water in the fuel system only when the aircraft is fueled, since this is the only time the system can collect moisture.

17. T F Float-type carburetor systems provide more even fuel distribution and faster throttle response than do fuel injection systems, but they are less efficient.

18. T F The carburetor's float mechanism seals the chamber and prevents further fuel from entering.

19. T F The engine ignition system of most general aviation airplanes is called dual because it operates independently of other airplane systems.

20. T F Central to the airplane's ignition is the alternator, which typically runs off the accessory drive pad and which produces a high-voltage electrical pulse for the spark plugs.

21. T F With a fixed-pitch propeller airplane, engine power is registered on the tachometer.

22. T F The red line on a tachometer indicates a maximum RPM reading that may be exceeded only in straight-and-level flight.

23. T F Carburetor icing almost always occurs simultaneously at the needle valve and in the float chamber.

24. T F On a warm, sunny day, if the oil pressure does not reach the green arc within 30 seconds after starting the engine, the engine should be shut down.

25. T F One result of permitting an airplane engine to idle for a long period of time while on the ground is that the spark plugs may become fouled.

26. T F If an airplane engine continues to run after the ignition switch is turned to the OFF position, the probable cause is a broken magneto ground wire.

27. T F Applying carburetor heat results in more air going through the throttle valve.

28. T F In case of electrical fire, you should first turn off the master switch.

29. T F The main reason to avoid long engine runups on the ground is to help avoid excessive vibration caused by air moving over the control surfaces.

30. T F During long descents, you should gradually increase the air/fuel mixture.

31. Central to the airplane ignition system is the _____, which typically runs off the engine accessory drive pad and which produces a high-voltage electrical pulse.
    1--alternator
    2--battery
    3--generator
    4--magneto

32. Which of the following is not part of the airplane engine's lubrication system?
    1--Connecting rods.
    2--Pressure sensor.
    3--Sump.
    4--Temperature sensing device.

33. With a constant-speed propeller airplane,
    1--propeller speed should be increased before power is added.
    2--propeller speed should be increased before power is reduced.
    3--propeller speed should be reduced before power is added.
    4--propeller speed should be reduced before power is reduced.

34. What part of the carburetor is most susceptible to ice?
    1--Accelerating pump.
    2--Float chamber.
    3--Mixture control.
    4--Throttle valve.

35. The carburetor heat system directs
    1--cold air away from the carburetor.
    2--moisture away from the carburetor.
    3--warm air to the carburetor.
    4--prewarmed fuel to the carburetor.

36. To properly shut down an airplane engine, first you
    1--pull the mixture control to full lean.
    2--switch the ignition switch to the OFF position.
    3--turn off the master switch.
    4--apply carburetor heat.

37. In what position should the ignition switch be during takeoff?
    1--Both.
    2--L.
    3--R.
    4--Start.

38. Suppose battery and alternator fail during flight. In this situation,
    1--avionics equipment would also fail.
    2--cylinder head temperature would increase and oil pressure would decrease.
    3--the engine-driven fuel boost pump would fail, leading to engine failure, as well as loss of all avionics equipment, lights, and AC instruments.
    4--the engine ignition system, fuel gauges, lighting system, and all avionics would fail.

39. Which of the following statements is correct?
    1--Carburetor icing most likely would form when the air temperature is between 20°F and 70°F, with visible moisture or high humidity.
    2--The carburetor heater is a de-icing device that heats the air after it enters the carburetor.
    3--The first indication of carburetor icing in a fixed-pitch propeller airplane is an increase in RPM, followed by a rapid decrease in RPM.
    4--Carburetor icing occurs whenever the temperature falls below freezing (32°F).

40. Which of the following statements about spark plug fouling is correct?
    1--Carbon fouling of the plugs is caused primarily by operating the engine at excessively high cylinder head temperatures.
    2--Excessive heat in the combustion chamber of a cylinder causes oil to form on the center electrode of the plug, causing it to preignite.
    3--Permitting the engine to idle for a long period of time on the ground is the best way to clean fouled spark plugs.
    4--Spark plug fouling results from operating with an excessively rich mixture.

41. Detonation in an airplane engine
    1--can be detected easily by a pinging sound, similar to the knocking one sometimes encounters in an automobile engine.
    2--is most likely to occur immediately after starting a cold engine.
    3--is usually caused by a fuel/air mixture that is too rich.
    4--may be caused by opening the throttle too abruptly when the engine is running at slow speeds.

42. A low air-to-fuel mixture ratio is called
    1--detonated.
    2--lean.
    3--preignited.
    4--rich.

43. The engine ignition system in most general aviation airplanes is called dual because
    1--each cylinder fires independently of every other cylinder.
    2--it has two separate and independent magneto systems.
    3--it is independent of other airplane systems.
    4--the magnetos are powered by the engine accessory drive pad.

44. The engine ignition system
    1--can be stopped by turning off the magnetos.
    2--can be stopped by stopping engine rotation.
    3--is independent of other airplane electrical systems.
    4--all of the above.

45. The typical general-aviation airplane cylinder has _____ piston(s) and _____ spark plug(s).
    1--one; one
    2--one; two
    3--two; one
    4--two; two

46. What part of the airplane's electrical system must be activated before any of the component electrical parts can be activated?
    1--Alternator.
    2--Battery.
    3--Circuit breaker.
    4--Master switch.

47. What part of the airplane's electrical system will automatically turn off a piece of equipment that is not functioning properly?
    1--Alternator.
    2--Ammeter.
    3--Circuit breaker.
    4--Voltage regulator.

48. With a fixed-pitch propeller airplane, what instrument registers engine power?
    1--Ammeter.
    2--Manifold pressure gauge.
    3--Suction gauge.
    4--Tachometer.

49. With a constant-speed propeller airplane, power should be _____ before propeller speed is _____.
    1--added; added
    2--added; reduced
    3--reduced; added
    4--reduced; reduced

50. In an airplane equipped with a constant-speed propeller and a float-type carburetor, the first indication of carburetor ice most likely would be
    1--a drop in oil temperature and cylinder head temperature.
    2--a drop in manifold pressure.
    3--engine roughness.
    4--a loss of RPM.

51. In case of electrical fire, first you should
    1--check the circuit breakers to determine if you have lost electrical
        power.
    2--continue to the nearest airport and land.
    3--declare an emergency.
    4--shut off the master switch.

FAA EXAM QUESTIONS

1. (FAA 1417) What is an advantage of a constant-speed propeller?
    1--Permits the pilot to select and maintain a desired cruising speed.
    2--Allows a higher cruising speed than possible with a fixed-pitch
        propeller.
    3--Provides a smoother operation with stable RPM and eliminates
        vibrations.
    4--Permits the pilot to select the blade angle for the most efficient
        performance.

2. (FAA 1416) How is engine operation controlled on an engine equipped
   with a constant-speed propeller?
   1--The throttle controls power output as registered on the manifold
      pressure gauge and the propeller control regulates engine RPM.
   2--The throttle controls power output as registered on the manifold
      pressure gauge and the propeller control regulates a constant blade
      angle.
   3--The throttle controls engine RPM as registered on the tachometer and
      the mixture control regulates the power output.
   4--The throttle controls engine RPM as registered on the tachometer and
       the propeller control regulates the power output.

3. (FAA 1418) A precaution for the operation of an engine equipped with a
   constant-speed propeller is to
   1--avoid high RPM settings with high manifold pressure.
   2--avoid high RPM settings with low manifold pressure.
   3--always use a rich mixture with high RPM settings.
   4--avoid high manifold pressure settings with low RPM.

4. (FAA 1419) When starting an airplane engine by hand propping, it is
   extremely important that a competent pilot
   1--call "contact" before touching the propeller.
   2--be at the controls in the cockpit.
   3--in the cockpit be in charge and call out all commands.
   4--turn the propeller and call out all commands.

5. (FAA 1420) The first action after starting an aircraft engine should be
   to
   1--adjust for proper RPM and check for desired indications on the engine
      gauges.
   2--place the magneto or ignition switch momentarily in the OFF position
      to check for proper grounding.
   3--test each brake and the parking brake.
   4--visually clear the area for people and obstacles.

6. (FAA 1421) What action can a pilot take to aid in cooling an engine
   that is overheating during a climb?
   1--Lean the mixture to best power condition.
   2--Increase RPM and reduce climb speed.
   3--Reduce rate of climb and increase airspeed.
   4--Increase RPM and climb speed.

7. (FAA 1422) What is one procedure to aid in cooling an engine that is
   overheating?
   1--Enrichen the fuel mixture.
   2--Increase the RPM.
   3--Reduce the airspeed.
   4--Use alternate air.

8. (FAA 1040) For internal cooling, reciprocating aircraft engines are
   especially dependent on
   1--a properly functioning thermostat.
   2--air flowing over the exhaust manifold.
   3--the circulation of lubricating oil.
   4--a lean fuel/air mixture.

9. (FAA 1038) An abnormally high engine oil temperature indication may be caused by
    1--the oil level being too low.
    2--operating with a too high viscosity oil.
    3--operating with an excessively rich mixture.
    4--the oil level being too high.

10. (FAA 1039) Excessively high engine temperatures, either in the air or on the ground, will
    1--cause damage to heat-conducting hoses and warping of the cylinder cooling fins.
    2--cause loss of power, excessive oil consumption, and possible permanent internal engine damage.
    3--not appreciably affect an aircraft engine in either environment.
    4--increase fuel consumption and may increase power due to the increased heat.

11. (FAA 1043) Detonation occurs in a reciprocating aircraft engine when
    1--the spark plugs are fouled or shorted out or the wiring is defective.
    2--hot spots in the combustion chamber ignite the fuel/air mixture in advance of normal ignition.
    3--there is too rich a fuel/air mixture.
    4--the unburned charge in the cylinders explodes instead of burning normally.

12. (FAA 1045) If the grade of fuel used in an aircraft engine is lower than specified for the engine, it will most likely cause
    1--a mixture of fuel and air that is not uniform in all cylinders.
    2--lower cylinder head temperatures.
    3--an increase in power which could overstress internal engine components.
    4--detonation.

13. (FAA 1044) If a pilot suspects that the engine (with a fixed-pitch propeller) is detonating during climb-out after takeoff, normally the corrective action to take would be to
    1--increase the rate of climb.
    2--retard the throttle.
    3--lean the mixture.
    4--apply carburetor heat.

14. (FAA 1046) The uncontrolled firing of the fuel/air charge in advance of normal spark ignition is known as
    1--combustion.
    2--pre-ignition.
    3--atomizing.
    4--detonation.

15. (FAA 1048) Which would most likely cause the cylinder head temperature and engine oil temperature gauges to exceed their normal operating ranges?
    1--Using fuel that has a lower-than-specified fuel rating.
    2--Using fuel that has a higher-than-specified fuel rating.
    3--Operating with higher-than-normal oil pressure.
    4--Operating with the mixture control set too rich.

16. (FAA 1049) What type fuel can be substituted for an aircraft if the recommended octane is not available?
    1--The next higher octane aviation gas.
    2--The next lower octane aviation gas.
    3--Unleaded automotive gas of the same octane rating.
    4--Unleaded automotive gas of the next higher rating.

17. (FAA 1042) Filling the tank after the last flight of the day is considered a good operating procedure because this will
    1--force any existing water to the top of the tank away from the fuel lines to the engine.
    2--prevent expansion of the fuel by eliminating airspace in the tanks.
    3--prevent moisture condensation by eliminating airspace in the tanks.
    4--eliminate vaporization of the fuel.

18. (FAA 1047) On aircraft equipped with fuel pumps, the practice of running a fuel tank dry before switching tanks is considered unwise because
    1--the engine-driven fuel pump or electric fuel boost pump may draw air into the fuel system and cause vapor lock.
    2--the engine-driven fuel pump is lubricated by fuel and operating on a dry tank may cause pump failure.
    3--any foreign matter in the tank will be pumped into the fuel system.
    4--the fuel pump is located above the bottom portion of the fuel tank.

19. (FAA 1031) The operating principle of float-type carburetors is based on the
    1--automatic metering of air at the venturi as the aircraft gains altitude.
    2--difference in air pressure at the venturi throat and the air inlet.
    3--increase in air velocity in the throat of a venturi causing an increase in air pressure.
    4--measurement of the fuel flow into the induction system.

20. (FAA 1108) Which condition is most favorable to the development of carburetor icing?
    1--Any temperature below freezing and a relative humidity of less than 50 percent.
    2--Temperature between 32°F and 50°F and low humidity.
    3--Temperature between 0°F and 20°F and high humidity.
    4--Temperature between 20°F and 70°F and high humidity.

21. (FAA 1109) The possibility of carburetor icing should always be considered when operating in conditions where the
    1--temperature is as high as 95°F and there is visible moisture.
    2--relative humidity range is from 25 percent to 100 percent, regardless of temperature.
    3--relative humidity is between 30 percent and 100 percent and the temperature is between 0°F and 32°F.
    4--temperature is as high as 70°F and the relative humidity is high.

22. (FAA 1035) If an aircraft is equipped with a fixed-pitch propeller and a float-type carburetor, the first indication of carburetor ice would most likely be
1--a drop in oil temperature and cylinder head temperature.
2--engine roughness.
3--an increase, then drop, in manifold pressure.
4--loss of RPM.

23. (FAA 1032) The presence of carburetor ice in an aircraft equipped with a fixed-pitch propeller can be verified by applying carburetor heat and noting
1--an increase in RPM and then a gradual decrease in RPM.
2--a decrease in RPM and then a constant RPM indication.
3--an immediate increase in RPM with no further change in RPM.
4--a decrease in RPM and then a gradual increase in RPM.

24. (FAA 1033) Applying carburetor heat will
1--result in more air going through the carburetor.
2--not affect the mixture.
3--enrich the fuel/air mixture.
4--lean the fuel/air mixture.

25. (FAA 1034) What change occurs in the fuel/air mixture when carburetor heat is applied?
1--A decrease in RPM results from the lean mixture.
2--No change occurs in the fuel/air mixture.
3--The fuel/air mixture becomes leaner.
4--The fuel/air mixture becomes richer.

26. (FAA 1036) The use of carburetor heat tends to
1--decrease engine output and increase operating temperature.
2--decrease engine output and decrease operating temperature.
3--increase engine output and increase operating temperature.
4--increase engine output and decrease operating temperature.

27. (FAA 1030) In comparison to fuel injection systems, float-type carburetor systems are generally considered to be
1--equally susceptible to icing as a fuel injection unit.
2--susceptible to icing only when visible moisture is present.
3--more susceptible to icing than a fuel injection unit.
4--less susceptible to icing than a fuel injection unit.

28. (FAA 1041) If the engine oil temperature and cylinder head temperature gauges have exceeded their normal operating range, the pilot may have been
1--operating with the mixture set too rich.
2--operating with higher-than-normal oil pressure.
3--using fuel that has a higher-than-specified fuel rating.
4--operating with too much power and with the mixture set too lean.

29. (FAA 1050) While cruising at 9,500 ft. MSL, the fuel/air mixture is properly adjusted. If a descent to 4,500 ft. MSL is made without readjusting the mixture control,
1--the fuel/air mixture may become excessively lean.
2--there will be more fuel in the cylinders than is needed for normal combustion, and the excess fuel will absorb heat and cool the engine.
3--the excessively rich mixture will create higher cylinder head temperatures and may cause detonation.
4--the fuel/air mixture may become excessively rich.

30. (FAA 1051) During the runup at a high-elevation airport, a pilot notes a slight engine roughness that is not affected by the magneto check but grows worse during the carburetor heat check. Under these circumstances, which of the following would be the most logical initial action?
1--Check the results obtained with a leaner setting of the mixture control.
2--Taxi back to the flight line for a maintenance check.
3--Reduce manifold pressure to control detonation.
4--Check to see that the mixture control is in the full-rich position.

31. (FAA 1052) The basic purpose of adjusting the fuel/air mixture control at altitude is to
1--decrease the amount of fuel in the mixture in order to compensate for increased air density.
2--decrease the fuel flow in order to compensate for decreased air density.
3--increase the amount of fuel in the mixture to compensate for the decrease in pressure and density of the air.
4--increase the fuel/air ratio for flying at altitude.

32. (FAA 1037) One purpose of the dual ignition system on an aircraft engine is to provide for
1--improved engine performance.
2--uniform heat distribution.
3--balanced cylinder head pressure.
4--easier starting.

ANSWERS AND EXPLANATIONS

Key Terms and Concepts, Part 1

1.	A	7.	E	13.	K	19.	F
2.	T	8.	Q	14.	D	20.	L
3.	H	9.	M	15.	R	21.	X
4.	J	10.	B	16.	G	22.	W
5.	C	11.	S	17.	N	23.	V
6.	O	12.	P	18.	I	24.	U

Key Terms and Concepts, Part 2

1. I	7. A	13. H	19. J
2. G	8. N	14. Q	20. M
3. P	9. T	15. D	21. U
4. C	10. B	16. S	22. V
5. R	11. O	17. K	23. W
6. L	12. E	18. F	24. X

Discussion Questions and Exercises

1. See Study Guide Main Point #1.

2. See Study Guide Main Point #2.

3. See Study Guide Main Point #3.

4. See Study Guide Main Point #5.

5. See Study Guide Main Points #6 and #10.

6. See Study Guide Main Point #6.

7. See Study Guide Main Point #8.

8. See Study Guide Main Points #9 and #10.

9. See Study Guide Main Point #9.

10. See Study Guide Main Point #11.

11. See Study Guide Main Point #12.

12. See Study Guide Main Point #12.

13. See Study Guide Main Point #13.

14. F--You can use a higher octane, but not a lower one.

15. T--Definition.

16. F--It should be checked before **every** flight.

17. F--Fuel injection systems distribute fuel more evenly and are faster in response to throttle changes.

18. T--Self-explanatory.

19. F--It is considered dual because it has two separate and independent magneto systems.

20. F--This defines the magneto, not the alternator.

21. T--Definition.

22. F—This is a value that should **never** be exceeded.

23. F—It almost always occurs near the throttle valve.

24. T—Something is probably amiss.

25. T—Spark plug fouling may occur due to the rich mixture used for most ground operations.

26. T—One reason for the runup is to make certain the magnetos are properly grounded; if they do **not** decrease in RPM when checked, they may be improperly grounded (that is, any movement of the propeller may cause the engine to start).

27. F—It causes the mixture to become richer. Since warm air is less dense than cold air, the mixture runs richer.

28. T—This causes **all** electrical systems to stop (except the ignition system), after which you can test them individually using the various circuit breakers.

29. F—One reason is to keep the engine from overheating; it also helps to prevent spark plug fouling.

30. T—As altitude decreases, air density increases, so you have to increase the amount of fuel in the mixture to compensate.

31. 4—Definition.

32. 1—Connecting rods are part of the crankshaft system.

33. 1—Increase RPM before adding power. Decrease power before decreasing RPM.

34. 4—The throttle valve (butterfly valve) is the most susceptible place for carburetor ice to form.

35. 3—This is the main function of the carb heat system. Remember that the air is unfiltered, so avoid using carb heat on the ground, particularly in dusty conditions.

36. 1—The first thing to do is to starve the cylinders of fuel by pulling the mixture control to full lean.

37. 1—Definition. Both magnetos must be used to provide the most efficient engine operation.

38. 1—Remember that the electrical system is independent of the ignition system. The ignition system would continue to function properly, but things such as the avionics, which are part of the electrical system, would fail.

39. 1—Carburetor ice is most likely to form in conditions of high humidity and when the temperature is between 20°F and 70°F.

40. 4--Excessively rich mixtures lead to spark plug fouling. Permitting the engine to idle for long periods of time also contributes. High cylinder head temperatures help prevent fouling.

41. 4--This is one cause of detonation. Control movements should be applied smoothly, not abruptly.

42. 4--Definition.

43. 2--Two magneto systems provide redundancy and lead to increased engine efficiency.

44. 4--All of these statements are true. Since the magnetos are tied to engine rotation, both effectively stop the engine. Further, the ignition system is totally independent of the other electrical systems on the airplane.

45. 2--Each cylinder has two spark plugs, part of the redundancy of the airplane's ignition system.

46. 4--The master switch activates the electrical system.

47. 3--This is the job of the circuit breakers (or fuses).

48. 4--Definition. With a constant-speed propeller airplane, engine power is registered on the manifold pressure gauge.

49. 4--When decreasing power, you should first decrease manifold pressure, then decrease propeller speed (RPM). When increasing power, you should first increase RPM, then increase manifold pressure.

50. 2--Manifold pressure would decrease first. In a fixed-prop airplane, the first indication would be a drop in RPM, which is a direct reflection of engine power.

51. 4--Since the master switch controls the airplane's electrical system (but not the ignition system), this should be shut down first until you can determine the origin of the problem.

FAA Exam Questions

1. 4--The propeller is an airfoil. Different angles of attack are best for various flight conditions. The pilot can adjust the blade angle to obtain the most efficient performance for the specific flight conditions.

2. 1--The throttle controls the power output by adjusting the flow of the fuel/air mixture to the cylinders. In a constant-speed propeller engine, the output is measured by the pressure in the manifold. The RPM is regulated by the propeller control and the governor.

3. 4--When the RPM is kept low by the governor and the manifold pressure of the fuel/air mixture is high, the internal pressures in the cylinders will be great. If the pressures caused by the burning of the fuel/air mixture are too

great, damage can occur to the cylinders and/or pistons. When increasing power, increase RPM first, then advance the throttle. When decreasing power, reduce the throttle first, then reduce RPM.

4. 2--Hand propping can be hazardous. Two persons are required, one to pull the prop and another in the cockpit to hold the brakes and operate the engine controls.

5. 1--After starting, the RPM must be adjusted to the recommended RPM; too low can cause vibration, too high may damage a cold engine. The gauges must be checked to ensure that pressures and temperatures are within limits. It is especially necessary to have adequate oil pressure for cooling and lubrication.

6. 3--Increased airspeed increases the cooling air flow around the cylinders. Reducing rate of climb while keeping a constant power setting will increase airspeed.

7. 1--Richer mixtures burn cooler.

8. 3--The oil lubricates the parts to reduce friction and takes away heat to be dissipated in the oil cooler.

9. 1--Oil serves to cool as well as lubricate. When the quantity is low, the transfer of heat from cylinders to oil then to the oil cooler is reduced.

10. 2--High engine temperatures can damage the metal of the engine which may permit oil to escape by the rings. Also power will be lost.

11. 4--Detonation occurs when the fuel/air mixture is too lean, causing excessive heat, or when using a lower grade of fuel than specified by the manufacturers.

12. 4--Higher grades of fuel burn normally at higher temperatures, lower grades burn at lower temperatures.

13. 2--Reducing power will reduce the heat.

14. 2--Preignition occurs when the ignition of fuel happens before the spark plugs fire.

15. 1--Lower grades of fuel burn at lower temperatures causing higher internal temperatures.

16. 1--Lower octane might cause detonation and damage, higher octane is safe.

17. 3--When air cools, moisture may condense. When fuel is low, there is more air to provide moisture.

18. 1--Vapor lock may occur when air is drawn into the fuel lines, blocking fuel/air flow to the cylinders.

19. 2--The acceleration of the air through the venturi reduces the pressure, which draws the fuel into the airstream.

20. 4--Moisture is required for icing. Even though the ambient air is well above freezing, within the carburetor the temperature is reduced because of the acceleration and expansion, plus the cooling as the fuel vaporizes.

21. 4--Moisture is required for icing. Even though the ambient air is well above freezing, within the carburetor the temperature is reduced because of the acceleration and expansion, plus the cooling as the fuel vaporizes.

22. 4--Carburetor ice restricts the air flow; the fuel/air mixture becomes richer.

23. 4--The increase of temperature melts the ice, and the water reduces performance, as does the less dense warmer air. After the melted water is gone, RPM will increase.

24. 3--The heated air is less dense, thus the mixture is richer.

25. 4--The heated air is less dense, thus the mixture is richer.

26. 1--Carburetor heat reduces air density, thus reducing output. Additionally, it increases the operating temperature.

27. 3--Since the fuel injection system mixes the fuel and air at the cylinder, icing is less likely.

28. 4--A lean mixture causes a higher temperature as does high power settings.

29. 1--As altitude decreases, the air density increases, thus the fuel/air mixture becomes lean.

30. 1--At high elevations the air is less dense, thus the fuel/air mixture may be excessively rich. Carburetor heat also makes the air less dense. Leaning the mixture will reduce the fuel portion of the mixture.

31. 2--At altitude, the air is less dense. Reducing the mixture reduces fuel portion of the mixture to compensate for the lesser air density.

32. 1--The two spark plugs in each cylinder provide better burning of the fuel/air mixture.

FLIGHT INSTRUMENTS

MAIN POINTS

1. Basic flight instruments are classified by what they do and by how they work. They provide information about the airplane's attitude, flight path, and performance.

2. The **pitot-static system** measures the pressure of air that hits the airplane head-on (ram air) and the pressure of the still air (static air). The **pitot tube** captures ram air and transmits that pressure to the **airspeed indicator**. The **static ports**, mounted at a 90° angle from the direction of flight, receive air at outside atmospheric pressure. Static pressure is used as a reference for determining the airplane's speed through the air. Static air is also routed to the **altimeter** and the **vertical-speed indicator**. Clogged pitot tubes or static ports will affect the readings.

3. The difference between pitot pressure and static pressure is **dynamic pressure**; it is represented on the airspeed indicator as **indicated airspeed (IAS)**. This is speed through the air, not over the ground, and is the same for takeoffs and landings, regardless of the airplane's altitude. **Calibrated airspeed (CAS)** is indicated airspeed corrected for erroneous pressures read by the static port. **True airspeed (TAS)** is airspeed corrected for altitude and temperature. True airspeed can be approximated by increasing indicated airspeed by about 2 percent per 1,000 ft. of altitude above mean sea level (MSL).

4. There are several airspeeds, or V (velocity) speeds, on the airspeed indicator. The **white arc** is the flap operating range. The low end of the scale represents V_{s0}, the stall speed in the landing configuration. The high end of the white arc represents V_{fe}, the maximum flap extension speed. The **green arc** indicates the normal operating range. V_{s1} is the stall speed in a specified configuration, normally with flaps and gear up, and is at the low end of the green arc. At the upper end is V_{no}, the maximum structural cruising speed. The **yellow arc** represents caution. You may operate in this range as long as there is no turbulence. The yellow arc ends at the **red line**

speed, or V_{ne}, which is the never-exceed speed. V_a, maneuvering speed, is not depicted on the airspeed indicator because it varies with the weight of the airplane; V_a is less for a light airplane.

5.   The altimeter measures the height of the airplane above some constant reference point (for example, sea level). It does not measure the height above the ground; but, by knowing the height of the terrain and the obstacles upon it, you can calculate the distance between you and the terrain. The altimeter is a barometer that measures changes in atmospheric pressure. As altitude increases, pressure decreases. Pressure also changes as the weather changes, and so it is important to keep adjusting the altimeter to reflect these changing conditions.

6.   There are several types of altitude. **Pressure-altitude** is the reading on the altimeter when the Kollsman window is set to standard sea level pressure of 29.92. **True altitude** is the height above **mean sea level** (MSL). **Indicated altitude** is what the altimeter reads at any point in time. The indicated altitude will be the same as true altitude at sea level and under standard conditions when the current altimeter setting is in the Kollsman window; at higher altitudes true and indicated altitudes are approximately the same. **Absolute altitude** is the airplane's altitude **above ground level**. The altimeter translates changes in pressure to changes in altitude. The conversion formula is approximately 1 in. of mercury decrease for each 1,000 ft. in elevation. Altimeters are not always perfect, however, due to inherent limitation such as scale error, friction error, and hysteresis. Finally, remember that as atmospheric conditions change, so does the barometric pressure, which in turn affects the altitude reading. The saying "From a high to a low, look out below" refers to the condition in which you fly from a high-pressure area to a low-pressure area. Unless you reset the value in the Kollsman window, the altimeter will indicate that you are higher than you in fact are, a condition that can have disastrous consequences when you get closer to an obstruction or the ground. The same saying also applies to changes that occur in the temperature along your route of flight.

7.   Closely allied to the altimeter is the **vertical-speed indicator** (VSI), which measures the rate of descent or climb, typically in feet per minute. Due to their construction, most VSIs lag behind the airplane's performance and should not be relied upon during the entry into a climb or descent.

8.   The **magnetic compass** indicates direction relative to magnetic north. Its primary practical value is a reference force for the heading indicator. There are several limitations to its use. First, it points to magnetic north rather than true north. This difference is called **variation** (to be discussed in a later chapter in detail). Second, it can be affected by other instruments and radios, referred to as **deviation** errors. Third, the compass will dip when the airplane accelerates or decelerates on easterly or westerly headings. A handy way to remember these **acceleration-deceleration** errors is ANDS--Accelerate-North; Decelerate-South. Fourth, there are **northerly-southerly turning** errors. When you turn from a **northerly** heading, the compass will initially indicate a turn in the **opposite** direction and continue to lag through the turn. When you turn from a **southerly** heading, it will register a turn in the **same** direction but at an accelerated rate. Finally, in turbulent air, the magnetic compass may be subject to **oscillation** error.

9. **Gyroscopic instruments** include the attitude indicator, turn coordinator, and heading indicator. A gyroscope operates according to two principles: rigidity in space and precession. The **attitude indicator** or **artificial horizon** is a graphic display of the airplane, sky, and ground. It represents the airplane with reference to the horizon and indicates changes exactly when they occur, as when the airplane banks or pitches up or down. The **turn coordinator** indicates the rate of turn and provides information about yaw (inclinometer). The ball in the inclinometer indicates whether the airplane is slipping or skidding in a turn. A **slip** results when the rate of turn is too slow for the angle of bank. A **skid** results when the rate of turn is too fast for the angle of bank. Corrections can be effected by "stepping on the ball" with the appropriate rudder pedal. The **heading indicator**, or **directional gyro**, displays the airplane's heading. It must be set by reference to an established heading such as the magnetic compass either on the ground or in straight-and-level flight.

10. Airplane gyro instruments are typically powered by either electrical power or vacuum (air pressure) systems. In most airplanes, the turn coordinator and attitude indicator are powered independently so that if one system fails, the pilot still has a backup source of information, referred to as the concept of **redundancy**.

11. Most instrument panels have a **T arrangement** with the attitude indicator in the middle, flanked on either side by the airspeed indicator and altimeter. The heading indicator completes the leg of the **T**. It is typically flanked by the turn coordinator and vertical-speed indicator. The process of checking and rechecking instruments against one another is called **cross-check**. It is important to safe flight, but it is not a substitute for constantly referring to what is going on outside the airplane. Checking back and forth between the outside world and the flight instruments is called **composite flying**.

KEY TERMS AND CONCEPTS, PART 1

Match each term or concept (1-24) with the appropriate description (A-X) below. Each item has only one match.

___ 1. deviation
___ 2. V_{fe}
___ 3. magnetic compass
___ 4. indicated altitude
___ 5. altimeter
___ 6. precession
___ 7. north
___ 8. cross-check
___ 9. variation
___ 10. ram air
___ 11. composite flying
___ 12. absolute altitude
___ 13. 1,000
___ 14. knots
___ 15. gyroscope
___ 16. vertical-speed indicator
___ 17. pitot-static system
___ 18. true airspeed
___ 19. V_{s0}
___ 20. V_{ne}
___ 21. static ports
___ 22. Kollsman window
___ 23. south
___ 24. oscillation errors

A. maximum flap extension speed
B. altitude of an airplane above ground level (AGL)
C. movement of a gyro's spin axis due to some external force
D. turning the airplane from this heading causes the magnetic compass to initially indicate a turn in the opposite direction
E. what the altimeter indicates at any point in time
F. air that impacts the airplane head-on
G. modern aviation uses this to measure speed and distances
H. instrument that measures altitude
I. instrument that measures the rate of climb or descent
J. magnetic compass errors due to metallic or electrical cockpit components
K. process of checking and rechecking flight instruments against one another
L. system that measures and displays information about differential air pressure
M. 1 in. of mercury equals a change in altitude of _____ ft.
N. angle between magnetic north and true north
O. a mass spinning about an axis
P. cross-referencing the world outside the cockpit with the flight instruments
Q. instrument that measures the airplane's heading with respect to magnetic north
R. receptacles where air at outside atmospheric pressure enters
S. stall speed in the landing configuration
T. errors in magnetic compass readings during turbulent flight
U. speed through the air, corrected for altitude and temperature
V. never-exceed airspeed
W. direction the magnetic compass turns when decelerating
X. window on altimeter that displays barometric pressure correction values

KEY TERMS AND CONCEPTS, PART 2

Match each term or concept (1-20) with the appropriate description (A-T) below. Each item has only one match.

___ 1. pitot tube
___ 2. heading indicator
___ 3. barometer
___ 4. airspeed indicator
___ 5. turn coordinator
___ 6. indicated airspeed
___ 7. gimbals
___ 8. calibrated airspeed
___ 9. redundancy
___ 10. attitude indicator
___ 11. inclinometer
___ 12. pressure-altitude
___ 13. true altitude
___ 14. acceleration-deceleration
___ 15. 75
___ 16. skid
___ 17. vacuum system
___ 18. northerly turning error
___ 19. 3° per second
___ 20. slip

A. difference between ram air pressure and static air pressure
B. altitude read from the altimeter when it is set at 29.92
C. another name for the artificial horizon
D. gyroscopic instrument that displays the airplane's heading
E. the magnetic compass indicates a turn in the opposite direction
F. airspeed corrected for pitot-static vent position and other mechanical losses
G. results when the rate of turn is too fast for the angle of bank
H. instrument at the heart of most altimeters
I. number of feet of tolerance suggested by the FAA in altitude difference between the altimeter and field elevation
J. instrument that tells how fast you are moving through the air
K. object's height above mean sea level (MSL)
L. power system that converts engine motion to air pressure
M. interconnected frames used to suspend a rotating mass
N. device that captures ram air
O. concept: two independent systems performing the same function
P. instrument that provides the pilot with yaw information
Q. ball in the turn coordinator that indicates skids and slips
R. magnetic compass errors that occur during changes in airspeed
S. standard rate turn
T. results when the rate of turn is too slow for the bank angle

DISCUSSION QUESTIONS AND REVIEW EXERCISES

1. What flight instruments require pitot air pressure to operate? Which ones require static pressure? Which ones require both?

2. T F Airspeed is not the same as groundspeed.

3. What is the difference between pitot pressure and static pressure? How is this related to calibrated airspeed?

4. What happens to air pressure as measured by the static ports as altitude increases? Why?

5. Name and define the four types of altitude necessary for the safe operation of an airplane.

6. Suppose you depart Denver (elevation 5,280 ft. MSL) and fly to Vinland Valley, Kansas (elevation 890 ft. MSL). The altimeter reads 29.96 when you depart Denver and 29.96 when you land at Vinland. How many feet have you gained or lost in actual altitude during your trip due to changes in atmospheric conditions?

7. Suppose in Question #6 Vinland Valley had a barometric reading of 28.74 when you landed. Had you not changed your altimeter to reflect this change, something that is _required_ by the FAA, what would your altimeter have read when you landed at Vinland Valley?

8. Suppose in Question #6 the temperature in Denver was 95°F when you left and 67°F at Vinland Valley when you landed. Would your altimeter have registered higher or lower when you landed? Why?

9. What does the vertical-speed indicator measure? What is its major limitation?

10. What are the two fundamental properties of a gyroscope? Name three major gyroscopic instruments and describe their functions.

11. What are two major functions of the magnetic compass? Define each of the following magnetic compass errors: acceleration-deceleration error, northerly-southerly turn error, variation, deviation, and oscillation.

12. Why do most general aviation airplanes have both a vacuum power system
and an electrical system for their instruments?   •

13. What is the concept of **cross-check**? How is it related to the basic T
formation of airplane instruments? Be sure to state what instruments are
included in the basic T and why they are aligned the way they are. Drawing a
picture may help you visualize the answer.

14. Static ports are aligned _____ the line of flight.
     1--at a 45° angle away from
     2--directly away from
     3--directly into
     4--perpendicular to

15. Total pressure (from the pitot head) less static pressure (from the
static ports), when corrected for minor installation and mechanical errors,
yields a measure of the airplane's
     1--calibrated airspeed.
     2--dynamic airspeed.
     3--indicated airspeed.
     4--true airspeed.

16. Which of the following instruments rely on the pitot-static system as a
source of pressure? A--airspeed indicator; B--altimeter; C--heading
indicator; D--magnetic compass; E--turn coordinator; F--vertical-speed
indicator.
     1--A only.
     2--A, B, and F.
     3--B, D, and E.
     4--C and E only.

17. Atmospheric pressure _____ as altitude _____.
    1--decreases; decreases
    2--increases; decreases
    3--increases; increases
    4--remains constant; increases

18. When flying from air that is warm to air that is cold, the airplane will be _____ the altitude indicated on the altimeter.
    1--higher than
    2--lower than
    3--equal to
    4--impossible to predict since air pressure does not change consistently with changes in temperature.

19. Suppose while flying over Cleveland, OH (field elevation 1,850 ft.), you set your altimeter to 29.04 based on radio contact with Cleveland Flight Service Station. Your altimeter reads 4,500 ft. This would be defined as
    1--absolute altitude.
    2--indicated altitude.
    3--pressure-altitude.
    4--true altitude.

20. Suppose while flying over Cleveland, OH (field elevation 1,850 ft.), you set your altimeter to 29.04 based on radio contact with Cleveland Flight Service Station. Your altimeter reads 4,500 ft. Next, suppose you had a second altimeter and set it to 29.92. What would the second altimeter show?
    1--3,620 ft.
    2--4,500 ft.
    3--5,380 ft.
    4--Impossible to determine since we do not know Cleveland's true altitude.

21. Suppose while flying over Cleveland, OH (field elevation 1,850 ft.), you set your altimeter to 29.04 based on radio contact with nearby Cleveland FSS. Your altimeter reads 4,500 ft. Upon landing at Cleveland, you notice that your altimeter reads 1,975 ft. You check with Cleveland FSS again and find that the current altimeter is still 29.04. What should you do?
    1--Change your altimeter to 1,850 ft. since that is the true altitude and does not change with changes in atmospheric conditions.
    2--Have your altimeter checked since the discrepancy is outside FAA tolerance limits.
    3--Ignore the discrepancy since it is well within the tolerance limits set by the FAA.
    4--Leave your altimeter at 1,975 ft. and report the discrepancy to the nearest FSS Station so they can issue a Notice to Airmen (NOTAM).

22. Suppose you depart from Superior, WI (barometer 29.34), and fly direct to Minot, ND (field elevation 1,800 ft.). As you approach Minot at an indicated altitude of 6,500 ft. you receive a new altimeter setting of 29.62. When you change your altimeter to the new setting, approximately what indicated altitude will your altimeter read?
    1--4,420 ft.   4--6,220 ft.
    2--4,700 ft.   5--6,500 ft.
    3--4,980 ft.   6--6,780 ft.

23. Which of the following instruments is used to indicate changes in an airplane's pitch? A--Attitude indicator; B--Turn coordinator; C--Heading indicator; D--Magnetic compass.
    1--A only.
    2--A and B.
    3--C and D.
    4--B, C, and D.

24. Which of the following instruments constitute the basic **T** arrangement? A--attitude indicator; B--vertical speed indicator; C--altimeter; D--heading indicator; E--magnetic compass; F--airspeed indicator; G--turn coordinator.
    1--A, C, D, and F.
    2--A, D, F, and G.
    3--A, B, C, D, and F.
    4--C, D, F, and G.
    5--A, B, C, D, E, F, and G.

25. Total pressure from the pitot head, less static pressure from the static ports, yields a measure of the airplane's forward speed. This speed
    1--is an accurate measure of the airplane's movement through the air only in nonwind conditions.
    2--is defined as indicated airspeed.
    3--is the same as calibrated airspeed when corrected for wind conditions.
    4--all of the above.

26. What instrument is at the heart of most altimeters?
    1--Barometer.
    2--Gyroscope.
    3--Pitot tube.
    4--Vacuum pump.

27. Suppose the current altimeter setting is 30.07 and your altimeter reads 6,150 ft. Directly below you is a smokestack whose surveyed altitude is 2,480 ft. MSL. What is your absolute altitude with respect to the smokestack?
    1--2,480 ft.
    2--3,520 ft.
    3--3,670 ft.
    4--6,000 ft.

28. Suppose the current altimeter setting is 30.07 and your altimeter reads 6,150 ft. Directly below you is a smokestack whose surveyed altitude is 2,480 ft. MSL. What is your indicated altitude in this example?
    1--3,520 ft.
    2--3,670 ft.
    3--6,000 ft.
    4--6,150 ft.

29. Suppose the current altimeter setting is 30.07 and your altimeter reads 6,150 ft. Directly below you is a smokestack with a surveyed altitude of 2,480 ft. MSL. What is your pressure-altitude in this example?
    1--3,520 ft.
    2--3,670 ft.
    3--6,000 ft.
    4--6,150 ft.

30. What instrument is at the heart of the heading indicator?
    1--Gyroscope.
    2--Inclinometer.
    3--Magnet.
    4--Venturi.

31. Suppose the current altimeter setting is 30.07 and your altimeter reads 6,150 ft. Directly below you is a smokestack whose surveyed altitude is 2,480 ft. MSL. What is the true altitude of the smokestack in this example?
    1--2,350 ft.
    2--2,480 ft.
    3--2,630 ft.
    4--Impossible to determine, since true altitude changes with changing atmospheric conditions, and we cannot be sure at any moment what those exact conditions are.

32. Suppose you have just departed Jasper, AL (current altimeter 29.78), and fly direct to Plains, GA (field elevation 1,240 ft.). As you approach Plains at an indicated altitude of 4,500 ft., you receive a new altimeter setting of 29.90. When you change your altimeter to the new setting, what indicated altitude will the altimeter read?
    1--3,140 ft.
    2--3,260 ft.
    3--3,380 ft.
    4--4,380 ft.
    5--4,500 ft.
    6--4,620 ft.

33. Suppose you have just departed Jasper, AL (current altimeter 29.78), and fly direct to Plains, Georgia (field elevation 1,240 ft.). As you approach Plains at an indicated altitude of 4,500 ft., you receive a new altimeter setting of 29.90. If you fail to change your altimeter (a violation of FAA regulations) and land at Plains, what would your altimeter read on touchdown?
    1--1,120 ft.
    2--1,240 ft.
    3--1,360 ft.
    4--4,380 ft.
    5--4,500 ft.
    6--4,620 ft.

34. Which of the following instruments uses a gyroscope as the basis for its operation?
    1--Airspeed indicator.
    2--Magnetic compass.
    3--Turn coordinator.
    4--Vertical-speed indicator.

35. A standard-rate turn is performed at ___ per second.
    1--3°
    2--6°
    3--10°
    4--30°

36. How many seconds does it take to complete a 360° standard-rate turn?
    1--60.
    2--120.
    3--180.
    4--360.

37. During turbulence or rapid flight maneuvers, the magnetic compass card may swing back and forth. These changes are referred to as _____ errors.
    1--acceleration-deceleration
    2--deviation
    3--oscillation
    4--variation

38. Which of the following instruments is not typically involved in primary cross-check during straight-and-level flight?
    1--Attitude indicator.
    2--Airspeed indicator.
    3--Altimeter.
    4--Turn coordinator.

FAA EXAM QUESTIONS

(Note: All FAA Figures are located in Appendix C)

 1. (FAA 1068) The pitot system provides impact pressure for only the
    1--airspeed indicator, vertical-speed indicator, and altimeter.
    2--altimeter and vertical-speed indicator.
    3--vertical-speed indicator.
    4--airspeed indicator.

 2. (FAA 1082) Which instrument(s) will become inoperative if the pitot tube becomes clogged?
    1--Altimeter.
    2--Vertical speed.
    3--Airspeed.
    4--Altimeter and airspeed.

 3. (FAA 1083) Which instrument(s) will become inoperative if the static vents become clogged?
    1--Airspeed only.
    2--Altimeter only.
    3--Airspeed and altimeter only.
    4--Airspeed, altimeter, and vertical speed.

 4. (FAA 1081) If the pitot tube and outside static vents or ports were clogged, which instrument or instruments would be affected?
    1--The airspeed indicator, altimeter, and turn-and-slip indicator.
    2--The altimeter, vertical-speed indicator, and airspeed indicator would provide inaccurate instrument readings.
    3--The only instruments that would provide erroneous indications would be the airspeed indicator and altimeter.
    4--The airspeed indicator would indicate excessively high airspeeds.

5. (FAA 1065) Refer to the color-coded marking on the airspeed indicator in Figure 5. What is the normal flap operating range for the airplane?
   1--60 to 100 MPH.
   2--65 to 165 MPH.
   3--60 to 208 MPH.
   4--165 to 208 MPH.

6. (FAA 1073) Refer to the airspeed indicator in Figure 5. Which of the color-coded markings identifies the normal flap operating range?
   1--The lower limit of the white arc to the upper limit of the green arc.
   2--The green arc.
   3--The white arc.
   4--The yellow arc.

7. (FAA 1072) Refer to the airspeed indicator in Figure 5. What is the maximum flaps-extended speed?
   1--165 MPH.
   2--100 MPH.
   3--65 MPH.
   4--60 MPH.

8. (FAA 1074) Refer to the airspeed indicator in Figure 5. Which of the color-coded markings identifies the power-off stalling speed with wing flaps and landing gear in the landing configuration?
   1--Upper A/S limit of the green arc.
   2--Upper A/S limit of the white arc.
   3--Lower A/S limit of the green arc.
   4--Lower A/S limit of the white arc.

9. (FAA 1071) Refer to the airspeed indicator in Figure 5. Which color-coded marking identifies the power-off stalling speed in a specified configuration?
   1--Upper A/S limit of the green arc.
   2--Upper A/S limit of the white arc.
   3--Lower A/S limit of the green arc.
   4--Lower A/S limit of the white arc.

10. (FAA 1075) Refer to the airspeed indicator in Figure 5. What is the maximum structural cruising speed?
    1--208 MPH.
    2--165 MPH.
    3--100 MPH.
    4--There is no colored arc indicating the airspeed.

11. (FAA 1066) Refer to the color-coded markings on the airspeed indicator in Figure 5. What is the caution range of the airplane?
    1--0 to 60 MPH.
    2--100 to 165 MPH.
    3--165 to 208 MPH.
    4--60 to 100 MPH.

12. (FAA 1069) Refer to the airspeed indicator in Figure 5. The maximum speed at which the airplane can be operated in smooth air is
1--100 MPH.
2--165 MPH.
3--65 MPH.
4--208 MPH.

13. (FAA 1067) The red line on an airspeed indicator means a maximum airspeed that
1--may be exceeded only if gear and flaps are retracted.
2--may be exceeded if abrupt maneuvers are not attempted.
3--may be exceeded only in smooth air.
4--should not be exceeded.

14. (FAA 1070) Refer to the airspeed indicator in Figure 5. Which of the color-coded markings on the airspeed indicator identifies the never-exceed speed?
1--Lower A/S limit of the yellow arc.
2--Upper A/S limit of the white arc.
3--Upper A/S limit of the green arc.
4--The red radial line.

15. (FAA 1076) What is an important airspeed limitation that is not color coded on airspeed indicators?
1--Never-exceed speed.
2--Maximum structural cruising speed.
3--Maneuvering speed.
4--Maximum flaps-extended speed.

16. (FAA 1079) Altimeter C in Figure 6 indicates
1--9,500 ft.
2--10,950 ft.
3--15,940 ft.
4--19,500 ft.

17. (FAA 1077) What altitude does altimeter A in Figure 6 indicate?
1--5000 ft.
2--1,500 ft.
3--10,500 ft.
4--15,000 ft.

18. (FAA 1078) Altimeter B in Figure 6 indicates
1--1,500 ft.
2--4,500 ft.
3--14,500 ft.
4--15,500 ft.

19. (FAA 1080) Which altimeter(s) in Figures 6 indicate(s) more than 10,000 ft.?
1--A, B, and C.
2--A and B only.
3--A only.
4--B only.

20. (FAA 1001)   What is true altitude?
    1--Actual height above sea level corrected for all errors.
    2--Altitude above the surface.
    3--Altitude reference to the standard datum plane.
    4--Altitude shown on a radar altimeter.

21. (FAA 1002)   Absolute altitude is the
    1--altitude read directly from the altimeter.
    2--altitude above the surface.
    3--altitude reference to the standard datum plane.
    4--indicated altitude corrected for instrument error.

22. (FAA 1003)   Density altitude is the
    1--altitude reference to the standard datum plane.
    2--pressure altitude corrected for nonstandard temperature.
    3--altitude read directly from the altimeter.
    4--altitude above the surface.

23. (FAA 1004)   Pressure altitude is the
    1--altitude read directly from the altimeter.
    2--altitude corrected for position and installation error.
    3--indicated altitude corrected for nonstandard pressure.
    4--true altitude corrected to the standard datum plane.

24. (FAA 1005)   Altimeter setting is the value to which the scale of the
    pressure altimeter is set so the altimeter indicates
    1--density altitude at field elevation.
    2--absolute altitude at field elevation.
    3--true altitude at field elevation.
    4--pressure altitude at field elevation.

25. (FAA 1009)   Under which condition(s) will pressure altitude be equal to
    true altitude?
    1--When the atmospheric pressure is 29.92" Hg.
    2--When standard atmospheric conditions exist.
    3--When indicated altitude is equal to the pressure altitude.
    4--When the OAT (outside air temperature) is standard for that altitude.

26. (FAA 1010)   Under what condition is pressure altitude and density
    altitude the same value?
    1--At sea level, when the temperature is 0°F.
    2--When the altimeter has no installation error.
    3--When the altimeter setting is 29.92.
    4--At standard temperature.

27. (FAA 1011)   Under what condition is the indicated altitude the same as
    true altitude?
    1--If the altimeter has no mechanical error.
    2--When at sea level under standard conditions.
    3--When at 18,000 ft. with the altimeter set at 29.92.
    4--At any altitude if the indicated altitude is corrected for
       nonstandard sea level temperature and pressure.

28. (FAA 1012) Under what condition will true altitude be lower than
    indicated altitude with an altimeter setting of 29.92 even with an
    accurate altimeter?
    1--In colder than standard air temperature.
    2--In warmer than standard air temperature.
    3--When density altitude is higher than indicated altitude.
    4--Under higher than standard pressure at standard air temperature.

29. (FAA 1013) Which condition would cause the altimeter to indicate a
    lower altitude than actually flown (true altitude)?
    1--Air temperature lower than standard.
    2--Atmospheric pressure lower than standard.
    3--Pressure altitude the same as density altitude.
    4--Air temperature warmer than standard.

30. (FAA 1014) If a flight is made from an area of low pressure into an
    area of high pressure without the altimeter setting being adjusted and a
    constant indicated altitude is maintained, the altimeter would indicate
    1--the actual altitude above sea level.
    2--higher than the actual altitude above sea level.
    3--lower than the actual altitude above sea level.
    4--the actual altitude above ground level.

31. (FAA 1015) If a flight is made from an area of high pressure into an
    area of lower pressure without the altimeter setting being adjusted and
    a constant indicated altitude is maintained, the altimeter would
    indicate
    1--lower than the actual altitude above sea level.
    2--higher than the actual altitude above sea level.
    3--the actual altitude above ground level.
    4--the actual altitude above sea level.

32. (FAA 1024) If a pilot changes the altimeter from 30.11 to 29.96, what
    is the approximate change in indication?
    1--Altimeter will indicate .15" Hg. higher.
    2--Altimeter will indicate 1.5" Hg. lower.
    3--Altimeter will indicate 150 ft. lower.
    4--Altimeter will indicate 150 ft. higher.

33. (FAA 1027) If it is necessary to set the altimeter from 29.15 to 29.85,
    what change occurs?
    1--70-foot increase in indicated altitude.
    2--700-foot increase in indicated altitude.
    3--70-foot increase in density altitude.
    4--700-foot increase in true altitude.

34. (FAA 1029) How do variations in temperature affect the altimeter?
    1--Pressure levels are raised on warm days and the indicated altitude is
       lower than true altitude.
    2--Higher temperatures expand the pressure levels and the indicated
       altitude is higher than true altitude.
    3--Lower temperatures lower the pressure levels and the indicated
       altitude is lower than true altitude.
    4--Indicated altitude varies directly with the temperature.

35. (FAA 1060) Deviation in a magnetic compass is caused by
    1--presence of flaws in the permanent magnets of the compass.
    2--the difference in the location between true north and magnetic north.
    3--magnetic ore deposits in the Earth distorting the lines of magnetic
       force.
    4--magnetic fields within the aircraft distorting the lines of magnetic
       force.

36. (FAA 1062) In the Northern Hemisphere, a magnetic compass will normally
    indicate initially a turn toward the west if
    1--a left turn is entered from a north heading.
    2--a right turn is entered from a north heading.
    3--an aircraft is decelerated while on a south heading.
    4--an aircraft is accelerated while on a north heading.

37. (FAA 1057) In the Northern Hemisphere, a magnetic compass will normally
    indicate a turn toward the north if
    1--a right turn is entered from an east heading.
    2--a left turn is entered from a west heading.
    3--an aircraft is decelerated while on an east or west heading.
    4--an aircraft is accelerated while on an east or west heading.

38. (FAA 1061) In the Northern Hemisphere, the magnetic compass will
    normally indicate a turn toward the south when
    1--a left turn is entered from an east heading.
    2--a right turn is entered from a west heading.
    3--the aircraft is accelerated while on an east heading.
    4--the aircraft is decelerated while on a west heading.

39. (FAA 1058) In the Northern Hemisphere, if an aircraft is accelerated or
    decelerated, the magnetic compass will normally indicate
    1--a turn momentarily, with changes in airspeed on any heading.
    2--correctly when on a north or south heading while either accelerating
       or decelerating.
    3--a turn toward the south while accelerating on a west heading.
    4--a turn toward the north while decelerating on an east heading.

40. (FAA 1063) In the Northern Hemisphere, a magnetic compass will normally
    indicate initially a turn toward the east if
    1--an aircraft is decelerated while on a south heading.
    2--an aircraft is accelerated while on a north heading.
    3--a right turn is entered from a north heading.
    4--a left turn is entered from a north heading.

41. (FAA 1064) During flight, when are the indications of a magnetic
    compass accurate?
    1--Only in straight-and-level unaccelerated flight.
    2--As long as the airspeed is constant.
    3--During turns if the bank does not exceed 18°.
    4--In all conditions of flight.

42. (FAA 1053) The proper adjustment to make on the altitude indicator, Figure 2, during level flight is to align the
1--horizon bar to the level-flight indication.
2--horizon bar to the miniature airplane.
3--miniature airplane to the horizon bar.
4--banking indicator to the zero-bank indication.

43. (FAA 1056) To receive accurate indications during flight from a heading indicator, Figure 4, the instrument must be
1--set prior to flight on a known heading.
2--calibrated on a compass rose at regular intervals.
3--adequately powered so that it seeks the proper direction.
4--periodically realigned with the magnetic compass as the gyro precesses.

44. (FAA 1054) How should a pilot determine the direction of bank from an attitude indicator such as illustrated in Figure 2?
1--The direction of deflection of the banking scale (A).
2--The direction of deflection of the horizon bar (B).
3--The direction of deflection of the miniature airplane (C).
4--The relationship of the miniature airplane (C) to the deflecting horizon bar (B).

45. (FAA 1055) The turn coordinator, Figure 3, provides an indication of
1--the movement of the aircraft about the yaw and roll axes.
2--the angle of bank up to but not exceeding 30°.
3--attitude of the aircraft with reference to the longitudinal axis.
4--motion of the aircraft about the lateral and vertical axes.

ANSWERS AND EXPLANATIONS

Key Terms and Concepts, Part 1

1. J	7. D	13. M	19. S
2. A	8. K	14. G	20. V
3. Q	9. N	15. O	21. R
4. E	10. F	16. I	22. X
5. H	11. P	17. L	23. W
6. C	12. B	18. U	24. T

Key Terms and Concepts, Part 2

1. N	6. A	11. Q	16. G
2. D	7. M	12. B	17. L
3. H	8. F	13. K	18. E
4. J	9. O	14. R	19. S
5. P	10. C	15. I	20. T

Discussion Questions and Review Exercises

1. See Study Guide Main Point #2.

2. T--Airspeed is speed relative to the air.

3. See Study Guide Main Point #3.

4. See Study Guide Main Point #5.

5. See Study Guide Main Point #6.

6. None, since the barometric conditions are the same in both places.

7. 2,100 ft. Since you are flying from high pressure to low pressure without changing the altimeter setting, actual MSL altitude would be lower than the altimeter reading. 29.96 - 28.74 = 1.22 in. of mercury. Since 1 in. = 1,000 ft., the altimeter would be off by 1,220 ft., and it would have registered 2,100 ft. when you landed! Further, had you used your altimeter to enter the pattern (1,880 ft. MSL), you would have come in contact with the ground before you ever reached the pattern. "When flying from a high to a low, look out below!"

8. It would have registered higher, since moving from high to low temperature results in your being lower than your altimeter indicates.

9. See Study Guide Main Point #7.

10. See Study Guide Main Point #9.

11. See Study Guide Main Point #8.

12. See Study Guide Main Point #10.

13. See Study Guide Main Point #11.

14. 4--So as not to be affected by ram air, the static ports are located at a 90° angle to the line of flight.

15. 1--This defines calibrated airspeed.

16. 2--The altimeter, vertical speed indicator, and airspeed indicator all rely on static air pressure to operate accurately. The airspeed indicator relies on ram air from the pitot tube. If both sources are clogged, these instruments will provide inaccurate information.

17. 2--The lower you go, the greater the pressure exerted by the air.

18. 2--The altimeter reads erroneously high when you fly from warm to cold air, or from high pressure to low pressure.

19. 2--This is indicated altitude. If you landed at Cleveland, your altimeter would read Cleveland's actual height above sea level, assuming there were no mechanical problems with the altimeter.

20. 3--It would indicate higher than you are by about 880 ft. (29.92 - 29.04 = .88 in. of mercury). Since 1 in. of mercury equals 1,000 ft., .88 in. equals 880 ft.

21. 2--Tolerance suggested by the FAA is plus or minus 75 ft. between the surveyed altitude and the height indicated on your altimeter when corrected for current ground level atmospheric conditions. Since the altimeter is off by 125, it is outside of the tolerance limits set by the FAA.

22. 6--Your altimeter would indicate that you are lower than you actually are by (29.62 - 29.34 = .28) x 100 = 280 ft. So, when you change the altimeter setting, the altimeter will read 6,780 ft.

23. 1--Pitch, or movement about the airplane's lateral axis, is indicated on the attitude indicator, as is the degree of bank (roll, or movement about the longitudinal axis).

24. 1--The attitude indicator, altimeter, heading indicator, and airspeed indicator define the basic T. The attitude indicator is at the center.

25. 2--This defines indicated airspeed, which is a measure of the airplane's speed through the air.

26. 1--The barometer provides information about air pressure.

27. 2--Since you have set your altimeter to the current setting, indicated altitude will be the same as true altitude. To calculate your absolute altitude, subtract the height of the smokestack from your indicated altitude.

28. 4--Indicated altitude is what your altimeter reads.

29. 3--To calculate pressure-altitude, set 29.92 in the Kollsman window of the altimeter. That is, 30.07 - 29.92 = .15 in. of mercury, which translates to a difference of 150 ft. Since you are moving from high pressure to low pressure, subtract 150 from indicated altitude.

30. 1--The heading indicator operates on gyroscopic principles.

31. 2--True altitude is actual height above the ground.

32. 6--Since you are flying from lower to higher pressure, your altimeter will indicate that you are lower than you actually are by (29.90 - 29.78 = .12 in.) x 100 = 120 ft.

33. 1--Since you flew from lower to higher pressure, indicated altitude will be lower than you actually are by 120 ft. [(29.90 - 29.78 = .12 in.) x 100 = 120 ft.], so the altimeter will register 1,240 - 120 = 1,120 ft.

34. 3--The turn coordinator operates on gyroscopic principles.

35. 1--At 3° per second, the standard rate turn takes 120 seconds, or 2 minutes, to complete.

36. 2--At 3° per second, the standard rate turn takes 120 seconds, or 2 minutes, to complete.

37. 3--These define oscillation errors.

38. 4--The attitude indicator is at the center of the basic T. It is flanked
on either side by the airspeed indicator and altimeter. The leg of the T is
the heading indicator.

FAA Exam Questions

1. 4--Only the airspeed indicator uses impact or ram air pressure.

2. 3--If the pitot tube is clogged, there will be no ram air pressure to the
airspeed indicator.

3. 4--If the static vents are clogged, all three of the pitot-static
instruments will be inoperative.

4. 2--When both pitot and static sources are clogged, all pitot-static
instruments will show erroneous readings.

5. 1--The white arc indicates the normal flap operating range.

6. 3--The white arc indicates the normal flap operating range.

7. 2--The upper limit of the white arc is V_{fe}, maximum flap-extended speed.

8. 4--The lower limit of the white arc is V_{s0}, the power-off stalling speed
in the landing configuration.

9. 3--The lower limit of the green arc is V_{s1}, the power-off stalling speed
in a specified configuration (usually gear and flaps up).

10. 2--The upper limit of the green arc is V_{no}, which should be exceeded only
in smooth air.

11. 3--The yellow arc indicates the caution range.

12. 4--The yellow arc indicates the caution range, in which the airplane may
be operated in smooth air. The red line, V_{ne} is at the top of the yellow arc.

13. 4--The red line indicates V_{ne}, the never-exceed speed.

14. 4--The red radial line is V_{ne}, the never-exceed speed.

15. 3--Maneuvering speed, V_a, is the speed above which structural damage may
occur when you make abrupt control inputs. You should use speeds below V_a in
turbulent air. V_a is not color coded because it varies with the weight of the
aircraft; V_a is lower for lighter aircraft.

16. 1--The shortest hand indicates less than 10,000 ft; the medium hand
indicates between 9,000 and 10,000 ft; the longest hand indicates 500 ft.

17.   3--The shortest hand points just past 10,000 ft; the medium length hand indicates less than 1,000 ft; the longest hand is pointing to 500 ft.

18.   3--The shortest hand indicates between 10,000 ft and 20,000 ft; the medium length hand indicates between 4,000 ft. and 5,000 ft.; the longest hand points to 500 feet.

19.   2--The shortest hand indicates 10s of thousands of feet. Both A and B show altitudes of more than 10,000 ft.

20.   1--This is the definition of true altitude.

21.   2--Absolute altitude is the distance from the aircraft to the surface over which it is flying. It can be determined by subtracting the true elevation of the surface from the true altitude of the aircraft.

22.   2--This is the definition of density altitude. Under standard conditions, pressure altitude and density altitude will be the same. However, you will seldom have standard temperature, pressure and humidity, thus corrections will usually be necessary to determine density altitude.

23.   3--When the standard pressure (29.92" Hg) exists, pressure altitude and indicated altitude is the same. But the pressure is seldom 29.92" Hg. To find pressure altitude, apply a correction for nonstandard pressure.

24.   3--When the setting in the Kollsman window matches the local altimeter setting, the indicated altitude will be the same as true altitude.

25.   2--Pressure altitude is the same as true altitude when standard atmospheric conditions of 29.92" Hg and 15°C (at sea level) exist.

26.   4--When temperature is standard, pressure altitude and density altitude are equal.

27.   2--At sea level, under standard conditions, when the current altimeter setting is in the Kollsman window, indicated and true altitudes will be the same.

28.   1--True altitude is less than indicated altitude when the temperature is colder than standard or when pressure is less than that of the altimeter setting in the Kollsman window. Answer 3 is incorrect because a higher density altitude could be caused by warmer than standard conditions and/or less pressure.

29.   4--When the air temperature is warmer than standard, you will be higher than indicated, thus the altimeter will read low. (When flying from high to low, look out below!)

30.   3--When flying from a low to a high pressure area, without changing the Kollsman setting, the altimeter will read low. (Low to high, you're in the sky.)

31.   2--When flying from a high to a low, without changing the Kollsman setting, you will be low, and the altimeter will read high.

32. 3--When changing from a high to a lower setting, the altimeter will show a decrease in altitude. Atmospheric pressure decreases by about 1 inch of mercury per 1,000 feet. 30.11 - 29.96 = .15 inch, 150 ft.

33. 2--When changing from a low to a higher altimeter setting, the altimeter will show an increase. 29.85 - 29.15 = .70 for a 700 ft. increase.

34. 1--Warmer temperatures increase pressure levels. You will be higher than indicated.

35. 4--The metals and electrical equipment of an aircraft distort the lines of the magnetic force.

36. 2--When turning from a north direction, the northerly turning error causes the magnetic compass to initially indicate a turn in the opposite direction, then lag the actual heading until reaching an east or west heading.

37. 4--Acceleration or deceleration causes dip errors when on an east or west heading. Acceleration causes an indication of a turn toward the north, deceleration indicates a turn toward the south. Remember the acronym ANDS.

38. 4--Acceleration or deceleration causes dip errors when on an east or west heading. Acceleration causes an indication of a turn toward the north, deceleration indicates a turn toward the south. Remember the acronym ANDS.

39. 2--There is no error when accelerating or decelerating while on a north or south heading.

40. 4--When turning from a north direction, the northerly turning error causes the magnetic compass to initially indicate a turn in the opposite direction, then lag the actual heading until reaching an east or west heading.

41. 1--When not in straight-and-level, unaccelerated flight, northerly turning error and dip cause erroneous readings.

42. 3--In level flight the miniature airplane's wings will overlap the horizon. The altitude indicator must be adjusted for each pilot's line of vision.

43. 4--Precession causes the heading indicator to drift.

44. 4--The relationship of the miniature airplane with the artificial horizon bar provides information on the airplane's attitude: nose high, low or level; bank angle left, right or level.

45. 1--The turn coordinator shows rate of turn, roll and yaw.

AIRPLANE WEIGHT AND BALANCE

MAIN POINTS

1. A teeter-totter is a lever on either side of a **fulcrum**. The length of the lever is called the **arm**. The force of a weight acting at the end of the arm is called a **moment**. Arm, moment, and weight are related such that Weight x Arm = Moment, Arm = Moment/Weight, or Weight = Moment/Arm.

2. Airplanes balance at a single point called the **center of gravity (CG)**, around which all moments are equal. The CG must be kept within certain limits to maintain control stability.

3. The reference point from which moment arms are measured is called the **datum** or **datum line**. The datum in most planes is located near the firewall. The CG and location of all components in the plane are measured in inches from the datum. Positions in the aircraft are sometimes referenced as station numbers. These are expressed in inches from the datum. For example, Station 140 is 140 inches aft of the datum. Weight times distance from the datum yields a moment. The sum of the airplane's empty weight plus everything else you put in it is called **gross weight**. If you sum the moments and divide the gross weight, you have the new CG location relative to the datum.

4. **Empty weight** is the airplane's weight with all listed equipment, hydraulic fluid, undrainable engine oil, and unusable fuel (fuel not available to the engine due to aircraft design). **Basic empty weight** is empty weight plus full oil. Gas weighs 6 lb. per gal., and oil weigh 7.5 lb. per gal. **Useful load** includes usable fuel and the payload (occupants, cargo, and baggage). **Maximum ramp weight** is the manufacturer's maximum ground maneuvering weight. **Maximum takeoff weight** is the maximum for the start of the takeoff run. **Maximum landing weight** is the maximum weight approved for touchdown. Most Pilot's Operating Handbooks list a **maximum gross weight** that is acceptable for all ground and flight operations.

5. The two basic questions you must ask as a pilot are: Is gross weight within allowable limits? Is the CG within allowable limits? After determining how much useful load you have and where it will go, you use the Pilot's Operating Handbook to determine the fuselage station number (arm) for

each item, which is listed conveniently in inches from the datum. Multiply weight by its arm and you have the moment; add all moments and divide by the gross weight to obtain the new CG. The Flight Manual for your airplane provides specific total moment limits for each airplane load condition.

6. There are two common formats for solving weight and balance problems: tabular and graphical. Both methods require that you first figure the **zero fuel condition**, then the **fuel loading**, which together yield the **ramp condition**. The **takeoff condition** compensates for fuel burned during taxi and runup. The **landing condition** takes into account fuel burned during flight. The tabular format refers you to a table of moment limits versus weight to determine if you are within an acceptable range of CG values. With the tabular format, you may have to **interpolate** between the numbers listed in the table. The graphical method presents moment values as index units for each compartment of the plane. The sum of the moments and weights is used to determine if you fall within the **CG envelope**.

7. Changing the weight and/or CG changes the airplane's performance characteristics. For example, high gross weights require a greater angle of attack to maintain level flight. Thus, the airplane will stall at higher airspeeds and have poorer climb and cruise performance. Forward CGs make the plane more stable, but extra elevator pressure is required to hold a desired attitude. Also, the airplane will stall at a slightly higher airspeed since the added nose-down moment adds to the lift required from the wings and tail. An aft CG makes the plane less stable and increases the chances of serious stalls or spins. Since the tail provides less download, the wind operates at a lower angle of attack, which in turn reduces stalling speed. An aft CG also increases fuel efficiency. All of these changes are minor and acceptable when the airplane is loaded **within** the limits defined in the Flight Manual, but they become extremely dangerous when those limits are exceeded.

8. Good pilots make weight and balance planning a **habit**! Although it may be a chore to rearrange the payload or embarrassing to ask someone for their actual weight, remember that your safety and the safety of your passengers is at stake. Finally, remember that most people, particularly those who are overweight, tend to **underestimate** their weight. Adding 10 percent to the reported weight typically compensates for this discrepancy.

KEY TERMS AND CONCEPTS

Match each term or concept (1-16) with the appropriate description (A-P) below. Each item has only one match.

___ 1. ramp weight   ___ 9. useful load
___ 2. arm   ___ 10. fuselage station number
___ 3. empty weight   ___ 11. maximum gross weight
___ 4. moment   ___ 12. usable fuel
___ 5. payload   ___ 13. datum
___ 6. takeoff condition   ___ 14. fulcrum
___ 7. CG envelope   ___ 15. zero fuel condition
___ 8. landing condition   ___ 16. center of gravity (CG)

A. reference point from which all moments are measured
B. ramp condition, less fuel used for taxi and runup
C. number of inches a fuselage position is from datum
D. weight of fuel aboard that is available to the engine
E. airplane's weight with all equipment and unusable fuel (but no oil)
F. weight of cargo, occupants, and baggage
G. weight of an item times its distance from the datum (arm)
H. takeoff condition, less fuel burned in flight
I. weight and moment of an airplane with payload, but no fuel load
J. point in an aircraft about which all moments are equal
K. distance of a station or item from the datum
L. occupants, cargo, baggage, and usable fuel
M. maximum weight to which an aircraft is certified by the FAA
N. support point of a level
O. weight and moment of an airplane with payload and fuel included
P. range of weight and balance operating limits

DISCUSSION QUESTIONS AND REVIEW EXERCISES

1. What is the relationship among arm, moment, and weight? How does this apply to general aviation aircraft?

2. What are the two major factors about the airplane's weight and balance that a pilot must attend to before the airplane flies?

3. What is **basic empty weight**? How is it different from **empty weight**?

4. Name three effects of each of the following on the airplane's flight characteristics:

a. high gross weight

b. operation with a forward CG

c. operation with an aft CG

Table 5.1 -- Excerpt from a Pilot's Operating Handbook

Aircraft designation: Four-place, single-engine, land monoplane
Engine operating limits: 150 horsepower at 2,700 RPM
Fuel system: Float-type carburetor
Fuel capacity: Standard tanks--42 gal., 38 usable
               Long-range tanks--52 gal., 48 usable
Oil capacity: 8 qt. (not included in licensed empty weight)
Propeller: Fixed-pitch
Landing gear: Fixed tricycle gear
Wing flaps: Electrically operated, 0-40°
Licensed empty weight: 1,364 lb.
Maximum gross weight: 2,300 lb.
Maximum weight in baggage compartment: 120 lb.

5. To answer questions a-e, refer to Table 5.1. Assume the airplane is loaded as follows:

Pilot	160 lb.
Front seat passenger	148 lb.
Rear seat passenger	122 lb.
Rear seat passenger	176 lb.
Baggage	80 lb.
Oil	Full
Fuel (standard tanks)	Full

a. How is the airplane loaded with respect to maximum gross weight?

b. Assume that you plan to load the airplane with 120 lb. of baggage, 8 qt. of oil, and four persons whose total weight is 698 lb. What is the total amount of usable fuel (standard tanks) that can be aboard without exceeding the maximum certified gross weight?

c. What is the combined maximum weight of four persons and baggage that can be loaded without exceeding maximum certified gross weight if the airplane is serviced to capacity with oil and fuel (including long-range tanks)?

d. Suppose you have filled the airplane's long-range fuel tanks to capacity and there are 8 qt. of oil in the engine. You wish to carry four persons whose total weight is 680 lb. There will be no baggage aboard. How close would the airplane be to maximum certified gross weight limits?

e. During the preflight inspection, you notice that there are 8 qt. of oil in the engine and the standard tanks are filled to capacity. The total weight of the pilot and passengers is 670 lb. What is the total weight of the baggage, if any, that can be loaded aboard without exceeding the maximum certified gross weight of the airplane?

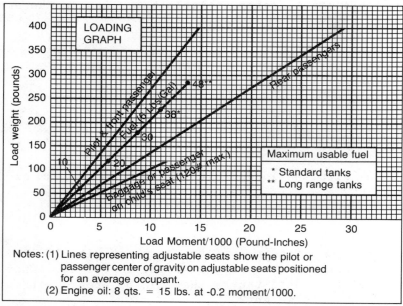

Figure 5.1

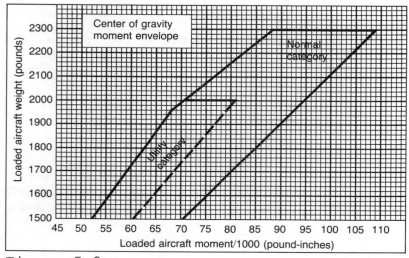

Figure 5.2

Table 5.2 -- Mesacruiser Weight and Balance Chart

Mesacruiser N100S -- Licensed Empty Weight: 1,454
                       Empty Moment: 60.6
                       Standard fuel tanks only   38 gal.

(Notes: (1) With these graphs, it is not necessary to divide total
moment by total weight to determine the exact CG. Use the CENTER OF
GRAVITY-MOMENT envelope to determine if you are within limits. (2) The
Mesacruiser CLIMB DATA chart shows that you must plan to use 1.0 gallons for
ground operations (start, taxi, runup, and takeoff). For takeoff weight and
balance calculations, you should <u>not</u> reduce the fuel by this amount.)

6. Use Figures 5.1 and 5.2 and the **Mesacruiser** weight and balance chart (Table 5.2) to answer questions a-e.

a. Calculate the moment/1000, the location of the center of gravity with this load, and whether the weight and CG are within limits.

	WEIGHT (lb.)	MOM/1000
Empty weight	1,454	60.6
Pilot and front passenger	300	_____
Rear passengers	200	_____
Baggage	60	_____
Fuel (full)	_____	_____
Oil	_____	_____
TOTAL	_____	_____

i. Is the weight within limits? _____

ii. Is CG within limits for Normal Category operations? _____

iii. Is CG within limits for Utility Category operations? _____

b. For your flight you expect to use a total of 20 gallons of fuel (including ground operations). Determine weight and balance for landing.

	WEIGHT (lb.)	MOM/1000
Empty weight	1,454	60.6
Pilot and front passenger	300	_____
Rear passengers	200	_____
Baggage	60	_____
Fuel (___ gallons)	_____	_____
Oil	_____	_____
TOTAL	_____	_____

i. Is the weight within limits? _____

ii. Is CG within limits for Normal Category operations? _____

iii. Is CG within limits for Utility Category operations? _____

c. After landing in problem #6b, the two rear passengers leave the airplane, taking with them 50 lb. of baggage. Calculate the new takeoff weight and balance.

	WEIGHT (lb.)	MOM/1000
Empty weight	1,454	60.6
Pilot and front passenger	300	_____
Rear passengers	_____	_____
Baggage	_____	_____
Fuel (18.0 gallons)	_____	_____
Oil	_____	_____
TOTAL	_____	_____

i.   Is the weight within limits? _____

ii. Is CG within limits for Normal Category operations? _____

iii. Is CG within limits for Utility Category operations? _____

d. You are now operating a lighter Mesacruiser. Calculate the location of the CG, the moment/1000, and whether the weight and CG are within limits. If the load is not within limits, state what you could do to bring it within limits.

	WEIGHT (lb.)	MOM/1000
Empty weight	1,300	51.7
Pilot (150 lb.) and front passenger (100 lb.)	250	_____
Rear (250 lb., 150 lb.) passengers	400	_____
Baggage	100	_____
Fuel (full)	_____	_____
Oil	_____	_____
TOTAL	_____	_____

i.   Is the weight within limits? _____

ii. Is CG within limits for Normal Category operations? _____

iii. Is CG within limits for Utility Category operations? _____

5 - 8

e. What action can you take to get within limits. Calculate the weight and balance for the decision you make.

	WEIGHT (lb.)	MOM/1000
Empty weight	1,300	51.7
Pilot (___ lb.) and front passenger (___ lb.)	_____	_____
Rear (___ lb., ___ lb.) passengers	_____	_____
Baggage	_____	_____
Fuel (full)	_____	_____
Oil	_____	_____
TOTAL	_____	_____

    i. Is the weight within limits? _____

  ii. Is CG within limits for Normal Category operations? _____

 iii. Is CG within limits for Utility Category operations? _____

7. If a camera bag originally in the front of the plane is moved to the baggage compartment aft of the cabin, how would this affect the airplane's center of gravity?
   1--The CG would change unpredictably as flight attitude changed.
   2--The CG would move aft.
   3--The CG would move forward.
   4--The CG would remain the same.

8. If you have a 40-lb. weight and an 80-in. arm, what is the moment?
   1--2 lb.-in.
   2--32 lb.-in.
   3--120 lb.-in.
   4--3,200 lb.-in.

9. The point in an airplane around which all moment-arms are equal is the
   1--ballast.
   2--center of gravity.
   3--datum.
   4--point of equilibrium.

10. The set of weight and balance operational restrictions assigned to your airplane is called the
   1--CG envelope.
   2--fuselage station number.
   3--load limit.
   4--moment limit.

11. Which of the following would probably increase stalling speed?
     1--An increased angle of bank.
     2--Operation at a high gross weight.
     3--Operation with a forward CG.
     4--All of the above would tend to increase stalling speed.

12. Of the following preflight planning procedures, which should be considered **first** in completing a weight and balance form?
     1--Payload.
     2--Fuel loading.
     3--Fuel to destination.
     4--Ramp condition.

13. If baggage originally stored in the baggage compartment (located aft of the cabin) was moved to the cabin area, how would this affect the airplane's center of gravity (CG)?
     1--The CG would change unpredictably as flight attitude changed.
     2--The CG would move aft.
     3--The CG would move forward.
     4--The CG would remain the same.

14. Which of the following formulae correctly expresses the relationship between arm, moment, and weight?
     1--arm = moment/weight.
     2--arm = weight/moment.
     3--moment = arm/weight.
     4--moment = weight/arm.

15. The reference point in an airplane from which all moment-arms are measured is called the
     1--ballast.
     2--center of gravity.
     3--datum.
     4--equilibrium point.

16. The weight of an airplane with all equipment, hydraulic fluid, full engine oil, and unusable fuel is called the
     1--basic empty weight.
     2--gross weight.
     3--maximum useful weight.
     4--useful weight.

17. The place where each item is assumed to concentrate its weight, expressed in inches from the datum, is called the
     1--CG envelope.
     2--fulcrum.
     3--fuselage station number.
     4--moment index.

18. Which of the following conditions would make an airplane **least** stable?
     1--An increased angle of bank.
     2--Operation at high gross weight.
     3--Operation with an aft CG.
     4--Operation with a forward CG.

19. What corrective action will you probably have to take with an airplane that has a forward CG?
    1--More right rudder, since torque will be higher.
    2--Less right rudder, since torque will be lower.
    3--More elevator trim to keep the tail down.
    4--Less elevator trim to keep the tail up.

20. What corrective action will you probably have to take with an airplane that has an aft CG?
    1--Use more right rudder, since torque will be higher.
    2--Use less right rudder, since torque will be lower.
    3--Use the elevator trim to trim the nose up.
    4--Use the elevator trim to trim the nose down.

FAA EXAM QUESTIONS

(Note: All FAA Figures are located in Appendix C)

1. (FAA 1373) Which of the following items are included in the empty weight of an aircraft?
   1--Hydraulic fluid and usable fuel.
   2--Only the airframe, powerplant, and equipment installed by the manufacturer.
   3--Full fuel tanks and engine oil to capacity, but excluding crew and baggage.
   4--Unusable fuel and optional equipment.

2. (FAA 1374) An aircraft is loaded 100 lb. over maximum certificated gross weight. If fuel (gasoline) is drained to bring the aircraft weight within limits, how much fuel should be drained?
   1--16.2 gal.
   2--18.4 gal.
   3--15.7 gal.
   4--17.1 gal.

3. (FAA 1375) If an aircraft is loaded 90 lb. over maximum certificated gross weight and fuel (gasoline) is drained to bring the aircraft weight within limits, how much fuel should be drained?
   1--9 gal.
   2--12 gal.
   3--6 gal.
   4--15 gal.

4. (FAA 1376) Given:

	WEIGHT (LB.)	ARM (IN.)	MOMENT (LB.-IN.)
Empty weight	1,495	101.4	151,593.0
Pilot and passengers	380	64.0	24,320
Fuel (30 gal. usable no reserve)	180	96.0	17,280

6 lb/gal

2055   193,193

The CG is located how far aft of datum?

1--92.44.
2--94.01.
3--119.8.
4--135.0.

5. (FAA 1380) Determine the moment/1000 with the following data using the graphs in Figure 33.

	WEIGHT (LB.)	MOM/1000
Empty weight	1,350	51.5
Pilot and front passenger	340	--
Fuel (std. tanks)	Capacity	--
Oil 8 qt.	--	--

1--38.7 lb.-in.
2--69.9 lb.-in.
3--74.9 lb.-in.
4--77.0 lb.-in.

6. (FAA 1381) Calculate the CG and determine the plotted position on the CG moment envelope graphs in Figure 33.

	WEIGHT (LB.)	MOM/1000
Empty weight	1,350	51.5
Pilot and front passenger	380	--
Fuel 48 gal.	288	--
Oil 8 qt.	--	--

1--CG 38.9, out of limits forward.
2--CG 39.9, utility category.
3--CG 38.9, normal category.
4--CG 39.9, normal category.

7. (FAA 1377) What is the maximum amount of baggage that may be loaded aboard the airplane for the CG to remain within the loading envelope? (See Figure 33.)

graph

	WEIGHT (LB.)	MOM/1000
Empty weight	1,350	51.5
Pilot and front passenger	250	9.2
Rear passengers	400	29.2
Baggage	(105)	12.0
Fuel (30 gal.) @ 6 lb/gal	180	8.7
Oil (8 qt.) @ 7½ lb/gal	15	-0.2

108.4

1--120 lb.
2--105 lb.
3-- 90 lb.
4-- 60 lb.

2300 MAX

5 - 12

8. (FAA 1378) Calculate the loaded aircraft moment/1000 of the airplane loaded as follows and determine which category when plotted on the CG moment envelope (See Figure 33.)

	WEIGHT (LB.)	MOM/1000
Empty weight	1,350	51.5
Pilot and front passenger	310	--
Rear passengers	96	--
Fuel (38 gal.)	--	--
Oil (8 qt.)	--	- 0.2
	------	------

1--79.2, utility category.
2--80.8, utility category.
3--81.2, normal category.
4--82.0, normal category.

9. (FAA 1379) What is the maximum amount of fuel that may be aboard the airplane on takeoff if it is loaded as follows? (See Figure 33.)

	WEIGHT (LB.)	MOM/1000
Empty weight	1,350	51.5
Pilot and front passenger	340	--
Rear passengers	310	--
Baggage	45	--
Oil (8 qt.)	--	--
	--------	------

1--24 gal.
2--32 gal.
3--40 gal.
4--46 gal.

10. (FAA 1384) Calculate the weight and balance and determine if the CG and the weight of the airplane are within limits. (See Figures 34 and 35.)

Front seat occupants	350 lb.
Rear seat occupants	325 lb.
Baggage	27 lb.
Fuel	35 gal.

1--81.7, out of limits forward.
2--83.4, within limits.
3--84.1, within limits.
4--84.8, out of limits aft.

11. (FAA 1382) Determine if the airplane weight and balance is within limits (See Figures 34 and 35.)

Front seat occupants	340 lb.
Rear seat occupants	295 lb.
Fuel	44 gal.
Baggage	56 lb.

1--Within limits.
2--20 lb. overweight, CG within limits.
3--Weight within limits, CG out of limits forward.
4--39 lb. overweight, CG out of limits forward.

12. (FAA 1386) Determine if the airplane weight and balance is within
limits. (See Figures 34 and 35.)

		ARM	MOM
A/C	2015	—	1554
Front seat occupants	415 lb.	.85	353.75
Rear seat occupants	110 lb.	1.21	133
Fuel, main and aux. tanks	63 gal.(x 6) .75		305
Baggage	32 lb.	1.4	45
	2950		2390

1--19 lb. overweight, CG within limits.
2--19 lb. overweight, CG out of limits forward.
③-Weight within limits, CG out of limits.
4--Weight and balance within limits.

13. (FAA 1383) Which is the maximum amount of baggage that can be carried
when the airplane is loaded as follows? (See Figures 34 and 35).

Front seat occupants   387 lb.
Rear seat occupants   293 lb.
Fuel   35 gal.

1--45 lb.
2--63 lb.
3--220 lb.
4--255 lb.

14. (FAA 1385) Upon landing, the front passenger (180 lb.) departs the
airplane. A rear passenger (204 lb.) moves to the front passenger
position. What effect does this have on the CG if the airplane
weighed 2,690 lb. and the MOM/100 was 2,260 just prior to the
passenger transfer? (See Figures 34 and 35.)
1--The weight changes, but the CG is not affected.
2--The CG moves forward approximately 0.1 in.
3--The CG moves forward approximately 2.4 in.
4--The CG moves forward approximately 3 in.

15. (FAA 1387) Which action can adjust the airplane's weight to maximum
gross weight and the CG within limits for takeoff? (See Figures 34
and 35.)

Front seat occupants   425 lb.
Rear seat occupants   300 lb.
Fuel, main tanks   44 gal.

1--Drain 12 gal. of fuel.
2--Drain 9 gal. of fuel.
3--Transfer 12 gal. of fuel from the main tanks to the auxiliary tanks.
4--Transfer 19 gal. of fuel from the main tanks to the auxiliary tanks.

16. (FAA 1388) With the airplane loaded as follows, what action can be taken to balance the airplane? (See Figures 34 and 35.)

```
Front seat occupants      411 lb.
Rear seat occupants       100 lb.
Main wing tanks            44 gal.
```

1--Drain 5 gal. of fuel.
2--Fill the auxiliary wing tanks.
3--Transfer 10 gal. of fuel from the main tanks to the auxiliary tanks.
4--Add a 100-pound weight to the baggage compartment.

17. (FAA 1389) What affect does a 35-gallon fuel burn have on the weight and balance if the airplane weighed 2,890 lb. and the MOM/100 was 2,452 at takeoff? (See Figures 34 and 35.)
1--Weight is reduced by 210 lb. and the CG is unaffected.
2--Weight is reduced to 2,680 lb. and the CG moves forward.
3--Weight is reduced to 2,855 lb. and the CG moves aft.
4--Weight is reduced by 210 lb. and the CG is aft of limits.

18. (FAA 1102) What determines the longitudinal stability of an airplane?
1--The location of the CG with respect to the center of lift.
2--The effectiveness of the horizontal stabilizer, rudder, and rudder trim tab.
3--The relationship of thrust and lift to weight and drag.
4--The dihedral, angle of sweepback, and the keep effect.

19. (FAA 1103) What causes an airplane (except a T-tail) to pitch nosedown when power is reduced and controls are not adjusted?
1--The CG shifts forward when thrust and drag are reduced.
2--The downwash on the elevators from the propeller slipstream is reduced and elevator effectiveness is reduced.
3--When thrust is reduced to less than weight, lift is also reduced and the wings can no longer support the weight.
4--The upwash on the wings from the propeller slipstream is reduced and angle of attack is reduced.

20. (FAA 1105) Loading an airplane to the most aft CG will cause the airplane to be
1--less stable at slow speeds, but more stable at high speeds.
2--less stable at high speeds, but more stable at low speeds.
3--more stable at all speeds.
4--less stable at all speeds.

21. (FAA 1104) An airplane has been loaded in such a manner that the CG is located aft of the aft CG limit. One undesirable flight characteristic a pilot might experience with this airplane would be
1--a longer takeoff run.
2--the inability to recover from a stalled condition.
3--stalling at higher-than-normal airspeed.
4--the inability to flare during landings.

ANSWERS AND EXPLANATIONS

Key Terms and Concepts

1. O	5. F	9. L	13. A
2. K	6. B	10. C	14. N
3. E	7. P	11. M	15. I
4. G	8. H	12. D	16. J

Discussion Questions and Review Exercises

1. See Study Guide Main Points #1, 2, and 3.

2. See Study Guide Main Point #5.

3. See Study Guide Main Point #4.

4. See Study Guide Main Point #7.

5. a. 2,293, or 7 lb. under gross weight. Empty weight (1,364), pilot and front seat passenger (298), baggage (80), oil (8 qt. = 2 gal. x 7.5 lb. per gal. = 15), and fuel (38 x 6 = 228).

   b. 17.1 gal. Use the data in question 5a. The total left for fuel is 103 lb., or 17.1 gal. at 6 lb. per gal.

   c. 633 lb. Use the total in question 5a. Fuel: 48 x 6 = 288; 2,300 less fuel (288), less oil (15), less empty weight (1,364) equals 633 lb.

   d. 47 lb. over maximum certified gross weight. Use the data in question 5a and make the appropriate substitutions.

   e. 23 lb. are left for baggage. Again, use the data in question 5a and make the appropriate substitutions.

6. a.

	WEIGHT (lb.)	MOM/1000
Empty weight	1,454	60.6
Pilot and front passenger	300	11.2
Rear passengers	200	14.6
Baggage	60	5.7
Fuel (full)	228	11.0
Oil	15	-0.2
TOTAL	2,257	102.9

   i. Is the weight within limits? YES
   ii. Is CG within limits for Normal Category operations? YES
   iii. Is CG within limits for Utility Category operations? NO

b.

	WEIGHT (lb.)	MOM/1000
Empty weight	1,454	60.6
Pilot and front passenger	300	11.2
Rear passengers	200	14.6
Baggage	60	5.7
Fuel (18.0 gallons)	108	5.1
Oil	15	-0.2
TOTAL	2,130	97.0

 i. Is the weight within limits? YES
 ii. Is CG within limits for Normal Category operations? YES
 iii. Is CG within limits for Utility Category operations? YES

c.

	WEIGHT (lb.)	MOM/1000
Empty weight	1,454	60.6
Pilot and front passenger	300	11.2
Rear passengers	0	0.0
Baggage	10	0.5
Fuel (18.0 gallons)	108	5.1
Oil	15	-0.2
TOTAL	1,887	77.2

 i. Is the weight within limits? YES
 ii. Is CG within limits for Normal Category operations? YES
 iii. Is CG within limits for Utility Category operations? YES

d.

	WEIGHT (lb.)	MOM/1000
Empty weight	1,300	51.7
Pilot (170 lb.) and front passenger (80 lb.)	250	9.1
Rear (250 lb., 150 lb.) passengers	400	28.8
Baggage	100	9.5
Fuel (full)	228	11.0
Oil	15	-0.2
TOTAL	2,293	110.0

 i. Is the weight within limits? YES
 ii. Is CG within limits for Normal Category operations? NO
 iii. Is CG within limits for Utility Category operations? NO

e. It makes the most sense to move the 250 lb. passenger from the rear seat to the front and move the 80 lb. passenger to the rear. You could also leave a passenger and/or baggage behind or you could move some of the baggage to the laps or feet of the passengers, but this is not a particularly safe procedure. Finally, draining fuel will not help, since the fuel is almost on the center of gravity. Try draining some fuel to see what happens. Assuming you have switched the passengers as mentioned above, the new weight and balance data look like this:

	WEIGHT (lb.)	MOM/1000
Empty weight	1,300	51.7
Pilot (150 lb.) and front passenger (250lb.)	400	14.5
Rear (150 lb., 100 lb.) passengers	250	17.8
Baggage	100	9.5
Fuel (full)	228	11.0
Oil	15	-0.2
TOTAL	2,293	104.3

i.   Is the weight within limits? **YES**
ii. Is CG within limits for Normal Category operations? **YES**
iii. Is CG within limits for Utility Category operations? **NO**

7. 2--CG changes any time weight is shifted. If weight moves back, the CG moves back.

8. 4--Moment = Arm x Weight. In this case, moment = 80 x 40, or 3,200 lb.-in.

9. 2--This defines the center of gravity (CG).

10. 1--This defines the CG envelope, a range of values for relating weights and balances.

11. 4--As you may recall, increasing the angle of bank increases stalling speed. Operation with a high gross weight or a forward CG destroys lift, which in turn increases stalling speed. A forward CG also makes it more difficult to recover from a stall.

12. 1--The first thing to figure is payload and empty condition.

13. 3--Any change in weight affects the CG. In this case, it moves forward.

14. 1--Arm = Moment/Weight.

15. 3--This defines the datum.

16. 1--This defines basic empty weight.

17. 3--This defines the fuselage station number.

18. 3--An aft CG makes the airplane least stable.

19. 3--A forward CG will cause the nose to go down and the tail up, so elevator trim will be required to keep the tail down.

20. 4--An aft CG will cause the nose to go up and the tail to go down, so elevator trim will be required to keep the nose down.

FAA Exam Questions

1. 4--Empty weight includes the airplane, powerplant, installed equipment, hydraulic fluid, and unusable fuel.

2. 2--Fuel weighs about 6 lb. per gallon. 100 lb. divided by 6 lb. per gallon = 18.3 gallons.

3. 4--Fuel weighs about 6 lb. per gallon. 90 lb. divided by 6 lb. per gallon = 15 gallon.

4. 2--Find total weight and total moment.

	WEIGHT (LB.)	ARM (IN.)	MOMENT (LB.-IN.)
Empty weight	1,495	101.4	151,593.0
Pilot and passengers	380	64.0	24,320.0
Fuel (30 gal)	180	96.0	17,280.0
TOTAL	2,055		193,193.0

Center of gravity is the average arm or total moment divided by total weight. 193,193 / 2,055 = 94.01 inches aft of datum.

5. 3--With this type of loading graph, you do not deal with ARM and no multiplication is necessary to find moment. Start with the LOADING GRAPH. For each load item, find the weight on the vertical left scale, proceed horizontally to the intersection with the diagonal line for the load item, then down vertically to find the load moment (divided by 1000 for simplicity). Add the individual weights and moments to find the loaded aircraft weight and moment. See Note: "The empty weight of this airplane DOES NOT INCLUDE the weight of the oil." Now move to the CENTER OF GRAVITY MOMENT ENVELOPE. Draw a horizontal line from the left loaded aircraft weight scale; if it is at or below the dark line at the top of the envelope, you are within maximum gross weight limits. Draw a vertical line from the loaded aircraft moment scale. If the intersection of the two lines is within the envelope, you are within CG. Note that there is a smaller envelope for operations in the UTILITY CATEGORY where up to 4.4 G's are permitted rather than the 2.8 G's of the NORMAL CATEGORY.

	WEIGHT (LB.)	MOM/1000
Empty weight	1,350	51.5
Pilot and front passenger	340	12.6
Fuel (std)	228	11.0
Oil (8 qt)	15	-0.2
	1,933	74.9

6. 3--See FAA Answer #5. Note that there is a smaller envelope for operations in the UTILITY CATEGORY.

	WEIGHT (LB.)	MOM/1000
Empty weight	1,350	51.5
Pilot and front passenger	380	14.0
Fuel (48 gal.)	288	13.8
Oil (8 qt.)	15	-0.2
	------	------
	2,033	79.1

The loaded weight and moment are within the NORMAL category envelope. To find CG, divide total moment by weight, remember to multiply total weight by 1,000. 79.1 x 1,000 = 79,100. 79,100 / 2,033 = 38.9

7. 2--See FAA Answer #5. Note that there is a smaller envelope for operations in the UTILITY CATEGORY.

	WEIGHT (LB.)	MOM/1000
Empty weight	1,350	51.5
Pilot and front passenger	250	9.3
Rear passengers	400	29.2
Baggage	------	------
Fuel (30 gal.)	180	8.5
Oil (8 qt.)	15	-0.2
	------	------
Total Wt.	2,195	Total Mom 98.3

These are within weight and CG limits. Maximum weight is 2,300 lb. 2,300-2,195 = 105 lb. which can be added.

	2,195	98.3
Baggage	105	10.2
	----	-----
New wt.	2,300	Mom 108.5

Check the envelope. These are at the upper limits of weight and CG for the NORMAL CATEGORY.

8. 2--See FAA Answer #5. Note that there is a smaller envelope for operations in the UTILITY CATEGORY.

	WEIGHT (LB.)	MOM/1000
Empty weight	1,350	51.5
Pilot and front passenger	310	11.5
Rear passenger	96	7.0
Fuel (38 gal.)	228	11.0
Oil (8 qt.)	15	-0.2
	------	------
	1,999	80.8

The loaded weight and moment are just within the upper limits of UTILITY CATEGORY.

9. 3--See FAA Answer #5. Note that there is a smaller envelope for operations in the UTILITY CATEGORY.

	WEIGHT (LB.)	MOM/1000
Empty weight	1,350	51.5
Pilot and front passenger	340	12.6
Rear passenger	310	22.6
Baggage	45	4.2
Oil (8 qt.)	15	-0.2
	------	------
	2,060	90.7

Maximum weight 2,300 - 2,060 = 240 lb. of fuel which can be carried. 240 lb. divided by 6 lb. per gal. = 40 gal.

10. 2--With these tables, multiplication is not necessary to find moment; however, you may have to interpolate. If the position weight exceeds that listed, break the weight down into smaller components and find the moment for each--example: for 340 lb., add the moments for 140 lb. and 200 lb.; or, you may multiply weight times arm. The empty weight and moment of the aircraft are given. Note that oil is included in the empty weight; do not add it in. All moments have been divided by 100. After you find the total weight and total moment, check the weight line on Figure 35 to determine if the total moment is within the limits for that total weight.

	WEIGHT (LB.)	MOM/100
Empty weight	2,015	1,554.0
Front (350)	200	170.0
Front	150	128.0
Rear (325)	160	194.0
Rear	165	200.0
Baggage	27	37.8
Fuel	210	158.0
	-----	-------
	2,929	2,441.8

The total moment is within the limits for 2,930 lb. of 2,399 - 2,483. CG is (2,441.8 x 100) / 2,929 = 83.4.

11. 2--See FAA Answer #10. We'll use the arm/100 to determine front and rear passenger moments.

	WEIGHT (LB.)	ARM	MOM/100
Empty weight	2,015		1,554.0
Front passengers	340	0.85	289.0
Rear passengers	295	1.21	357.0
Fuel 44 gal.	264		198.0
Baggage	56		78.4
	-----		-------
	2,970		2,476.4

Maximum weight is 2,950; you are 20 lb. heavy. The acceptable moment for 2,950 lb. is 2,422 to 2,499. To fly, you must reduce total weight by 20 lb., then rework the weight and balance problem to ensure you are within limits.

12. 3--See FAA Answer #10. Note: the main fuel tanks hold 44 gal. and the aux tank holds 19 gal. We'll use the arm/100 to determine front and rear passenger moments.

	WEIGHT (LB.)	ARM	MOM/100
Empty weight	2,015		1,554.00
Front	415	0.85	352.75
Rear	110	1.21	133.10
Fuel-main (44 gal.)	264		198.00
Fuel-aux (19 gal.)	114		107.00
Baggage	32		44.80
	-----		--------
	2,950		2,389.65

The moment limits for 2,950 lb. are 2,422 - 2,499, the CG is forward of limits.

13. 1--See below.

	WEIGHT (LB.)
Empty weight	2,015
Front	387
Rear	293
Fuel (35 gal.)	210

	2,905

Figure 35 shows the maximum weight to be 2,950 lb.; 2,950 - 2,905 = 45 lb. which can be added.

14. 4--With these tables, multiplication is not necessary to find moment; however, you may have to interpolate. All moments have been divided by 100. Start with the total weight and moment before the passenger transfer. Subtract the weight and the moment of the departing passenger. Then subtract the moving passengers old moment and add the new moment. Find the moment on Figure 34.

Old total weight	2,690	Mom	2,260.0
Departing front passenger	- 180		-153.0
	-----		-------
New total	2,510		2,107.0
Rear passenger moves	-(204)		-246.8
To front	+(204)		+173.2
	------		-------
New total	2,510		2,033.4

Old CG = (2,260 x 100) / 2,690 = 84.0 New CG = (2,033 x 100) / 2,510 = 80.9
CG shifts 3.1" forward

15. 2--See FAA Answer #10.

	WEIGHT (LB.)	ARM	MOM/100
Empty weight	2,015		1,554.00
Front	425	0.85	361.25
Rear	300	1.21	363.00
Fuel (44 gal.)	264		198.00
	-----		---------
	3,004		2,476.25

Total 3,004 - max 2,950 = 54 lb. overweight. 54 / 6 lb. per gal. = 9 gal.

16. 4--See FAA Answer #10.

	WEIGHT (LB.)	ARM	MOM/100
Empty weight	2,015		1,554.00
Front	411	0.85	349.35
Rear	100	1.21	121.00
Fuel (44 gal.)	264		198.00
	------		---------
	2,790		2,222.35

The moment limits for 2,790 lb. are 2243 - 2374. The CG is forward of the limits. You must shift some weight, add weight aft, or reduce forward weight. Try each possible answer.

a.	Total weight	2,790	Mom	2,222
	drain 5 gal.	30		22
		----		-----
		2,760		2,200

Moment limits for 2,760 is 2,210 - 2,350, out of limits.

b.	Total weight	2,790	Mom	2,222
	fill aux (19 gal.)	114		107
		-----		-----
		2,904		2,329

Moment limits for 2,900 lb. are 2,365 - 2,460, out of limits.

c.	Total weight	2,790	Mom	2,222
	drain 10 gal. main	-60	Mom	-45
	add 10 gal. aux.	+60		+56
		-----		-----
		2,790		2,233

Still out of limits.

d.	Total weight	2,790	Mom	2,222
	Baggage	100		140
		-----		-----
		2,890		2,362

Moment limits for 2,890 lb. are 2,354 - 2,452. Within limits at last!

17. 4--With these tables, multiplication is not necessary to find moment; however, you may have to interpolate. All moments have been divided by 100. After you find the total weight and total moment, check the weight line on Figure 35 to determine if the total moment is within the limits for that total weight. Subtract the weight and moment of fuel burned.

```
Total weight    2,890   Mom 2,452
35 gal. burned    210         158
                -----       -----
                2,680       2,294
```

Old CG = (2,452 x 100) / 2,890 = 84.84. New CG = (2,294 x 100) / 2,680 = 85.59. CG moves aft. Moment limits for 2,680 lb. are 2,123 - 2,287. CG is out of limits aft.

18. 1--The location of the CG determines longitudinal stability. When the CG is ahead of the center of lift, you have positive stability; when the nose is displaced upward, the forward CG causes it to tend to pitch down to the trimmed condition.

19. 2--When power is reduced on the airplane, the downwash over the horizontal stabilizer/elevators provides the negative lift to keep the tail down to balance the normal nose down effects of CG. When the downwash is reduced, the nose pitches down.

20. 4--When the CG is forward, the nose tends to pitch down when displaced upward. With an aft CG, the airplane is less stable and the nose may not tend to pitch down when displaced. Excessive elevator force may be required to effect stall recovery.

21. 2--When the CG is forward, the nose tends to pitch down when displaced upward. With an aft CG, the airplane is less stable and the nose may not tend to pitch down when displaced. Excessive elevator force may be required to effect stall recovery.

PERFORMANCE: MEASURING AN AIRPLANE'S CAPABILITIES

V_x – BEST ANGLE OF CLIMB SPEED

USUAL → V_y – BEST RATE OF CLIMB SPEED (67

MAIN POINTS

1. The **demonstrated** capability of an airplane appears in the Performance Section of the Pilot's Operating Handbook (POH). These data were obtained with new airplanes flown under favorable conditions by experienced pilots.

2. Atmospheric conditions influence both flight instruments and flight characteristics. **Atmospheric pressure** decreases as altitude increases due to the reduction of the density of the air. A 1000-ft. change in altitude corresponds to about a 1-in. change in mercury. Air temperature also decreases as altitude increases. The reference for measuring air properties is the **International Standard Atmosphere (ISA)**. Standard sea level conditions are 59°F (15°C) and 29.92 in. of mercury. When you set your altimeter to 29.92 and read the elevation from the altimeter, you have **pressure-altitude**, which is the altitude above a pressure level of 29.92. The higher the barometric pressure, the lower the pressure-altitude.

3. **Density-altitude** reflects three variables: pressure, temperature, and humidity. Warm temperatures make air expand and thus produce a higher density-altitude, as do actual increases in altitude. Water vapor displacing air molecules also makes air less dense. A cold, dry day at sea level would have a low density-altitude, while a warm, humid day in Mexico City (field elevation over 5,000 ft. MSL) would have a high density-altitude. Pressure-altitude is necessary to compute exact density-altitude. Figure 6.2 shows a chart relating outside air temperature (OAT) and pressure-altitude to density-altitude. The solid diagonal line from upper left to lower right represents ISA values.

4. Atmospheric factors affect performance. Less air density (higher density-altitude) means longer takeoff and landing runs and slower climb rates since there is less thrust and less lift. The pilot must calculate these effects of density-altitude on the takeoff run. Another atmospheric variable is the wind. Headwinds decrease takeoff and landing distances and tailwinds increase them. Airplane and runway characteristics also affect takeoff performance. As mentioned in an earlier chapter, more lift is required as

weight is increased and when the plane is loaded toward the forward CG limit; thus, both increase takeoff distance. Flaps, when partially extended, may increase lift and may be recommended for some airplanes for departing from soft fields to decrease the takeoff roll. The slope of the runway will also affect takeoff distance. A downhill slope decreases it and an uphill slope increases it. Rain, snow, and ice may also affect the takeoff distance, as will your technique as a pilot.

5. The indicated airspeed for takeoffs and landings remains the same regardless of changes in pressure and/or altitude. For the purpose of calculating takeoff performance, we will use indicated airspeed (uncorrected for errors in the instrument itself). First, determine pressure-altitude, either by setting the altimeter at 29.92 and reading it directly from the altimeter, or by computing it from the pressure and altitude data available. For example, in Lawrence, Kansas (field elevation 852 ft.), an atmospheric condition of 30.06 would have a pressure-altitude of 852 + ([-30.06 + 29.92] x 1,000) = 852 - 140, or 712 ft. Another way to determine pressure-altitude is to look it up on a pressure-altitude correction chart. Next, you need to calculate the effect of the wind. Runways are numbered according to their magnetic direction; and, for the purposes of takeoff and landing, surface wind directions are given as coming from a magnetic heading. Note: wind directions are always given as a true direction, except for purposes of takeoffs and landings. Using a wind components chart (see Figure 6.1), find the angle between the wind direction and flight path and the wind velocity to determine headwind and crosswind components. Finally, using a takeoff distance chart such as that shown in Figure 6.3, integrate the effects of density-altitude, gross weight, wind components, and obstacle heights to determine the takeoff distance.

6. **Interpolation.** Aircraft performance charts describe the performance of an aircraft under given conditions or ground rules. It is impossible for the aircraft manufacturer to provide the data for every possible condition; instead, performance under selected conditions is calculated and verified by flight testing. It is seldom that the actual conditions are identical to one of those listed. To determine your aircraft's approximate performance under existing conditions, you must sometimes use **interpolation.**

7. There are two airspeeds you must know: V_x, the best angle-of-climb, which yields the greatest altitude per distance traveled; and V_y, the best rate-of-climb, which gives you the greatest increase in altitude per unit of time. There are performance charts to help calculate climb performance. Once obstacles are cleared, use the recommended cruise climb speed to help prevent engine overheating.

8. Cruise speed depends upon your objective: maximum speed, maximum range, or maximum endurance (best ratio of fuel burned per unit of time). Fuel mixture should be leaned as recommended in the POH to enhance engine performance and to realize the best fuel consumption. Once aloft, winds remain a factor whether headwind, tailwind, or crosswind. Actual speed through the air is called **true airspeed (TAS)**; it is near **indicated airspeed (IAS)** at low altitudes but higher than IAS at high altitudes. Once again, there are graphs and charts to help you determine true airspeed at various power settings and density-altitudes. There are also graphs and charts that enable you to calculate range and endurance under different pressure-altitudes and power settings.

9. Fuel efficiency can be improved by keeping your airplane clean, loading it lightly, loading it near (but not beyond) the aft CG limit, keeping ground operations to a minimum, climbing directly on course, leaning the engine as recommended, and using shallow glide paths.

10. One key to effective landings is to establish the proper final approach airspeed and attitude early. The use of flaps, for example, requires considerable planning because the airplane responds more sluggishly when flaps are extended. A typical landing chart is shown in Figure 6.4.

11. Actual performance seldom is as good as that calculated using the performance data provided by the manufacturers. The prudent pilot assumes that performance will be 10-20% <u>less</u> than that calculated.

KEY TERMS AND CONCEPTS

Match each term or concept (1-16) with the appropriate description (A-T) below. Each item has only one match.

__	1. humidity	__	9. indicated airspeed (IAS)
__	2. short field	__	10. pressure-altitude
__	3. best rate-of-climb	__	11. maximum endurance
__	4. atmospheric pressure	__	12. ISA sea level
__	5. tailwind	__	13. best angle-of-climb
__	6. true airspeed (TAS)	__	14. magnetic north
__	7. crabbing	__	15. density-altitude
__	8. crosswind	__	16. maximum range

A. limited length runway with an obstacle at the departure end
B. actual speed through the air
C. best ratio of fuel consumed per unit of time
D. reference for surface wind directions given by a control tower
E. wind condition that will increase the landing distance
F. amount of water vapor the air contains
G. pressure exerted by the air
H. altitude read by setting the altimeter at 29.92
I. airspeed that produces the greatest altitude gain per unit of time
J. wind from any other direction but on the nose or tail
K. flying with the nose at an angle to the ground track into the wind
L. altitude corrected for nonstandard air temperature and pressure
M. dry air, 59°F (15°C) at a barometer setting of 29.92
N. airspeed that produces the greatest altitude gain for distance traveled
O. airspeed uncorrected for density-altitude or instrument error
P. best ratio of nautical miles per gallon of fuel consumed

DISCUSSION QUESTIONS AND EXERCISES

1. Define each of the following terms:

   a. atmospheric pressure

   b. International Standard Atmosphere (ISA)

   c. pressure-altitude

   d. density-altitude

2. State how each of the following affects density-altitude:

   a. air pressure

   b. temperature

   c. humidity

3. How and why does density-altitude affect the takeoff run? Give an example and state what you should do to take into account the effect of density-altitude. Finally, briefly describe how and why each of the following affects the takeoff run:

   a. headwind

b. tailwind

c. gross weight

d. runway gradient

e. CG

4. **Interpolation** is simply a process to compute intermediate values between a series of stated conditions. For aircraft performance, interpolation is used to compute values for actual conditions between those listed in a table. When performance is critical, an accurate determination of the performance value is the only acceptable means to ensure safe flight. Guessing to determine these values should be avoided.

The sample performance chart for your aircraft's takeoff data is shown below. But, your aircraft actually weighs 2,400 lb. So, you will have to use interpolation to determine exactly how far the ground roll will be.

Gross weight	Ground roll
2,200	1,000
2,600	1,600

The steps for interpolating are:

(1) Determine the fraction of the way between the two table values at which you existing condition is located:

```
  2,600                    2,400
 -2,200                   -2,200
 ------                   -----
    400 (between table values)    200    (difference between your value and
                                          the lower table value)
```

200 divided by 400 = 1/2

Your value (2,400) is 1/2 of the distance from the lesser value (2,200) to the greater value (2,600).

(2) Determine the distance between the performance data for the two table values: 1,600 - 1,000 = 600

(3) Multiply the distance of step 2 by the fraction of step 1 to obtain the correction amount for the performance data:

    600 x 1/2 = 300

    Your takeoff distance will be 300 ft. longer than that for a 2,200 lb aircraft and 300 ft. less than for a 2,600 lb. aircraft.

(4) Apply this difference to the lesser distance from the table. This is the takeoff distance for your weight of 2,400 lb.

    1,000 + 300 = 1,300

    Let's look at another example using the same table. Determine the takeoff distance for an aircraft weighing 2,300 lb.

(1)   2,600   2,300
        -2,200   -2,200
        -----   -----
          400   100   100/400 = 1/4

(2)   1,600 - 1,000 = 600

(3)   600 x 1/4 = 150

(4)   1,000 + 150 = 1,150, the takeoff distance for a 2,300 lb. aircraft.

Caution: Be sure to apply the correction from the proper value in the proper direction. The computed data will <u>always</u> be between the two given values.

    Now, it is your turn to solve the following problems.

a. <u>Table</u>

head wind	ground roll
0	1,025
15	875
30	700

Find the ground roll for 5 kts. of head wind.

b. <u>Table</u>

weight	rate of climb (feet per minute)
2,100	1,470
2,400	1,210
2,650	1,030

Find the rate of climb for 2,450 lb.

c. <u>Table - ground roll</u>

Airplane		Airport Elevation	
Weight	Sea level	2,500 ft.	5,000 ft.
2,100	1,055	1,270	1,525

Find the ground roll for a field elevation of 3,000 ft.

d. Is there a <u>safe</u> alternative to interpolation? Explain.

5.   The wind components chart (Figure 6.1) has several uses. First, for any given wind report, you can determine the magnitude of the crosswind component. Second, you can determine the maximum velocity for a given crosswind angle. Finally, you can determine which runway is best suited for a takeoff or landing without exceeding the maximum crosswind component. Use Figure 6.1 to answer the following questions.

a. What is the crosswind component for a landing on Rwy 18 if the tower reports the wind at 220° at 30 kts.?

b. What is the headwind component for a landing on Rwy 18 if the tower reports the wind at 220° at 30 kts.?

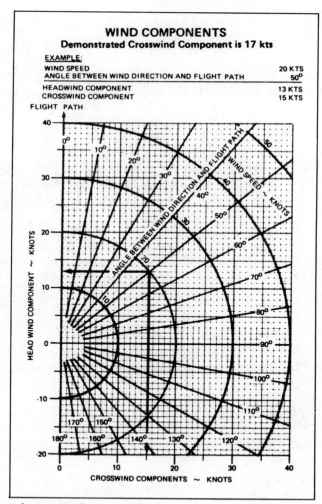

Figure 6.1

c. What is the maximum wind velocity for a 30° crosswind if the maximum crosswind component for an airplane is 12 kts.?

d. Determine the maximum wind velocity for a 45° crosswind if the maximum crosswind component for your airplane is 25 kts.?

e. With a reported wind from the north at 20 kts., which runway (6, 14, 24, or 32) is appropriate for an airplane with a 13-kt. maximum crosswind component?

f. With a reported wind from the west at 25 kts., which runway (6, 14, 24, or 32) is appropriate for an airplane with a 13-kt. maximum crosswind component?

6. To answer questions a-b, refer to Figure 6.2.

a. If the outside air temperature is 90° F in Denver, Colorado (elevation 5,330 ft.), and the altimeter setting is 30.30, what is the density-altitude?

b. Assume you are departing Rapid City (South Dakota) Regional Airport (field elevation 3,182 ft.), where the air temperature is 85°F and the altimeter is 29.60. What is the density-altitude?

7. When an airport tower controller reports that "the wind is 120 at 15," exactly what is the controller saying?

8. Define **indicated airspeed**. How is it different from **true airspeed**? How does the relationship between the two change as altitude increases?

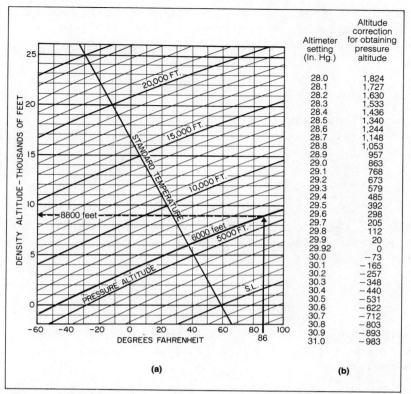

Figure 6.2

9. What is the difference between the best angle-of-climb airspeed and the best rate-of-climb speed?

10. Use the takeoff distance data in Figure 6.3 and the landing data in Figure 6.4 to solve the following problems. Also, you may need to refer to Figure 6.1 to calculate wind components.

    a. Suppose your airplane (2,800 lb. gross weight) is about to depart Rwy 31 at South Lake Tahoe (field elevation 4,870 ft., hard surface runway). Winds are reported at 340° at 18 kts., the temperature is 22°C, and the barometer is 29.32. Calculate how much runway will you need to get off the ground.

b. Determine that total takeoff distance necessary to clear a 50-ft. obstacle with a standard OAT, a pressure-altitude of 4,000 ft., a takeoff weight of 2,800 lb., and a headwind component of 20 kts.

c. What is the approximate ground roll distance for takeoff with an OAT of 100°F, a pressure-altitude of 2,000 ft., a takeoff weight of 2,950 lb., and calm wind conditions?

d. What is the total distance for a takeoff to clear a 50-ft. obstacle with an OAT of 59°F, a pressure-altitude of sea level, a takeoff weight of 2,700 lb., and a tailwind of 10 kts.?

e. Determine the approximate ground roll distance for takeoff with an OAT of 90°F, a pressure-altitude of 2,000 ft., a takeoff weight of 2,500 lb., and a 20-kt. headwind.

f. Determine the total distance to land the airplane over a 50-ft. obstacle with a standard OAT, a pressure-altitude of 2,000 ft., a landing weight of 2,500 lb., and calm winds.

g. What is the approximate ground roll distance after landing with an OAT of 90°F, a pressure-altitude of 4,000 ft., a landing weight of 2,800 lb., and a tailwind of 5 kts.?

h. What is the total landing distance over a 50-ft. obstacle with an OAT of 85°F, a pressure-altitude of 3,000 ft., a landing weight of 2,850 lb., and a headwind of 25 kts.?

TAKE-OFF DISTANCE

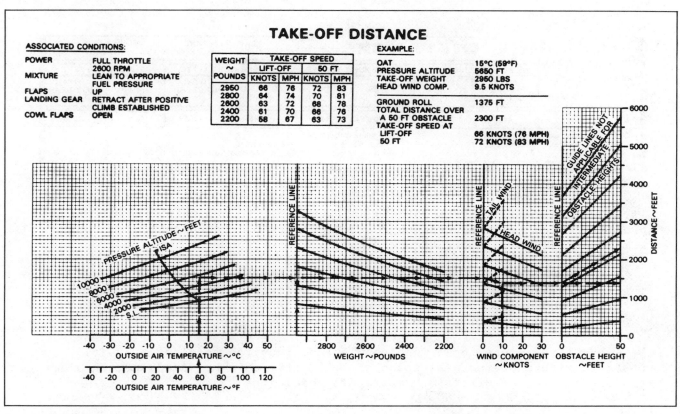

ASSOCIATED CONDITIONS:

POWER	FULL THROTTLE
	2600 RPM
MIXTURE	LEAN TO APPROPRIATE
	FUEL PRESSURE
FLAPS	UP
LANDING GEAR	RETRACT AFTER POSITIVE
	CLIMB ESTABLISHED
COWL FLAPS	OPEN

WEIGHT ~ POUNDS	TAKE-OFF SPEED			
	LIFT-OFF		50 FT	
	KNOTS	MPH	KNOTS	MPH
2950	66	76	72	83
2800	64	74	70	81
2600	63	72	68	78
2400	61	70	66	76
2200	58	67	63	73

EXAMPLE:

OAT	15°C (59°F)
PRESSURE ALTITUDE	5650 FT
TAKE-OFF WEIGHT	2950 LBS
HEAD WIND COMP.	9.5 KNOTS
GROUND ROLL	1375 FT
TOTAL DISTANCE OVER A 50 FT OBSTACLE	2300 FT
TAKE-OFF SPEED AT	
LIFT-OFF	66 KNOTS (76 MPH)
50 FT	72 KNOTS (83 MPH)

Figure 6.3

LANDING DISTANCE

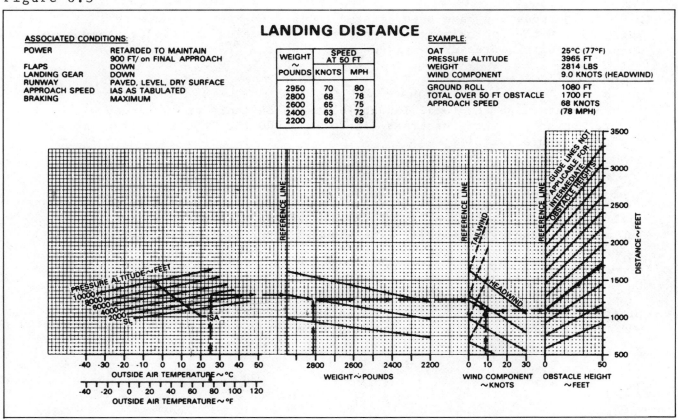

ASSOCIATED CONDITIONS:

POWER	RETARDED TO MAINTAIN
	900 FT/ on FINAL APPROACH
FLAPS	DOWN
LANDING GEAR	DOWN
RUNWAY	PAVED, LEVEL, DRY SURFACE
APPROACH SPEED	IAS AS TABULATED
BRAKING	MAXIMUM

WEIGHT ~ POUNDS	SPEED AT 50 FT	
	KNOTS	MPH
2950	70	80
2800	68	78
2600	65	75
2400	63	72
2200	60	69

EXAMPLE:

OAT	25°C (77°F)
PRESSURE ALTITUDE	3965 FT
WEIGHT	2814 LBS
WIND COMPONENT	9.0 KNOTS (HEADWIND)
GROUND ROLL	1080 FT
TOTAL OVER 50 FT OBSTACLE	1700 FT
APPROACH SPEED	68 KNOTS (78 MPH)

Figure 6.4

LANDING DISTANCE			FLAPS LOWERED TO 40° - POWER OFF HARD SURFACE RUNWAY - ZERO WIND							

GROSS WEIGHT LBS.	APPROACH SPEED, IAS, MPH	AT SEA LEVEL & 59° F.		AT 2500 FT. & 50° F.		AT 5000 FT. & 41° F.		AT 7500 FT. & 32° F.	
		GROUND ROLL	TOTAL TO CLEAR 50 FT. OBS	GROUND ROLL	TOTAL TO CLEAR 50 FT. OBS	GROUND ROLL	TOTAL TO CLEAR 50 FT. OBS	GROUND ROLL	TOTAL TO CLEAR 50 FT. OBS
1600	60	445	1075	470	1135	495	1195	520	1255

NOTES:
1. Decrease the distances shown by 10% for each 4 knots of headwind.
2. Increase the distance by 10% for each 60°F. temperature increase above standard.
3. For operation on a dry, grass runway, increase distances (both "ground roll" and "total to clear 50 ft. obstacle") by 20% of the "total to clear 50 ft. obstacle" figure.

Figure 6.5

11. Use the landing-distance data in Figure 6.5 to complete the following problems. You may also have to refer to Figure 6.1 to compute wind components.

a. Determine the landing ground roll with a pressure-altitude at sea level, standard temperature, and an 8-kt. headwind.

b. What is the total landing distance required to clear a 50-ft. obstacle with a pressure-altitude of 7,500 ft., an 8-kt. headwind, on a dry grass runway under standard temperature conditions?

c. Suppose you have been cleared to land on Rwy 7. The wind is 100° at 28. What is the approximate landing roll distance under standard temperature conditions with a pressure-altitude of 3,750 ft.?

d. Determine the total landing distance on a dry grass runway with a 50-ft. obstacle? The pressure-altitude is 5,000 ft., the wind is calm, and the temperature is 101°F.

e. Determine the total distance required to land over a 50-ft. obstacle with a pressure-altitude of 5,000 ft. and standard temperature conditions. You will be landing on Rwy 35. The wind is reported "010 at 34."

f. What is the approximate landing ground roll distance with a pressure-altitude of 1,250 ft. under standard temperature conditions? You will be landing on Rwy 7. The winds are reported "360 at 24."

CRUISE PERFORMANCE
STANDARD DAY
AVERAGE CRUISE WEIGHT = 1600 POUNDS

ALTITUDE FEET	THROTTLE SETTING RPM	FUEL FLOW GPH	IAS KNOTS	TAS KNOTS
2500	2700	8.0	101	105
	2500	6.4	94	97
	2400	5.7	90	93
	2300	5.2	85	88
3500	2700	7.8	100	105
	2500	6.3	92	97
	2400	5.7	88	93
	2300	5.2	84	88
4500	2700	7.7	99	105
	2500	6.3	91	97
	2400	5.6	87	93
	2300	5.1	82	88
5500	2700	7.6	97	105
	2500	6.2	89	97
	2400	5.5	85	92
	2300	5.0	81	87
6500	2700	7.4	96	105
	2500	6.1	88	97
	2400	5.4	84	92
	2300	5.0	79	87
7500	2500	6.0	86	96
	2400	5.3	82	91
	2300	4.9	77	86
8500	2500	5.8	85	96
	2400	5.3	80	91
	2300	4.9	76	85
9500	2500	5.7	83	95
	2400	5.2	79	90
	2300	4.8	74	85
10500	2500	5.6	81	95
	2400	5.1	77	90
	2300	4.7	72	84
11500	2500	5.5	80	94
	2400	5.0	75	89
	2300	4.7	70	82

Cruise performance is based on best power mixture. Lean to maximum rpm for best performance.

Figure 6.6

12. Refer to Figure 6.6. Suppose you are cruising at 6,500 ft. under standard temperature conditions. You have the throttle set at 2,500 RPM. What is your fuel flow, your indicated airspeed, and your true airspeed?

13. Refer to Figure 6.7. What is your maximum range at 2,400 RPM with a pressure-altitude of 8,000 ft.?

14. Refer to Figure 6.8. What is your maximum endurance at 2,400 RPM with a pressure-altitude of 8,000 ft.?

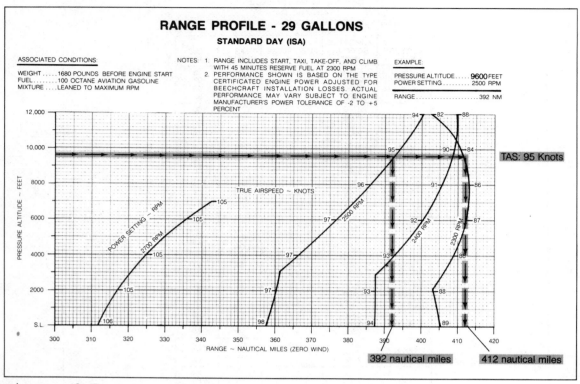

Figure 6.7

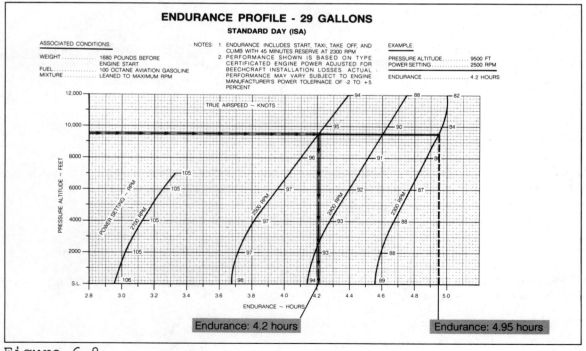

Figure 6.8

15. Name five things you can do as a pilot to conserve fuel.

16. What is one of the most important factors that contributes to a safe and efficient landing?

17. T F When landing at an airport with a high density-altitude, a pilot should add extra speed to the final-approach indicated airspeed to compensate for the thinner air.

Explain your answer.

CRUISE POWER SETTINGS

75% MAXIMUM CONTINUOUS POWER (OR FULL THROTTLE)
2800 LBS

| PRESS ALT. | ISA −20°C (−36°F) | | | | | | STANDARD DAY (ISA) | | | | | | ISA +20°C (+36°F) | | | | | |
| | IOAT | | ENGINE SPEED | MAN. PRESS | FUEL FLOW PER ENGINE | TAS | | IOAT | | ENGINE SPEED | MAN. PRESS | FUEL FLOW PER ENGINE | TAS | | IOAT | | ENGINE SPEED | MAN. PRESS | FUEL FLOW PER ENGINE | TAS | |
FEET	°F	°C	RPM	IN HG	PSI	GPH	KTS	MPH	°F	°C	RPM	IN HG	PSI	GPH	KTS	MPH	°F	°C	RPM	IN HG	PSI	GPH	KTS	MPH
SL	27	−3	2450	23.1	8.2	13.6	156	180	63	17	2450	23.8	8.2	13.6	159	183	99	37	2450	24.4	8.2	13.6	162	186
2000	19	−7	2450	22.8	8.2	13.6	158	182	55	13	2450	23.5	8.2	13.6	162	186	93	34	2450	24.2	8.2	13.6	165	190
4000	12	−11	2450	22.6	8.2	13.6	161	185	50	10	2450	23.3	8.2	13.6	165	190	86	30	2450	23.9	8.2	13.6	168	193
6000	7	−14	2450	22.3	8.2	13.6	164	189	43	6	2450	23.0	8.2	13.6	167	192	79	26	2450	23.4	8.0	13.4	170	196
8000	0	−18	2450	21.8	8.0	13.3	166	191	36	2	2450	21.8	7.6	12.8	167	192	72	22	2450	21.8	7.2	12.3	168	193
10000	−8	−22	2450	20.3	7.2	12.3	164	189	28	−2	2450	20.3	6.8	11.8	165	190	64	18	2450	20.3	6.5	11.4	166	191
12000	−15	−26	2450	18.8	6.4	11.3	162	186	21	−6	2450	18.8	6.2	10.9	163	188	57	14	2450	18.8	5.8	10.6	163	188
14000	−22	−30	2450	17.4	5.9	10.5	159	183	14	−10	2450	17.4	5.6	10.1	160	184	50	10	2450	17.4	5.3	9.8	160	184
16000	−29	−34	2450	16.1	5.3	9.7	156	180	7	−14	2450	16.1	5.1	9.4	156	180	43	6	2450	16.1	4.9	9.1	155	178

NOTES: 1. Full throttle manifold pressure settings are approximate.
2. Shaded area represents operation with full throttle.

Figure 6.9

18. Refer to Figure 6.9 to answer the following questions.

a. What is the expected fuel consumption for a 1,000-mi. flight at a pressure-altitude of 8,000 ft. with calm winds and a temperature of -18°C? Manifold pressure is 21.8" Hg.

b. What is the expected fuel consumption for a 500-mi. flight at a pressure-altitude of 4,000 ft. with calm winds and a temperature of +30°C? Manifold pressure is 23.9" Hg.

c. What fuel flow should a pilot expect at 8,500 ft. on a standard day with 75 percent maximum continuous power?

d. Determine the approximate fuel flow at 75 percent maximum continuous power at 6,500 ft. with a temperature of 36°F higher than standard.

19. Climb Performance. Figure 6.10 provides information to determine time, distance, and fuel to climb. Enter the chart for airport temperature in degrees Celsius, proceed vertically to the pressure-altitude line, then move horizontally. When you intercept the fuel, time, and distance lines, proceed vertically to determine the fuel, time, and distance required. If the climb begins at some elevation above sea level, determine the data for a climb from sea level to the cruise altitude. Then, you must subtract the data that would have been required to climb from sea level to the starting elevation/altitude. Use Figure 6.10 for the following problems.

a. Airport temperature is forecast to be +30°C. For a climb from sea level to 7,000 ft., determine fuel required, time to climb and distance to climb.

b. Airport temperature is forecast to be -10°C. For a climb to 9,000 ft. from a takeoff at an airport with an elevation of 3,000 ft., determine fuel to climb, time to climb, and distance to climb.

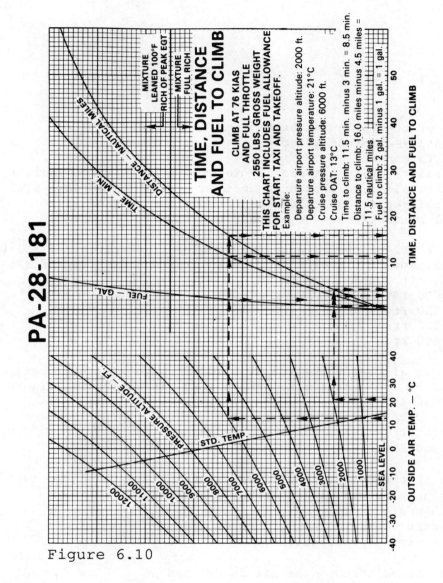

Figure 6.10

20. An airplane takes off into a direct 20-kt. headwind. The stalling speed of the airplane is 50 kts., and its indicated airspeed in a climb is 65 kts. If the pilot turns the airplane downwind and the 20-kt. headwind becomes a 20-kt. tailwind, will the airplane stall? Explain why or why not.

21. Which of the following statements is correct?
    1--Density-altitude affects takeoff performance, but not landing performance.
    2--Density-altitude typically increases as altitude increases.
    3--Extra airspeed should be used to land at an airport with a high density-altitude to compensate for the thinner air.
    4--All of the above are correct.

22. Refer to Figure 6.2. Assuming an airport elevation of 3,165 feet, an outside air temperature of 93°F, and an altimeter setting of 30.10, what is the density-altitude?
    1--3,000 ft.
    2--3,850 ft.
    3--5,800 ft.
    4--6,800 ft.

23. Given an airport elevation of 3,700 ft., an altimeter setting of 29.60, and an OAT of 75°F, determine the density-altitude using Figure 6.2.
    1--1,000 ft.
    2--3,950 ft.
    3--5,200 ft.
    4--5,950 ft.

24. Which of the following will increase the length of the takeoff roll?
    1--Using a runway with a downhill gradient.
    2--A headwind.
    3--A soft field.
    4--Increasing gross weight.

25. Actual speed through the air is defined as _____ airspeed.
    1--calibrated
    2--indicated
    3--relative
    4--true

26. If the barometer is 30.32 and you are at 120 MSL, pressure-altitude is
    1-- -280 ft.
    2-- 80 ft.
    3-- 100 ft.
    4-- 520 ft.

27. Refer to Figure 6.6. Given a barometric setting of 29.22 and indicated altitude of 5,800 ft., what is your true airspeed and fuel flow at 2,500 RPM?
    1--92 kts.; 5.4 gal./hr.
    2--92 kts.; 6.1 gal./hr.
    3--97 kts.; 6.1 gal./hr.
    4--97 kts.; 5.4 gal./hr.

28. Refer to Figures 6.7 and 6.8. Assume a pressure-altitude of 8,000 ft. and 2,400 RPM. What is your maximum range and maximum endurance under these conditions?
    1--385 NM; 4.1 hr.
    2--405 NM; 4.5 hr.
    3--425 NM; 4.7 hr.
    4--450 NM; 4.1 hr.

29. Refer to Figure 6.7. How much could you extend your range at a pressure-altitude of 6,400 ft. if you were to reduce the throttle from 2,400 RPM to 2,300 RPM?
    1--6 NM.
    2--8 NM.
    3--11 NM.
    4--15 NM.

30. Dry air that is 15°C and has a pressure of 29.92 in. of mercury defines
    1--atmospheric pressure.
    2--density-altitude.
    3--International Standard Atmosphere (ISA).
    4--pressure-altitude.

31. Which of the following leads to a high density-altitude?
    1--High air pressure.
    2--Low relative humidity.
    3--High temperature.
    4--All of the above.

32. Which of the following leads to a high density-altitude?
    1--Low air pressure.
    2--High relative humidity.
    3--High temperature.
    4--All of the above.

33. If you plan to land at an airport where the elevation is 7,500 ft., the indicated approach speed should be
    1--higher than that used at a sea level airport.
    2--higher than that used at a sea level airport, and some power should be
        used until touchdown.
    3--lower than that used at a sea level airport.
    4--the same as that used at a sea level airport.

34. Which of the following combinations of atmospheric conditions will have the most adverse effect on airplane takeoff and climb performance?
    1--High temperature and high relative humidity.
    2--High temperature and low relative humidity.
    3--Low temperature and high relative humidity.
    4--Low temperature and low relative humidity.

35. Refer to Figure 6.1. If the elevation of an airport is 5,480 ft., the altimeter setting is 29.90, and the outside air temperature is 80°F, what is the density-altitude at that airport?
     1--2,800 ft.
     2--5,400 ft.
     3--8,100 ft.
     4--9,200 ft.

36. Refer to Figure 6.1. Outside air temperature is 90°F, the altimeter 30.20, and airport elevation is 4,725 ft. What is the density-altitude?
     1--1,700 ft.
     2--4,400 ft.
     3--7,400 ft.
     4--7,800 ft.

37. While on the ground at an airport, you can determine the pressure-altitude by
     1--setting the altimeter to the field elevation and reading the value in the altimeter setting window.
     2--setting the altimeter to zero and reading the value in the altimeter setting window.
     3--setting 29.92 in the airplane's altimeter setting window and reading the altitude indicated on the altimeter.
     4--setting the field elevation in the altimeter setting window and reading the altitude indicated on the altimeter.

38. If the barometer is 29.32 and you are at 8,240 ft. MSL, what is the pressure-altitude?
     1--7,640 ft.
     2--8,180 ft.
     3--8,300 ft.
     4--8,840 ft.

39. If the barometer is 29.90 and you are at 8,900 ft. MSL, what is the pressure-altitude?
     1--8,700 ft.
     2--8,880 ft.
     3--8,920 ft.
     4--9,100 ft.

40. Refer to Figure 6.6. Given a barometric setting of 28.92 and an indicated altitude of 3,500 ft., what is your true airspeed and your fuel flow per hour if you maintain 2,300 RPM?
     1--84 kts.; 5.2 gal./hr.
     2--85 kts.; 5.7 gal./hr.
     3--88 kts.; 5.2 gal./hr.
     4--88 kts.; 5.7 gal./hr.

41. Refer to Figure 6.7 and 6.8. Assume a pressure-altitude of 4,000 ft. and 2,400 RPM. What is your maximum range and maximum endurance?
     1--348 NM; 3.6 hr.
     2--366 NM; 3.8 hr.
     3--382 NM; 4.0 hr.
     4--393 NM; 4.3 hr.

42. Refer to Figure 6.7. How much could you extend your range at a pressure-altitude of 10,000 ft. if you were to reduce the throttle from 2,500 RPM to 2,400 RPM?
     1--12 NM.
     2--15 NM.
     3--20 NM.
     4--24 NM.

47. Refer to Figure 6.8. How much could you extend your endurance at a pressure-altitude of 5,000 ft. if you were to reduce the throttle from 2,400 RPM to 2,300 RPM?
     1--0.2 hr.
     2--0.4 hr.
     3--0.6 hr.
     4--0.8 hr.

FAA EXAM QUESTIONS

(Note: All FAA Figures are located in Appendix C)

1. (FAA 1003) Density altitude is the
    1--altitude reference to the standard datum plane.
    2--pressure altitude corrected for nonstandard temperature.
    3--altitude read directly from the altimeter.
    4--altitude above the surface.

2. (FAA 1006) What effect does high density altitude have on aircraft performance?
    1--It increases engine performance.
    2--It reduces an aircraft's climb performance.
    3--It will decrease the runway length required for takeoff.
    4--It increases lift because the light air exerts less force on the airfoils.

3. (FAA 1007) Which factor would tend to increase the density altitude at a given airport?
    1--Increasing barometric pressure.
    2--Increasing ambient temperature.
    3--Decreasing relative humidity.
    4--Decreasing ambient temperature.

4. (FAA 1008) What effect does high humidity have on aircraft performance?
    1--Increase in rate of climb.
    2--Landing speed will be higher.
    3--Decrease in takeoff run.
    4--Indicated cruise speed will be faster.

5. (FAA 1025) If the outside air temperature at a given altitude is warmer than standard, the density altitude is
1--lower than pressure altitude, but approximately equal to the true altitude.
2--higher than true altitude, but lower than pressure altitude.
3--higher than the pressure altitude.
4--lower than true altitude.

6. (FAA 1026) Which combination of atmospheric conditions will reduce aircraft takeoff and climb performance?
1--Low temperature, low relative humidity, and low density altitude.
2--High temperature, low relative humidity, and low density altitude.
3--High temperature, high relative humidity, and high density altitude.
4--Low temperature, high relative humidity, and high density altitude.

7. (FAA 1028) What effect does higher density altitude have on propeller efficiency?
1--Increased efficiency due to less friction on the propeller blades.
2--Reduced efficiency because the propeller exerts less force than at lower density altitudes.
3--Reduced efficiency due to the increased force of the thinner air on the propeller.
4--Increased efficiency because the propeller exerts more force on the thinner air.

8. (FAA 1017) Determine the pressure altitude with an indicated altitude of 1,380 ft. with an altimeter setting of 28.22" Hg. at standard temperature. (See Figure 1.)
1--250 ft.
2--1,373 ft.
3--2,303 ft.
4--2,800 ft.

9. (FAA 1022) Determine the pressure altitude at an airport that is 1,386 ft. MSL with an altimeter setting of 29.97. (See Figure 1.)
1--1,451 ft.
2--1,562 ft.
3--1,684 ft.
4--1,341 ft.

10. (FAA 1019) Determine the pressure altitude at an airport that is 3,563 ft. MSL with an altimeter setting of 29.96. (See Figure 1.)
1--3,527 ft.
2--3,556 ft.
3--3,639 ft.
4--3,507 ft.

11. (FAA 1018) Determine the density altitude for the following conditions: (See Figures 1.)

Altimeter setting	29.25
Rwy temperature	+81°F
Airport elevation	5,250 ft.

1--4,600 ft.   2--5,877 ft.
3--8,500 ft.   4--7,700 ft.

12. (FAA 1021) Determine the density altitude for the following conditions:
(See Figure 1.)

Altimeter setting	30.35
Rwy temperature	+25°F
Airport elevation	3,894 ft.

1--2,900 ft.
2--3,500 ft.
3--3,800 ft.
4--2,000 ft.

13. (FAA 1016) What is the effect of a temperature increase from 25° to
50° F on the density altitude if the pressure altitude remains at
5,000 ft.? (See Figure 1.)
1--1,650-foot increase.
2--1,400-foot increase.
3--1,200-foot increase.
4--1,000-foot increase.

14. (FAA 1020) What is the effect of a temperature increase from 30° to
50° F on the density altitude if the pressure altitude remains at
3,000 ft.? (See Figure 1.)
1--900-foot increase.
2--1,100-foot decrease.
3--1,500-foot increase.
4--1,300-foot increase.

15. (FAA 1023) What is the effect of a temperature decrease and a pressure
altitude increase on the density altitude from 90°F and 1,250 ft.
pressure altitude to 60°F and 1,750 ft. pressure altitude?
(See Figure 1.)
1--500-foot increase.
2--1,300-foot decrease.
3--1,300-foot increase.
4--500-foot decrease.

16. (FAA 1331) What is the headwind component for a landing on Rwy 18 if
the tower reports the wind as 220° at 30 kts.? (See Figure 24.)
1--19 kts.
2--23 kts.
3--26 kts.
4--30 kts.

17. (FAA 1336) What is the crosswind component for a landing on Rwy 18 if
the tower reports the wind as 220° at 30 kts.? (See Figure 24.)
1--19 kts.
2--23 kts.
3--30 kts.
4--34 kts.

18. (FAA 1332) Determine the maximum wind velocity for a 45° crosswind if
the maximum crosswind component for the airplane is 25 kts. (See Figure
24.)

1--18 kts.   2--25 kts.
3--29 kts.   4--35 kts.

19. (FAA 1334) What is the maximum wind velocity for a 30° crosswind if the maximum crosswind component for the airplane is 12 kts.? (See Figure 24.)
    1--13 kts.
    2--17 kts.
    3--21 kts.
    4--24 kts.

20. (FAA 1333) With a reported wind of north at 20 kts., which runway (6, 14, 24, or 32) is appropriate for an airplane with a 13-knot maximum crosswind component? (See Figure 24.)
    1--Rwy 6.
    2--Rwy 14.
    3--Rwy 24.
    4--Rwy 32.

21. (FAA 1335) With a reported wind of south at 20 kts., which runway (6, 14, 24, or 32) is appropriate for an airplane with a 13-knot maximum crosswind component? (See Figure 24.)
    1--Rwy 6.
    2--Rwy 14.
    3--Rwy 24.
    4--Rwy 32.

22. (FAA 1355) With the following conditions, determine the landing ground roll from the Landing Distance Chart. (See Figure 29.)

    Pressure altitude   Sea level
    Headwind   4 kts.
    Temperature   Std.

    1--356 ft.   2--401 ft.
    3--490 ft.   4--534 ft.

23. (FAA 1356) What is the total landing distance required to clear a 50-foot obstacle with the following conditions using the Landing Distance Chart? (See Figure 29.)

    Pressure altitude   7,500 ft.
    Headwind   8 kts.
    Temperature   Std.
    Runway   Dry grass.

    1--1,004 ft.   2--1,205 ft.
    3--1,506 ft.   4--1,757 ft.

24. (FAA 1357) Determine the approximate landing ground roll distance from the Landing Distance Chart. (See Figure 29.)

    Pressure altitude   3,570 ft.
    Headwind   12 kts.
    Temperature   Std.

    1--193 ft.   2--338 ft.
    3--483 ft.   4--816 ft.

25. (FAA 1358) What is the total landing distance required to clear a 50-foot obstacle with the following conditions using the Landing Distance Chart? (See Figure 29.)

Pressure altitude	5,000 ft.
Headwind	8 kts.
Temperature	41°F
Runway	Hard surface

1--837 ft.   2--956 ft.
3--1,076 ft.   4--1,554 ft.

26. (FAA 1359) Determine the total distance required to land over a 50-foot obstacle from the Landing Distance Chart. (See Figure 29.)

Pressure altitude	5,000 ft.
Headwind	Calm
Temperature	101°F

1--239 ft.   2--1,099 ft.
3--1,291 ft.   4--1,314 ft.

27. (FAA 1360) What is the approximate landing ground roll distance using the Landing Distance Chart? (See Figure 29.)

Pressure altitude	1,250 ft.
Headwind	8 kts.
Temperature	Std.

1--275 ft.   2--366 ft.
3--470 ft.   4--549 ft.

28. (FAA 1351) Determine the total distance to land the airplane under the following conditions. (See Figure 28.)

OAT	32°F
Pressure altitude	8,000 ft.
Weight	2,600 lb.
Headwind component	20 kts.
Obstacle	50 ft.

1--850 ft.   2--1,400 ft.
3--1,750 ft.   4--2,100 ft.

29. (FAA 1352) Determine the total distance to land the airplane under the following conditions. (See Figure 28.)

OAT	Std.
Pressure altitude	2,000 ft.
Weight	2,300 lb.
Wind component	Calm

1--850 ft.   2--1,250 ft.
3--1,450 ft.   4--1,700 ft.

30. (FAA 1353) What is the approximate ground roll distance after landing under the following conditions? (See Figure 28.)

OAT	90°F
Pressure altitude	4,000 ft.
Weight	2,800 lb.
Tailwind component	10 kts.

1--1,200 ft.   2--1,575 ft.
3--1,725 ft.   4--1,950 ft.

31. (FAA 1354) What is the total landing distance under the following conditions? (See Figure 28.)

OAT	90°F
Pressure altitude	3,000 ft.
Weight	2,900 lb.
Headwind component	10 kts.
Obstacle	50 ft.

1--1,300 ft.   2--1,450 ft.
3--1,550 ft.   4--1,725 ft.

32. (FAA 1367) Determine the total distance for a takeoff to clear a 50-foot obstacle. (See Figure 31.)

OAT	Std.
Pressure altitude	4,000 ft.
Takeoff weight	2,800 lb.
Headwind component	Calm

1--1,250 ft.   2--1,500 ft.
3--1,750 ft.   4--1,900 ft.

33. (FAA 1368) What is the approximate ground roll distance for takeoff under the following conditions? (See Figure 31.)

OAT	100°F
Pressure altitude	2,000 ft.
Takeoff weight	2,750 lb.
Headwind component	Calm

1--1,150 ft.   2--1,300 ft.
3--1,800 ft.   4--2,000 ft.

34. (FAA 1369) What is the total distance for takeoff to clear a 50-foot obstacle under the following conditions? (See Figure 31.)

OAT	Std.
Pressure altitude	Sea level
Takeoff weight	2,700 lb.
Headwind component	Calm

1--1,000 ft.   2--1,400 ft.
3--1,700 ft.   4--1,900 ft.

35. (FAA 1370) Determine the approximate ground roll distance for takeoff under the following conditions. (See Figure 31.)

OAT   90°F
Pressure altitude   2,000 ft.
Takeoff weight   2,500 lb.
Headwind component   20 kts.

1--650 ft.   2--800 ft.
3--1,000 ft.   4--1,250 ft.

36. (FAA 1337) What is the expected fuel consumption for a 1,000-nautical mile flight under the following conditions? (See Figure 25.)

Pressure altitude   8,000 ft.
Temperature   -19°C
Manifold pressure   19.5" Hg.
Wind   Calm

1--41.9 gal.   2--63.5 gal.
3--71.4 gal.   4--73.2 gal.

37. (FAA 1338) What is the expected fuel consumption for a 500-nautical mile flight under the following conditions? (See Figure 25.)

Pressure altitude   4,000 ft.
Temperature   +29°C
Manifold pressure   21.3" Hg.
Wind   Calm

1--31.4 gal.   2--36.1 gal.
3--40.1 gal.   4--43.2 gal.

38. (FAA 1339) What fuel flow should a pilot expect at 11,000 ft. on a standard day with 65 percent maximum continuous power? (See Figure 25.)
1--10.6 gal./hr.
2--11.2 gal./hr.
3--11.8 gal./hr.
4--12.1 gal./hr.

39. (FAA 1340) Determine the approximate manifold pressure setting with 2,450 RPM to achieve 65 percent maximum continuous power at 6,500 ft. with a temperature of 36°F higher than standard? (See Figure 25.)
1--19.8" Hg.
2--21.0" Hg.
3--20.8" Hg.
4--20.4" Hg.

40. (FAA 1341) Approximately what true airspeed should a pilot expect with 65 percent maximum continuous power of 9,500 ft. with a temperature of 36°F below standard? (See Figure 25.)
1--178 MPH.
2--181 MPH.
3--183 MPH.
4--186 MPH.

ANSWERS AND EXPLANATIONS

Key Terms and Concepts

1. F	5. E	9. O	13. N
2. A	6. B	10. H	14. D
3. I	7. K	11. C	15. L
4. G	8. J	12. M	16. P

Discussion Questions and Review Exercises

1. See Study Guide Main Points #2 and #3.

2. See Study Guide Main Point #3.

3. See Study Guide Main Points #3 and #4.

4.

   a. 975 ft. 5 kts. is 1/3 of the way into the interval. 1/3 of the difference between (,1025 - 875 = 150) is 50 ft., which you then <u>subtract</u> from 1025. For planning, you could have used the ground roll for 0 kt. (1,025 ft.)

   b. 1,174 ft./min. 2,450 lb. is 1/5 of the way into the interval. 1/5 of the difference between (1,210 - 1,030 = 180) is 36 ft./min., which you <u>subtract</u> from 1210. The more adverse condition of 2,650 lbs. shows a lesser rate of 1,030 ft./min.

   c. 1,321 ft. 3,000 ft. is 1/5 of the way into the interval. 1/5 of the difference between (1,525 - 1,270 = 255) is 51 ft., which you <u>add</u> to 1,270. If you had used the more adverse condition of 5,000 ft. elevation, you would have used 1,525 ft. for planning purposes. You cannot use the more adverse condition when the performance margin is close. In this problem, your landing runway is only 1500 ft. in length. Simply using the more adverse condition would indicate that you have insufficient runway for these conditions. Do not guess that you can safely land because the actual elevation is less than 5000 ft. In this case, you <u>must</u> use interpolation to determine the actual requirements of 1,321 ft. for the landing roll. Thus, according to the manufacturers' data, you have enough runway for landing (<u>barely</u>).

   d. There is a safe alternative to interpolation; you may use the performance for a more <u>adverse</u> condition.

5.

   a. 19 kt. The angle between the runway and wind is 40°. Read out the diagonal 40° line until you intersect the **curved** line that represents a wind speed of 30 kt. Now read **down** vertically to the crosswind component.

   b. 23 kt. The angle between the runway and wind is 40°. Read out the diagonal 40° line until you intersect the **curved** line that represents a wind speed of 30 kt. Now read horizontally **across** to the headwind component.

   c. 21 kt. Use the same procedure outlined for answer 5d.

d. 35 kt. This will require some estimation on your part. First, find 25 kt. on the crosswind component scale. Go up until you intersect a point equidistant between 40° and 50° on the line that represents the angle between wind direction and flight path. Now you must **imagine** a curved line somewhere between 30 and 40 kt. As it so happens, the point is almost exactly equidistant between the two lines, or 35 kt.

e. Rwy 32 is the most appropriate, but there are two correct answers to this problem. First, logic tells us that we should take off **into** the wind, unless there is some extenuating circumstance that would dictate otherwise. The runway with a heading closest to north is Rwy 32; and, by checking the wind components in Figure 6.1 for a 40° angle at a wind velocity of 20 kt., we are barely within the airplane's crosswind limits. But, let's also look at Rwy 14. This would involve a departing tailwind; but, with a 40° crosswind (the difference between Rwy 14 and a tailwind at 180°), the airplane is still within limits.

f. Rwy 24 would be the most appropriate. An analysis of Figure 6.1 also reveals that the airplane would be within its crosswind limits.

6.
  a. 8,100 ft. Find the altimeter setting of 30.3 on the chart in Figure 6.2. Read across to find the altitude correction (-348 ft.), which you subtract from 5,330 ft. to arrive at pressure-altitude, 4,982 ft. Read up the 90°F line until you intersect the diagonal 5,000 pressure-altitude line. Read over to the density-altitude scale, approximately 8,100 ft.

  b. 3,480 ft. Use the same procedure described for 6a above.

7. The wind is coming **from** 120° (magnetic) at 15 kt.

8. See Study Guide Main Point #8.

9. See Study Guide Main Point #7.

10.
  a. 1,200 ft. This is not an easy question. Nor is the chart particularly easy to read. We strongly suggest that you use a straightedge to help you read the chart accurately. If your answers are a little different from ours, it is probably due to reading errors. Differences of 100 ft. or so are common. Now to the details. First, you need to determine the pressure-altitude. Go to Figure 6.2 and make the altitude correct for 29.30 (579 ft.), which must be added to the field elevation of 4,870 ft. The resulting pressure-altitude is 5,449 ft. Second, you must use Figure 6.1 to calculate the headwind component. The angle between the runway and the wind is 30°. The headwind component is 14°. Third, refer to Figure 6.3. Read up the chart from 22°C until you intersect a pressure-altitude corresponding to 5,449 ft. (estimate it). Now read **over** to the reference line. Read down, parallel to the shaded lines, until you intersect 2,800 lb. Read over to the next reference line. Again, staying parallel to the solid headwind lines, read diagonally until you intersect 14 kt. Now read over to the last reference line. If there were an obstacle at the end of the runway, you would have to read up, parallel to the diagonal lines. However, there is no obstacle, so read directly across to the distance axis.

b. 1,500 ft. Use the same procedure to read Figure 6.3 as described in answer 10a.

c. 1,300 ft. Use the same procedure to read Figure 6.3 as described in answer 10a.

d. 1,700 ft. Use the same procedure to read Figure 6.3 as described in answer 10a.

e. 650 ft. Use the same procedure to read Figure 6.3 as described in answer 10a.

f. 1,500 ft. Now it is time to use Figure 6.4. The procedure for reading it is the same as the procedure you just practiced on Figure 6.3. To review, read up from the temperature scale until you intersect the pressure-altitude line. Read over to the reference line. Parallel the weight line until you intersect the airplane weight. Read over to the next reference line. Depending upon whether you have a headwind or a tailwind, read down or up the chart, parallel to the wind line. Read over to the next reference line. At this point, if there is no obstacle, read directly across to the distance scale. If there is an obstacle, read up, parallel to the solid lines, until you intersect the distance axis. If you are still having trouble, follow through with the example provided in the figure.

g. 1,575 ft. See answer 10f.

h. 1,300 ft. See answer 10f.

11.

a. 356 ft. The ground roll will be reduced by 20 percent due to the headwind. 445 – (.2 x 445) = 445 – 89 = 356. Another way to compute this is to multiply 445 x 0.8.

b. 1,205 ft. This requires you to reduce the landing roll by 20 percent due to the headwind (1,255 – 257 = 1,004). Then, you must add back in 20 percent of the "total to clear 50-ft. obstacle" figure (1,004 + 201 = 1,205).

c. 193 ft. First, compute the headwind component from Figure 6.1. The angle is 30° and the headwind component is 24 kt. In this answer you must interpolate between 5,000 and 2,500 ft. It just so happens that 3,750 is exactly between them so you take half of the difference between 495 and 470 (12.5 ft.) and add it to 470 to arrive at a landing distance under standard conditions of 482.5 ft. The landing distance, however, will be reduced by 60 percent due to the headwind component, or 289.5 ft. The difference between 482.5 – 289.5 = 193 ft.

d. 1,577 ft. In this answer you must first add 10 percent to compensate for 60°F above standard conditions. Then, add 20 percent to the total to compensate for the dry grass runway. So, you multiply 1,195 x 1.1 = 1,314; then multiple 1,314 x 1.2 = 1,577 ft.

e. 239 ft. Again, you must compute the headwind component from Figure 6.1. The angle is 20° and the headwind component is 32 kt. Next, take the strong headwind into account by subtracting 0.8 x 1,195 ft. = 956 ft. from 1,195. The answer is 239 ft.

f. 366 ft. Again, you must compute the headwind component from Figure 6.1. The angle is 70° and the calculated headwind component is 8 kt. Next, you must interpolate between sea level and 2,500 ft., which again happens to be exactly in between the two values on the chart (445 and 470). 445 + ([470 − 455]/2) = 457.5 ft. Next, correct for the 8 kt. headwind by subtracting 20 percent (91.5) to arrive at a landing distance of 366 ft.

12. Read directly from Figure 6.6. Fuel flow is 6.1 gal./hr. IAS is 88 kt. and TAS is 97 kt.

13. 406 mi. Read over on the chart from a pressure-altitude of 8,000 ft. until you intersect the 2,400 RPM line. Now, read down to the range axis.

14. 4.5 hr. Read over on the chart from a pressure-altitude of 8,000 ft. until you intersect the 2,400 RPM line. Now, read down to the endurance axis.

15. See Study Guide Main Point #9.

16. See Study Guide Main Point #10.

17. False. Indicated airspeed does not change with changes in altitude. True airspeed will be higher with higher density-altitudes, but indicated airspeed remains the same.

18.

a. 69.6 gal. First, determine the duration by dividing 1,000 mi. by 191 kt. (TAS). Find the ISA − 20°C portion of the table. Read over on the pressure-altitude = 8,000 ft. line to find both TAS and fuel flow (13.3). Divide 1,000 by 191 to obtain 5.235 hr. Now, multiply 5.235 hr. x 13.3 = 69.6 gal.

b. 35.2 gal. Use the same logic as presented in answer 18a. Divide trip distance (500 mi.) by 193 to obtain 2.59 hr. Multiply 2.59 x 13.6 gal./hr. to arrive at 35.2 gal. In this answer, you will use the far right (ISA + 20°C) portion of the figure.

c. 12.55 gal./hr. In this answer, you will use the middle panel of the figure (Standard Day). Fuel flow **decreases** as you go higher, so the amount will be less than that required at 8,000 ft. (12.8). A pressure-altitude of 8,500 ft. is 25 percent of the distance between 8,000 and 10,000 ft., so multiply the difference between 12.8 and 11.8 gal./hr x .25 = .25 gal./hr. Now, **subtract** .25 from 12.8 to arrive at 12.55 gal./hr.

d. 13.1 gal./hr. For this answer, you will use the right panel in Figure 6.9 (ISA + 36°F). 13.4 − 12.3 = 1.1 gal./hr. difference between 6,000 ft. and 8,000 ft. Take 25 percent of the difference to arrive at the value you must **subtract** from the 6,000 ft. value.

19.

    a. Fuel required is 3.3 gal., time to climb is 18 min., and distance to climb is 25.5 nm.

    b.

	SL to 9000	SL to 3000	3000 to 9000
Fuel required	3.0 gal.	1.0 gal.	2.0 gal.
Time to climb	17 min.	4 min.	13 min.
Distance to climb	25 nm	5 nm	20 nm

20. No. Stalling speed has to do only with speed through the air. It is not affected by the speed of the wind over the ground.

21. 2--As altitude increases, air pressure decreases, which in turn leads to a higher density-altitude. IAS for approaches should stay the same. You should remember, however, that at high density-altitudes, you will be moving faster relative to the ground at the same IAS. Finally, density-altitude affects both takeoff and landing performance.

22. 3--First, correct for the altimeter setting by subtracting 165 ft. from the field elevation. Use the right panel of Figure 6.2. Next, read up from the Degrees F axis at 93° until you intersect the diagonal pressure-altitude line at 3,000 ft. Now read over to the density-altitude axis to find 5,800 ft.

23. 4--First, correct for the altimeter setting by adding 298 ft. to the field elevation. Next, read up the 75°F line until you intersect the pressure-altitude line that represents 4,000 ft. Now read over to the density-altitude axis to find approximately 5,950 ft.

24. 3--A soft field provides more resistance for the wheels and thus will increase the takeoff roll, as will increasing the gross weight, taking off uphill or with tailwinds, moving the CG forward, and increasing the density-altitude.

25. 4--This defines true airspeed.

26. 1--([29.92 - 30.32] x 1,000) + true altitude = (-0.4 x 1,000) + 120 = -400 + 120 = -280 ft.

27. 3--First, figure the pressure-altitude (29.92 - 29.22) = .7 x 1,000 = 700 ft. + 5,800 ft. = 6,500 ft. Use a pressure-altitude of 6,500 ft. as an approximation. Fuel flow is about 6.1 gal./hr. and TAS is 97 kt.

28. 2--On Figure 6.7 read over from a pressure-altitude of 8,000 ft. to the 2,400-RPM line and then down to the range, which in this question is 405 mi. On Figure 6.8 read over from a pressure-altitude of 8,000 ft. until you intersect 2,400 RPM, then read down to endurance, which in this question is 4.5 hr. or 4 hr. and 38 min.

29. 3--Read over on the pressure-altitude line representing 6,400 ft. until you intersect each RPM line. The difference is approximately 11 mi.

30. 3--This defines indicated airspeed (ISA).

31. 3--Density-altitude increases with increases in temperature, altitude, and relative humidity.

32. 4--Density-altitude increases with increases in temperature, altitude, and relative humidity.

33. 4--Density-altitude affects both takeoffs and landings. It increases with increases in altitude, relative humidity, and temperature. Finally, you should use the same indicated altitude regardless of the airport's altitude above sea level.

34. 1--Density-altitude affects both takeoffs and landings. It increases with increases in altitude, relative humidity, and temperature. Finally, you should use the same indicated altitude regardless of the airport's altitude above sea level.

35. 3--First, determine the pressure-altitude by adding 20 ft. to the indicated altitude (obtained from the right panel of Figure 6.1). Next, read up the 80°F line until you intersect the diagonal pressure-altitude line representing 5,500 ft. Read across to the density-altitude axis to obtain 8,100 ft.

36. 3--First, determine the pressure-altitude (4,468 ft.) by adding 257 ft. to the field elevation (obtained from the right panel of Figure 6.1). Next, read up the 90°F line until you intersect the curved pressure-altitude line representing 4,468 ft. Finally, read across to the density-altitude axis to obtain 7,400 ft.

37. 3--This defines pressure-altitude.

38. 4--8,240 + ([29.92 - 29.32] x 1,000) = 8,240 + (0.6 x 1,000) = 8,840 ft.

39. 3--8,900 + ([29.92 - 29.90] x 1,000) = 8,900 + (0.02 x 1000) = 8,920 ft.

40. 3--First, compute the pressure-altitude. 3,500 ft. + ([29.92 - 28.92] x 1,000) = 3,500 - 1,000 = 2,500. Now, refer to the chart in Figure 6.6. For a pressure-altitude of 2,500 ft., read across the 2,300-RPM line to find 5.2 gal./hr. and 88 kt. TAS.

41. 4--Read across the 4,000-ft. pressure-altitude line on each chart until you intersect the 2,400-RPM line and read down to the range and endurance axes.

42. 2--Read across the 10,000-ft. pressure-altitude line in Figure 6.7 until you intersect the 2,400-ft. line. Read across the same line until you intersect the 2,500-ft. line. Subtract the distances obtained on the range axis to obtain 15 NM.

43. 2--Read across the 5,000 ft. pressure-altitude line in Figure 6.8 until you intersect the 2,300-ft. line. Read across the same line until you intersect the 2,400-ft. line. Subtract the endurance values obtained on the hours axis to obtain approximately 0.4 hr.

1. 2--This is the definition of density-altitude. Under standard conditions, pressure-altitude and density-altitude will be the same. However, you will seldom have standard temperature, pressure and humidity, thus corrections will usually be necessary to determine density-altitude.

2. 2--Under high density-altitude conditions the air is less dense. Lift is decreased and engine performance is less. The climb rate is decreased and the takeoff and landing distances are longer.

3. 2--High density-altitude is caused by low pressure, high temperature and/or high humidity.

4. 2--With higher density-altitude, the true airspeed will be more than indicated airspeed. While the indicated airspeed for landing is the same under all density-altitude conditions, the true airspeed and the groundspeed will be greater.

5. 3--Warmer than standard temperature contributes to higher density altitude.

6. 3--High density-altitude reduces aircraft performance. High temperature, high relative humidity and high altitude (low pressure) cause high density-altitude.

7. 2--In the less dense air, the propeller has a smaller mass of air on which to act.

8. 4--To find pressure-altitude, apply the appropriate Pressure Altitude Conversion Factor from the right column, interpolating when necessary. The conversion factor for 28.20" is +1,630 ft. (the + is not written). For 28.30" it is +1,533 ft. Use interpolation: 1,630 - 1,533 = 97; 0.2 x 97 = 19.4; 1,630 - 19.4 = 1,611 ft. (conversion factor). Pressure-altitude 1,380 ft. + 1,611 ft. conversion factor = 2,991 ft. Answer 4 is the closest.

9. 4--To find pressure-altitude, apply the appropriate Pressure Altitude Conversion Factor from the right column, interpolating when necessary. The conversion factor for 29.90" is +20 ft. (the + is not written). For 30.00 it is -73 ft. Use interpolation: +20 - (-73) = -93; 0.7 x 93 = 65; 20 - 65 = -45 ft. (conversion factor). Pressure-altitude 1,386 - 45 = 1,341 ft.

10. 1--Use the scale at the right of Figure 1. You will have to interpolate. The conversion for 29.90 is +20; for 30.00 it is -73. 0.6 x 93 = 55.8; +20 - 56 = -36, the altitude conversion factor. 3,563 - 36 = 3,527.

11. 3--Find the pressure-altitude from Figure 1 (right side). You will have to interpolate. 29.20 is 673; 29.30 is 579. 0.5 x 94 = 47, the altitude conversion factor. 673 - 47 = 626; 5,250 + 626 = 5,876. Use the graph to find density-altitude when pressure-altitude and temperature are known. Start at the bottom of the temperature scale. Proceed vertically to the diagonal line for the given pressure altitude. From that intersection, follow the horizontal line to the left scale. Find 81°F on the chart and go vertically to a position between the diagonal 5,000 and 6,000 pressure-altitude lines (5,876). Proceed horizontally to find density-altitude of 8,400 ft.

12.   4--Find the pressure-altitude from Figure 1 (right side). You will to interpolate. 30.30 is -348; 30.40 is -440. 0.5 x 92 = 46, the altitude conversion factor. -348 - 46 = -394. The pressure-altitude is 3,894 - 394 = 3,500. Use the graph to find density-altitude when pressure-altitude and temperature are known. Start at the bottom of the temperature scale. Proceed vertically from 25° to the diagonal line for the given pressure-altitude (judge between the 3,000 and 4,000 lines for 3,500). Move horizontally to find density-altitude of 2,000 ft.

13.   1--Use the graph to find density-altitude when pressure-altitude and temperature are known. Start at the temperature scale at the bottom, and proceed vertically to the diagonal line for the given pressure altitude of 5,000 ft. From the intersection of these lines, proceed horizontally to the left scale for density-altitude of 3,850 ft. The density-altitude for 50°F is 5,500 ft.

14.   4--Use the graph to find density-altitude when pressure-altitude and temperature are known. Start at the bottom of the temperature scale. Proceed vertically from 30° to the diagonal line for the given pressure-altitude of 3,000 ft. From the intersection of these lines, proceed horizontally to the left scale for density-altitude of 1,650 ft. For 50°, the density-altitude is 3,000 ft.

15.   2--Use the graph to find density-altitude when pressure-altitude and temperature are known. Start at the temperature scale at the bottom, and proceed vertically from 90° to the diagonal line for the given pressure of 1,250 ft. From the intersection of these lines, proceed horizontally to the left scale for density-altitude of 3,600 ft. For 60° and 1,750 ft. pressure-altitude, the density-altitude is 2,300 ft.

16.   2--The wind is 40° from the runway heading. Find the intersection of the 40° diagonal line and the 30 kt. arc. Go horizontally to the left to find the headwind component of 23 kt.

17.   1--The wind is 40° from the runway heading. Find the intersection of the 40° diagonal line and the 30 kt. arc. Proceed vertically down from the intersection of the 40° diagonal and 30 kt. arc to find the 19 kt. crosswind component.

18.   4--Locate 25 kt. on the crosswind component line. Proceed vertically to the 45° diagonal wind line. Interpolate between the wind arcs for 35 kt. maximum crosswind velocity at 45° crosswind.

19.   4--Proceed vertically up the 12 kt. crosswind component line to the 30° diagonal. Interpolate between the 20 kt. and 30 kt. arcs for 24 kt.

20.   4--Determine the crosswind angle for each runway for a wind from 000°. Rwy 6 = 60° (headwind), Rwy 14 = 40° (tailwind) Rwy 24 = 60° (tailwind), Rwy 32 = 40° (headwind). Rwy 32 has a headwind with the least crosswind component. Confirm that this wind is within limits by finding crosswind component by finding the intersection of the 40° diagonal wind line and the 20 kt. arc. Proceed vertically down to find the crosswind component - 13 kt.

21. 2--Determine the crosswind angle for each runway for a wind from 180°.
Rwy 6 = 60° (tailwind), Rwy 14 = 40° (headwind), Rwy 24 = 60° (headwind), Rwy
32 = 40° (tailwind). Rwy 14 has a headwind with the least crosswind
component. Confirm that this wind is within limits by finding the crosswind
component. Find the intersection of the 40° diagonal and the 20 kt. arc and
proceed vertically down to find the crosswind component - 13 kt.

22. 2--Read all of the notes on the charts. Note 1: Decrease the distances
shown by 10% for each 4 kt. of headwind. SEA LEVEL GROUND roll is 445 ft.
10% x 445 ft. = 44.5. 445 - 44.5 = 400.5 ft.

23. 2--On the 7,500 ft. table, find TOTAL TO CLEAR 50 FT. OBS of 1,255.
Note 1: Decrease the distance shown by 10% for each 4 kt. of headwind. Note
3: For operation on a dry grass runway, increase distance (both "ground roll"
and "total to clear 50 ft. obstacle") by 20% of the "total to clear 50 ft.
obstacle" figures. First correct for the headwind: 1,255 - (20% x 1,255) 251
= 1,004. Now correct for the grass runway: 1,004 + (20% x 1,004) 200.8 =
1,204.8.

24. 2--You must interpolate for 3,750 ft. between the 2,500 ft. and 5,000 ft.
tables. 495 - 470 = 25, 25 divided by 2 = 12.5, 470 + 12.5 = 482.5 ft. ground
roll at 3,750 ft. (calm wind). Note 1: Decrease the distance shown by 10% for
each 4 knots of headwind. The wind correction for 12 kt. is -30%; 482.5 x 0.7
= 337.5 ft.

25. 2--See Note 1: Decrease the distance shown by 10% for each 4 knots of
headwind. TOTAL TO CLEAR 50 FT. OBSTACLE is 1,195 x 80% = 956 ft.

26. 4--See Note 2: Increase distance by 10% for each 60°F temperature
increase above standard. Standard temperature for 5,000 ft. is 41°F, thus
101°F is 60°F above standard. 1,195 x 110% = 1,314.5.

27. 2--Interpolate for 1,250 ft. 470 - 445 = 25, 25 divided by 2 = 12.5, 445
+ 12.5 = 4,577.5. See Note 1: Decrease the distance shown by 10% for each 4
kt. of headwind. 457.5 x 80% = 366 ft.

28. 2--This graph is actually 4 separate graphs linked together. The easiest
way to use these is to first draw in vertical lines for the given values on
each of the charts. For this problem, draw lines for 32°F temperature, 2600
lb. weight, 20 kt. headwind and 50 ft. obstacle. Start at the intersection of
the 32°F vertical line and the 8,000 ft. pressure-altitude diagonal. Now move
horizontally to the vertical weight reference line, then move diagonally down
remaining the same relative distance between the weight diagonal lines to the
vertical 2,600 lb. line. Move horizontally to the vertical wind reference
line, then diagonally down between reference lines to the vertical 20 kt.
headwind. Move horizontally to the vertical obstacle reference line, then
diagonally up between the reference lines to the vertical 50 ft. obstacle line
to 1,400 ft.

29. 1--This graph is actually 4 separate graphs. The easiest way to use them
is to first draw in vertical lines for the given values on each chart. For
this problem, draw a line for 2,300 lb. weight. With standard temperature,
start at the intersection of the ISA diagonal and the 2,000 ft.
pressure-altitude diagonal. Move horizontally to the vertical weight

reference line, then diagonally down, remaining the same relative distance
between lines, to the vertical 2,300 lb. line. With calm wind and no
obstacle, move horizontally through the wind and obstacle graphs to 850 ft.

30. 4--This graph is actually 4 separate graphs. To use them, draw in
vertical lines for the given values on each chart. For this problem, draw
lines for 90°F temperature, 2800 lb. weight, and 10 kt. tailwind. Start at
the intersection of the 90°F vertical line and the 4,000 ft. pressure-altitude
diagonal. Now move horizontally to the vertical weight reference line, then
move diagonally down, remaining the same relative distance between lines, to
the vertical 2,800 lb. line. Move horizontally to the vertical wind reference
line, then diagonally up between reference lines to the vertical 20 kt.
tailwind line. With no obstacle, move horizontally through the obstacle graph
for 1,950 ft.

31. 4--This graph is actually 4 separate graphs. To use them, draw in
vertical lines for the given values on each chart. For this problem, draw
lines for 90°F temperature, 2900 lb. weight, 10 kt. headwind and 50 ft.
obstacle. Start at the intersection of the 90°F vertical line and the 3,000
ft. pressure-altitude diagonal. Now move horizontally to the vertical weight
reference line, then move diagonally down, remaining the same relative
distance between lines, to the vertical 2,900 lb. line. Move horizontally to
the vertical wind reference line, then diagonally down between reference lines
to the vertical 10 kt. headwind line. Move horizontally to the vertical
obstacle reference line, then diagonally up between the diagonal reference
line to the vertical 50 ft. obstacle line to 1,725 ft. With the weight at the
maximum, proceed from the vertical weight reference line directly horizontal
through the weight graph to the wind reference line.

32. 3--This graph is actually 4 separate graphs. To use them, draw in
vertical lines for the given values on each chart. For this problem, draw
lines for 2,800 lb. weight and 50 ft. obstacle. With standard temperature,
start at the intersection of the ISA diagonal line and the 4,000 ft.
pressure-altitude diagonal. Now move horizontally to the vertical weight
reference line, then move diagonally down, remaining the same relative
distance between lines, to the vertical 2,800 lb. line. With calm wind, move
horizontally through the wind graph to the vertical wind reference line, then
diagonally up between the diagonal reference line to the 50 ft. obstacle line
for 1,750 ft.

33. 1--This graph is actually 4 separate graphs. To use them, draw in
vertical lines for the given values on each chart. For this problem, draw
lines for 100°F temperature and 2,750 lb. weight. Start at the intersection
of the 100°F vertical line and the 2,000 ft. pressure altitude diagonal. Now
move horizontally to the vertical weight reference line, then diagonally down,
remaining the same relative distance between the reference lines, to the 2,750
lb. line. With calm wind and no obstacle, move horizontally through the wind
and obstacle graphs to 1,150 ft.

34. 2--This graph is actually 4 separate graphs. To use them, draw in
vertical lines for the given values on each chart. For this problem, draw
lines for 2,700 lb. weight and 50 ft. obstacle. With standard temperature
start at the intersection of the ISA diagonal line and the Sea Level
pressure-altitude diagonal. Now move horizontally to the vertical weight
reference line, then diagonally down, remaining the same relative distance

between the references lines, to the vertical 2,700 lb. line. With calm wind, move horizontally to the obstacle reference line, then diagonally up between the reference line to the 50 ft. vertical line for 1,400 ft.

35.   1--This graph is actually 4 separate graphs. To use the, draw in vertical lines for the given values on each chart. For this problem, draw lines for 90°F temp., 2,500 lb. weight, and 20 kt. headwind. Start at the intersection of the 90°F vertical line and the 2,000 ft. pressure-altitude diagonal. Now move horizontally to the vertical weight reference line, then diagonally down, remaining the same relative distance between lines, to the 2,600 lb. line. Move horizontally to the vertical wind reference line, then diagonally down between reference lines to the vertical 20 kt. headwind. With no obstacle, move horizontally through the obstacle graph for 650 ft.

36.   4--Use the left chart for ISA - 20°C. On the 8,000 ft. line find fuel flow of 11.5 gph (gallons per hour) and TAS 157 kt. To find the time of the flight, divide distance by speed. 1,000 / 157 = 6.4 hours. Multiply time, 6.4 hr., by fuel flow, 11.5 gph, to obtain fuel consumption of 73.2.

37.   2--The standard temperature at 4,000 ft. would be 7°C (15°C standard at sea level minus 2° per 1,000 ft.). With temperature 22° above standard, use the right chart. Fuel flow is 11.5 gph and TAS is 159 kt. The flight time is 500 nm divided by 159 kt. = 3.1 hr. 3.1 hr. x 11.5 gph = 36.1 gal.

38.   2--For a standard day, use the center chart. For 11,000 ft., interpolate between 10.9 gph for 12,000 ft. and 11.5 gph for 10,000 ft. 11.5 - 10.9 = .6, .6 / 2 = .3, 11.5 - .3 = 11.2 gph.

39.   2--Use the right chart, ISA +20°C (+36°F). Manifold pressure for 6,000 ft. is 21.0 in. Hg.

40.   3--Use the left chart for ISA -20°C (-36°F). TAS at 9,500 ft. is slightly less than the 10,000 ft. TAS of 184 mph.

[handwritten annotations in top margin: "X-WIND", "UPWIND", "DOWNWIND", "FINAL APPROACH", "ABEAM", "BASE", "TRAFFIC PATTERN", "LAND STRIP", "ALTITUDE", "ROT. BCN", "SERVICE", "LIGHTS", "370L45 - CONCRETE RWY C1000'", "BLUE-NO TD"]

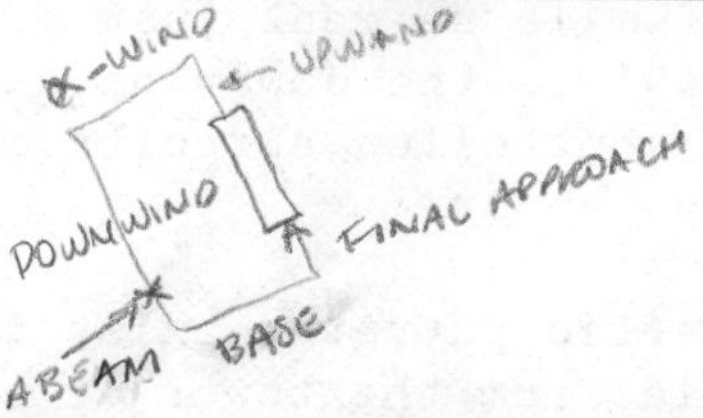

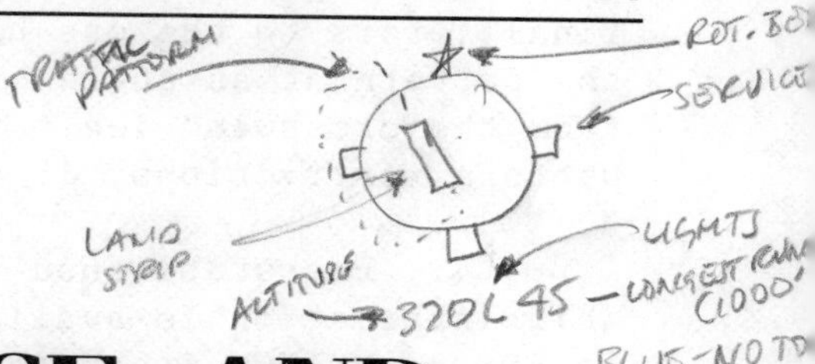

AIRPORTS, AIRSPACE, AND LOCAL FLYING

MAIN POINTS

1. Airports with towers are **controlled**; those without towers are **uncontrolled**. Controlled airports have an **airport traffic area (ATA)** with specific procedures. The local flying area is a zone up to 25 NM from the airport.

2. **Runways** are represented by one- or two-digit numbers corresponding to the nearest magnetic heading divided by 10. For example, a runway with a magnetic heading of 214° is Rwy 21, and its reciprocal (when used in the opposite direction) is Rwy 3 (a heading of 034°). L (left), R (right), and C (center) are used to denote parallel runways. A **basic runway** has a white number with a dashed centerline. A nonprecision instrument **approach runway** displays threshold markings (broad parallel stripes) before the runway number. **Precision approach runways** have more sophisticated markings, including side stripes and a touchdown zone marker. **Displaced thresholds** are marked by a series of chevrons at the end of the runway, the clearance area, which may be used for takeoff, and for rollout when landing in the opposite direction. A wide band of chevrons running up the center of the area before the threshold indicates an **overrun** area that should not be used for any aircraft operation except in an emergency. An **X** is used to mark a closed runway. **Taxiways** are marked with a yellow centerline. **Holding lines** are solid yellow lines perpendicular to the taxiway; do not cross them at controlled airports until cleared by the tower. Under category II operations, the tower may tell you to stop at Cat II holding lines (two lines connected by bars). At night, airports are identified by a rotating beacon with alternating green and white lights at night (a double-flashing white between green flashes indicates a military airfield). If the beacon is rotating during the day, it means the weather is below VFR minimums. If present, green lights indicate the threshold, red lights the departure end, white lights side boundaries, and blue lights taxiways and taxiway turnoffs. By pilot control of lighting, runway lights may be turned on by clicking the microphone.

3. Unless authorized by the FAA, the standard traffic pattern consists of left turns (except at entry). The legs of a pattern are **upwind** or **takeoff**, to about 300-400 ft. AGL; **crosswind**, 90° to the upwind leg and usually not to

be entered until crossing the departure end of the runway; **downwind**, parallel to the runway but in the opposite direction (typically flown at 1,000 ft. AGL, the **traffic pattern altitude**); **base**, parallel to the crosswind leg but at the opposite end of the field; and **final**, upwind, in line with the landing runway. The term **long final** refers to that portion just after turning from base; **short final** refers to the one-half-mile segment just prior to the threshold. Enter the pattern at an angle of 45° to the downwind leg, depart at a 45° turn away from the crosswind leg. At controlled airports, the tower will tell you what pattern restrictions, if any, apply.

4. Preestablished traffic patterns exist for operating at all airports. This information is available from the tower at controlled airports and from an FSS or UNICOM frequency, or from the **segmented circle** at uncontrolled airports. The segmented circle may have base to final approach indicators, and it may have a tetrahedron, wind sock, or wind tee in the middle to indicate the direction for landing. An amber light in the segmented circle, on the control tower, or on an adjoining building indicates that a right-hand pattern is in effect. An **X** in the circle means the field is closed.

5. The normal **glide path** (glide slope) is about 3° to the horizon. Many airports have a **visual approach slope indicator** (VASI) consisting of two sets of basic lights (white and red). A safe, correct approach is one where red is over white. Red/red indicates the airplane is too low, and white/white indicates it is too high. Remember the sayings: "Red over white, you're alright; red over red, you're dead; white over white, you'll fly all night."

6. An **uncontrolled airport** may have a facility designated an **Aeronautical Advisory Station** (ASS) and operate a private radio service called UNICOM. Typical UNICOM frequencies are 122.8 and 123.0. All airports have a **Common Traffic Advisory Frequency (CTAF)**. Specific frequencies are shown on aeronautical charts and in the Airport/Facility Directory. UNICOM is not used for air traffic control, but rather for pilots to advise one another of taxiing, pattern, departure, and arrival intentions. When flying into airports with no control tower, FSS, or UNICOM, use MULTICOM (122.9) for communication at and around the airport. Private airports use either 122.725 or 122.75. Flight Service Stations (FSS) provide weather information, flight plan filing services, and airport advisory services if they are located at uncontrolled fields. When calling an FSS, it is referred to as "radio." For example, you might call Kansas City **Radio.**

7. **Controlled airports** require two-way radio communication for any movement on the ground or in the **airport traffic area (ATA)**. The airport traffic area extends from the ground up to, but not including, 3,000 ft. AGL, with a radius of 5 statute miles (SM) around the airport. The ATA is in effect **only** when the tower is operating. The speed limit in the ATA is 180 MPH (156 kts.). At many busier airports, prerecorded information is available via **Automatic Terminal Information Service** (ATIS). You should use it before you contact the tower (in flight) or ground control (prior to taxi). In the event of a radio failure, light signals are used to give the pilot directions.

8. In good weather, all aircraft operate under the principle of **visual separation.** The FAA specifies minimum weather conditions that must be met for **visual flight rules** (VFR). Poor weather, referred to as **instrument meteorological conditions** (IMC), has a set of rules that govern flight called **instrument flight rules** (IFR). The purpose of **controlled airspace** is to

separate VFR and IFR traffic. Areas over which ATC has no control are called **uncontrolled airspace**. In VFR weather, also called **visual meteorological conditions (VMC)**, no contact with ATC is required in most controlled airspace below 18,000 ft. In IFR weather, all aircraft **must** have clearance from ATC to fly in controlled airspace.

9. **VFR weather minimums.** In uncontrolled airspace, you need 1-mi. visibility and must remain clear of clouds **below 1,200 ft. AGL**. Between 1,200 ft. AGL and 10,000 ft. MSL, you must have 1-mi. visibility and you must stay 500 ft. below, 1,000 ft. above, or 2,000 ft. horizontally from clouds. At or **above 10,000 ft. MSL, and above 1,200 ft. AGL**, you must have 5-mi. visibility and remain at least 1,000 ft. below, 1,000 ft. above, or 1-mi. horizontally from clouds. In controlled airspace, there are two altitude divisions. Below 10,000 ft. MSL, you need 3-mi. visibility and must remain 500 ft. below, 1,000 ft. above, or 2,000 ft. horizontally from clouds. **At or above 10,000 feet MSL and above 1,200 ft. AGL**, you need 5-mi. visibility and must remain at least 1,000 ft. below, 1,000 ft. above, or 1-mi. horizontally from clouds. To learn this, draw a picture for each type of airspace.

10. There are a variety of types of **controlled airspace**. The **positive control area (PCA)** exists from 18,000 ft. MSL to FL 600, where FL means flight level and FL 600 refers to 60,000 ft. pressure altitude. It is IFR territory and requires transponder and two-way radio. The **continental control area** (14,500 ft. MSL and up) covers the 48 states and parts of Alaska. VFR flight is permitted in the continental control area, but added equipment is required. **Control zones** help separate VFR from IFR traffic when instrument conditions prevail and exist around airports with instrument approach capability. They extend from the surface to the base of the continental control area or other controlled airspace. They extend outward at least 5 mi. from the airport and may have a keyhole appearance to accommodate instrument approaches. Flight in a control zone requires 3-mi. visibility and a ceiling of at least 1,000 ft. A ceiling is the height of the base of the clouds covering one-half or more of the sky. Special VFR clearance may be obtained in a control zone if you have 1-mi. visibility and can stay clear of clouds. Special VFR is issued at night only if you have an instrument rating. A control zone marked by T's on the chart means no special VFR is allowed. **Transition areas** around airports are indicated by magenta boundaries on sectional charts and have a floor of 700 ft. AGL. They extend up to the base of the continental control areas and are also designed to help separate VFR and IFR aircraft. **Control areas** around federal airways extend 4 mi. on either side of the airway and from 1,200 ft. AGL up to the overlying continental control area. Flights over charted U.S. Wildlife Refuges, parks, and forest service areas are required to remain 2,000 ft. above the surface.

11. The distinction between a **control zone** and an **airport traffic area** is important. While the size of a control zone can vary, an ATA is always 5 mi. in radius and 3,000 ft. tall. An ATA places a communication requirement on aircraft, whereas a control zone has a weather requirement. ATAs are in effect **only** when there is an operating control tower. On aeronautical charts, a control zone is depicted by dashed blue lines. An airport that can have an ATA has a blue symbol and has a control tower frequency in the data block.

12. **Special-use airspace** defines areas within which activities occur that require restrictions to aircraft operations. Flight is not permitted in **Prohibited Areas** without special permission. **Restricted Areas** contain unseen hazards; you must obtain permission to enter these areas. **Warning Areas** contain the same types of hazards as Restricted Areas, but are located outside the territorial limits of the country. You do not need permission to enter a Warning Area, but is is not wise to enter without knowledge of the activities.

Military Operations Areas (MOA) are used to separate certain military training activities from IFR traffic; VFR pilots may contact an FSS within 100 miles for information on activity in a MOA. **Alter Areas** may contain a high volume of pilot training. **Military Training Routes (MTR)** are established for training operations above 1,500 feet AGL. IR routes are for IFR operations in both good and bad weather and VR operations are conducted only under VFR rules. Beware of low, fast movers on these routes.

13. Another service available at some airports is **radar**, whereby the controller can monitor progress and give specific approach and departure instructions. **Terminal Radar Programs** are available in two stages, II and III, depending upon the degree of control over IFR and VFR aircraft. At very busy airports, the control area is expanded to include a larger area of airspace called a **Terminal Control Area (TCA)**. Shaped like an upside-down wedding cake, it requires positive control when you operate within it. TCAs are of two types, I and II. **Group II TCAs** require a 4096-code transponder, altitude encoding altimeter, two-way radio, navigation radio, and compliance with ATC instructions. **Group I TCAs** have the same requirements as Group II TCAs; in addition, student pilots flying solo are not permitted to land at the primary airport. **Airport Radar Service Areas (ARSAs)** are the most recent addition to the radar service sector. ARSAs typically have an inner zone that extends from the surface to 4,000 ft. AGL with a radius of 5 naut miles and an outer zone that covers a radius of 10 naut miles from 1,200 ft. AGL to 4,000 ft. AGL. Two-way radio communication must be established before entering an ARSA. Aircraft may depart a **satellite** airport without prior ATC approval, but must establish and maintain two-way radio communications with ATC as soon as practicable. Takeoffs and landings at satellite airports must comply with FAA approved arrival and departure traffic patterns.

14. Radio communications occur on VHF frequencies between 118.000 and 135.975 megahertz (MHz). Most modern VHF radios have the transmitter and receiver combined in one unit, a transceiver. Talking on the radio involves natural conversational tone and knowledge of the **phonetic alphabet**. There is no easy way to learn the phonetic alphabet except to use it. Learn how to spell your name phonetically. Practice it in other settings, such as asking for stock quotations. Some **numbers** are also pronounced in special ways. For example, nine is pronounced "niner." Multidigit numbers are given by saying each number individually (for example, "heading two zero zero"). When a decimal is present, it is referred to as "point" (for example, UNICOM might be "one two three point zero"). One exception to the decimal rule is barometric pressure, which is read without a decimal (for example, "three zero zero six"). Altitudes below 10,000 are read in thousands and hundreds (for example, "seven thousand two hundred" for 7,200). From 10,000 to FL 180, the thousand digit is stated separately, followed by the hundreds (for example, "one three thousand four hundred" for 13,400). **Time** is given with reference to the Greenwich meridian (zulu time), commonly called coordinated universal time (abbreviated UTC). UTC uses military standards established for the

24-hour clock (0000-2400). **Airplane call signs** are used to identify each
aircraft and are given without the prefix N (for example, Cessna N5009G would
be identified "Cessna five zero zero niner gulf"). Always include your call
sign or abbreviated call sign in each transmission to leave no doubt as to who
is talking with ATC. Finally, ATC uses the **clock position reference system** to
identify the position of airborne traffic relative to a given plane. The nose
of the plane points toward 12 o'clock and the tail points toward 6 o'clock. A
plane at 9 o'clock would be off your left wing.

15.   The following sequence is customary for initiating radio
communication: (1) ground facility being called, (2) aircraft call number,
(3) location and altitude, (4) intentions, and (5) other information (for
example, ATIS received).

16.   **Night flying** has special characteristics and considerations. Night
vision is different from daylight vision. Your eyes require a lengthy
adaptation period (20-30 min.) to adjust, and this adjustment can easily be
disrupted by sudden bursts of light. Cockpit illumination, whether red or
white, should be kept at a minimum. Since night vision is concentrated in the
eye's _peripheral_ area, you may need to glance at objects quickly and
indirectly several times to identify them correctly. Sometimes oxygen is
recommended to maintain the pilot's visual acuity. You should also be aware
that illusions are much more prevalent at night than during the day. More
information on the physiology of night flying is discussed in Chapter 15.

17.   Airplane lights include an **anticollision light** system (beacons or
strobe lights), **position** or **navigation lights** (red, left wing; green, right
wing; white, tail) required for night flight, and **landing lights**. You can
tell the relative angle of an aircraft by the position lights that are
visible. If you are looking at the left rear quarter, you will see the red
and white lights. If you are looking at the left front quarter, you will see
only the red light. If you see both red and green lights, you are directly in
front of the aircraft. Landing or position lights can be used to signal the
control tower at night in the event of a radio failure. When flying at night,
it is wise to carry a flashlight in the event the lights fail. Finally, when
flying at night, rely primarily on your instruments and not your senses for
the airplane's attitude, altitude, vertical speed, and airspeed. Instruments
seldom lie, except when they malfunction; your senses frequently do,
particularly at night.

18.   You should follow all published noise abatement procedures, unless
compliance compromises the aircraft's safety. Also, there are areas over
which you should exercise caution and stay within published limits such as
parks and wildlife preserves.

19.   Planning a flight, even one in which you simply practice takeoffs
and landings, requires considerable attention to details, such as the
airplane, the weather (required by the FAA), and runway conditions. That is
why normal procedures are conducted by reference to checklists. The **preflight
inspection** includes an examination of various parts of the airplane. **Ground
operations** require coordinating your attention between events outside the
cabin and indicators inside the cabin. Once you take off, the **in-flight
checklist** becomes relevant. Next, there is a **landing checklist**. Finally,
there is a **postflight checklist** to complete before leaving the aircraft. Use
these lists as "check" lists, not "do" lists.

20. **Taxiing** can be tricky, particularly if the wind is blowing. When surface winds are high, position the ailerons **into** the wind when taxiing into a quartering headwind and **away** from the wind when the wind is coming from the rear quarter. In triangle gear airplanes, keep the elevator neutral when the wind is coming from in front of you and down when it is coming from the rear. In tail wheel type airplanes, the elevator control should be in the aft position to keep the tail down for headwinds and in the forward position for tailwinds.

KEY TERMS AND CONCEPTS, PART 1

Match each term or concept (1-20) with the appropriate description (A-T) below. Each item has only one match.

___ 1. civil airport at night
___ 2. departure
___ 3. words twice
___ 4. prime meridian
___ 5. ceiling
___ 6. airport traffic area
___ 7. IMC
___ 8. threshold
___ 9. ARSA
___ 10. Group II TCA

___ 11. crosswind
___ 12. prohibited area
___ 13. flashing white
___ 14. control area
___ 15. ATIS
___ 16. vector
___ 17. UTC
___ 18. restricted airspace
___ 19. VMC
___ 20. clear

A. do not enter this pattern leg after takeoff before crossing the departure end of the runway
B. point beyond which landing aircraft can contact the runway
C. exists at controlled airports with specific flight procedures--5-mi. radius and up to but not including 3,000 ft. AGL
D. alternating green and white beacon
E. red lights mark this end of the runway at night
F. repeat each key word or phrase twice
G. line that runs through Greenwich, England
H. area in which radar service operates; two-way radio communication with ATC is required to enter one, but no other special equipment is required
I. airspace in which aircraft operation is forbidden
J. airspace that may contain unseen hazards such as a military gunnery range
K. lowest layer of clouds classified as broken or overcast
L. designated airspace such as a VOR federal airway
M. universal coordinated time
N. instrument meteorological conditions
O. two-way radio, 4096-code transponder, mandatory ATC control, and an encoding altimeter are required
P. being given a heading and altitude to fly
Q. prerecorded airport information available at busier controlled airports
R. light signal used to indicate "return to starting point on airport"
S. visual meteorological conditions
T. word you should yell before engaging the starter

KEY TERMS AND CONCEPTS, PART 2

Match each term or concept (1-20) with the appropriate description (A-T) below. Each item has only one match.

___ 1. glide slope
___ 2. tetrahedron
___ 3. call sign
___ 4. taxiway turnoff
___ 5. Rwy 19
___ 6. Group I TCA
___ 7. FSS
___ 8. vector
___ 9. UNICOM
___ 10. verify

___ 11. control zone
___ 12. holding line
___ 13. 1700
___ 14. ARTCC
___ 15. one mile
___ 16. positive control area
___ 17. final
___ 18. uncontrolled
___ 19. VHF communications
___ 20. 3 o'clock

A. where you file flight plans and receive weather information
B. 122.8 and 123.0 are typical VHF radio frequencies
C. angle of descent on final approach
D. portion of the pattern flown after the base leg
E. three-dimensional triangle used as wind direction indicator
F. place on taxiway where you must stop at a controlled airport
G. reciprocal of Rwy 1
H. student pilots flying solo may not land at the primary airport
I. airport without an operating tower to control ground and air traffic
J. horizontal distance you must maintain from clouds at or above 10,000 ft. MSL in both controlled and uncontrolled airspace
K. blue lights mark this point on a runway at night
L. double-check the accuracy of the transmission
M. falls within these radio frequencies: 118.00 to 135.975 MHz
N. heading issued to an aircraft to provide navigational radar guidance
O. UTC time when many people leave work in the afternoon
P. provides air traffic control to IFR flight along controlled airways
Q. 18,000 ft. MSL to FL 600
R. controlled airspace (typically at least 5-mi. radius from the airport) upward from the surface to 14,500 ft. MSL
S. aircraft identification number--for example, N7017G
T. where you would find an aircraft reported off your right wing

Match each term or concept (1-20) with the appropriate description (A-T) below. Each term has only one match.

___ 1. wind **T**
___ 2. Stage III radar
___ 3. upwind
___ 4. squelch
___ 5. short final
___ 6. rock your wings
___ 7. local flying area
___ 8. steady red
___ 9. 45
___ 10. flashing red

___ 11. read back
___ 12. magenta
___ 13. transponder
___ 14. MULTICOM
___ 15. transmitter
___ 16. **X**
___ 17. three
___ 18. position lights
___ 19. segmented circle
___ 20. nonprecision instrument approach runway

A. positive radar separation of all **participating** VFR and IFR traffic
B. radio device that sends out a signal when it detects a radar wave
C. signal used to let the control tower know you have received a signal when your radio is inoperative
D. light signal used to indicate "give way to other aircraft; continue to circle"
E. light signal used to indicate "airport unsafe--do not land"
F. color used on aeronautical charts to depict uncontrolled airports and their legends
G. 122.9, one frequency used for air-to-air radio transmissions
H. a flight path parallel to the landing runway in the direction of landing
I. normal glide slope angle (in degrees)
J. portion of the traffic pattern one-half mile prior to the threshold
K. airport display used to indicate approach to final legs
L. markings that indicate a runway is closed
M. angle at which you should enter the downwind leg
N. runway with a heading number, dashed centerline, and broad parallel stripes
O. area up to approximately 25 mi. from a given airport
P. transceiver control that balances volume and static
Q. a type of landing direction indicator
R. lights on the wingtips and tail
S. repeat all the transmission that has just been received
T. portion of a radio that broadcasts

KEY TERMS AND CONCEPTS, PART 4

Match each term or concept (1-20) with the appropriate description (A-T) below. Each item has only one match.

___ 1. anticollision lights   ___ 11. UHF communications
___ 2. transition area   ___ 12. engine starting checklist
___ 3. chevrons   ___ 13. active
___ 4. downwind   ___ 14. Stage II radar service
___ 5. controlled airport   ___ 15. MOA
___ 6. overrun area   ___ 16. reciprocal
___ 7. basic runway   ___ 17. continental control area
___ 8. base   ___ 18. flashing green
___ 9. wind sock   ___ 19. Group I and II TCA requirements
___ 10. transceiver   ___ 20. peripheral vision

A. airspace designated for military operations
B. field of vision to either side of the eyes
C. controlled airspace at an airport with an instrument approach that extends upward from 700 ft.
D. airspace over the 48 states and parts of Alaska from 14,500 ft. MSL upward
E. two-way radio, an encoding altimeter, and mandatory ATC control
F. radar sequencing of arriving VFR and IFR traffic; advisories for departing VFR traffic
G. light signal used to indicate "clear to taxi"
H. a direction 180° from a given direction
I. airport with an operating tower to control ground and air traffic
J. beacon or strobe system on fuselage
K. area of a runway marked by a wide band of chevrons indicating that this area should not be used for any normal aircraft operations
L. pattern leg parallel to the active runway but in the opposite direction from it
M. pattern leg parallel to crosswind but at the opposite end of the field
N. radio transmitter and receiver combined in a single unit
O. markings on a runway indicating a displaced threshold
P. runway with only a heading number and dashed centerline
Q. initial oil pressure check occurs with reference to this checklist
R. runway being used for takeoffs and landings
S. radio frequencies used mostly for military communications
T. wind indicator whose short end points **away from** the wind

DISCUSSION QUESTIONS AND REVIEW EXERCISES

1. What is the difference between a controlled airport and an uncontrolled airport? What is the difference between an airport traffic area (ATA) and the local flying area?

2. Briefly characterize each of the following:

   a. basic runway

   b. runway heading indicator

   c. nonprecision instrument approach runway

   d. displaced threshold

   e. closed runway

   f. taxiway

   g. holding line

   h. overrun area

3. Draw Rwy 14. Indicate altitudes and directions of flight for a
right-hand pattern with a pattern altitude of 800 ft. AGL. Field elevation is
2,000 ft. MSL.

4. Draw a segmented circle for the following airport: Rwy 18-36 with right
traffic for 18 and left traffic for 36; Rwy 9-27 with right traffic for 9 and
left traffic for 27. The wind is 240° at 15. Draw a wind sock in the middle
of the circle indicating the wind direction.

    a. If you were landing here, what runway would you use and what would
the traffic pattern be?

b. Suppose you decide to practice some touch and go's here. The wind is still 240° at 15. The pattern altitude is 1000 ft., field elevation is 2720 ft., and the barometric pressure is 29.54. Describe how you will fly the pattern, indicating for each leg the direction of flight (you do not need to adjust for the crab angle), altitude AGL, and altitude on the altimeter.

5. Briefly describe the standard runway lighting, taxi lighting, and beacon configuration at civilian and military airports.

6. Briefly describe the meanings of the color components of the two-light visual approach slope indicator (VASI).

7. Characterize each of the following including special restrictions, communication

a. UNICOM

b. CTAF

c. MULTICOM

d. FSS

e. ATA

f. ATIS

g. Stage II radar service

h. Stage III radar service

i. Group I TCA

j. Group II TCA

k. ARSA

l. Airport Advisory Service

8. Indicate what each of the following light signals means.

a. steady green

b. flashing green

c. steady red

d. flashing red

e. flashing white

f. alternating red and green

9. Distinguish between visual meteorological conditions and instrument meteorological conditions. What type of rules apply to each condition?

10. What is the difference between controlled and uncontrolled airspace?

11. What weather minimums apply to each of the following airspaces:

a. uncontrolled--below 1,200 ft. AGL

b. uncontrolled--between 1,200 ft. AGL and 10,000 ft. MSL

c. uncontrolled--at or above 10,000 ft. MSL and above 1,200 ft. AGL

d. controlled--below 10,000 ft. MSL

e. controlled--at or above 10,000 ft. MSL

12. Briefly describe each of the following.

a. positive control area

b. continental control area

c. control zone

d. transition area

e. prohibited area

f. control area around a federal airway

13. You will need to learn the phonetic alphabet. After studying the letters and their names, reproduce as many as you can from memory in the space below. Try starting with the letters in your name. Once you have done as many as you can, complete the table, by referring to the text. This exercise will help you learn the alphabet and will serve as a handy reference for review.

14. How do you say each of these using standard radio communication language:

a. Tripacer N2497C

b. a heading of 290°

c. an altitude of 3,120 ft.

d. an altitude of 15,800 ft.

e. 2240 UTC

f. Kansas City ARTCC

g. Tulsa FSS

h. Repeat the transmission that was just received.

i. Double-check the accuracy of the transmission.

j. The message has been received and understood.

k. 123.6

l. a barometer reading of 30.09

m. position of an aircraft directly in front of you

15. List the five things you should state when initiating radio contact.

16. Suppose you are flying in a Cessna 172 (N7280Q) equipped with a two-way radio and transponder (squawking 1200) over Marietta, Georgia, at 5,500 ft. on a heading of 170°. You intend to land at Peachtree-DeKalb Airport and have carefully listened to ATIS, information Echo. Write out exactly what you would say when contacting Atlanta Approach Control.

17. Identify four extra precautions you should take when preparing for a night flight. Why should you not use anticollision lights while you are on the ground.

18. Briefly describe the function and location of each of the following airplane lights:

    a. anticollision lights

    b. position (navigation) lights

    c. landing lights

19. What lights should you use to signal a control tower if your radio fails on a flight at night? How should these lights be used?

20. Suppose you are flying at night and in the distance you spot another aircraft at is approaching you?

21. Briefly describe the position the ailerons and elevator should be in when taxiing under the following conditions:

    a. strong headwind

    b. quartering headwind from the right

    c. quartering headwind from the left

    d. quartering tailwind from the right

e. quartering tailwind from the left

f. strong tailwind

22. Which of the following wind indicators has its small end pointing <u>into</u> the direction of the wind?
    1--Tetrahedron.
    2--Tetrahedron, wind cone.
    3--Tetrahedron, wind T.
    4--Wind cone, wind T.

23. Solid yellow lines that run perpendicular to the taxiway are called
    1--displaced thresholds.
    2--holding lines.
    3--stopways.
    4--thresholds.

24. Unless otherwise indicated, a magenta boundary around a control area means that it has a floor of
    1--700 ft. AGL.
    2--1,200 ft. AGL.
    3--3,000 ft. AGL.
    4--14,500 ft. MSL.

25. Lights installed on the wingtips and tail of an airplane are called
    1--anticollision lights.
    2--directional lights.
    3--position lights.
    4--taxiing lights.

26. Which of the following wind indicators has its small end pointing <u>away from</u> the wind?
    1--Tetrahedron, wind cone.
    2--Tetrahedron, wind T.
    3--Wind cone, wind T.
    4--Wind T.

27. Runways 13 and 31 at Topeka, KS, indicate that the runway is oriented
    1--013° and 031° magnetic.
    2--013° and 031° true.
    3--130° and 310° magnetic.
    4--130° and 310° true.

28. What leg(s) of a standard traffic pattern is (are) flown perpendicular to the downwind leg?
    1--Base, crosswind.
    2--Base, final.
    3--Crosswind, final.
    4--Final only.

29. What leg(s) of a standard traffic pattern is (are) flown parallel to the downwind leg?
    1--Base, crosswind.
    2--Base, final.
    3--Crosswind, final.
    4--Final only.

30. At what angle does one typically enter the downwind leg or depart the crosswind leg?
    1--30°
    2--45°
    3--60°
    4--90°

31. A VOR federal airway is considered a
    1--control area.
    2--control zone.
    3--positive control area.
    4--transition area.

32. What is the correct way to state a radio frequency of 122.95?
    1--One two two niner five.
    2--One two two point niner five.
    3--One hundred two two point niner five.
    4--Twenty-two niner five.

33. What is the correct way to state an altitude of 6,100 ft.?
    1--Six one zero zero.
    2--Sixty one hundred.
    3--Six thousand one hundred.
    4--Six thousand one hundred zero zero.

34. What is the correct way to identify Piper N431AQ?
    1--Piper Alpha Quebec.
    2--Piper four three one A Q.
    3--Piper four three one Alpha Quebec.
    4--Piper four thirty one A Q.

35. Which of the following terms means that a transmission has been received and understood?
    1--Affirmative.
    2--Over.
    3--Roger.
    4--Verify.

36. What color of lights marks the departure end of a runway at night?
    1--Blue.
    2--Green.
    3--Red.
    4--White.

37. What color of lights marks the approach end of a runway at night?
    1--Blue.
    2--Green.
    3--Red.
    4--White.

38. T F An aircraft may enter an ARSA without prior ATC approval if the pilot has activated the aircraft's Mode C altitude encoding transponder and that transponder is transmitting altitude and location information.

39. T F An aircraft may depart a **satellite** airport within an ARSA only after the pilot has received approval from ATC.

FAA EXAM QUESTIONS

(Note: All FAA Figures are located in Appendix C)

 1. (FAA 1440) An airport's rotating beacon operated during the daylight hours indicates
    1--there are obstructions on the airport.
    2--that weather in the control zone is below basic VFR weather minimums.
    3--the Airport Traffic Area is not in operation.
    4--the airport is temporarily closed.

 2. (FAA 1444) How can a military airport be identified at night?
    1--Alternate white and green beacon light flashes.
    2--Dual peaked (two quick) white flashes between green flashes.
    3--White flashing beacon lights with steady green at the same location.
    4--Alternate white and red beacon light flashes.

 3. (FAA 1441) Airport taxiway edge lights are identified at night by
    1--white directional lights.
    2--blue omnidirectional lights.
    3--white and red lights.
    4--a green, yellow, and white rotating beacon.

 4. (FAA 1443) To set the high intensity runway lights on medium intensity, the pilot should click the microphone seven times, then click it
    1--one time.
    2--three times.
    3--five times.
    4--seven times.

5. (FAA 1454) That portion of the runway identified by the letter A in
   Figure 45
   1--may be used for taxiing but should not be used for takeoffs or
      landings.
   2--may be used for taxiing or takeoffs but not for landings.
   3--may be used for taxiing, takeoffs, and landings.
   4--may not be used except in an emergency.

6. (FAA 1455) Which statement is true, according to the airport diagram
   shown in Figure 45?
   1--Takeoffs may be started at position D on Rwy 30, and the landing
      portion of this runway begins at position E.
   2--The takeoff and landing portion of Rwy 12 begins at position B.
   3--Rwy 30 is equipped at position E with emergency arresting gear to
      provide a means of stopping military aircraft.
   4--Takeoffs may be started at position A on Rwy 12, and the landing
      portion of this runway begins at position B.

7. (FAA 1460) The arrows that appear on the end of the north/south runway
   as shown in Figure 46 indicate that the area
   1--may be used only for taxiing.
   2--is usable for taxiing, takeoff, and landing.
   3--cannot be used for landing, but may be used for taxiing and takeoff.
   4--is available for landing at the pilot's discretion.

8. (FAA 1456) What is the difference between area "A" and area "E" on the
   airport depicted in Figure 45?
   1--"A" may be used for taxi and takeoff; "E" may be used only as an
      overrun.
   2--"A" may be used for all operations except heavy aircraft landings;
      "E" may be used only as an overrun.
   3--"A" may be used only for taxiing; "E" may be used for all operations
      except landing.
   4--"A" may be used only for an overrun; "E" may be used only for taxi
      and takeoff.

9. (FAA 1457) Area C on the airport depicted in Figure 45 is classified as
   1--a blast pad.
   2--a stabilized area.
   3--a multiple heliport.
   4--a closed runway.

10. (FAA 1461) The numbers 9 and 27 on a runway indicate that the runway is
    oriented approximately
    1--090° and 270° magnetic.
    2--009° and 027° true.
    3--090° and 270° true.
    4--009° and 027° magnetic.

11. (FAA 1436) The segmented circle shown in Figure 43 indicates that the
    airport traffic is
    1--left-hand for Rwy 17 and right-hand for Rwy 35.
    2--right-hand for Rwy 9 and left-hand for Rwy 27.
    3--right-hand for Rwy 35 and right-hand for Rwy 9.
    4--left-hand for Rwy 35 and right-hand for Rwy 17.

12. (FAA 1437) The traffic patterns indicated in the segmented circle
    depicted in Figure 43 have been arranged to avoid flights over an area
    to the
    1--south of the airport.
    2--north of the airport.
    3--southeast of the airport.
    4--northwest of the airport.

13. (FAA 1438) The segmented circle depicted in Figure 43 indicates that a
    landing on Runway 26 will be with a
    1--right-quartering headwind.
    2--left-quartering headwind.
    3--right-quartering tailwind.
    4--left-quartering tailwind.

14. (FAA 1439) Which runway and traffic pattern should be used as indicated
    by the wind cone in the segmented circle depicted in Figure 43?
    1--Right-hand traffic on Rwy 8.
    2--Right-hand traffic on Rwy 17.
    3--Left-hand traffic on Rwy 35.
    4--Left-hand traffic on Rwy 26.

15. (FAA 1458) Select the proper traffic pattern and runway for a landing
    as indicated on the airport diagram in Figure 46.
    1--left-hand traffic and Rwy 18.
    2--right-hand traffic and Rwy 18.
    3--left-hand traffic and Rwy 22.
    4--left-hand traffic and Rwy 36.

16. (FAA 1459) If the wind is as shown by the landing direction indicator
    in Figure 46, the pilot should land to the
    1--north on Rwy 36 and expect a crosswind from the right.
    2--south on Rwy 18 and expect a crosswind from the right.
    3--southwest on Rwy 22 directly into the wind.
    4--northeast on Rwy 4 directly into the wind.

17. (FAA 1445) When approaching to land on a runway serviced by a VASI, the
    pilot shall
    1--intercept and remain on the glide slope until touchdown only if the
       aircraft is operating on an instrument flight plan.
    2--maintain an altitude that captures the glide slope at least 2 miles
       down wind from the runway threshold.
    3--maintain an altitude at or above the glide slope.
    4--remain on the glide slope and land between the 2-light bar.

18. (FAA 1451) Illustration A in Figure 44 indicates that an aircraft is
    1--off course.
    2--below the glide slope.
    3--on the glide slope.
    4--above the glide slope.

19. (FAA 1452) While on final approach to a runway equipped with a standard
    2-bar VASI, the lights appear as shown by Illustration D in Figure 44.
    This means that the pilot is
    1--receiving an erroneous light indication.
    2--above the glide slope.
    3--below the glide slope.
    4--on the glide slope.

20. (FAA 1453) VASI lights appearing as shown by Illustration C in Figure
    44 would indicate that an airplane is
    1--off course to the left.
    2--on the glide slope.
    3--below the glide slope.
    4--above the glide slope.

21. (FAA 1446) An on glide slope indication from a tricolor VASI is
    1--a white light signal.
    2--a green light signal.
    3--an amber light signal.
    4--a pink light signal.

22. (FAA 1447) An above glide slope indication from a tricolor VASI is
    1--a white light signal.
    2--a green light signal.
    3--an amber light signal.
    4--a pink light signal.

23. (FAA 1448) A below glide slope indication from a tricolor VASI is
    1--a pink light signal.
    2--a green light signal.
    3--an amber light signal.
    4--a red light signal.

24. (FAA 1449) A slightly high glide slope indication from a precision
    approach path indicator is
    1--four white lights.
    2--three white lights and one red light.
    3--two white lights and two red lights.
    4--one white light and three red lights.

25. (FAA 1450) A below glide slope indication from a pulsating approach
    slope indicator is a
    1--pulsating white light.
    2--steady white light.
    3--alternating red and white light.
    4--pulsating red light.

26. (FAA 1474) Prior to entering an airport advisory area, a pilot
    1--must obtain a clearance from Air Traffic Control.
    2--should monitor ATIS for weather and traffic advisories.
    3--should contact approach control for vectors to the traffic pattern.
    4--should contact the local FSS for airport and traffic advisories.

27. (FAA 1472) What are the horizontal limits of an Airport Chart Area?
1--3 SM from the airport boundary.
2--5 SM from the airport boundary.
3--5 SM from the geographical center of the airport.
4--3 SM from the geographical center of the airport.

28. (FAA 1473) The vertical limit of an Airport Traffic Area is from the surface up to
1--but not including 1,500 ft. AGL.
2--and including 2,000 ft. AGL.
3--but not including 3,000 ft. AGL.
4--the base of the overlying control area.

29. (FAA 1475) ATIS is the continuous broadcast of recorded information
1--alerting pilots of radar-identified aircraft when their aircraft is in dangerous proximity to terrain or an obstruction.
2--concerning nonessential information to reduce frequency congestion.
3--concerning noncontrol information in selected high activity terminal areas.
4--concerning sky conditions limited to ceilings below 1,000 ft. and visibility is less than 3 mi.

30. (FAA 1507) Who should the pilot contact to receive a special VFR departure clearance in a control zone collocated with an Airport Traffic Area?
1--FSS
2--Airport control tower.
3--Air route traffic control center.
4--Approach control.

31. (FAA 1611) Unless otherwise specified, Federal airways extend from
1--1,200 ft. above the surface upward to, but not including, 14,500 ft. MSL and are 16 NM wide.
2--700 ft. above the surface upward to the Continental Control Area and are 10 NM wide.
3--1,200 ft. above the surface upward to, but not including, 18,000 ft. MSL and are 8 NM wide.
4--The surface upward to 18,000 ft. MSL and are 4 NM wide.

32. (FAA 1612) Within the contiguous United States, a control zone extends from the surface upward to the base of
1--an Airport Traffic Area.
2--the Continental Control Area.
3--a Transition Area.
4--a Terminal Control Area.

33. (FAA 1462) Under what condition, if any, may civil pilots enter a restricted area?
1--For takeoff and landing to take care of official business.
2--With the controlling agency's authorization.
3--On airways with ATC clearance.
4--Under no condition.

34. (FAA 1463) When operating VFR in a MOA, a pilot
    1--must obtain a clearance from the controlling agency prior to entering
       the MOA.
    2--may operate only on the airways that transverse the MOA.
    3--should exercise extreme caution when military activity is being
       conducted.
    4--must operate only when military activity is not being conducted.

35. (FAA 1464) Who is responsible for collision avoidance in an alert area?
    1--The controlling agency.
    2--All pilots, without exception.
    3--Only the pilots transitioning the area.
    4--All pilots except those participating in the training operations.

36. (FAA 1465) What minimum altitude is requested for aircraft over
    national wildlife refuges?
    1--500 ft. AGL.
    2--1,000 ft. AGL.
    3--2,000 ft. AGL.
    4--3,000 ft. AGL.

37. (FAA 1466) Basic radar service in the terminal radar program is best
    described as
    1--traffic advisories and limited vectoring to VFR aircraft.
    2--mandatory radar service provided by the ARTS program.
    3--windshear warning at participating airports.
    4--sequencing and separation service to IFR aircraft.

38. (FAA 1468) From whom should a departing VFR aircraft request Stage II
    Terminal Radar Advisory Service during ground operations?
    1--The nearest FSS.
    2--Clearance delivery.
    3--Tower controller, just before takeoff.
    4--Ground control, on initial contact.

39. (FAA 1467) Stage III service in the terminal radar program provides
    1--IFR separation (1,000 ft. vertical and 3 mi. lateral) between all
       aircraft.
    2--warning to pilots when their aircraft are in unsafe proximity to
       terrain, obstructions, or other aircraft.
    3--sequencing and separation for participating VFR aircraft.
    4--service to aircraft principally during the in route phase of flight.

40. (FAA 1469) If radar traffic information is desired, which action should
    the pilot take prior to entering a TRSA?
    1--Prior to entering the TRSA, contact approach control on the
       appropriate frequency.
    2--Contact the tower and request permission to enter the TRSA.
    3--Maintain an altitude below 2,000 ft. AGL prior to entering the TRSA.
    4--Maintain an altitude at or below 3,000 ft. AGL until entering the
       airport control zone, then make initial contact with approach
       control for radar service.

41. (FAA 1470)   All operations within an Airport Radar Service Area (ARSA) must
1--be conducted under instrument flight rules.
2--be in compliance with ATC clearances and instructions.
3--be in an aircraft equipped with a 4096 transponder with Mode C capability.
4--file a flight plan prior to arrival or departure.

42. (FAA 1471)   Under what condition may an aircraft operate from a satellite airport within an Airport Radar Service Area (ARSA)?
1--The pilot must file a flight plan prior to departure.
2--The pilot must monitor ATC until clear of the ARSA.
3--The pilot must contact ATC as soon as practicable after takeoff.
4--The pilot must secure prior approval from ATC before takeoff from the satellite airport.

43. (FAA 1609)   The normal radius of the outer area of an Airport Radar Service Area (ARSA) is
1--5 SM.
2--5 NM.
3--15 NM.
4--20 NM.

44. (FAA 1610)   The vertical limit of an Airport Radar Service Area (ARSA) is
1--1,200 ft. AGL.
2--3,000 ft. AGL.
3--4,000 ft. above the primary airport.
4--up to, but not including, 14,500 ft.

45. (FAA 1212)   When flying EASY N2959S, the proper phraseology for initial contact with Buffalo Approach Control is "BUFFALO APPROACH,
1--EASY NOVEMBER TWO NINE FIVE NINE ESS."
2--EASY FIVE NINE SIERRA."
3--EASY TWENTY-NINE FIFTY-NINE SIERRA."
4--EASY TWO NINER FIVE NINER SIERRA."

46. (FAA 1213)   When flying HAWK N666CB, the proper phraseology for initial contact with McAlester FSS is
1--"MC ALESTER RADIO, HAWK SIX SIX SIX CHARLIE BRAVO."
2--"MC ALESTER STATION HAWK SIX SIX SIX CEE BEE."
3--"MC ALESTER FLIGHT SERVICE STATION, HAWK NOVEMBER SIX CHARLIE BRAVO."
4--"MC ALESTER RADIO, HAWK TRIPLE SIX CHARLIE BRAVO."

47. (FAA 1214)   When flying BREEZY N55899, the proper phraseology for initial contact with Seattle EFAS is
1--"SEATTLE RADIO, BREEZY FIVE FIVE EIGHT NINE NINE."
2--"SEATTLE ADVISORY SERVICE, BREEZY NOVEMBER EIGHT NINE NINE."
3--"SEATTLE FLIGHT WATCH, BREEZY FIVE FIVE EIGHT NINER NINER."
4--"SEATTLE EN ROUTE SERVICE, BREEZY FIFTY-FIVE EIGHT NINETY-NINE."

48. (FAA 1215)   The correct method of stating 4,500 ft. MSL to ATC is
1--"FORTY-FIVE HUNDRED FEET."
2--"FOUR POINT FIVE."
3--"FORTY-FIVE HUNDRED FEET MSL."
4--"FOUR THOUSAND FIVE HUNDRED."

49. (FAA 1216) The correct method of stating 10,500 ft. MSL to ATC is
    1--"TEN THOUSAND, FIVE HUNDRED FEET."
    2--"TEN POINT FIVE."
    3--"ONE ZERO THOUSAND, FIVE HUNDRED."
    4--"ONE ZERO FIVE HUNDRED FEET MSL."

50. (FAA 1211) In radio communications, the phrase "HAVE NUMBERS" indicates
    that the pilot has
    1--all the information in the current ATIS broadcast.
    2--the wind, runway, and altimeter setting at the airport.
    3--all of the ATIS information except the alphabetical code and runway
       in use.
    4--understood previous heading and altitude instructions from ATC.

51. (FAA 1479) An ATC radar facility issues the following advisory to a
    pilot flying on a heading of 090°: "TRAFFIC 3 O'CLOCK, 2 MILES,
    SOUTHBOUND..." Where should the pilot look for this traffic?
    1--East.
    2--South.
    3--West.
    4--North.

52. (FAA 1480) An ATC radar facility issues the following advisory to a
    pilot flying on a heading of 360°: "TRAFFIC 10 O'CLOCK, 2 MILES,
    SOUTHBOUND..." Where should the pilot look for this traffic?
    1--Northwest.
    2--Northeast.
    3--Southwest.
    4--Southeast.

53. (FAA 1481) An ATC radar facility issues the following advisory to a
    pilot during a local flight: "TRAFFIC 2 O'CLOCK, 5 MILES,
    NORTHBOUND..." Where should the pilot look for this traffic?
    1--Directly ahead.
    2--Between directly ahead and 90° to the left.
    3--Between directly behind and 90° to the right.
    4--Between directly ahead and 90° to the right.

54. (FAA 1482) An ATC radar facility issues the following advisory to a
    pilot flying north in a calm wind: "TRAFFIC 9 O'CLOCK, 2 MILES,
    SOUTHBOUND..." Where should the pilot look for this traffic?
    1--East.
    2--South.
    3--West.
    4--North.

55. (FAA 1477) After landing at a tower-controlled airport, where should
    the pilot contact ground control?
    1--Prior to turning off the runway.
    2--After reaching a taxiway that leads directly to the parking area.
    3--After leaving the runway and crossing the runway holding lines.
    4--When advised by the tower to do so.

56. (FAA 1478) If instructed by ground control to taxi to Rwy 9, the pilot
may proceed
1--via taxiways and across runways to, but not onto, Rwy 9.
2--to the next intersecting runway where further clearance is required.
3--via taxiways and across runways to Rwy 9, where an immediate takeoff
   may be made.
4--via any route at the pilot's discretion onto Rwy 9 and hold until
   cleared for takeoff.

57. (FAA 1434) VFR approaches to land at night should be made
1--at a higher airspeed.
2--low and shallow.
3--with a steep descent.
4--the same as during daytime.

58. (FAA 1431) What is the general direction of movement of the other
aircraft during a night flight if you observe a steady red light and a
flashing red light ahead and at the same altitude?
1--the other aircraft is crossing to the left.
2--the other aircraft is crossing to the right.
3--the other aircraft is approaching head-on.
4--the other aircraft is headed away from you.

59. (FAA 1432) What is the general direction of movement of the other
aircraft if during night flight you observe a steady white light and a
flashing red light ahead and at the same altitude?
1--the other aircraft is crossing to the left.
2--the other aircraft is crossing to the right.
3--the other aircraft is approaching head-on.
4--the other aircraft is headed away from you.

60. (FAA 1433) What is the general direction of movement of the other
aircraft if during a night flight you observe steady red and green
lights ahead and at the same altitude?
1--the other aircraft is crossing to the left.
2--the other aircraft is crossing to the right.
3--the other aircraft is approaching head-on.
4--the other aircraft is headed away from you.

61. (FAA 1413) Prior to every flight, a pilot should at least
1--check the operation of the ELT.
2--drain fluid from each quick drain.
3--perform a walk-around inspection of the aircraft.
4--check the required documents aboard the craft.

62. (FAA 1414) What special check should be made on an aircraft during
preflight after it has been stored an extended period of time?
1--ELT batteries and operation.
2--Condensation in the fuel tanks.
3--Damage or obstructions caused by animals, birds, or insects.
4--Lubrication of control systems and proper movement of control
   surfaces.

63. (FAA 1415) The use of a written checklist for preflight inspection in starting the engine is recommended
1--as an excellent crutch for those pilots with a faulty memory.
2--for memorizing the procedures in an orderly sequence.
3--as a procedure to instill confidence in the passengers.
4--to ensure that all necessary items are checked in a logical sequence.

64. (FAA 1124) Which aileron positions should a pilot generally use when taxiing in strong quartering headwinds?
1--Aileron up on the side from which the wind is blowing.
2--Aileron down on the side from which the wind is blowing.
3--Neutral.
4--Aileron up on the downwind side.

65. (FAA 1123) When taxiing with strong quartering tail winds, which aileron positions should be used?
1--Aileron down on the downwind side.
2--Neutral (streamline position).
3--Aileron up on the side from which the wind is blowing.
4--Aileron down on the side from which the wind is blowing.

66. (FAA 1119) How should the controls be held while taxiing a tricycle-gear equipped airplane into a left quartering headwind as depicted by A in Figure 9?
1--Left aileron up, neutral elevator.
2--Left aileron down, neutral elevator.
3--Left aileron up, down elevator.
4--Left aileron down, down elevator.

67. (FAA 1120) How should the controls be held while taxiing a tricycle-gear equipped airplane with a left quartering tailwind as depicted by C in Figure 9?
1--Left aileron up, neutral elevator.
2--Left aileron down, neutral elevator.
3--Left aileron up, down elevator.
4--Left aileron down, down elevator.

68. (FAA 1121) While taxiing a tailwheel equipped airplane into a right quartering headwind as depicted by B in Figure 9, the right aileron should be held
1--up and the elevator up.
2--down and the elevator neutral.
3--up and the elevator down.
4--down and the elevator down.

69. (FAA 1122) While taxiing a tailwheel equipped airplane with a right quartering tailwind, as depicted by D in Figure 9, the right aileron should be held
1--up and the elevator neutral.
2--down and the elevator neutral.
3--up and the elevator down.
4--down and the elevator down.

70. (FAA 1125) Which wind condition would be most critical when taxiing a
    nosewheel equipped high-wing airplane?
    1--Direct headwind.
    2--Direct crosswind.
    3--Quartering headwind.
    4--Quartering tailwind.

ANSWERS AND EXPLANATIONS

Key Terms and Concepts, Part 1

1.	D	6.	C	11.	A	16.	P
2.	E	7.	N	12.	I	17.	M
3.	F	8.	B	13.	R	18.	J
4.	G	9.	H	14.	L	19.	S
5.	K	10.	O	15.	Q	20.	T

Key Terms and Concepts, Part 2

1.	C	6.	H	11.	R	16.	Q
2.	E	7.	A	12.	F	17.	D
3.	S	8.	N	13.	O	18.	I
4.	K	9.	B	14.	P	19.	M
5.	G	10.	L	15.	J	20.	T

Key Terms and Concepts, Part 3

1.	Q	6.	C	11.	S	16.	L
2.	A	7.	O	12.	F	17.	I
3.	H	8.	D	13.	B	18.	R
4.	P	9.	M	14.	G	19.	K
5.	J	10.	E	15.	T	20.	N

Key Terms and Concepts, Part 4

1.	J	6.	K	11.	S	16.	H
2.	C	7.	P	12.	Q	17.	D
3.	O	8.	M	13.	R	18.	G
4.	L	9.	T	14.	F	19.	E
5.	I	10.	N	15.	A	20.	B

Discussion Questions and Review Exercises

1. See Study Guide Main Point #1.

2. See Study Guide Main Point #2.

3.   Takeoff leg: fly a heading of 140°, climb to at least 300 ft. AGL (2,300 ft. on the altimeter), and make certain you are past the departure end of the runway. Crosswind: turn right to a heading of 230° and continue your climb. Downwind: turn right to a heading of 320° and continue your climb to 2,800 ft. MSL (800 ft. AGL). Base leg: turn right to a heading of 50° and continue your descent. Final: continue your descent and turn right to a heading of 140°.

4.

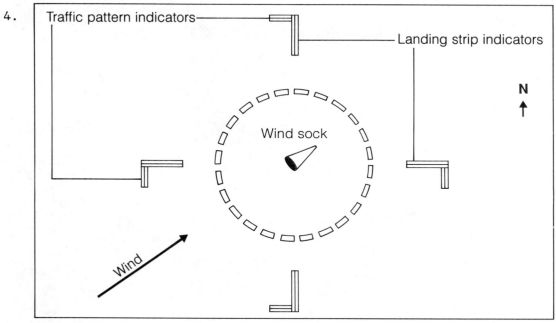

Figure 7.1

   a. Since the wind is only 30° off Rwy 27, you would land to the west on this Rwy. Enter the downwind leg of the pattern at a 45° angle (heading 045°) to intercept a heading of 090°. Begin you descent. Base leg: turn left to a heading of 360° and continue your descent. Final: continue your descent and turn left to a heading of 270°.

   b. Takeoff leg: fly a heading of 270°, climb to at least 300 ft. AGL (3,020 ft. on the altimeter), and make certain you are past the departure end of the runway. Crosswind: turn left to a heading of 180° and continue your climb. Downwind: turn left to a heading of 090° and continue your climb to 3,720 ft. MSL (1,000 ft. AGL). Base leg: turn left to a heading of 360° and continue your descent. Final: continue your descent and turn left to a heading of 270°. If you have set your altimeter (as required by the FAA) to 29.54, it will correspond to current conditions, and no further altitude corrections will have to be made.

5.   See Study Guide Main Point #2.

6.   See Study Guide Main Point #5.

7.   See Study Guide Main Points #4, #6, #7, #11, and #12.

8.   See text Table 7.1.

9.   See Study Guide Main Point #8.

10.   See Study Guide Main Point #8.

11.   See Study Guide Main Point #9.

12.   See Study Guide Main Points #10 and #11.

13.   For some practice, try the authors of this Study Guide, "George Semb and Don Taylor." Gulf echo oscar romeo gulf echo Sierra echo mike bravo alpha november delta Delta oscar november Tango alpha yankee lima oscar romeo.

14.   a.   "Tripacer two four niner seven charlie"
      b.   "Heading two niner zero"
      c.   "Three thousand one hundred twenty feet"
      d.   "One five thousand eight hundred feet"
      e.   "Two two four zero zulu"
      f.   "Kansas City Center"
      g.   "Tulsa Radio"
      h.   "Say again"
      i.   "Verify"
      j.   "Acknowledge"
      k.   "One two three point six"
      l.   "Three zero zero nine" (no decimal)
      m.   "12 o'clock"

15.   See Study Guide Main Point #15.

16.   You would initiate the call with, "Atlanta Approach, this is Cessna seven two eight zero quebec." They might respond, "Cessna eight zero quebec, Atlanta Approach, go ahead. You would respond, "Cessna eight zero quebec is over Marietta at five thousand five hundred, squawking one two zero zero, in bound for landing at Peachtree with information echo."

17.   See Study Guide Main Point #16.

18.   See Study Guide Main Point #17.

19.   You would use landing or position lights to let the tower know of a radio failure. You would then blink them in response to light-gun signals the tower issued.

20.   See Study Guide Main Point #17.

21.   See Study Guide Main Point #20.

22.   1--The tetrahedron's small end points into the wind; for the wind cone and the wind T, the large end points into the wind.

23.   2--These are called holding lines. At airports with an operating control tower, they indicate that you should stop and wait for further instructions.

24.   1--A magenta boundary indicates 700 ft. and a blue boundary indicates 1,200 ft. The upper boundary is 14,500 ft. MSL.

25.   3--Position lights are located on the wingtips and tail.

26. 3--Both the wind cone and the wind **T** have their small ends pointing away from the direction of the wind.

27. 3--Runways are aligned in the approach direction and are rounded to the nearest <u>magnetic</u> heading divided by 10. For example, a runway with a magnetic heading of 133° would be called Rwy 13 (133° is closest to 130°, which when divided by 10 gives Rwy 13).

28. 1--Base and crosswind are flown perpendicular to downwind.

29. 4--Final is flown parallel to the downwind leg.

30. 2--45° is the standard angle for entering the downwind leg or departing the crosswind leg.

31. 1--Federal airways are considered control areas.

32. 2--Include the decimal ("point").

33. 3--For altitudes below 10,000 ft., state the thousands first, followed by the hundreds.

34. 3--State each number and phonetic letter separately. Do not state the N ("November").

35. 3--"Roger" means that a transmission has been received and understood.

36. 3--Red lights mark the departure end of the active runway at night.

37. 2--Green lights mark the approach end of the active runway at night.

38. F--Two-way radio communication is required to enter an ARSA.

39. F--Departure from a satellite airport requires conformity to FAA-approved traffic patterns. Two-way radio communication with ATC must be initiated as soon as practicable.

FAA Exam Questions

1. 2--The rotating beacon is operated in the day time when the weather is below VFR minimums--ceiling 1,000 ft., visibility 3 statute miles.

2. 2--Military airfields are distinguished by two quick white flashes between the green flashes.

3. 2--Taxiway edge lights are blue.

4. 3--Clicking the mike 7 times within 5 seconds sets the lights to the highest intensity available, 5 clicks within 5 seconds will then set medium or lower intensity. The Airport/Facility Directory legend gives procedures.

5.   2--Arrows mark displaced thresholds which are established to keep the approach path above obstacles or other areas under the flight path. The area may be used for taxi and takeoff, but you must land beyond it. The beginning of the landing area is marked by one or more lines across the runway.

6.   4--Arrows mark displaced thresholds which are established to keep the approach path above obstacles or other areas under the flight path. The area may be used for taxi and takeoff, but you must land beyond it. The beginning of the landing area is marked by one or more lines across the runway.

7.   3--Arrows mark displaced thresholds which are established to keep the approach path above obstacles or other areas under the flight path. The area may be used for taxi and takeoff, but you must land beyond it. The beginning of the landing area is marked by one or more lines across the runway.

8.   1--Arrows mark displaced thresholds which are established to keep the approach path above obstacles or other areas under the flight path. The area may be used for taxi and takeoff, but you must land beyond it. Chevrons mark overruns which are to be used only in emergency situations.

9.   4--X's mark closed runways.

10.   1--Runways are numbered based on magnetic courses. The magnetic course is rounded to the nearest 10° and the last digit (zero) is left off.

11.   4--The segmented circle is a traffic pattern indicator. The traffic patterns are arranged to keep landing traffic away from certain areas. The leg of each L pointing toward the circle represents the landing runway, the other leg indicates the base leg.

12.   3--The segmented circle is a traffic pattern indicator. The traffic patterns are arranged to keep landing traffic away from certain areas. The leg of each L pointing toward the circle represents the landing runway, the other leg indicates the base leg.

13.   1--The open end of the wind sock is into the wind. This wind sock shows the wind from about 315°.

14.   3--The segmented circle is a traffic pattern indicator. The leg of each L pointing toward the circle represents the landing runway, the other leg indicates the base leg. The open end of the wind sock is into the wind. The wind sock shows the wind from about 315°. The open end of Runway 35 has the least crosswind.

15.   2--With tetrahedron the pointed end is into the wind. The wind is from 220°. Runway 22 is closed, thus Runway 18 is most into the wind. The segmented circle is a traffic pattern indicator. The leg of each L pointing toward the circle represents the landing runway, the other leg indicates the base leg. The segmented circle shows right traffic for Runway 18.

16.   2--With tetrahedron the pointed end is into the wind. The wind is from 220°. Runway 22 is closed, thus Runway 18 is most into the wind. The segmented circle is a traffic pattern indicator. The leg of each L pointing toward the circle represents the landing runway, the other leg indicates the base leg. The segmented circle shows right traffic for Runway 18.

17.   3--FAR 91.87 requires that when approaching to land on a runway served by a VASI, you must maintain an altitude at or above glide path until a lower altitude is necessary for a safe landing.

18.   3--The two bar VASI is the most common. Each bar has its own glide slope indication, red is low, white is high. On the proper approach glide slope, the far bar will be red and the near bar white. "Red over white, you're alright."

19.   3--The two bar VASI is the most common. Each bar has its own glide slope indication, red is low, white is high. On the proper approach glide slope, the far bar will be red and the near bar white. "Red over red, you're dead."

20.   4--The two bar VASI is the most common. Each bar has its own glide slope indication, red is low, white is high. On the proper approach glide slope, the far bar will be red and the near bar white. "White over white, you'll fly all night."

21.   2--A tricolor VASI has a single light unit projecting amber (high), green (on glide slope) and red (low) lights.

22.   3--A tricolor VASI has a single light unit projecting amber (high), green (on glide slope) and red (low) lights.

23.   4--A tricolor VASI has a single light unit projecting amber (high), green (on glide slope) and red (low) lights.

24.   2--The precision approach path indicator uses a single row of two or four red/white light units. 4 white lights is high, 3 white and 1 red is slightly high, 2 white and 2 red is on glide slope, 1 white and 3 red is slightly low, all red is low.

25.   4--With a pulsating VASI, on glide slope is steady white, high is pulsating white and low is pulsating red.

26.   4--An airport advisory area is the area within 10 miles of an airport without an operating control tower and on which a Flight Service Station is located. The FSS does not control traffic, but provides advisories on known traffic and traffic patterns.

27.   3--An Airport Traffic Area exists when the airport has an operating control tower. An ATA normally is a 5 statute mile circle about the center of the airport and extends up to, but not including 3,000 ft. AGL.

28.   3--An Airport Traffic Area exists when the airport has an operating control tower. An ATA normally is a 5 statute mile circle about the center of the airport and extends up to, but not including 3,000 ft. AGL.

29.   3--Automatic Terminal Information Service provides noncontrol information. It reduce controller workload and relieves frequency congestion by providing continuous repetitive information.

30. 2--Special VFR may be requested when the airport with an operating control tower has weather below the VFR minimum of 1,000 ft. ceiling and 3 SM visibility, but at least 1 SM visibility and the aircraft can remain clear of clouds. The control tower provides the clearance.

31. 3--Federal airways normally extend from 1,200 ft. above the surface up to, but not including, 18,000 ft. MSL and extends 4 nm either side of centerline.

32. 2--Control zones extend from the surface to the Continental Control Area.

33. 2--Restricted areas contain unseen hazards. You must receive permission from the controlling authority to enter active restricted areas.

34. 3--Military Operating Areas are used for certain military training activities. You do not need permission to enter, but should exercise extreme condition.

35. 2--Alert areas may contain a high volume of pilot training. As always, pilots are responsible for collision avoidance.

36. 3--While not a specific requirement, pilots are requested to maintain a minimum altitude of 2,000 ft. above the surface of national wildlife refuges. This is wise because of the bird hazards.

37. 1--The basic radar service provides traffic advisories and limited vectoring (on a workload permitting basis) to VFR aircraft.

38. 4--Stage II provides sequencing for arriving and departing traffic. Pilots of departing VFR aircraft are encouraged to request radar information by notifying ground control on initial contact.

39. 3--Stage III provides separation between all participating VFR aircraft and all IFR aircraft.

40. 1--Pilots should contact approach control before entering the Terminal Radar Service Area.

41. 2--ARSA's consist of controlled airspace about one or more airports. Permission is not required to operate in an ARSA, but you must establish and maintain two way communications. The FARs require compliance with ATC clearances and instruction.

42. 3--ARSA's consist of controlled airspace about one or more airports. When departing from a satellite airport, you may not have radio contact with ATC on the ground. You must contact ATC as soon as practicable.

43. 4--The normal radius of the outer area of an ARSA is 20 NM. The vertical limits are normally 4,000 ft. above the primary airport.

44. 3--The normal radius of the outer area of an ARSA is 20 NM. The vertical limits are normally 4,000 ft. above the primary airport.

45. 4--On initial contact the aircraft type and entire serial (less N when within the United States) is used. Speak each digit with NINER used for NINE.

46.   1--The call sign for an FSS is RADIO. Use the aircraft type and all digits and letters (except N).

47.   3--The call sign for Enroute Flight Advisory Service is FLIGHTWATCH.

48.   4--Altitudes are read in thousands and hundreds of feet.

49.   3--Above 10,000 feet, each digit of the tens of thousands is spoken plus the hundreds of feet.

50.   2--"HAVE NUMBERS" indicates that the pilot has wind, runway, and altimeter information. "INFORMATION SIERRA (or other letter) RECEIVED" means the entire ATIS broadcast was copied.

51.   2--Imagine a clock. Your nose points at 12; 3 is off your right wing.

52.   1--Imagine a clock. Your nose points at 12; 10 is just ahead of your left wing.

53.   4--Imagine a clock. Your nose points at 12; 2 is just ahead of your right wing.

54.   3--Imagine a clock. Your nose points at 12; 9 is off your left wing.

55.   4--You should not leave tower frequency until advised to do so.

56.   1--Clearance to taxi to a runway includes authorization to use taxiways and to cross all runways enroute to the takeoff runway.

57.   4--The airplane flys the same at night as it does in the daytime. The approach speeds should be the same.

58.   1--Position lights are: red on left wing tip, green on right wing tip and white on the tail; each may be seen only for a 180° arc, i.e. red from directly aft through left side to directly forward, white from rear only, green from right only. Thus red and green may both be seen only from directly ahead or directly aft (with white). The anticollision light may be a rotating red beacon or flashing white strobes, or both, and is seen from all directions. In this situation, you are seeing the left wing light and the rotating beacon.

59.   4--Position lights are: red on left wing tip, green on right wing tip and white on the tail; each may be seen only for a 180° arc, i.e. red from directly aft through left side to directly forward, white from rear only, green from right only. Thus red and green may both be seen only from directly ahead or directly aft (with white). The anticollision light may be a rotating red beacon or flashing white strobes, or both, and is seen from all directions. In this situation, you are directly behind the tail.

60.   3--Position lights are: red on left wing tip, green on right wing tip and white on the tail; each may be seen only for a 180° arc, i.e. red from directly aft through left side to directly forward, white from rear only, green from right only. Thus red and green may both be seen only from directly

ahead or directly aft (with white). The anticollision light may be a rotating red beacon or flashing white strobes, or both, and is seen from all directions.

61. 3--Pilots should perform a walk-around inspection of the aircraft before each flight to be sure there is no damage and no fluid leaks.

62. 3--Animals can cause damage to aircraft. Cows have eaten airplane fabric. Birds have built nests in engine areas and wheel wells. Insects can clog the pitot-static system.

63. 4--Pilots who trust to memory may forget things. Also beware of interruptions when using a checklist; when resuming the preflight, you may skip one or more items.

64. 1--For tricycle-gear airplanes in a quartering headwind, the aileron into the wind should be up to keep the wing down, and the elevator should be in the neutral position.

65. 4--For tricycle-gear airplanes in a quartering tailwind, the aileron into the wind should be down, and the elevator should be down to keep the nose down.

66. 1--For tricycle-gear airplanes in a quartering headwind, the aileron into the wind should be up to keep the wing down, and the elevator should be in the neutral position.

67. 4--For tricycle-gear airplanes in a quartering tailwind, the aileron into the wind should be down, and the elevator should be down to keep the nose down.

68. 1--For tailwheel airplanes, in a quartering headwind, the aileron into the wind should be up to keep the wing down, and the elevator should be up to keep the tail down.

69. 4--For tailwheel airplanes in a quartering tailwind, the aileron into the wind should be down, and the elevator should be down.

70. 4--Tailwinds can turn over a high-wing airplane. You should keep the wing into the wind down with down aileron and keep the elevator in the down position.

METEOROLOGY: A PILOT'S VIEW OF WEATHER

MAIN POINTS

1.   **Air** consists primarily of nitrogen (78 percent), oxygen (21 percent), other gases, and varying amounts of water vapor. The **atmosphere** contains air and **particulate matter** such as pollen and pollutants that can affect precipitation as well as pilot visibility. The three levels of the atmosphere are the **troposphere** (surface to 29,000 ft. near the poles and 54,000 ft. near the equator), where most weather occurs; the **stratosphere** (29,000-54,000 ft. to 40-60 mi.), where the atmosphere is stable; and the **ionosphere** (upward to about 300 mi.).

2.   Atmospheric pressure can be measured: (1) in inches of mercury--the International Standard Atmosphere is the pressure at sea level, 29.92" Hg.; (2) in pounds per square inch (**psi**)--the sea level standard is 14.7 psi.; and (3) in millibars (**mb**)--the standard is 1013.2 mb. One inch of mercury equals about 34 mb. Millibar pressures are common on weather charts. Atmospheric pressure decreases as altitude increases at a decreasing rate; that is, lower altitudes lose pressure more quickly than do higher altitudes.

3.   As water vapor increases, **condensation** (for example, clouds) or **precipitation** (discharge of moisture) may occur. Precipitation is affected by temperature (warm air can hold more moisture than can cold air) and the presence of particles on which moisture can condense. **Relative humidity** refers to the percentage of water vapor present compared to the amount it could hold under current conditions. When this value is 100 percent, the air is called **saturated**. The temperature at which saturation occurs is called the **dew point**. Because condensation is more likely to occur as the temperature of the air decreases, it is important to monitor both the current temperature and the dew point. When the spread between OAT and dew point is within 4°F and narrowing, condensation (for example, fog or low clouds) should be expected. Formation of water droplets also depends on particles in the air called **condensation nuclei**. Two ways by which water changes to gas are **evaporation** (water to gas) and **sublimation** (solid to gas).

4. The surface of the earth absorbs and releases heat, depending upon its color and texture. For example, the land both absorbs and releases heat more quickly than water, which accounts for many weather patterns in coastal areas. The amount of radiation reaching a place on earth is affected by the rotation of the earth on its axis and its revolution about the sun. No solar radiation touches a place at night and less is available during winter months.

5. Air loses temperature at an average rate of 2°C per 1,000 ft. in the troposphere (called the **standard lapse rate**), but this can be affected by many variables. It is important to know how the air and the surface below it are heated. **Radiation** heats the air and surface as it strikes them. **Conduction** refers to heating by direct contact, as when molecules collide with each other. **Convection** refers to currents set up as hot air rises or cool air falls. Horizontal transfer of heat (for example, a moving air mass) is called **advection**.

6. The principles of heat exchange affect the global circulation of the atmosphere, as does Earth's rotation. The apparent motion of the air is due to the **Coriolis force**, and it imparts a lateral component to the flow of winds. Generally, in the Northern Hemisphere, polar winds are from the east (**polar easterlies**); middle latitudes have **prevailing westerlies**; and, as you approach the equator, northeast winds (**northeast trades**) prevail. As polar easterlies meet prevailing westerlies, **circulation** begins, always in a counterclockwise direction around low-pressure regions and in a clockwise direction around high-pressure regions in the Northern Hemisphere.

7. Weather charts have lines of equal pressure called **isobars**. An elongated high-pressure area is called a **ridge**, and an elongated low-pressure area is called a **trough**. Winds above the friction level tend to flow parallel to the isobars. Rotational winds are called cyclones when associated with lows and anticyclones when associated with highs. How close together the isobars are (called the **pressure gradient**) indicates the intensity of the winds. A steep gradient (isobars close together) indicates higher winds.

8. The three **weather zones** are (a) the equator to 30° latitude--a belt of high pressure straddles the 30° line, (b) 30° to 60°--a belt of prevailing westerlies but much mixture of air from north and south, and (c) 60° to the pole--low pressure along 60° latitude. Other forces operating on the atmosphere include gravity, friction (for example, mountains), and centrifugal force. Gravity causes the air near the surface to be more dense. Friction causes wind near the surface to flow across isobars toward low-pressure areas. Centrifugal force causes wind speed to decrease near the center of a low and to increase near the center of a high.

9. The **ceiling** is defined as the height above the ground of the lowest layer of clouds, provided clouds cover more than half the sky. Sky cover is defined as **clear** (0 to 10 percent), **scattered** (10 to 50 percent), **broken** (60 to 90 percent), or **overcast** (90 to 100 percent). **Visibility** refers to horizontal distance and is normally given in miles. Several conditions contribute to limited visibility.

10. **Fog**, a cloud on or near the ground, is dangerous because it limits visibility severely. It is most likely to occur when relative humidity is high, condensation nuclei are present, and the air is cooling (as in the early evening after the sun sets). Four types of fog are **radiation fog**, or ground

fog, which occurs under clear skies and calm winds; **advection fog**, which occurs when moist air moves over a cool surface, as in coastal areas; **upslope fog**, which occurs when moist air moves up to a cool region, as against a mountain; and **frontal fog**, which occurs when evaporating rain is lifted.

11.   **Precipitation** also affects visibility (snow more than light rain). Other **obscurations** (for example, dust and smog) limit visibility and may lead to reports of sky obscured or sky partially obscured since no ceiling can be accurately defined.   If clouds or part of the sky may be seen above the obscuration, it is reported as a partial obscuration.   The terms used to refer to weather conditions are **visual meteorological conditions (VMC)**, which means that flight can be maintained by the use of outside references, and **instrument meteorological conditions (IMC)**, which means that visual flight is not possible.   These terms are not the same as VFR and IFR, both of which are a set of **flight rules**, not weather conditions.   Finally, the most significant measure of visibility aloft is **slant range** ("over the nose").

12.   For **ice** to form, there must be (a) visible moisture and (b) temperature below freezing.   Ice that forms from a sublimation process (water vapor turns directly into a solid) is called **frost**.   Frost on the airplane affects drag and lift and may prevent the airplane from becoming airborne. **Icing** is most likely to occur when there is visible moisture, OAT is between −5° and +3°C, and the aircraft skin is at or below freezing.   VFR pilots should stay out of clouds and away from freezing rain.   Structural ice comes in two varieties: **clear ice**, which is smooth-looking and clear; and **rime ice**, which is opaque and granular-looking.   Ice reduces lift, increases the airplane's weight, decreases thrust, increases drag, and increases stalling speed.

13.   Vertical motion of the air can lead to unstable atmospheric conditions and turbulence.   Dry air is more stable than moist air, and the **adiabatic lapse rate** is about 3°C per 1,000 ft. for dry air as compared to 1.1-2.8°C for moist air.   As mentioned earlier, the **standard lapse rate** is 2°C per 1,000 ft.; it is the average of lapse rates for dry and moist air.

14.   **Convection currents** (or thermals) develop as different shades and densities of the land differentially absorb and reflect heat, leading to vertical air movement.   Around large bodies of water, convective currents produce **onshore winds** (sea breezes) during the day as cool air over the ocean moves in to replace warm air over the land and **offshore winds** (land breezes) at night as this process reverses.

15.   **Surface obstructions** also affect turbulence.   Even small buildings, hangars, and trees can affect the flow of the wind (referred to as land flow turbulence) and can be particularly disruptive as the wind increases in velocity.

16.   Flying near mountains can also be dangerous due to updrafts and downdrafts created by mountain flow.   These vertical movements are also accentuated by an increase in the wind's velocity and can sometimes be identified by **lenticular** (almond- or lens-shaped) **clouds** on the leeward (downwind) side of the mountain.   **Wind shear,** common near thunderstorms and mountains, is a sudden change in the wind's horizontal or vertical movement. It is common when there is a reversal of the lapse rate (**temperature**

inversion) or when low-altitude winds are different from surface winds. Finally, there is **clear air turbulence (CAT)**, which is difficult to predict. It typically occurs at higher altitudes.

17. Clouds are visible moisture and come in a variety of different forms and sizes. They are classified by how they are formed and by their altitudes. **Cumulus (piled up) clouds** are formed by vertical currents of unstable air and have a fluffy appearance. **Stratus (layered) clouds** are formed by the cooling of a stable layer of air and have a sheetlike appearance. **Cirrus clouds** are thin, wispy clouds that occur at high altitudes. Additional descriptive words include **alto** (middle), **nimbo** (rain), and **fracto** (broken). Low clouds typically have bases less than 6,500 ft. AGL, middle clouds (alto) are found between 6,500 ft. and 16,500 ft. AGL, and high clouds (cirriform) occur between 16,500 ft. and 45,000 ft. AGL. The basic types of cumulus clouds are cumulus, alto cumulus, stratocumulus, and cumulonimbus. The stratus group includes stratus, altostratus, and nimbostratus. The cirrus group includes cirrus, cirrostratus, and cirrocumulus.

18. Of special note are **cumulonimbus** clouds, which are also referred to as Cbs, TRWs, or thunderstorms. They are extremely dangerous. A product of exaggerated vertical movement and instability, Cbs come in a variety of types, such as **orographic** (upslope lifting of moist air as it approaches a mountain range) and **frontal** (one air mass lifts another). Thunderstorms develop in three stages: **cumulus**, with rapid vertical development; **mature**, marked by updrafts and heavy downdrafts out from the center with rain and sometimes hail; and **dissipating**, identified by the classic anvil-shaped cirriform top that develops at the apex. Cbs can produce hail, lightning, updrafts and downdrafts, tornados, and severe icing. Navigating around Cbs requires great care: Give them a berth of at least 20 miles. Due to severe vertical movement, flying under them is dangerous because of downdrafts and damaging hail. If you are caught in or near a thunderstorm, do not turn back, maintain maneuvering speed, and control the airplane's **attitude**. Attempt to keep pitch and bank as level and constant as possible.

19. An **air mass** is an extensive body of air with fairly consistent stability, temperature, and moisture content. As an air mass begins to move along a pressure gradient, it behaves in a predictable way. The line of discontinuity between two differing air masses is called a **front**. The four main air mass sources are: **arctic**, the coldest regions, from the poles; **polar**, cold regions, high-pressure systems; **tropical**, a warm region, low-pressure systems; and **equatorial**, the warmest region, low pressure and calm winds. Masses that form over water are called **maritime** and contain more moisture than those that form over land, called **continental**. Air masses are classified as cold or hot in reference to the ground over which they pass. A cold air mass, designated **k** on a surface weather map, is a body of air that is colder than the ground over which it passes, while a warm air mass (**w**) is warmer than the surface over which it is moving. Cold air moving over a warm surface produces convective current (hot air rises) and is unstable, while warm air moving over cold surfaces is stable. **Maritime Polar air masses** are moist, unstable, and conducive to Cb buildups. **Continental Polar air masses** tend to be stable, dry, and characterized by cirrus clouds. **Maritime Tropical air masses** are typically humid, internally stable, and characterized by stratiform clouds. **Continental Tropical air masses** are dry, unstable, and not

likely to produce much precipitation. In the United States, polar and arctic air moves from the northwest and tropical air from the southwest. In general, cold air masses move faster than warm ones do.

20. **Fronts** are lines of discontinuity between two differing air masses. They are named for the **advancing** air mass. A **warm front** is a mass of warm air replacing cold air; a **cold front** is a mass of cold air supplanting warm air. In an **occluded front**, a cold front outraces a slower-moving air mass and moves it aloft. In a **stationary front**, the two fronts are balanced and the zone of discontinuity remains relatively constant geographically. **Frontogenesis** refers to the creation of a front, as when one air mass overtakes another. When the air masses normalize, the front dissipates (**frontolysis**). Frontal passage is typically characterized by simultaneous changes in temperature, barometric pressure, wind direction, and cloud formation.

21. **Warm air masses** tend to be moist and to climb over retreating cold air masses. As a warm air mass climbs over the cold air, its temperature decreases and condensation begins, usually in the form of drizzle or light rain. The frontal zone is usually stable and is preceded by high cirriform clouds. As the front passes, the wind changes from southeast to southwest, the barometer is steady or changes only slightly, the temperature rises, and frontal weather dissipates. Warm fronts typically have extensive cloud cover ahead of the front and low cloud cover near the front, things important for VFR pilots to remember in making flight plans.

22. **Cold air masses** move faster than warm fronts and tend to push themselves under warm air masses. This gives rise to cumulus clouds, turbulence, and thunderstorms. **Squall lines**, tightly knit lines of discontinuity, often precede the front and are characterized by highly unstable conditions. As the front passes, visibility improves, the wind shifts, the temperature drops, and the barometer dips as the front passes, then rises. Flying the front is not advisable.

23. **Occluded air masses** are ones that have been overtaken from behind by faster-moving cold fronts and forced aloft. Thunderstorms almost always occur in the stratiform cloud layers; the most activity is found in the area closest to the low, typically the northernmost 50-100 mi. Pilots should avoid occluded fronts.

24. **Stationary air masses** move very slowly, if at all. Winds associated with the frontal zone usually run parallel to the line of discontinuity. Such fronts are characterized by low cloud layers, drizzle, and an occasional thunderstorm. Sometimes frontal waves develop as cold and warm air begin to rotate, creating a miniature low-pressure cell (cyclogenesis).

25. As a VFR pilot, you should: (1) familiarize yourself with every relevant aspect of each flight, as required by FAR 91.5; (2) decide ahead of time when, during the course of your flight, you will make weather-related decisions; (3) avoid marginal conditions, no matter how important it is to arrive at your destination; (4) remember to lower your airspeed to give yourself extra time if you encounter bad weather; and, (5) remember that a 180° turn is usually the best and quickest route out of danger.

KEY TERMS AND CONCEPTS, PART 1

Match each term or concept (1-24) with the appropriate description (A-X) below. Each item has only one match.

___ 1. adiabatic lapse rate   ___ 13. mature
___ 2. stratosphere   ___ 14. frontolysis
___ 3. VMC   ___ 15. cirrus
___ 4. troposphere   ___ 16. overcast
___ 5. visibility   ___ 17. station pressure
___ 6. temperature inversion   ___ 18. polar easterlies
___ 7. clear   ___ 19. condensation nuclei
___ 8. radiation   ___ 20. cumulonimbus
___ 9. ridge   ___ 21. isobars
___ 10. onshore   ___ 22. fog
___ 11. maritime   ___ 23. cirrostratus
___ 12. ceiling   ___ 24. sublimation

A. extends from 54,000 ft. at the equator to about 40-60 mi. above the earth
B. dissipation of a front
C. Cb stage with heavy downdrafts out of the center
D. reversal of the normal lapse rate
E. wind typically encountered on the beach during the day
F. flight can be maintained by use of outside references
G. horizontal distance you can see
H. lowest layer of clouds covering more than one-half of the sky
I. high-pressure area that takes an elongated form
J. winds flowing from the North Polar regions
K. temperature change of mechanically lifted dry air of about 3°C per 1,000-ft. change in elevation
L. particles such as pollen suspended in the air
M. pressure to which you set your altimeter before taking off
N. extends from the surface to 29,000 ft. over the poles
O. air mass that forms over water
P. clouds that have a wispy, horsehair appearance
Q. form of icing that is difficult to detect
R. condition of the sky when 95 percent covered by clouds
S. heat derived directly from the sun's rays
T. ice changes directly into water vapor
U. layer of cirrus clouds
V. clouds that are lying on or near the ground
W. continuous equal pressure lines on a weather chart
X. raining cumulus cloud

KEY TERMS AND CONCEPTS, PART 2

Match each term or concept (1-24) with the appropriate description (A-X) below. Each item has only one match.

___ 1. advection fog

___ 2. counterclockwise

___ 3. offshore

___ 4. anticyclones

___ 5. trough

___ 6. ionosphere

___ 7. scattered

___ 8. atmosphere

___ 9. radiation fog

___ 10. 14.7

___ 11. IMC

___ 12. convection

___ 13. 29.92" Hg

___ 14. evaporation

___ 15. squall line

___ 16. dissipating

___ 17. angle of incidence

___ 18. wind shear

___ 19. precipitation

___ 20. prevailing westerlies

___ 21. dew point

___ 22. northeast trades

___ 23. conduction

___ 24. relative humidity

A. direction wind moves around a low-pressure system

B. circulatory motion of the air caused by heat transfer

C. angle at which the sun's rays strike the earth

D. discharge of moisture from the atmosphere

E. ISA inches of mercury at sea level

F. air, water vapor, and particulate matter

G. outer layer of the atmosphere

H. tightly knit line of discontinuity that sometimes precedes a cold front

I. Cb stage in which an anvil-shaped cloud forms at the apex

J. sudden change in wind speed or direction

K. wind typically encountered on the beach at night

L. flight cannot be maintained by use of outside references

M. fog caused by the ground's cooling at night

N. condition of the sky when 30 percent covered by clouds

O. low-pressure area that takes an elongated form

P. winds flowing between 30° and 60° latitude

Q. high-pressure areas and their associated rotational winds

R. water changes from a liquid to a gas

S. ISA pounds per square inch (psi) at sea level

T. fog caused by moist air moving over a cold surface; common in coastal areas

U. ratio of water vapor in the air to the maximum amount it could hold

V. heat transferred directly from one molecule to another

W. winds flowing from 30° to the equator

X. temperature at which condensation or precipitation occurs

KEY TERMS AND CONCEPTS, PART 3

Match each term or concept (1-20) with the appropriate description (A-T) below. Each item has only one match.

___ 1. standard lapse rate   ___ 11. cold air mass
___ 2. rime   ___ 12. slant range
___ 3. 1013.2   ___ 13. stratus
___ 4. front   ___ 14. clockwise
___ 5. upslope   ___ 15. occluded front
___ 6. pressure gradient   ___ 16. cyclones
___ 7. continental   ___ 17. obscuration
___ 8. broken   ___ 18. advection
___ 9. saturated   ___ 19. thermals
___ 10. cumulus   ___ 20. warm front

A. body of air that is colder than the surface it is passing over
B. clouds that are formed in layers
C. form of ice composed of small, brittle particles
D. fog caused when a moist air mass is lifted; common in and around mountains
E. condition of the sky when 75 percent covered by clouds
F. low-pressure areas and their associated rotational winds
G. direction wind moves around a high-pressure system
H. horizontal transfer of heat within an air mass as it passes over a surface
I. temperature decrease of 2°C per 1,000 ft. in elevation
J. air that has a relative humidity of 100 percent
K. ISA millibars (mb) at sea level
L. occurs when an advancing mass of warm air supersedes a cold air mass
M. air mass that forms over land
N. a rapidly moving cold front forces a slower moving air mass aloft
O. line of discontinuity between two differing air masses
P. clouds that appear to be piled up
Q. convective currents caused by differential heat reflection and absorption of the ground
R. "over-the-nose" visibility
S. condition that limits visibility, such as smog
T. pressure changes perpendicular to the isobars

DISCUSSION QUESTIONS AND REVIEW EXERCISES

1. What is the difference between air and the atmosphere? Why is the distinction important?

2. State two characteristics of each of the three layers of the atmosphere identified below.

    a. stratosphere

    b. ionosphere

    c. troposphere

3. What are the three common ways to report air pressure? For each, state the value associated with standard conditions.

4. How does the **rate of change** in air pressure change as altitude increases? Give an example.

5. What two things control precipitation in addition to the water vapor itself? Explain how and why each affects precipitation.

6. Define each of the following terms:

   a. relative humidity

   b. dew point

   c. condensation nuclei

   d. evaporation

   e. sublimation

7. Explain how each of the following affects air temperature:

   a. the earth's rotation

   b. unequal heating of land and water

   c. the earth's revolution around the sun

8. Characterize the following lapse rates:

   a. standard lapse rate

   b. adiabatic lapse rate (dry air)

8 - 10

c. adiabatic lapse rate (moist air)

9. Briefly describe the Coriolis force. How is it important in understanding global circulation patterns?

10. Briefly describe the three zones or cells that affect global circulation in the Northern Hemisphere and their associated weather conditions.

11. State in what direction winds circulate around high-pressure and low-pressure systems in the Northern Hemisphere.

12. Define each of the following terms:

    a. ridge

    b. trough

    c. cyclone

d. anticyclone

e. pressure gradient

13. Briefly state how each of the following factors affects the wind:

a. gravity

b. friction

c. centrifugal force

14. Define each of the following sky cover conditions and draw the symbol that is used to represent each one:

a. clear

b. scattered

c. broken

d. overcast

15. What is fog? What three conditions are necessary for its formation?

16. Describe each of the following types of fog and state where you would be likely to encounter each:

   a.   radiation

   b.   advection

   c.   upslope

   d.   frontal

17.   What is an obscuration? Give an example. Distinguish between reports of sky obscured and sky partially obscured.

18.   Distinguish among VMC, VFR, IMC, and IFR.

19.   What two conditions are necessary for the formation of ice? Briefly distinguish between rime ice and clear ice. What is the best way for VFR pilots to avoid icing conditions?

20. State how turbulence is related to each of the following:

    a. adiabatic lapse rate

    b. convective currents

    c. sea breezes

    d. offshore winds

    e. mountain flow

    f. wind shear

    g. temperature inversion

21. What is clear air turbulence? Why is it so difficult to deal with this phenomenon?

22. Characterize each of the following cloud types, including a description of what each looks like, what weather each is associated with, and the altitudes at which each is likely to be encountered:

    a. stratus

    b. cumulus

c. cirriform

d. stratocumulus

e. nimbostratus

f. cirrocumulus

23. Why are cumulonimbus clouds considered particularly dangerous? Characterize the three stages of the Cb life cycle.

24. <u>Why</u> is it dangerous to fly underneath a line of thunderstorms?

25. What is the most important thing you should do if you are caught in a thunderstorm cloud? Name three other things you should also do.

26. Characterize the four air mass source regions.

27. Distinguish between continental and maritime air masses. How do they typically differ in temperature and moisture content?

28. Distinguish between warm and cold air masses.

29. Describe each of the following air mass types:

    a. maritime Polar

    b. continental Polar

c. maritime Tropical

d. continental Tropical

30. Characterize each of the following:

a. warm front

b. cold front

c. occluded front

d. stationary front

e. cyclogenesis

31. What should VFR pilots do when the weather begins to "close in"?

32. T F The layer of the atmosphere that gives rise to northern lights is the ionosphere.

33. T F The atmosphere gains pressure less quickly as altitude increases.

34. T F One factor in the intensity of solar radiation is the sun's rotation around the earth.

35. T F The direction of circulation around a region of low pressure in the Northern Hemisphere is counterclockwise.

36. T F The steeper the pressure gradient is, the more likely high velocity winds are.

37. T F Wind speed along the isobars decreases as the center of a low-pressure area approaches and increases as the center of a high-pressure area approaches.

38. T F Fog caused by cooling of the ground at night (common under clear skies with calm winds) is called advection fog.

39. T F VMC and VFR refer to identical weather conditions.

40. T F Clear ice will accumulate rapidly in flight when the temperature is between freezing and -15°C and you are flying in cumuliform clouds.

41. T F Frost may form in flight when a cold aircraft descends from a zone of subzero temperatures to a zone of above-freezing temperatures and high relative humidity.

42. T F Onshore winds are common during the day, while offshore winds are common during the night.

43. T F Convection currents become less intense as the surface temperature increases.

44. T F An almond- or lens-shaped cloud that appears stationary but that may contain winds of 50 kts. or more is called a lenticular cloud.

45. T F A temperature inversion often develops near the ground on clear, cool nights in calm wind conditions.

46. T F The overhanging anvil of a thunderstorm points in the direction from which the storm has just moved.

47. T F Hail may be found in any level within a thunderstorm but not in the clear air outside the storm cloud.

48. T F A cold air mass is colder than the surface over which it passes.

49. T F A squall line is typically associated with a fast-moving warm front.

50. T F Warm fronts are frequently associated with low ceilings and limited visibility.

51. Which of the following numbers represents International Standard Atmosphere conditions in pounds per square inch (psi) at sea level?
    1--14.7.
    2--29.92
    3--123.6.
    4--1013.2.

52. On a weather map, isobars that are close together represent a steep
    1--anticyclone.
    2--pressure gradient.
    3--ridge.
    4--trough.

53. If 80 percent of the sky is covered by clouds, it is classified as
    1--broken.
    2--clear.
    3--overcast.
    4--scattered.

54. The type of ice that forms on an airplane surface depends on
    1--an inversion aloft.
    2--an increase in flight altitude.
    3--the size of the water drops that strike the airplane surface.
    4--the temperature/dew point spread.

55. What aerodynamic effects will structural icing have on an airplane?
    1--Drag increases; thrust will not be affected.
    2--Lift decreases; weight increases.
    3--Stall speed decreases; thrust increases.
    4--Weight increases; lift is not affected if drag and thrust remain
       constant.

56. Dry air is _____ stable and loses heat _____ rapidly than moist air.
    1--less; less
    2--less; more
    3--more; less
    4--more; more

57. Gray, uniform, sheetlike clouds lurking at 2,000 ft. AGL would be classified as
    1--altocumulus.
    2--cumulus.
    3--nimbostratus.
    4--stratus.

58. _____ _____ air masses are typically dry, stable, and characterized by sparse precipitation and excellent visibilities.
    1--Continental Polar
    2--Continental Tropical
    3--Maritime Polar
    4--Maritime Tropical

59. The atmospheric pressure reported for an airport or other geographic
location is called
     1--density-altitude.
     2--indicated pressure.
     3--station pressure adjusted to sea level.
     4--true pressure.

60. The temperature at which condensation or precipitation occurs is called
     1--the dew point.
     2--the evaporation level.
     3--the saturation level.
     4--the sublimation level.

61. Particles in an air mass around which moisture collects are called
     1--condensation nuclei.
     2--dew points.
     3--particulate matter.
     4--precipitation particles.

62. Horizontal transfer of heat is called
     1--advection.
     2--conduction.
     3--convection.
     4--radiation.

63. Which of the following components of windflow in the Northern Hemisphere
is in error?
     1--Arctic northerlies.
     2--Northeast trades.
     3--Prevailing westerlies.
     4--Polar easterlies.

64. Winds along the isobars typically _____ as the center of a low-pressure
area approaches and _____ as the center of a high-pressure area approaches.
     1--decrease; decrease
     2--decrease; increase
     3--increase; decrease
     4--increase; increase

65. Fog that occurs when moist air is lifted into a cooler region, as when
moist air moves up against the side of a mountain, is called
     1--advection fog.
     2--frontal fog.
     3--radiation fog.
     4--upslope fog.

66. A condition that limits visibility from the surface upward, such as smog,
is called a/an
     1--advection layer.
     2--indefinite ceiling.
     3--obscuration.
     4--virga.

67. Gray or blue clouds at 5,000 ft. AGL with individual rolls that are associated with light showers and strong, gusty surface winds would be classified as
    1--altostratus.
    2--nimbostratus.
    3--stratus.
    4--stratocumulus.

68. Gray, fibrous clouds at 10,000 ft. AGL characterized by light, continuous precipitation, poor surface visibility, and smooth air would be classified as
    1--altostratus.
    2--cumulonimbus.
    3--nimbostratus.
    4--stratocumulus.

69. Moist, unstable air masses that are typically characterized by thunderstorms are called
    1--Continental Polar.
    2--Continental Tropical.
    3--Maritime Polar.
    4--Maritime Tropical.

70. When two air masses are so well balanced that neither prevails, it is referred to as a/an
    1--discontinuous front.
    2--frontolysis.
    3--occluded front.
    4--stationary front.

71. When a rapidly moving cold front outraces a slower front and pushes it aloft, it is referred to as a/an
    1--discontinuous front.
    2--frontolysis.
    3--occluded front.
    4--stationary front.

72. Warm smooth air, low ceilings, poor visibility and multilayered overcast is typical of
    1--cyclogenetic fronts.
    2--fast-moving fronts.
    3--occluded fronts.
    4--stationary fronts.

FAA EXAM QUESTIONS

1. (FAA 1771) What are the standard temperature and pressure values for sea level?
    1--15°C and 29.92" Hg.
    2--59°C and 1013.2 millibars.
    3--50°F and 29.92 millibars.
    4--15°C and 1013.2" Hg.

2. (FAA 1775) What is meant by the term dewpoint?
   1--The temperature at which condensation and evaporation is equal.
   2--The temperature at which dew will always form.
   3--The temperature to which air must be cooled to become saturated.
   4--The spread between actual temperature and the temperature during
      evaporation.

3. (FAA 1776) The amount of water vapor air can hold largely depends on
   1--the dewpoint.
   2--air temperature.
   3--stability of air.
   4--relative humidity.

4. (FAA 1777) What are the processes by which moisture is added to
   unsaturated air?
   1--Heating and sublimation.
   2--Evaporation and sublimation.
   3--Heating and condensation.
   4--Supersaturation and evaporation.

5. (FAA 1774) If the temperature/dewpoint spread is small and decreasing,
   and the temperature is 62°F, what type weather is most likely to
   develop?
   1--Freezing precipitation.
   2--Thunderstorms.
   3--Fog or low clouds.
   4--Rain showers.

6. (FAA 1779) Clouds, fog, or dew will always form when
   1--water vapor condenses.
   2--water vapor is present.
   3--relative humidity reaches or exceeds 100 percent.
   4--the temperature and dewpoint are equal.

7. (FAA 1769) Every physical process of weather is accompanied by, or is
   the result of,
   1--the movement of air.
   2--a pressure differential.
   3--a heat exchange.
   4--moisture.

8. (FAA 1770) What causes variations in altimeter settings between
   weather reporting points.
   1--Unequal heating of the Earth's surface.
   2--Variation of terrain elevation creating barriers to the movement
      of an air mass.
   3--Coriolis force reacting with friction.
   4--Friction of the air with the Earth's surface.

9. (FAA 1780) Which of the following measurements can be used to determine
   the stability of the atmosphere?
   1--Atmospheric pressure.
   2--Actual lapse rate.
   3--Surface temperature.
   4--Wind velocity.

10. (FAA 1781) Which of the following would decrease the stability of an air mass?
1--Warming from below.
2--Cooling from below.
3--Decrease in water vapor.
4--Sinking of the air mass.

11. (FAA 1783) What is a characteristic of stable air?
1--Stratiform clouds.
2--Unlimited visibility.
3--Fair weather cumulus clouds.
4--Temperature decreases rapidly with altitude.

12. (FAA 1784) Moist, stable air flowing upslope can be expected to
1--produce stratus type clouds.
2--produce a temperature inversion.
3--cause showers and thunderstorms.
4--develop convective turbulence.

13. (FAA 1796) A stable air mass is most likely to have which characteristics?
1--Showery precipitation.
2--Turbulent air.
3--Smooth air.
4--Cumuliform clouds.

14. (FAA 1800) Steady precipitation, in contrast to showery activity, preceding a front is an indication of
1--cumuliform clouds with moderate turbulence.
2--stratiform clouds with moderate turbulence.
3--cumuliform clouds with little or no turbulence.
4--stratiform clouds with little or no turbulence.

15. (FAA 1785) If an unstable air mass is forced upward, what type clouds can be expected?
1--Layer-like clouds with a temperature inversion.
2--Layer-like clouds with little vertical development.
3--Layer-like clouds with considerable associated turbulence.
4--Clouds with considerable vertical development and associated turbulence.

16. (FAA 1794) A moist, unstable air mass is characterized by
1--cumuliform clouds and showery precipitation.
2--poor visibility and smooth air.
3--stratiform clouds and continuous precipitation.
4--fog and drizzle.

17. (FAA 1795) What are characteristics of unstable air?
1--Turbulence and good surface visibility.
2--Turbulence and poor surface visibility.
3--Nimbostratus clouds and good surface visibility.
4--Nimbostratus clouds and poor surface visibility.

18. (FAA 1797)   An unstable air mass is most likely to have which
    characteristics?
    1--Stratiform clouds and fog.
    2--Turbulent air.
    3--Continuous precipitation.
    4--Fair to poor visibility to haze and smoke.

19. (FAA 1786)   What is the approximate base of the cumulus clouds if the
    temperature at 1,000 ft. MSL is 70°F and the dewpoint is 48°F?
    1--3,000 ft. MSL.
    2--4,000 ft. MSL.
    3--6,000 ft. MSL.
    4--8,000 ft. MSL.

20. (FAA 1787)   At approximately what altitude above the surface would the
    pilot expect the base of cumuliform clouds if the surface air
    temperature is 82°F and the dewpoint is 38°F?
    1--8,000 ft. AGL.
    2--9,000 ft. AGL.
    3--10,000 ft. AGL.
    4--11,000 ft. AGL.

21. (FAA 1765)   What feature is associated with a temperature inversion?
    1--A stable layer of air.
    2--An unstable layer of air.
    3--Chinook winds on mountain slopes.
    4--Air mass thunderstorms.

22. (FAA 1766)   The most frequent type of ground or surface based
    temperature inversion is that produced by
    1--terrestrial radiation on a clear, relative still night.
    2--warm air being lifted rapidly aloft in the vicinity of mountainous
       terrain.
    3--the movement of colder air under warmer air, or the movement of warm
       air over cold air.
    4--widespread sinking of air within a thick layer aloft resulting in
       heating by compression.

23. (FAA 1767)   A temperature inversion would most likely result in which
    weather condition?
    1--Clouds with extensive vertical development above an inversion aloft.
    2--Good visibility in the lower levels of the atmosphere and poor
       visibility above an inversion aloft.
    3--An increase in temperature as altitude is increased.
    4--A decrease in temperature as altitude is increased.

24. (FAA 1768)   Which weather conditions should be expected beneath a
    low-level temperature inversion layer when the relative humidity is
    high?
    1--Smooth air and poor visibility due to fog, haze, or low clouds.
    2--Light wind shear and poor visibility due to haze and light rain.
    3--Turbulent air and poor visibility due to fog, low stratus type
       clouds, and showery precipitation.
    4--Updrafts and turbulence due to surface heating, fair visibility, and
       cumulus clouds developing at the top of the inversion.

25. (FAA 1772) Winds at 5,000 ft. AGL on a particular flight are southwesterly while most of the surface winds are southerly. This difference in direction is primarily due to
1--a stronger pressure gradient at higher altitudes.
2--friction between the wind and the surface.
3--stronger Coriolis force at the surface.
4--the influence of pressure systems at the lower altitudes.

26. (FAA 1764) Ceiling, as used in weather reports, is defined as the height above the Earth's surface of the
1--lowest reported obscuration and the highest layer of clouds reported as overcast.
2--lowest layer of clouds reported as broken or overcast and not classified as thin.
3--lowest layer of clouds reported as scattered, broken, or thin.
4--highest layer of clouds reported as broken or thin.

27. (FAA 1821) What situation is most conducive to the formation of radiation fog?
1--Warm, moist air over low, flatland areas on clear, calm nights.
2--Moist, tropical air moving over cold, offshore water.
3--The movement of cold air over much warmer air.
4--Light wind moving warm, moist air upslope during the night.

28. (FAA 1823) In which situation is advection fog most likely to form?
1--A warm, moist air mass on the windward side of mountains.
2--An air mass moving inland from the coast in winter.
3--A light breeze blowing colder air out to sea.
4--Warm, moist air settling over a warmer surface under no-wind conditions.

29. (FAA 1822) Low level turbulence can occur and icing can become hazardous in
1--advection fog.
2--rain-induced fog.
3--upslope fog.
4--steam fog.

30. (FAA 1806) One in-flight condition necessary for structural icing to form is
1--cumuliform clouds.
2--small temperature/dewpoint spread.
3--stratiform clouds.
4--visible moisture.

31. (FAA 1807) In which environment is aircraft structural ice most likely to have the highest accumulation rate?
1--Cumulus clouds.
2--Freezing drizzle.
3--Stratus clouds.
4--Freezing rain.

32. (FAA 1809) Which conditions result in the formation of frost?
    1--The freezing of dew.
    2--The collecting surface's temperature is at or below freezing and
       small droplets of moisture fall on the collecting surface.
    3--The temperature of the collecting surface is at or below the dewpoint
       of the adjacent air and the dewpoint is below freezing.
    4--Small drops of moisture falling on the collecting surface when the
       surrounding air temperature is at or below freezing.

33. (FAA 1808) Why is frost considered hazardous to flight?
    1--The increased weight requires a greater takeoff distance.
    2--Frost changes the basic aerodynamic shape of the airfoil.
    3--Frost decreases control effectiveness.
    4--Frost causes early airflow separation resulting in a loss of lift.

34. (FAA 1810) Frost which has not been removed from the lifting surfaces
    of an airplane before flight
    1--may prevent the airplane from becoming airborne.
    2--will change the camber (curvature of the wing) thereby increasing
       lift during the takeoff.
    3--may cause the airplane to become airborne with a lower angle of
       attack and at a lower indicated airspeed.
    4--would present no problems since frost will blow off when the airplane
       starts moving during takeoff.

35. (FAA 1106) Frost on the wings of an airplane may
    1--cause the airplane to become airborne with a lower angle of attack
       and at a lower indicated airspeed.
    2--make if difficult or impossible to become airborne.
    3--present no problems since frost will blow off when the airplane
       starts moving during takeoff.
    4--change the camber (curvature of the wing) thereby increasing lift
       during takeoff.

36. (FAA 1778) The presence of ice pellets at the surface is evidence that
    1--there are thunderstorms in the area.
    2--a cold front has passed.
    3--there is freezing rain at a higher altitude.
    4--the pilot can climb to a higher altitude without encountering more
       than light icing.

37. (FAA 1790) An almond or lens-shaped cloud which appears stationary, but
    which may contain winds of 50 kts. or more, is referred to as
    1--an inactive frontal cloud.
    2--a funnel cloud.
    3--a lenticular cloud.
    4--a stratus cloud.

38. (FAA 1802) Crest of standing mountain waves may be marked by
    stationary, lens-shaped clouds known as
    1--cumulonimbus mamma clouds.
    2--standing lenticular clouds.
    3--roll clouds.
    4--rotor clouds.

39. (FAA 1804) Possible mountain wave turbulence would be anticipated when winds of
    1--20 kts. or greater blow across a mountain ridge, and the air is unstable.
    2--40 kts. or greater blow across a mountain ridge, and the air is stable.
    3--40 kts. or greater blow down a mountain valley, and the air is unstable.
    4--50 kts. or greater blow parallel to a mountain peak, and the air is stable.

40. (FAA 1805) A pilot can expect a wind shear zone in a temperature inversion, whenever the windspeed at 2,000 to 4,000 ft. above the surface is at least
    1--5 kts.
    2--10 kts.
    3--15 kts.
    4--25 kts.

41. (FAA 1803) Hazardous wind shear is commonly encountered near the ground
    1--near thunderstorms and during periods when the wind velocity is stronger than 35 kts.
    2--during periods when the wind velocity is stronger than 35 kts. and near mountain valleys.
    3--during periods of strong temperature inversion and near thunderstorms.
    4--near mountain valleys and on the windward side of a hill or mountain.

42. (FAA 1820) Upon encountering severe turbulence, which condition should the pilot attempt to maintain?
    1--Constant altitude.
    2--Constant airspeed (VA).
    3--Level flight attitude.
    4--Constant altitude and constant airspeed.

43. (FAA 1791) Clouds are divided into four families according to their
    1--origin.
    2--outward shape.
    3--height range.
    4--composition.

44. (FAA 1792) Which clouds have the greatest turbulence?
    1--Towering cumulus.
    2--Cumulonimbus.
    3--Nimbostratus.
    4--Altocumulus castellanus.

45. (FAA 1793) Which cloud types would indicate convective turbulence?
    1--Altocumulus standing lenticular clouds.
    2--Nimbostratus clouds.
    3--Towering cumulus clouds.
    4--Cirrus clouds.

46. (FAA 1789) The suffix nimbus, used in naming clouds, means
    1--a cloud with extensive vertical development.
    2--a rain cloud.
    3--a middle cloud containing ice pellets.
    4--an accumulation of clouds.

47. (FAA 1817) Which weather phenomenon is always associated with a
    thunderstorm?
    1--Lightning.
    2--Heavy rain showers.
    3--Supercooled raindrops.
    4--Hail.

48. (FAA 1814) What conditions are necessary for the formation of
    thunderstorms?
    1--Lifting force, high humidity, and unstable conditions.
    2--High humidity, high temperature, and cumulus clouds.
    3--Low pressure, high humidity, and cumulus clouds.
    4--Lifting force, high temperature, and unstable conditions.

49. (FAA 1782) The conditions necessary for the formation of cumulonimbus
    clouds are a lifting action and
    1--unstable air containing an excess of condensation nuclei.
    2--unstable, moist air.
    3--either stable or unstable air.
    4--stable, moist air.

50. (FAA 1811) What feature is normally associated with the cumulus stage
    of a thunderstorm?
    1--Roll cloud.
    2--Continuous updraft.
    3--Frequent lightning.
    4--Beginning of rain at the surface.

51. (FAA 1812) Which weather phenomenon signals the beginning of the mature
    stage of a thunderstorm?
    1--The appearance of an anvil top.
    2--Precipitation is beginning to fall.
    3--Growth rate of cloud is maximum.
    4--Strong turbulence in the cloud.

52. (FAA 1815) During the life cycle of a thunderstorm, which stage is
    characterized predominately by downdrafts?
    1--Cumulus.
    2--Dissipating.
    3--Mature.
    4--Anvil.

53. (FAA 1816) Thunderstorms reach their greatest intensity during the
    1--updraft stage.
    2--mature stage.
    3--downdraft stage.
    4--cumulus stage.

54. (FAA 1819) A nonfrontal, narrow band of active thunderstorms, that often develop ahead of a cold front, is known as
1--an occlusion.
2--a prefrontal system.
3--a squall line.
4--a shear line.

55. (FAA 1813) Thunderstorms which generally produce the most intense hazard to aircraft are
1--air mass thunderstorms.
2--steady-state thunderstorms.
3--warm front thunderstorms.
4--squall line thunderstorms.

56. (FAA 1818) If there is thunderstorm activity in the vicinity of an airport at which you plan to land, which hazardous and invisible atmospheric phenomenon might be expected on the landing approach?
1--St. Elmo's fire.
2--Wind shear turbulence.
3--Tornadoes.
4--Virga.

57. (FAA 1801) What is indicated when a current SIGMET forecasts embedded thunderstorms?
1--Thunderstorms have been visually sighted.
2--Severe thunderstorms are embedded within a squall line.
3--Thunderstorms are dissipating and present no serious problem to IFR flight.
4--Thunderstorms are obscured by massive cloud layers and cannot be seen.

58. (FAA 1798) One weather phenomenon which will always occur when flying across a front is
1--a change in the wind.
2--a large precipitation area, if the frontal surface is steep.
3--a large temperature change, especially at high altitudes.
4--the presence of clouds, either ahead of or behind the front.

59. (FAA 1799) One of the most easily recognized discontinuities across a front is
1--temperature.
2--wind.
3--pressure.
4--dewpoint.

Key Terms and Concepts, Part 1

1.	K	7.	Q	13.	C	19.	L
2.	A	8.	S	14.	B	20.	X
3.	F	9.	I	15.	P	21.	W
4.	N	10.	E	16.	R	22.	V
5.	G	11.	O	17.	M	23.	U
6.	D	12.	H	18.	J	24.	T

Key Terms and Concepts, Part 2

1.	T	7.	N	13.	E	19.	D
2.	A	8.	F	14.	R	20.	P
3.	K	9.	M	15.	H	21.	X
4.	Q	10.	S	16.	I	22.	W
5.	O	11.	L	17.	C	23.	V
6.	G	12.	B	18.	J	24.	U

Key Terms and Concepts, Part 3

1.	I	6.	T	11.	A	16.	F
2.	C	7.	M	12.	R	17.	S
3.	K	8.	E	13.	B	18.	H
4.	O	9.	J	14.	G	19.	Q
5.	D	10.	P	15.	N	20.	L

Discussion Questions and Review Exercises

1. See Study Guide Main Point #1.

2. See Study Guide Main Point #1.

3. See Study Guide Main Point #2.

4. See Study Guide Main Point #2.

5. See Study Guide Main Point #3.

6. See Study Guide Main Point #3.

7. See Study Guide Main Points #4 and #5.

8. See Study Guide Main Points #5 and #13.

9. See Study Guide Main Point #6.

10. See Study Guide Main Point #8.

11. See Study Guide Main Point #6.

12. See Study Guide Main Point #7.

13. See Study Guide Main Point #8.

14. See Study Guide Main Point #9.

15. See Study Guide Main Point #10.

16. See Study Guide Main Point #10.

17. See Study Guide Main Point #11.

18. See Study Guide Main Point #11.

19. See Study Guide Main Point #12.

20. See Study Guide Main Points #13, #14, and #16.

21. See Study Guide Main Point #16.

22. See Study Guide Main Point #17.

23. See Study Guide Main Point #18.

24. See Study Guide Main Point #18.

25. See Study Guide Main Point #18.

26. See Study Guide Main Point #19.

27. See Study Guide Main Point #19.

28. See Study Guide Main Points #21 and #22.

29. See Study Guide Main Point #19.

30. See Study Guide Main Points #20, #21, #22, #23, and #24.

31. See Study Guide Main Point #25.

32. T--This is due to the ionosphere's properties.

33. F--It loses pressure as altitude increases.

34. T--It depends upon the earth's rotation around the sun as well as the earth's daily rotation and the angle of incidence.

35. T--And clockwise around a system of high pressure.

36. T--Steep pressure gradients mean rapid pressure changes that are typically associated with high winds.

37. T--Precisely!

38. F--This is called radiation fog.

39. F--VMC specifies the weather and VFR specifies the rules that govern actual flight.

40. T--Cumuliform clouds produce large water droplets that are especially prone to produce clear ice.

41. T--Such conditions may lead to frost.

42. T--At night, water retains heat while the land cools quickly, leading to offshore winds. During the day, the land warms more rapidly than the water, leading to onshore breezes as the cold air over the water moves in to replace the warm air.

43. F--It is just the opposite.

44. T--These are evidence of turbulent mountain waves on the leeward (downwind) side of the mountain.

45. T--This occurs because the ground cools at a rapid rate.

46. F--It points in the direction the storm is moving.

47. F--They may be thrown upward and outward as far as 5 mi.

48. T--Air masses are defined by the temperature of the mass in relation to the surface over which it travels.

49. F--It is associated with fast-moving cold fronts.

50. T--Warm fronts typically move slowly and cover a large area.

51. 1--14.7 psi is the ISA standard at sea level.

52. 2--The closeness of the isobars indicates the intensity of the pressure gradient.

53. 1--Clear (0-9 percent); scattered (10-49 percent); broken (50-89 percent); overcast (90-100 percent).

54. 3--The type of droplet will determine what type of ice will form, clear or rime.

55. 2--Drag increases, weight increases, lift decreases, thrust is reduced, and stall speed increases.

56. 4--Dry air is more stable than moist air, and it loses heat more rapidly than does moist air. The dry lapse rate is 3°C per 1,000 ft., while the moist rate is 1.1-2.8°C per 1,000 ft.

57. 4--This defines stratus clouds.

58. 1--Continental Polar air masses have cold surface temperatures, low moisture content, and great stability in lower layers, especially in the source region.

59.   3--The atmospheric pressure reported for an airport or other geographic location is the station pressure adjusted to sea level.

60.   1--This defines dew point.

61.   1--Condensation nuclei are particles in the air around which moisture collects.

62.   1--Advection is the horizontal transfer of heat.

63.   1--There are no arctic northerlies; the other three are correct.

64.   2--Wind speed along the isobars typically decreases as the center of a low approaches and increases as the center of a high approaches.

65.   4--This defines how upslope fog forms.

66.   3--This defines an obscuration.

67.   4--Stratocumulus clouds would be found at 5,000 ft. AGL and are characterized by light showers and strong, gusty winds.

68.   1--Altostratus clouds would be found at 10,000 ft. AGL and are characterized by light, continuous precipitation, poor surface visibility, and smooth air.

69.   3--Maritime polar air masses are typically moist, unstable, and characterized by thunderstorms.

70.   4--A stationary front is one in which two air masses are so well balanced that neither prevails.

71.   3--An occluded front occurs when a rapidly moving cold front outraces a slower front and pushes it aloft. Occluded fronts are almost always characterized by thunderstorms.

72.   4--Stationary fronts are typically characterized by warm, smooth air, low ceilings, poor visibility, and multilayered overcast.

FAA Exam Questions

1.   1--The International Standard Atmosphere (ISA) is 15°C (59°F) and 29.92" Hg. (1013.2 mb).

2.   3--Definition.

3.   2--In warm air the air expands and there is more capacity for water vapor.

4.   2--Water is changed from liquid to vapor by evaporation, from solid directly to vapor by sublimation.

5.   3--When the air temperature is cooled to the dewpoint (100% relative humidity) further cooling will result in condensation if condensation nuclei are present, resulting in clouds, fog, or dew.

6.   1--When water vapor condenses, clouds, fog, or dew appears. Condensation occurs when air is cooled past saturation (100% relative humidity) AND condensation nuclei are present.

7.   3--As with engines, heat exchange drives weather. The difference in heating causes pressure differences and cloud formation.

8.   1--The unequal heating causes pressure differences.

9.   2--Lapse rate is the rate at which air loses temperature as altitude increases. Stability is determined by the difference between the adiabatic rate of the parcel of air and the lapse rate of the surrounding air.

10.   1--Warm air rises, giving instability.

11.   1--Moist, stable air may bring stratiform clouds and poor visibility.

12.   1--Moist, stable air may produce stratus type clouds.

13.   3--Stable air has little or no vertical currents.

14.   4--Stratus clouds are normally continuous, thus there is no break in precipitation as the clouds move over you. There is little or no turbulence in the stable conditions which produce stratus clouds.

15.   4--Moist, unstable air may produce vertical development (cumulus clouds) and turbulence.

16.   1--Moist, unstable air may bring cumuliform clouds covering part of the sky. Thus, precipitation will be showery as successive clouds pass over you.

17.   1--The vertical currents of unstable air produce turbulence and clear away the pollutants.

18.   2--The vertical currents of unstable air produce turbulence.

19.   3--Estimate the height of the bases of cumulus clouds by computation. The average rate of decrease is 4.4°F per 1,000 ft. of altitude increase. Divide the difference between temperature and dew point by 4.4 to find the height in thousands of feet. 70°F - 48°F = 22° / 4.4 = 5.   5,000 ft. + 1,000 ft. = 6,000 ft.

20.   3--Estimate the height of the bases of cumulus clouds by computation. The average rate of decrease is 4.4°F per 1,000 ft. of altitude increase. Divide the difference between temperature and dew point by 4.4 to find the height in thousands of feet. 82°F - 38°F = 44° / 4.4 = 10 x 1,000 = 10,000 ft.

21.   1--With an inversion, a layer of warm air is above a layer of cooler air. Warm air does not rise past the inversion, thus stability.

22. 1--With an inversion, a layer of warm air is above a layer of cooler air. On a clear night, the ground may cool faster than the air above.

23. 1--An inversion exists when the temperature of the air increases with altitude instead of decreasing.

24. 1--With stable air, typical of inversions, there are few vertical currents to cause turbulence and carry away pollutants. If the humidity is high, you may have fog or low clouds.

25. 2--While the Coriolis force affects the winds aloft, surface friction slows the wind near the surface, reducing the Coriolis affect.

26. 2--Definition.

27. 1--Fog occurs when surface air is cooled past the dewpoint. Radiation fog forms when warm, moist air is cooled from below.

28. 2--Fog occurs when surface air is cooled past the dewpoint. Advection fog, formed when moist air moves over a cooler surface, deepens with wind increases to about 15 kts.

29. 4--Steam fog may occur with turbulence and thunderstorms; they may also occur with rain-induced fog, but AC-006A says steam fog is the answer.

30. 4--The two conditions for the formation of ice are: viable moisture and temperature at the aircraft skin below freezing.

31. 4--The heaviest icing is usually found at or slightly above the freezing level where supercooled drops freeze on impact.

32. 3--Frost forms when the dewpoint is below freezing and the temperature at the surface is at or below that dewpoint.

33. 4--Frost does not significantly change the shape of the wing or add much weight; it does create a rough surface which causes early airflow separation. Stall speed may increase by 5% to 10%.

34. 1--Frost causes early airflow separation and increases minimum speed to attain sufficient lift for flight.

35. 2--Frost causes a rough surface on the upper wing. This disrupts the smooth flow of air and causes early separation.

36. 3--The water started out at altitude as rain, then froze as it passed through colder air.

37. 3--A lens-shaped cloud is called a lenticular cloud. It may contain strong winds.

38. 2--Lens-shaped lenticular clouds appear to remain stationary, but in fact are continually forming in the updrafts and dissipating in the down drafts.

39. 2--Possible mountain wave turbulence should be anticipated whenever winds of 40 kts. or greater blow across the mountains.

40.   4--When the wind is 25 kts. or more at 2,000 ft. to 4,000 ft. in an inversion, you can expect wind shear.

41.   2--Strong temperature inversions cause wind shear near the ground, as do the strong vertical currents of thunderstorms.

42.   3--In severe turbulence, try to hold attitude, accepting airspeed and altitude variations, within limits.

43.   3--High (cirriform), middle (alto), low, and those with extensive vertical development through more than one of these height ranges.

44.   2--Cumulus clouds, formed by vertical currents of unstable air, produce turbulence. Cumulonimbus clouds have the strongest currents.

45.   3--Cumulus clouds, formed by vertical currents of unstable air, produce turbulence.

46.   2--Nimbus means rain.

47.   1--Without thunder, there is no thunderstorm. Without lightning, there is no thunder.

48.   1--Lifting force, high humidity and unstable conditions.

49.   2--Unstable air, moisture and lifting action.

50.   2--Stages: cumulus, mature, and dissipating. The cumulus (building) stage has continuous updrafts.

51.   2--Stages: cumulus, mature, and dissipating. When the condensed moisture is heavy enough to overcome updrafts, precipitation begins, bringing downdrafts.

52.   2--Definition.

53.   2--Stages: cumulus, mature, and dissipating. The mature stage with side-by-side updrafts and downdrafts is the most intense.

54.   3--A squall line is a nonfrontal narrow band of thunderstorms.

55.   4--Squall line thunderstorms are frequently severe.

56.   2--Wind shear between updrafts and downdrafts or between downdrafts and areas of no vertical movement may produce very hazardous wind shear.

57.   4--Embedded thunderstorms are especially dangerous because they are hidden by less hazardous cloud types.

58.   1--A front is a zone between two different air masses. When you fly across a front, expect changes in temperature, temperature/dewpoint spread, wind, and pressure.

59.   1--Although all four of the answers are discontinuities across a front, temperature is normally the most easily recognized.

USING AVIATION WEATHER SERVICES

MAIN POINTS

1. The **National Weather Service (NWS)** gathers information about the weather from such sources as direct observations, balloons, radar, and pilot reports. <u>**Flight Service Stations (FSS)** provide aviation weather briefing</u> services.

2. **Surface Analysis Charts** depict current pressure patterns, fronts, surface winds, temperature and dew points, and visibility restrictions at the surface. Fortunately, Surface Analysis Charts have legends so you will not have to memorize the many symbols that appear on them. Station models are used to depict weather by symbols. Cloud cover is represented by a circle that is progressively filled for greater amounts of cover. Wind direction is represented by a wind arrow whose tail points into the wind; wind velocity is indicated by feathers (5 or 10 kts. per) or a pennant (50 kts.). Isobars are represented in millibars (last two digits) and are spaced at 4-mb intervals. New surface analysis charts are issued every 3 hr., and the data displayed on them when they are first issued may be as much as 1 hr. old.

3. **Weather Depiction Charts** shade all IFR areas (visibility below 3 mi. and/or a ceiling of less than 1,000 ft.). Marginal VFR areas (visibility 3-5 mi. and/or a ceiling of 1,000 to 3,000 ft.) are enclosed by a solid line.

4. A **Significant Weather Prognosis Chart (Prog)** is a prognosis or forecast of how aviation weather may change. They are issued for low levels (surface to 24,000 ft.) and high levels (24,000 to 63,000 ft.). The typical low-level chart contains two successive 12-hr. estimates for surface and low-level conditions. Solid lines enclose IFR areas, scalloped lines enclose areas of marginal VFR, broken lines represent areas of moderate or greater turbulence, dotted lines depict surface freezing, and dashed lines represent freezing aloft. Shaded areas on the surface portion indicate areas of precipitation.

5. The **Radar Summary Chart** shows areas of precipitation, not cloud cover, which typically is more widespread. The chart indicates precipitation trends and intensities.

6. Weather reports are important in terms of both time frame and difference in relative accuracy between actual observations and future estimates based on those observations. Several reports can be used in flight planning.

7. The **Surface Aviation Weather Report (SA)**, or sequence report, is given every hour and contains the following information:

(1) station identifier, a three-letter code
(2) type of report--for example, hourly or special
(3) time of report, given in UTC or zulu
(4) sky condition and ceiling: measured (M), estimated (E), indefinite (W), or variable (V)
(5) visibility, given in statute miles
(6) present weather and obstructions to vision
(7) sea level pressure, given in millibars (no decimal, initial 9 or 10 omitted)
(8) temperature, in Fahrenheit
(9) dew point, in Fahrenheit
(10) wind direction (true) and speed in knots
(11) altimeter setting, last three digits only
(12) remarks--for example, pilot reports (PIREPs) and Notices to Airmen (NOTAMs)
(13) the report may also contain **runway visual range** data, the slant range visibility at airports equipped with instrument landing aids

8. PIREPs alert other pilots to in-flight situations, while NOTAMs alert pilots to closed runways, inoperable VOR stations, unusual airspace activity, and so forth. To file a PIREP, call FSS on the radio as soon as you detect an unusual or changing situation.

9. **Terminal Forecasts (FTs)**, prepared three times daily for selected large airports, contain a 24-hr. forecast similar to sequence reports. They include ceilings, cloud heights, sky cover, visibility, weather, surface winds, and forecast weather over a large area which includes several states. **Area Forecasts (FAs)** are released three times a day and consist of a 12-hr. forecast with additional 6-hr. outlook. **Winds and Temperatures Aloft Forecasts (FDs)** are important for performance and navigation calculations. Wind directions are reported with respect to true (not magnetic) north and temperatures are reported in Celsius.

10. Several in-flight advisories are issued. Advisories are identified by a phonetic letter, and each area issuing these reports numbers them sequentially. A SIGMET (WS) or significant meteorological advisory is an advisory issued for all aircraft pilots; it refers to severe weather developments such as turbulence or icing. A **convective SIGMET (WST)** refers to thunderstorm activity. An **AIRMET (WA)** or airmen's meteorological advisory is an advisory issued primarily to pilots of light aircraft and pilots flying VFR. Hurricane advisories (WH), convective outlooks (AC), severe weather watch bulletins (WW), and special flight forecasts are also issued.

11. Some Flight Service Stations have continuous aviation weather information available by telephone or radio. One type of telephone service is called Pilot's Automatic Weather Answering Service (PATWAS). Transcribed Weather Broadcasts (TWEB) provide continuous aviation weather information on

selected navigation radio aids for the area within 250 mi. of the station; in some locations this information is also available by telephone. Recorded general weather information is often provided by National Weather Service (NWS) facilities. Many Flight Service Stations have become automated, using a Voice Response System (VRS) to provide weather information to users with touch-tone telephones. The appropriate telephone numbers may be found in the Airport/Facility Directory or in the local telephone directory. You must learn how to copy weather information read to you over the telephone or radio circuits; a good way to practice this is to copy recorded information.

12. FAR 91.5 requires you to familiarize yourself with weather information prior to any flight outside the local area (typically defined as a 25-mi. radius). When recorded aviation weather information is available, you should copy this before contacting FSS or NWS specialists. When you contact the live FSS/NWS person, advise him/her if you have copied recorded information, then provide the following information in this order:

    Type of flight (VFR or IFR)
    Aircraft identification or pilot's name
    Aircraft type
    Departure point
    Route of flight
    Destination
    Altitude
    Estimated time of departure (ETD)
    Estimated time en route (ETE) or estimated time of arrival (ETA)

FAA-P-8740-30A, How to Obtain a Good Weather Briefing, appears at the end of this chapter. It provides details on weather briefings and includes a copy of the FAA Flight Planner form.

13. Once airborne, you should periodically obtain weather updates. Sectional and Terminal Control Area charts provide information on navigation radio aids (VORs and NDBs) which have TWEBS. Weather may be obtained by contacting FSS. Enroute Flight Advisory Service (EFAS) provides aviation weather on a common frequency; call Flight Watch on 122.0 MHz to talk to and receive from a specialist weather information and recommendations.

14. It is your responsibility to obtain a weather briefing. The FSS/NWS briefer can only provide information and recommendations; it is your decision on how to proceed based on that information. Remember "WHEN IN DOUBT, WAIT IT OUT."

KEY TERMS AND CONCEPTS

Match each term or concept (1-24) with the appropriate description (A-X) below. Each term has only one match.

___ 1. TWEB
___ 2. Winds Aloft Forecast
___ 3. Area Forecasts
___ 4. ceiling
___ 5. PIREP
___ 6. ATIS
___ 7. severe weather watch
___ 8. 122.0
___ 9. EFAS
___ 10. FSS
___ 11. VRS
___ 12. Surface Aviation Weather Reports

___ 13. AIRMET
___ 14. PATWAS
___ 15. SIGMET
___ 16. station model
___ 17. echo
___ 18. true north
___ 19. RVR
___ 20. isobars
___ 21. convective SIGMET
___ 22. Terminal Forecast
___ 23. Radar Summary Chart
___ 24. Significant Weather Prognosis Chart

A. height of the lowest layer of clouds above the earth's surface when the total coverage is more than 50 percent
B. in-flight pilot report on weather conditions
C. significant meteorological advisory pertaining to all aircraft
D. forecasts of winds at selected altitudes; issued every 6 hr.
E. hourly sequence report
F. short-term forecast of dangerous weather for small aircraft issued by NWS
G. provides aviation weather briefing services
H. chart that depicts precipitation through "echoes"
I. significant meteorological advisory about thunderstorms
J. expected weather for the next 12 hr. for a large geographical area; issued every 6 hours
K. continuous recording of current and forecast weather along certain flight routes available by telephone
L. continuous broadcast of meteorological information from a radio navigation facility
M. forecasts for specific airports issued three times daily
N. wind directions are given with respect to this in Surface Analysis Weather Reports and in Winds and Temperature Aloft Forecasts
O. appearance on a radar indicator of energy returned from a target such as a storm cell
P. EFAS radio frequency
Q. four-panel NWS charts for surface and significant weather estimates
R. voice response system used at some FSS stations to provide weather information by telephone
S. horizontal range along an identified runway at instrument-equipped airports
T. provides timely weather information at pilot request
U. lines on a surface analysis chart joining points of equal barometric pressure
V. in-flight advisory issued by National Severe Storms Forecast Center
W. grouping of weather information around a station on a surface analysis chart
X. continuous broadcast of recorded noncontrol information in selected terminal areas

DISCUSSION QUESTIONS AND REVIEW EXERCISES

1. State what the initials below stand for and describe the weather advisory function each performs:

    a. NWS

    b. FSS

    c. PATWAS

    d. ATIS

    e. TWEB

    f. EFAS

    g. SIGMET

    h. AIRMET

    i. PIREP

    j. VRS

2. Outline what you should tell a weather specialist when you call for a briefing.

3. What is a station model? How is it used on a Surface Analysis Chart?

4. What is the chief value to pilots of a Weather Depiction Chart?

5. How are the Significant Weather Prognosis Chart and the Surface Analysis Chart related? How are they different?

6. Of what value to pilots is a Radar Summary Chart?

7. Outline the information contained in a Surface Aviation Weather Report.

8. What are the three ways to determine a station's ceiling? How are they coded on Surface Analysis Charts?

9. How are Area Forecasts different from Terminal Forecasts?

10. Of what value to pilots are Winds And Temperatures Aloft Forecasts?

11. Indicate how each of the following would be shown on a surface weather map, including a statement as to how they are color-coded:

a. cold front aloft

b. squall line

c. ridge

d. stationary front

e. occluded front

f. trough

g. warm front

h. high-pressure center

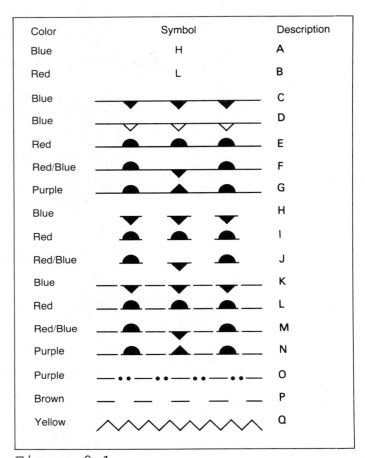

Figure 9.1

12. Refer to Figure 9.1. Weather conditions associated with symbol "O" are
   1--an area of thunderstorms.
   2--a squall line.
   3--rain, drizzle, and fog.
   4--stratiform clouds and haze.

13. Refer to the weather symbols in Figure 9.1. Which one properly identifies a stationary front?
   1--E.
   2--F.
   3--G.
   4--I.

14. Refer to the weather symbols in Figure 9.1. If symbol "E" is shown on a surface weather map, it indicates that
   1--a cold air mass has caught up with a warm air mass and the air masses have closed together to form an occluded front.
   2--a cold air mass is overtaking and replacing a warm air mass.
   3--neither a cold air mass nor a warm air mass is being replaced, and the front is stationary.
   4--a warm air mass is moving in and replacing colder air.

15. Refer to Figure 9.1. What symbol indicates a cold front aloft?
   1--D.
   2--F.
   3--H.
   4--K.

16. Refer to Figure 9.1. What symbol depicts the leading edge of cold air overtaking and replacing warmer air at the surface?
   1--C.
   2--D.
   3--F.
   4--I.

17. Refer to Figure 9.1. What symbol identifies an occluded front?
   1--D.
   2--F.
   3--G.
   4--Q.

18. A Radar Summary Chart helps a pilot in planning a safe flight because it graphically displays a collection of radar reports about
   1--clouds and ceiling heights.
   2--clouds and in-flight visibilities.
   3--fog and other obscurations.
   4--the intensity and movement of precipitation.

19. In a Winds and Aloft Forecast, the coded group 9900+00 means
   1--there is no forecast available for wind and temperature at that prescribed level.
   2--wind is from 90° at 9 kts., temperature 0°C.
   3--winds in excess of 90 kts., temperature 0°F.
   4--winds light and variable, temperature 0°C.

20.   Which chart would be most useful in preflight planning to identify the movement of a particular thunderstorm cell?
      1--Prog Chart.
      2--Radar Summary Chart.
      3--Surface Weather Map.
      4--Weather Depiction Chart.

21.   In Area Forecasts, cloud heights are given in reference to
      1--density-altitude.
      2--ground level.
      3--pressure-altitude.
      4--mean sea level, unless otherwise noted.

22.   The freezing level and areas of probable icing conditions aloft can be determined best by referring to
      1--Area Forecasts.
      2--Aviation Sequence Reports.
      3--Terminal Forecasts.
      4--Winds and Temperatures Aloft Forecasts.

23.   The height of a cloud base, as given in aviation weather reports, is reported as height above
      1--mean sea level at the station of observation.
      2--the highest terrain within a radius of 5 mi. of the observation station.
      3--the pressure altitude elevation of the station at the time of the observation.
      4--the surface at the station of observation.

24. FAR 91.5 states that you familiarize yourself with all available weather information before any flight outside the local area. This FAR is a
      1--suggestion for safe flight.
      2--requirement that applies only when IFR or marginal VFR conditions exist.
      3--requirement for student pilots and a suggestion for pilots who hold at least a Private Pilot Certificate.
      4--requirement for all pilots.

25.   A ceiling reported by a pilot flying at the base of a layer of clouds is referred to as a/an
      1--estimated ceiling.
      2--indefinite ceiling.
      3--measured ceiling.
      4--reported ceiling.

26.   An IFR pilot encounters clear ice at 8,000 ft. in clouds and calls FSS to report the situation. FSS prepares a message and broadcasts it to other pilots. This is an example of a/an
      1--AIRMET.
      2--NOTAM.
      3--PIREP.
      4--SIGMET.

27. The advisory that estimates the potential for severe and general thunderstorms over a 24-hr. period is called a/an
     1--AIRMET.
     2--convective outlook (AC).
     3--severe weather watch bulletin (WW).
     4--SIGMET.

28. A weather map that provides a means of locating pressure systems and fronts and an overview of winds and temperatures is called a
     1--Prognostic Chart.
     2--Radar Summary Chart.
     3--Surface Weather Map.
     4--Weather Depiction Chart.

FAA EXAM QUESTIONS

          (Note: All FAA Figures are located in Appendix C)

  1. (FAA 1865) Of what value is the depiction chart in Figure 54 to the pilot?
     1--To determine general weather conditions on which to base flight planning.
     2--For a forecast of cloud coverage, visibilities, and frontal activity.
     3--To determine the frontal trends and air mass characteristics.
     4--For an overall view of thunderstorm activity and forecast cloud heights.

  2. (FAA 1866) The IFR weather in eastern Texas in Figure 54 is due to
     1--intermittent rain.
     2--fog.
     3--dust devils.
     4--sandstorm.

  3. (FAA 1867) What weather phenomenon is causing IFR conditions along the coast of Oregon and California? (See Figure 54.)
     1--Squall line activity.
     2--Low ceilings.
     3--Heavy rain showers.
     4--Drizzle.

  4. (FAA 1868) What is the status of the front that extends from New Mexico to Indiana as depicted in Figure 54?
     1--Stationary.   2--Occluded.
     3--Retreating.   4--Dissipating.

  5. (FAA 1869) According to the depiction chart in Figure 54, the current weather for a flight from central Arkansas to southeast Alabama is
     1--broken clouds at 2,500 ft.
     2--visibility from 3-5 mi.
     3--broken to scattered clouds at 25,000 ft.
     4--fog and low ceilings to move in from the gulf.

6. (FAA 1871) For what phase of flight planning are the Significant
   Weather Progs designed? (See Figure 55.)
   1--A complete set of weather forecasts for overall planning.
   2--Information to avoid areas and/or altitudes of the freezing level and
      turbulence.
   3--An analysis of frontal activity, cloud coverage, and areas of
      precipitation.
   4--Overall depiction of current ceilings and visibilities with fronts
      and icing levels.

7. (FAA 1870) What weather is forecast for the Gulf Coast area just ahead
   of the cold front during the first 12 hr.? (See Figure 55.)
   1--Marginal VFR to IFR with intermittent thundershowers and rain
      showers.
   2--IFR with moderate or greater turbulence over the coastal areas.
   3--Thunderstorm cells moving northeastward ahead of the front.
   4--Rain and drizzle dissipating, clearing along the front.

8. (FAA 1872) Interpret the weather symbol depicted in lower California on
   the 12-hour Significant Weather Prog in Figure 55.
   1--Moderate turbulence, surface to 18,000 ft.
   2--Thunderstorm tops at 18,000 ft.
   3--Base of clear air turbulence, 18,000 ft.
   4--Moderate turbulence, 180 mb level.

9. (FAA 1873) The band of IFR weather associated with the cold front in
   the western states as depicted in Figure 55 is forecast to move
   1--southeast at 30 kts. with moderate snow showers.
   2--northeast at 12 kts. with the front and producing snow showers.
   3--eastward at 30 kts. with the low and producing snow showers.
   4--eastward at 30 kts. with continuous snow.

10. (FAA 1874) At what altitude is the freezing level found over
    southeastern Oklahoma on the 24-hour Significant Weather Prog? (See
    Figure 55.)
    1--Surface.
    2--4,000 ft.
    3--8,000 ft.
    4--12,000 ft.

11. (FAA 1840) What information is provided by the Radar Summary Chart that
    is not shown on other weather charts?
    1--Lines and cells of hazardous thunderstorms.
    2--Ceilings and precipitation between reporting stations.
    3--Types of precipitation between reporting stations.
    4--Areas of cloud cover and icing levels within the clouds.

12. (FAA 1885) What is the direction and speed of movement of the radar
    return at A in Figure 58?
    1--020° at 20 kts.
    2--East at 15 kts.
    3--Northeast at 22 kts.
    4--Southwest at 15 kts.

13. (FAA 1886) What does the dashed line enclose at B in Figure 58?
    1--Areas of heavy rain.
    2--Weather watch area.
    3--Areas of hail 1/4 inch in diameter.
    4--Convective outlook area.

14. (FAA 1887) What type of weather is occurring in radar return C in
    Figure 58?
    1--Thunderstorms.
    2--Continuous rain.
    3--Thunderstorms and rain showers.
    4--Heavy rain showers.

15. (FAA 1888) What is the direction and speed of movement of the radar
    return at D in Figure 58?
    1--East at 22 kts.
    2--Southeast at 30 kts.
    3--Northeast at 20 kts.
    4--West at 30 kts.

16. (FAA 1889) The maximum cloud top at D in Figure 58 is
    1--2,000 ft.   2--22,000 ft.
    3--30,000 ft.   4--50,000 ft.

17. (FAA 1843) Radar weather reports are of special interest to pilots
    because they indicate
    1--large areas of low ceilings and fog.
    2--location of precipitation along with type, intensity, and trend.
    3--location of broken to overcast clouds.
    4--icing conditions.

18. (FAA 1854) Where are the current conditions depicted for Chicago Midway
    Airport (MDW) in Figure 52?
    1--Thin overcast, measured ceiling 700 ft., overcast 1,100 ft.,
       visibility 2 mi. in rain plus fog.
    2--Sky partially obscured, measured ceiling 700 overcast, visibility
       1-1/2, heavy rain, fog.
    3--Thin overcast, measured 700 ft. overcast, visibility 1-1/2, heavy
       rain, fog.
    4--Sky partially obscured, measured ceiling 700 overcast, visibility 11,
       occasionally 2, with rain and heavy fog.

19. (FAA 1855) Which of the reporting stations in Figure 52 have VFR
    weather?
    1--All.
    2--All except JFK.
    3--All except JFK and MDW.
    4--INK only.

20. (FAA 1856) The wind direction and velocity at JFK (Figure 52) is from
    1--180° at 40 kts.
    2--040° variable 22 to 30 kts.
    3--180° at 4 kts.
    4--018° at 4 to 6 kts.

21. (FAA 1857) What are the wind conditions at Wink, Texas (INK)? (See Figure 52.)
1--Calm.
2--111°, 2 kts. gusting to 18 kts.
3--011°, 12 kts. gusting to 18 kts.
4--110°, 12 kts. gusting to 18 kts.

22. (FAA 1858) In Figure 52, the remarks section for MDW has RF2 and RB12 listed. These two entries mean
1--rain and fog are covering two-tenths of the sky and the barometer has risen 1.2 in. HG in the last hour.
2--rain and fog have reduced visibility to 2 SM and rain began at 1812Z.
3--rain and fog are obscuring two-tenths of the sky and rain began at 1812Z.
4--freezing rain has reduced visibility to 2 SM and the barometer has risen .12 in. Hg.

23. (FAA 1880) The base and tops of the overcast layer reported by a pilot in Figure 57 are
1--1,200 ft. AGL and 5,500 ft. AGL.
2--1,200 ft. MSL and 5,500 ft. MSL.
3--7,200 ft. AGL and 8,900 ft. AGL.
4--7,200 ft. MSL and 8,900 ft. MSL.

24. (FAA 1882) If the field elevation is 614 ft. MSL, what is the height above ground level of the base of the ceiling in Figure 57?
1--586 ft. AGL.   2--1,200 ft. AGL.
3--6,586 ft. AGL.   4--7,200 ft. AGL.

25. (FAA 1881) The winds and temperature at 12,000 ft. MSL as reported by a pilot in Figure 57 are
1--090° at 21 kts. and -9°C.
2--010° at 20 kts. and 1°F.
3--009° at 121 MPH and 90°F.
4--100° at 2 MPH and 12°F.

26. (FAA 1883) The intensity of turbulence reported by the pilot in Figure 57 is
1--light.   2--moderate.
3--severe.   4--extreme.

27. (FAA 1884) The intensity and type of icing reported by the pilot in Figure 57 is
1--light rime.
2--light to moderate clear.
3--moderate rime.
4--moderate to severe clear.

28. (FAA 1844) From which primary source should information be obtained regarding expected weather at the estimated time of arrival at your destination?
1--Low Level Prog Chart.
2--Weather Depiction Chart.
3--Terminal Forecast.
4--Radar Summary and Weather Depiction Chart.

29. (FAA 1859) According to the Terminal Forecast for Oklahoma City (OKC) in Figure 53, the cold front should pass through
1--between 21Z and 02Z the next day.
2--by 21Z.
3--between 1515Z and 18Z.
4--after 09Z the next day.

30. (FAA 1860) What wind conditions are expected at Hobart (HBR) at 16Z? (See Figure 53.)
1--Calm.
2--115° at 15 kts.
3--300° at 10 kts.
4--320° at 15 kts. gusting to 25 kts.

31. (FAA 1861) What ceiling is forecast for Gage (GAG) between 16Z and midnight Z? (See Figure 53.)
1--5,000 scattered.
2--6,000 scattered.
3--1,000 broken.
4--10,000 broken.

32. (FAA 1864) When is the wind forecast to shift at Tulsa (TUL)? (See Figure 53.)
1--15Z.
2--By 23Z.
3--Between 23Z and 09Z the next day.
4--After 09Z the next day.

33. (FAA 1862) What is the outlook for weather conditions at McAlester (MLC)? (See Figure 53.)
1--Ceilings 2,000-3,000 ft. with southerly winds.
2--Ceiling 700 ft., sky obscured, visibility 1/2 mi. in the thundershowers.
3--VFR except in the thundershowers, peak wind gusts 40 kts.
4--Marginal VFR due to low ceilings and thundershowers.

34. (FAA 1863) The wind condition in the Terminal Forecast Outlook for Ponca City (PNC) in Figure 53 is
1--missing.
2--for velocities of 25 kts. or stronger.
3--for a wind shift from south to northwest.
4--for the wind to change from a gusty condition to calm.

35. (FAA 1828) To best determine forecast weather conditions between weather reporting stations, the pilot should refer to
1--pilot reports.   2--prognostic charts.
3--weather maps.   4--Area Forecasts.

36. (FAA 1829) To determine the freezing level and areas of probable icing aloft, the pilot should refer to the
1--Radar Summary Chart.
2--Weather Depiction Chart.
3--Area Forecast.
4--Surface Analysis.

37. (FAA 1842) The section of the Area Forecast entitled SIG CLDS AND WX contains a
1--summary of cloudiness and weather significant to flight operations broken down by states or other geographical areas.
2--summary of forecast sky cover, cloud tops, visibility, and obstructions to vision along specific routes.
3--statement of AIRMET's and SIGMET's still in effect at the time of issue.
4--summary of only those clouds and weather considered adverse to safe flight operations.

38. (FAA 1845) What hazards are forecast in the Area Forecast (Figure 50) for Tennessee (TN), Alabama (AL), and the coastal waters?
1--Ceilings 3,000 to 5,000 ft. and visibilities 3 to 5 mi. in fog.
2--Thunderstorms with severe or greater turbulence, severe icing, and low level wind shear.
3--Moderate rime icing above the freezing level to 10,000 ft.
4--Moderate turbulence from 25,000 to 38,000 ft. due to the jetstream.

39. (FAA 1847) What sky condition and type obstructions to vision, if any, are forecast fore all the area except TN from 1040Z until 2300Z? (See Figure 50.)
1--None of any significance, VFR is forecast.
2--Ceilings 3,000 to 5,000 ft. broken, visibility 3 to 5 mi. in fog.
3--8,000 ft. scattered to clear except visibility below 3 mi. in fog until 15Z over south-central Texas.
4--Generally ceilings 3,000 to 8,000 ft. to clear with visibilities sometimes below 3 mi. in fog.

40. (FAA 1846) What type obstructions to vision, if any, are forecast for the entire area from 2300Z until 0500Z the next day? (See Figure 50.)
1--None of any significance, VFR is forecast.
2--Visibility 3 to 5 mi. in fog.
3--Visibility below 3 mi. in fog over south-central Texas.
4--Visibilities sometimes below 3 mi. in fog.

41. (FAA 1848) The forecast ceiling and visibility for the entire area in Figure 50 from 2300Z through 0500Z is ceiling
1--less than 500 ft. and/or visibility less than 1 SM.
2--500 to less than 1,000 ft. and/or visibility 1 to less than 3 SM.
3--1,000 to 3,000 ft. and/or visibility 3 to 5 SM.
4--greater than 3,000 ft. and visibility greater than 5 SM.

42. (FAA 1841) What values are used for Winds Aloft Forecasts?
1--Magnetic direction and knots.
2--Magnetic direction and miles per hour.
3--True direction and knots.
4--True direction and miles per hour.

43. (FAA 1849) What wind is forecast for St. Louis (STL) at 18,000 ft.? (See Figure 51.)
1--030° at 56 kts.
2--235° at 06 kts.
3--230° at 56 kts.
4--235° at 06 gusting to 16 kts.

44. (FAA 1850) Determine the wind and temperature aloft forecast for Denver (DEN) at 30,000 ft. (See Figure 51.)
1--023° at 53 kts., temperature 47° C.
2--230° at 53 kts., temperature -47° C.
3--235° at 34 kts., temperature -7° C.
4--235° at 34 kts., temperature -47° F.

45. (FAA 1851) Interpret the wind and temperature aloft forecast for 3,000 ft. at Kansas City (MKC). (See Figure 51.)
1--050° at 7 kts., temperature missing.
2--360° at 5 kts., temperature -7° C.
3--360° at 50 kts., temperature 7° C.
4--005° at 7 kts., temperature missing.

46. (FAA 1853) What wind is forecast for St. Louis (STL) at 34,000 ft.? (See Figure 51.)
1--073° at 6 kts.   2--730° at 61 kts.
3--306° at 19 kts.   4--230° at 106 kts.

47. (FAA 1852) When the term "light and variable" is used in reference to a Winds and Temperatures Aloft Forecast, the coded group and windspeed is
1--0000 and less than 7 kts.
2--9999 and less than 10 kts.
3--9900 and less than 5 kts.
4--7799 and less than 6 kts.

48. (FAA 1836) SIGMET's are issued as a warning of weather conditions hazardous
1--particularly to light aircraft.
2--to all aircraft.
3--only to light aircraft operations.
4--particularly to heavy aircraft.

49. (FAA 1837) AIRMET's are issued as a warning of weather conditions hazardous
1--to all aircraft.
2--particularly to light aircraft.
3--to VFR operations only.
4--particularly to IFR operations.

50. (FAA 1838) Which in-flight advisory would contain information on severe icing?
1--Convective SIGMET.   2--SIGMET.
3--AIRMET.   4--PIREP.

51. (FAA 1839) What information is contained in a convective SIGMET in the conterminous United States?
1--Tornadoes, embedded thunderstorms, and hail 3/4 in. or greater in diameter.
2--Severe icing, severe turbulence, or widespread dust storms lowering visibility to less than 3 mi.
3--Surface winds greater than 40 kts. or thunderstorms equal to or greater than VIP levels.
4--Moderate or greater turbulence and clear air turbulence.

52. (FAA 1830) To obtain a continuous transcribed weather briefing including winds aloft and route forecasts for a cross-country flight, a pilot should monitor
1--a TWEB on a low-frequency radio receiver.
2--a VHF radio receiver tuned to an ATIS frequency.
3--the regularly scheduled weather broadcast on a VOR frequency.
4--a high-frequency radio receiver tuned to the En Route Flight Advisory Service (Flight Watch) station.

53. (FAA 1831) Individual forecasts for specific routes of flight can be obtained from which weather service?
1--Transcribed Weather Broadcasts.
2--Terminal Forecasts.
3--Area Forecasts.
4--In-Flight Advisories.

54. (FAA 1832) TWEB's (Transcribed Weather Broadcasts) may be monitored by tuning the appropriate radio receiver to certain
1--FSS communications frequencies.
2--airport advisory frequencies.
3--VOR and NDB frequencies.
4--NDB frequencies only.

55. (FAA 1326) When telephoning a weather briefing facility for preflight weather information, pilots should
1--identify themselves as pilots.
2--tell the number of hours they have flown within the preceding 90 days.
3--state the number of occupants on board and the color of the aircraft.
4--state that they possess a current medical certificate.

56. (FAA 1328) When telephoning a weather briefing facility for preflight weather information, pilots should state
1--the full name and address of the formation commander.
2--that they possess a current pilot certificate.
3--whether they intend to fly VFR only.
4--the color of the aircraft and number of occupants on board.

57. (FAA 1327) When telephoning a weather briefing facility for preflight weather information, pilots should state
1--the full name and address of the pilot in command.
2--the intended route, destination, and type of aircraft.
3--the radio frequencies to be used.
4--the true airspeed and amount of fuel onboard.

58. (FAA 1833) To get a complete weather briefing for the planned flight, the pilot should request
1--an outlook briefing.
2--a general briefing.
3--an abbreviated briefing.
4--a standard briefing.

59. (FAA 1834) Which type of briefing should a pilot request to supplement mass disseminated data?
1--An outlook briefing.
2--A supplemental briefing.
3--An abbreviated briefing.
4--A standard briefing.

60. (FAA 1835) A weather briefing that is provided when the information requested is 6 or more hours in advance of the proposed departure time is
1--an outlook briefing.
2--a forecast briefing.
3--a prognostic briefing.
4--an abbreviated briefing.

61. (FAA 1329) How should contact be established with an EFAS (En Route Flight Advisory Service) station, and what service would be expected?
1--Call EFAS on 122.2 for routine weather, current reports on hazardous weather, and altimeter settings.
2--Call flight assistance on 122.5 for advisory service pertaining to severe weather.
3--Call Flight Watch on 122.0 for information regarding actual weather and thunderstorm activity along proposed route.
4--Call ARTCC on assigned frequency and ask for Flight Watch services.

62. (FAA 1330) What service should a pilot normally expect from an En Route Flight Advisory Service station?
1--Actual weather information and thunderstorm activity along the route.
2--Preferential routing and provide radar vectoring to circumnavigate severe weather.
3--Severe weather information, changes to flight plans, and receive routine position reports.
4--Radar vectors for traffic avoidance, routine weather advisories, and altimeter settings.

63. (FAA 1483) Below FL180, en route weather advisories should be obtained from an FSS on
1--122.1 MHz.
2--122.0 MHz.
3--123.6 MHz.
4--122.4 MHz.

ANSWERS AND EXPLANATIONS

Key Terms and Concepts

1.	L	7.	V	13.	F	19.	S
2.	D	8.	P	14.	K	20.	U
3.	J	9.	T	15.	C	21.	I
4.	A	10.	G	16.	W	22.	M
5.	B	11.	R	17.	O	23.	H
6.	X	12.	E	18.	N	24.	Q

Discussion Exercises and Review Questions

1. See Study Guide Main Points #1, #8, #10, #11, and #12.

2. See Study Guide Main Point #12.

3. See Study Guide Main Point #2.

4. See Study Guide Main Point #3.

5. See Study Guide Main Points #2 and #4.

6. See Study Guide Main Point #5.

7. See Study Guide Main Point #7.

8. See Study Guide Main Point #7.

9. See Study Guide Main Point #9.

10. See Study Guide Main Point #9.

11. See Study Guide Figure 9.1.

12. 2--This defines a squall line.

13. 2--This represents a stationary front.

14. 4--A warm front is replacing cooler surface air.

15. 1--This is called a cold front aloft.

16. 1--This is called a cold front.

17. 3--An occluded front is almost always associated with active
thunderstorms.

18. 4--Radar summary charts depict areas of precipitation, together with
their intensity and movement.

19. 4--The "9900" refers to light and variable winds; the "+00" refers to a
temperature of 0°C.

20. 2--Radar summary charts depict areas of precipitation, together with
their intensity and movement. Thunderstorms typically have significant
precipitation.

21. 4--Cloud heights are given in reference to MSL on area forecasts unless
otherwise noted.

22. 1--Area forecasts indicate freezing levels and areas of probable icing
conditions.

23. 4--The height of a cloud base is given in reference to the surface of the observation station.

24. 4--FAR 91.5 states that **all** pilots **must** familiarize themselves with all available weather information before any flight outside the local area.

25. 4--A pilot-reported ceiling is called a reported ceiling.

26. 3--This is an example of a pilot report, or PIREP.

27. 2--Convective outlooks estimate the potential for severe and general thunderstorms over a 24-hr. period.

28. 3--Surface weather maps provide a means of locating pressure systems and fronts and a general overview of winds and temperatures.

FAA Exam Questions

1. 1--Weather depiction charts provide a general overview of the weather in an easy-to-read format.

2. 2--On the TX-LA border is a hatched area outlined by a smooth line indicating IFR weather. The weather condition is indicated to the left of the sky cover circle. 2= means visibility 2 miles in fog.

3. 2--See the IFR hatched area on the west area of CA-OR; below the sky cover circles are the numbers 2 (in CA) and 3 (in OR), indicating ceilings of 200 ft. and 300 ft.

4. 1--Cold fronts - triangles (icicles), warm fronts - bubbles (blisters). When they alternate on opposite sides of the front, there is little or no movement.

5. 3--Center of ARK - sky cover symbol 3/4 black indicates broken coverage. The 250 below the symbol - clouds are forecast to be at 25,000 ft. In MISS - sky cover symbol is 1/4 filled indicating scattered clouds. Between these stations - broken to scattered.

6. 2--Provide a visual portrayal of forecast VFR/MVFR/IFR weather, turbulence, freezing levels, precipitation, and thunderstorms.

7. 1--Left panels - forecast weather for the first 12 hours of the period. Right panels - 24 hr. surface prog. Lower charts - surface forecast. Upper charts - surface to 24,000 ft. MSL. The lower charts show the location of the fronts and have dash-dot lines enclosing an area of showery precipitation within which are Cbs and rain. The left upper panel has a scalloped line from Mexico to Canada - marginal VFR; the solid line (LA and MI) indicates IFR.

8.   1--Upper left panel (surface to 24,000 ft. for 12 hr.) - area enclosed by a dashed line; single ^ = moderate turbulence. Base and tops - numbers under and above a horizontal line. 180 = tops at 18,000 ft.; lack of a number under the line = turbulence starts at the surface.

9.   4--Direction and speed - a number at the head of the arrow showing speed (see Utah). Two stars (Idaho and Mon.) = continuous snow.

10.   4--Freezing levels - dashed lines on the upper charts at 4,000 ft. intervals. OK has two dashed lines, at 8,000 ft. in the N and another at 12,000 ft. in the SE.

11.   1--Thunderstorms.

12.   2--Wind flags are used to show the direction and speed of movement of lines or areas of echos. Beside A, the shaft points east, the one long and one short barb indicate 15 kt.

13.   2--Heavy dashed lines (Radar Summary Charts) = severe weather watch areas.

14.   4--To the left of the C is RW+.
15.   3--Movement of a single cell is indicated by a direction arrow with a number for speed.

16.   2--Echo heights (or reported cloud heights in non-NWS radar areas) are shown by underlined numbers. Above D 220 (22,000 ft.) is underlined.

17.   2--Radar detects precipitation only.

18.   2--The SA report for MDW shows -X (sky partially obscured) M7 OVC (measured ceiling 700 ft. overcast) 1-1/2 R+F (visibility 1-1/2 mi. in heavy rain and fog).

19.   3--INK reports CLR 15 (VFR), BOI reports 150 SCT 30 (VFR). JFK reports W5 X 1/2 F (ceiling 500, visibility 1/2 mile) (less than VFR). MDW reports -X M7 OVC 1-1/2 R+F (ceiling 700 ft., visibility 1 1/2 mi.) (less than VFR).

20.   3--The JFK entry shows 1804 for the wind.

21.   4--The INK entry shows 1112G18 for the wind.

22.   3--RF2 = rain and fog covers 2/10 of the sky, RB12 = rain began 12 min. past the hour.

23.   4--The SK section gives sky cover. The first number is the base of clouds, followed by amount of cover, then a number for the top of that layer. All heights are MSL (what the pilot reads on the altimeter). SK 012 BKN 055/072 OVC 089/CLR ABV indicates two layers, a broken layer from 1,200 ft. MSL to 5,500+MSL, an overcast layer from 7,200 ft. MSL to 8,900 ft. MSL and clear above that.

24.   1--Ceiling = height above ground, but pilots report cloud height in MSL. Ceiling = cloud height - field elevation. 1,200 ft. MSL - 614 ft. MSL = 586 ft. AGL.

25. 1--The WV section gives the wind at the pilots flight level. WV 0921.
Temperature is indicated by TA-9. This is at 12,000 ft. MSL (FL 120).

26. 2--Turbulence is reported in the TB section: TB MDT 055-072.

27. 2--Icing is indicated by ICG. See ICG - LGT-MDT CLR 072-089.

28. 3--Terminal Forecasts (FTs) predict weather at selected airports.

29. 2--FTs--when changes of weather are expected; preceding weather ends
with a period, followed by time and new conditions. The OKC entry shows an
entry for 18Z. New conditions forecast: 21Z CFP 100 SCT.. CFP = cold front
passage.

30. 3--The HBR wind entry for 1500Z to 1700Z is 3010.

31. 4--The GAG sky condition and ceiling for 1600Z to 0100Z is C100 BKN.

32. 2--TUL - 15Z winds 1915G22 and 19Z winds 1815G25. 23Z CFP.... 3215G25
shows cold front passage by 2300Z with winds shifting.

33. 4--For MLC, the forecast reads 09Z MVFR CIG TRW = MVFR because of
ceilings 1000-3000 ft. and thundershowers. Visibility = VFR (> 5mi.) due to
entry of VIS.

34. 2--TUL outlook = 09Z VFR WIND. Ceiling and visibility forecast = VFR;
wind = 25 kt. or stronger.

35. 4--Area Forecasts (FAs) provide forecasts over large areas.

36. 3--FAs have sections on icing and freezing levels.

37. 1--This section forecasts significant clouds and weather in various
areas.

38. 4--The DFWT, turbulence, section includes the entry OCNL MDT TURBC
250-380 for TN AL AND CSTL WTRS.

39. 3--See DFWC, SGFNT CLOUD AND WX, section for OK AR TX LA MS AL and CSTL
wtrs: 80 SCT TO CLR EXCP VSBY BLO 3F TIL 15Z OVR PTNS S CNTRL TX.

40. 1--The period of 042300Z to 050500Z is covered in the outlook section.
OTLK...VFR = visibility > 5 mi. and ceiling > 3,000 ft.

41. 4--The period of 042300Z to 050500Z is covered in the outlook section.
OTLK...VFR = visibility > 5 mi. and ceiling > 3,000 ft.

42. 3--Wind direction (charts, reports, and forecasts) is TRUE. Wind
transmitted to pilots by towers is in MAGNETIC. Wind speed is always in
knots.

43. 3--The wind STL entry for 18,000 ft. is 2356. 23 means wind from 230°
true, 56 means wind speed of 56 kt.

44. 2--The DEN entry for 30,000 ft. is 235347 meaning wind from 230° true at a speed of 53 kt. The temperature is -47°C. The negative sign is left off of temperature entries above 24,000 ft. (see entry on third line: TEMPS NEG ABV 24,000)

45. 1--The MKC entry for 3,000 ft. is 0507 meaning wind from 050° true at 7 kt. Temperature are never forecast for 3,000 ft.

46. 4--The STL entry for 34,000 ft. is 730649. A wind direction entry greater than 36 (for 360) = wind speed is greater than 100 kts. Subtract 50 from the direction entry and add 100 to the speed. 73-50 = 23, wind direction 230; 100 to 6 = 106 kt.

47. 3--When the wind is forecast to be less than 5 kt., it is considered light and variable and is coded 9900.

48. 2--SIGMETs (WSs) are significant weather advisories for weather which may be hazardous to all aircraft.

49. 2--AIRMETs (WAs) advise of possible hazards to light aircraft and VFR only pilots.

50. 2--Severe icing is hazardous to all aircraft; SIGMETS (WS).

51. 1--A corrective SIGMET (WST) provides information on the possible serious hazards of tornadoes, embedded thunderstorms, and hail 3/4 in. or greater in diameter.

52. 1--TWEBs provide continuous weather information on many low and medium frequency (NDB) and VOR navigation facilities.

53. 1--TWEBs include information on routes near the radio facility.

54. 3--TWEBs provide continuous weather information on many low and medium frequency (NDB) and VOR navigation facilities.

55. 1--The FSS briefer needs to know only that you are a pilot. Number of occupants and aircraft color are part of a flight plan, not a weather briefing.

56. 3--The briefing will be tailored - IFR or VFR only. A current pilot certificate is not necessary. Aircraft color and occupants are not part of a weather briefing.

57. 2--Route, destination and type of aircraft.

58. 4--Definition.

59. 3-- An ABBREVIATED briefing supplements information from mass disseminated sources such as TWEB, PATWAS, VRS.

60. 1--An OUTLOOK briefing provides forecasts for periods beyond 6 hr. in advance of departure time.

61.   3--The call sign for EFAS is Flight Watch.   122.0 MHz is the common frequency for Flight Watch in the U.S.   Full current and forecast weather information is available.

62.   1--Flight Watch provides only weather services.

63.   2--Selected FSS's have En Route Flight Advisory Service on the common frequency of 122.0, call sign Flight Watch.

WEATHERWISE III: HOW TO OBTAIN A GOOD WEATHER BRIEFING

Here are some "tips" on how to get a *good* weather briefing. This handout complements the material contained in the FAA/GAMA/OSU slide-tape presentation "Weatherwise II: Go or No Go?" Additional copies of the Flight Planner Form (over and above the two blank copies contained in this handout) are available from your nearest General Aviation District Office (GADO) or Flight Service Station (FSS). Just ask for extra copies of FAA Form 8740-2.

THE "ANATOMY" OF A GOOD WEATHER BRIEFING

A good weather briefing starts with developing an awareness of the overall weather "big picture" before attempting to get a *detailed* weather briefing. At many locations, you can learn about the big picture by listening to the TWEB, an acronym for Transcribed Weather Broadcast; the PARWAS, for Pilot's Automatic Telephone Weather Answering Service; or by watching a good television weather report. The *Airport Facility Directory,* the AOPA *Handbook for Pilots,* and other aviation reference materials list the sources of weather information. When you are ready to call for a weather briefing, the telephone number for either the Federal Aviation Administration (FAA) or the National Weather Service (NWS) can be found in these same references.

In a telephone book, look under United States Government/Department of Transportation/ Federal Aviation Administration/Flight Service Station. If no FSS is listed, look under United States Government/Department of Commerce/National Oceanic and Atmospheric Administration/National Weather Service (NWS). Make sure your planned route of flight is worked out and your flight plan *partially* completed *before* you make the telephone call.

For your preflight briefing, give the briefer the following information:

- Your qualifications, e.g., student, private, commercial, and whether instrument rated.
- The type of flight contemplated, either VFR or IFR.
- The aircraft's N-number identification. If you don't know the N-number, the pilot's name.
- The aircraft type.
- Your departure point.
- Your proposed route-of-flight.
- Your destination.
- Your proposed flight altitude(s).
- Your estimated time of departure (ETD).
- Your estimated time en route (ETE) or, alternatively, your estimated time of arrival (ETA).

Request that the briefer provide you with a standard weather briefing. Then *LISTEN* to the briefer. The briefer will be following the instructions contained in the FAA's *Flight Service Handbook,* a handbook which prescribes procedures and phraseology for use by FAA personnel providing flight services. The briefer will advise you of any adverse conditions along your proposed route of flight. When a VFR flight is proposed and actual or forecast conditions make VFR flight questionable, the briefer will describe the conditions and may advise you that "VFR flight [is] not recommended." If this occurs, or if you feel that the weather conditions are clearly beyond your capabilities (or that of your aircraft or equipment), you should consider terminating the briefing. This will free the briefer to handle other incoming calls.

The briefer will usually summarize weather reports and forecasts. After the conclusion of the initial briefing, if there is *anything* that you do *not* understand about the weather briefing, let the briefer know. For example, if the briefer uses an abbreviation that you do not understand, ask him to explain it. If the briefer talks too fast, ask him to speak more slowly. The amount of detail in your weather briefing will depend upon how complicated the weather situation really is. Remember, if the weather situation really is "iffy," expect—and *insist* upon—a *detailed* weather briefing. It is both your legal responsibility and your prerogative as a pilot to do so.

STANDARD PREFLIGHT WEATHER BRIEFING

At a minumum, your preflight briefing should include the following elements:

- **Adverse Conditions**—significant meteorological and aeronautical information that might influence you, the pilot, to alter your proposed route of flight—or even cancel your flight entirely (e.g., hazardous weather, thunderstorms, icing, turbulence, low ceilings or visibilities, runway closures, or NAVAID outages). Expect the briefer to emphasize conditions that are particularly significant such as low level wind shear along the route of flight, embedded thunderstorms, reported icing, or frontal zones. Hazardous weather may be disseminated to you as SIGMETs, convective SIGMETs, or AIRMETs.
- **Weather Synopsis**—expect a brief statement as to the cause of the weather (e.g., fronts or pressure systems) which might affect your proposed route of flight.

- **Current Weather**—when your proposed time of departure is within 2 hours, a summary of the current weather applicable to your flight will be given.
- **The En Route Forecast**—expect the briefer to summarize en route weather conditions along your proposed route in a logical order, i.e., departure, climb-out, en route, and descent.
- **Destination Terminal Forecast**—the destination forecast for your planned ETA will be provided, including any significant changes within 1 hour before and after your planned time of arrival.
- **Winds Aloft**—The briefer will summarize forecast winds aloft for the proposed route. Temperature information will be provided on request.
- **Notices to Airmen (NOTAMS)**—"Current" NOTAMs pertinent to your proposed route of flight will be provided. However, information on military training routes and operational areas, along with *PUBLISHED* NOTAMs and Special Notices, must be specifically requested. (Note: NOTAMs of any type are *NOT* available from the NWS.)

SUMMARY—
The Preflight Briefing

In person or by phone from either a FSS or the NWS

Your preflight weather briefing should include:

- Adverse weather, including SIGMETs, convective SIGMETs, and AIRMETs
- Synopsis
- Current weather, including PIREPS
- En route weather forecast
- Destination weather forecast
- Alternate airport weather forecast
- Winds aloft forecast
- NOTAMS (not available from NWS)

Don't forget—first give the briefer the flight information he needs to compile a good briefing, then *listen* to the briefer.

Use your flight planner form to record the weather information provided, *then* ask questions if you don't understand of if you *need* more information.

WEATHER JUDGMENT

Judgment, which may be defined as the power of arriving at a wise decision, is the combined result of *knowledge, skills,* and *experience.* You can improve your "Go or No Go" weather judgment by setting personal weather minimums that are higher than the legal minimums. For instance, use a 2,000 foot ceiling and 5 miles visibility, instead of the legal 1,000 and 3, until you are familiar with flight under those conditions. You may *then* gradually reduce your personal minimums to whatever limits you find comfortable, at or above the legal limits.

Here are some obvious *DO NOTS* for everyone—beginner and pro alike:

- Do *NOT* fly in or near thunderstorms. Scattered thunderstorms may be safely circum-navigated but do not try to fly through or under one.
- Do not continue VFR into IFR weather conditions at *any* time unless you are IFR rated and have the appropriate Air Traffic Control (ATC) clearance. Wait it out or turn around if you find en route weather lowering to IFR conditions. Don't forget, there will be areas en route—or even near airports—which are below VFR minimums, whenever reporting stations are at or near VFR minimums. Be especially cautious when the temperature and dew point spread get within 4 degrees of each other—fog could result.
- Do not proceed "on-top," hoping to find a hole at the other end, or hoping to get ATC to "talk you down" if you get caught on top.
- Allow more margin for weather at night. Scud and lower clouds don't show up very far ahead, particularly when it's a really dark night.
- Do not fly into areas of rain when the air temperature is near freezing. Ice on the windshield and on the wings makes for poor VFR flying conditions. Remember too, flight into known icing conditions is prohibited for all aircraft not properly equipped.

And finally, if you do get caught in weather, tell a FSS or ATC facility. They will do their utmost to help you.

HOW TO USE THE FLIGHT PLANNER FORM

The flight planner form is intended as a *tool* to help you, the pilot, record *all* the necessary information you need to make an intelligent Go or No Go decision.

As much of the information as possible could be recorded on the form prior to calling the FSS or NWS for a briefing. This can be accomplished by listening to the TWEB or PATWAS or through the use of the Voice Response System (VRS), where available. Then, during your briefing, you will have only to fill in details.

Look for trends in the weather. Use this form as a checklist to assure yourself that you have received all the necessary weather information during your preflight briefing. Remember that regulations require that you familiarize yourself with current weather and forecasts **prior** to departing on any IFR flight or a VFR flight that is not in the vicinity of an airport.

Remember, also, it's **your** responsibility to make that final Go or No Go decision.

The Weather Briefing "Flow Chart"

Preliminary Flight Planning—
Getting the "Big Picture"
- Media:
  —AM Weather on public television stations (consult local TV listings for exact time).
  —Newspaper weather maps
  —TV and radio weather reports
- Transcribed Radio Broadcasts:
  —NOAA Weather Radio
  —Transcribed Weather Broadcasts (TWEBs) on non-directional, low-frequency radio navigational aids. Available by telephone at some locations (Tele-TWEB)
- Recorded Telephone Weather:
  —"VRS" for FAA's Voice Response System (telephone-computer interface)
  —Pilot's Automatic Telephone Weather Answering Service ("PAT-WAS")

The Preflight Weather Briefing
- In person from either:
  —A FSS, or
  —NWS briefer
- "Self-brief"; visit a FSS or NWS office and personally review the following:
  —Weather maps...analyses and forecasts, including the weather depiction chart
  —Area forecasts
  —Hazardous weather, including severe weather outlooks, SIGMETs/AIRMETs, and severe weather watches/warnings
  —Terminal forecasts
  —Sequence (i.e., hourly) weather reports
  —Radar summary charts
  —Weather radar observations
  —Freezing level chart
  —Winds and temperature aloft forecast
  —PIREPs
  —Stability chart
  —Satellite pictures
  NOTAMS (FSS only)
- By telephone, from either:
  A FSS briefer, or
  —A NWS meteorologist via "a ring-through" connection through FSS, or
  —contact the nearest NWS office directly

THE "GO" OR "NO GO" DECISION

THE "GO" DECISION

If You Don't Go...Your Alternatives
- Delay/postpone (and get a later preflight weather briefing), or
- Cancel

Destination/Arrival Weather
Destination weather can be obtained from the following sources:
- Via VHF radio, from:
  —En route Flight Advisory Service (EFAS)
  —FSS's or Control Facilities
  —Unicom
- Transcribed VHF radio broadcasts
  —ATIS
  —On-site automated weather observations

Inflight Weather Update—Sources of inflight weather include:
- Via VHF radio:
  —EFAS (i.e., "flight watch" on 122.0 MHZ for "real-time" weather)
  —FSSs
  —Air traffic control will broadcast a SIGMET alert once on all frequencies, upon receipt, and
  —To the extent possible, air traffic control will issue pertinent information on weather and assist pilots in avoiding hazardous weather areas, when requested.
- Transcribed radio broadcasts:
  —TWEBs
  —HIWAS

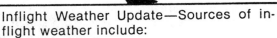

TIPS ON HOW TO USE THE FLIGHT PLANNER FORM

Refer to the completed flight planner form on page 5 as you read these tips.

① Before calling for a weather briefing you can fill out most of your flight plan. A check of your aircraft's cruise performance, as contained in your *Pilot's Operating Handbook (POH) or Flight Manual,* will provide you with a true airspeed value close enough for preflight planning purposes. A decision on your initial cruising altitude and your estimated time en route will depend on your preflight weather briefing of winds aloft, turbulence, and icing.

② Your route of flight should be planned out in detail in the preflight portion of the flight log. VIA is either an airway or direct. CRS is the direct magnetic course or VOR radial. DIST is the distance, in nautical miles. Enter your departure point in the first block and then each checkpoint (fix) in succeeding blocks.

③ Use this block to list the weather reporting stations nearest your departure and destination airports. Include your alternate if applicable. When weather conditions are doubtful, you may wish to add one or two other key locations along your route. You are now prepared to fill in the actual weather from recorded sources, or to ask the briefer for these specific reports following the preflight briefing. It is unlikely that there will be a need to record individual reports when the weather is VFR (i.e., ceiling 3000 feet or greater, and visibilities 5 miles or greater.) In this case, the notation "VFR" should suffice.

④ As the weather briefer describes the overall synoptic situation, sketch out the weather on the synoptic map. Be sure to note the "valid time" of your weather information. You can use the symbols on page 5 or your own if you so choose.

⑤ A summary of current weather can be written in this section.

⑥ A summary of forecast weather en route, and the terminal forecast for your destination(s) should be recorded here.

⑦ The winds and temperatures aloft forecast for your planned altitude(s) should be entered here.

⑧ Record any hazardous weather information in this block including SIGMETs, convective SIGMETs, AIRMETs, and Urgent PIREPs. Any significant NOTAMs should also be noted here.

⑨ Any additional forecast information can be noted in this area.

⑩ Just before departure, if new hourly weather reports have been issued and the weather situation *warrants* an update, you can enter the data in this column of the en route weather trend section.

⑪ You are now in a position to compare the weather from the first hour (Item #5) to the weather in a later hour (Item #10) and note if a trend has developed. The actual weather information and trend can then be compared to the forecast information to allow you to make your Go or No Go decision.

⑫ Use this checklist to be sure that you have received *all* of the important weather information.

⑬ Knowing the sky cover and ceiling, and whether you intend to go VFR or IFR, you can now select a cruising altitude. By using the winds aloft information and your estimated true airspeed, you can calculate your estimated time en route.

⑭ Keep track of the fuel consumed out of each tank by noting the time the tank was turned on and off and enter these data in the fuel management block. Column headings in this block can be "LO" for left outboard tank, "RI" for right inboard tank, and so forth.

⑮ Your departure time can be recorded in this block, as well as on your flight plan.

⑯ Upon levelling-off at your cruising altitude and having obtained a good check on your groundspeed, you can then make an inflight estimate for your next leg in this section of the flight log. GS stands for groundspeed, ETE is estimated time en route, and ETA is estimated time of arrival.

⑰ Actual groundspeed (GSZ), actual time en route (ATE), and actual time of arrival (ATA) can be noted in this section of the flight planner.

⑱ Clearances, frequencies, and other related flight information can be entered in this space.

⑲ An inflight weather update, including new sequence weather, can be posted in this column of the en route weather trend. Pilot report (PIREP) data can be recorded in the "Other Data" section.

⑳ At the conclusion of your flight, note your arrival time in the block and determine your total flight time. It's also a good practice to calculate your fuel consumption rate to gain an insight as to how effective (or ineffective) your fuel conservation procedures were.

FLIGHT INFORMATION PUBLICATIONS

MAIN POINTS

1. The FAA expects you to be a knowledgeable and prepared pilot. Familiarity with a number of publications will help to accomplish this task. The critical feature of each publication is its currency.

2. **Regulatory** and technical information publications include: **Federal Aviation Regulations (FARs)**, which establish and enforce aviation safety and standards and which will be discussed in great detail in Chapter 11; **Airworthiness Directives (ADs)**, which are notices about compulsory maintenance, repair, or inspection; and **FDC** Notams, which contain Flight Data Center regulatory information. There are also a number of nonregulatory and supplemental publications, some of which will be discussed later in this chapter. Finally, the **National Transportation Safety Board (NTSB)** publishes aviation statistics and accident and incident reports.

3. **Aeronautical charts** published by the National Ocean Survey (NOS) include sectional aeronautical charts (primarily for VFR navigation), world aeronautical charts (for high-flying, high-performance aircraft), VFR terminal area charts (large-scale charts that cover the area around a TCA or TRSA), and flight planning charts (large-area, small-scale charts that show the entire United States). Check the chart ledger.

4. The **Airman's Information Manual (AIM)** provides data on navigational aids (radio navaids, airport marking, and lighting aids), airspace restrictions, air traffic control (for example, ARTCC, FSS, and VFR advisory services; radio techniques; airport operations at controlled and uncontrolled airports; ATC clearance procedures; preflight activities such as weather briefings; pilot and controller responsibility; emergency procedures; and national security and interception procedures), flight safety procedures, good operating practices, aviation physiology, and terminology. The AIM is published every 112 days, and each issue indicates on the cover the next date of issue.

5. The <u>Airport/Facility Directory</u> is an integral tool for cross-country flying. It is published every 56 days and covers primarily airports and communication facilities. Refer to Figure 10.1 for a sample entry in the <u>Airport/Facility Directory</u> and its interpretation.

6. <u>Notices to Airmen</u> (<u>NOTAMs</u>) are divided into two classes. Class I <u>NOTAMs</u> are distributed via telecommunications and Class II are published every 14 days. Class II <u>NOTAMs</u> contain current flight safety bulletins. They are available for pilot briefings and are posted in FSS facilities. FDC <u>NOTAMs</u> provide regulatory information.

7. **Advisory Circulars (ACs)** are informative and explanatory in nature. They are not regulations; rather, they attempt to supplement the letter of the law with some guidance as to its intent and with techniques for operating safely within its framework. ACs are numbered to correspond with the topics covered by the FARs and are revised when necessary to reflect changing concepts, adoption of new equipment, or the approval of new regulations. The FAA also publishes informational pamphlets as part of the Accident Prevention Program. Most of this material is free. Your General Aviation District Office (GADO) has some of them; all are available by mail. Addresses are in the Postscript Chapter of this study guide.

KEY TERMS AND CONCEPTS

Match each term or concept (1-12) with the appropriate description (A-L) below. Each item has only one match.

____ 1. NOTAM--Class II   ____ 7. FARs
____ 2. FDC <u>NOTAM</u>   ____ 8. <u>A/F Directory</u>
____ 3. NTSB   ____ 9. ACs
____ 4. WAC   ____ 10. sectionals
____ 5. ADs   ____ 11. flight planning chart
____ 6. terminal area chart   ____ 12. AIM

A. a guidebook of airports
B. group that publishes aviation safety statistics and accident reports
C. publication that deals with navigation, ATC procedures, flight safety, and medical facts
D. navigational charts used primarily by high-flying, high-performance aircraft
E. large-scale navigational charts that cover the area around a TCA
F. rules establishing and enforcing aviation safety standards
G. large, small-scale, navigational charts that depict the entire United States
H. large-scale navigational charts used primarily by VFR pilots
I. notices of compulsory maintenance, repair, or inspection
J. Flight Data Center regulatory information
K. publications that contain information on flying safety
L. informative and explanatory FAA publications

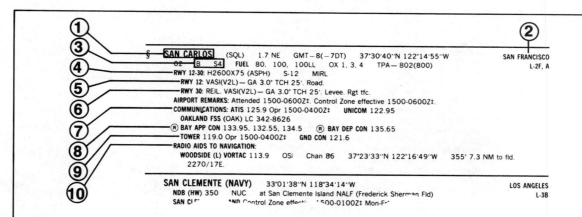

①—San Carlos Airport

②—Airport can be found on the San Francisco sectional chart.

③ { B There is a rotating beacon operating at the airport from dusk to dawn.
S4 Major airframe and power plant repairs are available.

④ {
RWY 12-30: Following information pertains to runways 12 and 30:

H is hard surfaced

2600 Length is 2600 feet.

X75 Width is 75 feet.

(ASPH) Surface is asphalt.

S-12 Capable of supporting single-wheel landing gear airplanes with
    maximum gross weight capacity of 12,000 pounds

MIRL Has medium-intensity runway lights

⑤—VASI A visual approach slope indicator system is available for runway 12.

⑥—REIL Runway 30 has runway-end identifier lights.

⑦ {
ATIS Information is available on frequency 125.9.
UNICOM Advisories available on frequency 122.95 MH.

⑧—Ⓡ BAY APP CON Radar approach control is available on the
    listed frequencies.

⑨ {
TOWER Tower control frequency is 119.0 MH.
GND CON Ground control frequency is 121.6 MH.

⑩ {
RADIO AIDS TO The airport is located on a 355° bearing, 7.3 nautical miles
NAVIGATION   away from the Woodside VORTAC.

Figure 10.1

§ **MONTEREY PENINSULA** (MRY) 3 SE UTC–8(–7DT) 36°35'17"N 121°50'53"W
244 B S4 **FUEL** 100, JET A OX 2, 4 LRA CFR Index C TPA—1744(1500)
RWY 10-28: H6597X150 (ASPH-PFC) S-100, D-160, DT-300 HIRL 1.4% up E
RWY 10: SSALR. Tree. RWY 28: REIL. VASI(V4L)—GA 3.5° TCH 47.3'. Trees. Rgt tfc.
RWY 06-24: H4001X150 (ASPH) S-60, D-110, DT-200 MIRL
RWY 06: Tree. RWY 24: Thld dsplcd 460'. Tree. Rgt tfc.
AIRPORT REMARKS: Attended continuously. Rwy 06-24 lgts off when twr clsd. Rwy 24 closed to ngt ldg; lights have not
been removed. Overngt tiedown fee at FBO. Ldg fee for acft over 8000 pounds. Flight Notification Service (ADCUS)
available. Control zone effective 1400-0700Z‡.
COMMUNICATIONS: CTAF 118.4 ATIS 119.25 UNICOM 122.95
SALINAS FSS (SNS) Toll free call, dial 800-372-6050. NOTAM FILE MRY
Ⓡ APP/DEP CON 133.5 (360°-096°) 133.0, 127.15 (096°-360°) (1400-0700Z‡)
OAKLAND CENTER APP/DEP CON 125.45 (0700-1400Z‡)
TOWER 118.4 (1400-0700Z‡) GND CON 121.9
STAGE III SVC ctc APP CON within 30 NM
RADIO AIDS TO NAVIGATION: NOTAM FILE SNS.
SALINAS (H) ABVORTAC 117.3 ■ SNS Chan 120 36°39'50"N 121°36'08"W 232° 12.7 NM to fld.
80/17E.
MUNSO NDB (LOM) 385 MR 36°37'15"N 121°56'15"W 098° 4.3 NM to fld. NOTAM FILE MRY.
Unusable 110°-160° beyond 7 NM.
ILS/DME 110.7 I-MRY Chan 44 Rwy 10 LOM MUNSO NDB (ILS/DME unmonitored when twr clsd.)
Glide Slope coupled approaches unusable 5.5-2 NM inbound.
ILS/DME 110.7 I-MTB Rwy 28 Chan 44 LOC only. (LOC/DME unmonitored when twr clsd.)
COMM/NAVAID REMARKS: IFR arrivals close flight plan with SNS FSS on Freq 118.4 when Monterey twr clsd. Stage III
svc not available within Salinas air traffic area.

SAN FRANCISCO
H-2E, L-2E, 2F
IAP

---

§ **OAKDALE** (O27) 3 SE UTC–8(–7DT) 37°45'23"N 120°48'01"W
234 B S4 **FUEL** 80, 100 OX 1 TPA—1226(1000)
RWY 10-28: H3020X66 (ASPH) S-20 MIRL
RWY 10: VASI(V2L)—GA 2.5° TCH 22'. Tower. RWY 28: P-line.
AIRPORT REMARKS: Attended dalgt hours. Nights on call.
COMMUNICATIONS: CTAF/UNICOM 122.8
SACRAMENTO FSS (SAC) Toll free call, dial 800-852-7036. NOTAM FILE SAC.
Ⓡ STOCKTON APP/DEP CON 123.85 (1400-0700Z‡) OAKLAND CENTER APP/DEP CON 126.85 (0700-1400Z‡)
RADIO AIDS TO NAVIGATION: NOTAM FILE SCK.
MANTECA (H) VORTAC 116.0 ECA Chan 107 37°50'01.2"N 121°10'13.3"W 087° 18 NM to fld. 40/17E.

SAN FRANCISCO
L-2F
IAP

OAKLAND

§ **METROPOLITAN OAKLAND INTL** (OAK) 4 S UTC–8(–7DT)
37°43'17"N 122°13'11"W
06 B S4 **FUEL** 80, 100, JET A OX 1, 2, 3, 4 TPA—See Remarks
LRA CFR Index D
RWY 11-29: H10,000X150 (ASPH-GRVD) S-200, D-200, DT-400, DDT-900 HIRL, CL
RWY 11: MALSR. Rgt tfc. RWY 29: ALSF1, TDZ
RWY 09R-27L: H6212X150 (ASPH) S-155, D-158, DT-253, DDT-525 HIRL
RWY 09R: VASI(V4L)—GA 3.0° TCH 46'. Tree.
RWY 27L: VASI(V4L)—GA 3.0° TCH 55'.
RWY 15-33: H3366X75 (ASPH) S-12.5, D-65, DT-100 HIRL
RWY 33: Rgt tfc.
RWY 09L-27R: H5453X150 (ASPH) S-100, D-115, DT-180 HIRL
RWY 09L: VASI(V4L)—GA 3.0° TCH 37.7'. Building. RWY 27R: MALSR. Building. Rgt tfc.
AIRPORT REMARKS: Attended continuously. Fee rwy 11-29 and overnight tiedown. Birds on and in vicinity of arpt. Rwy
09L-27R closed to air carrier acft except taxiway 09L and 27R for taxiing. Turbo-jet/fan turbo-prop acft with
certificated gross weight over 12,500 lbs & 4-engine reciprocating acft prohibited from takeoff 27R, 27L or landing
09L & 09R. This prohibition not applicable or effective in emergency or when rwy 11-29 is closed. Acft with
experimental or limited certification having over 1000 h.p or 4000 lbs are restricted to rwy 11-29 for all ops due to
maintenance, construction, or reasons of safety. Rwy 15-33 restricted to aircraft 12,500 lbs or less and is for 24
hour use. Rwy 09R-27L FAA gross weight strength DC 10-10 350,000 pounds, DC 10-30 450,000 pounds, L-1011
350,000 pounds. Rwy 11-29 FAA gross weight strength DC 10-10 600,000 pounds, DC 10-30 700,000 pounds,
L-1011 600,000 pounds. TPA—Rwy 27L 606(600), TPA—Rwy 27R 1006(1000). Flight Notification Service
(ADCUS) available.
COMMUNICATIONS: ATIS 126.0 (N. Complex), 128.5 (415-635-5850) (S. Complex) UNICOM 122.95
OAKLAND FSS (OAK) on arpt. 122.5, 122.2 Toll free call, dial 800-345-4546. NOTAM FILE OAK.
Ⓡ BAY APP CON 124.4 (S. Complex), 135.4 (N. Complex), 134.5
OAKLAND TOWER 118.3 (N. Complex) (1500-0600Z‡) 127.2 (S. Complex) 124.9
GND CON 121.75 (S. Complex), 121.9 (N. Complex) CLNC DEL 121.1
Ⓡ BAY DEP CON 120.9 (NW-E), 135.1 (SE-W)
STAGE III svc ctc APP CON 127.2
RADIO AIDS TO NAVIGATION: NOTAM FILE OAK.
OAKLAND (H) VORTAC 116.8 OAK Chan 115 37°43'34"N 122°13'21"W at fld. 10/17E
RORAY NDB (LMM) 341 AK 37°43'17"N 122°11'35"W at fld.
ILS 108.7 I-INB Rwy 29
ILS 111.9 I-AAZ Rwy 11
ILS 109.9 I-OAK Rwy 27R LMM RORAY NDB

SAN FRANCISCO
H-1A, 2E, L-2F, A
IAP

OAKLAND
(H) VORTAC 116.8 OAK Chan 115 37°43'34"N 122°13'21"W.
at Metropolitan Oakland Int'l. 10/17E. NOTAM FILE OAK.
VOR unusable 307-323° beyond 10 NM below 5000' 307-323° beyond 17 NM below 12,500'
DME unusable:
307-323° beyond 30 NM below 1500' 040-065° beyond 30 NM below 4100'
350-030° beyond 20 NM below 3500'
FSS (OAK) at Metropolitan Oakland Intl 122.5, 122.2 LC 527-9980

SAN FRANCISCO
H-1A, 2E, L-2F, A

Figure 10.2

DISCUSSION QUESTIONS AND REVIEW EXERCISES

1. What are **Airworthiness Directives**? Why should you be concerned with
them?

2. Using the excerpts from the Airport/Facility Directory in Figure 10.2 and
the legend in Appendix A, answer the following questions:

   a. How would you obtain information about current conditions and runway
in use for the following airports without calling to request such information.

   Monterey Peninsula (MRY) -

   Oakland Metropolitan (OAK) -

   b. Is 80 octane fuel available at the following airports?

   MRY -   Oakdale (027) -   OAK -

   c. During what hours is the control zone in effect at MRY?

   d. State how you would obtain a preflight weather briefing at:

   MRY -

   027 -

   OAK -

   e. What is the longest runway at the following airports?

   MRY -   027 -   OAK -

   f. What information do you know about Rwy 10 at 027?

g. Which runways at MRY have right traffic patterns?

h. State how you would obtain permission to take off or land at:

MRY -

027 -

OAK -

i. What is the field elevation of the following airports:

MRY -   027 -   OAK -

j. What is the normal pattern altitude at the following airports?

MRY -   027 -   OAK -

k. When flying to MRY, can approach control provide you with assistance? How?

l. Where is the Oakland VORTAC DME unusable?

m. What radio navaid serves 027? What is the frequency and identification? What is the bearing and distance from the navaid to the airport?

3. Suppose you want to learn more about the special techniques and hazards of flying at night. What publication would you expect to contain piloting tips and information on the physiology of night flying?

4. Before using **any** flight information **publication** for flight planning or navigation, what should you check first?

5. In what flight information document would you find a list of telephone numbers for an FAA Flight Service weather briefing?

6. Assume you are planning to arrive at Beals Airport at twilight. The following NOTAM is posted for Brule, Nebraska:

    BRULE, BEALS ARPT: for rwy lights rwy 8-26 key freq 121.7
    (10/84-2)

What does the NOTAM say and what operational procedures does it contain that are relevant to your arrival?

7. T F To determine if UNICOM is available at an airport without a control tower, you should refer to Notices to Airmen (NOTAMs).

8. T F Sectional charts for the conterminous United States are updated every six months.

9. What is the **Airman's Information Manual**? What types of information will you find in it?

10. Briefly describe what you should do when planning a VFR cross-country flight. Be sure to identify what planning aids you would use and what information you would obtain from each.

11. Which of the following publications is regulatory and/or technical in nature?
    1--Advisory Circular (AC).
    2--Airworthiness Directive (AD).
    3--National Transportation Safety Board publications.
    4--VFR terminal area charts.

FAA EXAM QUESTIONS

(Note: All FAA Figures are located in Appendix C)

1. (FAA 1490) Traffic patterns in effect at McCook Municipal (Figure 47) are
   1--left-hand on all runways.
   2--left-hand on Rwy 12, Rwy 21 and Rwy 30; right-hand on Rwy 03.
   3--right-hand on all runways.
   4--right-hand on the concrete runways and left-hand on the turf runways.

2. (FAA 1491) Where is Loup City Municipal located with relation to the city? (See Figure 47.)
   1--Northeast approximately 3 mi.
   2--Northwest approximately 1 mi.
   3--East approximately 10 mi.
   4--250°, 29.3 NM.

3. (FAA 1488) When approaching Lincoln Municipal (Figure 47) from the west at noon for the purpose of landing, the initial communications should be with
   1--Lincoln Approach Control on 124.0 MHz.
   2--Minneapolis Center Approach Control on 128.75 MHz.
   3--Lincoln Tower on 118.5 MHz.
   4--Lincoln Approach Control on 124.8 MHz.

4. (FAA 1489) Which type radar service is listed for Lincoln Municipal? (See Figure 47.)
   1--Radar advisory and sequencing service for IFR aircraft only.
   2--Radar advisory for VFR traffic and sequencing service for IFR aircraft.
   3--Radar sequencing and separation for participating VFR aircraft.
   4--Radar sequencing and separation service for all aircraft.

5. (FAA 1492) What is the recommended communications procedure for landing at Lincoln Municipal during the hours when the tower is not in operation? (See Figure 47.)
   1--Contact UNICOM on 122.95 MHz for traffic advisories.
   2--Monitor ATIS for airport conditions, then announce position on 122.95 MHz.
   3--Request advisories and sequencing from Minneapolis Center Approach control.
   4--Contact the Lincoln FSS on 118.5 MHz for traffic advisories.

6. (FAA 1508) FAA advisory circulars (some free, others at cost) are available to all pilots and are obtained by
1--distribution from the nearest FAA district office.
2--ordering those desired from the Government Printing Office.
3--subscribing to the Federal Register.
4--subscribing to FAR's.

ANSWERS AND EXPLANATIONS

Key Terms and Concepts

1. K	4. D	7. F	10. H
2. J	5. I	8. A	11. G
3. B	6. E	9. L	12. C

Discussion Questions and Review Exercises

1. See Study Guide Main Point #2.

2.

   a. MRY - Listen to ATIS on 119.25; OAK - Listen to ATIS on 128.5 or call (415) 635-5850.

   b. MRY - no; 027 - yes; OAK - no.

   c. 1400-0700Z.

   d. MRY - telephone Salinas FSS at (408) 372-6050; 027 - telephone Sacramento FSS at (800) 852-7036; OAK - since the FSS is on the field, you can visit the facility, contact them by telephone at (800) 345-4546, or contact FSS by radio on 122.5 or 122.2, but you should not tie up these frequencies for a preflight weather briefing.

   e. MRY - 10-28; 027 - 10-28; OAK - 11-19.

   f. 3020 ft. long, 66 ft. wide, hard surface (asphalt), medium intensity runway lighting, VASI available for Rwy 10 only, tower near Rwy 10.

   g. 24 and 28.

   h. MRY - call the tower, 118.4, when it is in operation; when not in operation, you clear yourself and advise others of your intentions on CTAF, 118.4. 027 - since there is no tower, you clear yourself and advise of intentions on CTAF/UNICOM, 122.8. OAK - call the tower, 118.3, 127.2, 124.9, as appropriate.

   i. Mry - 244 ft.; 027 - 234 ft.; OAK - 6 ft.

   j. MRY - 1,744 feet MSL (1,500 ft. AGL); 027 - 1,226 ft. MSL (1,000 ft. AGL); OAK - Rwy 27L - 606 ft. MSL (600 ft. AGL) and Rwy 27R - 1,006 ft. MSL (1,000 ft. AGL).

k. Approach control can provide STAGE III service, radar sequencing and separation service for participating VFR aircraft within the TRSA; contact them within 30 nm.

1. 307-323° beyond 30 nm below 1,500 ft.; 350-030° beyond 30 nm below 3,500 ft.; 040-065° beyond 30 nm below 4,100 ft.

m. Manteca VORTAC; 087°, 18 nm.

3. AIM.

4. Its currency.

5. Airport/Facility Directory.

6. For Beals Airport at Brule, Nebraska. Runway lights are available for Rwy 8-26 by keying the radio on 121.7 MHz.

7. F--You should refer to the appropriate Airport/Facility Directory.

8. T--See the sectional chart legend.

9. See Study Guide Main Point #4.

10. See Study Guide Main Points #3-#7.

11. 2--ADs are notices about compulsory maintenance, repair, or inspection.

FAA Exam Questions

1. 2--The runway information has the entry "Rgt tfc" for runway 03. The lack of such notations for the other runways indicates that they have the normal left traffic.

2. 2--On the top line is "1 NW" indicating that the airport is about 1 mile NW of the city.

3. 1--Stage III radar service. Contact approach control. The APT/DEP CON entry is 124.0 MHz when approaching from 170°-349° (1200-0600 Z); local time = UTC-6 (0600-0000).

4. 3--Stage III radar for sequencing and separating participating VFR aircraft.

5. 4--See the entry "LINCOLN FSS (LNK) on arpt." An Airport Advisory Area exists when the tower is not operating. FSS will provide only traffic advisories, not control. The CTAF is 118.5.

6. 2--Government Printing Office.

FEDERAL AVIATION REGULATIONS

MAIN POINTS

1. FAR PART 1: DEFINITIONS AND ABBREVIATIONS

    Airport: area of land or water used for takeoffs and landings.

    Airport traffic area (ATA): airspace from the ground up to but not including 3,000 feet AGL; 5-mile radius from the center of an airport with an operating control tower.

    Air traffic clearance: authorization to proceed within controlled airspace.

    Calibrated airspeed (CAS): airspeed corrected for position and installation errors.

    Ceiling: height AGL of the lowest layer of broken or overcast clouds.

    Controlled airspace: ATAs, control zones, transition areas, navigation routes, and the continental control area are examples.

    Flight crewmember: pilot, navigator, or engineer with assigned duty during flight time.

    Flight visibility: forward horizontal distance.

    IFR: Instrument Flight Rules, in effect when weather conditions are below VFR minimums.

    Indicated airspeed (IAS): pitot-static airspeed, pressure, uncorrected for airspeed system errors.

    Pilot in command: the pilot responsible for the operation and safety of an aircraft during flight time.

Positive control: control of all air traffic within designated airspace by air traffic control.

Prohibited area: no flight allowed.

Restricted area: restrictions to flight apply.

True airspeed (TAS): airspeed relative to undisturbed air.

2. FAR PART 61: CERTIFICATION: PILOTS AND FLIGHT INSTRUCTORS

Subpart A--General

61.3   (a) You must have your pilot's certificate and medical certificate in your possession to act as pilot-in-command.

61.15   Convicted drug dealers and users can have certificates or ratings revoked and are ineligible for certification for one year following conviction.

61.17   Temporary certificates are good for 120 days.

61.19   Student pilot certificates expire at the end of the 24th month after issue. Other pilot certificates are issued without a specific expiration date.

61.23   Third Class Medical Certificates, common for student and private pilots, expire at the end of the same calendar month in which they were issued, 24 mo. after the exam.

61.31   In general, you must receive instruction and hold a category and class rating for an airplane to act as pilot-in-command.

61.39   To qualify for the practical test, you must have passed the written test within two years, hold a current medical certificate, and have a CFI's written statement, issued within 60 days, stating that the candidate is prepared to take the practical test.

61.51   Reliable records of required flight time and experience must be kept. Student pilots must also carry logbooks on solo cross-country flights as evidence of the required instructor clearances and endorsements.

61.57   (a, b) Biennial Flight Reviews (BFR) by a CFI or other person designated by the Administrator are mandatory at least every 24 calendar months to act as pilot-in-command. They expire on the last day of the same calendar month two years after they are issued. The BFR includes questions on general operating procedures, flight rules, and flight maneuvers. (c) To act as pilot-in-command of an aircraft carrying passengers, you must have made at least three takeoffs and landings in the same category and class of aircraft within the prior 90 days. (d) To act as pilot-in-command of an aircraft carrying passengers during the period from one hour after sunset to one hour before sunrise, a person must have made at least three takeoffs and three full-stop landings during that period within the preceding 90 days.

61.60   A change of permanent mailing address must be reported to the FAA. If the change is not reported within 30 days after moving, a pilot may not exercise the privileges of the certificate.

Subpart B--Aircraft Ratings and Special Certificates

61.63   To receive additional ratings, the pilot must present a logbook endorsed by an authorized instructor and pass a practical test.

Subpart C--Student Pilots

61.83   The minimum age is 16, English language competency is required, and you must hold at least a Third Class Medical Certificate.

61.87   Solo flight requires an endorsement by your CFI that appropriate training has been given; it is good for 90 days.

61.89   Student pilots cannot carry passengers nor can they act as required crewmembers.

61.93   Cross-country flights (more than 25 NM) require a CFI's endorsement on the student pilot certificate and in the logbook for each cross-country flight.

Subpart D--Private Pilots

61.103   The minimum age is 17; you must have competence in the English language; you must hold at least a Third Class Medical Certificate; and you must pass the written test and the practical test.

61.109   To apply for a private pilot certificate, the applicant must have at least 20 hr. of flight instruction and 20 hr. of solo time, as outlined in Chapter 1.

61.118   Private pilots may not act as a pilot-in-command of an aircraft that is carrying passengers for compensation or hire. A private pilot may share operating expenses with passengers. A private pilot may also act as pilot-in-command to demonstrate an aircraft and for charitable airlifts if he/she is an aircraft salesperson with at least 200 hr. of logged flight time.

3.   FAR PART 67: MEDICAL STANDARDS AND CERTIFICATION

67.31   If a situation warrants it, the Administrator may request medical records.

4. FAR Part 91: GENERAL OPERATING AND FLIGHT RULES

Subpart A--General

91.3 The pilot-in-command is responsible for the aircraft. Deviations from a rule to meet an emergency must be reported to the Administrator in writing **only upon request.**

91.5 The pilot must consider weather and runway lengths before any flight not in the vicinity of an airport.

91.7 Fastened seatbelts are required of crewmembers when at stations. During takeoff and landing, shoulder harnesses (when available) must be used.

91.11 Alcohol cannot be consumed by the pilot-in-command within 8 hr. of a flight, nor can the pilot carry passengers who are obviously under the influence of alcohol or drugs, unless under medical supervision. Crewmembers can be tested to determine the percentage by weight of alcohol in the blood.

91.14 The pilot-in-command is responsible for ensuring that each person knows how to fasten and unfasten his/her safety belt and for instructing each person to fasten that belt prior to takeoff and landing.

91.21 Simulated instrument flights require the presence of an appropriately rated safety pilot.

91.22 Minimum fuel reserves are 30 min. for a day VFR flight and 45 min. for a night VFR flight.

91.24 Group I and II TCAs require a Mode 3/A 4096 code transponder as well as a Mode C encoding altimeter. While in controlled airspace, an aircraft equipped with an operable ATC transponder shall operate the transponder, including Mode C equipment if installed, and shall reply on the appropriate code or as assigned by ATC.

91.27 An airworthiness certificate must be openly displayed inside the aircraft.

91.31 The pilot must comply with the aircraft's operating limitations and have the following required documents on board: airworthiness certificate, registration, radio station operator's permit, operating limitations, and weight and balance data. A convenient way to remember these is to use the acronym ARROW.

91.32 Supplemental oxygen is required for the flight crew for flights of more than 30 min. between 12,500 and 14,000 feet MSL. For **any** flights above 14,000 feet MSL, the crew **must** use oxygen, and passengers must be provided with oxygen for flights above 15,000 feet MSL.

91.52 An operable emergency locator transmitter (ELT) is required for flights outside the local area.

91.67 (a) Vigilance shall be maintained (VFR, and IFR when weather permits) to see and avoid other aircraft. (b) An aircraft in distress has the right-of-way over all other aircraft. (c) The aircraft to the right has the right-of-way when two aircraft of the same category are converging. Balloons have the right-of-way over other categories. A glider has the right-of-way over airships, airplanes, and rotorcraft. An airship has the right-of-way over airplanes and rotorcraft. (d) When approaching head-on, alter course to the right. (e) An aircraft that is overtaking another aircraft shall give right-of-way and pass on the right. (f) Aircraft on final approach have the right-of-way over aircraft on the ground; also, aircraft at lower altitudes have the right-of-way on landing.

91.70 (a) The speed limit below 10,000 feet MSL and in TCAs is 250 kts. (288 MPH). (b) The ATA speed limit is 156 kts. (180 MPH) for reciprocating engine aircraft and 200 kts. (230 MPH) for turbine-powered aircraft. (c) The limit under overlying TCA airspace is 200 kts. (230 MPH).

91.71 Acrobatic flight is prohibited over congested areas or open-air assemblies, within control zones, on Federal airways, below 1,500 feet AGL, or when visibility is less than 3 miles.

91.73 Position lights are required for night operation (on the ground and in the air); anticollision lights are required for night flight.

91.75 Except in an emergency, the pilot must comply with ATC instructions. ATC should be notified of any deviations as soon as possible. ATC may request a written report of any emergency within 48 hr.

91.77 ATC light signals were covered in Chapter 7. If you cannot remember them, go back for review.

91.79 (a) Aircraft must always be operated at an altitude that would allow an emergency landing without undue hazard to people and property on the surface. (b) Over congested areas, aircraft must be at least 1,000 feet above the highest obstacle within 2,000 feet of the aircraft. (c) Over other than congested areas, maintain an altitude of 500 feet above the surface, except over sparsely populated areas, where aircraft must stay at least 500 feet away from people, structures, or vehicles.

91.81 For flights below 18,000 feet MSL, altimeters must be set to a station within 100 NM along the route or, if no station is within the prescribed area, to an appropriate current reported altimeter setting. If no radio is available, set in the field elevation of the departure airport.

91.83 Flight plans shall include the aircraft ID number; type of aircraft; pilot's name and address; time and point of departure; proposed route, altitude, and TAS; point of first landing and ETE; fuel on board; alternate airport (IFR only); and number of persons on board. (Note: VFR flight plans are optional but highly recommended, particularly for cross-country flights.

91.87   Pilots going to or from or operating on an airport with a control tower are to follow instructions issued by the controller. Two-way radio communication is mandatory unless other arrangements have been made in advance or the radio fails in flight. (Note: A clearance to "taxi to" the takeoff runway is a clearance to cross other runways, but not to taxi onto or cross any portion of the active runway.)

91.88   Within airport radar service areas (ARSAs), two-way radio communication must be established with ATC prior to entering the ARSA. Aircraft may depart a **satellite** airport (defined as an airport other than the primary airport within the ARSA) without prior approval, but must establish and maintain two-way radio communication with ATC as soon as practicable. Takeoffs and landings at a satellite airport within an ARSA must comply with FAA approved arrival and departure traffic patters.

91.90   Operating within a Group I TCA requires an operable VOR or TACAN receiver, an operable two-way radio with appropriate frequencies, ATC clearance, a Mode 3/A 4096 code transponder with a Mode C encoding altimeter, and an appropriate authorization. A private pilot's certificate is the minimum certificate required to land at or take off from the primary airport within a Group I TCA. Operation in a Group II TCA requires the same equipment and authorization; however, only a student pilot certificate is required to land at or take off from an airport within the TCA.

91.91   Special flight restrictions are issued as <u>N</u>otices <u>to</u> <u>Airmen</u> (<u>NOTAM</u>s).

Subpart B--Flight Rules: Visual Flight Rules

91.105   Cloud clearance and flight visibilities:

<u>Surface</u> <u>to</u> <u>1,200</u> <u>feet</u> <u>AGL</u>:

Controlled airspace: 3 mile visibility and 500 feet below, 1,000 feet above, and 2,000 feet horizontal cloud clearance.

Uncontrolled airspace: 1 mile visibility and clear of clouds.

<u>1,200</u> <u>feet</u> <u>AGL</u> <u>to</u> <u>10,000</u> <u>feet</u> <u>MSL</u>:

Controlled airspace: 3 mile visibility and 500 feet below, 1,000 feet above, and 2,000 feet horizontal cloud clearance.

Uncontrolled airspace: 1 statute mile visibility and the same cloud clearance as for controlled airspace.

<u>More</u> <u>than</u> <u>1,200</u> <u>feet</u> <u>AGL</u> <u>and</u> <u>at</u> <u>or</u> <u>above</u> <u>10,000</u> <u>feet</u> <u>MSL</u>:

Visibility of 5 statute miles and 1,000 feet above and below clouds with a 1 mile horizontal cloud clearance.

91.107 Special VFR weather minimums that apply in a control zone are: clear of clouds and 1 statute mile visibility. Special VFR at night requires both the airplane and the pilot to be capable of IFR flight.

91.109   VFR cruising altitudes for flights above 3,000 feet AGL:

Below 18,000 feet MSL: on **magnetic** courses of 0° to 179°: odd thousand foot MSL altitudes plus 500 feet; on **magnetic** courses of 180° to 359°: even thousand foot MSL altitudes plus 500 feet   (Remember **NEODD** - North or East, odd altitudes +500 feet; **SWEVEN** - South or West, even altitudes +500 feet.)

FL 180 to FL 290:   on **magnetic** courses of 0° to 179°:   any odd flight level plus 500 feet; on **magnetic** courses of 180° to 359°:   any even flight level plus 500 feet.

Subpart C--Maintenance, Preventive Maintenance, and Alterations

91.163 The owner or operator is responsible for maintaining the aircraft in an airworthy condition. Only authorized persons can perform certain maintenance and alterations.

91.165   Maintenance and inspections are the owner's/operator's responsibility.

91.167 Passengers may not be carried until an alteration or repair has been checked and entered in the aircraft log. There are two logs, one for the airframe and one for the engine.

91.169 (a) Annual inspections are required for all aircraft. (b) 100-hr. inspections are required for all aircraft that are operated for hire, including those used for flight instruction for hire. (c) Progressive inspections may be authorized to replace (a) and (b).

91.173 Records of inspections, alterations, total airframe time, and overhauls must be maintained by the owner or operator.

5.   PART 830:   NATIONAL TRANSPORTATION SAFETY BOARD RULES PERTAINING TO THE NOTIFICATION AND REPORTING OF AIRCRAFT ACCIDENTS OR INCIDENTS AND OVERDUE AIRCRAFT, AND PRESERVATION OF AIRCRAFT WRECKAGE, MAIL, CARGO, AND RECORDS

Subpart A--General

830.1 Accidents must be reported.

Subpart B--Initial Notification of Aircraft Accidents, Incidents, and Overdue Aircraft

830.5 The operator must report an accident to the NTSB at once. Other flight incidents that must be reported include flight control system failure or malfunction, inability of a required crewmember to perform normal duties due to injury or illness, in-flight fire, an airborne collision, or an aircraft that is overdue or is believed to have been involved in an accident.

Subpart C--Preservation of Aircraft Wreckage, Mail, Cargo, and Records

    830.10   Wreckage, cargo, and all records must be preserved.

Subpart D--Reporting of Aircraft Accidents, Incidents, and Overdue Aircraft

    830.15   Written reports are due within 10 days of an accident.   A report of an incident in 830.5 may also be requested.

DISCUSSION QUESTIONS AND REVIEW EXERCISES

1. T   F   An airport traffic area (ATA) extends from the surface to 12,000 feet MSL and for a radius of 5 miles from the control tower.

2. T   F   Calibrated airspeed (CAS) is indicated airspeed corrected for position and installation errors.

3. T   F   The ceiling is defined as the height above the ground of the lowest layer of clouds that are classified as broken or overcast.

4. T   F   Transition areas are examples of controlled airspace.

5. T   F   Indicated airspeed (IAS) refers to pitot-static airspeed corrected for airspeed system errors.

6. T   F   Flights in prohibited areas must be cleared by ATC in a manner identical to that for flights in other control zones.

7. What does each of the following acronyms mean?

    a. AGL

    b. ARSA

    c. ATC

    d. CAS

    e. IAS

    f. IFR

    g. MSL

h. TAS

i. V_x

j. V_y

k. VFR

8. T F To act as pilot-in-command of an airplane, you must have your pilot certificate and medical certificate in your possession.

9. T F Temporary certificates are typically good for six months from the day on which they were issued.

10. T F Student pilot certificates are issued without a specific expiration date.

11. T F FARs recommend but do not require student pilots to log their flight time.

12. T F FARs recommend but do not require private pilots to have a Biennial Flight Review once every two years.

13. T F To act as a pilot-in-command of a single-engine airplane carrying passengers, you must have made three takeoffs and landings in the past 30 days in the same category and class of aircraft.

14. T F Student pilots can carry passengers on local flights but not on cross-country flights, unless authorized by a CFI.

15. T F Obtaining weather information is mandatory only for cross-country flights that may encounter weather below IFR or marginal VFR minimums.

16. T F Alcohol cannot be consumed less than 8 hr. before you perform duties as a crewmember of a civil aircraft operated under FAR Part 91.

17. T F Each passenger is responsible for knowing how to fasten and unfasten safety belts.

18. T F Minimum fuel reserves for a daytime VFR flight of more than 2-hr. duration are 45 min.

19. T F Simulated instrument flights require the presence of an appropriately rated safety pilot.

20. What aircraft documents must you carry on board the airplane? They are represented by the letters ARROW.

21. Who has the right-of-way in the following circumstances?

    a. aircraft of the same category converging on your right

    b. two aircraft approaching head-on

    c. one aircraft overtaking another

    d. aircraft on final approach

22. Supplemental oxygen is required for the minimum flight crew of a civil aircraft if the flight exceeds 30 min. above a certain minimum cabin pressure altitude. What is that altitude? What is the minimum cabin pressure altitude at or above which the minimum flight crew must use oxygen continuously? At what minimum cabin pressure altitude must **every** occupant of the aircraft be provided with supplemental oxygen?

23. T F If two aircraft are on final approach, the aircraft at the lower altitude has the right-of-way.

24. T F The speed limit in a TCA below 10,000 feet MSL is 150 kts. (180 MPH).

25. T F Supplemental oxygen is required for all crewmembers for any flight over 30 min. at 10,000 feet MSL or higher.

26. T F Acrobatic flight is prohibited over congested areas, below 3,000 feet, and with visibility less than 1 mile.

27. T F Position lights are required for night flight but not for taxiing an aircraft from one place to another on the airfield at night.

28. T F Except in an emergency, the pilot must comply with ATC instructions when flying in an ATA.

29. T F Except for takeoffs and landings, aircraft must always be operated at an altitude that would allow an emergency landing without undue hazard to people and property on the surface.

30. T F Over sparsely populated areas, you must stay at least 1,000 feet away from people or structures.

31. T F Flight plans are required for VFR flights over 200 miles.

32. What are the minimum safe altitudes (except for takeoffs and landing) and horizontal clearance from obstacles required for operation over a congested area? What are the minimums over other than congested areas?

33. T F For flights below 18,000 feet MSL, the altimeter must be set to a station within 50 miles of the route of flight.

34. T F Flight plans are mandatory on any cross-country flight in which the pilot-in-command is a student pilot.

35. A controller clears you to "taxi to" the active runway. Between you and the active runway are several other intersecting runways. How will you proceed?

36. T F At airports without control towers, turns are typically made to the left unless markings (such as a segmented circle) indicate otherwise.

37. T F To land at or take off from the primary airport within a Group I TCA, the pilot must possess at least a private pilot's certificate and have at least 20 hr. of instrument flight instruction.

38. List the basic VFR flight visibilities and cloud clearances both within and outside of controlled airspace for flights:

a. at 1,200 feet or less AGL

b. at more than 1,200 feet AGL but less than 10,000 feet MSL

c. at more than 1,200 feet AGL and at or above 10,000 feet MSL

39. T   F   Special VFR minimums in a control zone include visibility of at least 3 miles and clear of clouds.

40. T   F   A private pilot may not act as pilot-in-command for hire or compensation, but he/she may share operating expenses of a flight with passengers.

41. T   F   An aircraft may enter an ARSA without prior ATC approval if the pilot has activated the aircraft's Mode C altitude encoding transponder and that transponder is transmitting altitude and location information.

42. T   F   An aircraft may depart a **satellite** airport within an ARSA only after the pilot has received approval from ATC.

43. What is an **ARSA**? What is required to enter an ARSA? If you are leaving a satellite airport within an ARSA, what are you required to do? Name at least two requirements.

(Note: All FAA Figures are located in Appendix C)

1. (FAA 1602) An Airport Traffic Area is automatically in effect when
   1--its associated control tower is in operation.
   2--the weather is below VFR minimums.
   3--nighttime hours exist.
   4--radar service is available.

2. (FAA 1603) The definition of nighttime is
   1--sunset to sunrise.
   2--30 min. after sunset to 30 min. before sunrise.
   3--1 hr. after sunset to 1 hr. before sunrise.
   4--from the end of evening civil twilight to the beginning of morning civil twilight.

3. (FAA 1601) After takeoff, which airspeed would permit the pilot to gain the most altitude in a given period of time?
   1--V_y.   2--V_x.
   3--V_a.   4--V_r.

4. (FAA 1604) Which would provide the greatest gain in altitude in the shortest distance during climb after takeoff?
   1--V_d.   2--V_a.
   3--V_x.   4--V_y.

5. (FAA 1607) Which V-speed indicates the maximum flap extended speed?
   1--V_{le}
   2--V_{lof}
   3--V_{fc}
   4--V_{fe}

6. (FAA 1608) Which V-speed indicates the maximum landing gear extended speed?
   1--V_{le}
   2--V_{lo}
   3--V_{fe}
   4--V_{lof}

7. (FAA 1606) V_{no} is defined by Federal Aviation Regulations as the
   1--normal operating range.
   2--never-exceed speed.
   3--normal glide range.
   4--maximum structural cruising speed.

8. (FAA 1605) V_{s0} is defined by Federal Aviation Regulations as the
   1--stalling speed or minimum steady flight speed in the landing configuration.
   2--stalling speed or minimum steady flight speed in a specified configuration.
   3--takeoff safety speed.
   4--maximum speed in level flight with maximum continuous power.

9. (FAA 1614) Private pilots acting as pilot in command, or in any other capacity as a required pilot flight crewmember, must have in their personal possession while aboard the aircraft
1--a current logbook endorsement to show that a flight review has been satisfactorily accomplished.
2--the current and appropriate pilot and medical certificates.
3--a current endorsement on the pilot certificate to show that a flight review has been satisfactorily accomplished.
4--the pilot logbook to show recent experience requirements to serve as pilot in command have been met.

10. (FAA 1616) What document(s) must be in your personal possession while operating as pilot in command of an aircraft?
1--A certificate showing accomplishment of a current flight review.
2--A certificate showing accomplishment of a checkout in the aircraft and a current flight review.
3--A pilot logbook with endorsements showing accomplishment of a current flight review and recency of experience.
4--An appropriate pilot certificate and a current medical certificate or statement.

11. (FAA 1617) A Third-Class Medical Certificate is issued on August 10, this year. To exercise the privileges of a private pilot certificate, the medical certificate will be valid until midnight on
1--August 10, 3 yr. later.
2--August 10, 2 yr. later.
3--August 31, 3 yr. later.
4--August 31, 2 yr. later.

12. (FAA 1618) A Third-Class Medical Certificate is issued on May 3, this year. To exercise the privileges of a Private Pilot Certificate, the medical certificate will be valid until midnight on
1--May 31, 1 yr. later.
2--May 31, 2 yr. later.
3--May 3, 1 yr. later.
4--May 3, 2 yr. later.

13. (FAA 1619) For private pilot operations, a Second-Class Medical Certificate issued on July 15, this year, will expire at midnight on
1--July 15, 1 yr. later.   2--July 31, 1 yr. later.
3--July 15, 2 yr. later.   4--July 31, 2 yr. later.

14. (FAA 1620) For private pilot operations, a First-Class Medical Certificate issued on October 21, this year, will expire at midnight on
1--April 21, next year.   2--October 30, next year.
3--October 21, 2 yr. later.   4--October 30, 2 yr. later.

15. (FAA 1622) Which aircraft requires that the pilot in command hold a type rating in that aircraft?
1--A turbojet-powered airplane.
2--A large airship.
3--A multiengine helicopter.
4--A turboprop airplane.

16. (FAA 1623) Which is a high-performance airplane?
    1--An airplane with more than 180 hp., retractable landing gear, and
       flaps.
    2--An airplane with retractable landing gear, flaps, and a controllable
       propeller.
    3--An airplane that can seat six or more passengers.
    4--An airplane with a normal cruise speed in excess of 200 kts.

17. (FAA 1624) Before a person holding a Private or Commercial Pilot
    Certificate may act as pilot in command of a high-performance airplane,
    that person must have
    1--passed a flight test in that airplane from an FAA inspector.
    2--passed an oral examination given by any flight instructor.
    3--an endorsement in that person's logbook that he/she is competent to
       act as pilot in command.
    4--received flight instruction from an authorized flight instructor who
       then endorses that person's logbook.

18. (FAA 1625) To act as pilot in command of an airplane that has more than
    200 hp., a person is required to do which of the following, if no
    pilot-in-command time in a high-performance airplane was logged prior to
    November 1, 1973?
    1--Make three solo takeoffs and landings in such an airplane.
    2--Receive flight instruction in an airplane that has more than 200 hp.
    3--Pass a flight test in such an airplane.
    4--Hold a 200-horsepower class rating.

19. (FAA 1628) To act as pilot in command of an aircraft, one must show by
    logbook endorsement the satisfactory (1) accomplishment of a flight
    review, or (2) completion of a pilot proficiency check within the
    preceding
    1--6 calendar months.   2--12 calendar months.
    3--24 calendar months.   4--36 calendar months.

20. (FAA 1629) The takeoffs and landings required to meet recency of
    experience requirements for carrying passengers in a tailwheel airplane
    1--may be touch-and-go in the same class airplane.
    2--must be touch-and-go in any class airplane.
    3--may be full stop in any class airplane.
    4--must be full stop in the same class airplane.

21. (FAA 1631) To act as pilot in command of an aircraft with passengers
    aboard, the pilot must have made at least three takeoffs and three
    landings in an aircraft within the preceding
    1--120 days.   2--90 days.
    3--24 calendar months.   4--12 calendar months.

22. (FAA 1632) To act as pilot in command of an aircraft carrying
    passengers, the pilot must have made the required takeoffs and landings
    for currency in an aircraft of the same
    1--make but not class.
    2--class but not type.
    3--category and class but not type.
    4--category, class, and type.

23. (FAA 1626) If recency of experience requirements for night flight are
not met and official sunset is 1830, the latest time passengers may be
carried is
1--1730.
2--1830.
3--1900.
4--1930.

24. (FAA 1627) To meet the flight experience requirements to act as pilot
in command carrying passengers at night, a pilot must have made at least
three takeoffs and three landings to a full stop within the preceding 90
days
1--in the same category and class of aircraft to be used.
2--in the same class of aircraft to be used.
3--in any aircraft, but must be accompanied by a certificated flight
   instructor who meets the recent experience for night flight.
4--in the same type of aircraft to be used.

25. (FAA 1630) The three takeoffs and landings to a full stop that are
required to act as pilot in command at night must be done during the
time period from
1--sunset to sunrise.
2--30 min. after sunset to 30 min. before sunrise.
3--1 hr. after sunset to 1 hr. before sunrise.
4--the end of evening civil twilight to the beginning of morning civil
   twilight.

26. (FAA 1633) When a certified pilot changes permanent mailing address and
fails to notify the FAA Airmen Certification Branch of the new address,
the pilot is entitled to exercise the privileges of the pilot
certificate for a period of only
1--30 days after the date of the move.
2--60 days after the date of the move.
3--90 days after the date of the move.
4--120 days after the date of the move.

27. (FAA 1634) No person may act as pilot in command of any aircraft towing
a glider unless that person has within the preceding
1--90 days made three actual glider tows.
2--12 mo. made three flights in a powered glider.
3--12 mo. made three actual or simulated glider tows while accompanied
   by a qualified pilot.
4--90 days made three actual or simulated glider tows while accompanied
   by a qualified flight instructor.

28. (FAA 1635) A certificated private pilot may not act as pilot in command
of an aircraft towing a glider unless there is entered in the pilot's
logbook a minimum of
1--100 hr. of pilot flight time in powered aircraft.
2--200 hr. of pilot flight time in powered aircraft.
3--100 hr. of pilot flight time in any aircraft.
4--10 flights as pilot in command of a glider.

29. (FAA 1636) In regard to general privileges and limitations, a private pilot may
    1--not be paid in any manner for the operating expenses of a flight.
    2--act as pilot in command of an aircraft carrying a passenger for compensation if the flight is in connection with a business or employment.
    3--share the operating expenses of a flight with a passenger.
    4--charge a reasonable rate for acting as pilot in command.

30. (FAA 1637) According to regulations pertaining to general privileges and limitations, a private pilot may
    1--not be paid in any manner for the operating expenses of a flight.
    2--be paid for the operating expenses of a flight if at least three takeoffs and three landings were made by the pilot within the preceding 90 days.
    3--share the operating expenses of a flight with the passengers.
    4--charge a reasonable fee for acting as pilot in command.

31. (FAA 1638) What exception, if any, permits a private pilot to act as pilot in command of an aircraft carrying passengers who pay for the flight?
    1--There is no exception.
    2--If the passengers pay all the operating expenses only.
    3--If a donation is made to a charitable organization for the flight.
    4--If the pilot acts as second in command of an aircraft requiring more than one pilot.

32. (FAA 1641) The final authority as to the operation of an aircraft is the
    1--FAA.
    2--pilot in command.
    3--owner or operator of the aircraft.
    4--inspector who performs the periodic check.

33. (FAA 1639) If an in-flight emergency requires immediate action, a pilot in command may
    1--deviate from FAR's to the extent required to meet the emergency, but must submit a written report to the Administrator within 24 hours.
    2--not deviate from FAR's unless prior to the deviation approval is granted by the Administrator.
    3--deviate from FAR's to the extent required to meet that emergency.
    4--not deviate from FAR's unless permission is obtained from Air Traffic Control.

34. (FAA 1642) When must a pilot who deviates from a rule during an emergency send a written report of that deviation to the Administrator?
    1--24 hr.   2--7 days.
    3--10 days.   4--Upon request.

35. (FAA 1646) Prior to each flight, the pilot in command must
    1--check the personal logbook for appropriate recent experience.
    2--become familiar with all available information concerning that flight.
    3--calculate the weight and balance of the aircraft to determine if the CG is within limits.
    4--check ATC for the latest traffic advisories and any possible delays.

36. (FAA 1644) Preflight action, as required by regulations for all flights away from the vicinity of an airport, shall include a study of the weather, taking into consideration fuel requirements and
1--an operational check of the navigation radios.
2--the designation of an alternate airport.
3--the filing of a flight plan.
4--an alternate course of action if the flight cannot be completed as planned.

37. (FAA 1645) In addition to other preflight actions for a VFR flight away from the vicinity of the departure airport, regulations require the pilot in command to
1--file a flight plan.
2--check each fuel tank visually to ensure that it is full.
3--check the accuracy of the omninavigation equipment and the emergency locator transmitter.
4--determine runway lengths of airports of intended use and the aircraft's takeoff and landing distance data.

38. (FAA 1643) Which preflight action is required for every flight?
1--Check weather reports and forecasts.
2--Determine runway length at airports of intended use.
3--Determine alternatives if the flight cannot be completed.
4--Check for any known traffic delays.

39. (FAA 1647) While at their stations, each required flight crewmember aboard an aircraft shall keep seatbelts fastened during
1--takeoff and landing, and while en route.
2--takeoff and landing.
3--the en route phase of flight.
4--the entire flight including during taxi operations.

40. (FAA 1648) While at their stations, each required flight crewmember aboard an aircraft shall keep shoulder harnesses fastened during
1--takeoff and landing, and while enroute.
2--takeoff and landing.
3--the en route phase of flight.
4--the entire flight including during taxi operations.

41. (FAA 1649) A person may not act as a crewmember of a civil airplane if alcoholic beverages have been consumed by that person within the preceding
1--8 hr.
2--12 hr.
3--24 hr.
4--48 hr.

42. (FAA 1651) No person may act as crewmember of a civil aircraft while having
1--any detectable alcohol in the blood.
2--taken any drug.
3--.04 percent by weight or more alcohol in the blood.
4--used a prescription medication.

43. (FAA 1650) Under what condition, if any, may a pilot allow a person who is obviously under the influence of intoxicating liquors or drugs to be carried aboard an aircraft?
1--Under no condition.
2--Only if the person is a medical patient under proper care or in an emergency.
3--Only if the person does not have access to the cockpit or pilot's compartment.
4--Only if a second pilot is aboard.

44. (FAA 1652) Objects may be dropped from an aircraft.
1--only in an emergency
2--if precautions are taken to avoid injury or damage to persons or property on the surface.
3--if prior permission is received from the FAA.
4--if passengers are not carried.

45. (FAA 1657) What obligation does a pilot in command have concerning the use of seatbelts?
1--The pilot in command's seatbelt must be fastened during the entire flight.
2--The pilot in command must brief the passengers on the use of seatbelts and notify them to fasten the seatbelts during takeoff and landing.
3--The pilot in command must instruct the passengers to keep seatbelts fastened for the entire flight except for brief rest periods.
4--The pilot in command must instruct the passengers on the use of seatbelts, but does not have the authority to require their use, except during an emergency.

46. (FAA 1653) Other than sport parachutists seated on the floor, passengers must have seatbelts properly secured about them
1--except during takeoffs and landings.
2--during taxi operations.
3--unless they have not reached their second birthday.
4--from engine start to engine shutdown.

47. (FAA 1655) Regulations require that seatbelts in an airplane be properly secured about the
1--occupants during takeoffs and landings.
2--crewmembers only, during takeoffs and landings.
3--occupants during flight in moderate or severe turbulence only.
4--passengers and crewmembers during the entire flight.

48. (FAA 1656) Seatbelts are required to be properly secured about which persons in an aircraft and when?
1--Pilot crewmembers only, during takeoffs and landings.
2--Occupants, during takeoffs and landings.
3--Each person on board the glider during the entire flight.
4--Occupants, during flight in moderate or severe turbulence only.

49. (FAA 1659) A chair-type parachute must have been packed by a certificated and appropriately rated parachute rigger within the preceding
1--30 days.   2--60 days.
3--90 days.   4--120 days.

50. (FAA 1658) When must each occupant of an aircraft wear an approved parachute?
1--When an aircraft is being tested after major repair.
2--When operating an aircraft in acrobatic flight.
3--When a door is removed from the aircraft to facilitate parachute jumpers.
4--When an intentional bank that exceeds 60° is to be made.

51. (FAA 1667) What is the fuel requirement for flight under VFR during daylight hours in an airplane?
1--Full fuel tanks.
2--Enough to complete the flight at normal cruising flight with adverse wind conditions.
3--Enough to fly to the first point of intended landing and to fly after that for 30 min. at normal cruising speed.
4--Enough to fly to the first point of intended landing and to fly after that for 45 min. at normal cruising speed.

52. (FAA 1666) What is the fuel requirement for flight under VFR at night in an airplane?
1--Full fuel tanks.
2--Enough to complete the flight at normal cruising flight with adverse wind conditions.
3--Enough to fly to the first point of intended landing and to fly after that for 30 min. at normal cruising speed. ← DAY
4--Enough to fly to the first point of intended landing and to fly after that for 45 min. at normal cruising speed.

53. (FAA 1669) An operable transponder is required in which airspaces?
1--Group I TCA's, ADIZ, and Positive Control Areas.
2--Group I and Group II TCA's only.
3--High-density Airport Traffic Areas and Group I TCA's.
4--Group I TCA's, Group II TCA's, and Positive Control Areas.

54. (FAA 1670) In addition to a valid Airworthiness Certificate, what documents or records must be aboard an aircraft during flight?
1--Aircraft engine and airframe logbooks and owner's manual.
2--Radio station license and repair and alternation forms.
3--Operating limitations and Registration Certificate.
4--Radio station license and owner's manual.

55. (FAA 1671) Who is responsible for determining if an aircraft is in condition for safe flight?
1--A certificated aircraft mechanic.
2--A certificated aircraft maintenance inspector.
3--The pilot in command.
4--The owner or operator.

56. (FAA 1672) An aircraft's operating limitations may be found
1--on the Airworthiness Certificate.
2--in the airplane flight manual, approved manual material, markings, and placards, or any combination thereof.
3--only in the FAA-approved airplane flight manual.
4--only in the owner's handbook published by the aircraft manufacturer.

57. (FAA 1674) Federal Aviation Regulations require that when operating an aircraft at cabin pressure altitudes above 12,500 ft. MSL up to and including 14,000 ft. MSL, supplemental oxygen shall be used
1--the entire flight time at those altitudes.
2--the time in excess of 10 min. at those altitudes.
3--the entire climb phase at those altitudes, but is not required for the descent at those altitudes.
4--that time in excess of 30 min. at those altitudes.

58. (FAA 1673) Unless each occupant is provided with supplemental oxygen, no person may operate a civil aircraft of U.S. registry above a maximum cabin pressure altitude of
1--15,000 ft. MSL.
2--14,000 ft. MSL.
3--12,500 ft. MSL.
4--10,000 ft. MSL.

59. (FAA 1675) Which is normally prohibited when operating a restricted category civil aircraft?
1--Flight under instrument flight rules.
2--Flight over a densely populated area.
3--Flight within a control zone.
4--Flight within the Continental Control Area.

60. (FAA 1676) No person may operate an aircraft that has an experimental certificate.
1--in a control zone.
2--in a congested airway.
3--over a populated area.
4--over an airport with a control tower.

61. (FAA 1678) Batteries in an ELT must be replaced or recharged, if rechargeable,
1--after any inadvertent activation of the transmitter.
2--when the transmitter has been in use for more than 1 cumulative hour.
3--when the ELT can no longer be heard over the airplane's communication radio receiver.
4--after an airframe and powerplant mechanic completes an inspection.

62. (FAA 1677) When are non-rechargeable batteries of an ELT (emergency locator transmitter) required to be replaced?
1--Every 24 mo.
2--When 50 percent of their useful life expires.
3--At the time of each 100-hour or annual inspection.
4--Annually.

63. (FAA 1680) No person may operate an aircraft in formation flight
1--when carrying passengers.
2--over a densely populated area.
3--in a control zone under special VFR.
4--except by prior arrangement with the pilot in command of each aircraft.

64. (FAA 1683) What action is required when two aircraft of the same category converge at the same altitude, but not head-on?
1--The more maneuverable aircraft shall give way.
2--The faster aircraft shall give way.
3--The aircraft on the left shall give way.
4--Each aircraft shall give way to the right.

65. (FAA 1685) Which aircraft has the right-of-way over the other aircraft listed?
1--Glider.
2--Airship.
3--Aircraft refueling other aircraft.
4--Helicopter.

66. (FAA 1681) An airplane and an airship are converging. If the airship is left of the airplane's position, which aircraft has the right-of-way?
1--The pilot of the airplane should give way; the airship is to the left.
2--The airship has the right-of-way.
3--Each pilot should alter course to the right.
4--The airplane has the right-of-way.

67. (FAA 1684) Which aircraft has the right-of-way over the other aircraft listed?
1--Airship.
2--Aircraft towing other aircraft.
3--Gyroplane.
4--Airplane.

68. (FAA 1686) Which action should be taken, if during a night flight, a pilot observes a steady green light and a flashing red light on another aircraft at the same altitude?
1--Exercise extreme caution, the other aircraft is in distress.
2--Give way to the right, the other aircraft is approaching head-on.
3--Be alert, the other aircraft should give way.
4--Give way to the left, the other aircraft is passing to the right.

69. (FAA 1687) What action should be taken if a glider and an airplane approach each other at the same altitude and on a head-on collision course?
1--The airplane should give way because the glider has the right-of-way.
2--The airplane should give way because it is more maneuverable.
3--Both should give way to the right.
4--The glider should give way because it is more maneuverable.

70. (FAA 1682) When two or more aircraft are approaching an airport for the purpose of landing, the right-of-way belongs to the aircraft
1--that has the other to its right.
2--that is the least maneuverable.
3--that is either ahead of or to the other's right regardless of altitude.
4--at the lower altitude, but it shall not take advantage of this rule to cut in front of or to overtake another.

71. (FAA 1688) Which aircraft has the right-of-way over all other air traffic?
1--A balloon.
2--An aircraft in distress.
3--An aircraft on final approach to land.
4--An aircraft towing or refueling another aircraft.

72. (FAA 1690) Unless otherwise authorized or required by Air Traffic Control, what is the maximum indicated airspeed at which a person may operate an aircraft below 10,000 ft. MSL?
1--156 kts.
2--180 kts.
3--200 kts.
4--250 kts.

73. (FAA 1691) Unless otherwise authorized or required by Air Traffic Control, the maximum indicated airspeed at which a reciprocating engine-equipped aircraft should be flown within an Airport Traffic Area is
1--156 kts.
2--180 kts.
3--200 kts.
4--230 kts.

74. (FAA 1689) When flying beneath the lateral limits of a Terminal Control Area, the maximum speed authorized is
1--250 kts.
2--200 kts.
3--180 kts.
4--156 kts.

75. (FAA 1692) The maximum indicated airspeed for a turbine-powered aircraft within an Airport Traffic Area within a TCA is
1--156 kts.
2--180 kts.
3--200 kts.
4--250 kts.

76. (FAA 1693) In which controlled airspace is acrobatic flight prohibited?
1--All controlled airspace.
2--Control zones and Federal airways.
3--Control zones, Federal airways, and control areas.
4--Control zones, Federal airways, control areas, and Traffic Control Areas.

77. (FAA 1694) No person may operate an aircraft in acrobatic flight
1--in a control area.
2--over an open-air assembly of persons.
3--in an Airport Traffic Area.
4--over a populated area.

78. (FAA 1695) No person may operate an aircraft in acrobatic flight when the flight visibility is less than
1--3 mi.   2--5 mi.
3--7 mi.   4--10 mi.

79. (FAA 1696) What is the lowest altitude permitted for acrobatic flight?
    1--1,000 ft. AGL.
    2--1,500 ft. AGL.
    3--1,000 ft. above the highest obstacle within 5 mi.
    4--1,500 ft. above the highest obstacle within 5 mi.

80. (FAA 1697) When an aircraft is being operated at night, except in
    Alaska, it must display lighted position lights during the period from
    1--1 hr. before sunset to 1 hr. after sunrise.
    2--30 min. after sunset to 30 min. after sunrise.
    3--30 min. before sunset to 30 min. after sunrise.
    4--sunset to sunrise.

81. (FAA 1698) Except in Alaska, during what time period should lighted
    position lights be displayed on an aircraft?
    1--30 min. after sunset to 30 min. before sunrise.
    2--End of evening civil twilight to be the beginning of morning civil
       twilight.
    3--1 hr. after sunset to 1 hr. before sunrise.
    4--Sunset to sunrise.

82. (FAA 1699) What action should be taken if a pilot receives a clearance
    that will cause a deviation from a rule?
    1--Accept the clearance, because the pilot is not responsible for the
       deviation.
    2--Accept the clearance and advise Air Traffic Control when deviation
       occurs.
    3--Refuse the clearance as stated and request that it be amended.
    4--Accept the clearance and advise Air Traffic Control that you believe
       a rule deviation will occur.

83. (FAA 1700) When may Air Traffic Control request a detailed report of an
    emergency even though a rule has not been violated?
    1--When priority has been given.
    2--Anytime an emergency occurs.
    3--When the emergency occurs in controlled airspace.
    4--Only when an accident results from the emergency.

84. (FAA 1701) What action, if any, is appropriate if the pilot deviates
    from an Air Traffic Control instruction during an emergency and is given
    priority?
    1--Take no special action since you are pilot in command.
    2--If requested, file a detailed report within 48 hr. to the chief of
       the Air Traffic Control facility.
    3--File a report to the FAA Administrator as soon as possible.
    4--File a report to the chief of that Air Traffic Control facility
       within 24 hr.

85. (FAA 1702) An Air Traffic Control clearance provides
    1--authorization for flight in uncontrolled airspace.
    2--priority over all other traffic.
    3--adequate separation from all traffic.
    4--authorization to proceed under specified traffic conditions in
       controlled airspace.

86. (FAA 1703) An alternating red and green light signal directed from the control tower to your aircraft in flight is a signal to
1--hold your position.
2--exercise extreme caution.
3--not land; the airport is unsafe.
4--return to the airport immediately.

87. (FAA 1704) While on the final approach for landing, an alternating green and red light followed by a flashing red light is received from the control tower. Under these circumstances, the pilot should
1--land and clear the runway in use as safely and quickly as possible.
2--discontinue the approach, fly the same traffic pattern and approach again, and land.
3--abandon the approach, realizing the airport is unsafe for landing.
4--abandon the approach, circle the airport to the right, and expect a flashing white light when the airport is safe for landing.

88. (FAA 1705) A steady green Air Traffic Control light signal directed to an aircraft in flight is a signal that the pilot
1--is cleared to land.
2--should give way to other aircraft and continue circling.
3--should return for landing.
4--should exercise extreme caution.

89. (FAA 1706) A flashing white light signal from the control tower to an aircraft taxiing is an indication
1--to taxi at a faster speed.
2--to taxi only on taxiways and not cross runways.
3--to return to the starting point on the airport.
4--that instrument conditions exist.

90. (FAA 1707) If the control tower uses a light signal to direct a pilot to give way to other aircraft and continue circling, the light will be
1--flashing red.
2--steady red.
3--alternating red and green.
4--flashing green.

91. (FAA 1708) Which light signal from a control tower clears a pilot to taxi?
1--Flashing green.
2--Steady green.
3--Flashing white.
4--Steady red.

92. (FAA 1710) Except when necessary for takeoff or landing, what is the minimum safe altitude for a pilot to operate an aircraft anywhere?
1--An altitude allowing, if a power unit fails, an emergency landing without undue hazard to persons or property on the surface.
2--An altitude of 500 ft. above the surface and no closer than 500 ft. to any person, vessel, vehicle, or structure.
3--An altitude of 500 ft. above the highest obstacle within a horizontal radius of 1,000 ft.
4--An altitude of 1,000 ft. above the highest obstacle within a horizontal radius of 2,000 ft.

93. (FAA 1711) Except when necessary for takeoff or landing, what is the
    minimum safe altitude required for a pilot to operate an aircraft over
    congested areas?
    1--An altitude allowing, if a power unit fails, an emergency landing
        without undue hazard to persons or property on the surface.
    2--An altitude of 1,000 ft. above any person, vessel, vehicle, or
        structure.
    3--An altitude of 500 ft. above the highest obstacle within a horizontal
        radius of 1,000 ft.
    4--An altitude of 1,000 ft. above the highest obstacle within a
        horizontal radius of 2,000 ft.

94. (FAA 1712) Except when necessary for takeoff or landing, what is the
    minimum safe altitude for a pilot to operate an aircraft over other than
    a congested area?
    1--An altitude allowing, if a power unit fails, an emergency landing
        without undue hazard to persons or property on the surface.
    2--An altitude of 500 ft. AGL except over open water or a sparsely
        populated area which requires 500 ft. from any person, vessel,
        vehicle, or structure.
    3--An altitude of 500 ft. above the highest obstacle within a horizontal
        radius of 1,000 ft.
    4--An altitude of 1,000 ft. above the highest obstacle within a
        horizontal radius of 2,000 ft.

95. (FAA 1709) Except when necessary for takeoff or landing, an aircraft
    may not be operated closer than what distance from any person, vehicle,
    or structure?
    1--600 ft.
    2--500 ft.
    3--200 ft.
    4--150 ft.

96. (FAA 1715) Prior to takeoff, the altimeter should be set to
    1--the current local altimeter setting, if available, or the departure
        airport elevation.
    2--the corrected density altitude of the departure airport.
    3--the corrected pressure altitude for the departure airport.
    4--29.92" Hg.

97. (FAA 1713) If an altimeter setting is not available before flight, to
    which altitude or setting should the pilot adjust the altimeter?
    1--To 29.92" Hg for flight below 18,000 ft. MSL.
    2--The elevation of the nearest airport corrected to mean sea level.
    3--The elevation of the departure area.
    4--Pressure altitude corrected for nonstandard temperature.

98. (FAA 1714) When is it first required that the altimeter be set to
    29.92" Hg. when climbing to cruising altitude or flight level?
    1--12,500 ft. MSL.
    2--14,500 ft. MSL.
    3--18,000 ft. MSL.
    4--24,000 ft. MSL.

99. (FAA 1716) What is the purpose of an Airport Traffic Area?
    1--To provide for the control of aircraft landing and taking off from
       an airport with an operating control tower.
    2--To provide for the control of all aircraft operating in the vicinity
       of an airport with an operating control tower.
    3--To provide for the control of air traffic within a control zone that
       has an operating control tower.
    4--To restrict aircraft without radios from operating in the vicinity
       of an airport with an operating control tower.

100. (FAA 1718) When is an Airport Traffic Area in effect?
    1--When the weather minimums are below basic VFR.
    2--When the associated control tower is in operation.
    3--When the associated FSS is in operation.
    4--From sunrise to sunset.

101. (FAA 1717) Unless otherwise authorized, two-way radio communications
    with Air Traffic Control are required for landing and takeoffs
    1--within control zones regardless of the weather conditions.
    2--at all tower controlled airports regardless of the weather
       conditions.
    3--at all tower controlled airports only when weather conditions are
       less than VFR.
    4--at tower controlled airports within control zones only when weather
       conditions are less than VFR.

102. (FAA 1721) When operating to an airport with an operating control
    tower, each pilot of an airplane approaching to land on a runway served
    by a visual approach slope indicator shall
    1--fly any safe final approach pattern.
    2--maintain a 3° glide to the runway.
    3--maintain an altitude at or above the glide slope.
    4--stay high until the runway can be reached in a power-off landing.

103. (FAA 1720) Which is the correct traffic pattern departure procedure to
    use at a noncontrolled airport?
    1--Depart in any direction consistent with safety, after crossing the
       airport boundary.
    2--Make all turns to the left.
    3--Comply with any FAA traffic pattern established for the airport.
    4--Depart as prearranged with other pilots using the airport.

104. (FAA 1722) Regardless of weather conditions, Air Traffic Control
    authorization is required prior to operating an aircraft within a
    1--control zone.
    2--Terminal Radar Service Area.
    3--Terminal Control Area.
    4--Transition Area.

105. (FAA 1724) What minimum pilot certification is required for operations
    through a Group I Terminal Control Area?
    1--Student Pilot Certificate with appropriate logbook endorsement.
    2--Private Pilot Certificate.
    3--Private Pilot Certificate with instrument rating.
    4--Commercial Pilot Certificate.

106. (FAA 1723) An operable 4096 code transponder and Mode C encoding
     altimeter are required in
     1--Group I and Group II Terminal Control Areas.
     2--an Airport Radar Service Area.
     3--a Group I Terminal Control Area.
     4--a Terminal Radar Service Area.

107. (FAA 1725) In which type of airspace are VFR flights prohibited?
     1--Terminal Control Area.
     2--Continental Control Area.
     3--Control zone.
     4--Positive Control Area.

108. (FAA 1728) VFR flight above 1,200 ft. AGL and below 10,000 ft. MSL
     requires a minimum visibility and vertical cloud clearance of
     1--3 SM., and 500 ft. below or 1,000 ft. above the clouds in controlled
        airspace.
     2--5 SM., and 1,000 ft. below or 1,000 ft. above the clouds at all
        altitudes.
     3--5 SM., and 1,000 ft. below or 1,000 ft. above the clouds only in the
        Continental Control Area.
     4--3 SM., and 1,000 ft. below or 2,000 ft. above the clouds at all
        altitudes within and outside of controlled airspace.

109. (FAA 1735) During operations within controlled airspace at altitudes of
     more than 1,200 ft. AGL, but less than 10,000 ft. MSL, the minimum
     distance above clouds requirement for VFR flight is
     1--500 ft.
     2--1,000 ft.
     3--1,500 ft.
     4--2,000 ft.

110. (FAA 1739) During operations within controlled airspace at altitudes of
     less than 1,200 ft. AGL, the minimum horizontal distance from clouds
     requirement for VFR flight is
     1--500 ft.   2--1,000 ft.
     3--1,500 ft.   4--2,000 ft.

111. (FAA 1727) During operations outside controlled airspace at altitudes
     of more than 1,200 ft. AGL, but less than 10,000 ft. MSL, the minimum
     flight visibility for VFR flight is
     1--1 SM.
     2--3 SM.
     3--5 SM.
     4--not specified by regulations.

112. (FAA 1734) What minimum visibility and clearance from clouds are
     required for VFR operations in uncontrolled airspace at 700 ft. AGL or
     below during daylight hours?
     1--1 mi. visibility and clear of clouds.
     2--3 mi. visibility and clear of clouds.
     3--1 mi. visibility, 500 ft. below, 1,000 ft. above, and 2,000 ft.
        horizontal clearance from clouds.
     4--3 mi. visibility, 500 ft. above, 1,000 ft. below, and 2,000 ft.
        horizontal clearance from clouds.

113. (FAA 1737) Outside controlled airspace, the minimum flight visibility requirement for VFR flight above 1,200 ft. AGL and below 10,000 ft. MSL during daylight hours is
1--1 SM.
2--3 SM.
3--5 SM.
4--7 SM.

114. (FAA 1738) During operations outside controlled airspace at altitudes of more than 1,200 ft. AGL, but less than 10,000 ft. MSL, the minimum distance below clouds requirement for VFR flight is
1--500 ft.
2--1,000 ft.
3--1,500 ft.
4--2,000 ft.

115. (FAA 1726) The minimum flight visibility required for VFR flights above 10,000 ft. MSL and more than 1,200 ft. AGL in controlled airspace is
1--1 SM.
2--3 SM. <10,000'
3--5 SM.
4--not specified by regulation.

116. (FAA 1729) For VFR flight operations above 10,000 ft. MSL and more than 1,200 ft. AGL outside of controlled airspace, the minimum horizontal distance from clouds required is
1--1,000 ft.
2--2,000 ft.
3--1 mi.
4--5 mi.

117. (FAA 1732) The minimum distance from clouds required for VFR operations on an airway below 10,000 ft. is
1--remain clear of clouds.
2--500 ft. below, 1,000 ft. above, and 2,000 ft. horizontally.
3--500 ft. above, 1,000 ft. below, and 2,000 ft. horizontally.
4--1,000 ft. above, 1,000 ft. below, and 1 mi. horizontally.

118. (FAA 1733) What minimum flight visibility is required for VFR flight operations on an airway below 10,000 ft.?
1--1 SM.
2--3 SM.
3--4 SM.
4--5 SM.

119. (FAA 1736) During operations at altitudes of more than 1,200 ft. AGL and at or above 10,000 ft. MSL, the minimum distance above clouds requirement for VFR flight is
1--500 ft.
2--1,000 ft.
3--1,500 ft.
4--2,000 ft.

120. (FAA 1730) No person may take off or land an aircraft at any airport in a control zone under basic VFR unless the
1--flight visibility at that airport is at least 1 SM.
2--ground visibility at that airport is at least 1 SM.
3--flight visibility at that airport is at least 3 SM.
4--ground visibility at that airport is at least 3 SM.

121. (FAA 1731) The basic VFR weather minimums for operating an aircraft beneath the ceiling within a control zone are
1--500-foot ceiling and 1 SM. visibility.
2--1,000-foot ceiling and 3 SM. visibility.
3--clear of clouds and 2 SM. visibility.
4--2,000-foot ceiling and 1 SM. visibility.

122. (FAA 1740) Except for a helicopter, a special VFR clearance authorizes the pilot of an aircraft to operate VFR while within a control zone
1--when the ceiling is less than 1,000 ft. and visibility less than 1 SM., if the aircraft does not exceed maneuvering speed.
2--if clear of clouds and the flight visibility is at least 1 SM.
3--with no minimum visibility requirements if clear of the clouds.
4--at or below cloud base with a flight visibility of 1 SM. or less, provided the aircraft remains below 1,000 ft. above the surface.

123. (FAA 1743) What is the minimum weather condition required for airplanes operating under special VFR in a control zone?
1--1 SM. flight visibility.
2--1 SM. flight visibility and 1,000-foot ceiling.
3--3 SM. flight visibility and 1,000-foot ceiling.
4--3 SM. flight visibility.

124. (FAA 1741) No person may operate an airplane within a control zone at night under special VFR unless
1--the flight can be conducted 500 ft. below the clouds.
2--an instructor is aboard.
3--the airplane is equipped for instrument flight.
4--the flight visibility is at least 3 SM.

125. (FAA 1742) What are the minimum requirements for airplane operations under special VFR in a control zone at night?
1--The minimum visibility is 3 SM., and the airplane must operate clear of clouds.
2--The airplane must be under radar surveillance at all times while in the control zone.
3--The airplane must be equipped for IFR and with an altitude reporting transponder.
4--The pilot must be instrument rated, and the airplane must be IFR equipped.

126. (FAA 1745) Which VFR cruising altitude is acceptable for a flight on a Victor airway with a magnetic course of 175°? The terrain is less than 1,000 ft.
1--4,000 ft.
2--4,500 ft.
3--5,000 ft.
4--5,500 ft.

127. (FAA 1746) Which VFR cruising altitude is acceptable for a flight on a Victor airway with a magnetic course of 185°? The terrain is less than 1,000 ft.
1--4,000 ft.   2--4,500 ft.
3--5,000 ft.   4--5,500 ft.

128. (FAA 1747) Each person operating an aircraft under VFR in level cruising flight at an altitude of more than 3,000 ft. above the surface, and below 18,000 ft. MSL, shall maintain an odd-thousand plus 500-foot altitude while on a
1--magnetic heading of 180° through 359°.
2--magnetic course of 0° through 179°.
3--true course of 180° through 359°.
4--true heading of 0° through 179°.

129. (FAA 1748) The responsibility for ensuring that an aircraft is maintained in an airworthy condition is primarily that of the
1--pilot in command of the aircraft.
2--owner or operator of the aircraft.
3--maintenance shop.
4--certified mechanic who signs the aircraft maintenance records.

130. (FAA 1749) An Airworthiness Certificate remains valid
1--until ownership is transferred.
2--provided the aircraft has not had major damage.
3--until surrendered, suspended, or revoked.
4--provided the aircraft is maintained and operated according to FAR's.

131. (FAA 1755) How long does the Airworthiness Certificate of an aircraft remain valid?
1--As long as the aircraft has a current Registration Certificate.
2--Indefinitely, unless the aircraft suffers major damage.
3--As long as the aircraft is maintained and operated as required by FAR's.
4--Indefinitely, unless the prescribed operating limitations are exceeded.

132. (FAA 1750) If an alteration or repair substantially affects an aircraft's operation in flight, that aircraft must be test flown by an appropriately-rated pilot and approved for return to service prior to being operated
1--by any private pilot.
2--with passengers aboard.
3--for compensation or hire.
4--away from the vicinity of the airport.

133. (FAA 1751) Before passengers can be carried in an aircraft that has been altered in a manner that may have appreciably changed its flight characteristics, it must be flight tested by an appropriately-rated pilot with at least a
1--Commercial Pilot Certificate and an instrument rating.
2--Private Pilot Certificate.
3--Commercial Pilot Certificate and a mechanic's certificate.
4--Commercial Pilot Certificate.

134. (FAA 1752) Completion of an annual inspection and the return of the aircraft to service should always be indicated by
1--the relicensing date on the Registration Certificate.
2--an appropriate notation in the aircraft maintenance records.
3--an inspection sticker placed on the instrument panel that lists the annual inspection completion date.
4--the issuance date of the Airworthiness Certificate.

135. (FAA 1753) An aircraft's last annual inspection was performed on July 12, this year. The next annual inspection will be due no later than
1--July 31, next year.
2--July 13, next year.
3--100 flight hours following the last annual inspection.
4--12 calendar months after the date shown on the Airworthiness Certificate.

136. (FAA 1754) To determine the expiration date of the last annual aircraft inspection, a person should refer to the
1--Airworthiness Certificate.
2--Registration Certificate.
3--aircraft maintenance records.
4--owner/operator manual.

137. (FAA 1756) What aircraft inspections are required for a rental aircraft also used for flight instruction?
1--Annual and 100-hour inspections.
2--Periodic and annual inspections of aircraft maintenance records.
3--100- and 50-hour inspections.
4--Annual and 50-hour inspections.

138. (FAA 1757) An aircraft had a 100-hour inspection when the tachometer read 1,259.6. When is the next 100-hour inspection due?
1--1,269.6 hr.   2--1,309.6 hr.
3--1,359.6 hr.   4--1,409.6 hr.

139. (FAA 1758) A 100-hour inspection was due at 3,302.5 hr. on the tachometer. The 100-hour inspection was actually done at 3,309.5 hr. When is the next 100-hour inspection due?
1--3,409.5 hr.   2--3,402.5 hr.
3--3,809.5 hr.   4--3,802.5 hr.

140. (FAA 1759) No person may use an ATC transponder unless it has been tested and inspected within the preceding
1--90 days.
2--6 calendar months.
3--12 calendar months.
4--24 calendar months.

141. (FAA 1760) Which record or documents shall the owner or operator of an aircraft keep to show compliance with an applicable Airworthiness Directive?
1--The aircraft maintenance records.
2--Airworthiness Certificate and owner's handbook.
3--Airworthiness and Registration Certificates.
4--Aircraft flight manual and owner's handbook.

142. (FAA 1763) Preventative maintenance has been performed on an aircraft. What paper work is required?
1--Record keeping is only required after major or minor repairs.
2--A full, detailed description of the work done must be entered in the airframe logbook.
3--The date the work was completed and the name of the person who did the work must be entered in the pilot's logbook.
4--The name of the person performing the work and a description of the work must be entered in the aircraft maintenance records.

143. (FAA 1761) Which operation would be described as preventative maintenance?
1--Changes in the aircraft empty weight.
2--Alteration of main seat support brackets.
3--Engine adjustments to allow auto gas to be used.
4--Servicing landing gear wheel bearings.

144. (FAA 1762) Which operation would be described as preventative maintenance?
1--Removing and installing glider wings.
2--Repair of landing gear brace struts.
3--Refinishing decorative coating of fuselage.
4--Repair of portions of skin sheets by making additional seams.

145. (FAA 1589) If an aircraft is involved in an accident which resulted in substantial damage to the aircraft, the nearest NTSB field office should be notified
1--immediately.
2--within 5 days.
3--within 7 days.
4--within 10 days.

146. (FAA 1590) Which would necessitate an immediate notification to the nearest NTSB field office?
1--An in-flight generator/alternator failure.
2--An in-flight fire.
3--An in-flight loss of VOR receiver capability.
4--Ground damage to the rotor or propeller blades.

147. (FAA 1591) Which incidents would require that an immediate notification be made to the nearest NTSB field office?
1--An overdue aircraft that is believed to be involved in an accident.
2--An in-flight radio (communication) failure.
3--An in-flight generator or alternator failure.
4--In-flight hail damage.

148. (FAA 1592) Which incident requires an immediate notification to the nearest NTSB field office?
1--A forced landing due to engine failure.
2--Landing gear damage, due to a hard landing.
3--Inability of any required crewmember to perform normal flight duties due to in-flight injury or illness.
4--Substantial aircraft ground fire with no intention of flight.

149. (FAA 1593) An aircraft is involved in an accident that results in substantial damage to the aircraft, but no injuries to the occupants. When must the pilot or operator of the aircraft notify the nearest NTSB field office of the occurrence?
1--Within 1 week.
2--Immediately.
3--Within 48 hr.
4--Within 10 days.

150. (FAA 1596) Prior to the time the NTSB takes custody of an aircraft wreckage, mail, or cargo, those items may
1--be moved by any law enforcement officer for any reason.
2--be moved to protect the wreckage from further damage.
3--not be moved under any circumstance.
4--not be moved except by the pilot in command.

151. (FAA 1594) The operator of an aircraft that has been involved in an accident is required to file an accident report within how many days?
1--3.
2--5.
3--7.
4--10.

152. (FAA 1595) The operator of an aircraft that has been involved in an incident is required to submit a report to the nearest field office of the NTSB
1--within 3 days.
2--within 10 days.
3--within 7 days.
4--only if requested to do so.

ANSWERS AND EXPLANATIONS

Discussion Questions and Review Exercises

1. F--It extends up to but does not include 3,000 feet AGL and for a 5-mile radius. See FAR 1.1.

2. T--See FAR 1.1.

3. T--See FAR 1.1.

4. T--See FAR 1.1.

5. F--This is called calibrated airspeed. See FAR 1.1.

6. F--Flights are prohibited in prohibited areas. See FAR 1.1.

7.

a. Above ground level.

b. Area Radar Service Area.

c. Air traffic control.

d. Calibrated airspeed.

e. Indicated airspeed.

f. Instrument Flight Rules.

g. Mean sea level.

h. True airspeed.

i. Best angle-of-climb airspeed.

j. Best rate-of-climb airspeed.

k. Visual Flight Rules.

8. T--See FAR 61.3.

9. F--They are good for 120 days. See FAR 61.17.

10. F--Student pilot certificates expire at the end of 24 mo. after they were issued. See FAR 61.17.

11. F--Student pilots must log flight time. See FAR 61.51.

12. F--BFRs are required every two years. See FAR 61.57.

13. F--You must have made three takeoffs and landings in the past 90 days in the same category and class. See FAR 61.57.

14. F--Student pilots cannot carry passengers. See FAR 61.89.

15. F--Obtaining weather information is mandatory on all IFR flight and for all flights not in the vicinity of the airport. See FAR 91.5.

16. T--See FAR 91.11.

17. F--It is the responsibility of the pilot-in-command to inform passengers how to fasten and unfasten their seat belts. See FAR 91.14.

18. F--The minimum fuel reserve for a daytime VFR flight is 30 min. The minimum for a night flight is 45 min. See FAR 91.22.

19. T--See FAR 91.21.

20. See FAR 91.31.

21. See FAR 91.57.

a. The aircraft on the right has the right-of-way.

b. Both aircraft must alter course to the right.

c. The aircraft being overtaken has the right-of-way.

d. The aircraft on final approach has the right-of-way.

22. See FAR 91.32.

23. T--See FAR 91.67.

24. F--The speed limit is 250 kts. (288 MPH). See FAR 91.70.

25. F--Supplemental oxygen is required of all crewmembers for any flight over 30 min. from 12,500 feet to 14,000 feet MSL; above 14,000 feet MSL, it is required for crewmembers at all times; and above 15,000 feet MSL, it is required for all occupants. See FAR 91.32.

26. F--Acrobatic flight is prohibited over congested areas, below 1,500 feet AGL, and when visibility is less than 3 miles. See FAR 91.71.

27. F--They are required for any night operation, on the ground or in the air. See FAR 91.73.

28. T--See FAR 91.75.

29. T--See FAR 91.79.

30. F--Over sparsely populated areas, you must stay at least 500 feet away from people or structures. See FAR 91.79.

31. F--Flight plans for VFR flights are optional, but highly recommended. See FAR 91.83.

32. See FAR 91.79

33. F--The station need only be within 100 miles, if one exists. See FAR 91.81.

34. F--Flight plans for VFR flights are optional, but highly recommended. See FAR 91.83.

35. Taxi to the approach end of the active runway. Clearance to "taxi to" authorizes you to cross the other runway. See FAR 91.87.

36. T--See FAR 91.89.

37. F--A private pilot's certificate is the minimum certificate required to land at or take off from an airport within the horizontal and vertical limits of a Group I TCA. A two-way radio, operable VOR or TACAN, Mode 3/A 4096 code transponder, and a Mode C encoding altimeter are required to operate within a Group I TCA. No instrument instruction is required. See FAR 91.90.

38. See FAR 91.105.

39. F--Special VFR minimums are clear of clouds and visibility of 1 mile. An instrument rating and an instrument-equipped aircraft is required for special VFR at night. See FAR 91.107.

40.   T--See FAR 61.118

41.   F--Two-way radio communication is required to enter an ARSA.

42.   F--Departure from a satellite airport requires conformity to FAA approved traffic patterns. Two-way radio communication with ATC must be initiated as soon as practicable.

43.   See FAR 91.88.

FAA Exam Questions

1. 1--FAR 1.

2. 4--FAR 1.

3. 1--FAR 1.

4. 3--FAR 1.

5. 4--FAR 1.

6. 1--FAR 1.

7. 4--FAR 1.

8. 1--FAR 1.

9. 2--FAR 61.3(a) and (c).

10. 4--FAR 61.3(a) and (c).

11. 4--FAR 61.23(c). A 3rd class medical certificate expires at the last day of the 24th month after the date of examination.

12. 2--FAR 61.23(c). A 3rd class medical certificate expires at the last day of the 24th month after the date of examination.

13. 4--FAR 61.23(b). A 2nd class medical certificate expires at the end of the 12th month after the date of the exam for commercial pilots, BUT on the last day of the 24th for private and student pilots.

14. 4--FAR 61.23(a). A 1st class medical certificate expires at the end of the 6th month for airline transport pilots, the 12th month for commercial, and the 24th month for private and student pilots.

15. 1--FAR 61.31(a). A type rating is required to be PIC in any turbojet and in large aircraft (over 12,500 lb.), lighter-than-air excepted.

16. 2--FAR 61.31(e). A high performance airplane is one with > 200 HP or one with retractable landing gear, flaps and a controllable prop.

17. 4--FAR 61.31(e).

18. 2--FAR 61.31(e).

19. 3--FAR 61.57(a).

20. 4--FAR 61.57(c). 3 takeoffs and 3 full stop landings within the preceding 90 days in a tailwheel airplane.

21. 2--FAR 61.57(c). 3 takeoffs and 3 landings in the preceding 90 days.

22. 3--FAR 61.57(c). They must be in the same category and class but not necessarily the same type (Cessna 150, Piper Archer, etc.).

23. 4--FAR 61.57(d). Night = 1 hour after sunset to 1 hour before sunrise.

24. 1--FAR 61.57(d). Same class and category are required.

25. 3--FAR 61.57(d). Night = 1 hour after sunset to 1 hour before sunrise.

26. 1--FAR 61.60.

27. 3--FAR 61.69.

28. 1--FAR 61.69.

29. 3--FAR 61.118(b).

30. 3--FAR 61.118(b).

31. 3--FAR 61.118(d).

32. 2--FAR 91.3(a).

33. 3--FAR 91.3(b) and (c). The PIC may deviate from the FARs in an emergency. A written report is not required unless requested.

34. 4--FAR 91.3(c). A report is required only if requested.

35. 2--FAR 91.5. The PIC must be familiar with all available information.

36. 4--FAR 91.5(a).

37. 4--FAR 91.5(a).

38. 2--FAR 91.5(b).

39. 1--FAR 91.7(a). Crewmembers MUST keep seatbelts fastened enroute, passengers MUST use them only for takeoff and landings.

40. 2--FAR 91.7(b) Shoulder harnesses must be secured only for takeoffs and landings.

41. 1--FAR 91.11(a) (1). Eight hours bottle to throttle.

42. 3--FAR 91.4(a) (1). The limits are .04 percent.

43. 2--FAR 91.11(b). It is not legal to carry persons under the influence of alcohol or drugs, unless under medical care.

44. 2--FAR 91.13.

45. 2--FAR 91.14(a)(1)(2).

46. 3--FAR 91.14(a)(3). Only during takeoffs and landings except for children less than 2 who are held by an adult.

47. 1--FAR 91.14(a)(3). Only during takeoffs and landings.

48. 2--FAR 91.14(a)(3). Only during takeoffs and landings.

49. 4--FAR 91.15(a).

50. 4--FAR 91.15(c). Parachutes are required for INTENTIONAL banks > 60°.

51. 3--FAR 91.22(a)(1).

52. 4--FAR 91.22(a)(2).

53. 4--FAR 91.24(b). Group I and II TCAs and in controlled airspace above 12,500 ft. MSL in the contiguous states. The PCA is controlled airspace.

54. 3--FAR 91.27 and 91.31. ARROW: A-Airworthiness certificate, R-Registration, R-Radio station license, O-Operating limitations, and W-Weight and balance data.

55. 3--FAR 91.29(b)

56. 2--FAR 91.31(b) The limitations must be available to the PIC.

57. 4--FAR 91.32(a). From 12,500-14,000 ft. MSL, no oxygen required for flights less than 30 min. (e.g., to cross a mountain range).

58. 1--FAR 91.32(a). Above 15,000 ft. cabin altitude - flight crew members must use it; passengers must be provided, but its use is optional.

59. 2--FAR 91.39(d)(1).

60. 2--FAR 91.39(d)(2).

61. 2--FAR 91.52(b)(1).

62. 2--FAR 91.52(b)(2).

63. 4--FAR 91.65(b).

64. 3--FAR 91.67(c). The aircraft on the other's right has the right of way.

65. 1--FAR 91.67(c)(2).

66. 2--FAR 91.67(c)(3).

67. 2--FAR 91.67(c)(3).

68. 3--FAR 91.67(c). You are seeing the right wing tip light and anti-collision light. You are on the right and have the right of way.

69. 3--FAR 91.67(d).

70. 4--FAR 91.67(f).

71. 2--FAR 91.67(b).

72. 4--FAR 91.70(a).

73. 1--FAR 91.70(b)(1).

74. 2--FAR 91.70(c).

75. 4--FAR 91.70.

76. 2--FAR 91.71.

77. 2--FAR 91.71.

78. 1--FAR 91.71.

79. 2--FAR 91.71.

80. 4--FAR 91.73.

81. 4--FAR 91.73.

82. 3--FAR 91.75. ATC clearance is not authorization to deviate from a rule. Advise ATC that it would violate a rule (e.g, a VFR flight is vectored into a cloud).

83. 1--FAR 91.75(d).

84. 2--FAR 91.75(c) and (d). If you deviate from a clearance in an emergency, you must notify ATC (not file a report) as soon as possible. If priority was given, you may be requested to file a detailed report within 48 hours.

85. 4--FAR 91.75, AIM. A clearance is an authorization to proceed, but it does not give priority nor ensure separation from nonparticipating traffic.

86. 2--FAR 91.77.

87. 3--FAR 91.77.

88. 1--FAR 91.77.

89. 3--FAR 91.77.

90. 2--FAR 91.77.

91. 1--FAR 91.77.

92. 1--FAR 91.79(a).

93. 4--FAR 91.79(b).

94. 2--FAR 91.79(c).

95. 2--FAR 91.79(c).

96. 1--FAR 91.81(a).

97. 3--FAR 91.81(a)(1).

98. 3--FAR 91.81(b).

99. 1--FAR 91.87(a). The term "vicinity" in answer 2 is too broad; the aircraft could be above the ATA. Control zones may exist where there is not an ATA.

100. 2--FAR 91.87.

101. 2--FAR 91.87(b).

102. 3--FAR 91.87(d)(3).

103. 3--FAR 91.89.

104. 3--FAR 91.90(a)(1).

105. 1--FAR 91.90(a)(2). While you must have at least a Private Pilot Certificate to TAKEOFF and LAND at an airport within a TCA any certificated pilot may fly THROUGH a Group I TCA.

106. 1--FAR 91.90(a)(3) and (b).

107. 4--91.97(a).

108. 1--FAR 91.105(a).

109. 2--FAR 91.105(a).

110. 4--FAR 91.105(a).

111. 1--FAR 91.105(a).

112. 1--FAR 91.105(a).

113. 1--FAR 91.105(a).

114. 1--FAR 91.105(a).

115. 3--FAR 91.105(a).

116. 3--FAR 91.105(a).

117. 2--FAR 91.105(a). An airway is controlled airspace.

118. 2--FAR 91.105(a). An airway is controlled airspace.

119. 2--FAR 91.105(a).

120. 4--FAR 91.105(d).

121. 2--FAR 91.105(c) and (d).

122. 2--FAR 91.607(b) and (c).

123. 1--FAR 91.107(c).

124. 3--FAR 91.107(e).

125. 4--FAR 91.107(e).

126. 4--FAR 91.109(a). In controlled airspace (3,000-18,000 ft. MSL), use an odd thousand +500 when the MC is 000°-179° (NEODD - due North or Easterly = ODD). When the MC is 180°-359°, use an even thousand +500 (SWEVEN - due South or Westerly = EVEN). Note: applies to magnetic COURSE, not magnetic or compass HEADING.

127. 2--FAR 91.109(a). In controlled airspace (3,000-18,000 ft. MSL), use an odd thousand +500 when the MC is 000°-179° (NEODD - due North or Easterly = ODD). When the MC is 180°-359°, use an even thousand +500 (SWEVEN - due South or Westerly = EVEN). Note: applies to magnetic COURSE, not magnetic or compass HEADING.

128. 2--FAR 91.109(a). In controlled airspace (3,000-18,000 ft. MSL), use an odd thousand +500 when the MC is 000°-179° (NEODD - due North or Easterly = ODD). When the MC is 180°-359°, use an even thousand +500 (SWEVEN - due South or Westerly = EVEN). Note: applies to magnetic COURSE, not magnetic or compass HEADING.

129. 2--FAR 91.163(a).

130. 4--FAR 21.182.

131. 3--FAR 21.182.

132. 2--FAR 91.167(b).

133. 2--FAR 91.167(b).

134. 2--FAR 91.169(a)(2).

135. 1--FAR 91.169(a). Last day of the 12th month after the inspection.

136. 3--FAR 91.169(a).

137. 1--FAR 91.169(b).

138. 3--FAR 91.169(b).   100 hr. on the tachometer.

139. 2--FAR 91.169(b).   The 100 hr. limitation may be exceeded by not more than 10 hours; however, that excess time may not be used in computing the next inspection.

140. 4--91.172.

141. 1--FAR 91.173.

142. 4--FAR 91.173.

143. 4--FAR 91.173.   Preventative maintenance is work accomplished before a problem occurs. It does not include alterations or changes.

144. 3--FAR 91.173.   Preventative maintenance is work accomplished before a problem occurs. It does not include alterations or changes.

145. 1--NTSB 830.5 requires immediate notification for an aircraft accident resulting in substantial damage.

146. 2--NTSB 830.5 requires immediate notification for an aircraft accident and for certain incidents including an inflight fire.

147. 1--NTSB 830.5 requires immediate notification for an aircraft accident and for certain incidents including an overdue aircraft thought to be involved in an accident.

148. 3--NTSB 830.5 requires immediate notification for an aircraft accident and for certain incidents including the inability of any required flight crewmember to perform duties because of injury or illness.

149. 2--NTSB 830.5 requires immediate notification for an aircraft accident resulting in substantial damage.

150. 2--NTSB 830.10 requires that wreckage not be disturbed EXCEPT to remove injured or trapped persons, to protect the wreckage from further damage, or to protect the public from injury.

151. 4--NTSB 830.15.

152. 4--NTSB 830.15.

BASICS OF AIR NAVIGATION

MAIN POINTS

The complete manual and instructions for the E6-B FLIGHT COMPUTER appear at the end of this chapter. You should study the use of the flight computer thoroughly before you do the flight computer problems in this chapter.

We would like to thank Aero Research Products, Inc., 11201 Hindry Ave,. Los Angeles, CA. 90045, for permission to reproduce the E6-B Flight Computer: Complete Instruction Manual) in this Study Guide.

1. All navigation problems share certain things in common. Before you go somewhere, you need to know exactly where you are. Determining your position on the Earth's surface is called a **fix**. A fix is made when two **lines of position (LOPs)** intersect. There are five basic methods of navigation: **pilotage**, reference to visual landmarks; **dead reckoning** (DR), figuring your position from time-distance computations using one or more LOPs; **radio navigation**, observing your bearings from a radio source; **celestial**, navigation by reference to the sun and stars; and **inertial**, navigation based on continuous computations performed by the airplane's instruments. Pilotage, dead reckoning, and radio navigation are the most common methods used by private pilots. Pilotage and dead reckoning are covered in this chapter. Radio navigation is covered in Chapter 13.

2. Lines that run between the poles are called **lines of longitude**, or **meridians**. Lines that run parallel to the equator are called **lines of latitude**, or **parallels**. Taken together, lines of latitude and lines of longitude provide a geographic coordinate system or grid. The **prime meridian** runs north and south through Greenwich, England, and lines to the east and west are numbered in degrees. The **equator** divides Northern and Southern Hemispheres and is 0° latitude. Latitude degrees increase as you approach the poles. For finer discriminations, latitude and longitude are further subdivided into 60 arc minutes per degree and 60 arc seconds per minute. A

nautical mile (NM) is one minute of latitude marked off vertically on a meridian. The shortest distance between two points on the earth's surface is along a **great circle**, one whose plane runs through the center of the Earth.

3. The earth is divided into 24 time zones of approximately 15° longitude each. Most aviation-related time is reported relative to a standard: **Coordinated Universal Time (UTC)** or **zulu time**. To convert from local time to UTC in the Western Hemisphere, add hours to local time depending on which time zone you are in and whether the area is observing standard or daylight savings time. Times are typically reported on the 24-hr. clock. Thus, 6 p.m. becomes (1200 + 600) or 1800. An a.m. time such as 4 a.m. becomes 0400. All UTC or zulu times are given on the 24-hr. clock. Because conversions to/from UTC may change dates, time may be expressed in six digits; for example, 8PM on the 20th is 202000.

4. The three most common types of VFR navigational charts are **sectional charts, terminal area charts, and world aeronautical charts**. Sectional charts are used primarily for low-altitude, low-airspeed flight by reference to visible landmarks. They contain three general types of information: (a) topographical features: cities, roads, obstructions (MSL with AGL given in parentheses), contour lines, lakes, and so on; (b) aeronautical data: airports, communication information, airspace restrictions, and so forth; and (c) legend and notes: airport directory, VFR rules, and so on. **Terminal area charts** are available for selected TCAs and are larger in scale than sectional charts. **World aeronautical charts (WACs)** are small scale charts that cover larger areas.

5. **Pilotage** requires little more than a clear day, a sectional chart, and a straightedge such as a **navigational plotter**. The plotter consists of a straightedge, mileage scales for sectional charts and WACs, and a protractor. To determine a course, select the appropriate chart, make a general inspection of the terrain, draw a true course line, and determine the **true course**, or TC. To determine the true course, use your plotter and a meridian line near the center of your course. Next, measure the distance you intend to travel. Divide the course into 10-20 mile or 5-10 minute intervals and select prominent landmarks (plainly visible ones that suggest direction as well as position) along the intended route of flight. Also select landmarks to either side of your intended route so as to **bracket** the course.

6. **Dead reckoning (DR)** begins with determining a true course line and then making corrections for wind and magnetic variation. The angle between the wind and your intended route of flight is called the **wind correction angle (WCA)**. When the value of the WCA is added to or subtracted from the true course, the result is called the **true heading (TH)**. Angular **variation (VAR)** between magnetic and geographic north is shown on the chart and is used to obtain the **magnetic heading (MH)**. Magnetic heading must be corrected for **compass deviation (CD)** to obtain the **compass heading (CH)**. Finally, determine **true airspeed (TAS)** by referring to you flight manual. After adjusting for the effects of the wind, you will know what your **groundspeed** will be, which is crucial in determining how fast you will travel from fix to fix.

7. Once you have completed all steps normally involved in pilotage, you perform numerous calculations for dead reckoning, all of which are facilitated by using a **mechanical flight computer** or **electronic flight calculator**. With a flight computer, you use the wind face to calculate both the wind correction

angle and groundspeed for any given true course, true airspeed, and wind condition (obtained from the Winds Aloft Forecast). Any crosswind component will affect your true course, and the effect is magnified as the crosswind component increases. Second, to determine the magnetic heading, you need to correct for the magnetic variation shown on the chart. **Isogonic lines** are lines of equal variation. (The line of no variation is referred to as the **agonic line**.) If the variation is to the west, you **add** it to the true heading; if it is to the east, you **subtract** it. To remember this, use the rhyme: "East is least (-) and west is best (+)." **Magnetic course (MC)** is the true course corrected for variation **without** taking wind into account; it is used by the FAA to regulate cruising altitudes. **Magnetic heading (MH)** is the true heading corrected for both wind (WCA) and variation (VAR). Because wind is given in True, WCA must be applied before variation. Once magnetic heading is corrected for compass deviation errors, you will have determined the compass heading you will need to hold in order to fly a desired track.

8. Your flight computer or electronic calculator will greatly simplify your ability to solve dead reckoning problems, but you should also understand the concepts behind each computation. Most computations are based on the relationship between distance (D), time (T), and rate (R) such that R = D/T. Endurance can be calculated by dividing fuel on board by fuel flow (measured in gallons per hour). The computer can be used to solve these and similar proportional problems. You will need to spend time with your computer to learn to read the scales accurately.

9. In addition to groundspeed, endurance, fuel flow, and time, the computer has a scale to convert calibrated airspeed into true airspeed (airspeed corrected for the effects of altitude and temperature on air density). TAS must be determined before the wind correction angle or groundspeed can be computed. During preflight planning, you will use an estimated TAS from the performance charts in the POH. To compute TAS in-flight, you need to know the pressure-altitude, temperature, and indicated airspeed.

10. The flight computer also allows you to compute true altitudes for nonstandard temperatures, density-altitude for a given temperature and pressure-altitude, and to make conversions such as statute miles to nautical miles, pounds of fuel to gallons, and Fahrenheit to Celsius.

11. The wind correction angle (WCA) is the number of degrees you must add or subtract from your true course to obtain a true heading that compensates for drift. Groundspeed is affected by both the speed and the direction of the wind. Both groundspeed and true heading can be derived from the computer by following specific instructions written on most computers. After you have done several practice exercises, these computations will become routine.

12. The choice of a flight computer or electronic calculator is an individual one. In either case, it is wise to understand the concepts and relationships so that you can intuitively arrive at an estimate of what the answer should be. The computer or calculator can then give you a precise answer.

13. If you use an electronic flight calculator during the FAA written test, any information printed on the case relating to regulations, ATC signals, and so forth must be obscured. Memory circuits must be cleared before and after the test, and a tape printout, if produced, must be surrendered at the end of the test. Finally, you cannot use the operations manual during the test, nor are you allowed to use prewritten programs.

14. The chapter concludes with a section on the use of the E6-B flight computer. There are several exercises and problems in the E6-B manual as well as several problems in study guide.

15. A tip for using a mechanical flight computer: put a light coating of petroleum jelly on the clear wind window. You can write through this with your pencil, but you will not have to use an eraser. Just rub lightly with your finger and the marks will disappear.

KEY TERMS AND CONCEPTS, PART 1

Match each term or concept (1-20) with the appropriate description (A-T) below. Each item has only one match.

___ 1. zulu
___ 2. inertial
___ 3. pilotage
___ 4. protractor
___ 5. equator
___ 6. latitude
___ 7. bracketing
___ 8. sectional chart
___ 9. longitude
___ 10. fix

___ 11. compass heading
___ 12. magnetic heading
___ 13. prime meridian
___ 14. celestial
___ 15. true heading
___ 16. plotter
___ 17. dead reckoning
___ 18. easterly
___ 19. agonic line
___ 20. terminal control area chart

A. TH plus or minus VAR
B. navigation by reference to visual landmarks
C. a typical one has a straightedge, two mileage scales, and protractor
D. line that runs through Greenwich, England
E. lines that run between the poles
F. selecting landmarks on both sides of a course line
G. MH corrected for compass deviation
H. navigation by reference to the sun and stars
I. large-scale aeronautical chart that depicts a TCA (scale of 1 in. = 4 mi.)
J. line parallel to the equator
K. point where two lines of position (LOPs) intersect
L. instrument used to measure angles
M. line that divides the earth into Northern and Southern Hemispheres
N. TC plus or minus the WCA
O. type of time used to make most weather reports and for filing flight plans
P. navigation by making time-distance computations along a line of position
Q. navigation based on computations performed by the airplane's instruments
R. chart used primarily for low-altitude, low-airspeed flight by reference to visual landmarks (scale of 1 in. = 8 mi.)
S. type of magnetic variation subtracted from TH to obtain MH
T. line of no variation

KEY TERMS AND CONCEPTS, PART 2

Match each term or concept (1-12) with the appropriate description below (A-L). Each item has only one match.

___ 1. groundspeed   ___ 7. true altitude
___ 2. indicated airspeed   ___ 8. wind correction angle
___ 3. pressure-altitude   ___ 9. magnetic course
___ 4. UTC   ___ 10. westerly
___ 5. true airspeed   ___ 11. calibrated airspeed
___ 6. magnetic variation   ___ 12. isogonic line

A. IAS corrected for pitot-static errors
B. true course corrected for magnetic variation but not wind effects
C. number of degrees added to or subtracted from TC to yield TH
D. lines of equal variation
E. airspeed corrected for density-altitude
F. difference between true north and magnetic north
G. type of magnetic variation added to TH to obtain MH
H. altitude read from the altimeter when 29.92" Hg. is set in the Kollsman window.
I. airspeed read directly from the airspeed indicator
J. actual height above mean sea level
K. TAS corrected for wind effects
L. universal time standard used for aviation time matters

DISCUSSION QUESTIONS AND REVIEW EXERCISES

1. What is the relationship between a line of position (LOP)and a fix?

2. Name the three basic methods of navigation commonly used by private pilots.

3. What does the expression 55°40'N, 104°20'W represent and how would it be interpreted by a pilot or navigator?

4. T F The prime meridian runs east and west while the equator runs north and south.

5. T F Longitude lines are of the same length, whereas lines of latitude decrease in length as the distance from the equator increases.

6. T F Longitude lines converge at the poles, whereas lines of latitude converge at the equator.

7. How are surface obstructions and terrain relief depicted on sectional charts? What information about them would you expect to find in a sectional chart?

8. Refer to your San Francisco sectional chart and the legend in Appendix A. What is the highest obstruction (above ground level) within a 5-NM radius of Hanford Airport (approximately 36°19'N, 119°38'W)? What kind of obstruction is it? How high is it above the ground?

9. Locate the quadrangle on your San Francisco sectional chart in which the city of Stockton is located (approximately 37°54'N, 121°15'W). At a quick glance, can you tell how high above sea level the highest obstruction is? How is this reported on the map?

10. Find Fresno Air Terminal on your San Francisco sectional chart (approximately 36°46'N, 119°43'W). Explain what each of the various numbers and symbols above and below the name mean.

11. Name two major limitations to pilotage as a primary means of air navigation.

12. What is bracketing? Explain why it is an important procedure to follow in pilotage.

13. Why is dead reckoning considered a means of coordinating other methods of navigation?

14. Given:

True course	280°
Variation	15° east
Cruising altitude	8,500 ft. MSL
Winds at 9,000 ft.	240° at 35 kts.
True airspeed	110 kts.

Find the magnetic heading, the correct wind angle, and the groundspeed.

15. Suppose you plan a flight of 225 statute miles at an anticipated groundspeed of 123 MPH. The airplane has 36 gal. of usable fuel on board and a fuel consumption rate of 9 gal./hr. How much fuel will you have left when you land at your destination? How much flying time does this represent?

16. Assume you depart Hays, KS (Central Time Zone) at 1330 CDT for a 2-hr. flight west to Colorado Springs, CO (Mountain Time Zone). What would be your landing time, expressed in UTC, or zulu time?

17.   Suppose the OAT is 68°F and you are flying at a CAS of 120 kts. at a pressure-altitude of 6,500 ft. MSL. What is your TAS in kts.? What is your TAS in MPH?

18. For this problem, refer to your San Francisco sectional chart. You are going to fly a cross-country trip from Salinas Airport (approximately 36°40'N, 121°36'W) to Fresno Chandler Airport.   Given:

Usable fuel	29 gal.
Fuel consumption	5.3 gal./hr.
Cruise altitude	7,500 ft.
TAS	91 kts.
Winds at 6,000 ft.	210° at 25 kts.
Winds at 9,000 ft.	230° at 35 kts.

   a.   How far is it from Salinas to Fresno?

   b.   What is your true course?

   c.   What is the wind correction angle?

   d.   What is your magnetic heading?

   e.   What is your groundspeed? How long will it take you to fly the trip?

   f.   How much fuel will you burn?

19.   Given the same conditions as in question 18, answer the following questions for a return trip to Salinas. Use a cruise altitude of 6,500 ft. and assume the winds at 6,000 ft. are representative of your proposed altitude.

   a.   What is your true course?

   b.   What is the WCA?

   c.   What is the magnetic heading?

   d.   What is your groundspeed? How long will it take you to fly the trip?

   e.   How much fuel will you burn?

20. Time and chart problems.

    a. Compute the Time Zone for the following latitudes; state your answer as UTC+ or UTC-.

147° W _____   122° W _____   27° E _____   74° W _____

178° E _____   132° E _____   27° W _____   92° E _____

    b. Convert the following UTC date/time groups to local date/time groups.

192100Z _____ (UTC+3)   210400Z _____ (UTC-8)   120600Z _____ (UTC-3)

011900Z _____ (UTC-5)   031100Z _____ (UTC-8)   312300z _____ (UTC-12)

    c. Convert the following local date/time groups to UTC date/time groups.

150400 (UTC+5) _____ Z   092105 (UTC-3) _____ Z   112220 (UTC-7) _____ Z

080820 (UTC+3) _____ Z   092300 (UTC-12) _____ Z   130400 (UTC+6) _____ Z

    d. Using the San Francisco sectional chart, draw the symbols used to depict the following:

Power lines _____   Isogonic lines _____   Railroads _____

Race track _____   Glider operations _____   Water tanks _____

Highways _____   Open air theater _____

    e. Using the San Francisco sectional chart, who controls Alert Area 251 (37°0'N, 120°20'W)? What are its hours of use?

    f. What is the symbol for an airport with facilities?

    g. What can be determined about an airport when runways are shown in the airport symbol?

    h. What does a star beside a frequency indicate?

    i. What color denotes airports with Airport Traffic Areas (ATAs)?

    j. What is the height (both MSL and AGL) of the obstruction located at 36°19'N., 119°44'W?

k. How are the Maximum Elevation Figures for an area indicated? Give an example and explain what the numbers mean.

1. Find the Monterey Peninsula Airport (36°35'N, 121°51'W).

What is the field elevation (MSL)?

Does the field have hard surface runways?

What is the length of the longest runway?

What does the letter "L" indicate?

What is the 119.25 MHz frequency?

What is the closest VOR?

m. What is located at? (Draw the symbol and write the name.)

36°36'N, 120°05'W. _____ _____

37°04'N, 121°08'W. _____ _____

37°24'N, 121°28'W. _____ _____

n. What is the geographic location of NAS Lemoore (near the lower right corner of the chart)?

o. What is the geographic location of Columbia Airport (near the upper edge, 1/4 of the way from right to left on the chart)?

p. What is the true course from NAS Lemoore to the Monterey Peninsula Airport? What is the magnetic course? What is the distance?

q. What is the true course from Columbia Airport to the Castle AFB, which is located 37°23'N, 120°34'W? What is the magnetic course? What is the distance?

21. <u>Magnetic compass exercises.</u>

Aircraft Compass Corrections

FOR(MH)	0	30	60	90	120	150	180	210	240	270	300	330
STEER(CH)	356	028	060	091	121	153	184	212	241	270	299	328

	True heading	Variation	Magnetic heading	Deviation	Compass heading
a.	054	14 W	____	____	____
b.	243	10 E	____	____	____
c.	189	____	164	____	____
d.	345	____	347	____	____
e.	____	4 W	308	____	____
f.	____	5 W	195	____	____
g.	____	6 E	____	____	015
h.	____	10 W	____	____	284

Flight Computer Exercises

Instructions for the **E6-B FLIGHT COMPUTER** appear at the end of this chapter. Study these or the instructions that came with you flight computer.

22. <u>Time/Speed/Distance Problems.</u>

	Speed (kts)	Distance (nm)	Time
a.	120 kts	56 nm	___+____
b.	90 kts	56 nm	___+____
c.	120 kts	240 nm	___+____
d.	120 kts	174 nm	___+____
e.	175 kts	1,892 nm	___+____
f.	100 kts	_____	0+14
g.	129 kts	_____	0+57
h.	105 kts	_____	2+15
i.	225 kts	_____	1+10
j.	65 kts	_____	+10
k.	_____	166 nm	2+00
l.	_____	600 nm	0+25
m.	_____	650 nm	3+40
n.	_____	225 nm	0+57
o.	_____	420 nm	2+40

23. <u>Fuel problems.</u>

	Fuel available	Consumption rate	Time	Speed	Range
a.	25 gal	12.5 gph	___+____	150 kts	____ nm
b.	12 gal	4.5 gph	___+____	130 kts	____ nm
c.	35 gal	15.0 gph	___+____	95 kts	____ nm
d.	8 gal	3.0 gph	___+____	110 kts	____ nm

Fuel used	Consumption	Time	Speed	Distance
a. 13 gal	_____ gph	1+30	224 kts	_____ nm
b. 10 gal	_____ gph	1+53	190 kts	_____ nm
c. 8 gal	_____ gph	0+53	139 kts	_____ nm
d. 12 gal	_____ gph	0+45	130 kts	_____ nm

Fuel required	Consumption	ETE	Speed	Distance
a. ___ gal	10.0 gph	__+_____	180 kts	270 nm
b. ___ gal	8.8 gph	__+_____	160 kts	187 nm
c. ___ gal	3.5 gph	__+_____	135 kts	429 nm
d. ___ gal	6.0 gph	__+_____	155 kts	142 nm

24. Conversions.

Statue miles	Nautical miles		Knots (kts)	Miles per hour (mph)
a. 340 sm	_____ nm	e.	150 kts	_____ mph
b. 200 sm	_____ nm	f.	100 kts	_____ mph
c. _____ sm	210 nm	g.	_____ kts	200 mph
d. _____ sm	340 nm	h.	_____ kts	180 mph

°F	°C		°F	°C
a. +20°	_____ °	d.	_____ °	-12°
b. -10°	_____ °	e.	_____ °	+12°
c. +80°	_____ °	f.	_____ °	+33°

25. True airspeed.

Calibrated airspeed (CAS)	Pressure-altitude (PA)	Outside air temperature (OAT)	True airspeed (TAS)
a. 135 kts	8000 feet	-10°C	_____ kts
b. 145 kts	10000 feet	-05°C	_____ kts
c. 165 kts	8000 feet	+10°C	_____ kts
d. 165 kts	8000 feet	-05°C	_____ kts
e. 150 kts	2500 feet	+10°C	_____ kts
f. _____ kts	6000 feet	-10°C	115 kts
g. _____ kts	7000 feet	+05°C	160 kts
h. _____ kts	5000 feet	-05°C	170 kts
i. _____ kts	2500 feet	+15°C	180 kts
j. _____ kts	7500 feet	-05°C	190 kts

26. Density-altitude.

OAT (C)	Pressure-altitude	Density-altitude
a. -10	8000 feet	_____ feet
b. -05	10000 feet	_____ feet
c. +10	8000 feet	_____ feet
d. -05	8000 feet	_____ feet
e. +15	2500 feet	_____ feet

27. Wind problems.

	Wind direction	Wind speed	True course	True airspeed	WCA (L or R)	True heading	Ground speed
a.	100	29	140	132	_____	_____	_____
b.	040	20	040	100	_____	_____	_____
c.	045	35	315	115	_____	_____	_____
d.	100	14	280	140	_____	_____	_____
e.	350	25	010	150	_____	_____	_____
f.	180	15	035	130	_____	_____	_____
g.	225	12	340	125	_____	_____	_____
h.	150	5	360	125	_____	_____	_____
i.	300	10	330	115	_____	_____	_____
j.	045	30	350	125	_____	_____	_____
k.	____	____	135	135	_____	140	130
l.	____	____	315	148	_____	305	155
m.	____	____	270	158	_____	268	148
n.	____	____	245	168	_____	238	174
o.	____	____	180	178	_____	187	174

28. "Best" wind problems. Use the wind information below to determine which altitude has the "best" winds for the flight direction; that is, the fastest groundspeed. First determine the TAS at each altitude, then determine which altitude has the most favorable winds. It is not necessary to do separate calculations for each altitude; make wind dots for all winds, then determine which one provides the fastest groundspeed and complete your calculations.

FT	3000	6000	9000	12000
SFO	2315	2720+03	0125-03	0330-09
FAT	1105	1320+03	1525-03	1530-09

(assume standard temperature at 3000 ft - +10)

a. CAS is 130.   TAS at 3000 ft _____   TAS at 9000 ft _____
                 TAS at 6000 ft _____   TAS at 12000 ft _____

b. Best winds in the vicinity of San Francisco (SFO):

True course	Best altitude	TAS	TH	GS	Var	Magnetic heading
280	_____	_____	_____	_____	16 E	_____
080	_____	_____	_____	_____	16 E	_____
180	_____	_____	_____	_____	16 E	_____

c. Best winds in the vicinity of Fresno (FAT):

True course	Best altitude	TAS	TH	GS	Var	Magnetic heading
100	_____	_____	_____	_____	16 E	_____
140	_____	_____	_____	_____	16 E	_____
320	_____	_____	_____	_____	16 E	_____

29. Navigation by figuring your position through reference to lines of position and time-distance computation is called
    1--celestial navigation.
    2--dead reckoning.
    3--inertial navigation.
    4--pilotage.

30. Contour lines placed on a sectional aeronautical chart are to show points of the same
    1--MSL elevation.
    2--latitude.
    3--longitude.
    4--variation.

31. A star (*) at the top of an airport symbol on a sectional chart means
    1--that high-performance airplanes are permitted to land.
    2--that it has a rotating beacon in operation from sunset to sunrise.
    3--that services and fuel are available.
    4--that this is a military airport.

32. Assume an airplane is serviced with 38 gal. of usable fuel, and an average groundspeed of 138 kts. is anticipated on a flight of 260 nautical miles. At a fuel consumption rate of 12 gal./hr., what would be the maximum flying time available with the fuel remaining after reaching your destination?
    1--1 hr., 2 min.
    2--1 hr., 17 min.
    3--2 hr., 5 min.
    4--2 hr., 30 min.

33. Refer to your San Francisco sectional chart. Given variation of 16° east, what is the **true course** from Monterey Peninsula to Watsonville?
    1--175°.
    2--355°.
    3--191°.
    4--011°.

34. Refer to your San Francisco sectional chart. Given variation of 16° east in this area, what is the **magnetic course** from Watsonville to Monterey Peninsula?
    1--011°.
    2--191°.
    3--175°.
    4--355°.

35. Refer to your San Francisco sectional chart. What is the approximate distance from Monterey Peninsula to Watsonville?
    1--82 NM.
    2--44 NM.
    3--21 NM.
    4--10 NM.

36.   Refer to your San Francisco sectional chart. Suppose you fly the traffic
pattern at 1,000 ft. AGL at Watsonville. If the altimeter is adjusted to the
latest altimeter setting, it would indicate a pattern altitude of
        1--1000 ft.
        2--1045 ft.
        3--1160 ft.
        4--1228 ft.

37.   Refer to your San Francisco sectional chart. Given a TAS of 130 kts.,
17° east variation, forecasted winds from 110° at 15 kts., what is the
magnetic heading and ground speed from Monterey Peninsula to Watsonville?
        1--009°, 131 kts.
        2--025°, 131 kts.
        3--018°, 129 kts.
        4--011°, 129 kts.

38.   Refer to your San Francisco sectional chart. Given a true airspeed of
109 kts., variation of 16° east, a compass deviation of +1°, and winds from
210° at 20 kts., calculate the compass heading and time en route from
Watsonville to Monterey Peninsula.
        1--181°, 18 min.
        2--179°, 14 min.
        3--018°, 25 min.
        4--011°, 18 min.

39.   The line you draw on a sectional or world aeronautical chart to fly
directly from one place to another defines the
        1--compass heading.
        2--magnetic course if measured from true north.
        3--magnetic heading.
        4--true course if measured from true north.

40.   The true heading plus or minus variations yields the
        1--compass heading.
        2--magnetic course.
        3--magnetic heading.
        4--true heading.

41.   The true course corrected for the effects of any crosswinds yields the
        1--compass heading.
        2--magnetic course.
        3--magnetic heading.
        4--true heading.

42.   Refer to Figure 12.1. The maximum elevation of the terrain and
obstructions such as towers within the quadrangle bounded by the ticked lines
of latitude and longitude is
        1--495 ft. AGL.
        2--880 ft. MSL.
        3--1,600 ft. AGL.
        4--1,600 ft. MSL.

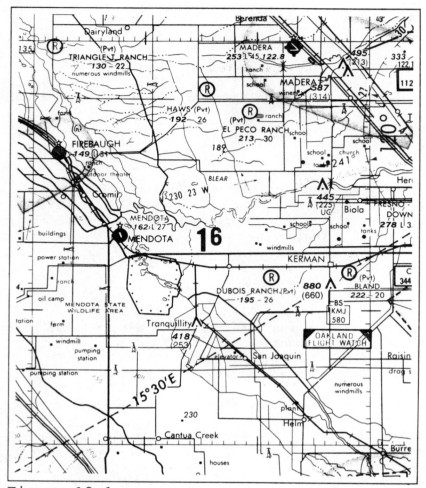

Figure 12.1

43. The large number (1^6) in the center of the quadrangle in Figure 12.1
    1--does not include the maximum elevation of vertical obstructions within
       the area.
    2--indicates the base of the controlled airspace over the area.
    3--is a maximum elevation figure, including terrain and obstructions.
    4--is the latitude and longitude coordinate of the area bounded by the
       ticked lines.

44. Refer to the obstruction near the town of Tranquillity in Figure 12.1.
The top of the obstruction is
    1--253 ft. AGL.
    2--253 ft. MSL.
    3--418 ft. AGL.
    4--1,600 ft. MSL.

45. Refer to the obstruction south of Kerman in Figure 12.1. Select the true statement regarding this obstruction.

    1--It is a free-standing tower with no guy wires. The base is 880 ft. MSL.
    2--The top of the obstruction is 660 ft. AGL.
    3--This is a group obstruction, the tops of which are 600 ft. AGL.
    4--This is a single obstruction with guy wires; its top is 880 AGL.

46. Refer to the obstructions near Madera in Figure 12.1. Which of the following statements is correct?

    1--Each of the these is a single obstruction, neither of which is more than 1,000 ft. MSL.
    2--This is a group obstruction; the base of one is 213 ft. AGL and the base of the other is 314 ft. AGL.
    3--This is a group obstruction; the tops are less than 1,000 ft. AGL.
    4--This is a group obstruction; the maximum top is 587 ft. MSL.

47. Refer to Figure 12.1. Assume you are flying over Madera from east to west. In accordance with regulations, which of the following altitudes would be the minimum safe altitude to fly over the highest obstruction shown?

    1--600 ft. AGL.
    2--1,000 ft. MSL.
    3--1,400 ft. AGL.
    4--3,000 ft. AGL.

48. Refer to Figure 12.1. What statement, if any, about Madera Airport is correct?

    1--FSS at this airport operates on 122.8.
    2--Landing lights are available on request.
    3--The airport is 253 ft. AGL.
    4--None of the statements is correct.

49. Refer to Figure 12.1. The following surface aviation weather report has been issued for Madera: MAD SA 1351 80 BKN 25 090/29/20/0000/975. At what indicated altitude above Madera would you expect the base of the clouds?

    1--800 ft. MSL.
    2--1,053 ft. MSL.
    3--8,000 ft. MSL.
    4--8,253 ft. MSL.

50. The magnetic heading plus or minus compass deviation yields the

    1--compass heading.
    2--magnetic course.
    3--true course.
    4--true heading.

51. When flying over a national wildlife refuge, pilots are requested to maintain what minimum altitude above the terrain?

    1--1,000 ft. AGL.
    2--1,500 ft. AGL.
    3--2,000 ft. AGL.
    4--3,000 ft. AGL.

52. Which of the following statements is correct?
1--Longitude lines are of the same length, while latitude lines decrease
in length as the distance from the equator increases.
2--Longitude lines converge at the pole, while latitude lines converge at
the equator.
3--The prime meridian is to latitude as the equator is to longitude.
4--All of the above statements are correct.

FAA EXAM QUESTIONS

(Note: All FAA Figures are located in Appendix C)

1. (FAA 1217) What is the approximate latitude and longitude of
Cooperstown Airport? (See Figure 13, Area B.)
1--47°25'N - 98°06'W.
2--47°55'N - 98°06'W.
3--47°25'N - 99°54'W.
4--47°55'N - 99°54'W.

2. (FAA 1218) Determine the approximate latitude and longitude of
Currituck County Airport. (See Figure 14, Area C.)
1--36°24'N - 76°01'45"W.
2--36°24'N - 75°58'15"E.
3--36°48'N - 76°01'45"W.
4--36°48'N - 75°58'15"E.

3. (FAA 1221) Determine the approximate latitude and longitude of Shoshone
County Airport. (See Figure 16.)
1--47°02'N - 116°41'W.
2--47°32'N - 116°41'W.
3--47°02'N - 116°11'W.
4--47°32'N - 116°11'W.

4. (FAA 1219) Which airport is located at approximately 47°45'N latitude
and 100°57'30"W longitude? (See Figure 15.)
1--Linrud.
2--Willoughby.
3--Johnson.
4--Washburn.

5. (FAA 1220) Which airport is located at approximately 47°21'N latitude
and 101°01'W longitude? (See Figure 15.)
1--Underwood.   2--Evenson.
3--Washburn.   4--Johnson.

6. (FAA 1191) Refer to Figure 12. An aircraft departs an airport in the
eastern daylight time zone at 0945 EDT for a 2-hour flight to an airport
located in the central daylight time zone. The landing should be what
coordinated universal time?
1--1145Z.   2--1345Z.
3--1445Z.   4--1545Z.

7. (FAA 1193)   Refer to Figure 12.   An aircraft departs an airport in the
   central standard time zone at 0845 CST for a 2-hour flight to an airport
   located in the mountain standard time zone.   The landing should be at
   what coordinated universal time?
   1--1345Z.
   2--1445Z.
   3--1545Z.
   4--1645Z.

8. (FAA 1195)   Refer to Figure 12.   An aircraft departs an airport in the
   Pacific standard time zone at 1030 PST for a 4-hour flight to an airport
   located in the central standard time zone.   The landing should be at
   what coordinated universal time?
   1--2030Z.
   2--2130Z.
   3--2230Z.
   4--2330Z.

9. (FAA 1192)   Refer to Figure 12.   An aircraft departs an airport in the
   central standard time zone at 0930 CST for a 2-hour flight to an airport
   located in the mountain standard time zone.   The landing should be at
   what time?
   1--0930 MST.
   2--1030 MST.
   3--1130 MST.
   4--1230 MST.

10. (FAA 1194)   Refer to Figure 12.   An aircraft departs an airport in the
    mountain standard time zone at 1615 MST for a 2-hour 15-minute flight to
    an airport located in the Pacific standard time zone.   What should be
    the estimated time of arrival at the destination airport?
    1--1630 PST.
    2--1730 PST.
    3--1830 PST.
    4--1930 PST.

11. (FAA 1196)   Refer to Figure 12.   An aircraft departs an airport in the
    mountain standard time zone at 1515 MST for a 2-hour 30-minute flight to
    an airport located in the Pacific standard time zone.   What is the
    estimated time of arrival at the destination airport?
    1--1645 PST.   2--1745 PST.
    3--1845 PST.   4--2345 PST.

12. (FAA 1198)   The Common Traffic Advisory Frequency (CTAF FSS) at
    Jamestown Airport (Area D in Figure 13) is
    1--121.1 MHz.   2--122.0 MHz.
    3--123.0 MHz.   4--123.6 MHz.

13. (FAA 1199)   What is the recommended communication procedure when inbound
    to land at McVille Airport?   (See Figure 13, Area A.)
    1--Broadcast intentions when 10 mi. out on 122.9 MHz.
    2--Contact UNICOM when 10 mi. out on 122.8 MHz.
    3--Circle the airport in a left turn prior to entering traffic.
    4--Broadcast intentions when 10 mi. out on 121.5 MHz.

14. (FAA 1200) What is the Common Traffic Advisory Frequency (CTAF) at Barnes County Airport? (See Figure 13, Area F.)
    1--121.5 MHz.
    2--122.0 MHz.
    3--122.8 MHz.
    4--123.6 MHz.

15. (FAA 1201) What is the recommended procedure for contacting Flight Watch in the area depicted by Figure 13 for En Route Flight Advisory Service?
    1--Contact the Jamestown Flight Watch on 123.6 MHz.
    2--Contact the Grand Forks Flight Watch on 122.0 MHz.
    3--Contact the Jamestown FSS on 123.0 MHz.
    4--Contact the Grand Forks Flight Watch on 121.5 MHz.

16. (FAA 1202) What is the recommended communications procedure for a landing at Currituck County Airport? (See Figure 14, Area C.)
    1--Contact Elizabeth City CGAS/MUNI CT for traffic advisories.
    2--Contact Elizabeth City FSS for airport advisory service.
    3--Request Stage III radar service from Norfolk TRSA.
    4--Transmit intentions on 122.9 MHz when 10 mi. out and give position reports in the traffic pattern.

17. (FAA 1203) On what frequency can a pilot receive a Transcribed Weather Broadcast in the area depicted by Figure 15?
    1--117.1 MHz.
    2--118.0 MHz.
    3--122.0 MHz.
    4--122.95 MHz.

18. (FAA 1204) On what frequency can a pilot receive Enroute Flight Advisory Service in the area depicted by Figure 15?
    1--117.1 MHz.
    2--118.0 MHz.
    3--122.0 MHz.
    4--122.95 MHz.

19. (FAA 1205) The CTAF frequency for Garrison Municipal (Area B in Figure 15) is
    1--122.0 MHz.
    2--122.8 MHz.
    3--122.9 MHz.
    4--123.6 MHz.

20. (FAA 1206) If Coeur D'Alene Tower is not in operation, which frequency should be used to self-announce position and intentions? (See Figure 16, Area B, and Figure 21.)
    1--122.1/108.8 MHz.   2--119.1 MHz.
    3--122.8 MHz.   4--122.9 MHz.

21. (FAA 1207) If Coeur D'Alene Tower is not in operation, which frequency should be used to monitor airport traffic? (See Figure 16, Area B, and Figure 21.)
    1--122.1/108.8 MHz.   2--119.1 MHz.
    3--122.8 MHz.   4--122.9 MHz.

22. (FAA 1208)   What is the correct frequency to be used at Coeur D'Alene to request fuel?   (See Figure 16, Area B, and Figure 21.)
1--122.1/108.8MHz.
2--119.1 MHz.
3--122.8 MHz.
4--122.95 MHz.

23. (FAA 1209)   If Hawthorne Tower is not in operation, which frequency should be used to monitor airport traffic?   (See Figure 19, Area C.)
1--118.4 MHz.
2--121.1 MHz.
3--122.8 MHz.
4--122.95 MHz.

24. (FAA 1210)   When approaching the Los Angeles area from the south, (see Figure 19) Los Angeles Approach control should be contacted on
1--121.3 MHz.
2--124.65 MHz.
3--125.5 MHz.
4--135.05 MHz.

25. (FAA 1222)   What hazards to aircraft may exist in areas like the Devils Lake East MOA?   (See Figure 13.)
1--Unusual, often invisible, hazards to aircraft such as artillery firing.
2--High density military training activities.
3--Parachute jump operations.
4--Controlled firing area.

26. (FAA 1197)   What is the recommended procedure for a flight from Jamestown VOR/DME northbound on V170 through Devils Lake East MOA when the MOA is activated?   (See Figure 13.)
1--Remain below 11,000 ft. MSL.
2--Contact Jamestown FSS for traffic advisories.
3--Fly at least 4 NM to the right or left of the center line of the airway.
4--Contact Grand Forks Flight Watch for flight-following service.

27. (FAA 1223)   The airspace overlying and within 5 SM. of Barnes County Airport (Area F in Figure 13) is
1--an Air Traffic Area from the surface to 3,000 ft. AGL.
2--a control zone from the surface to 14,500 ft. MSL.
3--uncontrolled airspace from the surface to 700 ft. AGL.
4--special use airspace from the surface to the overlying control area.

28. (FAA 1224)   Identify the airspace over Hoggarth Farm Airport that exists from the surface to 14,500 ft. (See Figure 13, Area C.)
1--Uncontrolled airspace - surface to 14,500 ft. MSL.
2--Uncontrolled airspace - surface to 700 ft. AGL, control area - 700 ft. AGL to 14,500 ft. MSL.
3--Uncontrolled airspace - surface to 1,200 ft. AGL, control area - 1,200 ft. AGL to 14,500 ft. MSL.
4--Control area - surface to 14,500 ft. MSL.

29. (FAA 1225) The visibility and cloud clearance requirements to operate VFR over Cooperstown Airport (Area B in Figure 13.) between 1,200 ft. AGL and 10,000 ft. MSL are
1--1 SM. and clear of clouds.
2--1 SM. and 1,000 ft. above, 500 ft. below, and 2,000 ft. horizontally from clouds.
3--3 SM. and 1,000 ft. above, 500 ft. below, and 2,000 ft. horizontally from clouds.
4--3 SM. and 1,000 ft. above, 1,000 ft. below, and 1 mi. horizontally from clouds.

30. (FAA 1226) The minimum altitude to be maintained above the Arrowwood National Wildlife Refuge (Area C in Figure 13) is
1--500 ft. AGL.
2--1,000 ft. AGL.
3--2,000 ft. AGL.
4--3,000 ft. AGL.

31. (FAA 1227) What hazards to aircraft may exist in warning areas such as Warning W-50? (See Figure 14.)
1--Unusual, often invisible, hazards such as aerial gunnery or guided missiles.
2--High volume of pilot training or unusual type of aerial activity.
3--Approach and departure area for military aircraft to and from the North Atlantic Control Area.
4--Overwater military training routes.

32. (FAA 1228) What minimum radio equipment is required to land and take off at Norfolk International? (See Figure 14, Area A.)
1--VHF transmitter and receiver.
2--Transponder and omnireceiver.
3--Transponder, omnireceiver, and DME.
4--Transponder, omnireceiver, DME, and VHF transmitter and receiver.

33. (FAA 1229) What type military flight operations should a pilot expect on IR 644? (See Figure 15.)
1--Area navigation training flights in IFR weather.
2--VFR training flights above 1,500 ft. AGL at speeds less than 250 kts.
3--Instrument training flights below 1,500 ft. AGL at speeds in excess of 150 kts.
4--IFR training flights above 1,500 ft. AGL at speeds in excess of 250 kts.

34. (FAA 1230) The visibility and cloud clearance requirements to operate VFR over County City Airport (Area A in Figure 16) at less than 1,200 ft. AGL are
1--3 SM and 1,000 ft. above, 1,000 ft. below, and 1 mi. horizontally from each cloud.
2--3 SM and 1,000 ft. above, 500 ft. below, and 2,000 ft. horizontally from each cloud.
3--1 SM and 1,000 ft. above, 500 ft. below, and 2,000 ft. horizontally from each cloud.
4--1 SM and clear of clouds.

35. (FAA 1231) The vertical limits of that portion of the Federal airway
    over Magee Airport (north of Area C in Figure 16) are
    1--1,200 ft. AGL to 7,500 ft. MSL.
    2--1,200 ft. AGL to 10,000 ft. MSL.
    3--7,500 ft. MSL to 12,500 ft. MSL.
    4--7,500 ft. MSL to 17,999 ft. MSL.

36. (FAA 1232) What is the upper limit of the Savannah TRSA? (See Figure
    17.)
    1--Up to but not including 3,000 ft. AGL.
    2--The base of the Continental Control Area.
    3--10,000 ft. MSL.
    4--18,000 ft. MSL.

37. (FAA 1233) The width of V114 (see Figure 18) from either side of the
    centerline is
    1--3 SM.
    2--4 NM.
    3--6 SM.
    4--10 NM.

38. (FAA 1234) Which cruising altitude is appropriate for a flight from
    Paris VORTAC to Quitman VORTAC? (See Figure 18.)
    1--4,000 ft. MSL.   2--4,500 ft. MSL.
    3--5,500 ft. MSL.   4--6,500 ft. MSL.

39. (FAA 1235) What minimum pilot certificate is required in order to fly
    from Area "A" to Area "C" in Figure 19 at 5,500 ft. MSL?
    1--Student.
    2--Private.
    3--Commercial.
    4--Airline Transport.

40. (FAA 1236) What minimum radio equipment is required to operate in the
    airspace below 7,000 ft. MSL and above 1,000 ft. AGL over Los Angeles
    International Airport? (See Figure 19.)
    1--Two-way radio communications equipment, transponder, and encoding
       altimeter.
    2--Two-way radio communications equipment and transponder.
    3--Transponder and encoding altimeter.
    4--Encoding altimeter and DME receiver.

41. (FAA 1237) What minimum radio equipment is required for operation into
    Ontario International Airport? (See Figure 19, Area E.)
    1--Two-way radio communications equipment, transponder, and DME.
    2--Two-way radio communications equipment and transponder.
    3--Transponder and DME.
    4--Two-way radio communications equipment.

42. (FAA 1238) The top of the ARSA at Ontario International Airport (Area E
    in Figure 19) is
    1--1,200 ft. AGL.
    2--3,000 ft. AGL.
    3--3,000 ft. above airport.
    4--4,000 ft. above airport.

43. (FAA 1239) The base of the outer circle of the ARSA at Ontario
    International Airport (Area E in Figure 19) is
    1--500 ft. AGL.
    2--700 ft. AGL.
    3--1,000 ft. AGL.
    4--1,200 ft. AGL.

44. (FAA 1240) The airspace overlying Fullerton Airport (Area D in Figure
    19) is
    1--uncontrolled from the surface to 700 ft. AGL.
    2--a TCA from the surface to 7,000 ft. MSL.
    3--a control zone from the surface to 14,500 ft. MSL.
    4--an Airport Traffic Area from the surface to 3,000 ft. MSL.

45. (FAA 1241) At which airport is fixed-wing special VFR not authorized in
    Figure 19?
    1--Burbank-Glendale-Pasadena Airport.
    2--Los Angeles International Airport.
    3--Long Beach Airport.
    4--Paradise Airport.

46. (FAA 1242) The airspace overlying Los Angeles International Airport
    (Area A in Figure 19) is
    1--a TCA.   2--an ARSA.
    3--a TRSA.   4--a CFA.

47. (FAA 1243) The flag symbol at Lake Drummond (Area B in Figure 14)
    represents
    1--a compulsory reporting point for the Norfolk TRSA.
    2--the recommended distance to contact Norfolk TRSA.
    3--a visual checkpoint used to identify position for initial callup to
       Norfolk TRSA.
    4--an outer limit where VFR traffic is not permitted to proceed further
       without radar contact with Norfolk TRSA.

48. (FAA 1244) The word CAUTION (Area A or Area E) denotes what hazard to
    aircraft? (See Figure 14.)
    1--Guy wires extending from radio or TV towers.
    2--Tall bridge over the inlet to the body of water.
    3--Powerlines crossing the body of water.
    4--Area contains aerial activities hazardous to nonparticipating
       traffic.

49. (FAA 1245) The elevation of the Chesapeake Municipal Airport (Area B
    in Figure 14) is
    1--sea level.   2--20 ft.
    3--36 ft.   4--360 ft.

50. (FAA 1246) The terrain elevation of the light tan area between Minot
    (Area A) and Audubon Lake (Area B in Figure 15) varies from
    1--sea level to 2,000 ft. MSL.
    2--2,000 ft. to 2,250 ft. MSL.
    3--2,000 ft. to 2,700 ft. MSL.
    4--2,600 ft. to 2,700 ft. MSL.

51. (FAA 1247) Which public use airports depicted in Figure 15 are indicated as having fuel and a rotating beacon?
1--Minot and Flying S.
2--Minot and Garrison Municipal.
3--Doyle and Washburn.
4--Flying S and Garrison Municipal.

52. (FAA 1248) Of what practical use, if any, are the private airports if a pilot does not have the owner's permission to use them?
1--Of no practical use.
2--Touch-and-go landing by permission from the nearest FSS.
3--To pick up or discharge passengers if intentions are broadcast on 122.9 MHz.
4--Landmark value for navigation and emergency use.

53. (FAA 1249) For information about the parachute jumping and glider operations at Henley Airport (Area B, Figure 16), refer to
1--notes on the border of the chart.
2--the Airport/Facility Directory.
3--the NOTAM's Directory.
4--AIM (Airman's Information Manual).

54. (FAA 1250) The flag symbols at Statesboro Airport, Claxton-Evans County Airport, and Ridgeland Airport in Figure 17 are
1--boundaries of the Savannah TRSA.
2--airports with special traffic patterns.
3--airports with remote communications outlets for Savannah TRSA.
4--visual checkpoints to identify position for initial callup to the Savannah TRSA.

55. (FAA 1251) What is the height of the lighted obstacle approximately 8 mi. southwest of Savannah International? (See Figure 17, Area C.)
1--1,500 ft. AGL.
2--1,532 ft. AGL.
3--1,531 ft. AGL.
4--1,549 ft. AGL.

56. (FAA 1252) The military air station at El Toro (Area B in Figure 19) can be identified by a rotating beacon that emits
1--white and green alternating flashes.
2--two quick, white flashes between the green flashes.
3--green, yellow, and white flashes.
4--green flashes.

57. (FAA 1253) What minimum altitude is necessary to vertically clear the antenna in the congested area approximately 10 NM southeast of MCAS El Toro? (See Figure 19, Area B.)
1--750 ft. MSL.   2--1,150 ft. MSL.
3--1,250 ft. MSL.   4--1,650 ft. MSL.

58. (FAA 1254) The top of the lighted stack approximately 14 mi. from the Savannah VORTAC on the 350 radial in Figure 17, Area C, is
1--305 ft. AGL.   2--400 ft. AGL.
3--430 ft. AGL.   4--830 ft. AGL.

59. (FAA 1255) What minimum altitude is necessary to vertically clear the obstacle on the northeast side of Airpark East Airport by 500 ft.? (See Figure 18, Area A.)
1--1,010 ft. MSL.
2--1,273 ft. MSL.
3--1,283 ft. MSL.
4--1,783 ft. MSL.

60. (FAA 1256) What minimum altitude is necessary to vertically clear the obstacle on the northeast side of Airpark East Airport by 500 ft.? (See Figure 18, Area A.)
1--821 ft. MSL.
2--1,013 ft. MSL.
3--1,401 ft. MSL.
4--1,513 ft. MSL.

61. (FAA 1257) Determine the magnetic course from McVille Airport (Area A) to Jamestown Airport (Area D). (See Figure 13.)
1--013°.
2--021°.
3--193°.
4--201°.

62. (FAA 1258) Determine the magnetic course from First Flight Airport (Area E) to Hampton Roads Airport (Area B). (See Figure 14.)
1--312°.
2--321°.
3--330°.
4--348°.

63. (FAA 1272) Determine the magnetic course from Airpark East Airport to Winnsboro Airport. (See Figure 18, Area A to B.)
1--075°.
2--082°.
3--091°.
4--256°.

64. (FAA 1260) Determine the magnetic heading for a flight from Hazen Airport (Area C) to Minot International (Area A). The wind is from 330 at 25 kts. and the TAS is 100 kts. (See Figure 15.)
1--351°.
2--002°.
3--012°.
4--021°.

65. (FAA 1261) What is the estimated time en route from Hazen Airport (Area C) to Minot International (Area A)? The wind is from 330 at 25 kts. and the TAS is 100 kts. Add 3-1/2 min. for departure and climbout. (See Figure 15.)
1--44 min.
2--48 min.
3--52 min.
4--56 min.

66. (FAA 1262) Determine the magnetic heading for a flight from County City Airport (Area A) to St. Maries Airport (Area D). The wind is from 215 at 25 kts. and the TAS is 125 kts. (See Figure 16.)
1--161°.
2--167°.
3--181°.
4--187°.

67. (FAA 1263) What is the estimated time en route from County City Airport (Area A) to St. Maries Airport (Area D)? The wind is from 215 at 25 kts. and the TAS is 125 kts. (See Figure 16.)
1--24 min.
2--27 min.
3--30 min.
4--34 min.

68. (FAA 1264) What is the magnetic heading for a flight from Priest River Airport (Area A) to Shoshone County Airport (Area C)? The wind is from 030 at 12 kts. and the TAS is 95 kts. (See Figure 16.)
1--116°.
2--123°.
3--130°.
4--136°.

69. (FAA 1265) Determine the time en route for a flight from Priest River Airport (Area A) to Shoshone County Airport (Area C). The wind is from 030 at 12 kts. and the TAS is 95 kts. Add 2 min. for climbout. (See Figure 16.)
1--23 min.
2--27 min.
3--31 min.
4--35 min.

70. (FAA 1266) Determine the magnetic heading for a flight from St. Maries Airport (Area D) to Priest River Airport (Area A). The wind is from 300 at 14 kts. and the TAS is 90 kts. (See Figure 16.)
1--319°.
2--325°.
3--331°.
4--339°.

71. (FAA 1267) What is the time en route for a flight from St. Maries Airport (Area D) to Priest River Airport (Area A)? The wind is from 300 at 14 kts. and the TAS is 90 kts. Add 3 min. for climbout. (See Figure 16.)
1--38 min.
2--43 min.
3--48 min.
4--51 min.

72. (FAA 1268) Determine the compass heading for a flight from Allendale County Airport (Area A) to Claxton-Evans County Airport (Area B). The wind is from 090 at 16 kts. and the TAS is 90 kts. (See Figure 17.)
1--200°.   2--205°.
3--211°.   4--229°.

73. (FAA 1269) What is the estimated time en route for a flight from Allendale County Airport (Area A) to Claxton-Evans County Airport (Area B)? The wind is from 090 at 16 kts. and the TAS is 90 kts. Add 2 min. for climbout. (See Figure 17.)
    1--33 min.
    2--37 min.
    3--41 min.
    4--45 min.

74. (FAA 1270) Determine the compass heading for a flight from Claxton-Evans County Airport (Area B) to Hampton Varnville Airport (Area A). The wind is from 290 at 18 kts. and the TAS is 85 kts. (See Figure 17.)
    1--034°.
    2--038°.
    3--042°.
    4--057°.

75. (FAA 1271) What is the estimated time en route for a flight from Claxton-Evans County Airport (Area B) to Hampton Varnville Airport (Area A)? The wind is from 290 at 18 kts. and the TAS is 85 kts. Add 2 min. for climbout. (See Figure 17.)
    1--36 min.
    2--39 min.
    3--43 min.
    4--46 min.

76. (FAA 1273) Determine the magnetic heading for a flight from Ontario International Airport (Area E) to Hawthorne Airport (Area C). The wind is from 150 at 21 kts., the TAS is 110 kts., and the magnetic variation is 14° east. (See Figure 19.)
    1--233°.
    2--248°.
    3--254°.
    4--276°.

77. (FAA 1274) What is the estimated time en route for a flight from Ontario International Airport (Area E) to Hawthorne Airport (Area C)? The wind is 150 at 21 kts., the TAS is 110 kts., and the magnetic variation is 14° east. (See Figure 19.)
    1--17 min.
    2--20 min.
    3--23 min.
    4--26 min.

78. (FAA 1259) En route to First Flight Airport (Area E), your flight passes over Hampton Roads Airport (Area B) at 1456 and then over Chespapeake Municipal at 1501. At what time should your flight arrive at First Flight? (See Figure 14.)
    1--1516.
    2--1521.
    3--1526.
    4--1531.

ANSWERS AND EXPLANATIONS

Key Terms and Concepts, Part 1

1.	O	6.	J	11.	G	16.	C
2.	Q	7.	F	12.	A	17.	P
3.	B	8.	R	13.	D	18.	S
4.	L	9.	E	14.	H	19.	T
5.	M	10.	K	15.	N	20.	I

Key Terms and Concepts, Part 2

1.	K	4.	L	7.	J	10.	G
2.	I	5.	E	8.	C	11.	A
3.	H	6.	F	9.	B	12.	D

Discussion Questions and Review Exercises

1. See Study Guide Main Point #1.

2. See Study Guide Main Point #1.

3. See Study Guide Main Point #2.

4. F--It is just the opposite.

5. T--Longitude lines are all the same length and converge at the poles, while lines of latitude are parallel to one another and become shorter as they approach the poles.

6. F--Lines of latitude do not converge; they run parallel to one another.

7. Refer to the San Francisco sectional chart and Study Guide Main Point #4.

8. The highest obstruction, twin towers, is 305 ft. AGL and 553 ft. MSL.

9. 3,700 ft. MSL, as indicated by the maximum elevation figures (MEF). MEFs use large numbers to represent thousands of feet and small numbers to represent hundreds of feet above MSL of the highest obstruction in the quadrangle bounded by the ticked lines of longitude and latitude.

10. The control tower frequencies are 118.2 and 128.1. Automatic Terminal Information Service (ATIS) is broadcast on 119.3 and 273.6. The field is 332 ft. above sea level (MSL), the longest runway is 9,200 ft., and UNICOM is available on 122.95. The FSS above the name indicates that there is a Flight Service Station located on the field.

11. See Study Guide Main Point #5.

12. See Study Guide Main Point #5.

13. See Study Guide Main Point #6.

14. The true heading is 280°. From that you subtract the wind correction angle (WCA) of -12° and the easterly variation (VAR) of -15° to obtain a magnetic heading (MH) of approximately 253°. Result obtained by electronic calculator.

15. On your trip, you will travel 1.83 hr. (225/123), or about 110 min. (1 hr., 50 min.), and you will burn 16.5 gal. (1.83 x 9) of fuel. The fuel remaining is 19.5 gal. (36 - 16.5), which represents about 2.17 hr. (19.5/9), or 2 hr., 10 min. To convert from a decimal representation of hours, such as 2.17, to hours and minutes, you need to multiply the decimal portion (.17) times 60 to determine the number of minutes.

16. Your UTC departure from Hays is 1330 + 5 hr., or 1830Z. You would land at Colorado Springs 2 hr. later, or 2030Z. To look at it another way, when you land at Colorado Springs, the local time would be 1330 + 2 hr. (flying time) - 1 hr. (time zone change), or 1430 local time, plus 6 hr. = 2030Z.

17. Converting 68°F to Celsius yields 20°C. TAS is 136 kts., which converts to 156 MPH.

18.
    a. 86 NM; use your plotter (NM on the sectional chart side).

    b. 87°; use your plotter and plot a true course.

    c. To determine the winds at 7,500 ft., interpolate between 6,000 and 9,000 ft. In this example interpolation is easy since 7,500 ft. is exactly halfway between. Use 220° at 30 kts. The wind correction (WCA) will be about 14° to correct for the effects of the southwesterly winds.

    d. To obtain your magnetic heading (MH), you must compute 87° (TC) + 14° (WCA) - 15° (VAR) to obtain 86° (MH).

    e. Use your navigation computer or electronic calculator to determine your groundspeed, 109 kts. Divide 87 kts. by 109 to find your estimated time en route, .80 hr. or about 48 min.

    f. Multiply .80 hr. x 5.3 gal./hr. to determine your fuel consumption, 4.2 gal.

19.
    a. 266°

    b. WCA = 13°

    c. 266° (TC) - 13° (WCA) - 15° (VAR) = 238° (MH).

    d. 75 kts.; 1.16 hr., or 1 hr., 10 min.

    e. 6.2 gal.

20.
a.	147° W	-10	122° W	-8	27° E	+2	74° W	-5
	178° E	+12	132° E	+9	27° W	-2	92° E	-6

b. 192100Z <u>200000</u> (UTC+3) 210400Z <u>202200</u> (UTC-8) 120600Z <u>120300</u> (UTC-3)

011900Z <u>011400</u> (UTC-5) 031100Z <u>030300</u> (UTC-8) 312300Z <u>311100</u> (UTC-12)

c. 150400 (UTC+5) <u>142300Z</u> 092105 (UTC-3) <u>100000Z</u> 112220 (UTC-7) <u>120520Z</u>

080820 (UTC+3) <u>080520Z</u> 092300 (UTC-12) <u>101100Z</u> 130400 (UTC+6) <u>122200Z</u>

d. See your San Francisco sectional chart.

e. There is no controlling agency; it is used from 0700-0200 (local), Monday through Friday.

f. See your San Francisco sectional chart.
g. It has a hard-surfaced runway of 1,500 ft. or greater length.
h. Part-time operation.
i. Blue.
j. 440 ft. MSL; 205 ft. AGL.
k. Large and medium blue numbers. For example, 4^7.

l. The field elevation is 244 ft. MSL. It has hard-surface runways, the longest of which is 6,600 ft. The letter "L" indicates that lighting is in operation from sunset to sunrise. 119.25 MHZ is the ATIS frequency. The closest VOR is Salinas.

m. 36°36'N, 120°05'W.   Power transmission line.
   37°04'N, 121°08'W.   Seaplane base.
   37°24'N, 121°28'W.   Mine or quarry.

n. The geographic location of NAS Lemoore is 36°20'N, 119°56'W.

o. Columbia Airport is located at 38°02'N, 120°25'W.

p. The true course from NAS Lemoore to the Monterey Peninsula Airport is 279°, the magnetic course is 263°, and it covers a distance of 92 nm.

q. The true course from Columbia Airport to the Castle AFB is 190°, the magnetic course is 174°, and the distance is 40 nm.

21. <u>Magnetic compass exercises</u>.

	True heading	Variation	Magnetic heading	Deviation	Compass heading
a.	054	14 W	068	0	068
b.	243	10 E	233	+1	234
c.	189	25 E	164	+3	167
d.	345	2 W	347	-3	344
e.	304	4 W	308	-1	307
f.	190	5 W	195	+3	198
g.	024	6 E	018	-3	015
h.	275	10 W	285	0	284

True +/- Variation = Magnetic +/- Deviation = Compass
(add west or subtract east)

22. Time/Speed/Distance Problems.

	Speed (kts)	Distance (nm)	Time
a.	120 kts	56 nm	0+28
b.	90 kts	56 nm	0+37
c.	120 kts	240 nm	2+00
d.	120 kts	174 nm	1+27
e.	175 kts	1,892 nm	10+49
f.	100 kts	23 nm	0+14
g.	129 kts	123 nm	0+57
h.	105 kts	238 nm	2+15
i.	225 kts	256 nm	1+10
j.	65 kts	11 nm	+10
k.	83 kts	166 nm	2+00
l.	1455 kts	600 nm	0+25
m.	176 kts	650 nm	3+40
n.	180 kts	225 nm	0+57
o.	159 kts	420 nm	2+40

23. Fuel problems.

	Fuel available	Consumption rate	Time	Speed	Range
a.	25 gal	12.5 gph	2+00	150 kts	300 nm
b.	12 gal	4.5 gph	2+40	130 kts	347 nm
c.	35 gal	15.0 gph	2+20	95 kts	228 nm
d.	8 gal	3.0 gph	2+40	110 kts	293 nm

	Fuel used	Consumption rate	Time	Speed	Distance
a.	13 gal	8.7 gph	1+30	224 kts	336 nm
b.	10 gal	5.3 gph	1+53	190 kts	358 nm
c.	8 gal	9.1 gph	0+53	139 kts	123 nm
d.	12 gal	16.0 gph	0+45	130 kts	97 nm

	Fuel required	Consumption	ETE	Speed	Distance
a.	15.0 gal	10.0 gph	1+30	180 kts	270 nm
b.	10.3 gal	8.8 gph	1+10	160 kts	187 nm
c.	11.2 gal	3.5 gph	3+11	135 kts	429 nm
d.	5.5 gal	6.0 gph	0+55	155 kts	142 nm

24. Conversions.

	Statue miles	Nautical miles		Knots (kts)	Miles per hour (mph)
a.	340 sm	295 nm	e.	150 kts	173 mph
b.	200 sm	174 nm	f.	100 kts	115 mph
c.	242 sm	210 nm	g.	174 kts	200 mph
d.	391 sm	340 nm	h.	156 kts	180 mph

	°F	°C		°F	°C
a.	+20°	−7°	d.	+10°	−12°
b.	−10°	−23°	e.	+54°	+12°
c.	+80°	+27°	f.	+91°	+33°

25. <u>True airspeed</u>.

	Calibrated airspeed (CAS)	Pressure altitude (PA)	Outside air temperature (OAT)	True airspeed (TAS)
a.	135 kts	8000 feet	−10°C	150 kts
b.	145 kts	10000 feet	−05°C	168 kts
c.	165 kts	8000 feet	+10°C	190 kts
d.	165 kts	8000 feet	−05°C	185 kts
e.	150 kts	2500 feet	+10°C	155 kts
f.	108 kts	6000 feet	−10°C	115 kts
g.	143 kts	7000 feet	+05°C	160 kts
h.	161 kts	5000 feet	−05°C	170 kts
i.	172 kts	2500 feet	+15°C	180 kts
j.	162 kts	7500 feet	−05°C	190 kts

26. <u>Density-altitude</u>.

	OAT (C)	Pressure-altitude	Density-altitude
a.	−10	8000 feet	7000 feet
b.	−05	10000 feet	10000 feet
c.	+10	8000 feet	9000 feet
d.	−05	8000 feet	7500 feet
e.	+15	2500 feet	3000 feet

27. <u>Wind problems</u>.

	Wind direction	Wind speed	True course	True airspeed	WCA (L or R)	True heading	Ground speed
a.	100	29	140	132	8 L	132	108
b.	040	20	040	100	0	040	80
c.	045	35	315	115	18 R	333	109
d.	100	14	280	140	0	280	154
e.	350	25	010	150	3 L	007	125
f.	180	15	035	130	4 R	039	142
g.	225	12	340	125	6 L	334	129
h.	150	5	360	125	1 R	001	129
i.	300	10	330	115	2 L	328	106
j.	045	30	350	125	11 R	001	105
k.	204	13	135	135	5 R	140	130
l.	205	27	315	148	10 L	305	155
m.	241	11	270	158	2 L	268	148
n.	136	22	245	168	7 L	238	174
o.	263	22	180	178	7 R	187	174

28. "Best" wind problems.

FT	3000	6000	9000	12000
SFO	2315	2720+03	0125-03	0330-09
FAT	1105	1320+03	1525-03	1530-09

(assume standard temperature at 3000 ft - +10)

a. CAS is 130. TAS at 3000 ft 136   TAS at 9000 ft 149
                TAS at 6000 ft 142   TAS at 12000 ft 156

b. Best winds in the vicinity of San Francisco (SFO):

True course	Best altitude	TAS	TH	GS	Var	Magnetic heading
280	12000	156	290	165	16 E	274
080	6000	142	078	162	16 E	062
180	12000	156	174	180	16 E	158

c. Best winds in the vicinity of Fresno (FAT):

True course	Best altitude	TAS	TH	GS	Var	Magnetic heading
100	12000	156	108	135	16 E	092
140	3000	136	139	132	16 E	123
320	12000	156	318	185	16 E	302

29. 2--LOPs and time-distance computations are the basis of dead reckoning.

30. 1--Contour lines indicate points of equal elevation above sea level (MSL).

31. 2--The star (*) means that the airport has a rotating beacon in operation from sunset to sunrise.

32. 2--Divide distance (260 nm) by speed (138 kts.) to determine time (1.88 hr.). Multiply time (1.88 hr.) by the fuel flow (12 gal./hr.) to determine total consumption (22.6 gal.). This leaves 15.4 gal, which divided by 12 gal./hr. leaves 1.28 hr. of unburned fuel. Converting .28 hr. to 17 min. (.28 x 60) yields an answer of 1 hr., 17 min. Another way to solve the problem is to figure total endurance (38 hr./12 gal./hr.), or 3.16 hr. (3 hr., 10 min.). Subtract 1.88 from 3.16 to get 1.28 hr.

33. 4--011°. Variation is applied to True to find magnetic.

34. 3--175°. (TC) 191 - 16 (E VAR) = 175 MC.

35. 3--Use your plotter to measure 21 NM. Be sure to use the sectional side of the plotter.

36. 3--The field elevation is 160 ft., to which you add 1,000 ft. to determine the indicated pattern altitude.

37.   1--Your TC is 011°, groundspeed is 131 kts., and the WCA is +7°.
018° (TC) + 7° (WCA) - 16° (VAR) = 009° (MH).

38.   2--TC is 191°, the wind is 20 kts., the WCA is +3°, and the groundspeed
is 90 kts.   191° (TC) + 3° (WCA) - 16° (VAR) = 178° (MH).   178° (MH) + 1°
(DEV) = 179° (CH).   Groundspeed (90 kts.) divided into distance (21 nm.)
yields roughly .23 hr., or 14 min.

39.   4--The true course line is the one initially plotted on a sectional or
world chart.

40.   3--Magnetic heading is the true heading corrected for variation.

41.   4--True heading is the true course corrected for the effects of any
crosswinds.

42.   4--Large numbers in the center of a quadrangle (referred to as the
maximum elevation figure, or MEF) indicate that the highest elevation is 1,600
ft. MSL.

43.   3--Large numbers in the center of a quadrangle (referred to as the
maximum elevation figure, or MEF) indicate the maximum elevation of terrain
and obstructions.

44.   1--MSL is indicated in bold figures; AGL is indicated in parentheses.

45.   2--MSL is indicated in bold figures; AGL is indicated in parentheses.
These may be guy wires extending outward.

46.   1--These are separate obstructions.   One is 495 MSL and (213) AGL; the
other is 587 MSL and (314) AGL.

47.   3--According to FARs, the minimum required altitude over an obstruction
is 1,000 ft.   The tallest obstruction is 314 ft. AGL, so 1,400 ft. AGL would
satisfy the requirement.

48.   4--No FSS facility is available at this airport (it would be indicated by
the letters FSS); landing lights are in operation from sunset to sunrise at
Madera and do not need to be requested; and the airport is 253 ft. MSL.

49.   4--The report indicates that the clouds are at 8,000 ft. and broken.
This measure of the cloud base is referenced to ground level, so you must add
field elevation (253 ft.) to determine the indicated altitude.

50.   1--Compass heading is the magnetic heading corrected for any compass
deviation errors.

51.   3--2,000 ft. AGL is the altitude requested for flight over a wildlife
refuge.   See notes on the sectional chart.

52.   1--Latitude lines do not converge; they run parallel to one another and
to the equator.   The prime meridian is to longitude as the equator is to
latitude.

1. 1--Cooperstown is 25 marks north of the 36° North line (or 5 marks south of 36°30'N) and 6 marks left of 98°W.

2. 1--Currituck County is 24 marks north of the 36°N line (or 6 marks south of 36°30'N) and almost 2 marks west of 76°W.

3. 4--Shoshone County is 2 marks north of the 47°02'N line and 11 marks west of 116°W.

4. 2--Plot the location indicated.

5. 3--Plot the location indicated.

6. 4--EDT is 4 hours behind UTC. Convert takeoff time to UTC: 0945 EDT + 4 = 1345Z. ETA is 1345 + 2 = 1545Z.

7. 4--CST is + 6 from UTC. Convert takeoff time to UTC: 0845 CST + 6 = 1445Z. ETA is 1445 + 2 = 1645Z.

8. 3--PST is + 8 to UTC. Convert takeoff time to UTC: 1030 PST + 8 = 1830Z. ETA is 1830 + 4 = 2230Z.

9. 2--CST is + 6 to UTC. MST is + 7 to UTC. Takeoff is at 0830 MST.

10. 2--MST is + 7 from UTC. PST is + 8 from UTC. Takeoff is at 1515 PST.

11. 1--MST is +7 to UTC. PST is +8. Takeoff is at 1415 PST.

12. 4--The AIM states that the CTAF may be a UNICOM, MULTICOM, FSS or tower frequency. This question asks for CTAF FSS. See the partial box for the VOR/DME/FSS in the extreme lower left - 123.6 MHz.

13. 1--McVille has no tower, FSS nor UNICOM. In such cases you must use the universal MULTICOM for airports without a tower, FSS or UNICOM, 122.9. The AIM states that you should monitor and communicate on CTAF from 10 miles to landing.

14. 3--Barnes Co. has a UNICOM of 122.8. This is used as CTAF.

15. 2--The box northeast of Jamestown shows that Grand Forks Flight Watch serves this area. NOTE: charts no longer list flight watch information; you are expected to remember the frequency. Since all Flight Watches are on the same frequency, you don't need to know which one serves your area. Simply call "Flight Watch" and the nearest will answer.

16. 4--Currituck County has no tower or UNICOM, thus you should use the universal MULTICOM, 122.9. The AIM states that you should monitor and communicate on CTAF from 10 miles to landing.

17. 1--The square in the lower right of the MINOT VORTAC indicates that TWEB is transmitted on the VOR frequency of 117.1.

18.   3--All Enroute Flight Advisory Services (Flight Watches) are on 122.0. The box near the top of the page shows that Grand Forks Flight Watch serves this area. NOTE: charts no longer list flight watch information; you are expected to remember the frequency. Since all Flight Watches are on the same frequency, you don't need to know which one serves your area. Simply call "Flight Watch" and the nearest will answer.

19.   3--Garrison has no tower, FSS nor UNICOM, thus you should use the universal MULTICOM, 122.9.

20.   2--When the tower is not in operation use CTAF (119.1). It is common for CTAF to be the same as the tower frequency.

21.   2--When the tower is not in operation use CTAF (119.1). It is common for CTAF to be the same as the tower frequency.

22.   3--UNICOM (122.8) is used to request services.

23.   2--Where there is a tower, CTAF is normally the same frequency. See the CT-121.1.

24.   2--See the box at the bottom: "Arriving VFR aircraft should approach control with 20 mi. or 124.65 343.9."

25.   2--Military Operations Areas are established to separate certain military training activities from IFR traffic.

26.   2--The AIM states that pilots should contact an FSS within 100 nm of a MOA for information on the activities.

27.   3--The magenta shaded circle indicates that controlled airspace (transition areas) starts at 700 ft. AGL.

28.   1--The sharp line on the Hoggarth Farm side of the blue shaded markings indicate that this is uncontrolled airspace from the surface to the Continental Control Area.

29.   2--The airspace above Cooperstown is uncontrolled from the surface to 12,500 ft. The VFR visibility minimum is 1 statute mile, the cloud clearance minimum above 1,200 ft. AGL is 500 ft. below, 1,000 ft. above and 2,000 ft. horizontally.

30.   3--Aircraft are requested to remain 2,000 ft. above the surface of various National parks, wildlife refuges, etc.

31.   1--Warning areas contain the same unusual, often invisible, hazards as the Restricted Areas, but are over international waters.

32.   1--Norfolk International has a control tower. AIM requires pilots to establish and maintain radio communications with the tower prior to entering and while operating in the ATA.

33.   4--IR's are Military Training Routes for operations above 1,500 ft. AGL under instrument flight rules regardless of weather.

34. 4--The airspace below 1,200 AGL is normally uncontrolled. The airspace over County City is uncontrolled to the CCA. The cloud clearance rules below 1,200 ft. in uncontrolled airspace are 1 sm. visibility and clear of clouds.

35. 4--Airways extend from the floor of controlled airspace to 17,999 ft. The chart shows that above Magee, the floor is 7,500 ft. MSL rather than the normal 1,200 ft. AGL within blue shaded areas.

36. 3--The upper "100" symbols indicate that the upper limit is 10,000 ft.

37. 2--Victor airways are 4 nm wide.

38. 3--The magnetic course from Paris VORTAC to Quitman VORTAC is 166°. When flying VFR on a North or Easterly course use an odd thousand +500 ft. (NEODD).

39. 1--This is within LA Group I TCA. A private pilot certificate is required to land a Group I TCA. Only a student pilot certificate is required for flight through a TCA.

40. 1--LAX is within the TCA denoted by the wide blue lines. In Group I & II TCAs, you must have two-way radio communications, transponder, and encoding altimeter. Note that when this chart was printed, the exact altitudes of the TCA over LAX were cut off. The markings were 25/SFC and 70/50 indicating a TCA from the surface to 2,500 ft. MSL and 5,000-7,000 MSL.

41. 4--Ontario International is within an ARSA where two way radio communications is required.

42. 4--The normal top of an ARSA is 4,000 ft. above the airport. Note that 50/SFC indicates that in this ARSA the top is 5,000 ft. MSL; with field elevation of 942 ft., the top is slightly above the normal 4,000 AGL (5,000 ft. MSL - 942 ft. elevation = 4,058 ft. AGL).

43. 4--The base of the outer area of an ARSA is normally 1,200 ft. AGL. Note that the base at Ontario (50/27) is specified as 2,700 ft. MSL.

44. 3--A control zone above Fullerton and other airports is marked by a dashed line. It extends upward from the surface to the CCA.

45. 2--When a control zone is marked by small Ts, fixed wing special VFR is not authorized.

46. 1--The solid blue lines denote a TCA.

47. 3--The flag is a visual checkpoint that is well known by ATC.

48. 3--In both areas there are powerline symbols crossing bodies of water.

49. 2--See chart: CHESAPEAKE MUNI
                    20   36   122.7

50. 2--Tan indicates terrain of 2,000 ft. MSL to 3,000 ft. MSL. Note that the highest OBSTACLE extends to 3,149 ft. MSL in this area.

51.   1--The availability of fuel is indicated by four small barbs on the round airport symbol. A rotating beacon is indicated by a star at the top of the airport symbol.

52.   4--The chart legend states "Non-public use having emergency or landmark value."

53.   2--The A/FD contains this type of information.

54.   4--The flag identifies a visual checkpoint that is well-known by ATC.

55.   2--Of the three obstacles in this area, one has a height of 1549 ft. MSL (1532 ft. AGL).

56.   2--Military airfields are distinguished by a split white plus green rotating beacon.

57.   4--FAR 91.79 requires that in congested areas, aircraft must be at least 1,000 ft. above the highest obstacle within 2,000 ft. The obstacle has a height of 650 ft. MSL (250 ft. AGL).

58.   2--The stack has a height of 430 ft. MSL (400 ft. AGL).

59.   2--The obstacle has a height of 773 ft. MSL. In other than congested areas, you must fly 500 ft. above the surface and no closer than 500 ft. to any structure.

60.   3--The obstacle has a height of 901 ft. MSL (321 ft. AGL). In other than congested areas, you must fly 500 ft. above the surface and no closer than 500 ft. to any structure.

61.   3--TC is 201°, variation is 8°E (see the vertical dashed line east of McVille). 201 - 8 = 193° M. Or you can use the magnetic compass rose around the Jamestown VOR/DME because the navaid is on the airport. NOTE: The latter method works only when the VOR is co- located with the navigation feature; very few VORs are on airports.

62.   3--True course is 321°, variation is 9°W. 322 + 8 = 330° M.

63.   1--TC 082°, variation is 6°30 min. E. 082°TC - 6.50 = 075.5° M.

64.   1--TC is 012°. Variation is 11°E. Solve the wind problem: WCA is 10°L. 012 - 10 = 002° T - 11 = 351°M.

65.   2--TC is 012°, distance is 60NM. Solve the wind problem. GS is 80 kt. 80 kt./60 = 60 NM/45 min. Add 3 1/2 min. for departure/climb.

66.   2--TC 181°. Solve the wind problem. WCA is +7. 181 + 7 = 188° T - 19°E variation = 167 MH.

67.   4--TC is 181°. Distance is 59NM. Solve the wind problem. WCA is +7. GS 104 kt. 104 kt./60 = 59 NM/34 min.

68.   1--TC is 142°, variation is 19°E. Solve the wind problem. WCA is -7. 142° TC - 7° WCA = 135° TH - 19°E = 116° MH.

69. 3--TC is 142°, distance is 47NM. Solve the wind problem. GS is 99 kt.
99 kt./60 = 47 NM/29 min. 29 min. + 2 min. climb = 31.

70. 1--TC is 344°, variation is 19°E. Solve the wind problem. WCA = 6L.
344° TC - 6L = 338° TH - 19°E = 319° MH.

71. 2--TC is 344°, distance is 54NM. Solve the wind problem. GS is 80 kt.
80 kt./60 = 64NM/40 min. 40 min. + 3 min. climb = 43 min.

72. 3--TC is 213°, variation is 3°W. Solve the wind problem. WCA is 9L.
213° TC - 9L = 204° TH + 3°W = 207° MH. Use the compass correction card, the
closest MH is 210°. The card shows: FOR (Magnetic) 210°, STEER (Compass)
214°. The correction from MH to CH is +4. 207 + 4 = 211° CH.

73. 2--TC is 213°, distance is 57NM. Solve the wind problem. GS is 98 kt.
98 kt./60 = 57 NM/35 min. 35 + 2 min. = 37.

74. 1--TC is 045°, variation is 3W. Solve the wind problem. WCA is 11L.
045°TC - 11° = 034° TH + 3°W. = 037° MH. From compass correction card: For MH
030°, fly CH 027° (-3° correction). 037° MH - 3 = 034° CH.

75. 2--TC is 045°, distance is 57NM. Solve the wind problem. GS is 91 kt.
91 kt./60 = 57 NM/37 min. 37 min. + 2 min. (climb) = 39.

76. 1--TC is 257°, variation is 14°E. Solve the wind problem. WCA is 10L.
257° TC - 10L = 247° TH - 14°E = 233 MH.

77. 2--TC is 257°, distance is 37.5NM. Solve the wind problem. GS is 116
kt. 116 kt./60 = 37.5NM/20 min.

78. 3--The distance between the airports is 10 NM, which you covered in 5
min. Find the actual GS: 10NM/5 min. = 120kt./60. The distance from
Chesapeake to First Flight is 49 NM. Find the ETE for this leg: 120 kt./60 =
49 NM./25 min. 1501 + 25 = 1526 ETA.

E6-B FLIGHT COMPUTER

AERO PRODUCTS RESEARCH, INC.

complete instruction manual

APR has many models of E6-B-type computers and although the instructions for use are essentially the same we have clarified the particular features you can expect to find in each model. The following table identifies the major features:

Special Features of APR's E6-B Computers

	Wallet Case	Pouch Case	Flush Dial	Attaching Bars	Slide Lock	Micro-set	Compress. Scale
E6-B*			X			X	
E6-B1			X				X
E6-B2		X		X		X	X
E6-B3		X				X	X
E6-B4		X				X	X
E6-B9			X				
E6-B6			X				
I-E6-B2	X		X		X	X	X
I-E6-B4	X					X	X

*E6-B model only available in quantities by special order. Contact APR direct.

compiled by the
Aviation Education Department

AERO PRODUCTS RESEARCH, INC.

11201 HINDRY AVE., LOS ANGELES, CALIF. CA 90045 (213) 641-7242

Table of Contents

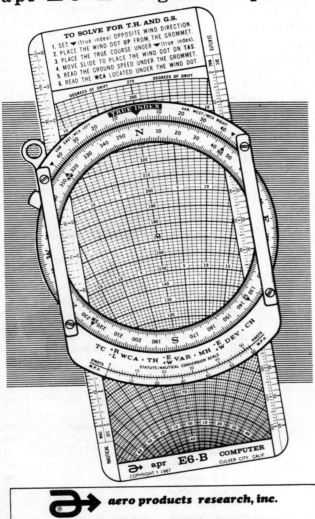

INSTRUCTIONS FOR USE

apr E6-B Flight Computer

TO SOLVE FOR T.H. AND G.S.
1. SET ▼ (true index) OPPOSITE WIND DIRECTION.
2. PLACE THE WIND DOT UP FROM THE GROMMET.
3. PLACE THE TRUE COURSE UNDER ▼ (true index).
4. MOVE SLIDE TO PLACE THE WIND DOT ON TAS.
5. READ THE GROUND SPEED UNDER THE GROMMET.
6. READ THE WCA LOCATED UNDER THE WIND DOT.

apr E6-B COMPUTER   CULVER CITY, CALIF.
COPYRIGHT 1967

aero products research, inc.

11201 HINDRY AVENUE, LOS ANGELES, CALIFORNIA 90045

a

FEATURES of APR E6-B FLIGHT COMPUTER

Calculator Side

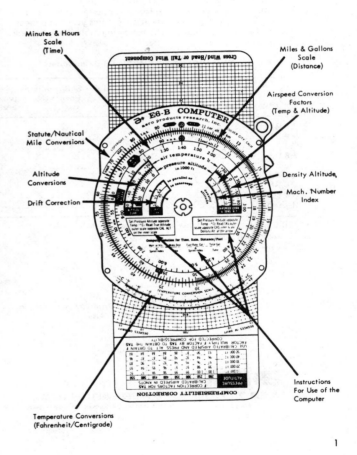

Minutes & Hours Scale (Time)

Miles & Gallons Scale (Distance)

Airspeed Conversion Factors (Temp & Altitude)

Statute/Nautical Mile Conversions

Altitude Conversions

Density Altitude

Mach. Number Index

Drift Correction

Instructions For Use of the Computer

Temperature Conversions (Fahrenheit/Centigrade)

1

Wind Side

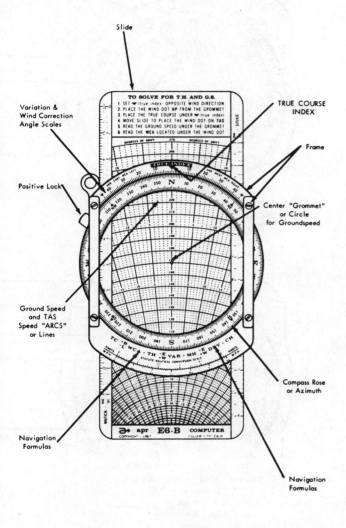

- Slide
- Variation & Wind Correction Angle Scales
- Positive Lock
- Ground Speed and TAS Speed "ARCS" or Lines
- Navigation Formulas

TO SOLVE FOR T.H. AND G.S.
1. SET ▼ (true index) OPPOSITE WIND DIRECTION
2. PLACE THE WIND DOT UP FROM THE GROMMET
3. PLACE THE TRUE COURSE UNDER ▼ (true index)
4. MOVE SLIDE TO PLACE THE WIND DOT ON TAS
5. READ THE GROUND SPEED UNDER THE GROMMET
6. READ THE WCA LOCATED UNDER THE WIND DOT

- TRUE COURSE INDEX
- Frame
- Center "Grommet" or Circle for Groundspeed
- Compass Rose or Azimuth
- Navigation Formulas

Computation — Calculator Side of E6-B

Time — Speed — Distance

The circular scales on the calculator face are like the scales of a slide rule, Figure 1. The same ratios hold good throughout the scale as shown:

$$\frac{20}{30} = \frac{40}{60} = \frac{60}{90}$$

Problems are solved by using these ratios for distance, time and speed, or for gallons, time and fuel consumption rate.

The outer scale is used for miles (or gallons), the middle scale represents minutes, and the inner scale hours.

First learn to read the values of the numbers on each scale. The number "10" may represent .10, 1.0, 10.0, 100 or 1000. The calibrations between numbers can also have different values. The first mark past "15" on the miles scale can equal 15.2, 152 and 1520, etc. The second mark past "30" equals 31. The first mark past "30" equals 30.5 or 305, etc. "150" minutes also equals 2 hours and 30 minutes.

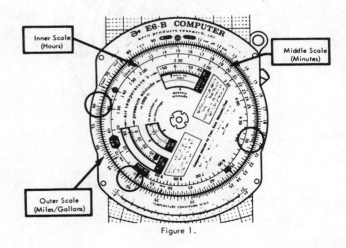

- Inner Scale (Hours)
- Middle Scale (Minutes)
- Outer Scale (Miles/Gallons)

Figure 1.

2

$$\frac{\text{Miles per hour}}{\blacktriangle} = \frac{\text{Distance}}{\text{Time}}$$
(One hour)

Figure 2.

Because of the relationship of scales of the computer, time, speed and distance problems are easily solved by using a proportion, Figure 2. To solve a problem, assume the speed to be 150 mph and time 36 minutes; to find the distance. The proportion would be:

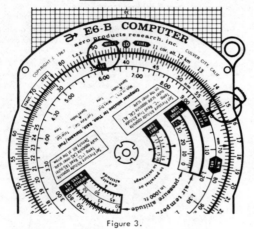

Figure 3.

$$\frac{150}{\blacktriangle} = \frac{\text{distance}}{36}, \text{ as shown in Figure 3.}$$
(1 hour)

Solution: Place 150 mph over the one hour index. (▲). Find 36 minutes on the minutes scale and opposite it read a distance of 90 miles on the miles scale.

Answer = 90 miles.

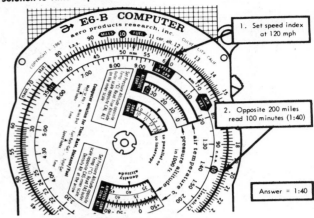

1. Set speed index at 120 mph

2. Opposite 200 miles read 100 minutes (1:40)

Answer = 1:40

Figure 4.

Given: Speed = 120 mph
Distance = 200 miles
Find: Time = _____
(See Figure 4 for solution.)

Answer: 1:40

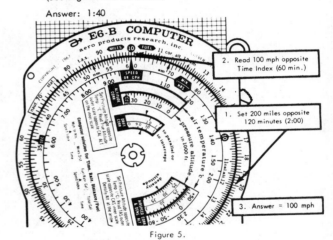

2. Read 100 mph opposite Time Index (60 min.)

1. Set 200 miles opposite 120 minutes (2:00)

3. Answer = 100 mph

Figure 5.

Given: Time = 2:00 (120 min.)
Distance = 200 miles
Find: Speed (mph) = _____
(See Figure 5 for solution.)

Answer: 100 mph.

4

5

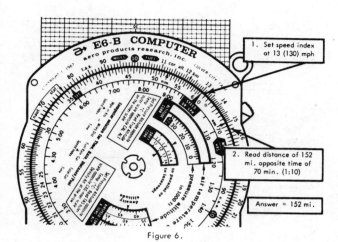

Figure 6.

Given: Speed = 130 mph
       Time = 1:10 (70 min.)
Find: Distance = _____ mi.
(See Figure 6 for solution.)

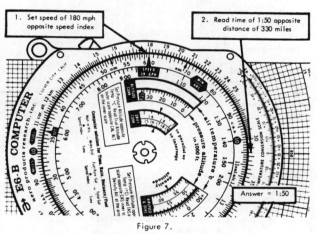

Figure 7.

Given: Speed = 180 mph
       Distance = 330 miles
Find: Time = _____
(See Figure 7 for solution.)

Answer: 1:50 (110 min.)

6

Practice Problems

	Speed	Time	Distance
1.		1:30	165 n.m.
2.	132 mph		198 mi.
3.	166 mph	1:50	
4.		2:10	206 mi.
5.	190 kts.		95 n.m.

Answers to Problems

	Speed	Time	Distance
1.	110 kts		
2.		1:30	
3.			305 mi.
4.	95 mph		
5.		:30	

Solution — Fuel Consumption Problems

Fuel consumption problems are solved like time, speed and distance problems, except that gallons are substituted for miles. The ratio used in these solutions is:

$$\frac{\text{gallons per hour}}{\text{Time} \blacktriangle \text{Index}} = \frac{\text{total gallons}}{\text{total time}}$$

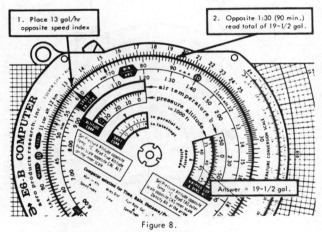

Figure 8.

Given: Fuel rate = 13 gal. per hour
       Time = 1:30 (90 min.)
Find: Total fuel = _____ gal.
(See Figure 8 for solution.)

Answer: 19-1/2 gallons.

7

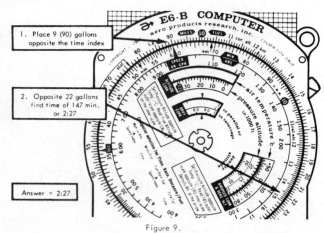

1. Place 9 (90) gallons opposite the time index

2. Opposite 22 gallons find time of 147 min. or 2:27

Answer = 2:27

Figure 9.

Given: Fuel rate = 9 gal. per hour
        Total fuel = 22 gallons
Find: Flight time = _____
(See Figure 9 for solution.)

Answer: 2:27 (147 min.)

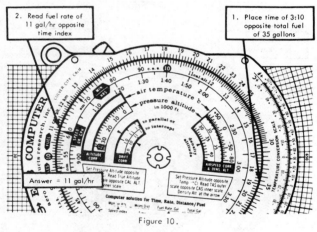

2. Read fuel rate of 11 gal/hr opposite time index

1. Place time of 3:10 opposite total fuel of 35 gallons

Answer = 11 gal/hr

Figure 10.

Given: Total gal. = 35 gal.
        Time = 3:10 (190 min.)
Find: Fuel rate = _____ gal/hr.
(See Figure 10 for solution.)

Answer: 11 gal/hour.

Practice Problems

	Fuel rate (gal/hr)	Time	Total Fuel
6.	18	1:50	
7.	14		21
8.		2:30	25
9.	13		40
10.	6	3:30	

Answers

	Fuel rate (gal/hr)	Time	Total Fuel
6.			33
7.		1:30	
8.	10		
9.		3:04	
10.			21

Conversions

True Airspeed

Indicated (or Calibrated) Airspeeds and True Airspeed are equal at sea level under standard conditions – pressure 29.92 inches Hg and temperature 15°C (59° F). As an airplane climbs to a higher altitude, pressure and temperature normally decrease. This change requires a correction to IAS to obtain TAS, since true airspeed increases with altitude.

Pressure Altitude is indicated on the altimeter when it is "set" to 29.92 inches Hg.

Conversion to TAS — Figure 11.

Given: Pressure Altitude = 10,000 feet
        Temperature = 0°C.
        Calibrated Airspeed = 150 mph.
Find: True Airspeed = _____
(See Figure 11 for solution.)

Answer: 176 mph.

To find Density Altitude, read it at the Index. In this case it is 10,500 feet.

8

9

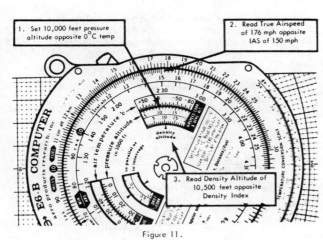

1. Set 10,000 feet pressure altitude opposite 0°C temp

2. Read True Airspeed of 176 mph opposite IAS of 150 mph

3. Read Density Altitude of 10,500 feet opposite Density Index

Figure 11.

Mach Number

To obtain the True Airspeed from a Mach Number, follow this procedure:

(a) Set Mach Number Index* opposite the true air temperature in degrees Centigrade.
(b) Read a Mach Number on the <u>minutes scale</u>.
(c) Opposite the Mach Number read true airspeed on the <u>miles scale</u>.

* Mach Number Index is at the end of the Pressure Altitude scale.

Practice Problems

	Temperature (°C)	Mach Number	True Airspeed
16.	0°C	0.9	_____ kts
17.	+20°C	0.45	_____ kts
18.	-10°C		190 kts
19.	+20°C	_____	_____ kts
20.	-20°C	_____	620 kts

Answers

	Mach Number	True Airspeed
16.		580 kts
17.		300 kts
18.	0.3	
19.		600 kts
20.	1.0	

True Airspeed Correction for Compressibility ("F" Factor)

When using True Airspeeds above 200 knots, these speeds may be corrected for compressibility. This procedure is illustrated by an example:

(1) Find the True Airspeed by the conventional procedure, using Pressure Altitude, Temperature (°C), and Calibrated Airspeed to find <u>uncorrected</u> TAS.

(2) Given: TAS = 250 knots (uncorrected)
Pressure Altitude = 20,000 feet

(3) Enter the "F" Correction Factor tabulation on the computer slide, Figure 12, find TAS of 250 knots and Pressure Altitude of 20,000 feet and read an "F" correction factor of .98. In some cases interpolation is necessary.

Practice Problems

	Pressure Altitude	Temperature	IAS	TAS	Density Altitude
11.	8000 ft.	-10°C	120 kts	_____	_____
12.	9000 ft.	+10°C	140 mph	_____	_____
13.	5000 ft.	+30°C	120 mph	_____	_____
14.	7000 ft.	-20°C	150 kts	_____	_____
15.	12000 ft.	-10°C	180 mph	_____	_____

Answers

	TAS	Density Altitude
11.	133 kts.	6900 ft.
12.	164 mph	10500 ft.
13.	135 mph	8000 ft.
14.	160 kts	4500 ft.
15.	216 mph	12000 ft.

10

11

(4) Correct TAS as follows:

```
     250 TAS (uncorrected)
×    .98 "F" factor
   ─────────
    2000
   2250
   ─────────
  245.00 = Corrected TAS
```

(5) 245 knots is the TAS corrected for compressibility.

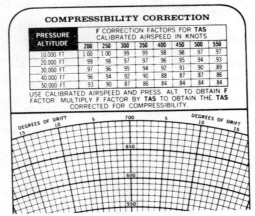

COMPRESSIBILITY CORRECTION

PRESSURE ALTITUDE	F CORRECTION FACTORS FOR TAS CALIBRATED AIRSPEED IN KNOTS							
	200	250	300	350	400	450	500	550
10,000 FT	1.00	1.00	.99	.99	.98	.98	.97	.97
20,000 FT	.99	.98	.97	.97	.96	.95	.94	.93
30,000 FT	.97	.96	.95	.94	.92	.91	.90	.89
40,000 FT	.96	.94	.92	.90	.88	.87	.87	.86
50,000 FT	.93	.90	.87	.86	.84	.84	.84	.84

USE CALIBRATED AIRSPEED AND PRESS. ALT. TO OBTAIN F FACTOR. MULTIPLY F FACTOR BY TAS TO OBTAIN THE TAS CORRECTED FOR COMPRESSIBILITY.

Figure 12.

Problems

	Uncorrected TAS	Pressure Altitude		Corrected TAS
21.	350 kts	10,000 ft	=	_____ kts
22.	325 kts	30,000 ft	=	_____ kts
23.	400 kts	30,000 ft	=	_____ kts
24.	500 kts	20,000 ft	=	_____ kts
25.	525 kts	25,000 ft	=	_____ kts

Answers

	Corrected TAS
21.	346 kts
22.	307 kts
23.	368 kts
24.	470 kts
25.	480 kts

12

Conversion to True Altitude

To convert Indicated (or Calibrated) Altitude to True Altitude, use the following procedure. Assume the airplane is flying at 8,000 feet "calibrated altitude" and the nearest ground station is at 5,000 feet altitude. Pressure altitude is 8,000 feet and True Air Temperature is -19°C.

(a) Find the difference between calibrated altitude and ground altitude; in this case 3,000 feet.
(b) Set pressure altitude opposite temperature °C on Altitude Computation scale, Figure 13.
(c) Find 3,000 feet on the middle scale and read 2,800 feet on the outer scale as true altitude correction, Figure 13.
(d) Add 2,800 feet to 5,000 feet and find true altitude of 7,800 feet.

(Figure 13 illustrates the problem on the E6-B Computer.)

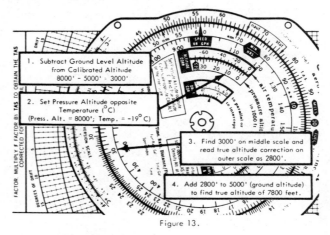

1. Subtract Ground Level Altitude from Calibrated Altitude 8000' - 5000' - 3000'

2. Set Pressure Altitude opposite Temperature (°C) (Press. Alt. = 8000'; Temp. = -19° C)

3. Find 3000 on middle scale and read true altitude correction on outer scale as 2800'.

4. Add 2800' to 5000' (ground altitude) to find true altitude of 7800 feet.

Figure 13.

Statute to Nautical Statute Miles

The E6-B Flight Computer has a conversion scale for converting statute to nautical (or nautical to statute) miles, Figure 14. Set statute miles on the middle scale under "stat" arrow, and read nautical miles on the middle scale opposite "naut" arrow. Reverse the process to read statute miles. The example in Figure 14 shows how to convert 115 statute miles to the equivalent nautical miles (100).

13

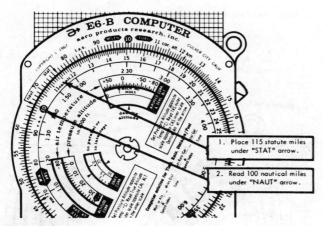

Figure 14.

Converting Speed to Statute MPH or Knots

On the E6-B, speeds (at the Speed Index) may be directly converted to statute mph or knots as shown in Figure 15. Assume the Speed Index is set to a speed of "120" and refer to the solution in Figure 15.

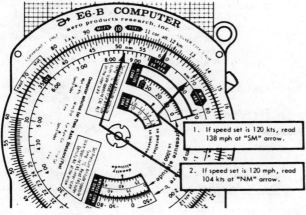

1. If speed set is 120 kts, read 138 mph at "SM" arrow.

2. If speed set is 120 mph, read 104 kts at "NM" arrow.

Figure 15.

14

Kilometers

When any value of statute or nautical miles is set opposite the "stat" or "naut" arrows, the distance in kilometers may be read opposite the "Km" arrow.

Minutes to Seconds

At 36 on the middle scale you will find an arrow which is labeled "SEC." To convert minutes to seconds:

(a) Place the Speed Index " ▲ " opposite minutes (on the outer scale).
(b) Read seconds opposite the "SEC" arrow.

Example: <u>8</u> minutes is equal to <u>480</u> seconds.

Problems

	Stat. Miles	Naut. Miles	Kilometers	Minutes	Seconds
26.	150		___		
27.		120	___		
28.				2.5	___
29.				___	300
30.			185		
31.	100	___			
32.	___		210		
33.	84	___			
34.					480
35.				3.5	___

Answers

	Stat. Miles	Naut. Miles	Kilometers	Minutes	Seconds
26.			241		
27.			222		
28.					150
29.				5	
30.		100			
31.		___	161		
32.	131				
33.		73			
34.				8	
35.					210

15

Conversion — Fahrenheit/Centigrade

The scale shown in Figure 16 is used to directly convert in either direction, Fahrenheit to Centigrade, or Centigrade to Fahrenheit temperatures.

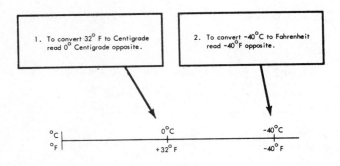

Figure 16.

Off-Course and Drift Correction

So called "Off-Course" problems are easily solved on the APR E6-B Flight Computer. The navigation factors which are used in the solution are:

(a) Distance off course.
(b) Distance flown.
(c) Distance remaining to be flown (distance to fly).

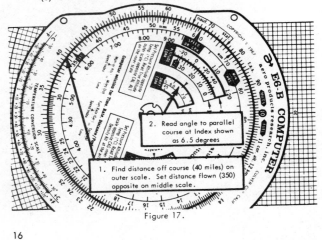

Figure 17.

A. Solution to Parallel the Original Course

Given: Distance off course = 40 miles
       Distance flown = 350 miles
Find: Angle to parallel course = _____ deg. (amount to turn).
(See solution of this part in Figure 17.)

B. Solution to Intercept Original Course

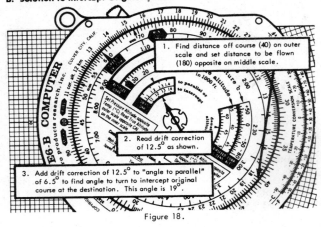

Figure 18.

Given: Distance off course = 40 miles (same as above).
       Distance to be flown = 180 miles
Find: (B) Angle to intercept course = _____ deg. (This value must be added to "angle to parallel course" as solved previously.)
     (A) Angle to parallel course was found to be 6.5° above.

Total correction to intercept = 6.5° + angle to intercept.
                    (called drift correction)

The solution is given in Figure 18.

Problems

	Distance Off Course	Distance Flown	Distance To Fly	Angle to Parallel	Drift Correction	Total Correction to Intercept Course
36.	30	244	105	_____	_____	_____
37.	22	70	85	_____	_____	_____
38.	10	100	100	_____	_____	_____
39.	35	300	150	_____	_____	_____
40.	20	180	120	_____	_____	_____

Answers *

	Angle to Parallel	Drift Correction	Total Correction To Intercept Course
36.	7.0°	16°	23°
37.	17.6°	14.5°	32.1°
38.	5.7°	5.7°	11.4°
39.	6.7°	13.2°	19.9°
40.	6.3°	9.5°	15.8°

* Notice that decimal points in answers must be adjusted to a value of about 1° off course in each 60 miles flown for each mile off course (at 60).

Slide Rule Mathematics

Multiplication

To multiply on the E6-B Flight Computer, use the following proportion:

$$\frac{Multiplier}{10 \; *} = \frac{Product}{Other \; factor}$$

* Use the 10 index and not the Speed Index of 60 (▲).

A sample problem would be:

$$2 \times 4 = 8$$

On the computer this problem would appear as:

$$\frac{2}{10} = \frac{X}{4} \qquad X = 8$$

This example is solved in Figure 19.

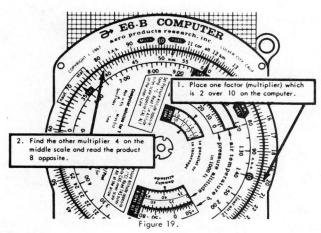

1. Place one factor (multiplier) which is 2 over 10 on the computer.

2. Find the other multiplier 4 on the middle scale and read the product 8 opposite.

Figure 19.

Division

To divide on the E6-B Flight Computer, use the following proportion:

$$\frac{Dividend}{Divisor} = \frac{Quotient}{10}$$

A sample problem would be:

$$8 \div 4 = 2$$

On the computer this problem would appear as:

$$\frac{8}{4} = \frac{2}{10} \; , \; \text{as shown in Figure 20.}$$

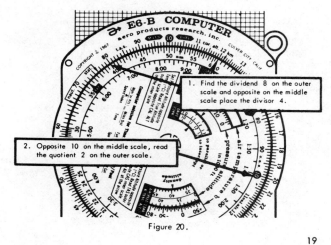

1. Find the dividend 8 on the outer scale and opposite on the middle scale place the divisor 4.

2. Opposite 10 on the middle scale, read the quotient 2 on the outer scale.

Figure 20.

18

19

Problems

41. 13 × 7 = _____
42. 300 ÷ 15 = _____
43. 19 × 5 = _____
44. 345 ÷ 15 = _____
45. 137 × 7 = _____

Answers

41. 91
42. 20
43. 95
44. 23
45. 959

Time and Distance to Radio Station

Time and/or distance from the airplane to a radio station can be computed very easily on the E6-B by proportion if the correct formulas are used.

Time to Radio Station

The formula to set up on the computer, after timing a radio bearing change, to find time to fly to the station is as follows:

$$\frac{\text{Time between bearings}}{\text{Degrees of bearing change}} = \frac{\text{Time to station}}{60 \ (\blacktriangle)}$$

Given: Time between bearings = 5 minutes
         Degrees of bearing change = 10 degrees
Find: Time to fly to station = _____ minutes.
(This problem is solved on the computer in Figure 21.)

Distance to Radio Station

The formula to set up on the computer to find distance to the station is as follows:

$$\frac{\text{Time between bearings}}{\text{Degrees of bearing change}} = \frac{\text{Distance to Station}}{\text{Airplane speed}}$$

Given: Time between bearings = 6 minutes
         Degree of bearing change = 10 degrees
         Airplane speed = 120 mph
Find: Distance to station = _____ miles.
(This problem is solved on the computer in Figure 22.)

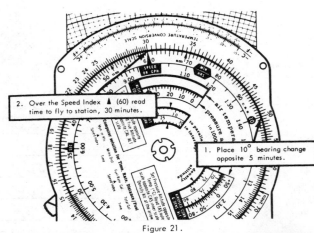

2. Over the Speed Index ▲ (60) read time to fly to station, 30 minutes.

1. Place 10° bearing change opposite 5 minutes.

Figure 21.

1. Place 6 minutes time over 10 degrees of bearing change.

2. Find airplane speed (120) on middle scale and read distance of 72 miles on outer scale.

Figure 22.

Problems

	Degrees of Bearing Change	Time Between Bearings	Airplane Speed	Time to Station	Distance to Station
46.	15°	5 min.		_____	
47.	12°	6 min.	120 mph		_____
48.	18°	6 min.		_____	
49.	15°	5 min.	180 mph		_____
50.	10°	5 min.		_____	

20

21

ADJUSTMENTS OF THE APR E6-B COMPUTER

It is possible to adjust the E6-B for both accuracy and tightness of parts.

A. To adjust the E6-B for "Accuracy:"

Although this APR Computer is the most accurate construction possible, some adjustment may be necessary at times.

1. To check the large slide for centering and alignment, align the center line with the grommet on the movable disc, at both ends of the slide. Turn the slide over and redo the test for the other centerline.

   (a) If both centerlines are aligned with the grommet you are ready to solve problems.

2. In case both centerlines of the slide do not align with the grommet, use this procedure:

   (a) Slightly loosen the 4 assembly screws until the slide will move.
   (b) Align the slide centerline with the grommet at both ends.
   (c) Tighten screws fairly snugly and again see if slide centerline is aligned with grommet, both ends and both sides.
   (d) When aligned, securely tighten the four screws.

B. To adjust the E6-B for "Tightness":

1. With bottom screws slightly loose, pull the bottom plate away slightly and test rotating disc for proper tension or tightness.

2. Gradually tighten the lower two screws until the disc is at the tension desired.

CAUTION AREAS OF THE E6-B COMPUTER

A. Do not expose the vinyl plastic model of the E6-B to temperatures above 140° F (which is 60° C) since high temperatures may warp the computer. Do not leave on the dash board of a car or airplane in direct sunlight or warping will occur.

B. Relative to the Positive Lock, do not forcibly move the slide while it is in the locked position or this may damage the slide. Release the lock before moving the slide.

C. Clean the plastic disc often when doing problems.

Lock must be left in "OFF" position when computer is not in use.

22

Wind and Wind Effect

If the air were absolutely still, relative to the earth's surface navigation of aircraft would be very simple. The pilot, merely by correcting for variation and deviation, could easily set the aircraft on any desired course. He could calculate ETA's and determine positions en route by using the true air speed. Or, if the science of meteorology were advanced to the point where the wind could always be forecast with complete accuracy, a flight could be planned on the ground and that plan could be used with complete confidence in flight.

Unfortunately, however, neither of these situations exists. Air masses are almost always moving, which is the phenomenon called wind. Meteorologists usually give accurate weather predictions but cannot always forecast winds with complete accuracy. And as a navigator, you will find that the wind is your main source of headaches. It has been said that navigation is "wind-finding," and this statement has much merit.

"Wind is the movement of an air mass over the earth's surface. Wind has both direction and speed." <u>Wind Direction (WD) is expressed as the direction from which the wind is blowing</u>, measured clockwise through 360° from true north. For example, if a wind is from the west, it is a west wind, and its direction is 270°. Keep in mind that Wind Direction differs from other directions used in navigation in that it is the direction from which, rather than the direction toward which, motion occurs. True Heading (TH), for example, is the direction toward which the aircraft is headed.

Wind Speed (WS) is the rate of movement of the air over the earth's surface. To maintain conformity, both meteorologists and pilots express Wind Speed in knots.

Wind Direction (WD) and Wind Speed (WS) together are expressed as Wind Velocity (WV) and should never be used independently, but rather as a unit. It is meaningless to speak of either the direction or speed of the wind alone. "WV (Wind Velocity) 180°/25k" means that the wind is <u>from</u> the south and that its speed is 25 knots. Remember: the term "velocity" implies both speed and direction.

The Effect of Wind on Aircraft

Any vehicle traveling on the ground, such as an automobile, moves in the direction in which it is steered or headed and is affected very little by wind. An aircraft, however, seldom travels in exactly the direction in which it is headed. You will understand this when you learn the effect of wind on the flight path. Consider first the effect of wind on a balloon which has no motion of its own. At 9:00 AM a balloon is launched into the air at point A. If the wind is from 270° at 20k (WV = 270°/20k), where is the balloon at 10:00 AM? You may

23

think of the balloon as floating in a body of air which moves from 270°
toward 90° at 20k. In one hour the body of air moves 20 nm and the
balloon moves with it. Thus, at 10:00 AM the balloon is at point B,
20 nm from point A in the direction of 90°. A balloonist never feels
any wind because he is suspended in the body of air and moves with it.
Consequently no air moves past him. A balloon in the air is just like
an empty bottle floating down a river; the bottle travels with the current.

Any free object in the air moves downwind with the speed of
the wind. This is just as true of an aircraft as it is of a balloon. If an
aircraft is flying in a 20k wind, the body of air in which it is flying
moves 20 nm in one hour. Therefore, the aircraft also moves 20 nm
downwind in one hour. This movement is in addition to the forward
movement of the aircraft through the body of air.

The path of an aircraft over the earth is determined by two independent factors: (1) the motion of the aircraft through the air, and
(2) the motion of the air across the earth's surface. The motion of the
aircraft through the air mass is directly forward in response to the pull
of the propellers or thrust of the jet units, and its rate of movement
through the air is True Air Speed (TAS). This motion takes place in
the direction of True Heading (TH). The motion of air across the
earth's surface may be from any direction and at any speed. The mea-
surement of movement is called wind and is expressed in direction and
speed (WV).

Drift is Caused by Wind

An aircraft's movement over the ground is comparable to a
boat crossing a river. If there is no current in the river, a boat starting at one shore of the river and rowed perpendicular to the river's
edge would end up at a point on the opposite shore directly across
from its starting point. However, if there is a current, the boat will
be carried downstream. Until the boat eventually reaches the opposite
shore, the displacement downstream is dependent upon the velocity of
the river current and the velocity of the boat.

The aircraft in Figure 23 departs from point X on a heading of
360° and flies for one hour in a wind of 270°/20k. The aircraft is
headed toward point M, directly north of X, so its True Heading is
represented by the line XM. If there were no wind, the aircraft would
be at point M at the end of the hour. However, there is a wind. The
body of air in which the aircraft is flying moves 20 nm toward the east
in the hour, and the aircraft moves downwind with it. Consequently,
at the end of the hour the aircraft is at point N, 20 nm downwind from
point M. Thus the line M is the path of the aircraft through the air;
the line NM shows the motion of the air itself; and the line XN is the
actual path of the aircraft over the earth (track). The effect, then, of
this wind on the aircraft is to cause it to follow a different path over
the ground than it does through the air mass. The path over the ground
is its Track (TR). At this time it might be well to differentiate be-

24

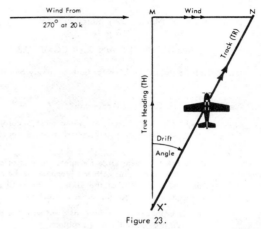

Figure 23.

tween the terms True Course (TC) and Track (TR). True Course (TC) is
the line on a chart representing the intended path of the aircraft over
the earth's surface. Track (TR) is the actual path that the aircraft
has flown over the earth's surface. The terms TC and TR are often considered synonymous. Remember, however, that in the actual workings
of navigation, True Course is considered to be future, while Track is
considered to be past. E.g.: a pilot intends to fly along a True
Course of 90°; however, due to unknown winds, he has drifted along
an actual Track of 100°.

The sideward displacement of the aircraft by the wind is called
Drift. Drift is the angle between the True Heading and the Track. As
shown in the preceding illustration, the aircraft has drifted to the
right. This is known as right drift. With a given wind, the amount of
drift will vary on different headings. A change of heading will also
effect the distance over the earth's surface that an aircraft will travel
in a given time. This rate traveled relative to the earth's surface is
known as Ground Speed (GS). Therefore, with a given wind, the
Ground Speed (GS) varies on different headings. Figure 24 shows the
effect of a 270°/20k wind on the Ground Speed and Track of an aircraft flying on headings of 000°, 090°, 180°, and 270°. The aircraft
flies on each heading from point X (the center of the circle) for one
hour at a constant True Air Speed.

Note that on a true heading of 000°, the wind causes right
drift, whereas on a true heading of 180°, the same wind causes left
drift. On the headings of 090° and 270°, there is no drift at all.
Note further that on a heading of 090°, the aircraft is aided by a tailwind and travels farther in an hour than it would without a wind; thus
its Ground Speed is increased by the wind. On the heading of 270°,
the headwind cuts down the distance traveled and also cuts down the
Ground Speed. On the headings of 000° and 180°, the Ground Speed
is somewhat increased.

25

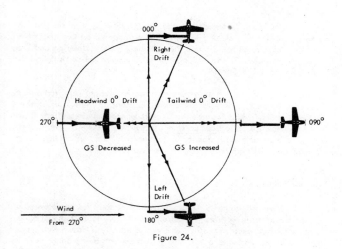

Figure 24.

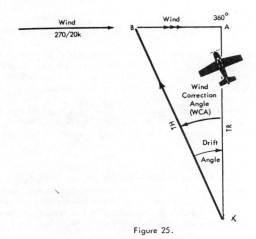

Figure 25.

Drift Correction Compensates for Wind

Thus far you have seen how the wind causes drift and affects the Track of an aircraft. But you have not seen how to adjust True Heading to allow for drift, and thus maintain a desired True Course.

In Figure 25, suppose you want to fly from point X to point A, a True Course of 360°, when the wind is 270°/20k. What should be the True Heading? Obviously, if you fly a True Heading of 360°, you will end up <u>not</u> at point A but at some point downwind from A. Therefore, you must head for some point <u>upwind</u> from point A and let the right drift bring you to A. If the aircraft is to be in the air for one hour, it will drift 20 nm downwind. Therefore, you must head for a point (B) 20 nm upwind from point A. Flying the heading XB, you will reach point A in one hour; the Track of the aircraft will be the line XA.

Heading an aircraft upwind in order to maintain the True Course is called correcting for drift. The angle AXB is called the Wind Correction Angle (WCA) and is always opposite to drift. If the aircraft drifts to the left, wind correction must be applied to the right. If the aircraft drifts to the right, wind correction must be applied to the left. In this case, drift is right and wind correction is to the left.

The amount of wind correction must be just enough to compensate for the amount of drift on the particular heading. Therefore, if the aircraft is on a heading of XB, the drift on the Wind Correction Angle must be equal to the drift angle. But if the drift is to the right, wind correction must be to the left or minus. Therefore, the Wind Correction Angle is measured in the opposite direction to the drift and given a sign of plus or minus.

Figure 26 shows the wind correction necessary in a 270°/20k wind if the aircraft is to make good a True Course of 360°, 090°, 180°, and 270°.

Note that to reach point B or D, the aircraft need make no wind correction. To reach point A or C, the aircraft must head upwind. This means that to reach point A, the aircraft must correct to the left or minus (–) wind correction, and to reach point C it must correct to the right, or plus (+) wind correction.

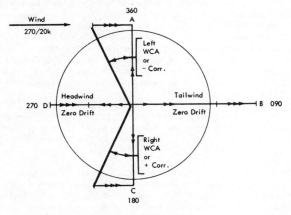

Figure 26.

26

27

Suppose an aircraft is flying from point X to point A, a True Course of 360°. Wind correction is left; hence, the True Heading is less than 360°. Therefore, the Wind Correction Angle which must be applied to the True Course to obtain the True Heading is minus in sign. Whenever the drift is right, you correct to the left, and the sign of the correction is minus. By considering a flight from point X to point C, you will see that the reverse is also true. Whenever the drift is left, you correct to the right, and the sign of the correction is plus.

You do not need to memorize these rules. In fact, you may become confused if you try to rely on some rule of thumb. Rather, you should visualize the situation, or draw a rough sketch, if necessary, and figure out the sign for yourself. Keep in mind a mental picture of the compass rose and how directions increase as you move clockwise.

Remember that after you have corrected for drift, the aircraft will still drift. All you have done is to head the aircraft off course so that the wind will cause it to drift along the course while maintaining a constant heading. This correction in the heading of the aircraft cannot, of course, have any effect on the wind itself. The wind is a natural element over which we have no control.

The Wind Triangle

In dead-reckoning navigation many problems involving speed and direction have to be solved. Primarily, you are concerned with Ground Speed, True Heading, True Air Speed, Wind Direction, Wind Speed, and True Course (or Track). Often you will know four of these six quantities and will need to determine the other two. For example, you may know True Heading, True Air Speed, Wind Direction, and Wind Speed, and need to know Track and Ground Speed. In order to solve such problems it is necessary to understand the relationships of these six quantities.

These quantities are represented by vectors. A vector is a quantity having both magnitude and direction. Though physics books treat of several others, the vector quantity of most importance in navigation is velocity.

Velocity is speed in a certain direction. As previously explained, Wind Velocity includes both Wind Speed and Wind Direction, not merely Wind Speed (WS) alone. Likewise, the velocity of an aircraft with relation to the earth's surface includes both Track and Ground Speed. And the velocity of an aircraft with relation to the air in which it is flying includes both True Heading and True Air Speed.

28

You have learned that the velocity of an aircraft over the earth's surface (Track and Ground Speed) depends on two quantities: (1) the velocity of the aircraft through the air (True Heading and True Air Speed), and (2) the velocity of the air over the earth (Wind Direction and Wind Speed).

A vector which thus results directly and entirely from two or more other vectors is said to be the resultant or vector sum of these other vectors. And two or more vectors whose sum or resultant is another vector are called components of this other vector. Two or more given components can produce only one resultant. A change in any component will cause a change in the resultant.

Vector Diagrams

A vector quantity, such as velocity, may be represented on paper by a straight line. The direction of the vector is shown by the line with reference to north. The vector usually is drawn like an arrow, with a head and a tail, so that there can be no doubt as to its direction. The magnitude of the vector is shown by the length of the line in comparison with some arbitrary scale. For example, you may let 1 inch equal 20 nm. Then a velocity of 50k in a certain direction is shown by a line 2-1/2 inches long in that direction, Figure 27.

When two or more vectors are components of a third vector, this relationship may be shown by means of a vector diagram. If the components are drawn tail to head in any order, a line from the tail of the first component to the head of the last component represents the resultant. Consequently, if you know the components, you can find the resultant. And if you know the resultant, and all but one of the components, you can find the missing component, Figure 28.

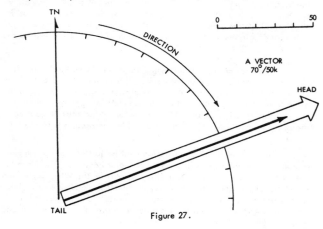

Figure 27.

29

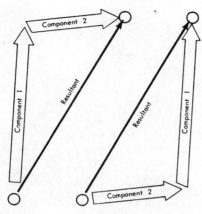

Figure 28.

A vector diagram showing the effect of the wind on the flight of an aircraft is called a wind triangle. One line is drawn to show the velocity of the aircraft through the air (True Heading and True Air Speed). This velocity is called the <u>true heading—true air speed vector</u> or <u>air vector</u>. Another line is drawn to the same scale and connected tail to head to show the velocity of the wind. This is the wind vector. A line connecting the tail of the first vector with the head of the second shows the resultant of these two velocities to the same scale; it shows the velocity of the aircraft over the earth (Track and Ground Speed). It is called the <u>track—ground speed vector</u> or <u>ground vector</u>. It does not matter which of the two components is drawn first; the resultant is the same, Figure 29.

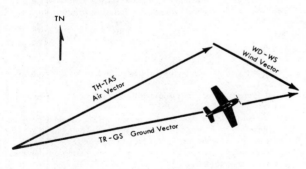

WIND TRIANGLE

Figure 29.

30

Take care to remember that True Air Speed is always in the direction of True Heading and that Ground Speed is always in the direction of Track. Also remember that the track—ground speed vector is the resultant of the other two; hence the true heading—true air speed vector and the wind vector are always drawn head to tail.

An easy way to remember this is to recall that the wind always blows the aircraft from the True Heading to the Track (TR).

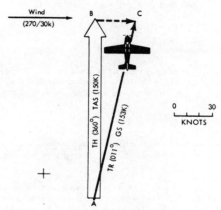

Figure 30.

Consider just what the wind triangle in Figure 30 shows. An aircraft departs from point A on a True Heading of 360° at a True Air Speed of 150k. In one hour, if there were no wind, the aircraft would reach point B at a distance of 150 nm. The line AB shows the direction and distance the aircraft would have flown under no wind conditions. Therefore, the length of AB shows the True Air Speed of the aircraft. Thus, AB represents the velocity of the aircraft through the air and is the air vector.

Imagine that at the end of the first hour the aircraft stops flying forward and remains suspended in mid-air at point B. Suppose then that the wind starts blowing from 270° at 30k. At the end of the second hour the aircraft is at point C, 30 miles downwind from B. The line BC shows the direction and distance the aircraft has moved with the wind, or the direction and distance the air has moved in an hour. Therefore, the length of BC represents the speed of the wind in the same scale as the True Air Speed. Thus, BC represents the wind velocity and is the wind vector.

31

As a result of the aircraft's forward motion and the effect of the wind during the same hour, the aircraft reaches C at the end of the first hour. It does not go to B and then to C. Instead, it goes directly by the line AC, since the wind carries it east at 30k at the same time that the propeller pulls it north at 150k. Therefore, the line AC shows the distance and direction the aircraft travels over the ground in one hour, and the length of AC represents the Ground Speed in the same scale as the True Air Speed and Wind Speed. Thus AC, which is the resultant of AB and BC, represents the velocity of the aircraft over the ground and is the ground vector.

Measuring the length of AC, you find that the Ground Speed is about 153k. Measuring the drift angle BAC and applying it to the True Heading of 360°, you find that the track is 011, or 11° to the right.

Wind Triangles on the Computer

The wind face of the computer has three basic parts: a frame, a transparent circular plate held in the frame in such a way that it can be rotated, and a grid which can be rotated up and down in the frame under the circular plate.

The frame has a reference mark called the true index. A drift scale is graduated 50° to the left and 50° to the right of the true index.

The circular plate has around its edge a compass rose in units of 1°. The position of the plate may be read, therefore, on the compass rose opposite the true index. Except for the edge, the circular plate is transparent, so that the markings on the grid may be seen through it. The center of the circular plate is marked by a small black circle called the grommet. Running the length of the grid is a center line, which falls beneath the true index and the grommet. The center line is cut at intervals of two units by arcs of concentric circles called speed circles; these are numbered at intervals of 10 units. The 60 at the bottom of the slide indicates that the origin of the center line and center of the speed circles are 60 units below the bottom of the slide.

On each side of the center line are drift lines at 1° intervals and are numbered at intervals of 5°. Thus, the 14° line on each side of the center line makes an angle of 14° with the center line at the origin. And the point where the 14° line intersects the speed circle marked "160" is 160 units from the origin.

In solving a wind triangle on the computer, you plot part of the triangle on the transparent surface of the circular plate. For the other parts of the triangle, you use the lines which are already drawn on the grid, Figure 31.

32

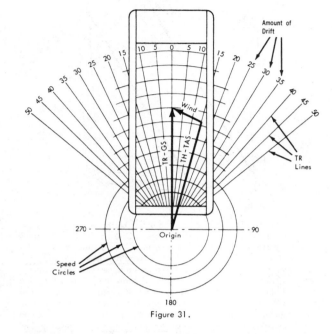

Figure 31.

Wind Solution — Wind Side of APR E6-B Flight Computer

The wind side of the E6-B Computer has the following significant components. Refer back to page 2 for illustration of the components.

(1) The frame with a True Index reference and variation scales 0° to 50°.
(2) A transparent, rotatable circular plate which has the following parts:
    (a) Azimuth scale for wind direction (also called Compass Rose).
    (b) Center "grommet" or circle for groundspeed.
    (c) A movable slide with speed curves and heading lines, or wind drift lines.
        (1) Where a curved line intersects the grommet it indicates groundspeed; otherwise it is used for airspeeds.

33

Positive Lock For Computer Slide

The new APR E6-B Computer has a unique feature in the form of a "positive lock" to prevent the Computer slide from moving (or falling out) of the Computer.

As illustrated in Figure 32, the lock can be secured by a flick of the finger to lock the slide in place. Another flick of the finger will unlock the slide for resetting when doing wind solutions.

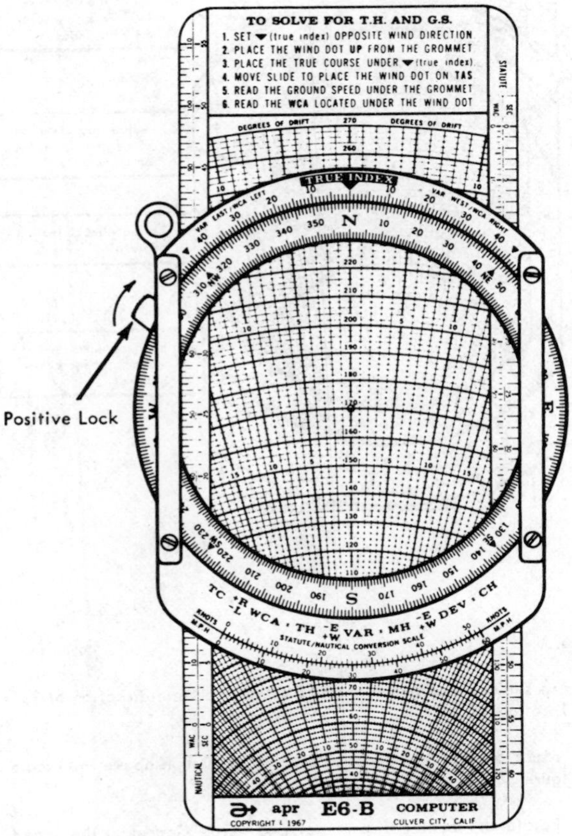

The graphical solution of a wind triangle is shown in Figure 33. In this illustration the center line represents the true course of 30°. The wind is blowing from 100° at 30 mph. The groundspeed (at the grommet) is at 150 mph, and the True Airspeed at the wind dot is 163 mph. The heading is 10° right of center, or 40°. The Wind Correction Angle is thus also 10° to the right.

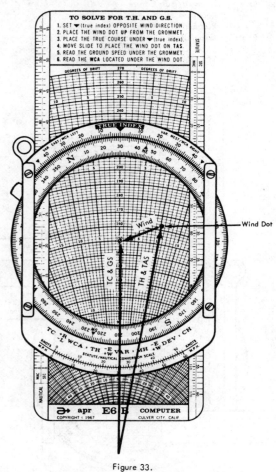

Figure 33.

All wind solutions can be graphically shown by a wind triangle similar to the one depicted in Figure 33.

Figure 32.

Flight Planning Type of Wind Solution

In this very common solution the reported wind is used with planned course and TAS to find the estimated groundspeed and heading.

Given: Planned True Course   = 340°
        Reported Wind   = 35° @ 30 mph
        Planned True Airspeed   = 140 mph
Find: Groundspeed   = _____ mph.
        Wind Correction Angle   = _____ degrees.
        True Heading   = _____ degrees.

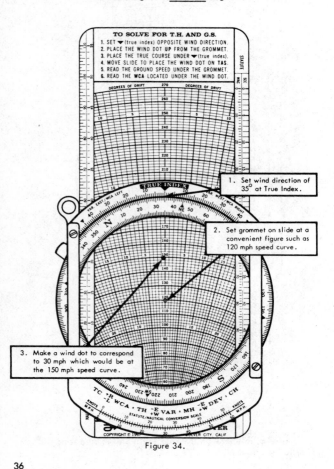

1. Set wind direction of 35° at True Index.

2. Set grommet on slide at a convenient figure such as 120 mph speed curve.

3. Make a wind dot to correspond to 30 mph which would be at the 150 mph speed curve.

Figure 34.

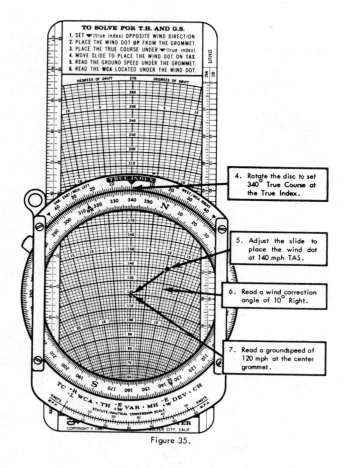

4. Rotate the disc to set 340° True Course at the True Index.

5. Adjust the slide to place the wind dot at 140 mph TAS.

6. Read a wind correction angle of 10° Right.

7. Read a groundspeed of 120 mph at the center grommet.

Figure 35.

Solution

As shown in Figures 34 and 35, set the wind direction of 35° at the True Index.

Mark a wind speed dot at a value of 30 mph above the grommet, Figure 34.

Rotate the center disc to set 340° True Course at the Speed Index, Figure 35.

36

37

Follow the balance of the procedure as given in Figure 35. Set the wind dot on the 140 mph airspeed curve by adjusting the slide, Figure 35. As shown in a continuation of the procedure, Figure 35, the groundspeed is 120 mph and the wind correction angle is 10° to the right.

If the true course is 340°, the true heading is 10° right, or 350°, which solves the problem.

Flight Planning Wind Problems

	True Course	Reported Wind	True Airspeed	WCA	True Heading	Ground-speed
51.	360°	40°@ 25 mph	160 mph			
52.	290°	240°@ 30 kts	130 kts			
53.	50°	190°@ 20 mph	150 mph			
54.	90°	320°@ 30 kts	145 kts			
55.	120°	120°@ 25 mph	170 mph			

Answers

	WCA	True Heading	Groundspeed
51.	6° R	006°	140 mph
52.	10° L	280°	109 kts
53.	5° R	55°	165 mph
54.	9° L	81°	163 kts
55.	0°	120°	145 mph

Variation Scales

The variation scales on the wind side of the E6-B Flight Computer are designed to convert magnetic courses to true courses for use in wind solution, since winds aloft are reported in true directions.

Solutions to determine the true course with easterly or westerly variation are illustrated in Figure 36.

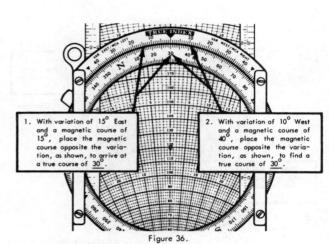

1. With variation of 15° East and a magnetic course of 15°, place the magnetic course opposite the variation, as shown, to arrive at a true course of 30°.

2. With variation of 10° West and a magnetic course of 40°, place the magnetic course opposite the variation, as shown, to find a true course of 30°.

Figure 36.

Enroute Wind Problems

This type of problem is useful for determining wind direction and velocity while flying "enroute" between two points. The data which must be known to solve this type of problem are:

Given: True Course
Groundspeed
True Heading
True Airspeed
To Find: Wind direction and velocity.

The same type wind triangle is used in the solution as the one illustrated in Figures 37 and 38.

Solution of Enroute Wind Problems

Given: True Course = 40°
Groundspeed = 145 mph
True Heading = 48°
Wind Correction Angle = 8° Right
True Airspeed = 166 mph
Find: Wind direction and velocity.

The solution to this problem is illustrated in Figures 37 and 38.

To read wind direction and velocity, use the procedure in Figure 38.

Thus, the answer to this problem is a wind direction of 90° and velocity of 30 mph. Use the same procedure to solve other enroute wind problems.

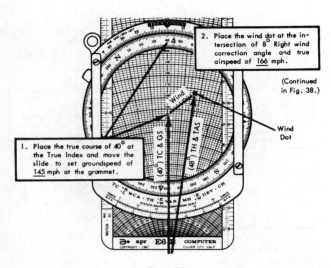

2. Place the wind dot at the intersection of 8° Right wind correction angle and true airspeed of 166 mph.

(Continued in Fig. 38.)

Wind Dot

1. Place the true course of 40° at the True Index and move the slide to set groundspeed of 145 mph at the grommet.

Figure 37.

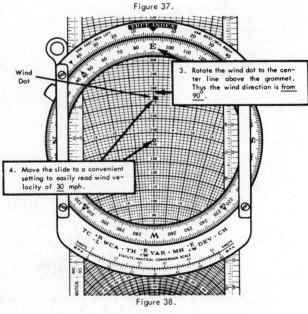

Wind Dot

3. Rotate the wind dot to the center line above the grommet. Thus the wind direction is from 90°.

4. Move the slide to a convenient setting to easily read wind velocity of 30 mph.

Figure 38.

	True Course	True Heading	Wind Correction Angle	Ground-speed	True Airspeed	Wind Direction	Velocity
56.	70°	77°	7° R	130 mph	147 mph	_____	@ _____
57.	340°	330°	10° L	144 kts	127 kts	_____	@ _____
58.	35°	42°	7° R	175 mph	160 mph	_____	@ _____
59.	75°	75°	0°	120 mph	140 mph	_____	@ _____
60.	110°	120°	10° R	153 kts	167 kts	_____	@ _____

Answers

	Wind Direction		Velocity
56.	118°	@	24 mph
57.	209°	@	29 kts
58.	164°	@	26 mph
59.	75°	@	20 mph
60.	178°	@	31 kts

WIND COMPONENTS (E6-B3, E6-B4, I-E6-B2, I-E6-B4 Only)

A wind component is that portion of an existing wind condition which acts in a definite direction with respect to the aircraft. That portion of the wind velocity which is pushing the aircraft sideways is called the "crosswind" component. That portion which retards its forward motion is the "headwind" component or that portion which reverses its forward motion is the "tailwind" component. A pilot may wish to know these components, particularly prior to landing.

The squared portion of the slide (bottom of the high speed scale) is used for solving wind component problems.

GIVEN: Wind Velocity 243° at 30 knots.
Runway heading 200° (magnetic).

FIND: Wind components.

SOLUTION

(1) Set the wind direction (243°) at the True Index (surface winds are magnetic).
(2) Set the grommet at "30" on the squared grid and make a "wind dot" at the intersection of the center line and the zero horizontal line.
(3) Set the runway heading (200°) at the True Index.
(4) If the wind dot is below the grommet, move the slide so that the grommet is over the intersection of the center line and the zero horizontal line. (This would be the case with a tailwind component.)
(5) In the example, the wind dot is above the grommet indicating that there is a headwind component. When this is the case, place the "wind dot" at the zero horizontal line.

(6)   For winds having tailwind components relative to heading, the tailwind and crosswind components are read under the "wind dot."

(7)   For winds having headwind components relative to heading, the speed of that component is read under the grommet, crosswind under the "wind dot." In the example, headwind component is 22 knots; crosswind component is from the right (left drift) at 20 knots.

Problems

	Runway Heading	Wind Dir.	Speed	Crosswind Component	Headwind Component	Tailwind Component
61.	195	310	20 kts	_____	_____	_____
62.	270	180	35 kts	_____	_____	_____
63.	080	120	40 kts	_____	_____	_____
64.	310	160	30 kts	_____	_____	_____
65.	130	080	20 kts	_____	_____	_____

Answers

	Crosswind Component	Headwind Component	Tailwind Component
61.	18 kts from Rt.	0	9 kts
62.	35 kts from L.	0	0
63.	26 kts from Rt.	30 kts	0
64.	15 kts from L.	0	26 kts
65.	15 kts from L.	13 kts	0

Problems

	MC	VAR	TC	IAS	°C Temp.	Press. ALT.	TAS	WCA	TH	GS	Wind DIR.	VEL.
66.	20°	10°E	____	135	0°C	7,000'					70°	20
67.	265°	15°W	____	158	-10°C	10,000'					200°	30
68.	____	10°E	90°	139	+10°C	8,000'			98°	147	____	____
69.	____	10°W	330°	160	-5°C	10,000'			323°	165	____	____
70.	65°	15°W	____	88	+10°C	5,000'					190°	20
71.	190°	10°E	____	151	+10°C	8,000'					260°	25
72.	____	12°W	310°	130	0°C	9,000'			303°	156	____	____
73.	____	15°E	180°	100	+20°C	8,000'			170°	99	____	____
74.	260°	10°E	____	115	0°C	8,000'					90°	30
75.	45°	15°W	____	134	-10°C	10,000'					330°	25

Answers

	MC	VAR	TC	IAS	°C Temp.	Press. ALT.	TAS	WCA	TH	GS	Wind DIR.	VEL.
66.			30°				150	5°R	35°	135		
67.			250°				182	7°L	243°	162		
68.	80°						160	8°R			153°	25
69.	340°						187	7°L			283°	31
70.			50°				96	9°R	59°	110		
71.			200°				174	7°R	207°	160		
72.	322°						150	7°L			198°	19
73.	165°						117	10°L			130°	26
74.			270°				130	0°	270°	160		
75.			30°				154	8°L	22°	140		

Glossary of Terms

Calibrated Airspeed (CAS): The Indicated Airspeed (IAS) corrected for instrument and position errors.

Calibrated Altitude (CA): The Indicated Altitude which has been corrected for installation errors.

Density Altitude (DA): The altitude which is "standard," and is used for computations of airplane and engine performance.

Groundspeed (GS): The speed of an airplane relative to the ground.

Indicated Airspeed (IAS): The speed of the airplane as shown on the Airspeed Indicator.

Mach Number (M): A number which relates the airplane speed to the speed of sound. The speed of sound is represented by Mach 1.0.

Magnetic Course (MC): The course of the airplane measured with reference to magnetic north.

Pressure Altitude (PA): The Indicated Altitude when the altimeter window (Kollsman) is set to 29.92 inches of Mercury. Used for navigation computations.

True Airspeed (TAS): The speed of an airplane relative to the air mass in which it is flying. True airspeed equals calibrated airspeed at sea level under standard atmospheric conditions.

True Altitude (TA): The absolute altitude above sea level, or actual altitude above the ground (called "absolute altitude").

True Course (TC): The course of an airplane measured with reference to True North.

True Heading (TH): The heading (longitudinal axis) of the airplane measured with reference to True North.

Wind Correction Angle (WCA): The angle equal to the difference between airplane heading and airplane track, which is equal to the wind drift.

RADIO NAVIGATION

MAIN POINTS

1. Radio navigation allows you to track predetermined LOPs and to fly to and from a radio source.

2. **Very-high-frequency (VHF) omnidirectional ranges** or VORs broadcast bearings called **radials** for all 360° of the compass. Stations using ultra-high frequencies (UHF) are called **tactical air navigation** stations, or TACAN, and are used by the military. They also have **distance measuring equipment or DME**. Most VOR and TACAN stations have been combined and are called **VORTACs**. Stations similar to commercial radio stations use low and medium frequencies to broadcast signals for direction-finding purposes. They are called **nondirectional beacons** or **NDBs** and are part of the **automatic direction finding (ADF)** system. Long-range navigation such as **LORAN** systems are becoming increasingly popular.

3. VORs transmit on frequencies between 108.0 and 117.95 MHz. Each radial is named for its magnetic course **from** the station. Magnetic course and the VOR radial are the same only when flying outbound from the station; when flying inbound to the station, the magnetic course is the reciprocal of the VOR radial. VHF airways, called **Victor airways**, connect VOR stations; Victor airways are 4 nm wide.

4. VOR cockpit controls include a tuning knob to obtain the desired frequency, an **omnibearing selector (OBS)** to obtain the desired radial, a **course deviation indicator (CDI)** to measure deviations from the radial, a **TO/FROM indicator** to determine whether the course selected takes you to or from the VOR, and an **Off flag**. The Off flag may indicate that the signal is too weak, that the station is off the air, that you are too far away, that you are passing directly overhead (the zone of confusion), or that you are 90° off the radial selected in the OBS. VOR receivers also have an audio channel with Morse code or voice identifiers. You should always verify that you have correctly tuned the receiver and that the station is operating by listening for its identifier.

5. VOR navigation provides a great deal of flexibility with its omnidirectional characteristics; it is relatively free from atmospheric interference, and it is relatively accurate (within 1° of the magnetic course), as long as the receiver is functioning properly. The main disadvantage of VOR navigation is that its signals operate on a line-of-sight basis, thus giving them a fairly limited range and necessitating a large network of stations.

6. There are a number of ways to use a VOR.

(a) Always tune and identify the station by selecting the desired frequency and listening to the Morse code or voice identifier. Monitor the station as long as you are using it. Select the desired OBS position and check the position of the Off flag.

(b) To simply fly to the station, turn the OBS until the CDI is centered and you have a TO indication. Then fly the magnetic heading indicated. When the needle moves off center, recenter it and select a new course with the OBS. This is called **homing**. It is not very efficient since it involves a curved flight path unless you have a direct headwind or tailwind.

(c) If you want to **proceed direct** to the station, center the CDI with a TO indication, fly the indicated heading, and then keep the CDI indicator centered. When the CDI moves off center (due to crosswind), turn the airplane into the wind (toward the CDI needle) to center the needle again. Make minor changes until have you have determined the amount of crosswind correction needed to keep the needle centered. This is called **tracking** and is the preferred method.

(d) To **intercept a radial** you need to establish an **intercept heading**. The angle the aircraft makes with the radial is called the **angle of interception**, and how fast you approach it is called the **rate of interception**. After setting the inbound course on the OBS with a TO indication, turn to the same heading as the inbound course. Note if the CDI points to the left or right and turn toward the needle to establish an intercept angle. If the CDI moves slowly, proceed slowly until you intercept it; if it moves rapidly, reduce the intercept angle to slow the needle's movement.

(e) To **intercept an outbound radial**, set the course and check for a FROM indication. Fly the heading of the outbound course to determine an intercept heading and follow the intercept procedures outlined above.

(f) Station passage occurs when you pass through the **cone of confusion** above the station. Station passage is confirmed when the TO/FROM indicator makes its first positive change from TO to FROM.

(g) **Time-distance checks** can also be made using the VOR by timing how long it takes to fly a 10° bearing change while heading approximately 90° to the radial. The time in seconds between bearings divided by the degree of bearing change (in this procedure, 10) tells you how many minutes you are from the station. You can calculate how far away the station is by working a time-distance-speed problem on your computer.

(h)   To **establish a VOR fix** once you have established a course with the CDI centered, tune and identify a second station.   Turn the OBS until the CDI is centered and the TO/FROM indicator states FROM.   Read the radial from the OBS and use it to establish your fix.   You can use any two stations to obtain a fix, but the fix may not be totally accurate unless you can use two VORs simultaneously.   If you know the distance from the station, you can use a single VOR to obtain a single-station fix.   Since you know the distance to the station, you can also calculate groundspeed by dividing the distance by how long it takes you to fly there.   Finally, to preflight your VOR equipment, many airports have **VOR test (VOT)** facilities.   VOT facilities are published in the Airport/Facility Directory.   Turn the OBS until the CDI is centered; it should read 000° with a FROM indication or 180° with a TO indication (plus or minus 4°).   If a VOT is not available, refer to the Airport/Facility Directory for airborne or ground checkpoints.

7.   **Distance measuring equipment (DME)** uses distance-fixing information from the VORTAC system.   It measures the slant range, not horizontal distance, from the source to the aircraft and is subject to line-of-sight restrictions.   DME is valuable not only for distance readings but also as a source of groundspeed calculations.

8.   **Automatic direction finding (ADF)** radio compasses use low frequencies (190 to 1750 kHz) to provide bearing information.   Unlike VHF and UHF signals, they are not limited to line-of-sight transmission.   A serious drawback to ADF navigation, however, is that the compasses are susceptible to interference.

(a)   A station that broadcasts a low-frequency navigation signal is called a **nondirectional beacon** or NDB.   ADF radios have a **bearing indicator**, an On-Off and volume control knob, and a selector knob.

(b)   The first step in ADF navigation is to tune and identify the station.   Magnetic bearing to the station is equal to the relative bearing indicated on the fixed card ADF plus the magnetic heading.   The **magnetic heading** is the heading indicated on the compass.   The **relative bearing** is the direction of the station relative to the nose of the airplane.   The **magnetic bearing** is the magnetic heading that would point the airplane directly toward the station.   Magnetic heading (MH) + relative bearing (RB) = magnetic bearing to the station (MB).   Some ADFs have movable cards that allow you to dial in the magnetic heading.   When the current magnetic heading is set, the needle shows magnetic bearing.

(c)   ADF homing is similar to VOR homing; it also involves a curved track to the station if there is any crosswind.   Interception of a bearing is similar to the procedure used for VOR.

(d)   ADF is usually used as a supplement to VOR navigation--for example, to establish fixes.

9.   Airway navigation does not always represent the shortest distance between destinations.   An alternative is **area navigation (RNAV)**, which involves creating phantom stations (waypoints) using VOR and/or DME information with special receiving equipment.

10. Radar allows air traffic controllers to monitor traffic on a radar screen. The system provides vectors to a destination, but the VFR pilot still has navigational responsibility (vital if a transponder fails or if service is terminated due to heavy IFR traffic). Radar navigation, rather than being a passive system on the pilot's part, involves several procedures, including VFR cloud and visibility minimums. The transponder has 4096 four-digit codes available for broadcast and several switches. **Standby** is used to warm up the system. **On** activates Mode A operation. **Alt** activates the Mode C encoding altimeter, if installed. **Reply** responds when the unit receives a signal from the ground. **Ident** broadcasts a special signal to the controller. Controllers use the word squawk to refer to airborne transponder transmissions. For example, squawk means to select the frequency requested by the controller, **squawk ident** means to push the Ident button, **squawk standby** means to turn the selector to Standby, and so on. General transmission codes are 1200 for VFR, 7500 for hijacking, 7600 for loss of two-way radio communication, and 7700 for airborne emergency. Use of precision approach radar (PAR) or airport surveillance radar (ASR) is reserved for IFR pilots or emergencies.

11. LORAN (LOng RAnge Navigation) is a system that uses signals from two ground stations to provide a fix (displayed as latitude and longitude). Most receivers can provide bearing and distance between any two fixes.

12. Some safety factors to consider in flight planning when using radio navigation include: checking minimum altitudes, since VORs transmit line-of-sight; checking the Airport/Facility Directory and NOTAMs; and checking equipment. Using one method of navigation to complement another (composite navigation) is both practical and, for many VFR flights, almost a necessity.

KEY TERMS AND CONCEPTS, PART 1

Match each term or concept (1-16) with the appropriate description (A-P) below. Each item has only one match.

___ 1. VOR
___ 2. homing
___ 3. rate of intercept
___ 4. Victor airway
___ 5. NDB
___ 6. CDI
___ 7. radio navigation
___ 8. magnetic bearing
___ 9. Off flag
___ 10. TACAN
___ 11. airways
___ 12. radial
___ 13. relative bearing
___ 14. TO/FROM
___ 15. omnibearing selector
___ 16. VORTAC

A. magnetic heading that would point the airplane directly toward an NDB
B. station that uses low or medium radio frequencies
C. part of the VOR cockpit display that shows the aircraft's deviation from a radial or course
D. how fast you encounter a desired course
E. direction of an NDB station relative to the airplane's nose
F. VHF omnidirectional range station
G. establishing courses and fixes by reference to radio signals broadcast from ground stations
H. part of the VOR cockpit display that designates whether the selected radial will take you to or from the VOR
I. a VHF airway connecting two VOR stations
J. bearings that run from one ground station to another
K. flying toward a radio source, always keeping the signal on the nose
L. UHF tactical air navigation station
M. part of the VOR cockpit display that indicates a weak signal
N. a LOP sent out by a VOR station
O. a combined VOR and TACAN station
P. part of the VOR cockpit display that allows you to select a radial

KEY TERMS AND CONCEPTS, PART 2

Match each term or concept (1-14) with the appropriate description (A-N) below. Each item has only one match.

___ 1. 1200
___ 2. cone of confusion
___ 3. ADF
___ 4. 7600
___ 5. squawk ident
___ 6. intercept heading
___ 7. station passage

___ 8. nondirectional beacon
___ 9. DME
___ 10. 7700
___ 11. composite navigation
___ 12. area navigation (RNAV)
___ 13. tracking
___ 14. LORAN

A. navigational system not limited by line-of-sight transmission
B. using one method of navigation to complement another
C. this is confirmed when the TO/FROM indicator makes its first positive change from TO to FROM
D. homing beacon that offers low-frequency navigation signal
E. activate the transponder to broadcast a special signal to air traffic control
F. VFR transponder code
G. heading used to get to a desired radial or course
H. area above a VOR station where radial signals cannot be interpreted correctly
I. uses UHF to fix distance from a VORTAC or VOR-DME station
J. transponder code to indicate an airborne emergency
K. navigation system in which phantom stations are created using VOR and/or DME information
L. transponder code used to indicate a loss of two-way radio communication capability
M. keeping the CDI needle centered by flying a heading to compensate for the wind
N. provides a fix, expressed in latitude and longitude

DISCUSSION QUESTIONS AND REVIEW EXERCISES

1. What are two major differences between VOR and TACAN radio transmissions? Explain.

2. How are signals from a VOR station radiated relative to actual headings?
What is the difference between TO and FROM bearings?

3. Briefly describe the VOR cockpit controls and their functions.

4. Name two advantages and two disadvantages of VOR as a navigation aid.

5. Outline the VOR procedure for each of the following:

    a. flying direct to the station

    b. intercepting a course inbound to the station

c.   intercepting a course outbound from the station

6. What is the cockpit indication that you have passed over a VOR station?

7. Outline how you can use a single VOR to obtain a time and distance check.

8. Briefly explain how distance measuring equipment (DME) works, where it derives radio information, and how station passage is indicated.

9. What is one major advantage of a low-frequency (ADF) navigation over a VOR? What is a low-frequency station's biggest disadvantage?

10. Given an ADF pointing to 190° and a magnetic compass indication of 135°, what is the magnetic bearing to the station? Assume 0° deviation for the heading.

11. Explain each of these as they relate to radar navigation:

   a. 4096

   b. Ident

   c. Standby

   d. squawk code 0413

   e. code 1200

   f. code 7500

   g. code 7600

   h. code 7700

   i. PAR and ASR for VFR pilots

12. Refer to Figure 13.1. Match each VOR indicator in the bottom of the figure with the appropriate airplane in the top of the figure. Some indicators may have more than one correct match. Assume the omnibearing selector (OBS) in all airplanes is set to read 190°.

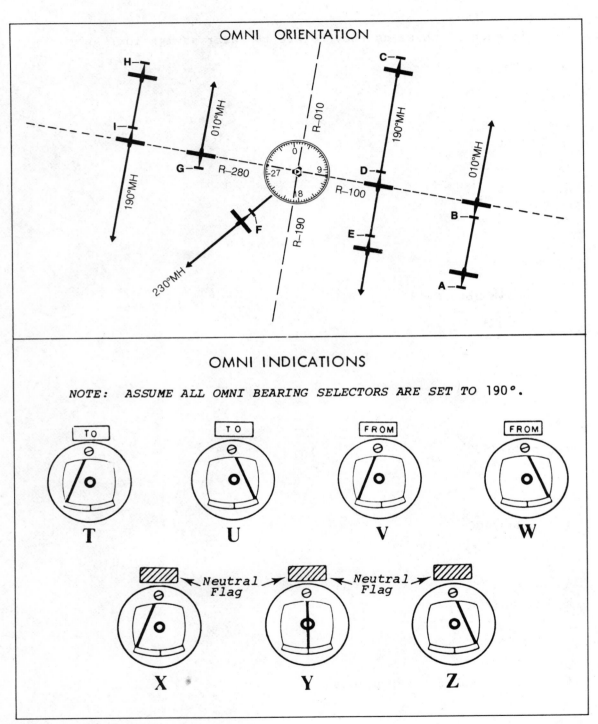

Figure 13.1

13. Refer to Figure 13.2. Match the correct ADF (fixed compass card) indication in the bottom of the figure with the airplanes shown in flight in the top of the figure for flight in the vicinity of a typical nondirectional radio beacon (NDB). Indicators may have no match, one match, or two matches.

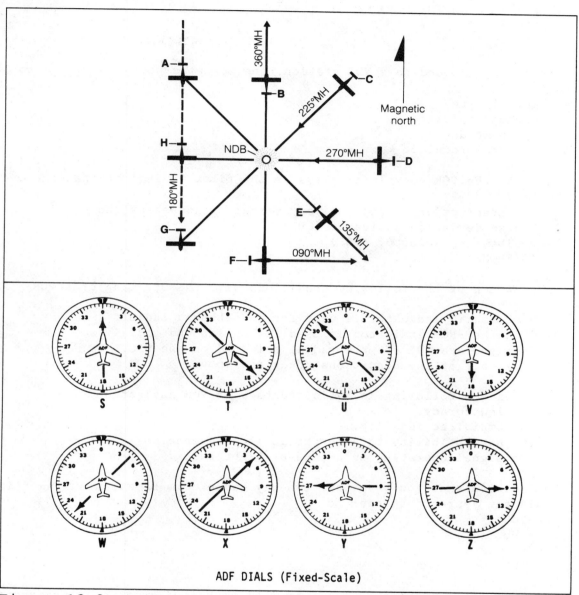

Figure 13.2

14. TACAN stations operate at _____ frequency.
    1--low
    2--medium
    3--very high
    4--ultra-high

15. Which of the following is **not** a frequency on which VORs transmit?
    1--107.8.
    2--113.2.
    3--116.0.
    4--117.85.

16. For flying inbound to a VOR station, the magnetic course is _____ to the VOR radial.
    1--parallel to
    2--perpendicular to
    3--the same as
    4--the reciprocal of

17. Which of the VOR cockpit displays is the first to indicate passage over a VOR station?
    1--An interruption in the auditory signal broadcast by the station.
    2--Course deviation indicator (CDI).
    3--Omnibearing selector (OBS).
    4--TO/FROM indicator.

18. Under which of the following conditions will the Off flag of a VOR receiver appear?
    1--When the TO indicator is used for an outbound radial.
    2--When the FROM indicator is used for an inbound radial.
    3--When you are 90° off the radial selected on the OBS.
    4--Under all of the conditions described above.

19. Which of the following is a disadvantage of VOR navigation?
    1--Its inaccuracy.
    2--Its omnidirectionality.
    3--Its susceptibility to atmospheric interference.
    4--Its signal operating on a line-of-sight basis.

20. To indicate that you have lost two-way radio communication during flight, you should set your transponder to
    1--1200.
    2--4096.
    3--7500.
    4--7600.

21. Which of the following is not a typical cockpit display on a transponder?
    1--CDI.
    2--Ident.
    3--Reply.
    4--Standby.

22. The use of phantom stations (waypoints) in which VOR and/or DME information is calculated for navigational purposes is part of a system referred to as
    1--area navigation (RNAV).
    2--ARTCC.
    3--TACAN.
    4--Victor airways.

23. NDBs broadcast at _____ frequency.
    1--low or medium
    2--high
    3--very high
    4--ultra-high

24. Which of the following is **not** a frequency on which VORs transmit?
    1--109.2.
    2--112.65.
    3--116.0.
    4--118.7.

25. For flying outbound from a VOR station, the magnetic course is _____ the VOR radial.
    1--parallel to
    2--perpendicular to
    3--the same as
    4--the reciprocal of

26. FAA-designated airways that connect VOR stations are called _____ airways.
    1--radio magnetic
    2--omnidirectional
    3--phantom
    4--Victor

27. The VOR cockpit display that indicates how far off a particular radial you are is called the
    1--course deviation indicator (CDI).
    2--Off flag.
    3--omni bearing selector (OBS).
    4--TO/FROM indicator.

28. Under which of the following conditions will the Off flag of a VOR receiver appear?
    1--When passing overhead, but slightly off course.
    2--When the TO indicator is used for an outbound radial.
    3--When you are 0° or 180° off the radial selected on the OBS.
    4--When all of the above conditions exist.

29. Which of the following is a frequency on which VORs transmit?
    1--114.0.
    2--118.1.
    3--120.9.
    4--123.6.

30. Keeping the CDI centered to fly to a VOR station is a VOR navigational procedure called
     1--homing.
     2--intercepting an inbound radial.
     3--intercepting an outbound radial.
     4--tracking.

31. VOR test facilities (VOTs) are listed
     1--in the Airman's Information Manual (AIM).
     2--in the Airport/Facility Directory.
     3--in NOTAMs.
     4--on sectional charts.

32. To indicate an emergency while in flight, you should tune your transponder to
     1--1200.
     2--4096.
     3--7500.
     4--7700.

33. Which of the following is not a typical cockpit display on a transponder?
     1--Ident.
     2--Off flag.
     3--Standby.
     4--Reply.

34. What indicator on the transponder flashes when the unit responds to a ground transmission?
     1--Alt.
     2--On.
     3--Reply.
     4--Standby.

35. Distance measuring equipment (DME) displays the airplane's _____ a VORTAC station.
     1--distance above
     2--ground distance from
     3--slant range distance from
     4--both (1) and (2) above

FAA EXAM QUESTIONS

        (Note: All FAA Figures are located in Appendix C)

   1. (FAA 1276) What is your approximate position on low altitude airway V1, southwest of Norfolk (Area A), if the VOR receiver indicates you are on the 340 radial of Elizabeth City VOR (Area C)? See Figure 14.)
     1--15 NM from Norfolk VORTAC.
     2--18 NM from Norfolk VORTAC.
     3--23 NM from Norfolk VORTAC.
     4--28 NM from Norfolk VORTAC.

2. (FAA 1277)   What course should be selected on the omnibearing selector to make a direct flight from Hazen Airport (Area C) to the Minot VORTAC with a TO indication? (See Figure 15.)
1--001°.
2--012°.
3--181°.
4--192°.

3. (FAA 1279)   What is the approximate position of the aircraft if the VOR receivers indicate the 310 radial of Savannah VORTAC and the 190 radial of Allendale VOR?   (See Figure 17.)
1--Town of Guyton.
2--Town of Springfield.
3--3 mi. east of Marlow.
4--Over the railroad 2 mi. southwest of Rincon.

4. (FAA 1280)   On what bearing should the VOR receiver (OBS) be set to navigate direct from Hampton Varnville Airport (Area A) to Savannah VORTAC (Area C)? (See Figure 17.)
1--005°.
2--185°.
3--200°.
4--360°.

5. (FAA 1281)   What is the approximate position of the aircraft if the VOR receivers indicate the 250 radial of Sulphur Springs VORTAC and the 130 radial of Blue Ridge VORTAC? (See Figure 18.)
1--Caddo Mills Airport.
2--Meadowview Airport.
3--3 mi. southeast of Caddo Mills Airport.
4--3 mi. northeast of Caddo Mills Airport.

6. (FAA 1282)   On what bearing should the VOR receiver (OBS) be set in order to navigate direct from Majors Airport to Quitman VORTAC? (See Figure 18, Area A to B.)
1--101°.
2--108°.
3--281°.
4--288°.

7. (FAA 1283)   The VHF navigation facility at Van Nuys (Area F in Figure 19) is a
1--TACAN.
2--VOR.
3--VORTAC.
4--VOR-DME.

8. (FAA 1284)   The VOR is tuned to Seal Beach VORTAC (Area D in Figure 19). The OBS is set on the 202 radial, with a TO indication, and a right CDI deflection. What is the aircraft's position from the VORTAC?
1--North.
2--East.
3--South.
4--West.

9. (FAA 1285) The VOR is tuned to Sulphur Springs VORTAC (Figure 18). The VOR has the indications shown in Dial H of Figure 22. What radial is the aircraft crossing?
1--300.
2--210.
3--120.
4--030.

10. (FAA 1286) The VOR is tuned to Jamestown VOR, and the aircraft is positioned over the town of Wembledon (Figure 13, Area C). Which VOR indication in Figure 22 is correct?
1--A.
2--D.
3--F.
4--G.

11. (FAA 1287) The VOR is tuned to Sulphur Springs VORTAC (Figure 18). The VOR receiver has the indications shown in Dial A in Figure 22. What is the aircraft's position from the station?
1--North.
2--East.
3--South.
4--West.

12. (FAA 1288) The VOR is tuned to Sulphur Springs VORTAC (Figure 18). The VOR receiver had the indications shown in Dial C in Figure 22. What is the aircraft's position from the station?
1--East.
2--On the 120 radial.
3--West.
4--On the 210 radial.

13. (FAA 1289) The VOR is tuned to Elizabeth City VOR, and the aircraft is positioned over Ferebee Private Airport (Figure 14, Area C). Which VOR indication in Figure 22 is correct?
1--E.
2--F.
3--G.
4--H.

14. (FAA 1290). The VOR is tuned to Blue Ridge VORTAC, and the aircraft is positioned over the town of Lone Oak, southeast of Majors Airport, (Figure 18). Which VOR indication in Figure 22 is correct?
1--A.
2--D.
3--F.
4--G.

15. (FAA 1278) While en route on V185, a flight crosses the 248 radial of Allendale VOR at 0951 and then crosses the 216 radial of Allendale VOR at 1000. What is the estimated time of arrival at Savannah VORTAC? (See Figure 17.)
1--1023.   2--1028.
3--1032.   4--1036.

16. (FAA 1275) When the CDI (course deviation indicator) needle is centered during an omnireceiver check using a VOT, the omnibearing selector and the TO/FROM indicator should read
1--180° FROM, only if the pilot is due north of the VOT.
2--0° TO or 180° FROM, regardless of the pilot's position from the VOT.
3--0° FROM or 180° TO, regardless of the pilot's position from the VOT.
4--0° TO, only if the pilot is due south of the VOT.

17. (FAA 1301) Refer to ADF Dial M in Figure 23. The relative bearing to the station is
1--090°.
2--180°.
3--270°.
4--360°.

18. (FAA 1300) Refer to ADF Dial M in Figure 23. The relative bearing to the station is
1--045°.
2--180°.
3--315°.
4--360°.

19. (FAA 1302) Refer to ADF Dial N in Figure 23. The relative bearing to the station is
1--090°.
2--180°.
3--270°.
4--360°.

20. (FAA 1303) Refer to ADF Dial O in Figure 23. On a magnetic heading of 320°, the magnetic bearing to the station is
1--005°.
2--185°.
3--225°.
4--320°.

21. (FAA 1304) Refer to ADF Dial P in Figure 23. On a magnetic heading of 035°, the magnetic bearing to the station is
1--035°.
2--180°.
3--215°.
4--360°.

22. (FAA 1305) Refer to ADF Dial Q in Figure 23. On a magnetic heading of 120°, the magnetic bearing to the station is
1--045°.
2--165°.
3--270°.
4--360°.

23. (FAA 1306) Refer to ADF Dial Q in Figure 23. If the magnetic bearing to the station is 240°, the magnetic heading is
1--045°.   2--105°.
3--195°.   4--285°.

24. (FAA 1307) Refer to ADF Dial R in Figure 23. If the magnetic bearing to the station is 030°, the magnetic heading is
1--060°.
2--120°.
3--270°.
4--300°.

25. (FAA 1308) Refer to ADF Dial S in Figure 23. If the magnetic bearing to the station is 135°, the magnetic heading is
1--135°.
2--270°.
3--315°.
4--360°.

26. (FAA 1291) Determine the magnetic bearing TO the station as indicated by ADF A in Figure 20.
1--030°.
2--180°.
3--210°.
4--330°.

27. (FAA 1292) What magnetic heading should the pilot use to fly to the station as indicated by ADF B in Figure 20?
1--010°.
2--145°.
3--190°.
4--316°.

28. (FAA 1293) Determine the approximate heading to intercept the 180° bearing TO the station using the information depicted by ADF B in Figure 20.
1--040°.
2--160°.
3--220°.
4--340°.

29. (FAA 1294) What is the magnetic bearing FROM the station as indicated by ADF C in Figure 20?
1--025°.
2--115°.
3--270°.
4--295°.

30. (FAA 1295) Which ADF indication in Figure 20 represents the aircraft tracking to the station with a right crosswind?
1--A.
2--B.
3--C.
4--D.

31. (FAA 1296) What outbound bearing is being crossed by the aircraft represented by ADF A in Figure 20?
1--030°.   2--150°.
3--180°.   4--210°.

32. (FAA 1291) Determine the magnetic bearing TO the station as indicated
    by ADF A in Figure 20.
    1--030°.
    2--180°.
    3--210°.
    4--330°.

33. (FAA 1298) What is the relative bearing to the station depicted by ADF
    B in Figure 20?
    1--315°.
    2--235°.
    3--190°.
    4--010°.

34. (FAA 1299) What is the relative bearing to the station depicted by ADF
    D in Figure 20?
    1--020°.
    2--060°.
    3--220°.
    4--340°.

35. (FAA 1502) If Air Traffic Control advises that radar service is being
    terminated when the pilot is departing a Terminal Radar Service Area,
    the transponder should be set to code
    1--0000.
    2--1200.
    3--4096.
    4--7700.

36. (FAA 1503) When making routine transponder code changes, pilots should
    avoid inadvertent selection of which codes?
    1--3100, 7600, 7700.
    2--7500, 7600, 7700.
    3--7000, 7600, 7700.
    4--4000, 7600, 7700.

37. (FAA 1504) In VFR conditions below 18,000 ft. MSL, what transponder
    code should be selected?
    1--Code 1200, and the IDENT feature should not be engaged.
    2--Code 1200, and the IDENT feature should be engaged.
    3--Code 1400, and the IDENT feature should not be engaged.
    4--Code 1400, and the IDENT feature should be engaged.

ANSWERS AND EXPLANATIONS

Key Terms and Concepts, Part 1

1.	F	5.	B	9.	M	13.	E
2.	K	6.	C	10.	L	14.	H
3.	D	7.	G	11.	J	15.	P
4.	I	8.	A	12.	N	16.	O

Key Terms and Concepts, Part 2

1. F	5. E	9. I	13. M
2. H	6. G	10. J	14. N
3. A	7. C	11. B	
4. L	8. D	12. K	

Discussion Questions and Review Exercises

1. See Study Guide Main Point #2.

2. See Study Guide Main Points #3 and #4.

3. See Study Guide Main Point #4.

4. See Study Guide Main Point #5.

5. See Study Guide Main Point #6.

6. See Study Guide Main Point #6.

7. See Study Guide Main Point #6.

8. See Study Guide Main Point #7.

9. See Study Guide Main Point #8.

10. 325°. The magnetic bearing to the station is equal to the heading plus the relative bearing.

11.
   a. number of available transponder codes.
   b. feature to send special coded signal.
   c. position where transponder is on but not transmitting.
   d. instruction to set code 0413, with transponder on.
   e. VFR code.
   f. code to indicate hijacking in progress.
   g. lost communication code.
   h. emergency code.
   i. Precision Approach Radar and Approach Surveillance radar may provide landing assistance to VFR pilots in emergencies.

12. Indicator matches:

   T--H.
   U--C.
   V--F.
   W--A, E. It doesn't matter where the nose of the airplane points.
   X--G, I. Remember, you are 90° off the radial.
   Y--   No match. You would have to be directly over the station in the zone of confusion to get this reading.
   Z--B, D.

13. ADF matches:

S--C, D.
T--No match.
U--A.
V--B, E.
W--G.
X--No match.
Y--F, H.
Z--No match.

14. 4--TACANs transmit UHF, or ultra-high frequency.

15. 1--VORs transmit on frequencies between 108.0 MHz and 117.95 MHz.

16. 4--The radial is its magnetic course **from** the station; all radials are from the station.

17. 4--The TO/FROM indicator denotes station passage when it makes its first positive change from TO to FROM.

18. 3--It will also appear when you are passing directly over the station (the cone of confusion), when the station is off, when it is out of the line-of-sight (you are too far away or there is an obstruction), and when you are 90° off the radial selected on the OBS.

19. 4--VORs are characterized by accuracy, omnidirectionality, and freedom from atmospheric interference. The major drawback is its restriction to line-of-sight transmission and reception.

20. 4--7600 is the transponder code for loss of two-way radio communication.

21. 1--The course deviation indicator (CDI) is part of the VOR cockpit display.

22. 1--RNAV uses phantom stations in which VOR and/or DME data is calculated for navigational purposes.

23. 1--Nondirectional beacons (NDBs) transmit on low or medium frequencies.

24. 4--VORs transmit on frequencies from 108.0 MHz to 117.85 MHz.

25. 3--The radial is its magnetic course **from** the station.

26. 4--They are called Victor (V) airways; for example, V 499. The Victor numbers **do not** refer to magnetic or true courses.

27. 1--The CDI displays how far off course you are.

28. 1--The Off flag will appear when you pass over a VOR, but slightly off course.

29. 1--VORs transmit on frequencies from 108.0 MHz to 117.85 MHz.

30. 4--Proceeding direct (also called tracking) involves keeping the CDI centered as you fly to a VOR station.

31. 2--VOTs are listed in the <u>Airport/Facility</u> <u>Directory.</u>

32. 4--7700 is the transponder code to use for an in-flight emergency.

33. 2--The Off flag is part of the VOR cockpit display.

34. 3--The Reply indicator flashes when it responds to a ground transmission.

35. 3--The DME displays slant range distance (from the nose of the airplane to the station). It does not measure ground distance or altitude.

FAA Exam Questions

1. 2--Plot the fix by using the line of position of 340° from the Elizabeth City VOR. Measure the distance to the Norfolk VORTAC.

2. 1--Line up a straight edge on the Minot VORTAC (at the airport) and Hazen. That line crosses the compass rose at the 180 position (180 radial). The inbound course is the reciprocal, 000° magnetic. 001° is the closest answer.

3. 1--Plot the position using lines through the compass roses of Savannah VORTAC and the Allendale VOR.

4. 2--Line up a straight edge on Hampton Varnville Airport and the Savannah VORTAC. Hampton Varnville is on the 005 radial. The inbound leading is 185° magnetic.

5. 2--Plot the position using the compass roses of the Sulphur Springs VORTAC and the Blue Ridge VORTAC.

6. 1--Line up a straight edge on Majors and Quitman VORTAC. Majors is on the 281 radial of Quitman. The course TO is 101° magnetic.

7. 4--The square symbol imposed on the VOR symbol indicates DME with the VOR.

8. 2--The OBS is set for 202 to take you to the VORTAC. If the CDI were centered, you would be on the 022 radial. The right deflection indicates you are left of course, somewhere in the easterly direction from the VORTAC.

9. 4--The OBS is set to 210 with the TO-FROM triangle pointing to TO, thus you are on the 030 radial.

10. 3--Wembledon is on the 026 radial of the Jamestown VOR. 030 FROM would take you away from the VOR as indicated on Dial F. The 2 dot right deflection of the CDI to the right indicates you are 4° left of the 030 radial.

11. 3--030 would take you TO the VOR, the CDI needle indicates you must fly left to get to this course. Full needle deflection indicates 10° or more off this course.

12. 2--Neither the TO nor FROM arrow is showing indicating either that you are not receiving the VOR or that you are in a position 90° off from the OBS setting. The CDI shows you are right of the 030 course. 030 + 090 = 120.

13. 4--FEREBEE is on the 030 radial. 210 magnetic would take you TO the VOR.

14. 4--Lone Oak is on the 125 radial. This is 90° off from all of the OBS settings, thus neither TO nor FROM will be showing. You are left of the 210 OBS.

15. 3--First, plot both positions on V-185 using the cross bearings from the Allendale VOR. Then measure the distance between the fixes of 11 NM. The time between fixes was 9 min. Use the flight computer to find the actual groundspeed: 11 NM/9 min = 73 kt./60. The distance from the second fix to Savannah VORTAC is 40 NM. 73 kt./60 = 40 NM/32 min. Time over last fix 1000 + 32 min. ETE = 1032 ETA.

16. 3--The VOR test facilities provide the same CDI reading no matter where the airplane is located.

17. 3--With a fixed card ADF indicator, the needle points to the Relative Bearing (RB).

18. 3--With a fixed card ADF indicator, the needle points to the Relative Bearing (RB).

19. 2--With a fixed card ADF indicator, the needle points to the Relative Bearing (RB).

20. 2--With a fixed card ADF indicator: Magnetic Bearing (MB) = Magnetic Heading (MH) + Relative Bearing (RB). If the result of the addition is more than 360°, subtract 360. MH 320 + RB 225 = MB 545 - 360 = MB 185°.

21. 1--With a fixed card ADF indicator: Magnetic Bearing (MB) = Magnetic Heading (MH) + Relative Bearing (RB). MH 035 + RB 000 = MB 035°.

22. 2--With a fixed card ADF indicator: Magnetic Bearing (MB) = Magnetic Heading (MH) + Relative Bearing (RB). MH 120 + RB 045 = MB 165°.

23. 3--In this problem magnetic BEARING is given, you must solve for magnetic HEADING. MB 240 - RB 045 = MH 195.

24. 2--In this problem magnetic BEARING is given, you must solve for magnetic HEADING. MB 030(+360) - RB 270 = MH 120°.

25. 4--In this problem magnetic BEARING is given, you must solve for magnetic HEADING. MB 135 - RB 135 = MH 000 (360)°.

26. 3--When the current magnetic heading is set on a moveable ADF indicator, the needle shows the magnetic bearing to the station.

27. 3--When the current magnetic heading is set on a moveable ADF indicator, the needle shows the magnetic bearing to the station.

28. 3--The easiest way to solve an ADF interception problem is to turn the aircraft to the desired inbound course and note the needle. If you turn to 180 MH, the needle will be 10° right of the course. You must turn right to intercept.

29. 2--With an RMI or moveable card ADF indicator, the tail indicates the bearing FROM the station.

30. 4--In a crosswind, the wind correction will be toward the wind, the needle will point opposite the wind. Indicator D shows a 20° right correction.

31. 1--With an RMI or moveable card ADF indicator the tail of the needle indicates the outbound bearing from the NDB.

32. 3--When the current magnetic heading is set on a moveable ADF indicator, the needle shows the magnetic bearing to the station.

33. 2--When the current magnetic heading is set on a moveable ADF indicator, the needle shows the magnetic bearing to the station. RB = MB - MH. In this problem you must add 360 to the MB. MB 190 + 360 - MH 315 = RB 235.

34. 4--When the current magnetic heading is set on a moveable ADF indicator, the needle shows the magnetic bearing to the station. RB = MB - MH. In this problem you must add 360 to the MB. MB 200 + 360 - MH 220 = RB 340.

35. 2--VFR flights use transponder code 1200, unless otherwise directed by ATC.

36. 2--Avoid the three emergency codes when changing squawks.

37. 1--VFR flights use transponder code 1200, unless otherwise directed by ATC. Use IDENT only when directed and release the button immediately.

COMPOSITE NAVIGATION: GOING CROSS-COUNTRY

MAIN POINTS

1.   This chapter, which describes the process of planning and executing a cross-country flight, draws on all the knowledge you have accumulated in the preceding chapters of this book, including preflight planning, dead reckoning, radio navigation, FARs, and weather. It concludes with an FAA Advisory Circular (AC No. 61-84B), "Role of Preflight Preparation."

2.   One of your tasks during this chapter will be to prepare a flight log for a proposed cross-country flight. The phases you will consider are general planning; preflight planning, including navigational computations; weather briefings and airport data; airplane preflight preparation; departure procedures; en route procedures; en route planning; arrival procedures; and postflight activities, including such items as closing your flight plan.

CROSS-COUNTRY EXERCISE

For this exercise, you will need a flight computer or electronic calculator, plotter, navigation log, San Francisco sectional chart, and excerpts from the Airport/Facility Directory (provided in Figure 14.1). Routing and weather information will be provided.

Note: Do not use the data and charts provided in this chapter for actual flight planning purposes! They are outdated. Only updated charts and information should be used. Furthermore, should you ever want to fly this particular cross-country trip, be sure to check with your local FBO, or others familiar with the airports, particularly Carmel Valley.

Your aircraft is a black and blue Starship U2 (N7118Q). You and your instructor will be going on a round-robin cross-country flight from Fresno Chandler Downtown (36°44'N, 119°49'W) to Pine Mountain Lake near Groveland (37°52'N, 120°11'W), then on to Carmel Valley golf course (36°29'N, 121°44'W), and finally back to Fresno. It is a warm Thursday in August; Pacific daylight time (PDT) is in effect.

CARMEL VALLEY (O62) 0 NE UTC–8(–7DT) 36°28'55"N 121°43'45"W SAN FRANCISCO
   450 TPA—1500(1050)
   RWY 11-29: H2475X35 (ASPH-DIRT)
     RWY 11: Thld dsplcd 665'. Trees. Rgt tfc.   RWY 29: Tree.
   AIRPORT REMARKS: Unattended. CAUTION—Dogs, horses, joggers and cars on rwy. Rwy 11-29 west 650' dirt
     remaining 1825' asph. No touch & go lndgs. Straight out departure Rwy 29, no turns below 1000'.
   COMMUNICATIONS: CTAF 122.9
     SALINAS FSS (SNS) LC 372-6050

- -

§ **FRESNO-CHANDLER DOWNTOWN** (FCH) 2 W UTC–8(–7DT) SAN FRANCISCO
   36°43'56"N 119°49'08"W   L-2E
   278 B S4 FUEL 100 OX 3, 4 TPA—1078(800)   IAP
   RWY 12R-30L: H3200X75 (ASPH) S-17 MIRL
     RWY 12R: REIL. Thld dsplcd 240'. Pole. Rgt tfc.
     RWY 30L: REIL. VASI(V2L)—GA 3.42°TCH 21'. Thld dsplcd 307'. Road.
   RWY 12L-30R: H3000X75 (ASPH) S-17
     RWY 12L: Thld dsplcd 198'. Road.   RWY 30R: Thld dsplcd 200'. Road. Rgt tfc.
   AIRPORT REMARKS: Attended 1600-0100Z‡. Fee for acft over 12,500 pounds gross weight. Fuel avbl 1600-0100Z‡
     daily. ACTIVATE MIRL, REIL Rwy 12R-30L and VASI Rwy 30L—123.0.
   COMMUNICATIONS: CTAF/UNICOM 123.0
     FRESNO FSS (FAT) LC 251-8269. NOTAM FILE FAT.
  Ⓡ APP CON–119.0, 119.6   Ⓡ DEP CON–119.0
   RADIO AIDS TO NAVIGATION: NOTAM FILE FAT.
     CLOVIS (H) ABVORTAC 112.9 ■ CZQ Chan 76 36°53'12"N 119°48'11"W 165°9.4 NM to fld. 360/15E.
     CHANDLER NDB (H-SAB) 344 • FCH 36°43'26"N 119°49'58"W at fld.
     NDB unusable 095-120° beyond 40 NM 200-235° beyond 35 NM
   COMM/NAVAID REMARKS: During tower closure, broadcast position/ Intentions/Advisories oh freq. 123.0.

- -

GROVELAND

PINE MOUNTAIN LAKE (Q68) 3 NE UTC–8(–7DT) 37°51'45"N 120°10'40"W SAN FRANCISCO
   2900 B S4 FUEL 80, 100 TPA—3700(800)   L-2F
   RWY 09-27: H3640X50 (ASPH) S-2 MIRL
     RWY 09: VASI(V2L)—GA 4.5°TCH 16'. Trees.   RWY 27: Tree. Rgt tfc.
   AIRPORT REMARKS: Attended irregular. Fuel available by request ctc-UNICOM. Be alert deer on and in vicinity of arpt
     especially Nov-Apr. Fee for overnight parking. Transient parking avbl.
   COMMUNICATIONS: CTAF/UNICOM 123.0
     SACRAMENTO FSS (SAC) Toll free call, dial 800-852-7036.
   RADIO AIDS TO NAVIGATION: NOTAM FILE MOD.
     MODESTO (H) VOR/DME 114.6 MOD Chan 93 37°37'39"N 120°57'25"W 052°39.7 NM to fld. 90/17E.

§ **LOS BANOS MUNI** (LSN) 1 W UTC–8(–7DT) 37°03'43"N 120°52'05"W SAN FRANCISCO
   119 B S4 FUEL 80, 100 TPA—919(800)   L-2F
   RWY 14-32: H3000X75 (ASPH) S-23 MIRL   IAP
     RWY 14: VASI(V4L)—GA 3.0°TCH 30'. Rgt tfc.   RWY 32: VASI(V4L)—GA 3.0°TCH 30'. Road.
   AIRPORT REMARKS: Attended 1600-0130Z‡. Avoid overflight of houses south. MIRL Rwy 14/32 preset low intensity until
     0800Z‡. To increase intensity and ACTIVATE MIRL and VASI Rwy 14-32—CTAF.
   COMMUNICATIONS: CTAF/UNICOM 122.8
     FRESNO FSS (FAT) Toll free call, dial 1-800-421-7112. NOTAM FILE FAT.
     PANOCHE RCO 122.1R 112.6T (FRESNO FSS)
  Ⓡ CASTLE APP/DEP CON 126.5 (Rwy 14) 124.8 (Rwy 32)
   RADIO AIDS TO NAVIGATION: NOTAM FILE FAT.
     PANOCHE (L) VORTAC 112.6 PXN Chan 73 36°42'56"N 120°46'40"W 333°21 NM to fld. 2060/16E.

Figure 14.1

Given

Aircraft identification	N7118Q
Transponder	4096 with Mode C
Two-way radio and VOR	Operable
Compass deviation	None
Proposed departure time--Fresno	0900 PDT
Fuel on board	23.0 gal.
Demonstrated crosswind component	17 kts.
IAS at 6,500 ft.	84 kts.
IAS at 7,500 ft.	82 kts.
TAS at 6,500 ft.	92 kts.
TAS at 7,500 ft.	91 kts.
Fuel flow at 6,500 ft.	5.4 gal./hr.
Fuel flow at 7,500 ft.	5.3 gal./hr.

Notes:

(1) Add 1 min. for each 1,000 ft. of climb to altitude to compensate for additional fuel burned and time spent to reach cruising altitude.

(2) Special equipment codes.

    /T - Transponder with no altitude encoding.
    /U - Transponder with altitude encoding.
    /B - DME and transponder, but no altitude encoding.
    /A - DME and transponder with altitude encoding.

Routing

Leg 1: Fresno Chandler Downtown (FCH) direct at 6,500 ft. MSL to Pine Mountain Lake at Groveland (Q68); 1-hr. stopover; proposed departure time 1100 PDT.

Leg 2: Pine Mountain Lake (Q68) direct at 6,500 ft. MSL to Los Banos (LSN); fly over checkpoint.

Leg 3: Los Banos (LSN) direct at 6,500 ft. MSL to Carmel Valley (062); 30 min. stopover; proposed departure time 1310 PDT.

Leg 4: Carmel Valley (062) direct at 7,500 ft. MSL to Panoche VOR (PXN); checkpoint.

Leg 5: Panoche VOR (PXN) at 7,500 ft. MSL direct to Fresno Chandler Downtown (FCH).

Weather Information (summarized)

Winds and temperature aloft:

    3,000 ft.: 240° at 15 kts.; 20°C
    6,000 ft.: 260° at 25 kts.; 15°C
    9,000 ft.: 260° at 25 kts.; 10°C

Fresno current: 8,000 broken, 10,000 overcast, visibility 10 mi., OAT 82°F,
                     dewpoint 67°F, barometer 29.76, surface winds 240° at 10 kts.

Modesto current: 12,000 scattered, visibility 12 mi., OAT 84°F, dewpoint
                     67°F, barometer 29.86, winds 200° at 20 kts.

Modesto forecast: clear, visibility 12 mi., OAT 88°F, dewpoint 68°F,
                     barometer 29.82, winds 240° at 20 kts.

Monterey current: field obscured, fog, visibility restricted, OAT 63°F,
                     dewpoint 63°F, barometer 29.62, winds calm.

Monterey forecast: clear, visibility 6 mi. and haze, OAT 70°F, dewpoint
                     63°F, barometer 29.76, winds 210° at 10 kts.

Fresno forecast: 6,000 scattered, visibility 10 mi., OAT 84°F, dewpoint
                     67°F, barometer 29.86, winds 270° at 20 kts.

DISCUSSION AND REVIEW EXERCISES

1. Complete the flight navigation log in Figure 14.2 for this cross-country trip.

     a. Are the altitudes appropriate for the routing and weather conditions? Why or why not?

     b. Calculate the headwind and crosswind components (Figure 6.1) for takeoffs and landings at:

          i.   Fresno (FHC) current; assume you will use Rwy 30L or Rwy 30R.

          ii. Pine Mountain Lake (Q68), both current and forecast; use Modesto for an approximation; assume you will use Rwy 27.

Figure 14.2

FLIGHT LOG

Aircraft number: _____
Proposed takeoff: _____
Actual takeoff: _____
Fuel GPH: _____

Route/Fix/Checkpoint	Alt.	IAS / Temp.	TAS	TC	Wind Dir. / Vel.	WCA / TH	Var. / MH	Dev. / CH	Ground Speed	Dist. / Dist. Rem.	Time ETE/ATE	ETA/ATA	Fuel Used	Rem.
Totals													

Airport Frequencies

Airport		
ATIS		
Cl. Del.		
Gnd.		
Twr.		
Dep.		
App.		
FSS		
UNICOM		

Airport/ATIS Advisories

Airport		
Cig.		
Vsby.		
Temp.		
Wind		
Alt.		
Rwy.		
NOTAMs		

Time in	
Time out	
Total Time	

Field Elevation MSL	
Departure	
Destination	

Remarks:

REMEMBER:
CLOSE YOUR FLIGHT PLAN
Freq. _____
Phone no. _____

14 - 5

iii. Carmel Valley (062); use the Monterey forecast; assume you will use Rwy 29.

iv. Fresno (FCH) forecast; assume you will use Rwy 30L or Rwy 30R.

c. Have you exceeded the demonstrated crosswind component in any of the above? Which, if any?

d. Pine Mountain Lake, as you discovered above, may present a problem in landing since the current Modesto conditions suggest that the demonstrated crosswind component might be exceeded. Should you change your flight plan at this point? Analyze the situation.

2. Your flight plan:

a. With whom will you file the plan? How will you contact them? Where are they located?

b. Complete a flight plan for this trip using Figure 14.3.

FLIGHT PLAN

DEPARTMENT OF TRANSPORTATION
FEDERAL AVIATION ADMINISTRATION

CIVIL AIRCRAFT PILOTS. FAR Part 91 requires you file an IFR flight plan to operate under instrument flight rules in controlled airspace. Failure to file could result in a civil penalty not to exceed $1,000 for each violation (Section 901 of the Federal Aviation Act of 1958, as amended). Filing of a VFR flight plan is recommended as a good operating practice. See also Part 99 for requirements concerning DVFR flight plans.

1. TYPE	2. AIRCRAFT IDENTIFICATION	3. AIRCRAFT TYPE/ SPECIAL EQUIPMENT	4. TRUE AIRSPEED	5. DEPARTURE POINT	6. DEPARTURE TIME		7. CRUISING ALTITUDE
VFR					PROPOSED (Z)	ACTUAL (Z)	
IFR							
DVFR			KTS				

8. ROUTE OF FLIGHT

9. DESTINATION (Name of airport and city)	10. EST. TIME ENROUTE		11. REMARKS
	HOURS	MINUTES	

12. FUEL ON BOARD		13. ALTERNATE AIRPORT(S)	14. PILOT'S NAME, ADDRESS & TELEPHONE NUMBER & AIRCRAFT HOME BASE	15. NUMBER ABOARD
HOURS	MINUTES			

16. COLOR OF AIRCRAFT

CLOSE VFR FLIGHT PLAN WITH_____FSS ON ARRIVAL

FAA Form 7233-1 (5-77)

Figure 14.3

c. How will you activate your flight plan on your departure from FCH?

3.   Departure and Leg 1:

a.   Given your proposed route of flight, to which runway will you probably be directed for takeoff? Why?

b.   After your runup, you are ready for takeoff. It is 0857 PDT. What do you do next?

c. How would you use your VOR to obtain a fix exactly 21 NM from Fresno Chandler (FCH) along your intended route of flight? What visual landmarks are also available at this point?

d. Use the road heading northwest out of Mariposa-Yosemite Airport as another checkpoint. A crosscheck is the 025° radial from the Merced (MCE) VOR. If it takes you 20 min. to get from the checkpoint in question 3c to the Mariposa-Yosemite checkpoint, what is your actual groundspeed? Why do you suppose it is different from your estimated groundspeed?

e. How would you call Pine Mountain to obtain an airport advisory?

f. Suppose Pine Mountain UNICOM reports that winds are 230° at 20 kts. Are you going to land? Explain.

g. How you would enter and fly the pattern at Pine Mountain? Include directions on the various legs of the pattern and compensation for the surface winds to keep the airplane in a rectangular pattern relative to the runway.

4. Leg 2:

a. What do you know about the **alert area** between Pine Mountain and Los Banos?

b. Since you will be flying over Castle Air Force Base, are you required to report your position to them? If so, where should you report?

c. Shortly after passing over Castle AFB, you notice, to your amazement, that the oil temperature gauge is near red line. What should you do?

d. As you approach Los Banos, the oil temperature continues to rise and is now on the red line. You and your instructor decide to land and have it checked. As you begin your descent, you need to check Los Banos. The winds are reported as 180° at 15 and Rwy 14 is the active runway. Describe how you will enter and fly the pattern, the direction on the various legs of the pattern, and what crabbing you will have to do to fly a rectangular pattern.

e. Suppose you decide to use VASI to aid you on your final approach. How will you get it turned on? How will you use it?

f. As your instructor and a mechanic analyze the problem (a faulty gauge), you decide to call FSS and file an amended flight plan that will allow an extra hour for lunch at Carmel Valley. How would you contact FSS and where is the station located?

g. After departing Los Banos, you climb to 6,500 ft. and proceed to Carmel Valley. Assume it takes you 12 min. to travel from V107 to V485. What is your groundspeed?

h. Briefly explain how you will make your approach to Carmel Valley, including a description of whom you will call and how you will fly the pattern.

5. Leg 3:

a. From studying the sectional chart, with what should you be concerned shortly after departing Carmel Valley? What do you plan to do?

b. How would you set your VOR to fly from Carmel Valley to Panoche VOR? Explain.

c. How would you set your VOR to fly from Panoche to Fresno Chandler? Explain.

d. Assume you decide to contact Fresno Chandler over Kerman. Whom would you call, what frequency would you use, and what would you say?

e. With whom would you close your flight plan? How would you contact them?

FAA EXAM QUESTIONS

(Note: All FAA Figures are located in Appendix C)

1. (FAA 1497) Prior to starting each maneuver, a pilot should
   1--check altitude, airspeed, and heading indications.
   2--visually scan the area below your aircraft in case of an accidental stall or spin.
   3--advise ATC of your intentions so as to receive timely traffic advisories.
   4--visually scan the entire area for collision avoidance.

2. (FAA 1498) What procedure is recommended when climbing or descending VFR on an airway?
   1--Advise the nearest FSS of the altitude changes.
   2--Offset 4 mi. or more from the centerline of the airway before changing altitude.
   3--Squawk 1400 on the transponder with Mode C selected.
   4--Execute gentle banks, left and right for continuous visual scanning of the airspace.

3. (FAA 1476) How should a VFR flight plan be closed at the completion of the flight at a controlled airport?
   1--The tower will automatically close the flight plan when the aircraft turns off the runway.
   2--The pilot must close the flight plan with the nearest FSS or other FAA facility upon landing.
   3--The tower will relay the instructions to the nearest FSS when the aircraft contacts the tower for landing.
   4--The pilot should close the flight plan with ground control while taxiing to the parking ramp.

4. (FAA 1499) If more than one cruising altitude is intended, which should be entered in Block 7 of the flight plan? (See Figure 48.)
   1--Initial cruising altitude.
   2--Highest cruising altitude.
   3--Lowest cruising altitude.
   4--Average of all cruising altitudes.

5. (FAA 1500) The information that should be entered in Block 9 (Figure 48) for a VFR day flight is the
   1--name of the airport of first intended landing.
   2--name of destination airport if no stopover for more than 1 hr. is anticipated.
   3--name of the airport where the aircraft is based.
   4--names of all the airports where landings are to be made.

6. (FAA 1501) What information should be entered in Block 12 (Figure 48) for a VFR day flight?
   1--The estimated time en route plus 30 min.
   2--The estimated time en route plus 45 min.
   3--The maximum endurance time as shown in the Pilot's Operating Handbook.
   4--The amount of usable fuel on board expressed in time.

ANSWERS AND EXPLANATIONS

Cross-Country Exercise

Note: Do not use the data and charts provided in this chapter for actual flight planning purposes! They are outdated. Only updated charts and information should be used. Furthermore, should you ever want to fly this particular cross-country trip, be sure to check with your local FBO, or others familiar with the airports, particularly Carmel Valley.

1. See Figure 14.4. Note that distances have been modified to account for time to climb to altitude by adding 1 min. for each 1,000-ft. increment.

   a. Yes, they meet FAA standards as far as the intended routes are concerned and they keep you away from adverse weather, assuming that Monterey clears as forecast.

Aircraft number: 7118Q

FLIGHT LOG

Proposed takeoff: 0900/1600Z
Actual takeoff: _____

Route/Fix/Checkpoint	Alt. / Temp.	IAS / TAS	TC	Wind Dir. / Vel.	WCA / TH	Var. / MH	Dev. / CH	Ground Speed	Dist. / Dist. Rem.	ETE / ATE	ETA / ATA	Used	Rem. (GPH: 54/5.5)
FCH ⇨ Q68	6,500 / +15	84 / 92	346	260 / 25	-16 / 330	-16 / 314	0 / 314	87	70 / 207	48+6	0854	4.9	18.1
Q68 ⇨ LSN	6,500 / +15	84 / 92	215	260 / 25	+11 / 226	-16 / 210	0 / 210	73	58 / 149	41+6		4.8	13.3
LSN ⇨ 062	6,500 / +15	84 / 92	230	260 / 25	+8 / 238	-16 / 222	0 / 222	69	54 / 95	47		4.2	9.1
062 ⇨ PXN (112.6)	7,500 / +12	82 / 91	073	260 / 25	-2 / 071	-16 / 055	0 / 055	116	48 / 47	25+1		2.9	6.2
PXN ⇨ FCH	1,500 / +12	82 / 91	089	260 / 25	+2 / 091	-16 / 075	0 / 075	116	47 / 0	25		2.2	4.0
Totals									277	3+31		19.0	4.0

Airport Frequencies

Airport	FCH	Q68	062
ATIS			
Cl. Del.			
Gnd.			
Twr.			
Dep.	119.0		
App.	119.0		
FSS	122.55		
UNICOM	123.0		

Airport/ATIS Advisories

Airport		
Cig.		
Vsby.		
Temp.		
Wind		
Alt.		
Rwy.		
NOTAMs		

Time in	
Time out	
Total Time	

Field Elevation MSL

Departure	Destination
FCH 278	Q68 2200
062 450	

Remarks:

STOPOVER Q68
1 HOUR
ETD 1100
STOPOVER 062
0+30
ETD 1310

REMEMBER:
CLOSE YOUR FLIGHT PLAN
Freq. 122.55
Phone no. 251-8269

Figure 14.4

b. Headwind and crosswind components for takeoff: Fresno current: headwind, 5 kts.; crosswind, 8.5 kts. Pine Mountain Lake current: assume you will use Rwy 27; headwind, 7 kts.; crosswind, almost 19 kts. Pine Mountain Lake forecast: headwind, 17 kts; crosswind, 10 kts. Carmel Valley forecast: assume you will use Rwy 29; headwind, 2 kts.; crosswind, almost 10 kts. Fresno forecast: assume you will use Rwy 30L and Rwy 30R; headwind, 17 kts.; crosswind, 10 kts.

c. Yes. Pine Mountain may have winds that exceed the demonstrated crosswind component, assuming Modesto is representative.

d. According to the Modesto forecast, the winds should become more favorable throughout the morning. It might be wise to call Pine Mountain, but the airport is unattended. You might also ask FSS for any pilot reports. The winds are a factor to monitor as your flight progresses but at present are not serious enough to warrant canceling that portion of the flight.

2. Your flight plan:

a. Fresno FSS, located at Fresno Air Terminal, can be reached by calling 251-8269 (local call). See Figure 14.1, the Airport/Facility Directory excerpt.

b. See Figure 14.5.

c. Call Fresno Radio on 122.55 or 123.65, or transmit on 122.1 and listen on the VOR (112.9). Refer to the sectional chart for frequencies. The small shaded box in the lower right corner of the FRESNO rectangle indicates TWEB is available.

3. Departure and Leg 1:

a. Since you will be departing to the northwest, you will probably be assigned to Rwy 30R to take into account the right traffic pattern. Rwy 30L has left traffic, which would take you away from your proposed flight route.

b. Call the tower on 121.1 and tell them you are ready to take off. Note: The sectional chart does not indicate that Chandler has an active control tower. However, the Airport/Facility Directory excerpt (Figure 14.1) states that there is a control tower and that it is operated from 1600-0400Z.

c. There are several options here. You can use the Panoche VOR (PXN, 112.6) and the 49° radial, or you can use the Merced VOR (MCE, 114.2) and the 94 radial, or you can use the Friant VOR (FRA, 115.6) and the 245° radial. The best one is the Friant VOR since it is approximately perpendicular to your line of flight in that region. A radial that is perpendicular to your route of flight is more accurate than one that runs at an obtuse or acute angle.

d. 27.5 NM in 20 min. (.33 hr.) yields a groundspeed of 82.5 kts., less than you estimated. Perhaps the winds are not as forecasted, or perhaps you are not following your course precisely. Finally, you should realize that, over relatively short distances, rounding errors may also account for some variance in your calculations.

1. TYPE	2. AIRCRAFT IDENTIFICATION	3. AIRCRAFT TYPE/ SPECIAL EQUIPMENT	4. TRUE AIRSPEED	5. DEPARTURE POINT	6. DEPARTURE TIME		7. CRUISING ALTITUDE

DEPARTMENT OF TRANSPORTATION
FEDERAL AVIATION ADMINISTRATION

FLIGHT PLAN

CIVIL AIRCRAFT PILOTS. FAR Part 91 requires you file an IFR flight plan to operate under instrument flight rules in controlled airspace. Failure to file could result in a civil penalty not to exceed $1,000 for each violation (Section 901 of the Federal Aviation Act of 1958, as amended). Filing of a VFR flight plan is recommended as a good operating practice. See also Part 99 for requirements concerning DVFR flight plans.

1. TYPE	2. AIRCRAFT IDENTIFICATION	3. AIRCRAFT TYPE/ SPECIAL EQUIPMENT	4. TRUE AIRSPEED	5. DEPARTURE POINT	6. DEPARTURE TIME PROPOSED (Z) / ACTUAL (Z)	7. CRUISING ALTITUDE
☒ VFR ☐ IFR ☐ DVFR	N7118Q	STARSHIP U-2	92 KTS	FCH	1600	6500

8. ROUTE OF FLIGHT

D→ Q68 D→ LSN D→ 062 D→ PXN D→ FCH

9. DESTINATION (Name of airport and city)	10. EST. TIME ENROUTE HOURS / MINUTES	11. REMARKS
FRESNO CHANDLER FRESNO	5 / 07	STOPOVERS Q68 (1+00) 062 (0+30)

12. FUEL ON BOARD HOURS / MINUTES	13. ALTERNATE AIRPORT(S)	14. PILOT'S NAME, ADDRESS & TELEPHONE NUMBER & AIRCRAFT HOME BASE	15. NUMBER ABOARD
4 / 00	N/A	IMA STUDENT 309 AIRPORT DR. FRESNO	2

16. COLOR OF AIRCRAFT
SKY BLUE & ROYAL BLUE

CLOSE VFR FLIGHT PLAN WITH ___FCH___ **FSS ON ARRIVAL**

FAA Form 7233-1 (5-77)

Figure 14.5

e. The sectional chart and <u>Airport/Facility Directory</u> both say it is 123.0 MHz.

f. You will be able to land, since the crosswind component is 13 kts., which is below the demonstrated crosswind component of 17 kts. Since this component is close to the airplane's limit, you must be sure to consider your own proficiency before deciding to attempt the landing.

g. You should plan a pattern altitude of 3,700 ft. MSL (800 ft. AGL), as described in the <u>Airport/Facility Directory.</u> Since you will be landing on Rwy 27, you should plan for a right-hand traffic pattern. Fly over the field, make a circle to the west, and enter downwind at a 45° angle midway along the runway. On downwind, you will be flying 090°, keeping in mind that you will have to crab to the south to maintain a straight downwind path. When you turn base (180°), the wind will retard you somewhat and also push you to the east, which means you will have to crab to the right. On final (270°), you will have to crab to the left to maintain a straight final approach.

4. Leg 2:

a. The alert area is in effect from 0700 to 0200 Monday through Friday from 1,000 to 4,000 ft. MSL. You will overfly the area, so there is no need for alarm. If you were flying through it, you would exercise extreme caution.

b. You are not required to contact them since the ATA extends from ground level up to but not including 3,000 ft. AGL. You are well above the ATA.

c. You might be tempted to land at Merced or Atwater, but since it is a hot day the high oil temperature might not be abnormal. You should check frequently to see if the temperature continues to rise, or if it is stable.

d. You are northeast of the field and will land on Rwy 14, which has a right-hand traffic pattern. As at Pine Mountain, you should fly over the field so you can enter the pattern on the southwest side of the field. Pattern altitude is 800 ft. AGL, so you will fly the pattern at 919 ft. MSL. The downwind leg will be 320° with a crab to the left; base will be 50° with crab to the right; and final will be 140° with a crab to the right.

e. Call on 122.8 and ask for it to be activated.

f. Use the telephone; ask the operator for Enterprise 14598, which will connect you with Fresno FSS (FAT).

g. It is 13 NM and it took you 0.2 hr., for a groundspeed of 65 kts., only slightly less than you estimated.

5. Leg 3:

a. Note that the elevation rises from 450 ft. MSL to 3,560 ft. MSL about 7 NM from Carmel Valley along your proposed route of flight. Make certain you check that you will be well above that altitude when you go over the mountains.

b. Set the VOR to 112.6 MHz, check for the identification (PXN), and fly TO 057°.

c. Fly FROM 072°.

d. Contact Chandler Tower on 121.1 and tell them where you are (over Kerman) and what your intentions are. Again, note that the sectional chart does not show a control tower at Chandler; but, according to the Airport/Facility Directory, there is one that operates from 1600-0400Z.

e. Fresno FSS.

FAA Exam Questions

1. 4--You should always be scanning for collision avoidance. It is especially necessary before starting turning and stalling maneuvers.

2. 4--When climbing or descending, the nose of the aircraft may block the view ahead and below. Gentle turns allow you to look to the side of the airplane.

3. 2--The pilot has the responsibility to close the flight plan. You should close it with the nearest FSS by radio or telephone, or if one is not available, you may request any ATC facility. Control towers do not automatically close VFR flight plans.

4. 1--Only the initial cruising altitude is entered.

5. 2--Enter the airport of landing at the end of the final entry in the route of flight block. Flight plans may include stopovers at intermediate airports, however, it is recommended that separate flight plans be filed when stops of over 1 hour are planned.

6. 4--Use your flight computer to determine flight time based on usable fuel on board and fuel consumption rate.

**U.S. Department
of Transportation**

**Federal Aviation
Administration**

Advisory
Circular

Subject: ROLE OF PREFLIGHT PREPARATION	Date: 3/18/85 Initiated by:AFO-840	AC No: 61-84B Change:

1. <u>PURPOSE</u>. This advisory circular (AC) modifies and updates the flight information available to pilots as a result of changes in the basic Airmen Information Manual format.

2. <u>CANCELLATION</u>. AC 61-84A dated December 1, 1980, is canceled.

3. <u>BACKGROUND</u>.

   a. One of the most often neglected acts of a pilot contemplating flight in an aircraft is that of proper preflight planning. While the reasons remain obscure, the facts are well supported by aircraft accident statistics. Although the number of general aviation accidents has shown a downward trend in recent years, the accident and fatality/serious injury statistics indicate an increase in the percentage of accidents during <u>takeoff</u>.

   b. Statistics taken from the National Transportation Safety Board files show that from 1979 through 1983, 728 persons died and 665 were seriously injured in 4,291 takeoff accidents. These accidents are significant to general aviation pilots--annually, they represent about 20 percent of all general aviation accidents and about 16 percent of all fatalities and serious injuries. Traditionally, pilots have emphasized the planning of the en route and approach/landing phases of flight; e.g., the route to be taken, en route and destination weather, en route and terminal facilities, applicable altitudes and fuel requirements. Accident data, however, indicate that too little preparation is made for the actual takeoff of the aircraft. In order for pilots to fulfill their responsibilities to ensure the safety of the entire flight, it is necessary that they have adequate knowledge of elements involved in preflight planning. It is also necessary that they take time to analyze the conditions and study the various factors which would affect the takeoff, en route, and landing phases of flight.

4. <u>KEY ELEMENTS OF PREFLIGHT PLANNING</u>.

   a. <u>Charts</u>.

   (1) A basic element of preflight preparation requires the use of current navigational charts on which pilots can mentally review their intended route of flight. They may or may not wish to draw a line on the chart representing the <u>true</u>

course. They should, however, review the projected path across the face of the chart for the location of good checkpoints, restricted areas, obstructions, other flight hazards, and suitable airports. For visual flight rule (VFR) pilot planning by either pilotage or dead reckoning, the Sectional Aeronautical Chart is an excellent choice. It is scaled at 1/500,000, or 8 miles to the inch. The physical characteristics of most landmarks, both cultural and geographic, are shown in great detail. The pilot should have little difficulty identifying the selected landmarks along the route of flight. Another popular chart is the World Aeronautical Chart (WAC). The scale of the WAC is 1/1,000,000, or 16 miles to the inch. Many states print aeronautical charts which are excellent for VFR navigation within their state boundaries. The pilot should realize, however, that all of these charts are designed primarily for VFR navigation and contain only limited information concerning radio aids and frequencies. The use of instrument flight rules (IFR) navigational charts for planning pilotage or dead reckoning VFR flights is not desirable for the following reasons:

(i) Many airports used by the VFR pilot are not depicted or listed on the IFR charts.

(ii) Very few geographic or cultural landmarks are provided.

(iii) The pilot should refer to the Airman's Information Manual - Basic Flight Information and Air Traffic Control Procedures (AIM) - for more precise coverage of this information.

(2) Most pilots are reluctant to admit to being disoriented or lost. Being lost can be an embarrassing and sometimes frightening experience. Pilots should carry appropriate and current aeronautical charts on all cross-country flights. The use of outdated charts may result in flights into airport traffic areas, control zones, or other restricted airspace without proper authorization. Having available the information contained in current charts will enhance the pilot's ability to complete the flight with greater confidence, ease, and safety.

b. Route. Since the shortest distance between two points is a straight line, a majority of pilots desire direct routes for most flights. Quite often there are factors that should be considered that may make a direct flight undesirable. Restricted and prohibited areas present obstacles to direct flights. In single-engine aircraft, pilots should give consideration to circumnavigating large, desolate areas. Pilots should also consider the single-engine service ceiling of multiengine aircraft when operating over high altitude terrain since the terrain elevation may be higher than the single-engine service ceiling of the multiengine aircraft being flown. An example of this is a multiengine aircraft with a single-engine service ceiling of 6,000 feet being flown over terrain of 9,000 feet elevation. Pilots should be aware that the only advantage they may have over a pilot flying a single-engine aircraft may be a wider latitude in selecting a suitable forced landing area.

c. Airman's Information Manual - Basic Flight Information and Air Traffic Control Procedures (AIM). Part 91 of the Federal Aviation Regulations (FAR) states, in part, that each pilot in command shall, before beginning a flight, become familiar with all available information concerning that flight. The AIM contains information concerning cross-country flight and basic fundamentals required for safe flight in the U.S. National Airspace System.

2

d. Airport/Facility Directory. The Airport/Facility Directory, published by the National Ocean Service, lists airports, seaplane bases, and heliports open to the public, communications data, navigational facilities, and certain special notices such as parachute jumping, Flight Service Station (FSS)/National Weather Service (NWS) telephone numbers, preferred routes, and aeronautical chart bulletins.

e. Notices to Airmen (Class II).

(1) Notices to Airmen (Class II) is issued biweekly and is divided into two sections. The first section contains those notices which are expected to remain in effect for at least 7 days after the effective date of the publication. National Flight Data Center (FDC) Notices to Airmen (NOTAMS) primarily reflect changes to standard instrument approach procedures. FDC NOTAMS also establish flight restrictions and correct data on aeronautical charts.

(2) The second section contains special notices that, either because they are too long or because they concern a wide or unspecified geographical area, are not suitable for inclusion in the first section. The content of these notices vary widely and there are no specific criteria for inclusion, other than their enhancement of flight safety.

f. Notices to Airmen (NOTAM). In addition to NOTAM information contained in the Notices to Airmen (Class II) publication, pilots should check with the nearest FSS for an update on the latest NOTAMS.

g. International Flight Information Manual. The International Flight Information Manual is published quarterly for use of private flyers, businessmen, and nonscheduled operators as a preflight and planning guide for flights outside the United States.

h. International Notices to Airmen.

(1) The International Notices to Airmen is a biweekly publication containing significant international NOTAM information and special notices which may affect a pilot's decision to enter or use certain areas of foreign or international airspace.

(2) Pilots should avail themselves of all appropriate charts and publications, including the AIM and NOTAMS.

i. Weather. A weather briefing is an important part of preflight planning. An overview of the synoptic situation and general weather conditions can be obtained from public media (radio, TV, etc.) or by telephone from recorded sources. This will help the pilot to better understand the overall weather picture when obtaining a complete briefing from the FSS, NWS, or other organization that provides this service. Information on public media and recorded weather sources is contained in the Meteorology chapter of the AIM. This chapter also provides information on how to obtain a complete weather briefing, what to look for, and what to ask of the briefer to ensure that the pilot has all the weather necessary for the flight. The weather information should be weighed very carefully in considering the go/no-go decision. This decision is the sole responsibility of the pilot and compulsion should never take the place of good judgment.

j. Navigation Log. Precise flight planning of log items, such as pre-computed courses, time and distance, navigational aids, and frequencies to be used will make en route errors in these items less likely. Special attention should be given to fuel requirements, keeping in mind the need for an ample reserve as well as location of refueling points available as the flight progresses.

k. Flight Plan (VFR). This is not required by FAR, but is dictated by good operating practice. A flight plan not only assures prompt search and rescue in the event the aircraft becomes overdue or missing, but it also permits the destination station to render better service by having prior knowledge of your flight. It costs only a few minutes of time to file a flight plan and may be the best investment the pilot ever makes.

l. Aircraft Manual. Aircraft manuals contain operating limitations, performance, normal and emergency procedures, and a variety of other operational information for the respective aircraft. Traditionally, aircraft manufacturers have done considerable testing to gather and substantiate the information in the aircraft manual. Pilots should become familiar with the manual and be able to refer to it for information relative to a proposed flight.

5. KEY ELEMENTS DURING TAKEOFF PHASE. The importance of thorough preflight preparation which considers possible hazards to takeoff cannot be over-emphasized. The following elements, which should be carefully considered, continue to emerge as factors in takeoff accidents:

a. Gross Weight.

(1) Maximum allowable gross weight is established for an aircraft as an operating limitation for both safety and performance considerations. The gross weight is important because it is a basis for determining the takeoff distance. If gross weight increases, the takeoff speed must be greater to produce the greater lift required for takeoff. The takeoff distance varies with the square of the gross weight. As an example, for an aircraft with a relatively high thrust-to-weight ratio, a 10 percent increase in takeoff gross weight would cause:

      (i)   a 5 percent increase in speed necessary for takeoff velocity;

      (ii)   at least a 9 percent decrease in acceleration; and,

      (iii)   at least a 21 percent increase in takeoff distance.

NOTE: For aircraft with relatively low thrust-to-weight ratios, the figures are slightly higher.

(2) Operations within the proper gross weight limits are outlined in each operator's manual. Gross weight and center of gravity (CG) limits should be considered during preflight preparation. Weight in excess of the maximum certificated gross weight may be a contributing factor to an accident, especially when coupled with other factors which adversely affect the ability of an aircraft to take off and climb safely. These factors may range from field elevation of the airport to the condition of the runway. The responsibility for considering these factors before each flight rests with the pilot.

4

b. Balance.

(1) A pilot must not only determine the takeoff weight of the aircraft, but also must assure that the load is arranged to fall within the allowable CG limits for the aircraft. Each aircraft manual provides instructions on the proper method for determining if the aircraft loading meets the balance requirements. The pilot should routinely determine the balance of the aircraft since it is possible to be within the gross weight limits and still exceed the CG limits.

(2) An airplane which exceeds the forward CG limits places heavy loads on the nosewheel and, in conventional landing gear airplanes, may, during braking, cause an uncontrollable condition. Furthermore, performance may be significantly decreased and the stall speed may be much higher.

(3) An airplane loaded in a manner that the CG exceeds the aft limit will have decreased static and dynamic longitudinal stability. This condition can produce sudden and violent stall characteristics and can seriously affect recovery.

(4) Pilots exceeding CG limits in helicopters may experience insufficient cyclic controls to safely control the helicopter. This can be extremely critical while hovering downwind with the helicopter load exceeding the forward CG limit.

c. Ice and Frost.

(1) Ice or frost can affect the takeoff performance of an aircraft significantly. Pilots should never attempt takeoffs with any accumulation of ice or frost on their aircraft. Most pilots are aware of the hazards of ice on the wings of an aircraft. The effects of a hard frost are much more subtle. This is due to an increased roughness of the surface texture of the upper wing and may cause up to a 10 percent increase in the airplane stall speed. It may also require additional speed to produce the lift necessary to become airborne.

(2) Once airborne, the airplane could have an insufficient margin of airspeed above stall such that gusts or turning of the aircraft could result in a stall. Accumulation of ice or frost on helicopter rotor blades results in potential rotor blade stalls at slower forward air speeds. It could also result in an unbalanced rotor blade condition which could cause an uncontrollable vibration.

d. Density Altitude.

(1) Aircraft instruments are calibrated to be correct under one set of conditions. Standard conditions represent theoretical sea level conditions, 59 degrees Farenheit and 29.92 in Hg. As higher elevations are reached, both temperature and pressure normally decrease. Thus, density altitude is determined by compensating for pressure and temperature variances from the standard conditions. A pilot must remember that as density altitude increases, there is a corresponding decrease in the power delivered by the engine and the propellers or rotor blades. For airplanes, this may cause the required takeoff roll to increase by up to 25 percent for every 1,000 feet of elevation above sea level. The most critical conditions of takeoff performance are the result of a combination of heavy loads, unfavorable runway conditions, winds, high temperatures, high airport elevations, and high humidity.

(2) The proper accounting for the pressure altitude (field elevation is a poor substitute) and temperature is mandatory for accurate prediction of takeoff data. The required information will be listed in the aircraft manual and should be consulted before each takeoff, especially if operating at a high density altitude or with a heavily loaded aircraft.

e. Effect of Wind.

(1) Every aircraft manual gives representative wind data and corresponding ground roll distances. A headwind which is 10 percent of the takeoff airspeed will reduce the no-wind takeoff distance by 19 percent. A tailwind which is 10 percent of the takeoff airspeed, however, will increase the no-wind takeoff distance by about 21 percent.

(2) Although this consideration is basic to a successful takeoff, the number of accidents involving the selection of the wrong runway for the existing wind and taking off into unfavorable wind conditions indicates a need for many pilots to reevaluate their preflight planning to ensure that the effect of wind is considered fully.

f. Runway Condition.

(1) There are more than 14,700 airports in the United States, each with runways having various surface compositions, slopes, and degrees of roughness. Takeoff acceleration is affected directly by the runway surface condition and, as a result, it must be a primary consideration during preflight planning.

(2) Most aircraft manuals list takeoff data for level, dry, hard-surfaced runways. The runway to be used, however, is not always hard-surfaced and level. Consequently, pilots must be aware of the effect of the slope or gradient of the runway, the composition of the runway, and the condition of its surface. Each of these can contribute to a failure to obtain/maintain a safe flying speed.

(3) The effective runway gradient is the maximum difference in the runway centerline elevation divided by the runway length. The FAA recognizes the effect of runway gradient on the takeoff roll of an aircraft and has published limits on the maximum gradients. For general aviation VFR airports the maximum longitudinal runway grade is 2 percent and the longitudinal runway grade change is 2 percent maximum. Furthermore, the takeoff length for a runway must be increased an additional 20 percent for each 1 percent of change in effective gradient to a maximum allowable effective gradient change of 2 percent.

(4) Since the runway gradient has a direct bearing on the component weight of the aircraft, a runway gradient of 1 percent would provide a force component along the path of the aircraft which is 1 percent of gross weight. In the case of an upslope, the additional drag and rolling friction caused by a 1 percent upslope can result in a 2 percent to 4 percent increase in the takeoff distance and subsequent climb.

(5) Frequently, the only runway at an airport has a slope. When determining which direction to use for takeoff, pilots must remember that a

direction uphill, but into a headwind, is generally preferred to a downwind takeoff on a downsloping runway. Factors such as steep slope, light wind, etc., however, make an uphill takeoff impractical.

(6) It is difficult to predict the retarding effect on the takeoff run that water, snow/slush, sand, gravel, mud, or long grass on a runway will have, but these factors can be critical to the success of a takeoff. Since the takeoff data in the aircraft manual is predicated on a dry, hard surface each pilot must develop individual guidelines for operations from other type surfaces.

g. Cold Weather Takeoffs. The following is an excerpt taken from AC 91-13C, Cold Weather Operation of Aircraft:

"Takeoffs in cold weather offer some distinct advantages, but they also offer special problems. A few points to remember are:

"(1) Do not overboost supercharged or turbine engines. Use the applicable power charts for the pressure altitude and ambient temperature to determine the appropriate manifold pressure or engine pressure ratio. Care should be exercised in operating normally aspirated engines. Power output increases at about 1 percent for each ten degrees of temperature below that of standard air. At -40 degrees F, an engine might develop 10 percent more than rated power even though RPM and MP limits are not exceeded.

"(2) On multiengine aircraft it must be remembered that the critical engine-out minimum control speed (Vmc) was determined at sea level with a standard day temperature. Therefore, Vmc will be higher than the published figure during a cold weather takeoff unless the power setting is adjusted to compensate for the lower density altitude.

"(3) With reciprocating engines, use carburetor heat as required. In some cases, it is necessary to use heat to vaporize the fuel. Gasoline does not vaporize readily at very cold temperatures. Do not use carburetor heat in such a manner that it raises the mixture temperature to freezing or just a little below. In such cases, it may be inducing carburetor icing. An accurate mixture temperature gauge is a good investment for cold weather operation. On some occasions in extremely cold weather, it may be advisable to use carburetor heat on takeoff.

"(4) If icing conditions exist, use the anti-ice and deice equipment as outlined in the Airplane Flight Manual. If the aircraft is turbine powered, use the appropriate power charts for the condition, bearing in mind that the use of bleed air will, in most cases, affect the aircraft's performance."

6. SUMMARY. Preflight preparation is the foundation of safe flying. Accident statistics of recent years indicate that adequate preflight preparation is lacking in many cases. As a result, while the number of general aviation accidents and approach and landing accidents has declined, takeoff accidents have increased. Statistics indicate that takeoff accidents occur because elements of the preflight preparation were:

a. not assigned the proper importance,

b. not incorporated into the preflight routine, or

c. pilots did not anticipate potential takeoff emergencies and the required procedures to follow.

7. <u>RECOMMENDATION</u>. To enhance the safety of flying, pilots are encouraged to:

a. form good preflight planning habits and review them continually,

b. be thoroughly knowledgeable of the hazards and conditions which would represent potential dangers, particularly during takeoff, and,

c. be aware of the capabilities and limitations of their aircraft.

William T. Brennan
Acting Director of Flight Operations

8

THE PHYSIOLOGY OF FLIGHT

MAIN POINTS

1. Flight has many effects on the human body; some are easy to understand and cope with, and others can produce serious consequences in a short period of time. This chapter explores both.

2. **Respiration** is the exchange of gases between your body and the environment. In particular, your body derives oxygen from the environment and expels carbon dioxide. As the amount of carbon dioxide increases, breathing becomes deeper and more frequent; as the amount of carbon dioxide decreases, breathing may become more shallow and sporadic. Furthermore, as altitude increases and atmospheric pressure decreases, less oxygen is available to the body. Gases inside the body also expand as altitude increases since they exert more pressure than is being exerted from the outside atmosphere. Thus it is sometimes necessary to clear your ears by yawning or blowing gently through your nose while pinching your nostrils (the **Valsalva** technique). Pilots should also remember that because underwater diving reverses the pressure gradient, diving should not be mixed with piloting--the body takes time to readjust.

3. Two oxygen-related disorders of particular interest to pilots are **hypoxia** (too little oxygen) and **hyperventilation** (too little carbon dioxide). Hypoxia, or oxygen deficiency, is a progressive condition characterized by impaired vision, euphoria, dizziness, hot and cold flashes, breathlessness, repeated thought patterns, headaches, slowed reaction time, tingling sensation, and perspiration. The time available from the onset of hypoxia to the point of inability to act is called the **time of useful consciousness** (**TUC**). As exposure to oxygen deficiency continues, the effects become more pronounced and may include increased respiration, inability to perform even simple computations, bluing of the skin (cyanosis), and finally, unconsciousness. The **rate** of onset increases dramatically with altitude. From sea level to 10,000 ft. (indifferent stage), vision may be affected, particularly at night. From 10,000 to 15,000 ft. (compensatory stage), pulse, respiration, and blood pressure increase. From 15,000 to 20,000 ft. (disturbance stage), TUC is 20 to 30 min., and from 20,000 to 25,000 ft. (critical stage), TUC can be as short as 3 to 5 min. Rapid decompression in a

pressurized cabin can produce extremely short (less than a minute) TUC. Furthermore, anything that affects the body's ability to get oxygen to the brain, such as hypertension or smoking, can increase the rate of onset. One way to counteract the effects of hypoxia is to descend at once to a lower altitude since recovery is rapid in an oxygen-rich environment. Oxygen should be used above 10,000 ft. during the day and above 5,000 ft. at night. FAR oxygen restrictions were discussed in Chapter 11.

4. **Hyperventilation**, or overbreathing, is an excessively fast rate of respiration that often occurs unknowingly in response to stress. Hyperventilation can cause the individual to pass out due to a severe shortage of carbon dioxide available to the voluntary respiration center. Symptoms include dizziness, tingling sensation, nausea, muscle tightness (tetany), cooling, and fainting. Hyperventilation can begin rapidly, particularly in anxiety-producing situations. Countermeasures are to reduce the rate of breathing or to breathe into an enclosed space, such as a bag, to increase the carbon dioxide content in the blood.

5. Because the symptoms of hypoxia and hyperventilation are similar, it is sometimes difficult to tell which one is occurring. One way to tell is to breathe oxygen (if it is available). If you are experiencing hypoxia, the symptoms should begin to go away almost immediately. If they do not, suspect hyperventilation as the culprit.

6. **Carbon monoxide poisoning** can be particularly insidious because the gas is odorless. Carbon monoxide (CO) deprives the brain of oxygen. Symptoms include a vague uneasy feeling, inability to concentrate, and headaches; if uncorrected, it will lead to unconsciousness and death. Effects can last for days because the blood's oxygen-carrying ability has been altered. Carbon monoxide usually enters the cabin through the heating system. If CO poisoning is suspected, close all heating vents, flood the cabin with air, and land at the nearest facility available.

7. The motion produced in an airplane also affects the body, in particular the motion associated with **acceleration** (changes in velocity). These changes are measured in gravity-level equivalents, or Gs. Forward- and aft-working Gs are called **transverse Gs**; side-force Gs are called **lateral Gs**; and up-and-down Gs are referred to as **positive** (those that push you down) or **negative** (those that push you up). Gs produced in varying combinations are called **asymmetric Gs**. Positive Gs tend to limit blood flow to the head and upper extremities, while negative Gs do just the opposite. The progressive effects of positive Gs are **grayout**, **blackout**, and unconsciousness because of the lack of oxygen. The effect of positive Gs, pushing blood to the lower extremities, can be counteracted by tightening the calf, thigh, and abdominal muscles. The effects of negative Gs, pushing blood to your head, are rare in general aviation and have no easy remedy.

8. The dynamics of flight can have a dramatic effect on spatial orientation. We receive special cues from three sources: eyes, motion sensors (the vestibular system) in the semicircular canals of the inner ear, and proprioceptive feedback from the postural system of touch, pressure, and tension. False cues may begin to develop, however, due to the motion produced in the cockpit, especially under conditions of low visibility. For the most

part, we have learned to trust our eyes; and, as long as VMC conditions prevail, they provide the quickest way to correct any false cues from the vestibular or postural senses.

9. **Spatial disorientation**, which is frequently referred to as **vertigo**, occurs when a pilot cannot orient the aircraft to the natural horizon. The condition is physiological, not learned, but understanding it will help you cope with it. By all means, if you suspect vertigo, **trust your aircraft instruments**. There are several motion-related disorientations. The **graveyard spiral** is a result of illusions in which the vestibular and postural systems adjust and stabilize to a spiral (power-on descending turn). Without reference to the appropriate instruments, you may be led to aggravate the situation by adding power and increasing the angle of bank. The **Coriolis illusion** occurs when you move your head quickly once the vestibular system has adjusted to constant conditions, such as a constant turn. It is your head that has moved, however, not the airplane. The **acceleration illusion** may occur when you experience transverse Gs due to a change in velocity. The sensation is that you are climbing, which may lead you to lower the nose of the airplane. The **oculogyral illusion** may occur when you perceive the visual field as moving, a condition that can be overcome by holding your head still and concentrating on the instrument panel. **Indefinite horizons** can be a problem at night when you confuse stars and ground lights or when angled cloud decks suggest a horizon. Staring at a stationary light may lead to **autokinesis**, in which the light source appears to move. This effect explains why many aviation lights such as beacons rotate, flash, or are arranged in patterns. Finally, **postural illusions** ("seat of the pants") can result from the various motions and G forces that act on the body. To prevent spatial disorientation, trust your eyes when you can see the horizon and your flight instruments when you cannot see it.

10. **Airsickness**, a sympathetic nervous system reaction to conflicting sensations, may have both physical components (for example, a warm, stuffy cockpit or changes in velocity) and psychological components (anxiety or anticipation of the possibility of becoming sick). The best way to cure airsickness is to prevent it. If it occurs or begins to occur, it is wise to scan the horizon or administer fresh air (or oxygen if it is available).

11. **Night vision** is less acute than daytime vision. It takes the eyes approximately 30 min. to fully adapt to a dark environment. Furthermore, the eyes are less sensitive to objects straight ahead at night, which means you may have to glance at cockpit instruments often and out of the side of your eye at night (peripheral vision). **Noise and vibration** also affect pilots, particularly over a long period of time. Sound, measured in **decibels**, can also become so intense that it produces pain or, in extreme cases, physical damage to the middle and inner ears. Persons who fly more than eight hours a week may want to wear ear plugs to help avoid hearing loss.

12. **Drugs and alcohol.** Even readily available cold remedies and pain relievers should not be taken until cleared by an Aviation Medical Examiner; many contain substances that dramatically affect bodily functions, and these effects may be exaggerated at high altitudes. Alcohol, which is a **depressant**, should be avoided 24 hr. before flight time, even though FARs only prohibit its use 8 hr. before flight. In addition to reduced judgment and a false

sense of capability, the effects of alcohol increase rapidly with altitude. Understand that when you exercise your rights as a pilot you also implicitly agree to submit to tests for drugs and/or alcohol in your blood.

13. Stress (psychological and bodily tensions) is a natural consequence of living. Not all stress is bad, nor is it necessarily produced from unpleasant things. Stress compels us to resolve certain situations and pushes us on to new endeavors. Extremely high levels of stress (such as panic) and extremely low levels of stress (such as sleep) both lead to low or ineffective performance. As stress increases (as in landing an airplane), our ability to perform increases up to a maximal level, after which performance capability decreases rapidly.

14. Stress has three sources: the environment, the body, and psychological processes. As you have probably experienced, the three sources frequently overlap and interact with one another. **Environmental stresses** of importance to pilots are apprehension, anxiety, and frustration. **Body stress** includes fatigue, both **acute** (short-lived) and **chronic** (continued). Chronic fatigue can have serious physiological effects on the body, such as slowed reactions and an ambivalent attitude. Diet also affects body stress, as do drugs and alcohol. The third type of stress, **psychological stress**, includes worry, job or marital difficulty, and anxiety. Reactions to stress, regardless of its source, include increases in pulse rate, blood pressure, perspiration, respiration, and muscle tension, all of which produce deleterious outcomes if they occur over a long period of time. One way to deal with stress is to learn to accommodate through relaxation.

15. **Panic**, a sudden, overpowering, and unreasoning fright, can seriously impede your ability to function and can be avoided, in part, by limiting your susceptibility to stress. This may be accomplished, for example, by relaxation exercises, by gaining more knowledge about your airplane, and by expanding your aviation experience.

16. Keeping your body in a general state of good health, knowing you are under stress or in a state of fatigue, and observing regulations about medication, alcohol, and drugs all will contribute to being a safe pilot. Finally, avoid the stress and fatigue associated with the **get-home** syndrome, the irrational desire to get home regardless of wind, weather, mechanical conditions, or physiological needs. A good way to judge your fitness is to use the I'M SAFE check: Illness, Medication, Stress, Alcohol, Fatigue, Emotions.

KEY TERMS AND CONCEPTS, PART 1

Match each term or concept (1-16) with the appropriate description (A-P) below. Each item has only one match.

___ 1. hyperventilation   ___ 9. TUC
___ 2. negative Gs   ___ 10. eustachian tube
___ 3. carbon dioxide   ___ 11. airsickness
___ 4. graveyard spiral   ___ 12. Valsalva technique
___ 5. positive Gs   ___ 13. hypoxia
___ 6. aviation physiology   ___ 14. respiration
___ 7. acceleration illusion   ___ 15. tetany
___ 8. stress   ___ 16. decibel

A. tube that connects the space behind the eardrum to the throat
B. time from the onset of oxygen deficiency to unconsciousness, also referred to as time of useful consciousness
C. blood begins to accumulate in the upper extremities as a result of these Gs
D. blood begins to accumulate in the lower extremities as a result of these Gs
E. science dealing with body functions in the flying environment
F. an excessively fast rate of respiration
G. blood gas your body uses to measure its need for oxygen; lack of this gas can lead to unconsciousness
H. illusion caused by transverse Gs
I. sympathetic reaction of the stomach to conflicting vestibular, visual, and postural sensations
J. pinching your nostrils and blowing gently through your nose
K. psychological, environmental, or body tension
L. constant descending turn that is the result of disorientation
M. condition in which the brain and body tissues receive too little oxygen
N. exchange of gas between you and the environment
O. muscle tightness
P. measure of sound intensity

KEY TERMS AND CONCEPTS, PART 2

Match each term or concept (1-16) with the appropriate description (A-P) below. Each item has only one match.

___ 1. vertigo
___ 2. transverse Gs
___ 3. acceleration
___ 4. oculogyral illusion
___ 5. alcohol
___ 6. fatigue
___ 7. vestibular
___ 8. oxygen

___ 9. panic
___ 10. Coriolis illusion
___ 11. carbon monoxide
___ 12. aviation medicine
___ 13. autokinesis
___ 14. lateral Gs
___ 15. alveoli
___ 16. cyanosis

A. branch of medicine that deals with body functions in flying environments
B. perceptual system located in the semicircular canals
C. believing that your field of vision is moving
D. a depressant drug that may lead to a false sense of confidence
E. the belief that the airplane is spinning in space
F. forward- and aft-working Gs
G. sudden, overpowering, and unreasoning fright
H. bluing of the skin
I. apparent movement of a stationary light after you have been staring at it
J. colorless, odorless, poisonous gas produced by internal combustion engines
K. air sacs in the lungs where oxygen and carbon dioxide are exchanged
L. gas your body needs to convert food to energy
M. any change in velocity
N. side-force Gs
O. illusion caused by a rapid head movement when in a constant-rate turn
P. caused by lack of sleep, stress, activity, or improper diet

DISCUSSION QUESTIONS AND REVIEW EXERCISES

1. What is respiration? Explain how blood chemistry regulates normal respiration?

2. Shortly after leveling off at 9,500 ft., a passenger with a mild cold begins to complain of a severe headache. What physiological disorder might you suspect and what action should you take?

3. Outline the effects of positive and negative Gs on the body's circulatory system?

4. What three body systems provide cues for spatial orientation? Which is most reliable in VMC conditions?

5. Name three sources of stress. What special types of flight-related stress may student pilots encounter? What effects do very high and very low levels of stress have on our ability to perform?

6. State what effects each of the following may have on your ability to perform as a pilot:

    a. fatigue

    b. diet

    c. alcohol

7. Explain the difference between acute fatigue and chronic fatigue. Which is more dangerous? Why?

8. What is the FAA regulation concerning the time between consuming alcohol and acting as a pilot-in-command? To what do you implicitly agree when exercising your privileges as a pilot?

9. Name at least five symptoms associated with hypoxia. How does the rate of onset vary with increasing altitude? What can you do to counteract it?

10. What is hyperventilation? Name at least four symptoms. How is it related to stress and how can it be counteracted?

11. What is carbon monoxide poisoning? Why is it so dangerous? What should you do if you suspect it while in flight?

12. What is airsickness? What action should you take if a passenger begins to complain of nausea during flight?

13. Briefly characterize each of the following motion-related disorientations and state what can be done to overcome them:

    a. vertigo

    b. graveyard spiral

    c. Coriolis illusion

    d. oculogyral illusion

e.   acceleration illusion

f.   autokinesis

g.   postural illusion

   h.   Two general rules for minimizing the occurrence and effects of
spatial disorientation

14.   What is panic?   How can it be avoided?

15.   How is night vision different from daytime vision?   Why is this
difference of particular importance to pilots?

16. Continued exposure to fatigue is called _____ fatigue.
    1--acute
    2--active
    3--chronic
    4--delayed

17. Which of the following is **not** a common reaction to alcohol?
    1--Improved reaction time.
    2--Increased self-confidence.
    3--Loss of visual acuity.
    4--Poor reasoning capability.

18. Which statement is true regarding alcohol in the human system?
    1--A common misconception is that coffee alters the rate at which the
       body metabolizes alcohol.
    2--An increase in altitude decreases its adverse effects.
    3--Alcohol increases judgment and decision-making abilities.
    4--Aspirin increases the rate the body metabolizes alcohol.

19. How can you combat the effects of positive Gs?
    1--Administer fresh air.
    2--Breathe gently through the nose while pinching the nostrils.
    3--Tighten your abdominal, thigh, and calf muscles.
    4--All of these are common, effective techniques.

20. Which of the following statements about hypoxia is correct?
    1--Hypoxia is a singular condition that typically strikes all at once.
    2--Hypoxia symptoms occur more rapidly as altitude increases,
       particularly above 10,000 ft. MSL.
    3--One of the most effective countermeasures for the effects of hypoxia
       is the Valsalva technique.
    4--All of the above are correct.

21. What blood gas controls the amount of oxygen in the blood?
    1--Carbon dioxide.
    2--Carbon monoxide.
    3--Nitrogen.
    4--Oxygen.

22. As cabin altitude increases, the amount of saturated oxygen in the blood
    1--decreases.
    2--increases.
    3--first decreases, then increases as the body's oxygen-carbon dioxide
       monitoring system begins to compensate.
    4--remains constant.

23. Pinching your nostrils and blowing gently through your nose (also known
as the Valsalva technique) is commonly used to counteract
    1--differential pressure in the eustachian tubes.
    2--hyperventilation.
    3--hypoxia.
    4--spatial disorientation.

24. How long should you wait after scuba diving before flying in an unpressurized airplane?
    1--One hour.
    2--One day.
    3--One week.
    4--It doesn't really matter since the body readjusts rapidly.

25. Which of the following perceptual systems provides the best sensory information for verifying an airplane's attitude when you can see the horizon?
    1--Auditory.
    2--Proprioceptive (postural).
    3--Vestibular.
    4--Visual.

26. How many hours does the FAA require under FAR 91.11(a) between the consuming of alcoholic beverages and acting as pilot-in-command?
    1--8.
    2--12.
    3--18.
    4--24.

27. Which of the following is **not** a common reaction to alcohol?
    1--Decreased self-confidence.
    2--Impaired reaction time.
    3--Loss of visual acuity.
    4--Poor reasoning capability.

28. Which of the following is **not** a common reaction to stress?
    1--Decreased blood pressure.
    2--Increased pulse rate.
    3--Increased respiration.
    4--Tetany (muscle tension).

29. A state of oxygen deficiency in the body tissues great enough to impair bodily functioning is called
    1--cyanosis.
    2--hyperventilation.
    3--hypoxia.
    4--tetany.

30. Which of the following gases is colorless, odorless, and extremely dangerous to your health, even if breathed over a short period of time?
    1--Carbon dioxide.
    2--Carbon monoxide.
    3--Nitrogen.
    4--Oxygen.

31. The illusion that a power-on turning descent has ended even though the airplane continues to turn and descend may lead to
    1--the acceleration illusion.
    2--the Coriolis illusion.
    3--a graveyard spiral.
    4--the oculogyral illusion.

32. The illusion produced by moving your head to the side while in a stabilized constant turn is called the
    1--acceleration illusion.
    2--Coriolis illusion.
    3--graveyard spiral.
    4--the oculogyral illusion.

33. During a night flight you begin to stare at a large spotlight in the distance. After you have stared at it for a few seconds, it appears to move. This is an example of
    1--autokinesis.
    2--the Coriolis illusion.
    3--the oculogyral illusion.
    4--the onset of a graveyard spiral.

34. Which of the following techniques is a common, effective way to combat airsickness?
    1--Administer fresh air.
    2--Breathe gently through your nose while pinching your nostrils.
    3--Tighten your abdominal, thigh, and calf muscles.
    4--All of the above are equally effective in combating airsickness.

35. A sudden, overpowering, and unreasoning fright is called
    1--anxiety.
    2--apprehension.
    3--frustration.
    4--panic.

36. Which of the following techniques will probably be the most effective in helping you overcome the effects of stress?
    1--Learning to adjust your intake of Valium to compensate for your intake of alcohol.
    2--Learning to relax.
    3--Learning to increase your blood pressure when you are under stress.
    4--Praying.

FAA EXAM QUESTIONS

1. (FAA 1576) To preclude the effects of hypoxia,
    1--avoid flying above 10,000 ft. MSL for prolonged periods without breathing supplemental oxygen.
    2--rely on your body's built-in alarm system to warn when you are not getting enough oxygen.
    3--try swallowing, yawning, or holding the nose and mouth shut and forcibly try to exhale.
    4--avoid hyperventilation which is caused by rapid heavy breathing and results in excessive carbon dioxide in the bloodstream.

2. (FAA 1151) What type of oxygen should be used to replenish an aircraft's oxygen system for high-altitude flights?
    1--Medical oxygen.   2--Therapeutic oxygen.
    3--Welder's oxygen.   4--Aviation breathing oxygen.

3. (FAA 1577) Rapid or extra deep breathing while using oxygen can cause a condition known as
    1--hypoxia.
    2--aerosinusitis.
    3--aerotitis.
    4--hyperventilation.

4. (FAA 1579) Which would most likely result in hyperventilation?
    1--Emotional tension, anxiety, or fear.
    2--The excessive consumption of alcohol.
    3--An extremely slow rate of breathing and insufficient oxygen.
    4--An extreme case of relaxation or sense of well-being.

5. (FAA 1578) A pilot should be able to overcome the symptoms or avoid future occurrences of hyperventilation by
    1--closely monitoring the flight instruments to control the airplane.
    2--slowing the breathing rate, breathing into a bag, or talking aloud.
    3--increasing the breathing rate in order to increase lung ventilation.
    4--refraining from the use of over-the-counter remedies and drugs such as antihistamines, cold tablets, tranquilizers, etc.

6. (FAA 1580) Large accumulations of carbon monoxide in the human body result in
    1--tightness across the forehead.
    2--loss of muscular power.
    3--an increased sense of well-being.
    4--being too warm.

7. (FAA 1581) Susceptibility to carbon monoxide poisoning increases as
    1--altitude increases.   2--altitude decreases.
    3--air pressure increases.   4--humidity of the air decreases.

8. (FAA 1584) A state of temporary confusion resulting from misleading information being sent to the brain by various sensory organs if defined as
    1--spatial disorientation.   2--hyperventilation.
    3--hypoxia.   4--motion sickness.

9. (FAA 1582) A pilot is more subject to spatial disorientation if
    1--ignoring or overcoming the sensations of muscles and inner ear.
    2--kinesthetic senses are ignored
    3--eyes are moved often in the process of cross-checking the flight instruments.
    4--body signals are used to interpret flight attitude.

10. (FAA 1583) A pilot experiences spatial disorientation during flight in a restricted visibility condition. The best way to overcome the effect is to
    1--depend on sensations received from the fluid in the semicircular canals of the inner ear.
    2--concentrate on any yaw, pitch, and roll sensations.
    3--consciously slow your breathing rate until symptoms clear and then resume normal breathing rate.
    4--rely upon the aircraft instrument indications.

11. (FAA 1586) The danger of spatial disorientation during flight in poor visual conditions may be reduced by

1--shifting the eyes quickly between the exterior visual field and the instrument panel.

2--having faith in the instruments rather than taking a chance on the sensory organs.

3--leaning in the opposite direction of the motion of the aircraft.

4--moving the head rapidly to equalize the fluid in the ear canals.

12. (FAA 1493) The most effective method of scanning for other aircraft for collision avoidance during daylight hours is to use

1--regularly spaced concentration on 3-, 9-, and 12-o'clock positions.

2--a series of short, regularly spaced eye movements to search each 30-degree sector.

3--peripheral vision by scanning small sectors and utilizing offcenter viewing.

4--rapid head and eye movement through a horizontal plane to cover the entire viewing area in a short time.

13. (FAA 1494) The most effective method of scanning for other aircraft for collision avoidance during nighttime hours is to use

1--regularly spaced concentration on the 3-, 9-, and 12-o'clock positions.

2--a series of short, regularly spaced eye movements to search each 10-degree sector.

3--peripheral vision by scanning small sectors and utilizing offcenter viewing.

4--rapid head and eye movements through a horizontal plane to cover the entire viewing area in a short time.

14. (FAA 1587) Which technique should a pilot use to scan for traffic to the right and left during straight-and-level flight?

1--Systematically focus on different segments of the sky for short intervals.

2--Concentrate on relative movement detected in the peripheral vision area.

3--Continuous sweeping of the windshield from right to left.

4--Concentrate on traffic ahead and to the right because traffic to the left must give right-of-way.

15. (FAA 1588) What effect does haze have on the ability to see traffic or terrain features during flight?

1--Haze causes the eyes to focus at infinity.

2--The eyes tend to overwork in haze and do not detect relative movement easily.

3--Contrasting colors become less distinct making objects easier to see.

4--All traffic or terrain features appear to be farther away than their actual distance.

16. (FAA 1585) What preparation should a pilot make to adapt the eyes for flying at night?

1--Wear sunglasses after sunset until ready for flight.

2--Avoid red light at least 30 min. before the flight.

3--Wear amber colored glasses at least 30 min. before the flight.

4--Avoid bright white lights at least 30 min. before the flight.

17. (FAA 1495) What is the most effective way to use the eyes during night flight?
1--Look only at far away, dim lights.
2--Scan slowly to permit offcenter viewing.
3--Blink the eyes rapidly when concentrating on an object.
4--Concentrate directly on each object for a few seconds.

18. (FAA 1435) The best method to use when looking for other traffic at night is to
1--stare directly at the object.
2--look to the side of the object and scan slowly.
3--scan the visual field very rapidly.
4--look to the side of the object and scan rapidly.

19. (FAA 1496) How can you determine if another aircraft is on a collision course with your aircraft?
1--The other aircraft will be pointed directly at your aircraft.
2--The other aircraft will always appear to get larger and closer at a rapid rate.
3--The nose of each aircraft is pointed at the same point in space.
4--There will be no apparent relative motion between your aircraft and the other aircraft.

ANSWERS AND EXPLANATIONS

Key Terms and Concepts, Part 1

1.	F	5.	D	9.	B	13.	M
2.	C	6.	E	10.	A	14.	N
3.	G	7.	H	11.	I	15.	O
4.	L	8.	K	12.	J	16.	P

Key Terms and Concepts, Part 2

1.	E	5.	D	9.	G	13.	I
2.	F	6.	P	10.	O	14.	N
3.	M	7.	B	11.	J	15.	K
4.	C	8.	L	12.	A	16.	H

Discussion Questions and Review Questions

1. See Study Guide Main Point #1.

2. See Study Guide Main Point #3.

3. See Study Guide Main Point #7.

4. See Study Guide Main Point #8.

5. See Study Guide Main Points #13 and #14.

6.   See Study Guide Main Point #14.

7.   See Study Guide Main Point #14.

8.   See Study Guide Main Point #12 and FAR 91.11 (Chapter 11).

9.   See Study Guide Main Point #3.

10. See Study Guide Main Points #3 and #4.

11. See Study Guide Main Point #6.

12. See Study Guide Main Point #10.

13. See Study Guide Main Point #9.

14. See Study Guide Main Point #15.

15. See Study Guide Main Point #11.

16. 3--Short exposure to fatigue is referred to as acute.

17. 1--Reaction time increases--that is, your reactions are slower.

18. 1--Your body metabolizes (burns) alcohol at a constant rate; there are no known ways to increase how fast it burns.

19. 3--This helps prevent blood from collecting in the lower extremities.

20. 2--Hypoxia is a progressive condition (not a single event); symptoms occur more rapidly at high altitudes.

21. 1--Carbon dioxide regulates the amount of oxygen in the blood.

22. 1--The oxygen level decreases as altitude increases.

23. 1--The Valsalva technique is used to reduce the pressure differential.

24. 2--You should wait at least a day to let your body readjust.

25. 4--If you can see the horizon, you should use visual cues. If you cannot see the horizon, rely on your flight instruments.

26. 1--The FAA requires 8 hours from "bottle to throttle." It is generally considered good practice to avoid alcohol for at least 24 hours prior to a flight.

27. 1--Alcohol leads to an increase in self-confidence, slower reaction times, poorer visual acuity, and less ability to reason.

28. 1--Stress increases blood pressure, as well as pulse rate, respiration, and tetany.

29. 3--Hypoxia results from oxygen deficiency.

30. 2--Carbon monoxide is extremely dangerous.

31. 3--This defines the conditions for a graveyard spiral.

32. 2--This defines the Coriolis illusion.

33. 1--This is an example of autokinesis.

34. 1--Fresh air is one way to combat airsickness.

35. 4--Panic is a sudden, overpowering, and unreasoning fright.

36. 2--Learning to relax is one of the best ways to combat STREEEEEEESSSSSS.

FAA Exam Questions

1. 1--FAR 91 REQUIRES that you use supplemental oxygen above 12,500 for that period longer than 30 minutes and continuously when above 14,000 ft. in unpressurized aircraft. Use of oxygen is RECOMMENDED above 10,000 ft. in the daytime and above 5,000 ft. at night.

2. 4--Aviation breathing oxygen is dry. Medical oxygen may contain moisture which could freeze and block valves and passages in the oxygen system.

3. 4--With rapid breathing, too much carbon dioxide is expelled.

4. 1--Stress or anxiety may cause an increased breathing rate. The anxiety of flight may be reduced by thorough planning for the flight and knowing your airplane and procedures.

5. 2--To overcome hyperventilation, you must decrease the intake of oxygen. You can do this by a reduced breathing rate or reducing the amount of oxygen available by rebreathing air in a paper bag. Talking reduces the breathing rate.

6. 2--Carbon monoxide reduces the oxygen carrying capacity of the blood. Loss of muscular power is one of the many effects.

7. 1--With less available oxygen at altitude, the susceptibility to carbon monoxide poisoning increases.

8. 1--The brain uses three body sensor systems to detect and monitor motion: vision, the inner ear, and the postural senses. Vision is the most used; when it is not available, as in clouds or on a dark night, the other body signals may provide misleading information. The condition is called spatial disorientation or vertigo.

9. 4--The brain uses three body sensor systems to detect and monitor motion: vision, the inner ear and the postural senses. Vision is the most used; when it is not available, as in clouds or on a dark night, the other body signals may provide misleading information. You cannot depend on the other body sensations, but must regain a visual reference, such as the artificial horizon provided by the gyro driven altitude indicator.

10. 4--The brain uses three body sensor systems to detect and monitor motion; vision, the inner ear, and the postural senses. Vision is the most used; when it is not available, as in clouds or on a dark night, the other body signals may provide misleading information. You cannot depend on the other body sensations, but must regain a visual reference, such as the artificial horizon provided by the gyro driven altitude indicator.

11. 2--The brain uses three body sensor systems to detect and monitor motion: vision, the inner ear, and the postural senses. Vision is the most used; when it is not available, as in clouds or on a dark night, the other body signals may provide misleading information. You cannot depend on the other body sensations, but must regain a visual reference, such as the artificial horizon provided by the gyro driven altitude indicator. Moving the head rapidly INCREASES the chances of vertigo.

12. 2--From AIM: Scanning should use a series of short, regularly spaced eye movements to bring successive areas of the sky into the central visual field. Each movement should not exceed 10 degrees, and each area should be observed for at least one second to enable detection.

13. 3--Because of the distribution of rods and cones, peripheral vision is very important for seeing objects at night.

14. 1--From AIM: Scanning should use a series of short, regularly spaced eye movements to bring successive areas of the sky into the central visual field. Each movement should not exceed 10 degrees, and each area should be observed for at least one second to enable detection.

15. 4--When items become less distinct to the eye, the brain perceives them as being further away. This can result in being closer to the traffic or terrain than you think you are.

16. 4--The eyes require about 30 min. to adapt to the dark after leaving white light.

17. 2--Because of the distribution of rods and cones, peripheral vision is very important for seeing objects at night.

18. 2--Night vision is a bit different than vision in daylight. The more important night vision receptors, the rods, are located around the periphery. When you stare at an object, it may disappear.

19. 4--From AIM: Any aircraft that appears to have no relative motion and stays in one scan gradient is likely to be on a collision course.

HANDLING AIRBORNE EMERGENCIES

MAIN POINTS

1. Emergency procedures are no different from normal operating procedures. They are simply encountered less frequently.

2. There are three general rules apply to airborne emergencies. First, and most importantly, <u>maintain control of the aircraft</u>. If you lose control of the aircraft, you won't have an opportunity to apply the other two. Second, attempt to locate the cause, analyze the situation, and take proper action. Third, land as soon as conditions permit. Specific procedures are found in your airplane's Pilot's Operating Handbook (POH). Learn them as if your life depended on it. It does.

3. Three factors cited most frequently in general aviation accidents are: (1) inadequate preflight procedures and/or planning; (2) failure to maintain flying speed; and (3) improper in-flight decision making.

4. Unless you are confronted with a real emergency, such as an engine fire, you should first confirm a suspected emergency with at least one other verifying indication. Pilot experience and confidence also play a factor in identifying and declaring an emergency. When more than one emergency exists at once, such as a radio/navigation failure in marginal weather conditions, it is referred to as a compound emergency. No matter what the emergency is, maintain control of the aircraft.

5. Equipment malfunctions can be diagnosed more readily if you are familiar with each instrument and how it is powered. For example, if you suspect an electrical malfunction, you should check the proper circuit breaker before taking further action. Again, no matter what the emergency is, maintain control of the aircraft.

6. Safety begins at home during preflight planning and inspections. Two important aspects of flight preparation are filing a flight plan and using flight-following services. Once you file a flight plan, follow it, or advise the nearest FSS if you make changes. When the flight is complete, close it!

7.   Emergency landing procedures are grouped into four categories: (1) land as soon as practicable means to land at the nearest suitable airport; (2) land as soon as possible means to land at the nearest airport regardless of facilities; (3) land immediately means that continued flight is inadvisable, as for example when there is an engine fire; and (4) forced landing, when the airplane will land very soon whether the pilot wishes it or not, as for example when there is a total engine failure.

8.   There are two types of forced landings, those that occur immediately after takeoff and those that occur after the airplane has gained a reasonable amount of altitude. When forced to land on the takeoff leg, land straight ahead! It is acceptable to make slight turns to avoid obstacles, but do not try to turn back to the runway because you will lose too much altitude in the turn. Remember, maintaining control of the aircraft is absolutely essential.

9.   Once the airplane has gained altitude, forced landing procedures include five phases. First, as outlined in your POH, there are several immediate actions you should take, including restarting procedures in case of engine malfunction. In any event, it is absolutely essential to maintain adequate airspeed. Establish a glide path aimed at maintaining as much altitude as possible and maintain control. If restart fails, set most light trainers as follows: mixture, idle cut off; fuel selector, off; ignition system, off; master switch, on (for radios and flaps). Maintain control. Second, select a landing site, preferably one with a hard surface that will allow you to land into the wind. Maintain control. Third, report your position and situation to the nearest facility, or use the standard emergency frequency. Maintain control. Fourth, in preparation for landing, secure seatbelts and shoulder harnesses (if provided) and stow loose items in the cabin. Maintain control. Fifth, maintain airspeed and avoid improvising at the last minute. Hold back pressure as long as possible after touchdown.

10. Know and use your **emergency locator transmitter (ELT)**. When activated, an ELT transmits on 121.5 or 243.0 MHz. If the ELT has been activated, you can monitor it on 121.5 MHz prior to engine shutdown. Operational tests of the ELT should be made only during the first 5 min. of the hour. Finally, the nonrechargeable batteries of an ELT need to be replaced when 50 percent of their useful life expires or when they have been in use for a cumulative period of one hour.

11. You should be familiar with ground-to-air signals in the event you land in a remote location. Stay near or in your airplane until you are located, unless you see a source of assistance. If you regularly fly in remote areas, you should carry a survival kit.

12. Being lost is an emergency. Remember the "four Cs": confess, communicate, climb, comply. **Confess** your problem. **Communicate** your situation over the appropriate radio channel. **Climb** when possible to improve radio communication, but maintain VFR conditions. **Comply** with controller instructions, again staying within VFR conditions. Radio assistance may include ATC directions if you have a transponder, or a direction-finding (DF) steer if you have a VHF transmitter and receiver.

13. The VHF emergency frequency, 121.5 MHz, is to be used **only** by an aircraft in distress. In an emergency, communicate your situation in plain English. State **mayday** three times (or **pan** if you are uncertain about the

situation). Next, repeat your airplane identification number three times.
Give your type of aircraft, position, heading, TAS, altitude, fuel remaining,
nature of distress, intentions, and request. Finally, hold your mike button
open for two consecutive 10-second intervals and then repeat your airplane ID
and say "over." If you have a transponder, squawk 7700 to indicate an
emergency.

15. If your communications receiver fails, you may still be able to
transmit and you may be able to receive over your navigation radio. If
neither appears to solve the problem, use the information you have already
learned about responding to controller light signals. If you have a
transponder, squawk 7600 to indicate two-way radio communication.

15. The **FAA Accident Prevention Program** has several guidelines for safe
piloting: know your limits, both physiological and technical; use a
checklist, particularly for routine tasks; preplan your flight: prepare, file,
open, fly, and close a flight plan; preflight your airplane; know your
airplane and its performance limits.

KEY TERMS AND CONCEPTS

Match each term and concept (1-12) with the appropriate description (A-L)
below. Each term has only one match.

___ 1. forced landing   ___ 7. 7600

___ 2. POH   ___ 8. maintain airplane control

___ 3. 7700   ___ 9. pan

___ 4. compound emergency   ___ 10. as soon as practicable

___ 5. 121.5 MHz   ___ 11. confess your problem

___ 6. mayday   ___ 12. as soon as possible

A. landing at the nearest airport with suitable facilities
B. first and most important thing you must do in an emergency situation
C. words used to indicate an actual airborne emergency
D. landing at once whether the pilot wishes it or not
E. more than one emergency condition occurs at the same time
F. transponder code that indicates two-way radio communication failure
G. VHF emergency frequency
H. where you find specific emergency procedures for your airplane
I. transponder code to squawk to declare an airborne emergency
J. what you must do when you are lost
K. words to use to notify the ground of a probable airborne emergency
L. landing at the nearest airport at once regardless of available facilities

DISCUSSION QUESTIONS AND REVIEW EXERCISES

1. Outline the three general rules for handling any airborne emergency.

2. What are three factors cited most frequently in general aviation accidents?

3. What is the primary way to distinguish between a suspected malfunction and an actual malfunction?

4. What are compound emergencies? Give an example illustrating how a pilot might help to create a compound emergency.

5. Suppose you have tried unsuccessfully several times to contact a nearby FSS station on your radio. Do you have a malfunctioning radio? How would you troubleshoot the situation?

6. Identify, describe, and give an example of each of the four types of emergency landings:

    a. land as soon as practicable

    b. land as soon as possible

    c. land immediately

    d. forced landing

7. Outline three immediate actions you should take in case of a sudden engine failure.

8. Name three criteria you should use in selecting a forced landing site.

9. What are the four Cs and how do they apply to being lost?

10. Identify the appropriate frequencies, code, or word for each of the following:

   a. VHF guard frequency

   b. ATC transponder code for an airborne emergency

   c. ATC transponder code for two-way radio failure

   d. international code for an airplane in distress

   e. international code word for a probable emergency

11. Refer to your San Francisco sectional chart and the cross-country exercise in Chapter 14. Suppose you are en route from Los Banos direct to Carmel Valley at 6,500 ft. You are 30 NM from Los Banos on course when your oil pressure skyrockets and the engine begins to run exceedingly rough. Use the data from the cross-country exercise in Chapter 14 to aid in your planning. Your airplane has a glide speed of 63 kts., which translates to about 1.3 NM per 1,000 ft. above the terrain.

   a. Where would you attempt to land? Why?

   b. What characteristics would you look for in selecting a landing site?

   c. Describe in detail what you would communicate over your radio.

12. Once activated, on what frequency does an ELT transmit? On what frequency can you monitor it? During what times can you make operational tests of an ELT? When should nonrechargeable batteries be replaced?

13. Briefly outline the six steps in the FAA Accident Prevention Program.

14. Which of the following things is most important in any airborne emergency?
    1--Contact air traffic control (ATC) and confess your problem.
    2--Contact the nearest FSS facility.
    3--Maintain aircraft control.
    4--Stay in VMC conditions.

15. Which of the following factors is cited least in general aviation accidents?
    1--Equipment malfunction.
    2--Failure to obtain or maintain flying speed.
    3--Improper in-flight decision making or planning.
    4--Inadequate preflight preparation and/or planning.

16. Where do you find specific guidance and procedures for emergency situations?
    1--AIM.
    2--Airport/Facility Directory.
    3--Pilot's Operating Handbook (POH).
    4--Rescue Coordination Handbook.

17. _____ means to locate the nearest airport and land at once regardless of available facilities.
    1--Forced landing
    2--Land as soon as practicable
    3--Land as soon as possible
    4--Land immediately

18. What is the transponder code for an airborne emergency?
    1--1200.   2--4096.
    3--7600.   4--7700.

19. The word to use to notify ground agencies of an urgent condition is
    1--help.   2--mayday.
    3--pan.   4--SOS.

20. The red line on an airspeed indicator means a maximum airspeed that
    1--may be exceeded only in an emergency situation.
    2--may be exceeded only if gear and flaps are retracted.
    3--may be exceeded only in smooth air.
    4--should not be exceeded.

21. The most important rule to remember in the event of a power failure after
becoming airborne is
    1--determining wind direction to plan for a forced landing.
    2--maintaining safe airspeed.
    3--quickly checking the fuel supply for possible fuel exhaustion.
    4--turning back immediately to the takeoff runway.

22. _____ means to land at the nearest airport that has suitable facilities
for your airplane and emergency condition.
    1--Forced landing
    2--Land as soon as practicable
    3--Land as soon as possible
    4--Land immediately

23. _____ refers to a condition in which continued flight is inadvisable, but
possible.
    1--Forced landing
    2--Land as soon as practicable
    3--Land as soon as possible
    4--Land immediately

24. What is the guard frequency for VHF communication?
    1--121.5 MHz.   2--122.8 MHz.
    3--123.6 MHz.   4--121.9 MHz.

25. What is the transponder code for two-way radio failure?
    1--1200.   2--4096.
    3--7600.   4--7700.

26. What is the international word to notify a ground agency of an actual
airborne emergency?
    1--Help.   2--Mayday.
    3--Pan.   4--SOS.

27. Which of the following things is most important in any airborne
emergency?
    1--Contact air traffic control (ATC) and confess your problem.
    2--Contact the nearest FSS facility.
    3--Land as soon as conditions permit.
    4--Maintain aircraft control.

FAA EXAM QUESTIONS

1. (FAA 1423) The most important rule to remember in the event of a power failure after becoming airborne is to
   1--quickly check the fuel supply for possible fuel exhaustion.
   2--determine the wind direction to plan for the forced landing.
   3--turn back immediately to the takeoff runway.
   4--maintain safe airspeed.

2. (FAA 1485) When activated, an ELT transmits on
   1--122.3 and 122.8 MHz.   2--123.0 and 119.0 MHz.
   3--121.5 and 243.0 MHz.   4--118.0 and 118.8 MHz.

3. (FAA 1486) Operational tests of the ELT should be made only
   1--during the first 5 min. of the hour.
   2--during the annual inspection.
   3--after one-half the shelf life of the battery.
   4--upon replacing the battery.

4. (FAA 1679) ELT transmitters may be tested
   1--anytime.
   2--at 15 and 45 min. past the hour.
   3--during the first 5 min. after any hour.
   4--at 30 min. past the hour and while airborne.

5. (FAA 1487) Which procedure is recommended to ensure that the ELT has not been activated?
   1--Turn off the aircraft ELT after landing.
   2--Ask the airport tower if they are receiving an ELT signal.
   3--Monitor 121.5 before engine shutdown.
   4--Have a certified repair station inspect the ELT.

6. (FAA 1505) The letters VHF/DF appearing in the Airport/Facility Directory for a certain airport indicate that
   1--this airport is designated as an airport of entry.
   2--the Flight Service Station has equipment with which to determine your direction from the station.
   3--this airport has a direct-line phone to the Flight Service Station.
   4--this airport is a defense facility.

7. (FAA 1506) To use VHF/DF facilities for assistance in locating an aircraft's position, the aircraft must have
   1--a VHF transmitter and receiver.
   2--an IFF transponder.
   3--a VOR receiver and DME.
   4--an ELT.

8. (FAA 1484) If the aircraft's radio fails, what is the recommended procedure when landing at a controlled airport?
   1--Observe the traffic flow, enter the patterns, and look for a light signal from the tower.
   2--Enter a crosswind leg and lock the wings.
   3--Flash the landing lights and cycle the landing gear while circling the airport.
   4--Select 7700 on the transponder and fly a normal traffic pattern.

ANSWERS AND EXPLANATIONS

Key Terms and Concepts

1. D	4. E	7. F	10. A
2. H	5. G	8. B	11. J
3. I	6. C	9. K	12. L

Discussion Questions and Review Exercises

1. See Study Guide Main Point #2.

2. See Study Guide Main Point #3.

3. See Study Guide Main Point #5.

4. See Study Guide Main Point #4.

5. See Study Guide Main Points #5 and #14.

6. See Study Guide Main Point #7.

7. See Study Guide Main Point #9.

8. See Study Guide Main Point #9.

9. See Study Guide Main Point #12.

10. See Study Guide Main Points #13 and #14.

11.

a. Given the winds aloft (240° at 25), it makes sense to turn around and glide to either Christensen Ranch (7.5 NM to the north) or Hollister (9.0 NM to the north). The glide ratio gives you 1.3 x 5.5, or about 7 NM in a no-wind situation with 1,000 ft. to spare when you reach your destination. Given the moderately favorable winds, you should be able to glide to Christensen Ranch. Furthermore, the topography between your present position and Christensen Ranch is relatively flat, which may give you even more options. Note that Christensen Ranch is a _private_ airport and cannot be used for normal operations without permission; however, private airports may be used for emergency landings.

b. If you do not make it to Christensen ranch, select the best landing site available, preferably one with a smooth, relatively flat surface of sufficient length without obstructions.

c. mayday, mayday, mayday.
Starship 7118Q, Starship 7118Q, Starship 7118Q.
Starship U2.
30 NM southwest of Los Banos, 7 south of Christensen.
steering 51° true.
true airspeed 97 kts.
6,500 ft. and descending.

with over 2 hr. fuel.
engine out.
proceeding direct to Christensen ranch.
notify Christensen ranch.
hold mike button for 10 seconds.
Starship 7118Q.
over.
If you have recently contacted FSS, call on that frequency.
Otherwise use 121.5 MHz, the VHF guard frequency.

12. See Study Guide Main Point #10.

13. See Study Guide Main Point #15.

14. 3--First and foremost, maintain aircraft control.

15. 1--Equipment malfunctions (for example, engine failure) play a minor role in general aviation accidents.

16. 3--Your POH contains **specific** emergency procedures.

17. 3--Land as soon as possible means that safety requires that the airplane be landed at once, without regard to available facilities.

18. 4--7700 is the emergency code.

19. 3--"Pan" is the word to use to indicate a probable emergency or urgent situation. "Mayday" is the word to use to indicate an airborne emergency.

20. 4--Red line indicates the speed that should not be exceeded.

21. 2--The most important rule is to maintain aircraft control.

22. 2--Land as soon as practicable means to land at the nearest airport that has suitable facilities for your airplane and emergency condition.

23. 4--Land immediately refers to a condition in which continued flight is inadvisable, but possible.

24. 1--121.5 MHz is the VHF guard frequency.

25. 3--The transponder code for radio failure is 7600, the code for an airborne emergency is 7700.

26. 2--"Mayday" is the international word for an emergency.

27. 4--Always maintain aircraft control.

FAA Exam Questions

1. 4--The first priority at all times is to fly the airplane: AVIATE, NAVIGATE, COMMUNICATE. This is particularly true in an emergency.

2. 3--An Emergency Locator Transmitter transmits on the emergency
frequencies of 121.5 MHz and 243.0 MHz.

3. 1--ELT tests should be conducted only during the first 5 minutes of the
hour to keep the emergency frequencies free for actual emergencies.

4. 3--ELT tests should be conducted only during the first 5 minutes of the
hour to keep the emergency frequencies free for actual emergencies.

5. 3--You may monitor the 121.5 MHz to find out if any ELT's are
transmitting in your vicinity. If so, it might be yours.

6. 2--VHF/DF is direction finding equipment by which an ATC facility can
determine your bearing from the station. DF from two stations provides a fix
on the transmitting aircraft's position.

7. 1--Only a VHF transmitter and receiver is required in the airplane for
VHF/DF. You will be asked to make a short, continuous transmission. The DF
station will determine your bearing and coordinate to get a fix.

8. 1--If your radio fails, remain outside or above the ATA until you have
determined the traffic pattern, then enter the pattern and look for light
signals.

POSTSCRIPT

MAIN POINTS

1. Congratulations on completing this private pilot instruction course.
Your aviation education should not end here, however. There are many ways to
continue your aviation education. Some of these include the following:

    a. Earn your instrument rating. This is required if you want to
become a professional pilot. But even if you only plan to fly for your
personal enjoyment, you will become a better pilot. You will learn to fully
utilize your airplane's equipment and you will qualify to fly in instrument
conditions.

    b. Take a few hours of aerobatic instruction. This is fun and you
will better understand the capabilities of airplanes.

    c. Take advanced courses. Many community colleges offer aviation
courses, at low cost, including weather, air traffic control, instrument
flying, commercial piloting, etc. Some have flight simulator training.

    d. Participate in the FAA Pilot Proficiency Award Program.
Distinctive wings are awarded to those meeting certain training requirements.
See Advisory Circular 61-91E at the end of this chapter for details.

    e. Visit FAA facilities. If these facilities are not in
your area, you might include these visits on cross-country flights.   These
include:

        (1) Control Towers. Most towers serving general
aviation welcome pilots, some have training programs for pilots. Contact
tower personnel for information on visits.

        (2) The General Aviation District Office or Flight Standards
District Office serving your area. The <u>Airport/Facility Directory</u> provides
the addresses and telephone numbers of the GADOs and FSDOs.

(3) A Flight Service Station. The <u>Airport/Facility Directory</u> provides the telephone numbers of the FSS. Call for information on visits and addresses.

(4) Terminal Radar Approach Control (TRACON) and Air Route Traffic Control Center (ARTCC). Many of these facilities have familiarization programs called Operation Raincheck. Contact the GADO/FSDO or the control facility for information on visits and on Operation Raincheck.

f. Attend FAA safety seminars. Information on these is available from the Accident Prevention Specialist at the nearest GADO/FSDO.

g. Obtain and study FAA publications such as Advisory Circulars and pamphlets. Many of these are available at no cost, others at low cost. Sources of government aviation publications are included at the end of this chapter.

h. Attend aviation seminars offered by commercial operators. You will probably be put on their mailing lists when your student pilot license is entered on file. Information on these may be found in aviation magazines and newspapers.

i. Read aviation magazines, newspapers, and books. In these you will find interesting articles, useful information, and information on ordering supplies and books by mail. Many libraries have some of these. You may want to subscribe to some of these magazines or newspapers.

j. View aviation videotapes. There are many interesting historical tapes. Additionally, there are an increasing number of videotapes with very useful information that can help you become a better pilot. Many sellers of these tapes advertise in aviation magazines and newspapers. Also some public libraries and commercial video rental shops have aviation videos available for loan or rent.

k. Join one or more pilot organizations. Local flying clubs offer the opportunity for you to share experiences and information with other pilots. National organizations offer many services; many include subscriptions to magazines or newsletters with your membership. Some have videotapes available for sale, rent, or loan.

2. The basic publication listing aviation publications available from the government is the "Guide to Federal Aviation Administration Publications." This 60 page book provides information on a large variety of government publications and order blanks for ordering them from the appropriate agencies. To obtain your free copy, order FAA-APA-PG-9 from: U.S. Department of Transportation, M-494.3, Washington, DC 20591. Specific types of publications of interest to private pilots discussed in this book are listed below.

a. Advisory circulars provide nonregulatory information. Some of these free publications are available at your GADO/FSDO. However, the main office is better able to supply the public. Order the Advisory Circular Checklist, AC 00-2.1, and specific ACs from: U.S. Department of Transportation, M-494.3, Washington, DC 20591.

b.   Flight Standards safety pamphlets, such as "Obtaining a Good Weather Briefing" (see chapter 9), are available only at GADOs or FSDOs. Ask about these when you visit your GADO/FSDO.

c.   In addition to the above free publications, there are educational and informational materials available at low cost. These include Pilot's Handbook of Aeronautical Knowledge, Aviation Weather, Flight Training Handbook, Instrument Flying Handbook, Medical Handbook for Pilots, the Practical Test Standards, pilot question books and military aviation history and pictures. Your local flight training school sells some of these, the Government Printing Office outlets in certain large cities stock some, or you may order them from Washington. For an illustrated pamphlet and order form, write for "U.S. Government Books Especially For Pilots" from: Superintendent of Documents, Government Printing Office, Washington DC 20402.

d.   Aviation charts and related navigation material are published by the National Ocean Service (NOS) component of the National Oceanic and Atmospheric Administration (NOAA) of the Department of Commerce. The most frequently used of these, such as sectional, TCA, and instrument charts, are available at private agencies at or near airports. For a free brochure on these materials and information on how to order charts directly from NOS and automatic distribution service, write for the "Catalog of Aeronautical Chart and Related Publications" from National Ocean Service, Distribution Branch (N/CG-33), 6501 Lafayette Avenue, Riverdale, MD 20737.

U.S. Department of Transportation

Federal Aviation Administration

Advisory Circular

Subject: PILOT PROFICIENCY AWARD PROGRAM	Date: 7/20/87	AC No: 61-91E
	Initiated by: AFS-810	Change:

1. PURPOSE. This advisory circular (AC) describes the Federal Aviation Administration's (FAA) Pilot Proficiency Award Program and outlines the eligibility requirements to qualify for Phase I through Phase VI awards.

2. CANCELLATION. AC 61-91D, Pilot Proficiency Award Program, dated 8/10/84, is cancelled.

3. OBJECTIVE. Regular proficiency training is essential to the safety of all pilots and their passengers. The objective of the Pilot Proficiency Award Program is to provide pilots with the opportunity to establish and participate in a personal recurrent training program.

4. WHO MAY PARTICIPATE. All pilots holding a private pilot certificate or higher and a current medical certificate, when required, may participate. Requests to participate in the program should be made to a flight instructor, an appointed Accident Prevention Counselor, or the Accident Prevention Specialist in the local FAA Flight Standards or General Aviation District Office.

5. INCENTIVE AWARDS - PILOT WINGS AND CERTIFICATE. Upon completion of each phase of the six-phase program, pilots become eligible to wear and are presented a distinctive lapel or tie pin (wings) and a certificate of completion. The Phase I wings are plain bronze tone, Phase II wings are silver tone with a star added, Phase III wings are gold tone with a star and wreath, Phase IV wings are gold tone and have a simulated ruby mounted in the shield, Phase V wings are gold tone with a rhinestone mounted in the shield, and Phase VI wings are gold tone with a simulated sapphire mounted in the shield. No complimentary wings will be given. All pilots, regardless of type of certificate, ratings, or position, must earn the right to wear the pilot proficiency wings.

6. PHASE I TRAINING REQUIREMENTS. Pilots may select the category and class of aircraft in which they desire to receive their operational training. All training requirements must be completed within 12 months after beginning training under the Pilot Proficiency Award Program. Certain training and flight maneuvers, with specified training minimums, have been established for airplanes, rotorcraft, gliders, and lighter-than-air. The training profile chosen represents those phases of operation for each category of aircraft that have been identified from accident reports as most likely to produce accidents.

a. Airplanes.

(1) One hour of flight training to include basic airplane control, stalls, turns, and other maneuvers directed toward mastery of the airplane.

(2) One hour of flight training to include precision approaches, takeoffs and landings, including crosswind, soft field, and short field techniques.

(3) One hour of instrument training in an airplane, instrument simulator, or training device.

b. Rotorcraft.

(1) One hour of ground training to include use of the rotorcraft flight manual to determine operating limitations, weight and balance computations, performance data, aircraft servicing, use of optional equipment, and normal emergency procedures.

(2) One hour of flight training to include airport and traffic pattern operations, including departures from a hover (helicopter only), normal and crosswind approaches and landings, maximum performance takeoffs, and steep approaches.

(3) One hour of flight training to include autorotative descents, power failure at a hover, settling-with-power, system or equipment malfunctions, slope takeoffs and landings, pinnacle/rooftop takeoffs and landings, and navigation procedures.

c. Gliders.

(1) One hour of ground training to include use of glider operating limitations, weight and balance computations, performance data, and normal emergency procedures.

(2) One hour or three flights to include launch procedures, proper position during tow, emergency procedures such as a slack line or tow rope failure, and tow release procedures.

(3) One hour or three flights to include safe thermalling procedures, including flight in close proximity to other aircraft, maneuvers at various performance speeds, demonstration of best lift over drag (L/D) and minimum sink, and precision approaches and landings.

d. Lighter-Than-Air.

(1) One hour of ground training to include fuel management, refueling, proper inflation procedures, review of the flight manual, and proper weather check.

(2) One hour of flight training to include precision approaches, touch-and-go, level flight, rapid descent and level out, and simulated landing in a congested area.

(3) One hour of flight training to include relighting the pilot light, simulated high wind/short field landings, and other simulated emergency situations.

e. Training Substitution. The 3 hours of required dual in each category of aircraft may be substituted by completion of a training program utilizing simulator and/or training devices, conducted by such organizations as FlightSafety International, Inc.; SimuFlite Training International, Inc.; and many of the nation's air carriers.

f. Safety Meetings.

(1) All applicants must attend at least one FAA or FAA-sanctioned aviation safety seminar or industry-conducted recurrent training program. FAA-sanctioned aviation safety seminars and recurrent training programs are conducted by such organizations as: Soaring Society of America, American Bonanza Society, and Balloon Federation of America.

(2) Attendance at an Accident Prevention Program aviation safety seminar must be verified in the pilot's logbook or other proficiency record. This verification must be signed by an FAA Accident Prevention Specialist, other FAA personnel, or any Accident Prevention Counselors involved in conducting the seminar.

(3) Attendance at a physiological training course conducted under the FAA, U.S. Air Force, or U.S. Navy training agreements at various military installations in the United States is also acceptable. AC Form 3150-7, Physiological Training Application/Agreement, is required for this training and is available from the local Accident Prevention Specialist or from the Mike Monroney Aeronautical Center, Aeromedical Education Branch, AAM-140, P.O. Box 25082, Oklahoma City, OK 73125. Students completing a physiological training course should present a completed FAA Form 3150-1, Physiological Training, to the Accident Prevention Specialist for verification of course completion.

7. PHASE II, III, IV, V, AND VI TRAINING REQUIREMENTS.

a. Phase II. Twelve months after the date of meeting the final requirements for the Phase I award, a pilot may initiate action to qualify for the Phase II award. To qualify for the Phase II award, a pilot must repeat the same requirements as stipulated for Phase I.

b. Phase III. Twelve months after the date of meeting the final requirements for the Phase II award, a pilot may initiate action to qualify for the Phase III award. To qualify for the Phase III award, a pilot must repeat the same requirements as stipulated for Phase I.

c. __Phase IV__. Twelve months after the date of meeting the final requirements for the Phase III award, a pilot may initiate action to qualify for the Phase IV award. To qualify for the Phase IV award, a pilot must repeat the same requirements as stipulated for Phase I.

d. __Phase V__. Twelve months after the date of meeting the final requirements for the Phase IV award, a pilot may initiate action to qualify for the Phase V award. To qualify for the Phase V award, a pilot must not have been involved in an aircraft accident within the past consecutive 5 years in which he or she was determined to be at fault, and must repeat the same requirements as stipulated for Phase I.

e. __Phase VI__. Twelve months after the date of meeting the final requirements for the Phase V award, a pilot may initiate action to qualify for the Phase VI award. To qualify for the Phase VI award, a pilot must not have been involved in an aircraft accident within the past consecutive 6 years in which he or she was determined to be at fault, and must repeat the same requirements as stipulated for Phase I.

8. __PILOT PROFICIENCY AWARD EARNED BY FLIGHT INSTRUCTORS__.

a. Pilot proficiency wings may be earned by certificated flight instructors, based upon the number of pilots they certify through the program and their participation in safety clinics. Certification that they have provided the training required for completion of steps (1), (2), and (3), outlined in paragraphs 6a, b, c, or d to three pilots (minimum of 9 hours instruction) earns the Phase I wings.

b. Certification of three additional pilots, as stated in subparagraph a, is required to earn Phase II wings, and another three pilots must be certified before earning the Phase III wings.

c. After completion of the Phase III requirements, Phase IV may be earned by successful completion of an evaluation or proficiency flight with a designated flight instructor examiner or an FAA operations inspector. Twelve months after the date of meeting the requirements for the Phase IV award, a certificated flight instructor may initiate action to qualify for the Phase V award.

d. To qualify for the Phase V award, a certificated flight instructor must not have been involved in an aircraft accident within the past consecutive 5 years in which he or she was determined to be at fault. The same requirements as stated in this paragraph for the Phase IV award must also be repeated.

e. To qualify for the Phase VI award, a certificated flight instructor must not have been involved in an aircraft accident within the past consecutive 6 years in which he or she was determined to be at fault. The same requirements as stated in this paragraph for the Phase IV award must also be repeated.

f. Flight instructors must also attend or participate in at least one FAA or FAA-sanctioned aviation safety seminar, attend an FAA-approved Flight Instructor Refresher Clinic, or attend a physiological training course as specified in paragraph 6f(3) to meet the requirements for each phase of the award. Attendance must also be verified in the flight instructor's logbook or other proficiency record. This verification must be signed by an Accident Prevention Specialist, other FAA personnel, or any Accident Prevention Counselors involved in conducting the above programs.

9. <u>AWARDING OF THE PILOT PROFICIENCY WINGS AND CERTIFICATE.</u>

a. As pilots complete each step of the training outlined in paragraph 6, their logbook or other proficiency record must be endorsed by the person who gave the instruction. That endorsement should read substantively as follows:

Mr./Ms._____, holder of pilot certificate
no._____, has satisfactorily completed the training requirements outlined in Advisory Circular 61-91E, paragraphs 6a, b, c, or d (state which).

/s/ J. Jones   652472   CFI   Exp. 7/31/88

b. The Pilot Proficiency Award Certificate and the appropriate wings will be awarded after the pilot's logbook or other proficiency record is presented to the Accident Prevention Specialist for verification of completion of training as stipulated in this advisory circular.

10. <u>SUMMARY.</u> Aviation safety is a cooperative effort of all members of the aviation community. We encourage each pilot to establish a regular recurrent training program and invite your participation in the Pilot Proficiency Award Program.

Robert L. Goodrich
Director of Flight Standards

APPENDIX A - FAA APPENDIX 2

DIRECTORY LEGEND

LEGEND

SECTIONAL AERONAUTICAL CHART
SCALE 1:500,000

Airports having Control Towers (Airport Traffic Areas) are shown in blue, all others in magenta. Consult Airport/Facility Directory (A/FD) for details involving airport lighting, controlled airspace, navigation aids, and services. For additional symbol information refer to the VFR Chart User's Guide.

AIRPORTS

○ Other than hard-surfaced runways

◁ Hard-surfaced runways 1500 ft. to 8000 ft. in length

◭ Hard-surfaced runways greater than 8000 ft.

⚓ Seaplane Base (SPB)

All recognizable hard-surfaced runways, including those closed, are shown for visual identification.

ADDITIONAL AIRPORT INFORMATION

Ⓡ Private "(Pvt)" Non-public use having emergency or landmark value.

Military – Other than hard-surfaced. All military airports are identified by abbreviations AFB, NAS, AAF, etc. For complete airport information consult DOD FLIP.

Ⓗ Heliport Selected

Ⓤ Unverified

⊗ Abandoned paved having landmark value

Ⓕ Ultralight Flight Park Selected

Services – fuel available and field tended during normal working hours depicted by use of ticks around basic airport symbol. Consult A/FD for service availability at airports with runways greater than 8000 ft.

★ Rotating light in operation Sunset to Sunrise

RADIO AIDS TO NAVIGATION AND COMMUNICATION BOXES

⊙ VHF OMNI RANGE (VOR)

◐ VORTAC

◎ VOR-DME

Non-Directional Radiobeacon

    R·Bn
    POINT LOMA
    302 · – · ·
    H+00 & ev 6m

⊙ Marine Radiobeacon

○ Other facilities, i.e., Commercial Broadcast Stations, FSS Outlets, RCO, etc.

```
OAKDALE
122.1R 122.6 123.6
┌──────────────┐
│ 362 116.8 OAK │ ⁝⁝
└──────────────┘
```

Underline indicates no voice on this freq

Square indicates TWEB, AWOS or HIWAS available at this NAVAID.

R – receive only

T – transmit only

122.1R
┌─────────┐
│ MIAMI   │
└─────────┘
Controlling FSS

Frequencies above thin line box are remoted to NAVAID site. Other freqs at controlling FSS may be available determined by altitude and terrain. Consult Airport/Facility Directory for complete information.

AIRPORT DATA

Indicates Flight Service Station on field.

```
FSS     CT – 118.3*
NAME    ATIS 124.9
        O3  92 122.95 ──► UNICOM
        VFR Advsy 125.3
        Airport of entry
```

Box indicates Special (See FAR 93) Traffic Area

FSS – Flight Service Station

CT – 118.3 – Control Tower (CT) – primary frequency

★ – Star indicates operation part time. See tower frequencies tabulation for hours of operation.

ATIS 124.9 – Automatic Terminal Information Service

UNICOM – Aeronautical advisory station

VFR Advsy – VFR Advisory Service shown where ATIS not available and frequency is other than primary CT frequency.

O3 – Elevation in feet

L – Lighting in operation Sunset to Sunrise

*L – Lighting available on request, part-time lighting, or pilot-controlled lighting.

92 – Length of longest runway in hundreds of feet; usable length may be less.

When facility or information is lacking, the respective character is replaced by a dash. All lighting codes refer to runway lights. Lighted runway may not be the longest or lighted full length. All times are local.

NFCT – Non Federal Control Tower

Heavy line box indicates Flight Service Station (FSS). Freqs 121.5, 122.2, 243.0 and 255.4 are normally available at all FSSs and are not shown above boxes. All other freqs are shown.

122.1R
┌──────────────┐
│ CHICAGO CHI │
└──────────────┘

For Airport Advisory Service use FSS freq 123.6

In Canada all available FSS frequencies are shown.

AIRPORT TRAFFIC SERVICE AND AIRSPACE INFORMATION

AIRSPACE INFORMATION

Only the controlled and reserved airspace effective below 18,000 ft MSL are shown on this chart. All times are local.

180° ──► V 3

Low Altitude Federal Airways are indicated by center line.

TA – Transition Area

The limits of controlled airspace are shown by tint bands (Vignette) and are color-coded in blue and magenta.

(black) Floor 700 feet above surface

(gray) Floor 1200 feet above surface

TCA – Terminal Control Area / Canadian Class C Airspace

ARSA – Airport Radar Service Area

TRSA – Terminal Radar Service Area

National Security Area

MTR – Military Training Routes

Floors other than 700 feet or 1200 feet above surface

Prohibited, Restricted, Warning and Alert Area

MOA – Military Operations Area

CZ – Control Zone

C Z – Extends upwards from the surface.

CZ within which fixed-wing special VFR Flight is prohibited Class C CZ (Canada)

⚷ Parachute Jumping Area See Airport/Facility Directory

Intersection – Arrows are directed towards facilities which establish intersection.

NAME (Red, Blue, or Black) Visual Check Point

Special Airport Traffic Areas (See F.A.R. Part 93 for details)

OBSTRUCTIONS

⋏ 1000 ft and higher AGL

⋀ below 1000 ft AGL

⋏ or ⋏ Group Obstruction

2049 ── Elevation of the top above mean sea level
(1149) ── Height above ground

UC – Under construction or reported; position and elevation unverified

CAUTION: Guy wires may extend outward from structures.

MISCELLANEOUS

–7°E ── Isogonic Line (1985 VALUE)

Glider Operations
Fl ★ Flashing Light
● Marine Light

Ultralight Activity

MILITARY TRAINING ROUTES (MTRs)

All IR and VR MTRs are shown, and may extend from the surface upwards. Only the route centerline, direction of flight along the route and the route designator are depicted – route widths and altitudes are not shown.

Since these routes are subject to change every 56 days, and the charts are reissued every 6 months, you are cautioned and advised to contact the nearest FSS for route dimensions and current status for those routes affecting your flight.

Routes with a change in the alignment of the charted route centerline will be indicated in the Aeronautical Chart Bulletin of the Airport/Facility Directory. Also, the VFR Wall Planning Chart is issued every 56 days and displays current route configurations and a composite tabulation of altitudes along these routes.

Military Pilots refer to Area Planning AP/1B Military Training Route North and South America for current routes.

TOPOGRAPHICAL INFORMATION

⟨⟨⟨ Roads
━⊙━ Road Markers
━━━ Railroad

Bridges And Viaducts

Power Transmission lines

Catenary; Height greater than 200 ft

Aerial Cable

⊙ Lookout Tower P-17 (Site Number)
618 (Elevation Base Of Tower)

CG Coast Guard Station

◆ Race Track

○ Tank–water, oil or gas

○ Oil Well ◆ Water Well

✕ Mines And Quarries

Mountain Pass
11823 (Elevation of Pass)

Outdoor Theater

⌁ Rocks

Shipwreck

Pier

Perennial Lake

Non-Perennial Lake

Dams

ATTENTION

THIS CHART CONTAINS MAXIMUM ELEVATION FIGURES (MEF). The Maximum Elevation Figures shown in quadrangles bounded by ticked lines of latitude and longitude are represented in THOUSANDS and HUNDREDS of feet above mean sea level. The MEF is based on information available concerning the highest known feature in each quadrangle, including terrain and obstructions (trees, towers, antennas, etc.).

Example: 12,500 feet 12⁵

CONTOUR INTERVAL 500 feet
Intermediate contour 250 feet

──── 500
──── 250

LEGEND 1.–Airport/Facility Directory.

DIRECTORY LEGEND
SAMPLE

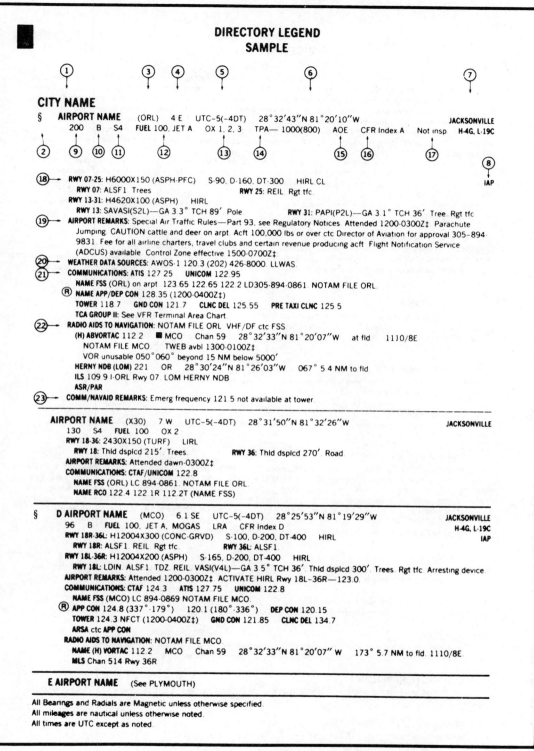

CITY NAME

§ AIRPORT NAME (ORL) 4 E UTC-5(-4DT) 28°32'43"N 81°20'10"W JACKSONVILLE

200 B S4 FUEL 100, JET A OX 1, 2, 3 TPA— 1000(800) AOE CFR Index A Not insp H-4G, L-19C

IAP

(18) RWY 07-25: H6000X150 (ASPH-PFC) S-90, D-160, DT-300 HIRL CL
RWY 07: ALSF1 Trees RWY 25: REIL Rgt tfc
RWY 13-31: H4620X100 (ASPH) HIRL
RWY 13: SAVASI(S2L)—GA 3.3° TCH 89' Pole RWY 31: PAPI(P2L)—GA 3.1° TCH 36' Tree Rgt tfc
(19) AIRPORT REMARKS: Special Air Traffic Rules—Part 93, see Regulatory Notices Attended 1200-0300Z‡ Parachute
Jumping. CAUTION cattle and deer on arpt Acft 100,000 lbs or over ctc Director of Aviation for approval 305-894-
9831. Fee for all airline charters, travel clubs and certain revenue producing acft Flight Notification Service
(ADCUS) available. Control Zone effective 1500-0700Z‡
(20) WEATHER DATA SOURCES: AWOS-1 120.3 (202) 426-8000. LLWAS.
(21) COMMUNICATIONS: ATIS 127.25 UNICOM 122.95
NAME FSS (ORL) on arpt 123.65 122.65 122.2 LD305-894-0861 NOTAM FILE ORL.
(R) NAME APP/DEP CON 128.35 (1200-0400Z‡)
TOWER 118.7 GND CON 121.7 CLNC DEL 125.55 PRE TAXI CLNC 125.5
TCA GROUP II: See VFR Terminal Area Chart
(22) RADIO AIDS TO NAVIGATION: NOTAM FILE ORL VHF/DF ctc FSS.
(H) ABVORTAC 112.2 ■ MCO Chan 59 28°32'33"N 81°20'07"W at fld 1110/8E
NOTAM FILE MCO TWEB avbl 1300-0100Z‡
VOR unusable 050°060° beyond 15 NM below 5000'
HERNY NDB (LOM) 221 OR 28°30'24"N 81°26'03"W 067° 5.4 NM to fld
ILS 109.9 I-ORL Rwy 07. LOM HERNY NDB
ASR/PAR
(23) COMM/NAVAID REMARKS: Emerg frequency 121.5 not available at tower.

AIRPORT NAME (X30) 7 W UTC-5(-4DT) 28°31'50"N 81°32'26"W JACKSONVILLE
130 S4 FUEL 100 OX 2
RWY 18-36: 2430X150 (TURF) LIRL
RWY 18: Thld dsplcd 215' Trees. RWY 36: Thld dsplcd 270' Road.
AIRPORT REMARKS: Attended dawn-0300Z‡
COMMUNICATIONS: CTAF/UNICOM 122.8
NAME FSS (ORL) LC 894-0861. NOTAM FILE ORL.
NAME RCO 122.4 122.1R 112.2T (NAME FSS)

---

§ D AIRPORT NAME (MCO) 6.1 SE UTC-5(-4DT) 28°25'53"N 81°19'29"W JACKSONVILLE
96 B FUEL 100, JET A, MOGAS LRA CFR Index D H-4G, L-19C
RWY 18R-36L: H12004X300 (CONC-GRVD) S-100, D-200, DT-400 HIRL IAP
RWY 18R: ALSF1. REIL Rgt tfc. RWY 36L: ALSF1.
RWY 18L-36R: H12004X200 (ASPH) S-165, D-200, DT-400 HIRL
RWY 18L: LDIN. ALSF1. TDZ. REIL. VASI(V4L)—GA 3.5° TCH 36'. Thld dsplcd 300'. Trees. Rgt tfc. Arresting device.
AIRPORT REMARKS: Attended 1200-0300Z‡. ACTIVATE HIRL Rwy 18L-36R—123.0.
COMMUNICATIONS: CTAF 124.3 ATIS 127.75 UNICOM 122.8
NAME FSS (MCO) LC 894-0869 NOTAM FILE MCO.
(R) APP CON 124.8 (337°-179°) 120.1 (180°-336°) DEP CON 120.15
TOWER 124.3 NFCT (1200-0400Z‡) GND CON 121.85 CLNC DEL 134.7
ARSA ctc APP CON
RADIO AIDS TO NAVIGATION: NOTAM FILE MCO.
NAME (H) VORTAC 112.2 MCO Chan 59 28°32'33"N 81°20'07"W 173° 5.7 NM to fld. 1110/8E.
MLS Chan 514 Rwy 36R

E AIRPORT NAME (See PLYMOUTH)

All Bearings and Radials are Magnetic unless otherwise specified.
All mileages are nautical unless otherwise noted.
All times are UTC except as noted.

LEGEND 2.–Airport/Facility Directory.

DIRECTORY LEGEND
LEGEND

This Directory is an alphabetical listing of data on record with the FAA on all airports that are open to the public, associated terminal control facilities, air route traffic control centers and radio aids to navigation within the conterminous United States, Puerto Rico and the Virgin Islands. Airports are listed alphabetically by associated city name and cross referenced by airport name. Facilities associated with an airport, but with a different name, are listed individually under their own name, as well as under the airport with which they are associated.

The listing of an airport in this directory merely indicates the airport operator's willingness to accommodate transient aircraft, and does not represent that the facility conforms with any Federal or local standards, or that it has been approved for use on the part of the general public.

The information on obstructions is taken from reports submitted to the FAA. It has not been verified in all cases. Pilots are cautioned that objects not indicated in this tabulation (or on charts) may exist which can create a hazard to flight operation.

Detailed specifics concerning services and facilities tabulated within this directory are contained in Airman's Information Manual, Basic Flight Information and ATC Procedures.

The legend items that follow explain in detail the contents of this Directory and are keyed to the circled numbers on the sample on the preceding page.

① CITY/AIRPORT NAME

Airports and facilities in this directory are listed alphabetically by associated city and state. Where the city name is different from the airport name the city name will appear on the line above the airport name. Airports with the same associated city name will be listed alphabetically by airport name and will be separated by a dashed rule line. All others will be separated by a solid rule line.

② NOTAM SERVICE

§—NOTAM "D" (Distance teletype dissemination) and NOTAM "L" (local dissemination) service is provided for airport. Absence of annotation § indicates NOTAM "L" (local dissemination) only is provided for airport. Airport NOTAM file identifier will be shown as "NOTAM FILE IAD" for all public-use airports. See AIM, Basic Flight Information and ATC Procedures for detailed descriptions of NOTAM.

③ LOCATION IDENTIFIER

A three or four character code assigned to airports. These identifiers are used by ATC in lieu of the airport name in flight plans, flight strips and other written records and computer operations.

④ AIRPORT LOCATION

Airport location is expressed as distance and direction from the center of the associated city in nautical miles and cardinal points, i.e., 4 NE.

⑤ TIME CONVERSION

Hours of operation of all facilities are expressed in Coordinated Universal Time (UTC) and shown as "Z" time. The directory indicates the number of hours to be subtracted from UTC to obtain local standard time and local daylight saving time UTC-5(-4DT). The symbol ‡ indicates that during periods of Daylight Saving Time effective hours will be one hour earlier than shown. In those areas where daylight saving time is not observed that (-4DT) and ‡ will not be shown. All states observe daylight savings time except Arizona and that portion of Indiana in the Eastern Time Zone and Puerto Rico and the Virgin Islands.

⑥ GEOGRAPHIC POSITION OF AIRPORT

⑦ CHARTS

The Sectional Chart and Low and High Altitude Enroute Chart and panel on which the airport or facility is located. Helicopter Chart locations will be indicated as, i.e., COPTER

⑧ INSTRUMENT APPROACH PROCEDURES

IAP indicates an airport for which a prescribed (Public Use) FAA Instrument Approach Procedure has been published.

⑨ ELEVATION

Elevation is given in feet above mean sea level and is the highest point on the landing surface. When elevation is sea level it will be indicated as (00). When elevation is below sea level a minus (–) sign will precede the figure.

⑩ ROTATING LIGHT BEACON

B indicates rotating beacon is available. Rotating beacons operate dusk to dawn unless otherwise indicated in AIRPORT REMARKS

⑪ SERVICING

S1   Minor airframe repairs.
S2   Minor airframe and minor powerplant repairs
S3   Major airframe and minor powerplant repairs
S4   Major airframe and major powerplant repairs

LEGEND 3.–Airport/Facility Directory.

DIRECTORY LEGEND

⑫ FUEL

CODE	FUEL
80	Grade 80 gasoline (Red)
100	Grade 100 gasoline (Green)
100LL	Grade 100LL gasoline (low lead) (Blue)
115	Grade 115 gasoline
A	Jet A—Kerosene freeze point–40° C.
A1	Jet A-1—Kerosene. freeze point–50° C.
A1+	Jet A-1—Kerosene with icing inhibitor, freeze point–50° C.
MOGAS	Automobile gasoline which is to be used as aircraft fuel.

CODE	FUEL
B	Jet B—Wide-cut turbine fuel, freeze point–50° C.
B+	Jet B—Wide-cut turbine fuel with icing inhibitor, freeze point–50° C.

NOTE: Automobile Gasoline. Certain automobile gasoline may be used in specific aircraft engines if a FAA supplemental type cetificate has been obtained. Automobile gasoline which is to be used in aircraft engines will be identified as "MOGAS", however, the grade/type and other octane rating will not be published.

Data shown on fuel availability represents the most recent informtion the publisher has been able to acquire. Because of a variety of factors, the fuel listed may not always be obtainable by transient civil pilots. Confirmation of availability of fuel should be made directly with fuel dispensers at locations where refueling is planned.

⑬ OXYGEN

OX 1 High Pressure
OX 2 Low Pressure
OX 3 High Pressure—Replacement Bottles
OX 4 Low Pressure—Replacement Bottles

⑭ TRAFFIC PATTERN ALTITUDE

Traffic Pattern Altitude (TPA)—The first figure shown is TPA above mean sea level. The second figure in parentheses is TPA above airport elevation.

⑮ AIRPORT OF ENTRY AND LANDING RIGHTS AIRPORTS

AOE—Airport of Entry—A customs Airport of Entry where permission from U.S. Customs is not required, however, at least one hour advance notice of arrival must be furnished.

LRA—Landing Rights Airport—Application for permission to land must be submitted in advance to U.S. Customs. At least one hour advance notice of arrival must be furnished.

NOTE: Advance notice of arrival at both an AOE and LRA airport may be included in the flight plan when filed in Canada or Mexico, where Flight Notification Service (ADCUS) is available the airport remark will indicate this service.This notice will also be treated as an application for permission to land in the case of an LRA. Although advance notice of arrival may be relayed to Customs through Mexico, Canadian, and U.S. Communications facilities by flight plan, the aircraft operator is solely responsible for insuring that Customs receives the notification. (See Customs, Immigration and Naturalization, Public Health and Agriculture Department requirements in the International Flight Information Manual for further details.)

⑯ CERTIFICATED AIRPORT (FAR 139)

Airports serving Department of Transportation certified carriers and certified under FAR, Part 139, are indicated by the CFR index; i.e., CFR Index A, which relates to the availability of crash, fire, rescue equipment.

FAR–PART 139 CERTIFICATED AIRPORTS

INDICES AND FIRE FIGHTING AND RESCUE EQUIPMENT REQUIREMENTS

Airport Index	Required No. Vehicles	Aircraft Length	Scheduled Departures	Agent + Water for Foam
A	1	≤90'	≥1	500#DC or 450#DC + 50 gal H₂O
AA	1	>90', ≤126'	<5	300#DC + 500 gal H₂O
B	2	>90', ≤126'	≥5	Index A + 1500 gal H₂O
		>126', ≤160'	<5	
C	3	>126', ≤160'	≥5	Index A + 3000 gal H₂O
		>160', ≤200'	<5	
D	3	>160', ≤200' >200'	≥5 <5	Index A + 4000 gal H₂O
E	3	>200'	≥5	Index A + 6000 gal H₂O

> Greater Than;   < Less Than;   ≥ Equal or Greater Than;   ≤ Equal or Less Than;   H₂O–Water;
DC–Dry Chemical.

LEGEND 4.–Airport/Facility Directory.

DIRECTORY LEGEND

NOTE: If AFFF (Aqueous Film Forming Foam) is used in lieu of Protein Foam, the water quantities listed for Indices AA thru E can be reduced 33$\frac{1}{3}$%. See FAR Part 139.49 for full details. The listing of CFR index does not necessarily assure coverage for non-air carrier operations or at other than prescribed times for air carrier. CFR index Ltd.—indicates CFR coverage may or may not be available, for information contact airport manager prior to flight.

⑰ FAA INSPECTION

All airports not inspected by FAA will be identified by the note: Not insp. This indicates that the airport information has been provided by the owner or operator of the field.

⑱ RUNWAY DATA

Runway information is shown on two lines. That information common to the entire runway is shown on the first line while information concerning the runway ends are shown on the second or following line. Lengthy information will be placed in the Airport Remarks.

Runway direction, surface, length, width, weight bearing capacity, lighting, gradient and appropriate remarks are shown for each runway. Direction, length, width, lighting and remarks are shown for sealanes. The full dimensions of helipads are shown, i.e., 50X150.

RUNWAY SURFACE AND LENGTH

Runway lengths prefixed by the letter "H" indicate that the runways are hard surfaced (concrete, asphalt). If the runway length is not prefixed, the surface is sod, clay, etc. The runway surface composition is indicated in parentheses after runway length as follows:

(AFSC)—Aggregate friction seal coat	(GRVD)—Grooved	(TURF)—Turf
(ASPH)—Asphalt	(GRVL)—Gravel, or cinders	(TRTD)—Treated
(CONC)—Concrete	(PFC)—Porous friction courses	(WC)—Wire combed
(DIRT)—Dirt	(RFSC)—Rubberized friction seal coat	

RUNWAY WEIGHT BEARING CAPACITY

Runway strength data shown in this publication is derived from available information and is a realistic estimate of capability at an average level of activity. It is not intended as a maximum allowable weight or as an operating limitation. Many airport pavements are capable of supporting limited operations with gross weights of 25-50% in excess of the published figures. Permissible operating weights, insofar as runway strengths are concerned, are a matter of agreement between the owner and user. When desiring to operate into any airport at weights in excess of those published in the publication, users should contact the airport management for permission. Add 000 to figure following S, D, DT, DDT and MAX for gross weight capacity:

    S—Runway weight bearing capacity for aircraft with single- wheel type landing gear, (DC-3), etc.
    D—Runway weight bearing capacity for aircraft with dual-wheel type landing gear, (DC-6), etc.
    DT—Runway weight bearing capacity for aircraft with dual-tandem type landing gear, (707), etc.
    DDT—Runway weight bearing capacity for aircraft with double dual- tandem type landing gear, (747), etc.

Quadricycle and dual-tandem are considered virtually equal for runway weight bearing consideration, as are single-tandem and dual-wheel.

Omission of weight bearing capacity indicates information unknown.

RUNWAY LIGHTING

Lights are in operation sunset to sunrise. Lighting available by prior arrangement only or operating part of the night only and/or pilot controlled and with specific operating hours are indicated under airport remarks. Since obstructions are usually lighted, obstruction lighting is not included in this code. Unlighted obstructions on or surrounding an airport will be noted in airport remarks. Runway lights nonstandard (NSTD) are systems for which the light fixtures are not FAA approved L-800 series: color, intensity, or spacing does not meet FAA standards. Nonstandard runway lights, VASI, or any other system not listed below will be shown in airport remarks.

Temporary, emergency or limited runway edge lighting such as flares, smudge pots, lanterns or portable runway lights will also be shown in airport remarks.

Types of lighting are shown with the runway or runway end they serve.

NSTD—Light system fails to meet FAA standards.	SALS—Short Approach Lighting System.
LIRL—Low Intensity Runway Lights	SALSF—Short Approach Lighting System with Sequenced Flashing Lights.
MIRL—Medium Intensity Runway Lights	
HIRL—High Intensity Runway Lights	SSALS—Simplified Short Approach Lighting System.
REIL—Runway End Identifier Lights	SSALF—Simplified Short Approach Lighting System with Sequenced Flashing Lights.
CL—Centerline Lights	
TDZ—Touchdown Zone Lights	SSALR—Simplified Short Approach Lighting System with Runway Alignment Indicator Lights.
ODALS—Omni Directional Approach Lighting System.	
AF OVRN—Air Force Overrun 1000' Standard Approach Lighting System.	ALSAF—High Intensity Approach Lighting System with Sequenced Flashing Lights
LDIN—Lead-In Lighting System.	ALSF1—High Intensity Approach Lighting System with Sequenced Flashing Lights, Category I, Configuration.
MALS—Medium Intensity Approach Lighting System.	
MALSF—Medium Intensity Approach Lighting System with Sequenced Flashing Lights.	ALSF2—High Intensity Approach Lighting System with Sequenced Flashing Lights, Category II, Configuration.
MALSR—Medium Intensity Approach Lighting System with Runway Alignment Indicator Lights.	VASI—Visual Approach Slope Indicator System.

NOTE: Civil ALSF-2 may be operated as SSALR during favorable weather conditions.

LEGEND 5.–Airport/Facility Directory.

DIRECTORY LEGEND
VISUAL INDICATORS GLIDESLOPE

VASI—Visual Approach Slope Indicator
SAVASI—Simplified Abbreviated Visual Approach Slope Indicator
PAPI—Precision Approach Path Indicator

P2R	2-identical light units placed on right side of runway
P2L	2-identical light units placed on left side of runway
P4R	4-identical light units placed on right side of runway
P4L	4-identical light units placed on left side of runway
S2L	2-box SAVASI on left side of runway
S2R	2-box SAVASI on right side of runway
V2R	2-box VASI on right side of runway
V2L	2-box VASI on left side of runway
V4R	4-box VASI on right side of runway
V4L	4-box VASI on left side of runway
V6R	6-box VASI on right side of runway
V6L	6-box VASI on left side of runway
V12	12-box VASI on both sides of runway
V16	16-box VASI on both sides of runway
*NSTD	Nonstandard VASI, VAPI, or any other system not listed above

PAPI/VASI approach slope angle and threshold crossing height will be shown when available; i.e., GA 3.5° TCH 37'.

PILOT CONTROL OF AIRPORT LIGHTING

Key Mike	Function
7 times within 5 seconds	Highest intensity available
5 times within 5 seconds	Medium or lower intensity (Lower REIL or REIL-Off)
3 times within 5 seconds	Lowest intensity available (Lower REIL or REIL-Off)

Available systems will be indicated in the Airport Remarks, as follows:

ACTIVATE MALSR Rwy 7, HIRL Rwy 7-25-122.8.
or
ACTIVATE MIRL Rwy 18-36-122.8.
or
ACTIVATE VASI and REIL, Rwy 7-122.8.

Where the airport is not served by an instrument approach procedure and/or has an independent type system of different specification installed by the airport sponsor, descriptions of the type lights, method of control, and operating frequency will be explained in clear text. See AIM, "Basic Flight Information and ATC Procedures," for detailed description of pilot control of airport lighting.

RUNWAY GRADIENT

Runway gradient will be shown only when it is 0.3 percent or more. When available the direction of slope upward will be indicated, i.e., 0.5% up NW.

RUNWAY END DATA

Lighting systems such as VASI, MALSR, REIL; obstructions; displaced thresholds will be shown on the specific runway end. "Rgt tfc"—Right traffic indicates right turns should be made on landing and takeoff for specified runway end.

⑲ AIRPORT REMARKS

Landing Fee indicates landing charges for private or non-revenue producing aircraft, in addition, fees may be charged for planes that remain over a couple of hours and buy no services, or at major airline terminals for all aircraft.

Remarks—Data is confined to operational items affecting the status and usability of the airport.

Parachute Jumping.—See "PARACHUTE" tabulation for details.

⑳ WEATHER DATA SOURCES

AWOS—Automated Weather Observing System

AWOS-1—reports altimeter setting, wind data and usually temperature, dewpoint and density altitude.
AWOS-2—reports the same as AWOS-1 plus visibility.
AWOS-3—reports the same as AWOS-1 plus visibility and cloud/ceiling data.
See AIM, Basic Flight Information and ATC Procedures for detailed description of AWOS.

SAWRS—identifies airports that have a Supplemental Aviation Weather Reporting Station available to pilots for current weather information.

LAWRS—Limited Aviation Weather Reporting Station where observers report cloud height, weather, obstructions to vision, temperature and dewpoint (in most cases), surface wind, altimeter and pertinent remarks.

LLWAS—indicates a Low Level Wind Shear Alert System consisting of a center field and several field perimeter anemometers.

HIWAS—See RADIO AIDS TO NAVIGATION

LEGEND 6.–Airport/Facility Directory.

DIRECTORY LEGEND

㉑ COMMUNICATIONS

Communications will be listed in sequence in the order shown below.

Common Traffic Advisory Frequency (CTAF), Automatic Terminal Information Service (ATIS) and Aeronautical Advisory Stations (UNICOM) along with their frequency is shown, where available, on the line following the heading "COMMUNICATIONS." When the CTAF and UNICOM is the same frequency, the frequency will be shown as CTAF/UNICOM freq.

Flight Service Station (FSS) information. The associated FSS will be shown followed by the identifier and information concerning availability of telephone service, e.g., Direct Line (DL), Local Call (LC-384-2341), Long Distance (LD 202-426-8800 or LD 1-202-555-1212) etc. The airport NOTAM file identifier will be shown as "NOTAM FILE IAD." Where the FSS is located on the field it will be indicated as "on arpt" following the identifier. Frequencies available will follow. The FSS telephone number will follow along with any significant operational information. FSS's whose name is not the same as the airport on which located will also be listed in the normal alphabetical name listing for the state in which located. Remote Communications Outlet (RCO) providing service to the airport followed by the frequency and name of the Controlling FSS.

FSS's provide information on airport conditions, radio aids and other facilities, and process flight plans. Airport Advisory Service is provided on the CTAF by FSS's located at non-tower airports or airports where the tower is not in operation.

(See AIM, Par. 157/158 Traffic Advisory Practices at airports where a tower is not in operation or AC 90 - 42C.)

Aviation weather briefing service is provided by FSS specialists. Flight and weather briefing services are also available by calling the telephone numbers listed.

Remote Communications Outlet (RCO)—An unmanned air/ground communications facility, remotely controlled and providing UHF or VHF communications capability to extend the service range of an FSS.

Civil Communications Frequencies—Civil communications frequencies used in the FSS air/ground system are now operated simplex on 122.0, 122.2, 122.3, 122.4, 122.6, 123.6; emergency 121.5; plus receive-only on 122.05, 122.1, 122.15, and 123.6.

    a. 122.0 is assigned as the Enroute Flight Advisory Service channel at selected FSS's.

    b. 122.2 is assigned to all FSS's as a common enroute simplex service.

    c. 123.6 is assigned as the airport advisory channel at non-tower FSS locations, however, it is still in commission at some FSS's collocated with towers to provide part time Airport Advisory Service.

    d. 122.1 is the primary receive-only frequency at VOR's. 122.05, 122.15 and 123.6 are assigned at selected VOR's meeting certain criteria.

    e. Some FSS's are assigned 50 kHz channels for simplex operation in the 122-123 MHz band (e.g. 122.35). Pilots using the FSS A/G system should refer to this directory or appropriate charts to determine frequencies available at the FSS or remoted facility through which they wish to communicate.

Part time FSS hours of operation are shown in remarks under facility name.

Emergency frequency 121.5 is available at all Flight Service Stations, Towers, Approach Control and RADAR facilities, unless indicated as not available.

Frequencies published followed by the letter "T" or "R", indicate that the facility will only transmit or receive respectively on that frequency. All radio aids to navigation frequencies are transmit only.

TERMINAL SERVICES

CTAF—A program designed to get all vehicles and aircraft at uncontrolled airports on a common frequency.

ATIS—A continuous broadcast of recorded non-control information in selected areas of high activity.

UNICOM—A non-government air/ground radio communications facility utilized to provide general airport advisory service.

APP CON—Approach Control. The symbol ⓡ indicates radar approach control.

TOWER—Control tower

GND CON—Ground Control

DEP CON—Departure Control. The symbol ⓡ indicates radar departure control.

CLNC DEL—Clearance Delivery.

PRE TAXI CLNC—Pre taxi clearance

VFR ADVSY SVC—VFR Advisory Service. Service provided by Non-Radar Approach Control.
  Advisory Service for VFR aircraft (upon a workload basis) ctc APP CON.

STAGE II SVC—Radar Advisory and Sequencing Service for VFR aircraft

STAGE III SVC—Radar Sequencing and Separation Service for participating VFR Aircraft within a Terminal Radar Service Area
  (TRSA)

ARSA—Airport Radar Service Area

TCA—Radar Sequencing and Separation Service for all aircraft in a Terminal Control Area (TCA)

TOWER, APP CON and DEP CON RADIO CALL will be the same as the airport name unless indicated otherwise

LEGEND 7.–Airport/Facility Directory.

DIRECTORY LEGEND

22 RADIO AIDS TO NAVIGATION

The Airport Facility Directory lists by facility name all Radio Aids to Navigation, except Military TACANS, that appear on National Ocean Service Visual or IFR Aeronautical Charts and those upon which the FAA has approved an Instrument Approach Procedure.

All VOR, VORTAC ILS and MLS equipment in the National Airspace System has an automatic monitoring and shutdown feature in the event of malfunction. Unmonitored, as used in this publication for any navigational aid, means that FSS or tower personnel cannot observe the malfunction or shutdown signal. The NAVAID NOTAM file identifier will be shown as "NOTAM FILE IAD" and will be listed on the Radio Aids to Navigation line. When two or more NAVAIDS are listed and the NOTAM file identifier is different than shown on the Radio Aids to Navigation line, then it will be shown with the NAVAID listing. Hazardous Inflight Weather Advisory Service (HIWAS) will be shown where this service is broadcast over selected VOR's.

NAVAID information is tabulated as indicated in the following sample:

```
          TWEB        TACAN/DME Channel      Geographical Position            Site Elevation

NAME (L) ABVORTAC  117 55  ▪ ABE   Chan 122(Y)  40°43'36"N 75°27'18"W  180°  4.1 NM to fld.  1110/8E.  HIWAS.

         Class  Frequency  Identifier

                                  Bearing and distance    Magnetic Variation   Hazardous Inflight
                                  facility to airport                          Weather Advisory Service
```

VOR unusable 020°-060° beyond 26 NM below 3500'

Restriction within the normal altitude/range of the navigational aid (See primary alphabetical listing for restrictions on VORTAC and VOR/DME).

Note: Those DME channel numbers with a (Y) suffix require TACAN to be placed in the "Y" mode to receive distance information.

HIWAS—Hazardous Inflight Weather Advisory Service is a continuous broadcast of inflight weather advisories including summarized SIGMETs, convective SIGMETs, AIRMETs and urgent PIREPs. HIWAS is presently broadcast over selected VOR's and will be implemented throughout the conterminous U.S.

ASR/PAR—Indicates that Surveillance (ASR) or Precision (PAR) radar instrument approach minimums are published in U.S. Government Instrument Approach Procedures.

RADIO CLASS DESIGNATIONS

Identification of VOR/VORTAC/TACAN Stations by Class (Operational Limitations):

Normal Usable Altitudes and Radius Distances

Class	Altitudes	Distance (miles)
(T)	12,000' and below	25
(L)	Below 18,000'	40
(H)	Below 18,000'	40
(H)	Within the Conterminous 48 States only, between 14,500' and 17,999'	100
(H)	18,000' FL 450	130
(H)	Above FL 450	100

(H) = High   (L) = Low   (T) = Terminal

NOTE: An (H) facility is capable of providing (L) and (T) service volume and an (L) facility additionally provides (T) service volume.

The term VOR is, operationally, a general term covering the VHF omnidirectional bearing type of facility without regard to the fact that the power, the frequency protected service volume, the equipment configuration, and operational requirements may vary between facilities at different locations.

AB ————————— Automatic Weather Broadcast (also shown with ▪ following frequency.)
DF ————————— Direction Finding Service.
DME ———————— UHF standard (TACAN compatible) distance measuring equipment.
DME(Y) —————— UHF standard (TACAN compatible) distance measuring equipment that require TACAN to be placed in the "Y" mode to receive DME.
H ———————————— Non-directional radio beacon (homing), power 50 watts to less than 2,000 watts (50 NM at all altitudes).
HH ——————————— Non-directional radio beacon (homing), power 2,000 watts or more (75 NM at all altitudes).
H-SAB ———————— Non-directional radio beacons providing automatic transcribed weather service.
ILS ————————— Instrument Landing System (voice, where available, on localizer channel).
ISMLS ———————— Interim Standard Microwave Landing System.
LDA ————————— Localizer Directional Aid.

LEGEND 8.–Airport/Facility Directory.

DIRECTORY LEGEND

LMM _____ Compass locator station when installed at middle marker site (15 NM at all altitudes)
LOM _____ Compass locator station when installed at outer marker site (15 NM at all altitudes)
MH _____ Non-directional radio beacon (homing) power less than 50 watts (25 NM at all altitudes)
MLS _____ Microwave Landing System
S _____ Simultaneous range homing signal and/or voice
SABH _____ Non-directional radio beacon not authorized for IFR or ATC. Provides automatic weather
                          broadcasts
SDF _____ Simplified Direction Facility
TACAN _____ UHF navigational facility-omnidirectional course and distance information
VOR _____ VHF navigational facility-omnidirectional course only.
VOR/DME _____ Collocated VOR navigational facility and UHF standard distance measuring equipment
VORTAC _____ Collocated VOR and TACAN navigational facilities
W _____ Without voice on radio facility frequency.
Z _____ VHF station location marker at a LF radio facility

LEGEND 9.–Airport/Facility Directory.

APPENDIX B - FAA PRIVATE PILOT EXAM CROSS-REFERENCE GUIDE

Appendix B lists all of the questions that appear in the Private Pilot Question Book (FAA-T-8080-1B). The questions that are cross-referenced apply to all aircraft, airplanes, and powered aircraft. These are the only questions that may be assigned on the Private Pilot Written Exam (Airplane). All other questions are designated "N.A." Each FAA exam question is cross-referenced to the appropriate chapter and item number in the study guide.

Periodically, the FAA publishes a list of items that are unusable for test purposes and that have been removed from the FAA Question Selection Sheets. Such items are underlined in the following list.

FAA	Ch Item	FAA	Ch Item	FAA	Ch Item	FAA	Ch Item
1001	4-20	1026	6-6	1051	3-30	1076	4-15
1002	4-21	1027	4-33	1052	3-31	1077	4-17
1003	4-22/6-1	1028	6-7	1053	4-42	1078	4-18
1004	4-23	1029	4-34	1054	4-44	1079	4-16
1005	4-24	1030	3-27	1055	4-45	1080	4-19
1006	6-2	1031	3-19	1056	4-43	1081	4-4
1007	6-3	1032	3-23	1057	4-37	1082	4-2
1008	6-4	1033	3-24	1058	4-39	1083	4-3
1009	4-25	1034	3-25	1059	N.A.	1084	2-1
1010	4-26	1035	3-22	1060	4-35	1085	2-3
1011	4-27	1036	3-26	1061	4-38	1086	2-2
1012	4-28	1037	3-32	1062	4-36	1087	2-4
1013	4-29	1038	3-9	1063	4-40	1088	2-17
1014	4-30	1039	3-10	1064	4-41	1089	2-6
1015	4-31	1040	3-8	1065	4-5	1090	2-5
1016	6-13	1041	3-28	1066	4-11	1091	2-13
1017	6-8	1042	3-17	1067	4-13	1092	2-14
1018	6-11	1043	3-11	1068	4-1	1093	2-15
1019	6-10	1044	3-13	1069	4-12	1094	2-16
1020	6-14	1045	3-12	1070	4-14	1095	2-31
1021	6-12	1046	3-14	1071	4-9	1096	2-9
1022	6-9	1047	3-18	1072	4-7	1097	2-18
1023	6-15	1048	3-15	1073	4-6	1098	2-10
1024	4-32	1049	3-16	1074	4-8	1099	2-11
1025	6-5	1050	3-29	1075	4-10	1100	2-12

FAA	Ch Item	FAA	Ch Item	FAA	Ch Item	FAA	Ch Item
1101	2-19	1126	N.A.	1151	15-2	1176	N.A.
1102	5-18	1127	N.A.	1152	N.A.	1177	N.A.
1103	5-19	1128	N.A.	1153	N.A.	1178	N.A.
1104	5-21	1129	N.A.	1154	N.A.	1179	N.A.
1105	5-20	1130	N.A.	1155	N.A.	1180	N.A.
1106	8-35	1131	N.A.	1156	N.A.	1181	N.A.
1107	2-32	1132	N.A.	1157	N.A.	1182	N.A.
1108	3-20	1133	N.A.	1158	N.A.	1183	N.A.
1109	3-21	1134	N.A.	1159	N.A.	1184	N.A.
1110	2-33	1135	N.A.	1160	N.A.	1185	N.A.
1111	2-7	1136	N.A.	1161	N.A.	1186	N.A.
1112	2-8	1137	N.A.	1162	N.A.	1187	N.A.
1113	2-35	1138	N.A.	1163	N.A.	1188	N.A.
1114	2-34	1139	N.A.	1164	N.A.	1189	N.A.
1115	2-21	1140	N.A.	1165	N.A.	1190	N.A.
1116	2-22	1141	N.A.	1166	N.A.	1191	12-6
1117	2-23	1142	N.A.	1167	N.A.	1192	12-9
1118	2-20	1143	N.A.	1168	N.A.	1193	12-7
1119	7-66	1144	N.A.	1169	N.A.	1194	12-10
1120	7-67	1145	N.A.	1170	N.A.	1195	12-8
1121	7-68	1146	N.A.	1171	N.A.	1196	12-11
1122	7-69	1147	N.A.	1172	N.A.	1197	12-26
1123	7-65	1148	N.A.	1173	N.A.	1198	12-12
1124	7-64	1149	N.A.	1174	N.A.	1199	12-13
1125	7-70	1150	N.A.	1175	N.A.	1200	12-14

FAA	Ch Item	FAA	Ch Item	FAA	Ch Item	FAA	Ch Item
1201	12-15	1226	12-30	1251	12-55	1276	13-1
1202	12-16	1227	12-31	1252	12-56	1277	13-2
1203	12-17	1228	12-32	1253	12-57	1278	13-15
1204	12-18	1229	12-33	1254	12-58	1279	13-3
1205	12-19	1230	12-34	1255	12-59	1280	13-4
1206	12-20	1231	12-35	1256	12-60	1281	13-5
1207	12-21	1232	12-36	1257	12-61	1282	13-6
1208	12-22	1233	12-37	1258	12-62	1283	13-7
1209	12-23	1234	12-38	1259	12-78	1284	13-8
1210	12-24	1235	12-39	1260	12-64	1285	13-9
1211	7-50	1236	12-40	1261	12-65	1286	13-10
1212	7-45	1237	12-41	1262	12-66	1287	13-11
1213	7-46	1238	12-42	1263	12-67	1288	13-12
1214	7-47	1239	12-43	1264	12-68	1289	13-13
1215	7-48	1240	12-44	1265	12-69	1290	13-14
1216	7-49	1241	12-45	1266	12-70	1291	13-26
1217	12-1	1242	12-46	1267	12-71	1292	13-27
1218	12-2	1243	12-47	1268	12-72	1293	13-28
1219	12-4	1244	12-48	1269	12-73	1294	13-29
1220	12-5	1245	12-49	1270	12-74	1295	13-30
1221	12-3	1246	12-50	1271	12-75	1296	13-31
1222	12-25	1247	12-51	1272	12-63	1297	13-32
1223	12-27	1248	12-52	1273	12-76	1298	13-33
1224	12-28	1249	12-53	1274	12-77	1299	13-34
1225	12-29	1250	12-54	1275	13-16	1300	13-18

FAA	Ch Item	FAA	Ch Item	FAA	Ch Item	FAA	Ch Item
1301	13-17	1326	9-55	1351	6-28	1376	5-4
1302	13-19	1327	9-57	1352	6-29	1377	5-7
1303	13-20	1328	9-56	1353	6-30	1378	5-8
1304	13-21	1329	9-61	1354	6-31	1379	5-9
1305	13-22	1330	9-62	1355	6-22	1380	5-5
1306	13-23	1331	6-16	1356	6-23	1381	5-6
1307	13-24	1332	6-18	1357	6-24	1382	5-11
1308	13-25	1333	6-20	1358	6-25	1383	5-13
1309	N.A.	1334	6-19	1359	6-26	1384	5-10
1310	N.A.	1335	6-21	1360	6-27	1385	5-14
1311	N.A.	1336	6-17	1361	N.A.	1386	5-12
1312	N.A.	1337	6-36	1362	N.A.	1387	5-15
1313	N.A.	1338	6-37	1363	N.A.	1388	5-16
1314	N.A.	1339	6-38	1364	N.A.	1389	5-17
1315	N.A.	1340	6-39	1365	N.A.	1390	N.A.
1316	N.A.	1341	6-40	1366	N.A.	1391	N.A.
1317	N.A.	1342	N.A.	1367	6-32	1392	N.A.
1318	N.A.	1343	N.A.	1368	6-33	1393	N.A.
1319	N.A.	1344	N.A.	1369	6-34	1394	N.A.
1320	N.A.	1345	N.A.	1370	6-35	1395	N.A.
1321	N.A.	1346	N.A.	1371	N.A.	1396	N.A.
1322	N.A.	1347	N.A.	1372	N.A.	1397	N.A.
1323	N.A.	1348	N.A.	1373	5-1	1398	N.A.
1324	N.A.	1349	N.A.	1374	5-2	1399	N.A.
1325	N.A.	1350	N.A.	1375	5-3	1400	N.A.

FAA	Ch Item	FAA	Ch Item	FAA	Ch Item	FAA	Ch Item
1401	N.A.	1426	2-27	1451	7-18	1476	14-3
1402	N.A.	1427	2-25	1452	7-19	1477	7-55
1403	N.A.	1428	2-29	1453	7-20	1478	7-56
1404	N.A.	1429	2-28	1454	7-5	1479	7-51
1405	N.A.	1430	2-30	1455	7-6	1480	7-52
1406	N.A.	1431	7-58	1456	7-8	1481	7-53
1407	N.A.	1432	7-59	1457	7-9	1482	7-54
1408	N.A.	1433	7-60	1458	7-15	1483	9-63
1409	N.A.	1434	7-57	1459	7-16	1484	16-8
1410	N.A.	1435	15-18	1460	7-7	1485	16-2
1411	N.A.	1436	7-11	1461	7-10	1486	16-3
1412	N.A.	1437	7-12	1462	7-33	1487	16-5
1413	7-61	1438	7-13	1463	7-34	1488	10-3
1414	7-62	1439	7-14	1464	7-35	1489	10-4
1415	7-63	1440	7-1	1465	7-36	1490	10-1
1416	3-2	1441	7-3	1466	7-37	1491	10-2
1417	3-1	1442	N.A.	1467	7-39	1492	10-5
1418	3-3	1443	7-4	1468	7-38	1493	15-12
1419	3-4	1444	7-2	1469	7-40	1494	15-13
1420	3-5	1445	7-17	1470	7-41	1495	15-17
1421	3-6	1446	7-21	1471	7-42	1496	15-19
1422	3-7	1447	7-22	1472	7-27	1497	14-1
1423	16-1	1448	7-23	1473	7-28	1498	14-2
1424	2-24	1449	7-24	1474	7-26	1499	14-4
1425	2-26	1450	7-25	1475	7-29	1500	14-5

FAA	Ch Item	FAA	Ch Item	FAA	Ch Item	FAA	Ch Item
1501	14-6	1526	N.A.	1551	N.A.	1576	15-1
1502	13-35	1527	N.A.	1552	N.A.	1577	15-3
1503	13-36	1528	N.A.	1553	N.A.	1578	15-5
1504	13-37	1529	N.A.	1554	N.A.	1579	15-4
1505	16-6	1530	N.A.	1555	N.A.	1580	15-6
1506	16-7	1531	N.A.	1556	N.A.	1581	15-7
1507	7-30	1532	N.A.	1557	N.A.	1582	15-9
1508	10-6	1533	N.A.	1558	N.A.	1583	15-10
1509	N.A.	1534	N.A.	1559	N.A.	1584	15-8
1510	N.A.	1535	N.A.	1560	N.A.	1585	15-16
1511	N.A.	1536	N.A.	1561	N.A.	1586	15-11
1512	N.A.	1537	N.A.	1562	N.A.	1587	15-14
1513	N.A.	1538	N.A.	1563	N.A.	1588	15-15
1514	N.A.	1539	N.A.	1564	N.A.	1589	11-145
1515	N.A.	1540	N.A.	1565	N.A.	1590	11-146
1516	N.A.	1541	N.A.	1566	N.A.	1591	11-147
1517	N.A.	1542	N.A.	1567	N.A.	1592	11-148
1518	N.A.	1543	N.A.	1568	N.A.	1593	11-149
1519	N.A.	1544	N.A.	1569	N.A.	1594	11-151
1520	N.A.	1545	N.A.	1570	N.A.	1595	11-152
1521	N.A.	1546	N.A.	1571	N.A.	1596	11-150
1522	N.A.	1547	N.A.	1572	N.A.	1597	1-1
1523	N.A.	1548	N.A.	1573	N.A.	1598	1-2
1524	N.A.	1549	N.A.	1574	N.A.	1599	1-3
1525	N.A.	1550	N.A.	1575	N.A.	1600	1-4

FAA	Ch Item	FAA	Ch Item	FAA	Ch Item	FAA	Ch Item
1601	11-3	1626	11-23	1651	11-42	1676	11-60
1602	11-1	1627	11-24	1652	11-44	1677	11-62
1603	11-2	1628	11-19	1653	11-46	1678	11-61
1604	11-4	1629	11-20	1654	N.A.	1679	16-4
1605	11-8	1630	11-25	1655	11-47	1680	11-63
1606	11-7	1631	11-21	1656	11-48	1681	11-66
1607	11-5	1632	11-22	1657	11-45	1682	11-70
1608	11-6	1633	11-26	1658	11-50	1683	11-64
1609	7-43	1634	11-27	1659	11-49	1684	11-67
1610	7-44	1635	11-28	1660	N.A.	1685	11-65
1611	7-31	1636	11-29	1661	N.A.	1686	11-68
1612	7-32	1637	11-30	1662	N.A.	1687	11-69
1613	N.A.	1638	11-31	1663	N.A.	1688	11-71
1614	11-9	1639	11-33	1664	N.A.	1689	11-74
1615	N.A.	1640	N.A.	1665	N.A.	1690	11-72
1616	11-10	1641	11-32	1666	11-52	1691	11-73
1617	11-11	1642	11-34	1667	11-51	1692	11-75
1618	11-12	1643	11-38	1668	N.A.	1693	11-76
1619	11-13	1644	11-36	1669	11-53	1694	11-77
1620	11-14	1645	11-37	1670	11-54	1695	11-78
1621	N.A.	1646	11-35	1671	11-55	1696	11-79
1622	11-15	1647	11-39	1672	11-56	1697	11-80
1623	11-16	1648	11-40	1673	11-58	1698	11-81
1624	11-17	1649	11-41	1674	11-57	1699	11-82
1625	11-18	1650	11-43	1675	11-59	1700	11-83

FAA	Ch Item	FAA	Ch Item	FAA	Ch Item	FAA	Ch Item
1701	11-84	1726	11-115	1751	11-133	1776	8-3
1702	11-85	1727	11-111	1752	11-134	1777	8-4
1703	11-86	1728	11-108	1753	11-135	1778	8-36
1704	11-87	1729	11-116	1754	11-136	1779	8-6
1705	11-88	1730	11-120	1755	11-131	1780	8-9
1706	11-89	1731	11-121	1756	11-137	1781	8-10
1707	11-90	1732	11-117	1757	11-138	1782	8-49
1708	11-91	1733	11-118	1758	11-139	1783	8-11
1709	11-95	1734	11-112	1759	11-140	1784	8-12
1710	11-92	1735	11-109	1760	11-141	1785	8-15
1711	11-93	1736	11-119	1761	11-143	1786	8-19
1712	11-94	1737	11-113	1762	11-144	1787	8-20
1713	11-97	1738	11-114	1763	11-142	1788	N.A.
1714	11-98	1739	11-110	1764	8-26	1789	8-46
1715	11-96	1740	11-122	1765	8-21	1790	8-37
1716	11-99	1741	11-124	1766	8-22	1791	8-43
1717	11-101	1742	11-125	1767	8-23	1792	8-44
1718	11-100	1743	11-123	1768	8-24	1793	8-45
1719	N.A.	1744	N.A.	1769	8-7	1794	8-16
1720	11-103	1745	11-126	1770	8-8	1795	8-17
1721	11-102	1746	11-127	1771	8-1	1796	8-13
1722	11-104	1747	11-128	1772	8-25	1797	8-18
1723	11-106	1748	11-129	1773	N.A.	1798	8-58
1724	11-105	1749	11-130	1774	8-5	1799	8-59
1725	11-107	1750	11-132	1775	8-2	1800	8-14

FAA	Ch Item	FAA	Ch Item	FAA	Ch Item	FAA	Ch Item
1801	8-57	1826	N.A.	1851	9-45	1876	N.A.
1802	8-38	1827	N.A.	1852	9-47	1877	N.A.
1803	8-41	1828	9-35	1853	9-46	1878	N.A.
1804	8-39	1829	9-36	1854	9-18	1879	N.A.
1805	8-40	1830	9-52	1855	9-19	1880	9-23
1806	8-30	1831	9-53	1856	9-20	1881	9-25
1807	8-31	1832	9-54	1857	9-21	1882	9-24
1808	8-33	1833	9-58	1858	9-22	1883	9-26
1809	8-32	1834	9-59	1859	9-29	1884	9-27
1810	8-34	1835	9-60	1860	9-30	1885	9-12
1811	8-50	1836	9-48	1861	9-31	1886	9-13
1812	8-51	1837	9-49	1862	9-33	1887	9-14
1813	8-55	1838	9-50	1863	9-34	1888	9-15
1814	8-48	1839	9-51	1864	9-32	1889	9-16
1815	8-52	1840	9-11	1865	9-1		
1816	8-53	1841	9-42	1866	9-2		
1817	8-47	1842	9-37	1867	9-3		
1818	8-56	1843	9-17	1868	9-4		
1819	8-54	1844	9-28	1869	9-5		
1820	8-42	1845	9-38	1870	9-7		
1821	8-27	1846	9-40	1871	9-6		
1822	8-29	1847	9-39	1872	9-8		
1823	8-28	1848	9-41	1873	9-9		
1824	N.A.	1849	9-43	1874	9-10		
1825	N.A.	1850	9-44	1875	N.A.		

DENSITY ALTITUDE CHART

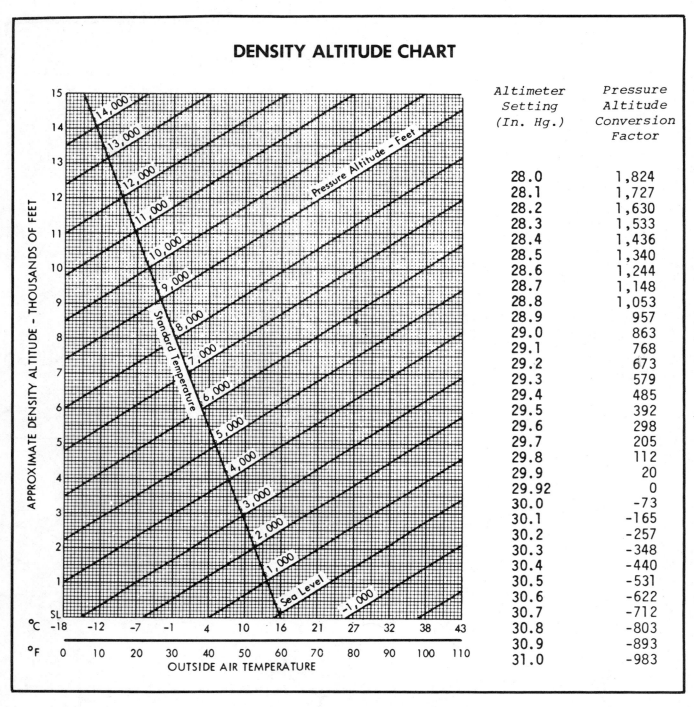

Altimeter Setting (In. Hg.)	Pressure Altitude Conversion Factor
28.0	1,824
28.1	1,727
28.2	1,630
28.3	1,533
28.4	1,436
28.5	1,340
28.6	1,244
28.7	1,148
28.8	1,053
28.9	957
29.0	863
29.1	768
29.2	673
29.3	579
29.4	485
29.5	392
29.6	298
29.7	205
29.8	112
29.9	20
29.92	0
30.0	-73
30.1	-165
30.2	-257
30.3	-348
30.4	-440
30.5	-531
30.6	-622
30.7	-712
30.8	-803
30.9	-893
31.0	-983

FIGURE 1.–Density Altitude Chart.

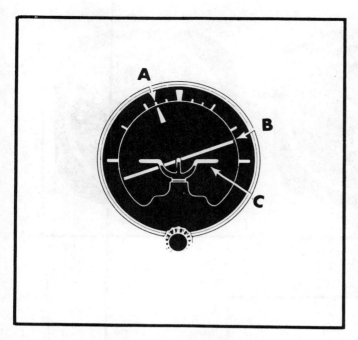

FIGURE 2.–Attitude Indicator.

FIGURE 4.–Direction Indicator.

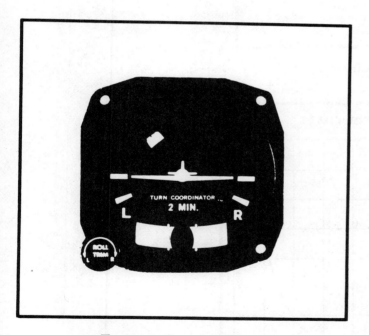

FIGURE 3.–Turn Coordinator.

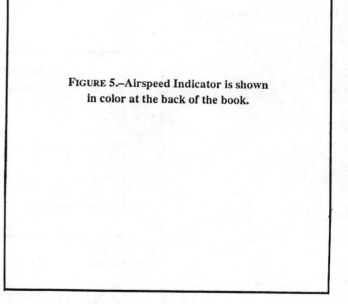

FIGURE 5.–Airspeed Indicator is shown
in color at the back of the book.

FIGURE 5.–Airspeed Indicator.

FIGURE 6.–Altimeter.

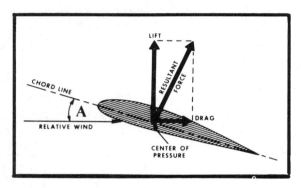

FIGURE 7.–Lift Vector.

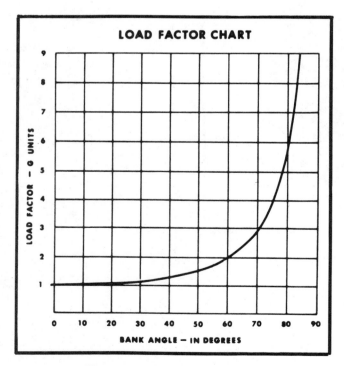

FIGURE 8.–Load Factor Chart.

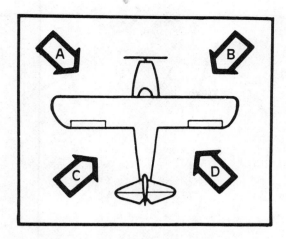

FIGURE 9.—Control Position for Taxi.

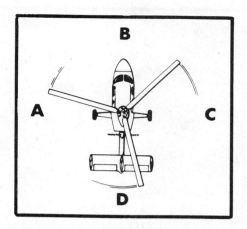

FIGURE 10.—Gyroplane Rotor Blade Position.

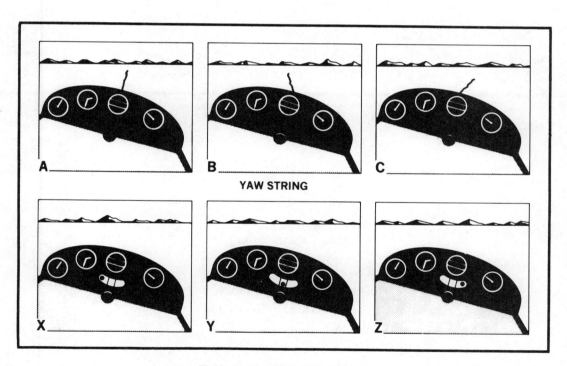

FIGURE 11.—Glider Yaw String.

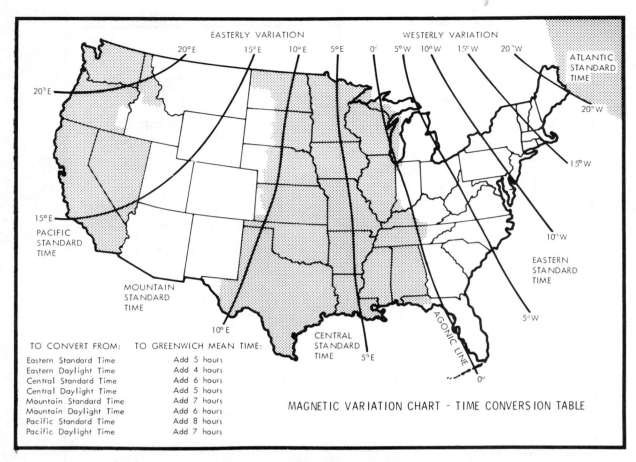

FIGURE 12.–Time Conversion Table.

The following figures are shown in color
at the end of the book:

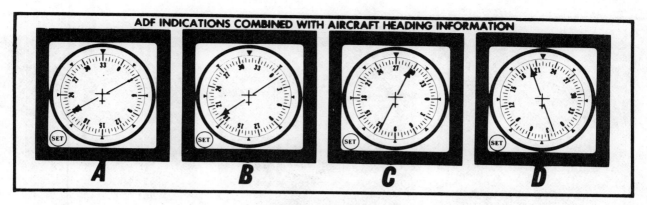

FIGURE 20.–ADF Indicator.

COEUR D'ALENE

§ **COEUR D'ALENE AIR TERM** (COE) 9 NW UTC-8(-7DT) 47°46'28"N 116°49'05"W | GREAT FALLS
2318 B S4 FUEL 80, 100, JET A | H-1B, L-9A
RWY 14-32: H5400X140 (ASPH) S-57, D-95, DT-165 | IAP
RWY 14: Fence. RWY 32: Fence.
RWY 05-23: H5400X140 (ASPH) S-57, D-95, DT-165 HIRL .7% up NE
RWY 05: MALSR. RWY 23: REIL. VASI(V4L)—GA 3.0°TCH 39'.
RWY 01-19: H5400X75 (ASPH) S-50, D-83, DT-150
RWY 01: Rgt tfc.
AIRPORT REMARKS: Attended dalgt hrs. ACTIVATE HIRL Rwy 05–23; MALSR Rwy 05—122.8. Rwy 14-32 no snow
removal. Ultralight activity permitted on the first 1000' of Rwy 14 with PPR from arpt manager call (208) 772-7838.
Control Zone effective 1500-0300Z‡ Mon-Fri.
COMMUNICATIONS: CTAF 119.1 UNICOM 122.8
SPOKANE FSS (SFF) LC 664-9891 NOTAM FILE COE
RCO 122.1R, 108.8T (SPOKANE FSS)
Ⓡ SPOKANE APP/DEP CON 125.8
TOWER 119.1 (1700-2300Z‡ weekends.) GND CON 121.8
RADIO AIDS TO NAVIGATION: NOTAM FILE COE.
SPOKANE (H) VORTAC 115.5 GEG Chan 102 47°33'54"N 117°37'33"W 048°35.1 NM to fld. 2760/21E.
NOTAM FILE GEG.
(T) VOR 108.8 COE 47°46'26"N 116°49'11"W at fld.
LEENY NDB (LOM) 347 CO 47°44'35"N 116°57'36"W 050°5.6 NM to fld.
ILS 110.7 I-COE Rwy 05 LOM LEENY NDB Glide slope unusable below 2470'.

FIGURE 21.–Airport/Facility Directory Excerpt.

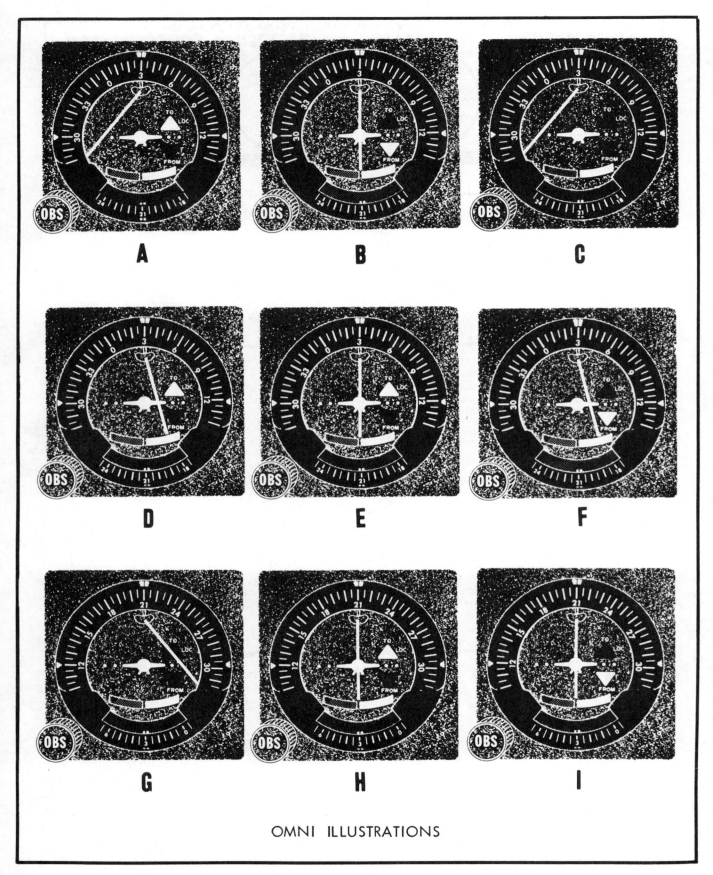

OMNI ILLUSTRATIONS

FIGURE 22.–Omni Illustrations.

Appendix C - 8

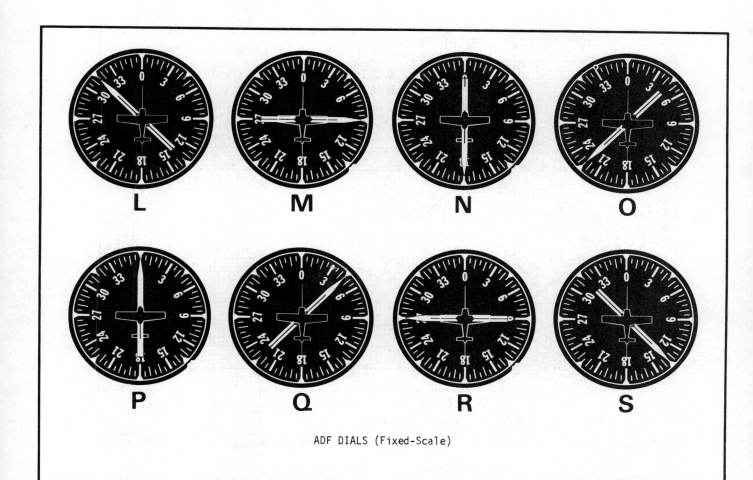

ADF DIALS (Fixed-Scale)

FIGURE 23.–ADF Dials.

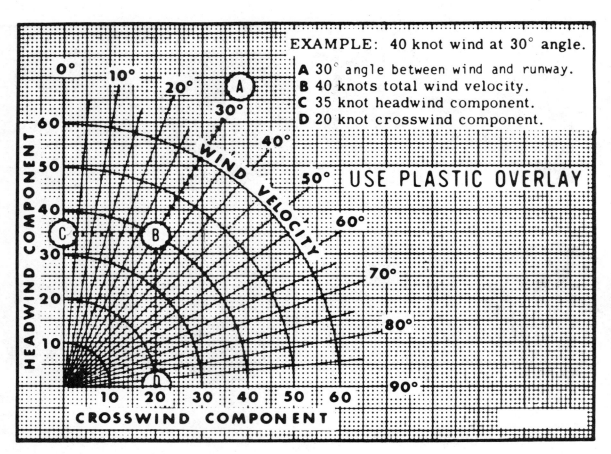

FIGURE 24.–Crosswind Component Graph.

CRUISE POWER SETTINGS

65% MAXIMUM CONTINUOUS POWER (OR FULL THROTTLE)
2800 LBS

PRESS ALT.	IOAT		ENGINE SPEED	MAN. PRESS	FUEL FLOW PER ENGINE		TAS		IOAT		ENGINE SPEED	MAN. PRESS	FUEL FLOW PER ENGINE		TAS		IOAT		ENGINE SPEED	MAN. PRESS	FUEL FLOW PER ENGINE		TAS	
FEET	°F	°C	RPM	IN HG	PSI	GPH	KTS	MPH	°F	°C	RPM	IN HG	PSI	GPH	KTS	MPH	°F	°C	RPM	IN HG	PSI	GPH	KTS	MPH
SL	27	-3	2450	20.7	6.6	11.5	147	169	63	17	2450	21.2	6.6	11.5	150	173	99	37	2450	21.8	6.6	11.5	153	176
2000	19	-7	2450	20.4	6.6	11.5	149	171	55	13	2450	21.0	6.6	11.5	153	176	91	33	2450	21.5	6.6	11.5	156	180
4000	12	-11	2450	20.1	6.6	11.5	152	175	48	9	2450	20.7	6.6	11.5	156	180	84	29	2450	21.3	6.6	11.5	159	183
6000	5	-15	2450	19.8	6.6	11.5	155	178	41	5	2450	20.4	6.6	11.5	158	182	79	26	2450	21.0	6.6	11.5	161	185
8000	-2	-19	2450	19.5	6.6	11.5	157	181	36	2	2450	20.2	6.6	11.5	161	185	72	22	2450	20.8	6.6	11.5	164	189
10000	-8	-22	2450	19.2	6.6	11.5	160	184	28	-2	2450	19.9	6.6	11.5	163	188	64	18	2450	20.3	6.5	11.4	166	191
12000	-15	-26	2450	18.8	6.4	11.3	162	186	21	-6	2450	18.8	6.1	10.9	163	188	57	14	2450	18.8	5.9	10.6	163	188
14000	-22	-30	2450	17.4	5.8	10.5	159	183	14	-10	2450	17.4	5.6	10.1	160	184	50	10	2450	17.4	5.4	9.8	160	184
16000	-29	-34	2450	16.1	5.3	9.7	156	180	7	-14	2450	16.1	5.1	9.4	156	180	43	6	2450	16.1	4.9	9.1	155	178

NOTES   1. Full throttle manifold pressure settings are approximate.
        2. Shaded area represents operation with full throttle.

FIGURE 25.–Airplane Power Setting Table.

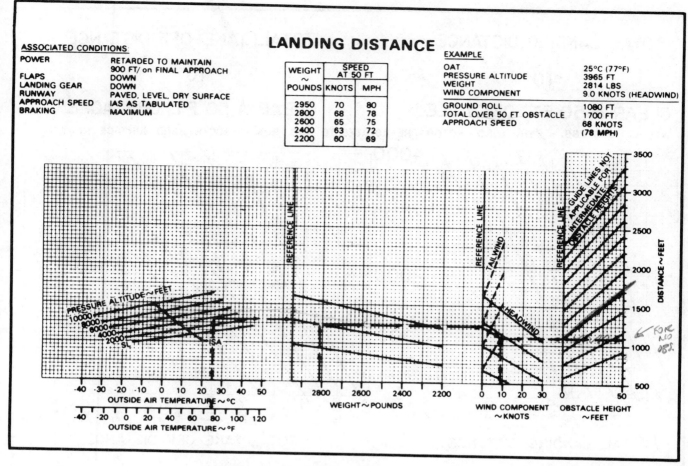

LANDING DISTANCE

WEIGHT ~ POUNDS	SPEED AT 50 FT KNOTS	SPEED AT 50 FT MPH
2950	70	80
2800	68	78
2600	65	75
2400	63	72
2200	60	69

EXAMPLE

OAT	25°C (77°F)
PRESSURE ALTITUDE	3965 FT
WEIGHT	2814 LBS
WIND COMPONENT	9 0 KNOTS (HEADWIND)
GROUND ROLL	1080 FT
TOTAL OVER 50 FT OBSTACLE	1700 FT
APPROACH SPEED	68 KNOTS (78 MPH)

FIGURE 28.–Airplane Landing Distance Graph.

LANDING DISTANCE		FLAPS LOWERED TO 40° - POWER OFF HARD SURFACE RUNWAY - ZERO WIND							
GROSS WEIGHT LBS.	APPROACH SPEED, IAS, MPH	AT SEA LEVEL & 59° F.		AT 2500 FT. & 50° F.		AT 5000 FT. & 41° F.		AT 7500 FT. & 32° F.	
		GROUND ROLL	TOTAL TO CLEAR 50 FT. OBS	GROUND ROLL	TOTAL TO CLEAR 50 FT. OBS	GROUND ROLL	TOTAL TO CLEAR 50 FT. OBS	GROUND ROLL	TOTAL TO CLEAR 50 FT. OBS
1600	60	445	1075	470	1135	495	1195	520	1255

NOTES: 1. Decrease the distances shown by 10% for each 4 knots of headwind.
2. Increase the distance by 10% for each 60°F. temperature increase above standard.
3. For operation on a dry, grass runway, increase distances (both "ground roll" and "total to clear 50 ft. obstacle") by 20% of the "total to clear 50 ft. obstacle" figure.

FIGURE 29.–Airplane Landing Distance Table.

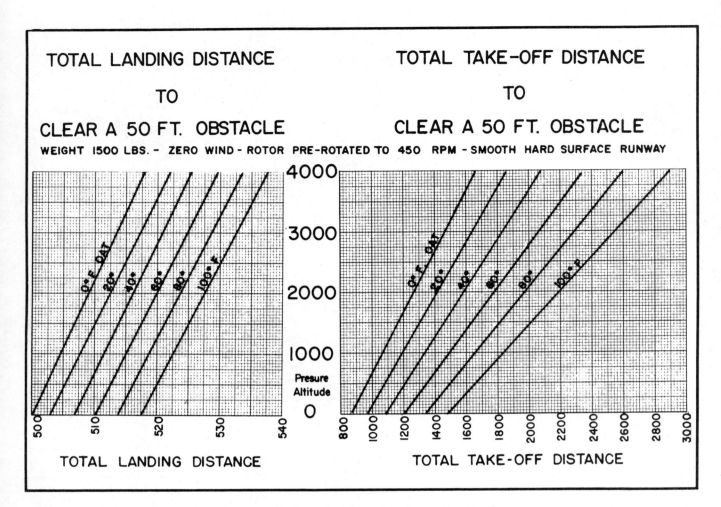

FIGURE 30.—Gyroplane Takeoff and Landing Graphs.

TAKE-OFF DISTANCE

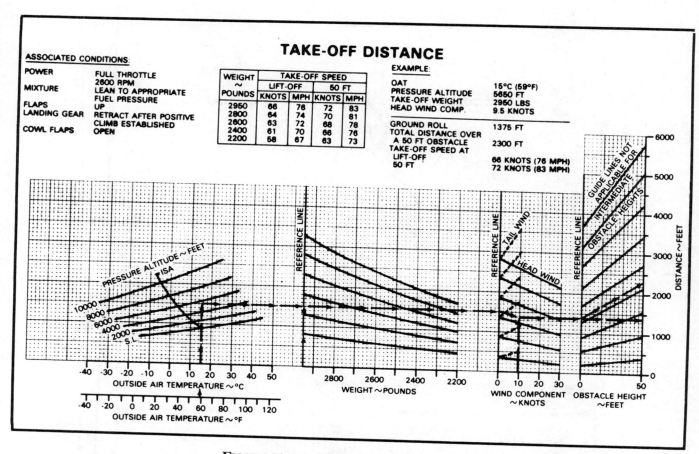

ASSOCIATED CONDITIONS:

POWER	FULL THROTTLE 2600 RPM
MIXTURE	LEAN TO APPROPRIATE FUEL PRESSURE
FLAPS	UP
LANDING GEAR	RETRACT AFTER POSITIVE CLIMB ESTABLISHED
COWL FLAPS	OPEN

WEIGHT ~ POUNDS	TAKE-OFF SPEED			
	LIFT-OFF		50 FT	
	KNOTS	MPH	KNOTS	MPH
2950	66	76	72	83
2800	64	74	70	81
2600	63	72	68	78
2400	61	70	66	76
2200	58	67	63	73

EXAMPLE:

OAT	15°C (59°F)
PRESSURE ALTITUDE	5650 FT
TAKE-OFF WEIGHT	2950 LBS
HEAD WIND COMP.	9.5 KNOTS
GROUND ROLL	1375 FT
TOTAL DISTANCE OVER A 50 FT OBSTACLE	2300 FT
TAKE-OFF SPEED AT LIFT-OFF	66 KNOTS (76 MPH)
50 FT	72 KNOTS (83 MPH)

FIGURE 31.–Airplane Takeoff Distance Graph.

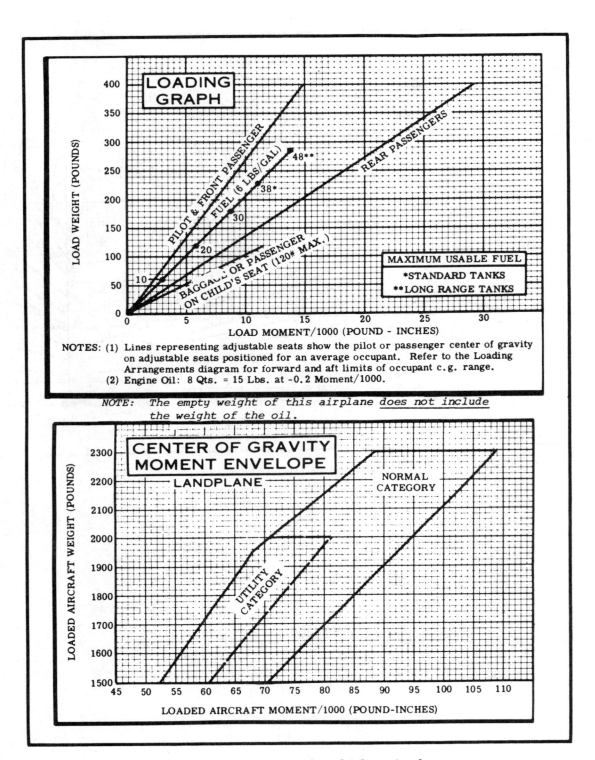

FIGURE 33.–Airplane Weight and Balance Graphs.

USEFUL LOAD WEIGHTS AND MOMENTS

OCCUPANTS

FRONT SEATS ARM 85		REAR SEATS ARM 121	
Weight	Moment/100	Weight	Moment/100
120	102	120	145
130	110	130	157
140	119	140	169
150	128	150	182
160	136	160	194
170	144	170	206
180	153	180	218
190	162	190	230
200	170	200	242

USABLE FUEL

MAIN WING TANKS ARM 75

Gallons	Weight	Moment/100
5	30	22
10	60	45
15	90	68
20	120	90
25	150	112
30	180	135
35	210	158
40	240	180
44	264	198

AUXILIARY WING TANKS ARM 94

Gallons	Weight	Moment/100
5	30	28
10	60	56
15	90	85
19	114	107

*OIL

Quarts	Weight	Moment/100
10	19	5

*Included in Basic Empty Weight

BAGGAGE OR 5TH SEAT OCCUPANT ARM 140

Weight	Moment/100
10	14
20	28
30	42
40	56
50	70
60	84
70	98
80	112
90	126
100	140
110	154
120	168
130	182
140	196
150	210
160	224
170	238
180	252
190	266
200	280
210	294
220	308
230	322
240	336
250	350
260	364
270	378

Empty Weight ~2015

MOM/100 ~1554

MOMENT LIMITS vs WEIGHT

Moment limits are based on the following weight and center of gravity limit data (landing gear down).

WEIGHT CONDITION	FORWARD CG LIMIT	AFT CG LIMIT
2950 lb. (take-off or landing)	82.1	84.7
2525 lb.	77.5	85.7
2475 lb. or less	77.0	85.7

FIGURE 34.–Airplane Weight and Balance Tables.

MOMENT LIMITS vs WEIGHT (Continued)

Weight	Minimum Moment 100	Maximum Moment 100	Weight	Minimum Moment 100	Maximum Moment 100
2100	1617	1800	2600	2037	2224
2110	1625	1808	2610	2048	2232
2120	1632	1817	2620	2058	2239
2130	1640	1825	2630	2069	2247
2140	1648	1834	2640	2080	2255
2150	1656	1843	2650	2090	2263
2160	1663	1851	2660	2101	2271
2170	1671	1860	2670	2112	2279
2180	1679	1868	2680	2123	2287
2190	1686	1877	2690	2133	2295
2200	1694	1885	2700	2144	2303
2210	1702	1894	2710	2155	2311
2220	1709	1903	2720	2166	2319
2230	1717	1911	2730	2177	2326
2240	1725	1920	2740	2188	2334
2250	1733	1928	2750	2199	2342
2260	1740	1937	2760	2210	2350
2270	1748	1945	2770	2221	2358
2280	1756	1954	2780	2232	2366
2290	1763	1963	2790	2243	2374
2300	1771	1971			
2310	1779	1980	2800	2254	2381
2320	1786	1988	2810	2265	2389
2330	1794	1997	2820	2276	2397
2340	1802	2005	2830	2287	2405
2350	1810	2014	2840	2298	2413
2360	1817	2023	2850	2309	2421
2370	1825	2031	2860	2320	2428
2380	1833	2040	2870	2332	2436
2390	1840	2048	2880	2343	2444
2400	1848	2057	2890	2354	2452
2410	1856	2065	2900	2365	2460
2420	1863	2074	2910	2377	2468
2430	1871	2083	2920	2388	2475
2440	1879	2091	2930	2399	2483
2450	1887	2100	2940	2411	2491
2460	1894	2108	2950	2422	2499
2470	1902	2117			
2480	1911	2125			
2490	1921	2134			
2500	1932	2143			
2510	1942	2151			
2520	1953	2160			
2530	1963	2168			
2540	1974	2176			
2550	1984	2184			
2560	1995	2192			
2570	2005	2200			
2580	2016	2208			
2590	2026	2216			

FIGURE 35.–Airplane Weight and Balance Tables.

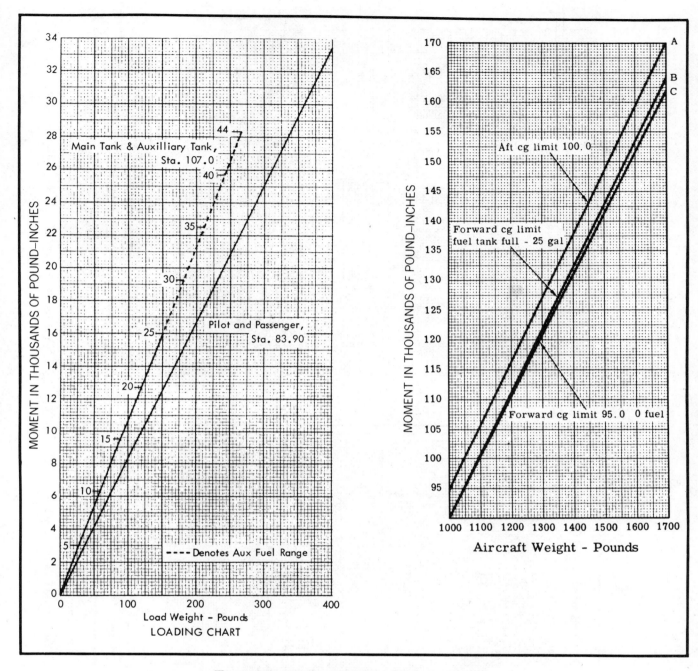

FIGURE 37.–Airplane Weight and Balance Graphs.

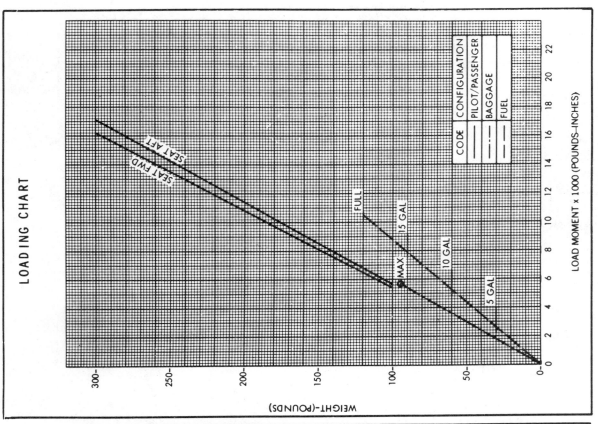

FIGURE 40.–Airplane Weight and Balance Graphs.

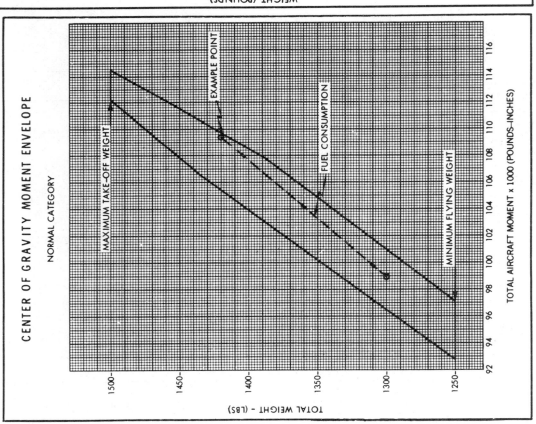

FIGURE 39.–Aiplane Weight and Balance Graphs.

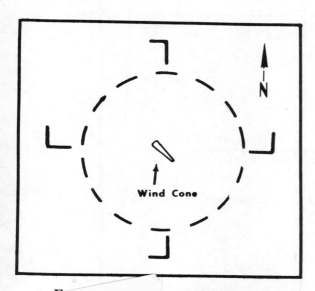

F... Landing Indicator.

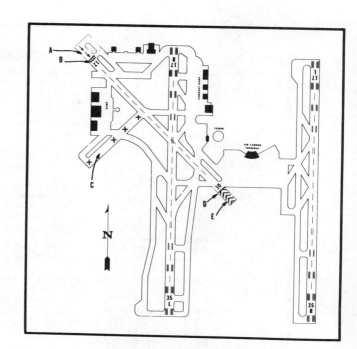

FIGURE 45.–Airport Diagram.

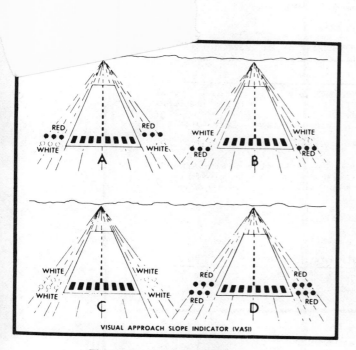

FIGURE 44.–VASI Illustrations.

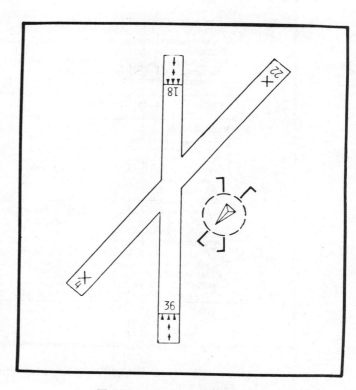

FIGURE 46.–Airport Diagram.

NEBRASKA

§ **LINCOLN MUNI** (LNK) 4 NW UTC–6(–5DT) 40°51′03″N 96°45′32″W **OMAHA**
H-1D, 3A, L-11B
IAP

1214 B S4 **FUEL** 100, 100LL, JET A1 TPA—3214 (2200) CFR Index C
RWY 17R-35L: H12901X200 (ASPH-CONC-AFSC) S-100, D-200, DT-400 HIRL
  RWY 17R: MALSR. VASI(V4L)—GA 3.0° TCH 55′. Rgt tfc. Arrest device.
  RWY 35L: MALSR. VASI(V4L)—GA 3.0° TCH 55′. Arrest device.
RWY 14-32: H8620X150 (ASPH-CONC-GRVD) S-80, D-170, DT-280 MIRL
  RWY 14: REIL. VASI(4VL)—GA 3.0°TCH 48′.
  RWY 32: VASI(4VL)—GA 3.0°TCH 53′. Thld dsplcd 442′. Pole.
RWY 17L-35R: H5500X100 (ASPH-CONC-AFSC) S-49, D-60 HIRL .8% up N
  RWY 17L: VASI(V4L)—GA 3.0°TCH 33′.
  RWY 35R: VASI(V4L)—GA 3.0°TCH 35′. Light standard. Rgt tfc.
AIRPORT REMARKS: Attended continuously. Arresting barrier located 2200′ in from thld 17R and 1500′ in from thld 35L.
  Arresting barrier in place departure end Rwy 17R-35L during military operations and approach end during
  emergencies. Airport manager advise 43000 lbs GWT single wheel Rwy 17L-35R. For MALSR Rwy 17R and 35L ctc
  Twr.; When Twr clsd MALSR Rwy 17R and 35L preset to Med intst.
WEATHER DATA SOURCES: LLWAS
COMMUNICATIONS: CTAF 118.5 **ATIS** 118.05 **UNICOM** 122.95
  LINCOLN FSS (LNK) on arpt. 122.2 LC 477-3929. Toll free call dial 1–800–WX–BRIEF. (1200-0300Z‡). NOTAM FILE
   LNK.
  COLUMBUS FSS (OLU) Toll Free call, dial 1–800–WX–BRIEF. (0300–1200Z‡)
  RCO 122.65 122.1R 116.1T (COLUMBUS FSS)
Ⓡ **APP/DEP CON** 124.0 (170°-349°) 124.8 (350°-169°) (1200-0600Z‡)
Ⓡ **MINNEAPOLIS CENTER APP/DEP CON** 128.75 (0600-1200Z‡)
  TOWER 118.5 125.7 (1200-0600Z‡) **GND CON** 121.9 **CLNC DEL** 120.7
  STAGE III ctc **APP CON**
RADIO AIDS TO NAVIGATION: NOTAM FILE LNK. VHF/DF ctc LINCOLN FSS
  (H) VORTAC 116.1 LNK Chan 108 40°55′26″N 96°44′30″W 185°3.8 NM to fld. 1370/9E
  LEMMS NDB (MHW/LOM) 385 LN 40°44′50″N 96°45′44″W 354°4.8 NM to fld. Unmonitored.
  ILS 111.1 I-OCZ Rwy 17R Unmonitored 0600–1200Z‡.
  ILS 109.9 I-LNK Rwy 35L LOM LEMMS NDB. LOM Unmonitored. ILS unmonitored 0600–1200Z‡.
COMM/NAVAID REMARKS: Freq 121.5 not available at tower.

LOUP CITY MUNI (NEØ3) 1 NW UTC–6(–5DT) 41°17′25″N 98°59′25″W **OMAHA**
L-11B

2070 B **FUEL** 100LL
RWY 15-33: H3200X50 (ASPH) S-8 LIRL
  RWY 33: Trees.
RWY 04-22: 2100X100 (TURF)
  RWY 04: Tree. **RWY 22:** Road.
AIRPORT REMARKS: Attended Mon-Sat 1500-1800Z‡. For svc other hours call 308-745-0328.
COMMUNICATIONS: CTAF 122.9
  COLUMBUS FSS (OLU) Toll free call dial 1–800–WX–BRIEF. NOTAM FILE OLU.
RADIO AIDS TO NAVIGATION: NOTAM FILE OLU.
  WOLBACH (H) VORTAC 114.8 OBH Chan 95 41°22′33″N 98°21′12″W 250°29.3 NM to fld. 2010/10E.

MARTIN FLD (See SO SIOUX CITY)

---

§ **McCOOK MUNI** (MCK) 2 E UTC–6(–5DT) 40°12′23″N 100°35′29″W **OMAHA**
H-1D, 3A, L-11A
IAP

2579 B S4 **FUEL** 100LL, JET A CFR Index A
RWY 12-30: H5998X100 (CONC) S-30, D-38 MIRL .6% up NW
  RWY 12: MALS. VASI(V4L)—GA 3.0°TCH 33.7′. Tree.   **RWY 30:** REIL. VASI(V4L)—GA 3.0°TCH 42′.
RWY 03-21: H3999X75 (CONC) S-30, D-38 MIRL
  RWY 03: VASI(V2L)—GA 3.0°TCH 26′. Rgt tfc.   **RWY 21:** VASI(V2L)—GA 3.0°TCH 26′.
RWY 17-35: 1350X200 (TURF)
AIRPORT REMARKS: Attended daylight hours. To ACTIVATE MALS Rwy 12 key 122.8 3 times for low, 5 times for Med, 7
  times for Hi. For VASI Rwy 12-30 Key 122.8 3 times. Control Zone effective 1100-0500Z‡. Except Holidays. Closed
  to air carrier operations of aircraft with seating capacity over 30 passengers except with prior approval, call arpt
  manager 308-345-2022; 24 hours in advance.
COMMUNICATIONS: CTAF/UNICOM 122.8
  COLUMBUS FSS (OLU) Toll free call dial 1–800–WX–BRIEF. NOTAM FILE MCK
  RCO 122.1R 110.0T (COLUMBUS FSS)
Ⓡ **DENVER CENTER APP/DEP CON** 132.7
RADIO AIDS TO NAVIGATION: NOTAM FILE MCK.
  (L) VOR/DME 110.0 MCK Chan 37 40°12′14″N 100°35′38″W at fld. 2550/11E.

FIGURE 47.–Airport/Facility Directory Excerpt.

U.S. DEPARTMENT OF TRANSPORTATION FEDERAL AVIATION ADMINISTRATION			(FAA USE ONLY) ☐ PILOT BRIEFING	☐ VNR	TIME STARTED	SPECIALIST INITIALS
FLIGHT PLAN			☐ STOPOVER			

Form Approved: OMB No. 2120-0026

1 TYPE	**2** AIRCRAFT IDENTIFICATION	**3** AIRCRAFT TYPE/ SPECIAL EQUIPMENT	**4** TRUE AIRSPEED	**5** DEPARTURE POINT	**6** DEPARTURE TIME		**7** CRUISING ALTITUDE
VFR IFR DVFR			KTS		PROPOSED (Z)	ACTUAL (Z)	

8 ROUTE OF FLIGHT

9 DESTINATION (Name of airport and city)	**10** EST. TIME ENROUTE		**11** REMARKS
	HOURS	MINUTES	

12 FUEL ON BOARD		**13** ALTERNATE AIRPORT(S)	**14** PILOT'S NAME, ADDRESS & TELEPHONE NUMBER & AIRCRAFT HOME BASE	**15** NUMBER ABOARD
HOURS	MINUTES			
			17 DESTINATION CONTACT/TELEPHONE (OPTIONAL)	

16 COLOR OF AIRCRAFT	CIVIL AIRCRAFT PILOTS. FAR Part 91 requires you file an IFR flight plan to operate under instrument flight rules in controlled airspace. Failure to file could result in a civil penalty not to exceed $1,000 for each violation (Section 901 of the Federal Aviation Act of 1958, as amended) Filing of a VFR flight plan is recommended as a good operating practice. See also Part 99 for requirements concerning DVFR flight plans.

FAA Form 7233-1 (8-82)   CLOSE VFR FLIGHT PLAN WITH_____ FSS ON ARRIVAL

FIGURE 48.–Flight Plan Form.

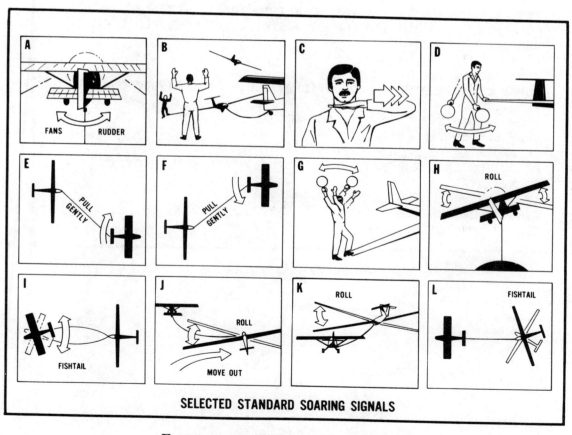

FIGURE 49.–Selected Standard Soaring Signals.

Appendix C - 21

```
DFWH FA Ø41Ø4Ø
HAZARDS VALID UNTIL Ø423ØØ
OK TX AR LA TN MS AL AND CSTL WTRS
FLT PRCTNS...TURBC...TN AL AND CSTL WTRS
          ...ICG...TN
          ...IFR...TX
TSTMS IMPLY PSBL SVR OR GTR TURBC SVR ICG AND LLWS
NON MSL HGTS NOTED BY AGL OR CIG
THIS FA ISSUANCE INCORPORATES THE FOLLOWING AIRMETS STILL IN
EFFECT...NONE.

DFWS FA Ø41Ø4Ø
SYNOPSIS VALID UNTIL Ø5Ø5ØØ
AT 11Z RDG OF HI PRES ERN TX NWWD TO CNTRL CO WITH HI CNTR
OVR ERN TX. BY Ø5Z HI CNTR MOVS TO CNTRL LA.

DFWI FA Ø41Ø4Ø
ICING AND FRZLVL VALID UNTIL Ø423ØØ
TN
FROM SLK TO HAT TO MEM TO ORD TO SLK
OCNL MDT RIME ICGIC ABV FRZLVL TO 1ØØ. CONDS ENDING BY 17Z.
FRZLVL 8Ø CHA SGF LINE SLPG TO 12Ø S OF A IAH MAF LINE.

DFWT FA Ø41Ø4Ø
TURBC VALID UNTIL Ø423ØØ
TN AL AND CSTL WTRS
FROM SLK TO FLO TO 9ØS MOB TO MEI TO BUF TO SLK
OCNL MDT TURBC 25Ø-38Ø DUE TO JTSTR. CONDS MOVG SLOLY EWD
AND CONTG BYD 23Z.

DFWC FA Ø41Ø4Ø
SGFNT CLOUD AND WX VALID UNTIL Ø423ØØ...OTLK Ø423ØØ-Ø5Ø5ØØ
IFR...TX
FROM SAT TO FSX TO BRO TO MOV TO SAT
VSBY BLO 3F TIL 15Z.
OK AR TX LA MS AL AND CSTL WTRS
8Ø SCT TO CLR EXCP VSBY BLO 3F TIL 15Z OVR PTNS S CNTRL TX.
OTLK...VFR.
TN
CIGS 3Ø-5Ø BKN 1ØØ VSBYS OCNLY 3-5F BCMG AGL 4Ø-5Ø SCT TO
CLR BY 19Z. OTLK...VFR.
```

FIGURE 50.–Area Forecast.

```
FD WBC 151745
BASED ON 151200Z DATA
VALID 1600Z FOR USE 1800-0300Z. TEMPS NEG ABV 24000
```

FT	3000	6000	9000	12000	18000	24000	30000	34000	39000
ALS			2420	2635−08	2535−18	2444−30	245945	246755	246862
AMA		2714	2725+00	2625−04	2531−15	2542−27	265842	256352	256762
DEN			2321−04	2532−08	2434−19	2441−31	235347	236056	236262
HLC		1707−01	2113−03	2219−07	2330−17	2435−30	244145	244854	245561
MKC	0507	2006+03	2215−01	2322−06	2338−17	2348−29	236143	237252	238160
STL	2113	2325+07	2332+02	2339−04	2356−16	2373−27	239440	730649	731960

FIGURE 51.–Winds Aloft Forecast.

```
INK SA 1854 CLR 15 106/77/63/1112G18/000
BOI SA 1854 150 SCT 30 181/62/42/1304/015
LAX SA 1852 7 SCT 250 SCT 6HK 129/60/59/2504/991
MDW RS 1856 −X M7 OVC 11/2R+F 990/63/61/3205/980/RF2 RB12
JFK RS 1853 W5 X 1/2F 180/68/64/1804/006/R04RVR22V30 TWR VSBY 1/4
```

FIGURE 52.–Surface Aviation Weather Reports.

```
OK FT 011447

GAG FT 011515 100 SCT 250 SCT 2610. 16Z 60 SCT C100 BKN 3315G22 CHC C50 BKN
    5TRW. 01Z 250 SCT 3515G25. 09Z VFR WIND..

HBR FT 011515 C120 BKN 250 BKN 3010. 17Z 100 SCT C250 BKN 3215G25 CHC C30 BKN
    3TRW. 00Z 250 SCT 3515G25. 092 VFR WIND..

MLC FT 011515 C20 BKN 1815 BKN OCNL SCT. 20Z C30 BKN 1815G22 CHC C20 BKN
    1TRW. 03Z C30 BKN 2015 CHC C7 X 1/2TRW+G40. 09Z MVFR CIG TRW..

OKC FT 011515 C12 BKN 140 BKN 1815G28 LWR BKN V SCT. 18Z C30 BKN 250 BKN
    2315G25 LWR BKN OCNL SCT CHC C7 X 1/2TRW+G40. 21Z CFP 100 SCT C250 BKN
    3315G25 CHC C30 BKN 5TRW−. 02Z 100 SCT 250 SCT 3515G25. 09Z VFR WIND..

PNC FT 011515 C100 BKN 250 BKN 1810. 16Z CFP 20 SCT C100 BKN 3115 SCT V BKN. 00Z
    250 SCT 3515G25. 09Z VFR WIND..

TUL FT 011515 C20 BKN 1915G22. 19Z C30 BKN 1815G25 CHC 3TRW. 23Z CFP C100 BKN
    250 BKN 3215G25 CHC C30 BKN 5TRW. 09Z VFR WIND..
```

FIGURE 53.–Terminal Forecast.

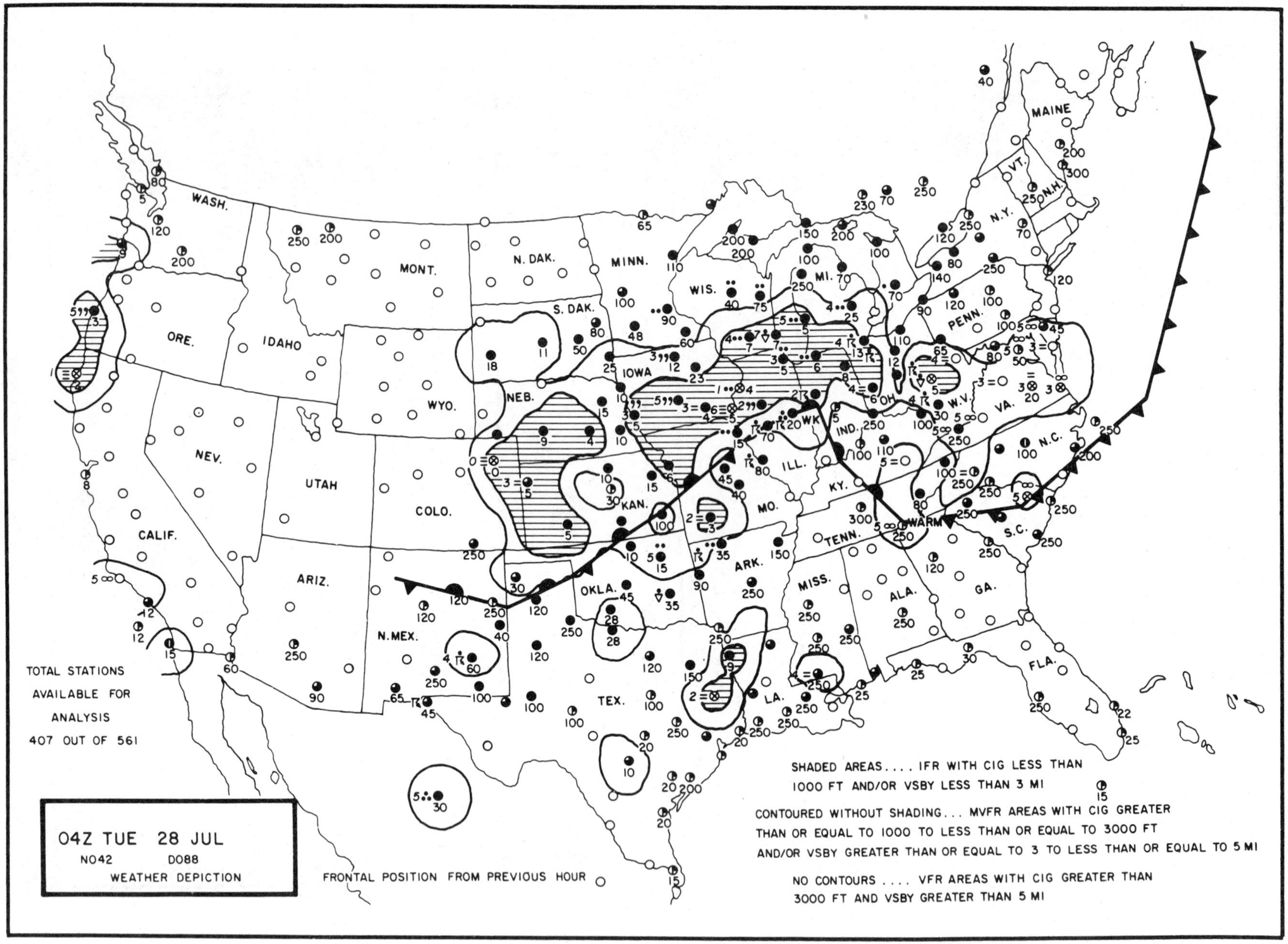

FIGURE 54.—Weather Depiction Chart.

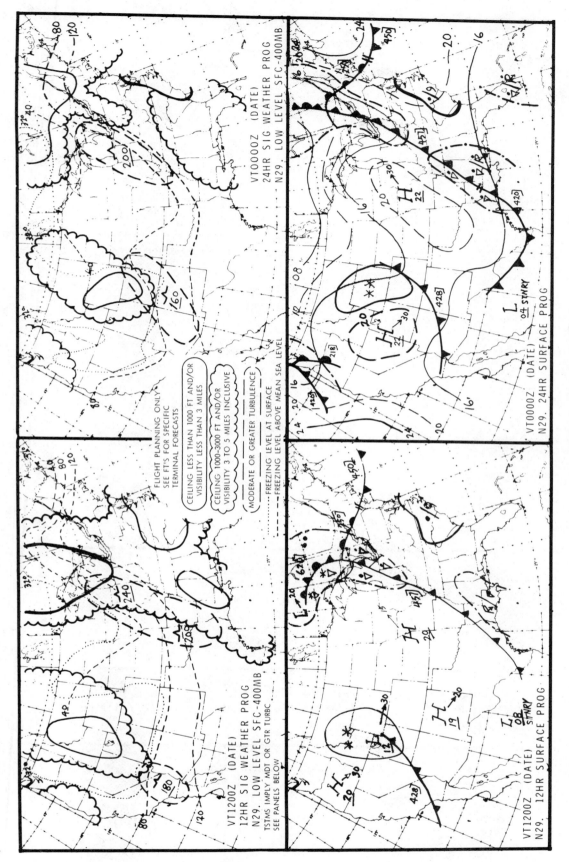

FIGURE 55.–Significant Weather Prognostic Chart.

This is a telephone weather briefing from the Dallas FSS for a local operation of gliders and lighter-than-air at Caddo Mills, Texas (about 30 miles east of Dallas). The briefing is at 13Z.

"There are no adverse conditions reported or forecast for today."

'A weak low pressure over the Texas Panhandle and eastern New Mexico is causing a weak southerly flow over the area.'

'Current weather here at Dallas is clear, visibility 12 miles, temperature 70, dew point 48, wind south 5 knots, altimeter 29 point 78.'

'By 15Z we should have a few scattered clouds at 5 thousand AGL, with higher scattered cirrus at 25 thousand MSL. After 20Z the wind should pick up to about 15 knots from the south.'

'The winds aloft are: 3 thousand 170 at 7, temperature 20; 6 thousand 200 at 18, temperature 14; 9 thousand 210 at 22, temperature 8; 12 thousand 225 at 27, temperature 0; 18 thousand 240 at 30, temperature -7.'

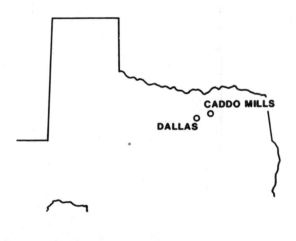

FIGURE 56.–Weather Telephone Briefing.

UA /OV OKC-TUL /TM 1800 /FL 120 /TP BE90 /SK Ø12 BKN Ø55 /
/Ø72 OVC Ø89 /CLR ABV /TA -9/WV Ø921/TB MDT Ø55-Ø72 /ICG LGT-MDT
CLR Ø72-Ø89.

FIGURE 57.–Pilot Weather Report.

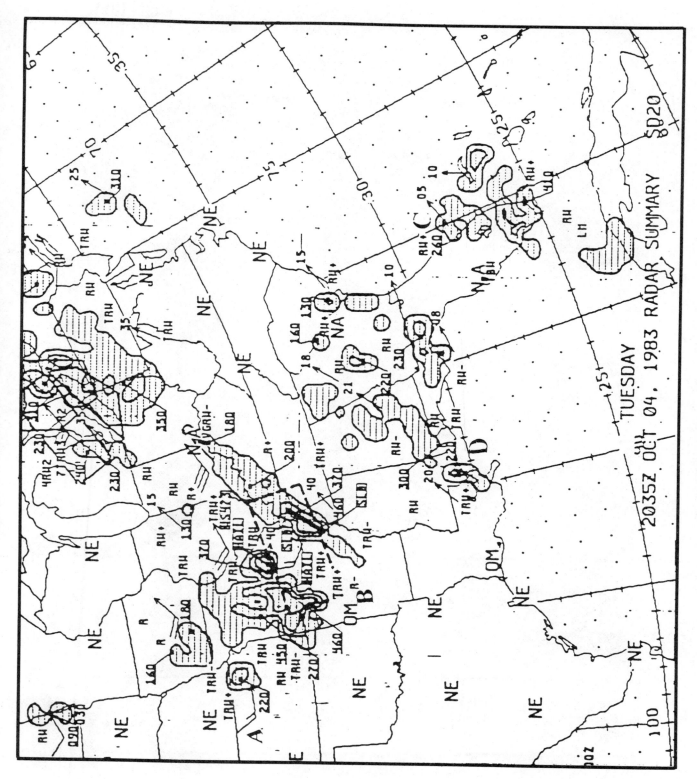

FIGURE 58.–Radar Summary Chart.

APPENDIX D - GENERAL INSTRUCTIONS, INTRODUCTION TO THE PRIVATE PILOT QUESTION BOOK, AND SUBJECT MATTER KNOWLEDGE CODES

GENERAL INSTRUCTIONS

MAXIMUM TIME ALLOWED FOR TEST: 6 HOURS

1. Read the instructions on page 1 of AC Form 8080–3, Airman Written Test Application, and complete the form on page 4.

2. The question numbers in this question book are numbered consecutively beginning with No. 1001. Refer to the question selection sheet to determine which questions to answer.

3. For each item on the answer sheet, find the appropriate question in the book.

4. Mark your answer in the space provided for that item on the answer sheet.

5. The supplementary material required to answer the questions will be found in appendixes 2 and 3.

6. Remember:

Read each question carefully and avoid hasty assumptions. Do not answer until you understand the question. Do not spend too much time on any one question. Answer all of the questions that you readily know and then reconsider those you find difficult. Be careful to make necessary conversions when working with temperatures, speeds, and distances.

If a regulation or operations procedure is changed after this question book is printed, you will receive credit until the affected questions are revised.

MATERIALS

Materials to be used with this question book when used for airman testing:

1. AC Form 8080–3 which includes the answer sheet.

2. Question selection sheet which identifies the questions to be answered.

3. Plastic overlay sheet which can be placed over performance charts for plotting purposes.

THE MINIMUM PASSING GRADE IS 70.

WARNING

§61.37 Written tests: Cheating or other unauthorized conduct.

(a) Except as authorized by the Administrator, no person may–
(1) Copy, or intentionally remove, a written test under this part;
(2) Give to another, or receive from another, any part or copy of that test;
(3) Give help on that test to, or receive help on that test from, any person during the period that test is being given;
(4) Take any part of that test in behalf of another person;
(5) Use any material or aid during the period that test is being given; or

(6) Intentionally cause, assist, or participate in any act prohibited by this paragraph.
(b) No person whom the Administrator finds to have committed an act prohibited by paragraph (a) of this section is eligible for any airman or ground instructor certificate or rating, or to take any test therefor, under this chapter for a period of 1 year after the date of that act. In addition, the commission of that act is a basis for suspending or revoking any airman or ground instructor certificate or rating held by that person.

INTRODUCTION TO THE
PRIVATE PILOT QUESTION BOOK

This question book follows the new concept in knowledge testing that was established in 1982 with the publication of the Private Pilot Question Book. All the new question books are dated to indicate their expiration date.

At an FAA testing center or an FAA designated written test examiner's facility, the applicant is issued a "clean copy" of this question book, an appropriate question selection sheet which indicates the specific questions to be answered, and AC Form 8080-3, Airman Written Test Application, which contains the answer sheet. The question book contains all the supplementary material required to answer the questions. This material will be found in appendixes 2 and 3.

Questions and Scoring

The test questions are of the multiple-choice type. Answers to questions listed on the question selection sheet should be marked on the answer sheet of AC Form 8080-3. Directions should be read carefully before beginning the test. Incomplete or erroneous personal information entered on this form delays the scoring process.

The answer sheet is sent to the Mike Monroney Aeronautical Center in Oklahoma City where it is scored by computer. The applicant will then be issued an AC Form 8080-2, Airman Written Test Report. This report must be presented for the practical test or for retesting in the event of written test failure. The applicant's AC Form 8080-2 will list the subject matter knowledge codes for the knowledge areas in which the applicant is found to be deficient. The written test subject matter knowledge codes, which list these knowledge areas by code, are located in this question book.

Taking the Test

The test may be taken at FAA testing centers, FAA written test examiners' facilities, or other designated places. After completing the test, the applicant must surrender the issued question book, question selection sheet, answer sheet, and any papers used for computations or notations, to the monitor before leaving the test room.

When taking the test, the applicant should keep the following points in mind:

1. Answer each question in accordance with the latest regulations and procedures.
2. Read each question carefully before looking at the possible answers. You should clearly understand the problem before attempting to solve it.

3. After formulating an answer, determine which of the alternatives most nearly corresponds with that answer. The answer chosen should completely resolve the problem.
4. From the answers given, it may appear that there is more than one possible answer; however, there is only one answer that is correct and complete. The other answers are either incomplete or are derived from popular misconceptions.
5. If a certain question is difficult for you, it is best to proceed to other questions. After the less difficult questions have been answered, return to those which gave you difficulty. Be sure to indicate on the question selection sheet the questions to which you wish to return.
6. When solving a computer problem, select the answer nearest your solution. The problem has been checked with various types of computers; therefore, if you have solved it correctly, your answer will be closer to the correct answer than to any of the other choices.
7. To aid in scoring, enter personal data in the appropriate spaces on the test answer sheet in a complete and legible manner. Enter the test number printed on the question selection sheet.

Retesting—FAR Section 61.49

Applicants who receive a failing grade may apply for retesting by presenting their AC Form 8080-2

1. after 30 days from the date the applicant failed the test; or
2. in case of the first failure, the applicant may apply for retesting before the 30 days have expired upon presenting a written statement from an authorized instructor certifying that the instructor has given ground instruction to the applicant and finds the applicant competent to pass the test.

DEPARTMENT OF TRANSPORTATION

FEDERAL AVIATION ADMINISTRATION

SUBJECT MATTER KNOWLEDGE CODES

To determine the knowledge area in which a particular question was incorrectly answered, compare the subject matter knowledge code(s) on AC Form 8080-2, Airmen Written Test Report, to the subject matter knowledge codes that follow. The total number of questions missed may differ from the number of subject matter knowledge codes shown on the AC Form 8080-2, since you may have missed more than one question in a certain subject matter knowledge code.

FAR 1   **Definitions and Abbreviations**

A01	General Definitions
A02	Abbreviations and Symbols

FAR 23   **Airworthiness Standards: Normal, Utility, and Acrobatic Category Aircraft**

A10	General

FAR 43   **Maintenance, Preventive Maintenance, Rebuilding and Alteration**

A15	General
A16	Appendixes

FAR 61   **Certification: Pilots and Flight Instructors**

A20	General
A21	Aircraft Ratings and Special Certificates
A22	Student Pilots
A23	Private Pilots
A24	Commercial Pilots
A25	Airline Transport Pilots
A26	Flight Instructors
A27	Appendix A: Practical Test Requirements for Airline Transport Pilot Certificates and Associated Class and Type Ratings
A28	Appendix B: Practical Test Requirements for Rotorcraft Airline Transport Pilot Certificates with a Helicopter Class Rating and Associated Type Ratings

FAR 63   **Certification: Flight Crewmembers Other Than Pilots**

A30	General
A31	Flight Engineers
A32	Flight Navigators

FAR 65   **Certification: Airmen Other Than Flight Crewmembers**

A40	General
A41	Aircraft Dispatchers

FAR 67   **Medical Standards and Certification**

A50	General
A51	Certification Procedures

FAR 71   **Designation of Federal Airways, Area Low Routes, Controlled Airspace, and Reporting Points**

A60	General
A61	Airport Radar Service Areas

FAR 73   **Special Use Airspace**

A70	General
A71	Restricted Areas
A72	Prohibited Areas

FAR 75   **Establishment of Jet Routes and Area High Routes**

A80	General

FAR 77   **Objects Affecting Navigable Airspace**

A90	General

FAR 91   **General Operating Rules**

B01	General
B02	Flight Rules
B03	Maintenance, Preventive Maintenance, and Alterations
B04	Large and Turbine-Powered Multiengine Airplanes
B05	Operating Noise Limits
B06	Appendix A: Category II Operations Manual, Instruments, Equipment, and Maintenance

FAR 103   **Ultralight Vehicles**

C01	General
C02	Operating Rules

FAR 108   **Airplane Operator Security**

C10	General

FAR 121   **Certification and Operations: Domestic, Flag and Supplemental Air Carriers and Commercial Operators of Large Aircraft**

D01	General
D02	Certification Rules for Domestic and Flag Air Carriers

M12   AC 121-25, Additional Weather Information: Domestic and Flag Air Carriers

M13   AC 121-195, Alternate Operational Landing Distances for Wet Runways; Turbojet Powered Transport Category Airplanes

M20   AC 125-1, Operations of Large Airplanes Subject to Federal Aviation Regulations Part 125

M30   AC 135-3, Air Taxi Operators and Commercial Operators

M31   AC 135-9, FAR Part 135 Icing Limitations

M32   AC 135-12, Passenger Information, FAR Part 135: Passenger Safety Information Briefing and Briefing Cards

M40   AC 150/5345-28, Precision Approach Path Indicator (PAPI) Systems

M50   AC 20-34, Prevention of Retractable Landing Gear Failures

American Soaring Handbook - Gliders

N01   A History of American Soaring
N02   Training
N03   Ground Launch
N04   Airplane Tow
N05   Meteorology
N06   Cross-Country and Wave Soaring
N07   Instruments and Oxygen
N08   Radio, Rope, and Wire
N09   Aerodynamics
N10   Maintenance and Repair

Soaring Flight Manual - Gliders

N20   Sailplane Aerodynamics
N21   Performance Considerations
N22   Flight Instruments
N23   Weather for Soaring
N24   Medical Factors
N25   Flight Publications and Airspace
N26   Aeronautical Charts and Navigation
N27   Computations for Soaring
N28   Personal Equipment
N29   Preflight and Ground Operations
N30   Aerotow Launch Procedures
N31   Ground Launch Procedures
N32   Basic Flight Maneuvers and Traffic Patterns
N33   Soaring Techniques
N34   Cross-Country Soaring

Taming The Gentle Giant - Balloons

O01   Design and Construction of Balloons
O02   Fuel Source and Supply
O03   Weight and Temperature
O04   Flight Instruments
O05   Balloon Flight Tips
O06   Glossary

Balloon Federation Of America - Flight Instructor Manual

O10   Flight Instruction Aids
O11   Human Behavior and Pilot Proficiency

O12   The Flight Check and the Designated Examiner

The Balloon Federation Of America Handbook - Propane Systems

O20   Propane Glossary
O21   Chemical and Physical Systems
O22   Cylinders
O23   Lines and Fittings
O24   Valves
O25   Regulators
O26   Burners
O27   Propane Systems - Schematics
O28   Propane References

The Balloon Federation Of America Handbook - Avoiding Powerline Accidents

O30   Excerpts

Balloon Flight Manual

O40   Excerpts

Airship Operations Manual

P01   Buoyancy
P02   Aerodynamics
P03   Free Ballooning
P04   Aerostatics
P05   Envelope
P06   Car
P07   Powerplant
P08   Airship Ground Handling
P09   Operating Instructions
P10   History

International Flight Information Manual

Q01   Passport and Visa
Q02   International NOTAM Availability and Distribution
Q03   National Security
Q04   International Interception Procedures
Q05   Intercept Pattern for Identification of Transport Aircraft
Q06   Flight Planning Notes
Q07   North Atlantic Minimum Navigation Requirements
Q08   North American Routes for North Atlantic Traffic
Q09   U.S. Aeronautical Telecommunications Services
Q10   Charts and Publications for Flights Outside the U.S.
Q11   Oceanic Long-Range Navigation Information

Aerodynamics For Naval Aviators, NAVWEPS 00-80T-80

R01   Wing and Airfoil Forces
R02   Planform Effects and Airplane Drag
R10   Required Thrust and Power
R11   Available Thrust and Power
R12   Items of Airplane Performance

R21	General Concepts and Supersonic Flow Patterns
R22	Configuration Effects
R31	Definitions
R32	Longitudinal Stability and Control
R33	Directional Stability and Control
R34	Lateral Stability and Control
R35	Miscellaneous Stability Problems
R40	General Definitions and Structural Requirements
R41	Aircraft Loads and Operating Limitations
R50	Application of Aerodynamics to Specific Problems of Flying
S01	Reserved
T01	Reserved
U01	Reserved
V01	Reserved
W01	Reserved
X01	Reserved
Y01	Reserved
Z01	Visual Flight Rules Chart Users Guide

NOTE: Most of the references and study materials listed in these subject matter knowledge codes are available through government outlets such as U.S. Government Printing Office bookstores. AC 00-2, Advisory Circular Checklist, transmits the status of all FAA AC's (advisory circulars), as well as FAA internal publications and miscellaneous flight information such as AIM, Airport/Facility Directory, written test question books, practical test standards, and other material directly related to a certificate or rating. To obtain a free copy of the AC 00-2, send your request to:

U.S. Department of Transportation
Utilization and Storage Section, M-443.2
Washington, DC   20590

APPENDIX E — ELECTRONIC STUDY GUIDE MANUAL

FAA Written Exam (Airplane)

Version 2.1

Developed for the IBM-PC

by

Jian Li, Kurt Look, Mike Merrill, John Schick, and George Semb
Trilogy Systems, Inc.
8020 Monrovia
Lenexa, Kansas 66215-2727
Phone: (913) 492-4541

~~~~~~

Contents

Overview

The Electronic Study Guide allows you to generate a test in a way similar to that used by the FAA, and then to take the test. On-screen menus prompt you every step of the way; answers and explanations are available after you answer each question. The computer keeps track of your performance on individual questions so you may return to the ones you missed for further study. It also keeps a running tally of your overall performance on the test, and it allows you to print out questions you may want to review more thoroughly. Finally, you can use the program to generate a test over specific areas of interest, such as weight and balance, VOR navigation, or flight physiology.

The enclosed set contains a *Program Diskette* and an *FAA Test Item Diskette* that contains all of the FAA questions (Airplane) that appear in the *Private Pilot Question Book* (FAA-T-8080-1B), together with answers to and explanations for every question.

The program has four options. First, *Make Test* allows you to create a test (there are several ways to do this, as described later in this manual), save a test to a disk file, or print the test on your printer. Second, *Take Test* presents the questions on the screen and allows you to respond to them. Correct answers and complete explanations follow each response. *Setup* allows you to configure the program for a particular computer or printer, and *Quit* is used to exit from the program and return to your operating system.

What if you don't have a computer? Let's face it. Aviation is becoming more and more computerized every day. This Electronic Study Guide is one application of that technology. If you have never used a computer, you owe it to yourself to find one and learn something about it. You might try a computer lab if one is available. Or you could go to a computer store and ask them to show you how one works--be sure to take this program with you. Or you could ask your friends or your instructor where you might find one. You owe it to yourself to find a computer and learn how to run this program.

System Requirements

(1) IBM-PC (or 100% compatible) with 256K of memory; (2) a two-360K floppy diskette drive system (or a hard drive); and (3) DOS 2.1 or higher.

Conventions

Throughout this manual we use <Enter> to denote the <Enter> key (on some keyboards this is the <Return> key), and <Esc> to denote the <Esc> key.

Installation

Before you go any further, *make copies of the master diskettes*. Store the master diskettes in a safe place and use the copies for everyday work.

The program comes installed to work on a two-360K floppy disk drive system with the first drive designated as Drive "A" and the second drive designated as Drive "B." When you run the program in this configuration, you *must* put the *Program Diskette* in Drive "A" and the *FAA Test Item Diskette* in Drive "B."

If you have a hard disk system, you must "install" the program. First, boot the system. Then, put the program diskette in the Drive "A" and at the A> prompt, type HDINSTAL. HDINSTAL creates a directory called "FAA-EXAM" and transfers the files to your hard disk. Just follow the on-screen instructions.

Demonstration

To see how the Electronic Study Guide works, you should run the demonstration (demo) program we have provided. To run this program, first boot your system. Then, put your working copy of the *Program Diskette* in Drive "A." At the A> prompt, type DEMO, and hit <Enter>. (If you have installed the program on a hard drive, change the directory to FAA-EXAM (e.g., C:CD\FAA-EXAM), type DEMO, and hit <Enter>.) Then, follow the on-screen instructions.

Running the Program

Boot the system. Then, put your working copy of the *Program Diskette* in Drive "A" and your working copy of the *FAA Test Item Diskette* in Drive "B." At A> type GO and hit <Enter>. (If you are using a hard disk, change the directory to FAA-EXAM (e.g., C:>CD\FAA-EXAM), type GO, and hit <Enter>.) The title menu appears and instructs you to hit any key to proceed. You will then see the opening menu with four choices: "Make Test," "Take Test," "Setup," and "Quit." In the upper left corner of the screen are the words `Test` : `<None>`. This prompt tells you which test file is currently open. When you first run the program, it will be empty. After you open a test the word "None" will be replaced with the name of the test you have opened.

At this point the "Make Test" option is highlighted. To select one of the other menu options, use the right arrow key and the left arrow key to move the highlight.

Make Test Menu

To select the **Make Test** option, move the highlight to Make Test and press <Enter>. A new menu appears:

        Edit/Make Test
        Open Test
        Save Test File
        Print Test to Paper
        Delete Test File

Open Test

Before you can edit, save, delete, or print a test, you must first "Open" a test file. Move the highlight to Open Test File and hit <Enter>. A large window will appear on the screen listing all existing tests. The prompt Open Test: will appear at the bottom of the screen where you can enter the test name. You will find it helpful to use names that are easy to remember, such as the subject of your test (e.g., VOR) or perhaps the date (41589). You can use a maximum of eight characters to name a test file name. After entering a test file name, hit <Enter>.

Edit/Make Test

Edit/Make Test allows you to create a new test or modify an old one. Move the highlight to "Edit/Make Test" and hit <Enter>. You will now see three new windows and a menu with these options:

        Make a Random Test
        Select a Range of Questions
        Select Individual Questions
        Delete a Question
        View Selected Questions

Total Questions: located in the upper right corner of the screen tells you how many questions you have selected for the test.

Now you are ready to select questions (or to have them selected for you). The highlighted option, Make a Random Test, allows you to produce a random test of, say, 50 questions from the FAA files. To see how this option works, hit <Enter>. The prompt "Number to Select" will appear at the bottom of the screen with the number 50 next to it. You can accept the number 50 by hitting the <Enter> key or you can type in another number and hit <Enter>. The program then randomly selects that number of questions from the pool. Once the test is generated, you are returned to the Make Test Menu, where you can select one of the other options.

(Note: The "random" selection procedure is designed to generate a "representative" test of all the areas in the FAA exam. It is similar to the question selection method we suspect the FAA uses. Thus, each random exam will be different, but it will emphasize what the FAA considers to be most important.)

Another way to create a test is to select specific areas for study. Move the highlight to Select Range of Questions and hit <Enter>. A new menu appears with several "chapter" names listed at the top of the screen and the following options at the bottom of the screen:

        Chapter:
        First Question:
        Last Question:
        Key Concept:
        Number to Select:

All FAA questions are cross-referenced to the appropriate chapter in the Study Guide. The chapters available are listed at the top of the screen. Use <PgUp> and <PgDn> to scroll through the chapter names. The percentages in parentheses next to the chapter names indicate the relative percentage of questions that will appear on randomly generated tests.

Enter the chapter number from which you want to select questions. If you chose a chapter that does not exist, an error message appears at the top of the screen and instructs you to press the <Esc> key or <Enter> to continue. Once you have entered the chapter number, the available questions within that chapter are displayed at the top of the screen. This will give you an idea of how many questions are available.

We have also provided a _Key Concept_ for every question. It is a key word or phrase that describes the content of the question. When the cursor moves to "Key Concept," all of the key concepts in the chapter are displayed at the top of the screen. You can use the <PgUp> and <PgDn> keys to move through the screens to see what concepts are available. If you want to select questions on the basis of a particular key concept, type in the name of the concept _exactly_ as it appears at the top of the screen. When you hit <Enter>, the name of the concept will appear in the lower left box. If you do not want to use "Key Concept" to select questions, simply leave the field blank and hit <Enter>.

The cursor will now be at **Number to Select**. The number shown on the screen will tell you how many questions are in the defined range. You can select the number shown by hitting <Enter> or type any number less than the number shown. The program will randomly select that number of questions from the range. You are returned to the previous menu after selecting the number of questions you want on the test.

Another way to create a test is to select individual questions. Move the highlight to _Select Individual Questions_ and hit <Enter>. The available chapters will again be displayed on the screen, together with a small window where you can specify the chapter number. Once you have entered the chapter number, you will be prompted to enter the question number. The window at the top of the screen lists the questions in the chapter.

To remove a question, move the highlight to _Delete a Question_ and hit <Enter>. You will now see the same window that you used to select questions. However, the question numbers you enter will be deleted from the test.

View Selected Questions removes the menu so that you can see all of the question numbers you have selected.

Save Test File

After you have created a test, return to the test submenu and _save your work_. Move the highlight to Save Test File and hit <Enter>. A window will open saying "Save Test" followed by the name of the test you currently have open. If you are satisfied with the name of the test, hit <Enter>. You will see a message stating that the test is to be written to a file that already exists.

You are given the option to continue or to stop. If you already have a test file with the same name, saving the new one to the same name will destroy the old test file. If you no longer want the old test, then continue with your save. If you want to keep your old test, type "N" to abort (cancel) the save. Then, save the new test to a new name.

Print Test to Paper

To send a test to your printer, move the highlight to Print Test to Paper and hit <Enter>. Before you do this, however, make sure that the "Open" test is the one you want to print. Once you start the printing process, the following message appears:

> Make sure your printer is on line, has enough
> paper, and the paper is properly aligned.
>
> Press Any Key (Esc to Exit) When Ready . . .

Press any key and the print job will start. While the job is printing, a menu will appear on the screen instructing you that if you want to abort the printing job, press the <Esc> key.

Delete Test File

Delete Test File lets you erase test files you no longer need. Be careful! When you delete a file, there is no way to recover it.

Take Test Menu

This menu allows you to take (or retake) a test. Move the highlight to "Take Test" and hit <Enter>. The following window will appear:

> Take Test
> Retake Test

Take Test

The Take Test option in the pull-down menu allows you to take the test on-screen. To use this option, move the highlight to "Take Test" and hit <Enter>. A window with the following information will appear in the middle of the screen: Reading : (test name you selected) (question counter). The counter displays the questions as they are read into memory. Next, the first question appears on the screen, together with a new menu of options.

> Answer Question
> Next Question
> Previous Question
> Go To (List) Questions

The highlight will be located on the word "Answer." Hit <Enter> and the cursor moves to the upper screen next to the word "Answer," where you can enter the number that corresponds to the answer you want to select. After you enter your answer, the program will display the correct response and ask if you want to see the explanation we have provided. After you respond to this prompt, you are returned to the menu pictured above. At this point you can answer the next question or select one of the other options.

If you decide to take a break or to stop working on the test, be sure to save your work! Use the Make Test pull-down menu to do this. When you return to continue taking the test, use Make Test to open the appropriate test, then move to the Take Test pull-down menu and select the "Take Test" option. (Note: Don't use the "Retake Test" option until you read how it works below.) After you select "Take Test" and hit <Enter>, you will begin where you left off during the previous session. All of your answers will still be there. If you do not save your work between sessions, however, your old work will be lost.

Previous Question and *Next Question* take you through the test one item at a time. The *Go To (List) Questions* option presents a screen that displays all of the test question numbers. It also tells you which questions you have already answered by placing a plus + in front of the questions you answered correctly and a minus – in front of the questions you answered incorrectly. You can use the *Go To (List) Questions* menu to return to questions you want to restudy.

Your score on the test is shown in the upper right corner of the screen both in terms of the number of correct responses out of the total number answered and the percentage of correct responses. When you have finished the test, hit <Esc> to return to the Take Test Menu.

(Note: Two other fields that appear on this screen are Main Point and Reference. The "Main Point" refers to the appropriate Chapter Main Point in the Study Guide. When needed, the "Reference" field refers to an FAA figure or chart from the *Private Pilot Question Book* (e.g., Fig 12.3). All of the FAA figures appear in Appendix C of this Study Guide.

Retake Test

The word *retake* means to take the test again from the beginning. It should not be confused with *continuing* to take a test. When you retake a test, the computer destroys your previous responses and you start over again from the beginning. If you want to continue to work a test you have only partially completed, use the "Take Test" option as described above. Only if you want to start over again from the beginning should you use the "Retake Test" option.

To use the Retake Test option, move the highlight to "Retake Test" and hit <Enter>. You can then retake all of the questions on the test. Once you are done retaking the test, hit <Esc> to return to the Take Test Menu. All of the options available in "Take Test" are also available in "Retake Test." A word of caution: When you use the Retake Test option, all of you previous answers are destroyed and you start from the beginning. Use this option *only* when you want to retake the entire test, not when you simply want to return to a test to continue working on it.

Setup Menu

The Setup Menu allows you to install the program for your particular computer. With the highlight at Change Setup hit <Enter>.

```
(F)loppy or (H)ard Drive      : F
Lines Per Page                : 66
Pause Between Pages (Y/N)      : N
Printer Init String           :
```

The "(F)loppy or (H)ard Drive" option tells your computer where files will be located. In the Floppy Drive configuration, you put the "Program Diskette" in Drive A and the "Test Question" diskette in Drive B. In the Hard Drive configuration, all files reside on your hard drive under "FAA-EXAM."

You are now given some options for your printer. "Lines Per Page" must be set to correspond with your printer's page limit. The program comes installed for 66 lines per page. Check your printer's manual to see if these settings are correct for your hardware. If not, make the necessary changes. "Pause Between Pages (Y/N)" allows you either to use continuous form feeds (No) or to have your printer stop after every page (Yes) so you can insert a new sheet of paper. You use "Printer Init String" to instruct your printer how to handle the output the program produces. Most of you will never have to attend to this annoying detail, but if you are unsure, consult your printer manual for details. (Note: We use two lines for the top and bottom margins, leaving 62 lines for actual printing. If you change the "Lines Per Page" option, we still maintain 2 lines for the top and bottom margins.)

To change any of the "Setup" settings, type the desired change, and hit <Enter>. The cursor then moves to the next setting. If you do not want to change a setting, hit <Enter>. The setting will remain as it is, and the cursor will move to the next setting. Once you have moved through all the "Setup" options, the message Save Changes to Disk (Y/N)? will appear. Hitting "Y" saves the changes permanently on your program disk. Hitting "N" makes the changes for the current session but does not write them to your program disk.

Quit Menu

To exit from the program, move the highlight to Quit, and hit <Enter>. If you have not made changes in any test files, you are returned to DOS. If you have made changes but have not saved them, you will be prompted to do so. If you want to save your work, hit "Y." A directory appears listing the available test files to assist you in selecting the file you want to save. After naming a file, hit <Enter>, and you will be returned to your operating system.

FIGURE 5
Airspeed Indicator

FIGURES 13–19
Color Sectional Charts

NEVER EXCEED
RED ~~BAR~~ LINE

CAUTION SPEED

MAX TURBULENCE SPEED

STALL SPEED
W/ FULL FLAPS BS1

POWER OFF STALL NO FLAPS
BS

NORMAL OPER. RANGE

MAX FLAP EXTENSION
SPEED

FIGURE 5.–Airspeed Indicator.

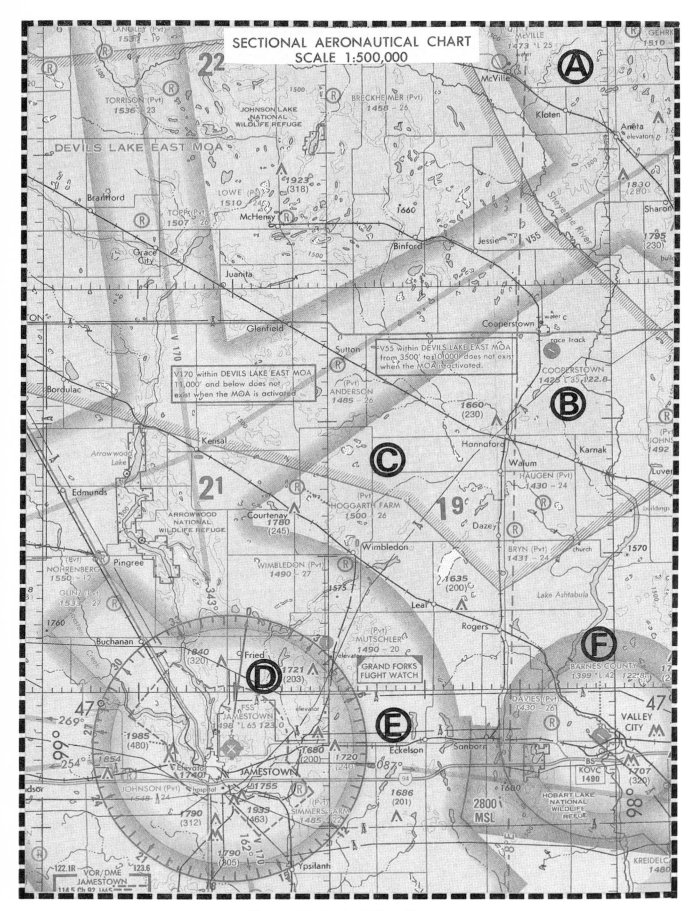

FIGURE 13.–Sectional Chart Excerpt.

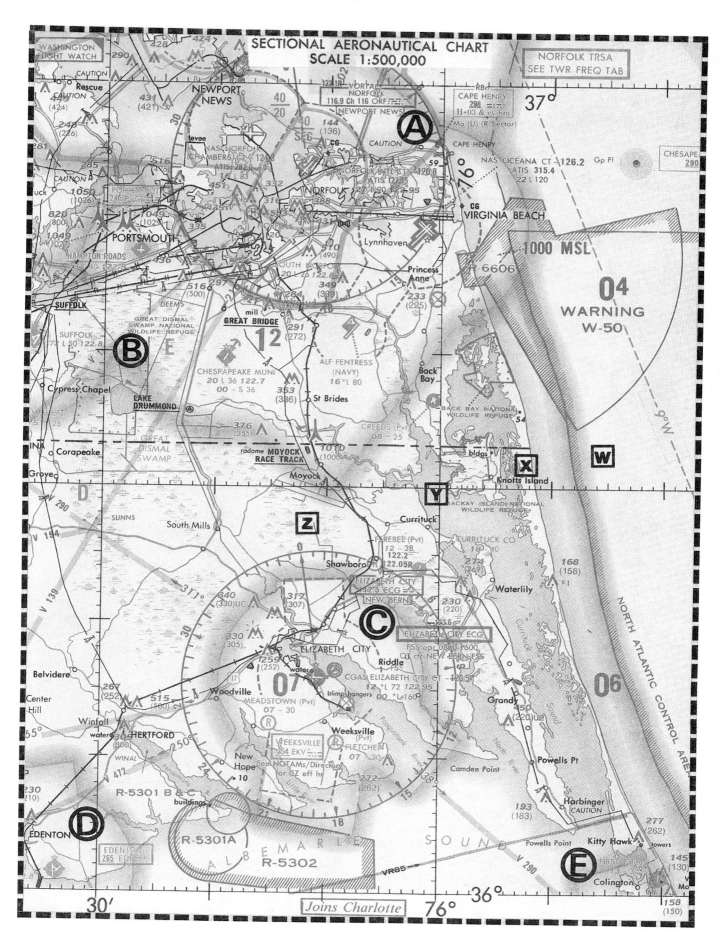

FIGURE 14.–Sectional Chart Excerpt.

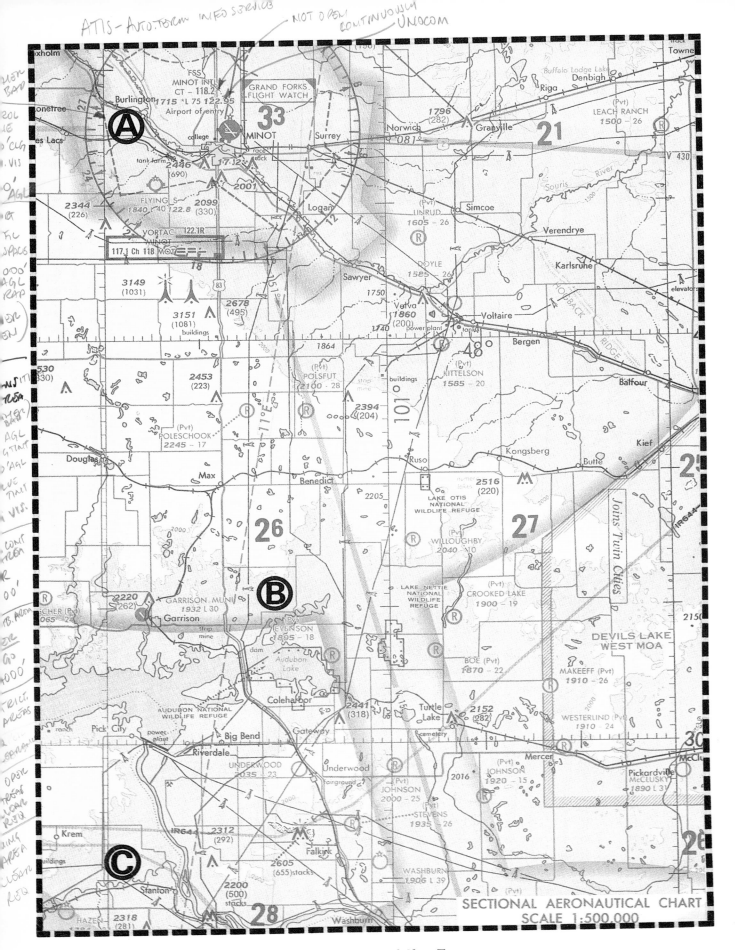

FIGURE 15.–Sectional Chart Excerpt.

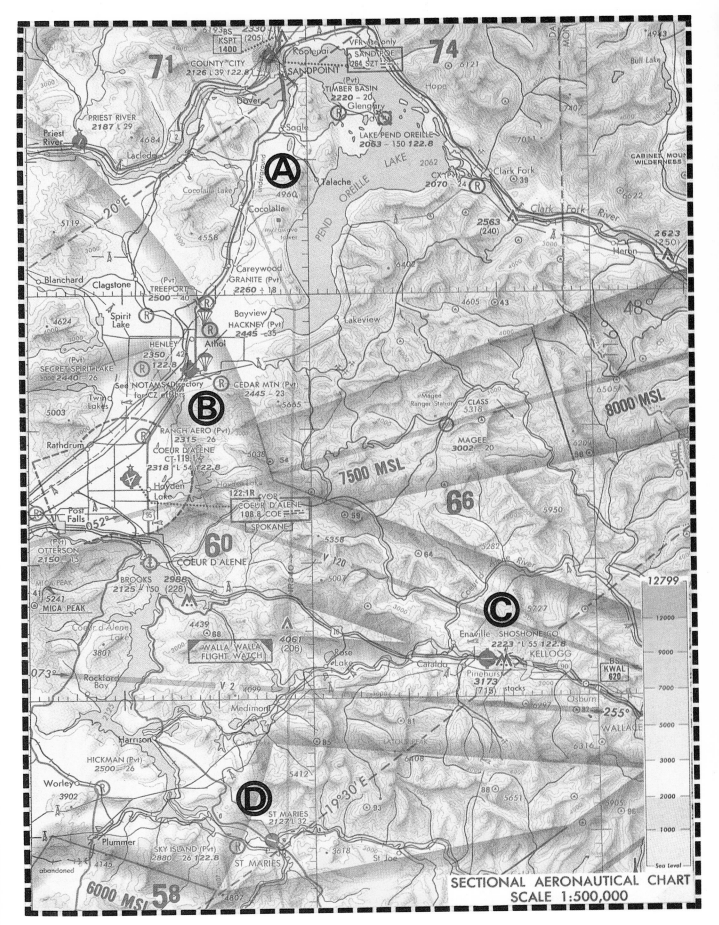

FIGURE 16.–Sectional Chart Excerpt.

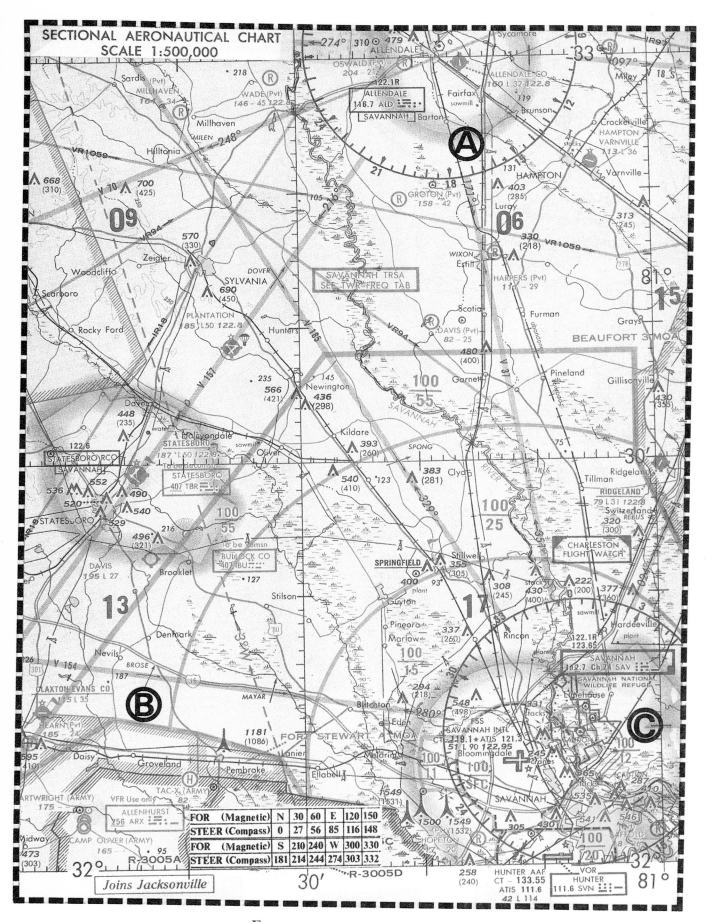

FIGURE 17.–Sectional Chart Excerpt.

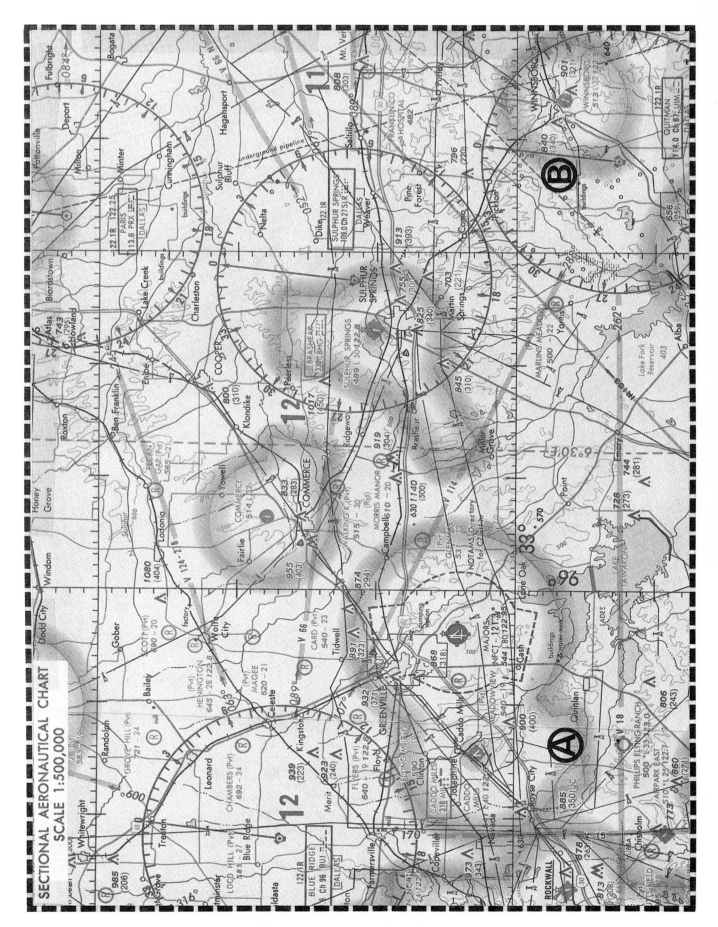

FIGURE 18.–Sectional Chart Excerpt.

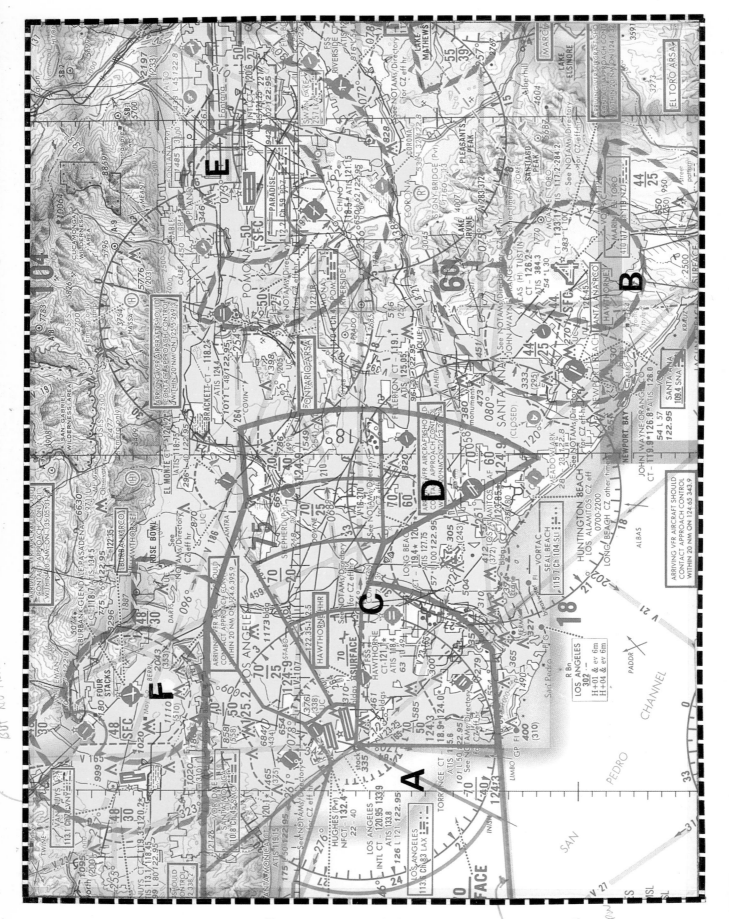

FIGURE 19.–Sectional Chart Excerpt.